D1568319

Text, Discourse, and Process

Toward a Multidisciplinary Science of Texts

ROBERT DE BEAUGRANDE

University of Florida

Volume IV in the Series
ADVANCES IN DISCOURSE PROCESSES
Roy O. Freedle, *Editor*

ABLEX Publishing Corporation
Norwood, New Jersey 07648

P
302
· D35

Printed in the United States of America

ISBN 0-89391-033-3   ISSN   0164-0224

ABLEX Publishing Corporation
355 Chestnut Street
Norwood, New Jersey 07648

Contents

Preface to the Series   vii
Acknowledgments   ix
0. Evolution and Development   xi

I. **Basic Issues** 1

    1. Systems and Models   *1*
    2. Levels in Models of Language   *7*
    3. Text Versus Sentence   *10*
    4. Textuality   *16*
    5. Textual Competence   *22*
    6. Text Utilization as Model-Building   *24*
    7. Overview of the Discussion   *31*

II. **Sequential Connectivity** 33

    1. Transformational Sentence Grammars   *33*
    2. Sequencing Operations   *39*

III. **Conceptual Connectivity** 60

    1. Meaning and Philosophy   *60*
    2. Meaning as Feature Clusters   *63*
    3. Meaning as Process   *65*
    4. Building the Text-World Model   *77*

IV. Informativity **103**

    1. Modifying Information Theory *103*
    2. Apperceptual Informativity *114*
    3. Informativity within the Sentence *118*
    4. A Newspaper Article *126*

V. Textual Efficiency **132**

    1. Motives for Efficiency *132*
    2. Recurrence *134*
    3. Definiteness *137*
    4. Co-Reference via Pro-Forms *144*
    5. Exophoric Reference *151*
    6. Ellipsis *155*
    7. Junction *159*

VI. Frames, Schemas, Plans, and Scripts **163**

    1. Global Perspectives on Knowledge *163*
    2. Frame Attachment *169*
    3. Schema Attachment *171*
    4. Plan Attachment *177*

VII. Further Issues in Text Processes **195**

    1. Text Types *195*
    2. The Production of Texts *200*
    3. Recalling Textual Content *220*

VIII. Conversation and Narration **242**

    1. Conversation *242*
    2. Narration *254*

IX. Applications for a Science of Texts **277**

    1. The Educational Enterprise *277*
    2. Traditional Grammar Versus Applied Linguistics *281*
    3. The Teaching of Reading *283*
    4. The Teaching of Writing *285*
    5. The Teaching of Foreign Languages *288*
    6. Translation Studies *290*
    7. Literary Studies *292*
    8. A Final Word *293*

X. Appendix **295**

References *298*
Table of Abbreviations *327*
Index of Names *329*
Index of Terms and Concepts *338*

Preface to the Series

Roy Freedle
Series Editor

This series of volumes provides a forum for the cross-fertilization of ideas from a diverse number of disciplines, all of which share a common interest in discourse—be it prose comprehension and recall, dialogue analysis, text grammar construction, computer simulation of natural language, cross-cultural comparisons of communicative competence, or other related topics. The problems posed by multisentence contexts and the methods required to investigate them, while not always unique to discourse, are still sufficiently distinct as to benefit from the organized mode of scientific interaction made possible by this series.

Scholars working in the discourse area from the perspective of socio-linguistics, psycholinguistics, ethnomethodology and the sociology of language, educational psychology (e.g., teacher–student interaction), the philosophy of language, computational linguistics, and related subareas are invited to submit manuscripts of monograph or book length to the series editor. Edited collections of original papers resulting from conferences will also be considered.

Volumes in the Series

Vol. I. Discourse production and comprehension. Roy O. Freedle (Ed.), 1977.

Vol. II. New directions in discourse processing. Roy O. Freedle (Ed.), 1979.

Vol. III. The pear stories: Cognitive, cultural, and linguistic aspects of narrative production. Wallace L. Chafe (Ed.), 1980.

Vol. IV. Text, Discourse, and Process: Toward a Multidisciplinary Science of Texts. Robert de Beaugrande, 1980.

Acknowledgments

This book has demonstrated, to my own satisfaction at least, the truth of my argument in Chapter VII.2.7 that text production is a process with no built-in point of completion. Sooner or later, the text producer is satisfied and terminates the process. I cannot enumerate the total number of versions the book, or parts of it, underwent in almost three years of constant work. But I can express my gratitude to those whose expertise, advice, and assistance guided my travels through this vast and often poorly mapped territory. I profited immensely from the chance to discuss various issues with Alan Baddeley, Bill Brewer, Jaime Carbonnel Jr., Wallace Chafe, Phil Cohen, Nick Colby, Max Cresswell, Teun van Dijk, Wolfgang Dressler, Charles Fillmore, Ken and Yetta Goodman, Paul Grice, Norbert Groeben, Peter Hartmann, Roland Harweg, Don Hirsch, Hans Hörmann, Wolfgang Iser, Walter Kintsch, Walter A. Koch, Bill Mann, Jim Meehan, Dieter Metzing, Bonnie Meyer, Maria Nowakowska, Barbara Partee, Dany Paul, János Petöfi, Wolfgang Prinz, Hannes Rieser, Roland Posner, Gert Rickheit, Siegfried J. Schmidt, Bob Shafer, Bob Simmons, Berhard Sowarka, Paul Weingartner, Harald Weinrich, Manfred Wettler, and Bill Woods. Professors Dressler, Hartmann, and Petöfi studied and commented on the entire penultimate version I circulated as a mimeograph. Special thanks are due to Mike Smith for bitching at me to replace my old numbering with mnemonic labels for my networks; and to Genevieve Miller and Zofia Solczak for discovering and eradicating thousands of typographical errors and inconsistencies in the manuscript (my own processing resources do not extend to accurate typing). Vivian Felix prepared the index of names. My chairpersons Dave Benseler of Ohio State and Ward Hellstrom and Mel New of the University of Florida were very considerate in not loading my teaching schedule. And finally, I learned immeasurably from the discussions following my guest lectures at the departments and institutes of Linguistics, Psychology, Communication Science, Education, and Computer Science in the Universities of Arizona, Berlin, Bielefeld, Bochum, Colorado, Florida, Munich, Saarbrücken, Texas, Trier, and Vienna.

0. Evolution and Development

1. Late in 1976, I embarked on the production of a new "introduction to text linguistics" in co-operation with Wolfgang Dressler, whose (1972a) introduction had been well received. I gradually came to appreciate the peculiar nature of the task: introducing people to a field which had not in fact been constituted and consolidated as a field at all. Professor Dressler's solution had been to extend the usual linguistic methodology to the domain of texts. But this approach seems too narrow from the perspective of 1980. It is now fairly clear that we cannot treat texts simply as units larger than sentences, or as sequences of sentences. The prime characteristic of texts is rather their *occurrence in communication,* and they might consist of a single word, a sentence, a set of fragments, or a mixture of surface structures. It follows that extending sentence studies to texts must miss a number of vital issues and raise serious empirical problems (cf. Beaugrande 1979k).

2. The present volume is the outcome of my attempts to define and lay out the field of text studies from the standpoint of *human activities.* I have essayed to integrate relevant research from such disciplines as cognitive psychology, sociology of language, and computer science (with its offshoot domain of artificial intelligence). The requirement of such a large-scale synthesis may have led me to make some unexpected uses of available research.[1] I must take full responsibility for the proposals and conclusions drawn here.

3. I can provide here only a bare outline of the evolution of text linguistics (for more details: cf. Petöfi 1971a; Dressler 1972a; Hartmann 1972, 1975;

---

[1] I use "cf." to cover many instances of citing the approximate ideas of research contributions.

Fries 1972; Schmidt 1973; Dressler & Schmidt [eds.] 1973; Kallmeyer, Klein, Meyer-Hermann, Netzer, & Siebert, 1974; Harweg 1974; Gülich & Raible 1977; Rieser 1978; Beaugrande & Dressler 1980). I would identify three main phases of the field with indistinct chronological boundaries (for a different division, see Rieser 1976). In the earliest phase, lasting into the later 1960's, we find only a few astute proposals that the text or the discourse ought to be the main object of linguistic study (e.g. Ingarden 1931; Bühler 1934; Hjelmslev 1943; Harris 1952; Pike 1954;[2] Coseriu 1955-56; Uldall 1957; Karlsen 1959; Slama-Cazacu 1961; Hartmann 1964; Weinrich 1966a). These arguments did not affect the mainstream of conventional linguistics, doubtless because the available methodologies pointed in contrary directions.The preoccupation with minimal units or isolated sentences naturally distracts from the study of whole texts.

4. Around 1968, linguists working mostly independently of each other converged on the notion of "linguistics beyond the sentence" (e.g. Heidolph 1966; Pike 1967; Crymes 1968; Dik 1968; Harweg 1968a; Hasan 1968; Palek 1968; Isenberg 1971; Koch 1971).[3] Attention focused on issues that could be stated in terms of sentence linguistics, but not satisfactorily resolved. The tendency was naturally to look at texts as sentence sequences (e.g. Waterhouse 1963; Harper 1965; Heidolph 1966; Wheeler 1967; Harper & Su 1969; Isenberg 1971). However, it has been pointed out later on that this perspective allows us to see only a fraction of the interesting properties of texts (cf. van Dijk 1972a: v; Harweg 1974: 100f.; Kintsch 1974: 79; Weinrich 1976: 148; van Dijk 1977a: 3). The greatest obstacle is that the *unity* of the text is left obscure.

5. The year 1968 also witnessed the rise of dissension among representatives of the then dominant "transformational" paradigm. It became evident that even the restricted range of issues under consideration could not be conclusively encompassed with the prevailing methodology. The counter-movements of "case grammar" (Fillmore 1968) and "generative semantics" (Lakoff 1968a, 1968b, 1968c; McCawley 1968a, 1968b) attested to the dissatisfaction with the usual treatment of meaning in grammar. But the basic tenets were retained. As Howard Maclay (1971: 178) remarks, the whole debate was carried on in terms of the general assumptions of Chomskian linguistics. The point of contention was the "autonomy" of syntax and its corollary of a syntactic "deep structure" (cf. II.1.17). But many other key issues, such as the expansion of study from sentences to texts, were hardly raised. For this reason, the situation has remained unsettled. A growing awareness of the inadequacies of transformational grammar has not led to

---

[2]Pike (1954) is now a part of Pike (1967).

[3]Isenberg (1971) is a revision of a paper originally published in *Replik* 2, 1968. Koch (1971) is a habilitation dissertation which was essentially complete as early as 1966.

anything but continual revisions, which try to preserve as much of the old theory as possible (e.g. the "extended standard theory"). Rumblings of discontent have become too noticeable to be overlooked. Robert P. Stockwell (1977: 196) concludes a book on transformational syntax with the ominous observation that "scholars will cling tenaciously to an explanation, or a principle, or a 'law' that they know to be wrong, because they do not have in hand an alternative explanation."

6. The year 1972 ushered in a new stage of research toward *alternative* theories of language rather than toward revisions of older theories. The new works were manifestly critical of the foundations of sentence grammars, leading to proposals for new departures (cf. Petöfi 1971a; van Dijk 1972a; Dressler 1972a; Gindin 1972; Kuno 1972; Schmidt 1973). Sociologists voiced their opposition to the context-free abstractness of older methods, and pointed out the importance of social interaction in language groups (cf. Gumperz & Hymes [eds.] 1972; Labov 1972a, 1972b). Computer scientists faced the exigencies of simulating human language processes on the computer (cf. Woods 1970; Simmons & Slocum 1971; Charniak 1972; Collins & Quillian 1972; Winograd 1972; Schank & K. Colby [eds.] 1973). Psychologists embarked on studies of memory (cf. Kintsch 1972; Tulving & Donaldson [eds.] 1972; Kintsch & Keenan 1973) that would eventually lead to concern for texts (cf. Kintsch 1974; Frederiksen 1975; Meyer 1975). This interdisciplinary demand for theories and models has been a major impetus in the development of text linguistics. It is clear that these disciplines want to do more than describe the structures of sentences; they are concerned with the *processes* by which language is *utilized by human beings.* My own discussions in this volume are intended to reflect this trend.

7. It would be distracting to offer a historical survey of individual projects and proposals, because it would remain unclear how all these might fit together. I recommend consulting surveys of this kind, however. For text linguistics proper, Dressler (1972a), Fries (1972), Schmidt (1973), Dressler & Schmidt (eds.) (1973), Kallmeyer et al. (1974), Harweg (1974, 1978), Hartmann (1975), Coulthard (1977), Gülich and Raible (1977), Jones (1977), Dressler (ed.) (1978), Gindin (1978), Grosse (1978), Kuno (1978), Nöth (1978), Rieser (1978), Beaugrande (1980a), and Beaugrande and Dressler (1980) can be consulted. For the psychology of language, I recommend Kintsch (1974, 1977a), Hörmann (1976, 1977), G. Loftus and E. Loftus (1976), H. Clark and E. Clark (1977), Freedle (ed.) (1977, 1979), Rosenberg (ed.) (1977). On language sociology, see Gumperz and Hymes (eds.) (1972), Dittmar (1976), and Viereck (ed.) (1976). On computer simulation of natural language processing, I recommend Schank and Colby (eds.) (1973), Minsky and Papert (1974), Bobrow and Collins (eds.) (1975), Charniak and Wilks (eds.) (1976), Goldstein and Papert (1977), Rumelhart (1977a), Wilks (1977b), Winston (1977), Walker (ed.) (1978), Findler (ed.) (1979), and the

proceedings of *TINLAP-2*. On philosophy and language, one can consult Cresswell (1973), Grewendorf and Meggle (eds.) (1974), Rüttenauer (ed.) (1974), and van Dijk (ed.) (1976).

8. In order to encompass the field at all, I was obliged to postpone or exclude some major research trends. I did not deal with the elaborate methodology of Hans Glinz (1952, 1973). I could not determine the role of "deconstructionist" work as exemplified by Jacques Derrida (1967a, 1967b, 1972, 1974) (a critical survey is found in Hempfer 1976). I could not go into the "universal grammar" derived from the writings of the late Richard Montague (1974) (an outline is presented in Löbner 1976).

9. Two further deficiencies must be mentioned. First, I restricted my explorations to English to avoid creating difficulties for readers who are not linguists. Many intriguing aspects of textuality in other languages, some of which are totally different from English in their organization, are discussed in Grimes (1975), Li (ed.) (1976), Longacre (1976), and Grimes (ed.) (1978). Second, I have not dealt in any concerted way with the undeniably crucial role of *text intonation* (cf. Halliday 1967c; Lehiste 1970; Brazil 1975). I surmise that text intonation would require the introduction of at least two further levels of networks. One would reflect the progression of intonation curves (cf. Halliday 1967c; Brazil 1975; Takefuta 1975). The other would capture the stress markings that arise from the need to show priorities of knowledge or contrasts (cf. Chafe 1976). I hope to return to these issues in later work, but for the time being, I have been experimenting and analyzing mostly with regard to written texts.

10. Today, text research is in progress literally all around the world. It is prominently represented in the appropriate faculties and departments of the Universities of Bielefeld, Konstanz, Amsterdam, and Bochum, with further chairs elsewhere (e.g. West Berlin, Abo Academy). Extensive contributions to "discourse analysis" have been forthcoming from the Cornell group directed by Joseph Grimes, the Lancaster group headed by John Sinclair, and the Summer Institute of Linguistics guided by Kenneth Pike and Robert Longacre. Text processing is being studied in the psychology departments of such institutions as the Universities of Colorado, Stanford, California (La Jolla), Illinois, Yale, Cambridge, and Carnegie-Mellon; in the computer science departments of such institutions as the Universities of Texas, Toronto, Massachusetts Institute of Technology, Yale, Carnegie–Mellon, Rochester, Southern California, California (Berkeley), California (Los Angeles), Illinois, Maryland, and Stanford. The work carried on at the Stanford Research Institute, the Xerox Palo Alto Research Center, the Center for the Study of Reading, and Bolt, Beranek, and Newman Inc. has been extremely enlightening.

11. The diversities among these various schools, and those between their work and the older methods of linguistics, should not imply that we do not all share a commitment to the joint scientific enterprise of exploring human

language. I would look to the conviction eminently expressed by Roman Jakobson (1973: 12):

> Like any age of innovative experimentation, the present stage of reflections on language has been marked by intensive contentions and tumultous controversies. Yet a careful, unprejudiced examination of all these sectarian creeds and vehement polemics reveals an essentially monolithic whole behind the striking divergencies in terms, slogans, and technical contrivances.

ROBERT DE BEAUGRANDE
University of Florida

I

Basic Issues

1. SYSTEMS AND MODELS

1.1 In many countries, the increasingly prominent role of text linguistics in the discipline of language study appears to signal a "paradigm shift" in the sense of Thomas Kuhn (1970). The older preoccupation with demonstration sentences isolated from communicative contexts is yielding to a new concern for the *naturally occurring manifestation* of language: the TEXT. Language occurrences may have the surface format of single words or sentences, but they occur *as texts:* meaningful configurations of language intended to communicate. The implications of this shift of investigation are far-reaching indeed. We are not simply moving from the exploration of shorter toward longer language samples. We are also replacing an emphasis on abstract forms with an interest in the UTILIZATION PROCESSES of language (cf. Hörmann 1976; H. Clark & E. Clark 1977).

1.2 The traditional restrictive confines of linguistics are gradually giving way to concerted interaction with other language-related disciplines: psychology, sociology, philosophy, computer science, semiotics, cybernetics, education, and literary studies. Unless linguistics is to disappear as a separate field (envisioned by Yngve 1969), it should become the pivotal science of discourse and communication envisioned by so many astute researchers (e.g., Lévi-Strauss 1958: 37; Dundes 1962: 96; Hymes 1962: 9; Piaget 1966: 25; Hartmann 1970: 53; Maclay 1971: 180f.; Jakobson 1973; Koch 1973/74: xi). The broad usefulness and applicability of linguistic theories and methods would then figure as a prominent goal and not, as in past times, an incidental by-product, or even a misunderstanding.

1

1.3 In this wide framework, text linguistics would constitute the *verbal domain of semiotics,* dealing with the entire range from one-word texts (e.g., 'Fire!')[1] to texts as vast as *The Divine Comedy.* The decisive trait of the text is its OCCURRENCE IN COMMUNICATION (Hartmann 1964), where it is produced by a single participant within some temporal limits (cf. Weinrich 1976: 187). A set of mutually relevant texts can be said to constitute DISCOURSE,[2] a progression of occurrences that may be continued at a later time (cf. van Dijk 1977a). The total constellation of mutually relevant discourses in a group or society can be called a UNIVERSE OF DISCOURSE (cf. Coseriu 1955-56; Pike 1967: 596; van Dijk 1977a: 127).

1.4 Human language is so complex in its organization and so diverse in its manifestations that the science of linguistics naturally remains in continual evolution. The linguist faces a formidable overabundance of data ranging from observable, face-to-face speaking to abstruse mathematical and philosophical speculations on language. In its early stages, linguistics was compelled to be highly selective and reductive in its treatment (Uhlenbeck 1973: 107; Grimes 1975: 3). Continued progress has rendered much of this attitude superfluous, though debates over admissible issues still rage. As our scope expands, we approach the time when linguistics may be able to meet the demands that society imposes upon a science of language (cf. Hartmann 1970).

1.5 However much data a researcher may gather and evaluate, data can be significant only with respect to the COGNITIVE INTERESTS of a discipline (cf. Kuhn 1970; Schmidt 1975): commitments to seeking certain kinds of knowledge. Especially in linguistics, what constitutes worthwhile data, or how data should be treated, is by no means self-evident. The cognitive interests expressed in this volume are devoted to texts as vehicles of HUMAN ACTIVITIES—a notion already envisioned by many founders of linguistics (e.g. Malinowski 1923; Jespersen 1924; Bühler 1934).

1.6 Using a term made current by Carl Hempel (quoted in Stegmüller 1969: 205), we can define the scientific treatment of data as SYSTEMIZA-TION: the imposition of a system upon obtainable evidence. A SYSTEM is considered to be a unity of mutually relevant ELEMENTS[3] whose FUNCTIONS are determined by their respective contributions to the workings of the whole. To account for data, researchers build a

---

[1] Throughout the book, I enclose linguistic samples cited within the running text in *single* quotes; punctuation is included inside only if part of the sample.

[2] The term "discourse analysis" has been variously used for beyond-the-sentence linguistics in general (Harris 1952) and for the study of conversation in particular (Coulthard 1977). In my scheme, both of those domains are only parts of a science of texts as actual communicative occurrences.

[3] I use the term "element" for any item whose occurrence or use is governed by SYSTEMIC (pertaining to a system) principles.

SYSTEMIC MODEL whose operations might yield such data (on the notion of the model, see Hartmann 1965; Gülich & Raible 1977). The correlation of the model with an empirical domain is regulated by BRIDGE PRINCIPLES (Hempel 1966) that state the degree of APPROXIMATION between the model and the domain (cf. Apostel 1961). Ideally, scientific progress continually reduces the degree of approximation and makes the model a more exact representation. However, the object of study may itself be FUZZY: characterized by structures and operations that are probabilistic and not exhaustively delimited. Such is the case with natural language communication.

1.7 The view of language as a system is well established (see for instance Saussure 1916; Weinreich 1954; Firth 1957; Halliday 1967a, 1969; Heger 1971; Labov 1971; Winograd 1972; Berry 1977; Clark & Clark 1977; van Dijk 1977a). The systems approach implies cognitive interest in the DYNAMICS of an entity (Hartmann 1963a, 1963b), such as CONTROL and INTERACTION among elements. Systems theory, which has become a discipline in its own right (cf. Boulding 1956; Bertalanffy 1962; Buckley [ed.] 1968), has found acceptance in research areas as diverse as psychology, sociology, behavioral science, design engineering, information science, computer science, factor analysis, thermodynamics, mathematical topology, and many more. The prevalence of the systems approach is heuristically enriching in allowing models to be shared and borrowed among disciplines. Of course, borrowed models have crucial effects upon research methods, and must be applied with caution.

1.8 Language is initially given as a MANIFESTATION: an occurrence or set of occurrences at least partly accessible to apperception (cf. Stegmüller 1969: 93). The observable aspects interact with non-observable ones in intricate and diverse ways. The total picture of a language must be gradually assembled via a sequence of systemizing tasks, for example:

1.8.1 IDENTIFYING a manifestation, its constituents, or its environment;

1.8.2 GENERALIZING about related or relevant manifestations;

1.8.3 DESCRIBING a set of manifestations methodically;

1.8.4 EXPLAINING the existence or occurrence of manifestations;

1.8.5 PREDICTING manifestations under statable conditions;

1.8.6 RECONSTRUCTING artificial correlates of the manifestations;

1.8.7 MANAGING the occurrence of manifestations.

1.9 This list of tasks is arranged in what I consider the order of increasing difficulty. Accomplishment of a given task presupposes prior achievement of those above it. In practice, however, we must often work provisionally without these prerequisites. For example, public education may require the management of language in absence of any thorough explanatory or predictive account.

1.10 In order to establish itself as a discipline, linguistics initially dissociated itself from the managerial ambitions of traditional grammar and sought to develop some objective, reliable tools for the more basic tasks of identification, generalization, and description. This early phase, usually entitled "descriptive linguistics," attained a sufficiently rigorous methodology to uncover the grammars of numerous hitherto unrecorded languages, even with no prior knowledge of their structure (especially via the "tagmemics" developed by Kenneth Pike [1967] and Robert E. Longacre [1964]). Emphasis was understandably placed upon the language aspects most accessible to observation: sounds, forms, and arrangements of utterances. The treatment of non-observable aspects, such as communicative strategies or psychological processes,[4] was informal and intuitive. Communication as a human activity was not viewed as a major object of study in its own right.

1.11 The "generative" approach to language study embarked on the more arduous tasks of explanation, prediction, and reconstruction (beginning with Hjelmslev 1943; compare Chomsky 1957). Generativists borrowed heavily on formal logic to build an idealized model of human language with severe restrictions on the object of study. The divergences between their model and the real data were sufficiently strong in some domains to cause an apparent antagonism between "model-oriented" and "data-oriented" studies (Liefrink 1973). However, the expansion of linguistics to new tasks remains an enduring contribution of the generative approach (cf. Dingwall 1971).

1.12 If models mediate between what we can apperceive and what we want to explain (motto attributed to Anaxagoras by Gülich & Raible 1977: 14; cf. Wagner 1974: 150), then the following situations would justify reliance on models (adapted from Apostel 1961):

1.12.1 when no known theory exists for a domain;

1.12.2 when a theory is known, but too complex to allow solving problems with currently available techniques;

1.12.3 when a theory is known and partly confirmed, but still incomplete;

1.12.4 when new research permits the correlation or integration of two or more known theories;

1.12.5 when the objects of investigation are too large, too small, too remote, or too arduous to allow direct observation and experimentation.

1.13 All of these situations obtain to some degree in linguistics:

1.13.1 Some areas are still without a workable theory, such as the interface of language with emotional states of communicative participants.

---

[4]Peter Hartmann (personal communication) comments that the notion of "observation" in these early discussions was somewhat out of place. The *actualization* of communicative strategies guarantees the potential for *objective* study, whether or not we are looking directly at the data in its most detailed form.

1.13.2 Some theories are available, such as Montague's (1974) grammar, but are too intricate to be useful in solving empirical language problems, at least with current technology.

1.13.3 The "generative" approach to language remains incomplete until it can explain how texts are actually produced and understood by humans.

1.13.4 Research on texts demands the integration of theories from many areas: sentence grammar, philosophy, computation, cognition, planning, and action.

1.13.5 Some aspects of language are too large (e.g. the totality of discourse in a whole society), too small (micro-impulses of nerve cells during language processing), too remote (storage of knowledge in the mind) or too arduous (relating every minimal feature of utterances to its social, psychological, and historical evolution) to be pursued in direct experimentation.

1.14 To sort out the regularities of language from the accidental details, one can distinguish between the SYSTEMIC aspects of language, styled "langue" or "competence," and the seemingly accidental or irrelevant aspects, designated "parole" or "performance." During the evolution of the discipline, the borderline between the two aspects shifts as domains once thought to be fortuitous are discovered to have a systemic nature after all. For instance, the sentence was assigned to "parole" by Saussure (1916: 172), only to become the primary entity of "competence" in transformational grammar since Chomsky (1957). I shall argue in I.5 that "textual competence" encompasses a markedly different domain from sentence competence (cf. also IV.1.24).

1.15 The respective limits of "langue" or "competence" influence and are influenced by the models and methods in use. Descriptivists broke down their sample evidence by extracting LEVELS of MINIMAL UNITS to be classified into a TAXONOMY: a scheme for sorting elements by distinctive features. If each level of minimal units was thought to be a system of mutual oppositions, the entire repertory of each system had to be exhaustively assembled, for example sounds (phonology) and forms (morphology); exhaustive treatment of meanings or situations was deemed impossible, and those domains were set aside. Later, the generativists preferred to begin at the other end with a GRAMMAR as a set of rules stipulating what does or does not belong to the language. The problem of exhaustiveness was suspended by postulating that all complex entities (however many there might be) could be derived from a limited set of simple ones (kernels) by using the proper rules. The rules were designed so as to produce an *infinite* set of sentences.

1.16 The generative approach is vastly more ambitious than the descriptive one, since it must not only systemize all occurrences: it must also preclude all non-occurrences (McCawley 1976). Strictly speaking, it is not a grammar of occurrences at all, because it professes to deal only with abstract potential. The empirical verification of such a grammar can be a major difficulty.

Outside the relatively small range of obvious, uncontroversial cases, people have trouble judging which utterances their native language should allow (cf. Labov 1966; Lakoff 1969; Carden 1970; Heringer 1970; Wedge & Ingemann 1970; Ringen 1975). Grammaticalness judgments are supposed to apply only to structure, not to context. But structures never occur naturally without context, and language users therefore do not possess the expertise needed to make consistent judgments. Informants are, in reality, trying to imagine possible contexts for each sample (Uhlenbeck 1973: 42; McCawley 1976: 155; van Dijk 1977c; Snow & Meijer 1977). The designation of "grammatical" is awarded to *banal* sentences whose occurrence is easy to imagine for everyone (Householder 1960: 340). For less banal cases, opinions are unstable and inconsistent. Heringer (1970) found that providing a context for such a simple sentence as 'John left until 6 P.M.' elicited a change in people's grammaticalness judgments of no less than 40%! People are still less able to decide about elaborate utterances, such as those which Robinson (1975: 141ff.) contests against Chomsky (1972).

1.17 The lack of empirical verification procedures for large sections of a language theory can lead to disquieting tactics (cf. Beaugrande 1979k):

1.17.1 *Circularity of proof:* the correct rules are those which generate only grammatical sentences; grammatical sentences are those generated by the rules (cf. critique in Dik 1967; Uhlenbeck 1973).

1.17.2 *Intuitions:* the linguist presents demonstration sentences which are (in his or her own intuition) grammatical or ungrammatical (criticism in Dik 1967: 372; J. Anderson 1976: 69; Schlesinger 1977: 210). The linguist becomes the informant and is free to exclude unfavorable examples at will (cf. Rieser 1978: 8), thus sacrificing both objectivity and generality.

1.17.3 *Appeals to the competence/performance distinction:* all data that the theory cannot treat are shunted off into the domain of "performance" and excluded from consideration as non-issues (criticism in van Dijk 1972a: 314). An egregious and anachronistic illustration is Dresher and Hornstein's (1976: 328) claim that "a study of competence abstracts away from the whole question of performance, which deals with problems of how language is processed in real time, why speakers say what they say, how language is used in various social groups, how it is used in communication, etc." A language user without all of that knowledge could be called "competent" only by a bizarre perversion of the whole notion in its commonsense usage.

1.18 If a language model can do no more than assign structural descriptions to sentences, then it deserves the old designation "structural descriptive linguistics" rather than "generative." To earn the latter designation, the model should suggest how utterances might actually *evolve* (J. Anderson 1976: 118; Simmons 1978: 2). Only then can we reasonably conduct empirical tests and agree on rational standards for evaluating, verifying, and accepting one account of language over any other.

2.   LEVELS IN MODELS OF LANGUAGE

2.1 A spoken or written text in English could appear to be or to consist of various things. One observer might notice a stream of sounds or forms following each other in the real time of speaking or of moving from left to right on a page. Another might notice that the text is intended to embody knowledge and meaning. Still another might notice that the text could be a vehicle for someone to get something done or to reach a goal. Each of these observers would be apperceiving a single, simultaneous aspect of the text: one of its LEVELS.[5] It seems reasonable that language science should attempt to extract and systemize these levels as a proper domain of investigation.

2.2 In its early phases, linguistics proceeded on the assumption that levels should be systemized independently of each other (e.g., Trager 1950). That outlook seemed to be successful for the description of sounds, though, as Kenneth Pike (1967: 362f.) notes, it was not fully upheld even by its defenders. Later, acute problems emerged when the borderline between morphology and syntax came into view. A distinction was drawn between the *paradigmatic* aspect that determined what items might fill a slot, and the *syntagmatic* aspect that determined the sequence of slots themselves.

2.3 The independence of syntax from meaning was maintained with considerable vigor (cf. Harris 1951; Chomsky 1957). Harris himself did find it expedient to use meaning as a short-cut for analyzing language, provided that a purely formal analysis of the *distribution* of language items would arrive at the same result. Harris, in effect, postulated that an item's meaning is the sum of all positions it can occupy in usage. This postulate is not in itself unreasonable, but for a model of either linguistic analysis or human language activities, it is unworkable. Meaning would remain undiscoverable until we had catalogued all distributions of a given item.

2.4 Rather than upholding the separation of syntax from meaning, Harris' postulate tends to suspend it. Meaning and syntax must interact in order for language items to have a given distribution. I shall argue, however, that we should go further and investigate the PROBABILITY of occurrences in systematic environments. The "well-formedness" (i.e., conformity with the grammar) of language sequences is not, taken by itself, a sufficient principle (cf. II.2.36ff.; IV.1.24).

2.5 Although reaffirming the independence of syntax from meaning, Chomsky's (1957) "transformational grammar" sought to escape the unworkability of Harris' postulate of distribution. Instead of analyzing the distributions of language items as such, Chomsky undertook to set up an

---

[5]The term "level" has been used indiscriminately in the past, often being conflated with such notions as "rank." I consider a "level" to be the total aspect of a participating language system; a "rank" is a unit of a given dimension in a hierarchy of size (e.g. word, sentence, etc.).

abstract rule system which could *produce* all allowable distributions of a language. Attention was transferred from the analysis of extensive samples toward the construction of rules. In essence, this transfer did not simplify linguistic research. Every counter-example to the previous rules called for new rules—a factor making the transformational model immune to falsification as a theory.

2.6 In semiotics, it is traditional to subsume all aspects of *formal arrangement* under the notion of SYNTAX, and all aspects of *meaning* under that of SEMANTICS; the *use* of language was subsumed under PRAGMATICS. To deal with an entire language, the "transformational" approach began with an autonomous set of syntactic rules; semantics was treated as an after-the-fact "interpretation" of syntactically produced strings. In some models, pragmatics was simply added as a further phase of "interpretation." Such an approach was obliged either to ignore the interaction of these three factors in the actual production and comprehension of utterances, or to reconstruct them all in terms of arbitrary syntactic rules. An alternative account in which meaning was given the key role from the outset was introduced as "generative semantics" (see. II.1.6). Quite aside from the detailed issues of rule constructing, this controversy pointed up a basic question concerning the building of language models. I shall examine the question here from a systems-oriented viewpoint.

2.7 In systems theory, we can distinguish the approaches of MODULARITY and INTERACTION (cf. Sussman 1973: 12f.; Winograd 1975: 192). The reliance upon formal logic and mathematics in generative grammar fosters modularity, in which system components are substantially independent, and operations are cumbersome (cf. Levesque & Mylopoulos 1978: 2). My outlook here will be directed toward interaction, without which the utilization of text would simply not be operational (cf. II.1; Walker [ed.] 1978).

2.8 Imagine for a moment a different kind of language model. We might start out with these two well-known levels:

2.8.1 SYNTAX PROPER is concerned with the abstract patterns and sequences which the grammar of a language stipulates independently of context.

2.8.2 SEMANTICS PROPER is concerned with "the relations between signs or symbols and what they denote or mean" (Woods 1975: 41). The repertory of signs and symbols with a statement of their meanings is contained in the LEXICON. If lexical items are defined according to their content, we have INTENSIONAL MEANING (e.g. 'blue is the color lying in the spectrum between green and violet'); if items are defined by their REFERENCE to entities, we have EXTENSIONAL MEANING (e.g. 'blue is the property shared by all blue things in the world'). The standards for judging the correctness of statements about some world and for combining statements in that perspective are set forth as TRUTH CONDITIONS. The extent to which a reference encompasses an object or class of objects is the issue of QUANTIFICATION (e.g. 'every person' or 'all persons'). The probability or necessity of a statement regarding some world is its MODALITY.

2.9 In the above definitions, syntax and semantics proper are indeed independent of each other. Formal sequences can be envisioned before deciding what specific lexical items might fit into them; and lexical meaning need not commit an expression to appearing in a given slot of a sequence. Yet no utterance could ever be produced without making these decisions and commitments, and none could be understood without recovering them. It follows that syntax proper and semantics proper as previously set forth are components of logical languages, *but not of natural languages in use*. Instead, let us envision two different levels of language use:

2.9.1 The SEMANTICS OF SYNTAX is concerned with how people utilize formal patterns and sequences to apply, convey, and recover knowledge and meaning. For example, noticing a noun–verb sequence might give rise to an expectation that an agent and an action are being expressed (cf. III.4.16.1).

2.9.2 The SYNTAX OF SEMANTICS is concerned with how concepts like agent, action, state, attribute, etc. are connected to yield the total meaning of a text. Semantics of syntax has a more predominant linear or sequential organization than does syntax of semantics. For instance, an action might be linked to an agent, a time, a location, a cause, and so on, while various linear arrangements would be possible for expression (cf. VII.2) (on grammars without fixed linearity, cf. Petöfi 1972).

2.10 These interfaced levels are not wholly novel here (compare Ihwe 1972: 339; Schank 1975b: 14f; Rieser 1976: 13). Their function is to co-ordinate operations people perform when utilizing meaning in connected utterances. I shall develop this direction by pursuing the notions of SEQUENTIAL CONNECTIVITY: how elements are arranged in the surface text; and CONCEPTUAL CONNECTIVITY: how underlying concepts and relations are put together.[6] The interaction of these two is controlled by MAPPING PROCEDURES (cf. Goldman, Balzer, & Wile 1977). The characteristic mapping procedures selected to produce a text yield the STYLE of the text.

2.11 When each language level is systemized, the entire language appears as an INTERSYSTEM the workings of which depend on the interaction of participating systems (cf. Halliday 1969; Berry 1977; Dressler 1979). Each system has INTERNAL CONTROLS that regulate the availability of options and the allowability of combinations; and EXTERNAL

---

[6]Compare the notion of "sense constancy" in Hörmann 1976, ch. 7.

CONTROLS which regulate that system's interaction with other systems.[7] Both kinds are indispensable to the production and utilization of texts, but external controls have received little attention in conventional linguistics.

2.12 Issues of control were largely assigned to the poorly explored domain of pragmatics, dealing with language use. In that line of reasoning, pragmatics becomes "meta-syntax" and "meta-semantics," that is, the self-awareness of decisions about arrangement and meaning. However, in order to attain a workable design, each system should have at least its own essential controls built right into it. Pragmatics is properly the domain of the human activities of PLANNING texts as vehicles of PURPOSIVE ACTIONS directed toward GOALS (Beaugrande 1979b). The theory of texts accordingly requires a different triad of domains than the old semiotic scheme:

SYNTAX → SEQUENTIAL CONNECTIVITY
SEMANTICS → CONCEPTUAL CONNECTIVITY
PRAGMATICS → ACTIONS, PLANS, GOALS

Each domain is subject to relevant controls during communication. The discrete items occur within a CONTINUITY which arises from the DIRECTIONALITY of CONTROL FLOW. Accordingly, we need a dynamic outlook for investigating not only the presence of structures in texts, but also the operations that can create, build, and utilize structures (cf. Hartmann 1963a; Mukařovský 1967: 11; Woods 1970; Winograd 1972; Koch 1976). If we define STRUCTURE as *a relation between at least two systemic elements in occurrence,* it is clear that a theory of language use should be centered upon the notion of CONNECTIVITY.

3.   TEXT VERSUS SENTENCE

3.1 Nearly all accounts of language structure set forth since classical antiquity have relied decisively on the notion of the SENTENCE. It is disquieting that this basic entity has been vaguely and inconsistently defined, even up to the present (O'Connell 1977; Glinz 1979). Different criteria for sentencehood have persisted without being explicitly recognized as divisive

---

[7]In his general systems theory, Luhmann (1970) stipulates that every system must have a "differentiation of internal and external," i.e. be distinguishable from its environment. Linguistics has been concerned with differentiating sets of system elements at the expense of operations, functions, and controls. As J. Anderson (1976: 80) notes, control has hardly been studied in cognitive theories.

rather than unifying standards, for example: (1) the expression of a "complete thought" (see Ivić 1965: 20); (2) a sequence of speech units followed by a pause (see Gardiner 1932: 207; Goldman-Eisler 1972); (3) a structural pattern with specified formal constituents (cf. Harris 1951; C. Fries 1952; Chomsky 1957). The functional implications of each of these criteria are radically distinct from the others. Empirical research makes it plain that people disagree with each other's judgments about what constitutes a sentence. When speech pauses were consulted, "many segments identified by this study as sentences would not be considered separate sentences by other criteria" (Broen 1971: 30). A still graver problem is that the boundaries of utterances are often marked by non-linguistic signals (Hörmann 1976: 329).

3.2 As O'Connell (1977) notes, linguists usually accept the sentence as a basic entity a priori, thus bypassing the methodological difficulties. In transformational grammar, language is in principle defined as a set of sentences. Whatever is not found as a sentence (e.g. a mere noun [Lees 1960]), must be converted into one by transformations and derivations. The sentence was inconsistently treated not only as a grammatical pattern, but also, whenever occasion arose, as a logical statement. But this duality is a property of logical languages, not natural languages. Entities such as "argument" and "predicate" are definable in terms of *logic,* but "noun phrase" and "verb phrase" are purely *grammatical* entities.

3.3 It appears that linguists tended to confuse *optional mapping* with *obligatory mapping.* The sentence provides no more than a grammatical format into which semantic and pragmatic unities *can* be mapped; some linguists treated the sentence as the format into which these unities *must* be mapped. This practice undermined the proclaimed autonomy of syntax, because many attributes assigned to the sentence actually belong to semantic and pragmatic unities. Consequently, the question of how humans DECIDE what to map onto what could hardly be raised. We can readily observe that people can make a wide range of decisions about syntactic formatting (cf. VII.2). As long as linguistics presupposes the sentence at the outset, such facts are difficult to treat; the linguist is compelled to retreat into a remote, reductive version of "ideal competence." An impasse has arisen beyond which linguistic theory cannot advance, because the most basic concepts are short-circuited across each other, rendering many vital realities of communication inadmissible issues.

3.4 I assert that the multi-level entity of language must be the TEXT, composed of FRAGMENTS which may or may not be formatted as sentences. I would cite the following essential distinctions between text and sentence:

3.4.1 The text is an ACTUAL SYSTEM, while sentences are elements of a VIRTUAL SYSTEM, as I shall explain in I.4.1.

3.4.2 The sentence is a purely grammatical entity to be defined only on the level of SYNTAX. The text must be defined according to the complete standards of TEXTUALITY as elaborated in section I.4.[8]

3.4.3 In a text, the grammatical constraints imposed upon abstract sentence structures can be OVERIDDEN by context-dependent motivations.[9] For example, elements easily recoverable from a situation via sensory apperception can be omitted or truncated by the speaker without damaging the communicativity of the text. Grammaticality should be treated not as a law, but as a DEFAULT: a standard assumed in absence of specific indications; or as a PREFERENCE: a standard to be selected over others when various options are open (cf. the notions of "default" and "most likely case" in Collins, Brown, & Larkin 1977: 17; and "preference" in Wilks 1975b, 1978).

3.4.4 The distinction between "grammatical" and "non-grammatical" is a *binary opposition* if one has an accurate and complete sentence grammar (R. Lakoff 1977) (which is not the case so far): one decides if a given entity is a sentence by matching it against the sequences produceable by grammatical rules. But the distinction between a "text" and a "non-text" is not decided by any such mechanical checking. Texts are ACCEPTABLE or NON-ACCEPTABLE according to a complex *gradation,* not a binary opposition, and contextual motivations are always relevant. It is well known, for example, that some respected literary texts are and must be beyond the range of any reasonable grammar (cf. S. Levin 1962; Thorne 1969; van Dijk 1972a, 1972b) (cf. IX.7.1ff.). Since the text is defined on the basis of its actual occurrence, the notion of a 'non-text" is a marginal concern.[10] Linguists who deliberately set out to construct non-texts are no longer participating in communication, and thus are not likely to explain the normal workings of the latter.

3.4.5 A text must be relevant to a SITUATION of OCCURRENCE, in which a constellation of STRATEGIES, EXPECTATIONS, and KNOWLEDGE is active. This wide environment can be called CONTEXT; the internal structuring of the text constitutes the CO-TEXT (on this

---

[8]Hence, it is pointless to debate whether sentences can have meaning inside or outside contexts (Bever vs. Olson, cited in Kintsch 1974: 15). The meaning belongs in any case to the *sentence-formatted text;* the format is at most a means to provide certain signals about the configurations of meaning (cf. III.4.16ff.).

[9]The phenomenon of ELLIPSIS (cf. V.6) is a good demonstration.

[10]The use of *counter-examples,* many of them bizarre and contrived, has been exaggerated in linguistic arguments, doubtless due to the striving for a categorical (context-free) well-formedness grammar. Counter-examples do not overthrow important regularities of a language (Wilks 1975a); cf. the samples indexed in footnote 14.

distinction, see Petöfi 1971b, 1975a; Petöfi & Rieser 1974).[11] One can design sentences, on the other hand, that might never occur spontaneously, being too long, too complex, too heavily embedded, too trite or inane semantically, or too pointless pragmatically. The rules for abstract sentence formation alone cannot stipulate some maximum length or complexity beyond which a sequence ceases to be a sentence.[12]

3.4.6 A text cannot be fully treated as a configuration of morphemes or symbols. It is the manifestation of a human ACTION in which a person INTENDS to create a text and INSTRUCTS the text receivers to build relationships of various kinds. As such, INSTRUCTION figures as the eliciting of processing actions (cf. Schmidt 1971c, 1971d, 1973; Weinrich 1976). Texts also serve to MONITOR, MANAGE, or CHANGE a SITUATION (cf. Kummer 1975; VI.4). The sentence is not an action, and hence has a limited role in human situations; it is used to instruct people about building syntactic relationships.

3.4.7 A text is a PROGRESSION between STATES (Chafe 1976: 27f.; Fowler 1977: 77): the knowledge state, emotional state, social state, etc. of text users are subject to CHANGE by means of the text (cf. "epistemic change" in van Dijk 1977a: 194). The production and comprehension of a text are enacted as progressive occurrences. At each point in those progressions, CURRENT CONTROLS apply which need not be identical with abstract formation principles. For example, the controls upon beginnings of texts differ from those upon continuations or endings (cf. Harweg 1968b). In contrast, sentences are to be viewed as elements of a STABLE SYNCHRONIC SYSTEM (i.e. a system seen in a single, ideal state free of time), so that controls apply CATEGORICALLY (obligatorily and correctly) or not at all.

3.4.8 SOCIAL CONVENTIONS apply more directly to texts than to sentences. People's social awareness applies to occurrences, not to grammatical rule systems. The social markedness of certain structures affects only a small portion of a total grammar and arises only through mediation of non-sentential factors in appropriate contexts.[13] To approach social issues via a sentence theory, William Labov (1969) was compelled to set up whole new provinces of rules designated "variable" as opposed to "categorical." An

[11]Petöfi's use of these terms is more rigorously defined. "Co-text" is said to subsume: grammatical components, syntax, intensional semantics, morphology, and phonology (or, in written texts, graphematics); "context" subsumes extensional semantics, and the production and reception of texts (Petöfi & Rieser 1974: vi; Petöfi 1975a: 1).

[12]Hence, sample (194) in VII.2.25 is grammatical, but hardly acceptable in communication.

[13]The doubling of sentence subjects with noun plus pronoun, for example, is probably due to processing strategies of the kind discussed in V.5.8.

empirically founded linguistics will discover, I suspect, that language rules are in principle variable in accordance with the demands of ongoing situations and with the motivations of text producers seeking special effects.[14]

3.4.9. PSYCHOLOGICAL FACTORS are more relevant to texts than to sentences (cf. van Dijk 1972a: 325; Ortony 1978a: 63). In mental processing, the sentence is one heuristic format among others for the wider purposes of communication (O'Connell 1977), such as expressing and recovering knowledge, or pursuing a goal. Sentence boundaries are decided late during text production and discarded early during comprehension (Bransford & Franks 1971). A theory of sentences, in contrast, is justified in treating as "irrelevant" such factors as "memory limitations, distractions, shifts of attention and interest," and so on (Chomsky 1965: 3f.). The wealth of experimentation purporting to explore sentences is in principle objectionable on these grounds; however, researchers conflated the sentence with so many other entities that their work has useful implications for the study of texts as well.

3.4.10 Texts PRESUPPOSE other texts in quite a different manner than sentences presuppose other sentences. To utilize sentences, language users rely on *grammatical* knowledge as a *general, virtual system.* To utilize texts, people need *experiential* knowledge of *specific, actual occurrences* (on virtual versus actual cf. I.4.1). This condition of INTERTEXTUALITY (cf. I.4.11.6) applies especially to summaries, protocols, continuations, replies, and parodies.

3.5 These fundamental differences between the text and the sentence as linguistic entities have important implications for the evolution of a linguistics of the text:

3.5.1 The confusion and conflation among entities like the sentence, the proposition, and the speech act must be replaced by investigation of the MAPPING PROCEDURES that control the interaction of entities on different language levels (cf. I.2.10).

3.5.2 The search for CATEGORICAL RULES must be redirected toward the DEFAULTS and PREFERENCES that apply with greater or lesser PROBABILITY in response to CONTEXT (on probabilities in "performance" theories, see Smith 1973). Text theory cannot state what *must* happen *all* the time, but rather what *is likely* to happen *most* of the time, given *current controls.*

3.5.3 Research cannot be based, nor can general conclusions be drawn, exclusively on DEMONSTRATION SENTENCES concocted by an investigator for a particular argument. The more convincing domain of samples is that of ACTUALLY OCCURRING TEXTS intended to

---

[14]Some examples of how people use language in unusual ways for effect can be found in II.1.8, IV.1.17, IV.1.19, V.2.3, V.3.13, V.4.3, V.4.11, V.4.12, and VII.2.32.

communicate (rather than to demonstrate grammatical rules). If we are unable to find spontaneous samples in a given case, we should be cautious about asserting the validity of our arguments. For example, sentence grammarians have expended great research and debate upon "multiple embeddings," which are extremely hard to discover in real communication (cf. II.2.27).

3.5.4. While "much of the success" of sentence theories "is due to the strategy of excluding unfavorable examples" (Rieser 1978: 8), the success of text linguistics depends on a broad empirical base. We must actively seek out a diversity of samples from all types of texts: stories, newspapers, magazines, conversations, plays, poems, science textbooks, novels, advertisements, and many others.

3.5.5 Text linguistics cannot have the task of providing an abstract grammar to generate all possible texts of a language and to exclude all non-texts. The domain to be generated is far too vast, and continually expanding. The notion of a "non-text" is not crucial, because the occurrence of non-texts usually signals a refusal or inability to communicate. A more essential task for text linguistics is rather to study the notion of TEXTUALITY as a factor arising from communicative procedures for text utilization.

3.5.6 The models which seem most suitable for workable OPERATION in TEXT UTILIZATION should be given the highest value as explanatory accounts. While abstract reconstructions that somehow crank out the desired structures may be very revealing, they should not claim to explain human language. They are at most auxiliary and intermediary artifacts to be discarded as soon as we move closer to a plausible model of human activities.

3.5.7 The notion of "competence" must receive a much more integrative scope than has been customary in sentence grammars (cf. I.1.17.3). We must seek to define the abilities that make people actually competent to produce and understand texts with consistent (though not universal) success. This kind of text theory will be both "mentalistic" in the basic sense (cf. Fodor, Bever, & Garrett 1974) and empirically verifiable or falsifiable.

3.5.8 Formalisms and representations must be developed that might plausibly be interpreted as PROCESSES, not just as self-sufficient designs of unexplained provenance (e.g., trees or formulas). A representation should suggest how the entities in question might be BUILT, CONTROLLED, and ACCESSED (Rumelhart & Norman 1975a: 35; J. Anderson 1976: 10; Hörmann 1976: 485; Loftus & Loftus 1976: 124; Levesque & Mylopoulos 1978: 3).

3.5.9 Whatever RULES are postulated should simultaneously embody possible PROCEDURES. For example, the rules which build sentences ought to represent tactics that work in real time under such normal conditions as span of memory and planning abilities (Rumelhart 1977a: 122).

3.5.10 Our efforts must above all be devoted to INTERDISCIPLINARY CO-OPERATION. Linguistics alone cannot provide the expertise needed to treat the psychological, social, and computational aspects of texts in use (cf. van Dikj 1972a: 161).

3.6 I hope to make a modest beginning here toward living up to these standards. I stress that my proposals must be tentative, pending more comprehensive research. But I have tried to work with insights that are at least reasonable in light of as much new research as I could assemble.

4.   TEXTUALITY

4.1 It should be noted that the general explication of the notion of "system" given in I.1.6 applies not only to a language level, but also to the entity TEXT (Hartmann 1963a: 85f.; Fowler 1977: 69). The intersystem of a natural language such as English is composed of VIRTUAL SYSTEMS: functional unities of elements whose potential is not yet put to use, e.g. the repertories of sounds, grammatical forms, sentence patterns, concept names, etc., which a particular language offers its users; in contrast to these repertories, a text is an ACTUAL SYSTEM: a functional unity created through processes of decision and selection among options of virtual systems (Hartmann 1963b: 96f.; Gülich & Raible 1977: 34ff.). The evolution of a text can therefore be termed ACTUALIZATION. This quality of occurrence, as I have stated in I.1.1f., is the essential criterion for identifying the text as such (Hartmann 1964). It follows that the text is *not* simply a larger "rank" than the sentence (Hasan 1978: 228), despite the views of some researchers (e.g., Pike 1967; Heger 1976; Jones 1977). A text may be no longer than a single word, and it may be composed of elements without sentence status (e.g. road signs, advertisements, telegrams, and so on).

4.2 Since Saussure, linguistics has been predominantly devoted to the study of virtual systems. Yet the knowledge of virtual systems would not be sufficient to enable people to communicate except in a very roundabout and inefficient way. People must know not only what options are offered, but also what options are relevant and useable for a given situation and purpose. The virtual aspects of mutual *opposition* and *differentiation* (following Saussure) and of *well-formedness* (following Chomsky) are incomplete guidelines. I hold any notion of competence to be incomplete which does not consider the strategies of actualization that humans apply to virtual systems. The fact that these strategies may lead to texts beyond the organization of the virtual systems has been noticed in studies of poetic texts (cf. Levin 1962; Mukařovský 1964; Thorne 1969; Beaugrande 1979e).

4.3 Actualization is a process we can explore in terms of CYBERNETIC REGULATION (cf. Breuer 1974; Clippinger 1977). A CYBERNETIC SYSTEM possesses an internal organization that enables it to adapt to ongoing occurrences by means of self-regulation (cf. Klaus 1963, 1972). The main objective of the system is STABILITY of states and operations. If the system is capable of adapting to a variety of occurrences, it is ULTRASTABLE; if it contains several ultrastable subsystems, it is a MULTISTABLE system (Klaus 1963: 125). The system can be still more effective if it maintains an INTERNAL MODEL of its environment, and if it can adapt along with the environment (a LEARNING system). All of these attributes are assignable to a language intersystem. The functionings of virtual systems are artifically stabilized in the abstract or synchronic viewpoint. Yet the environment of actualization requires constant adaptation of these subsystems according to context. As a result, the actualized text-system reflects not only the contributing virtual systems, but appropriate modifications and adaptations performed during the operations of actualization. The systems remain stable if they support UTILIZATION and CONTINUITY even though most texts in themselves are at least partly novel and occasionally contain greater or lesser discontinuities.

4.4 The STABILITY of the text as a cybernetic system thus depends upon the CONTINUITY of occurrences in participating systems. This continuity is not necessarily obvious: the stream of speech sounds or written symbols cannot reflect all of the relations that hold the textual system together. At most, the text is characterized by its CONNECTIVITIES, i.e. unbroken ACCESS among the occurring elements of the participating language systems. The text users may experience *continuity* as the FUZZINESS of the boundaries among the elements (cf. III.1.7); but the text itself can only offer *connectivities*. There should be a SEQUENTIAL CONNECTIVITY of GRAMMATICAL DEPENDENCIES in the SURFACE text (cf. Ch. II). The underlying meaning should have CONCEPTUAL CONNECTIVITY, e.g. relations of causality, time, or location (cf. Ch. III). The intentional arrangement of the DISCOURSE ACTIONS within texts (cf. III.4.26) should reflect a PLANNING connectivity, so that each component utterance is RELEVANT to some interactive or communicative plan, such as advising, requesting, agreeing, or just maintaining social solidarity (cf. VI.4; VIII.1). The context determines how many actual occurrences are needed for connectivity to prevail. In highly determinate contexts, people economize by omitting or compacting the actual occurrences in the surface structure of expression.

4.5 Illustrations of the regulatory operations I have outlined are not hard to find in regard to texts:

4.5.1 The compacting of surface structure in determinate contexts can be performed by the use of pro-forms and ellipsis (cf. V. 4 and V.6).

4.5.2 Decisions about the organization of a conceptual configuration elicit follow-up decisions about the organization of surface structure and vice versa (cf. III.4.16; VII.2.10ff.)

4.5.3 In the presence of ambiguities or disturbances, people can make intensified use of other cues to maintain textuality (see e.g. II.2.37; V.4.11).

4.5.4 When elements of a presented text are forgotten, the textual system in mental storage adjusts by compacting, rearranging, or reconstructing the remainder (see section VII.3).

4.5.5 Discrepancies and discontinuities do not normally cause a breakdown in communication, but only elicit regulatory operations from the hearer or reader (see I.6.9; IV.1.12; VIII.2.42ff.).

4.6 Most important of all is the regulatory nature of communicative systems among *individual participants*. Every person's knowledge and experience are in some ways unique, yet people normally communicate without difficulty. If a given person fails to utilize some language subsystem in the conventional way, regulatory occurrences generally become necessary: explaining, correcting misunderstandings, precluding alternative readings, restating, and even apologizing. People's actions and utterances are not governed by laws or categorical rules; but people must respect the operations of a system if they intend to use it effectively. Individual misuses are rare precisely because they elicit regulatory occurrences that damage efficiency if repeated very often.

4.7 Many texts are manifestly able to survive and be utilized long after their original contexts have been lost. If the virtual language systems undergo changes in the intervening time, readers need some mediation, such as the training needed today to read Old or Middle English. However, if the virtual systems remain generally stable, utilization is unproblematic. Texts are SELF-CONTEXTUALIZING because the actualization processes of writers and readers are geared toward continuity and regulation (cf. Halliday, McIntosh, & Strevens 1965: 246; R. Anderson 1977: 242). The higher the quality of a text, the greater its potential for later utilization: the decisions and selections made in production are especially well designed in enduring works (Winograd 1977a: 69). This factor accounts for the endurance of literary and poetic texts over other types (cf. VII.2.37ff.).

4.8 The possibility that different hearers or readers might make different uses of the same text is by no means unproblematic, as the lively debates over the role of the reader in literary theory attest (Warning [ed.] 1975). The stability of the text is derivative from the stability of participating virtual systems of communication, and the regulatory principles of actualization—a kind of "meta-stability" (E. D. Hirsch, personal communication). Linguistic discussions have often missed these considerations by dwelling extensively upon potential ambiguities or alternatives allowed by virtual systems, and giving little heed to the fact that real utterances are seldom misunderstood. The picture of language processing that emerges from those discussions is one of the language user floating in a sea of alternative readings and structures whose management in any reasonable time span seems miraculous. Thus, Chomsky (1975: 77) concludes: "the study of the capacity to use these structures and the exercise of this capacity, however, still seems to elude our understanding."

4.9 Transformational grammar is a pre-eminently virtual system that undertakes to state which sentences are categorically possible without regard for their occurrence. Linguists' samples are to some extent pseudo-occurrences, unless taken from spontaneously produced texts of non-linguists. Yet a grammar of pseudo-occurrences is a curious construction for a science, and its verification already a grave problem (cf. I.1.16ff.). Surely the enumeration of all possible sentences becomes a performance issue after the CORE of the grammar is systemized (cf. Grimes 1975: 198). People's competence is above all their limited, operational set of strategies for building and understanding sentences or texts that are *likely* to occur because they *make sense* and *are useful in getting things done.*

4.10 It is not surprising that linguists initially hoped to treat texts as virtual systems or system elements. Harris's (1952) attempt to uncover the distributional rules for texts suggests the assumption that virtual and actual systems were convergent. A pilot project largely inspired by transformational grammar was devoted to creating a rule apparatus to generate or derive a text by Bertolt Brecht (van Dijk, Ihwe, Petöfi, & Rieser 1972; see the debate between Ihwe & Rieser 1972 and Kummer 1972b, 1972c over the outcome). Thomas Ballmer (1975: 259) sees texts as nothing more than "well-formed sequences of morphemes" which can be treated by enlarging sentence grammar with "punctuation morphemes." These and similar experiments are all subject to the same principled objections: (1) they provide no plausible model of human activities; (2) they are operationally unworkable for any significantly large corpus of texts; and (3) they do not deal realistically with such issues as ungrammatical texts, better or worse style, interestingness, informativity, and communicative interaction.

4.11 I propose the following standards of TEXTUALITY to be the legitimate basis of the actualization and utilization of texts:

4.11.1 COHESION subsumes the procedures whereby SURFACE elements appear as progressive occurrences such that their SEQUENTIAL CONNECTIVITY is maintained and made recoverable. The means of cohesion include the grammatical formatting of phrases, clauses, and sentences (see Chapter II), and such devices as recurrence, pro-forms and articles, co-reference, ellipsis, and junction (see Chapter V).

4.11.2 COHERENCE subsumes the procedures whereby elements of KNOWLEDGE are activated such that their CONCEPTUAL CON-NECTIVITY is maintained and made recoverable. The means of coherence include: (1) logical relations such as causality and class inclusion; (2) knowledge of how events, actions, objects, and situations are organized; and (3) the striving for continuity in human experience. Cohesion is upheld by continual interaction of TEXT-PRESENTED KNOWLEDGE with PRIOR KNOWLEDGE OF THE WORLD (cf. VII.3.29ff.).

4.11.3 INTENTIONALITY subsumes the text producer's attitude that a given language configuration is INTENDED to be a cohesive and coherent text; and that such a text is an INSTRUMENT in following a PLAN toward a GOAL (cf. VI.4). There is a variable range of TOLERANCE where intentionality remains in effect even when the full standards of cohesion and coherence are not met, and when the plan does not actually lead to the desired goal. This tolerance is a factor of systemic regulation (I.4.3f.) mediating between language strategies at large and the exigencies of ongoing contexts.

4.11.4 ACCEPTABILITY subsumes the text receiver's attitude that a language configuration should be ACCEPTED as a cohesive and coherent text. Acceptability also has a tolerance range for cases where context brings disturbances, or where the receiver does not share the producer's goals (cf. II.2.37f.).

4.11.5 SITUATIONALITY subsumes the factors that make a text relevant to a current or recoverable SITUATION. The text figures as an ACTION that can both monitor and change a situation (cf. VI.4.2ff.). There may be only slight mediation toward the situation, as in face-to-face communication about directly apperceivable events; or substantial mediation, as in reading an old text of literary nature about events in an alternative world (e.g. *Gilgamesh* or *The Odyssey*) (cf. VII.1.8.4). The scope of situationality always implies the roles of at least two communicative participants, but they may not enter the focus of attention as persons.

4.11.6 INTERTEXTUALITY subsumes the relationships between a given text and other relevant texts encountered in prior experience, with or without mediation. A reply in conversation (cf. VIII.1) or a recall protocol of a text just read (cf. VII.3) illustrate intertextuality with very little mediation. More extensive mediation obtains when replies or criticisms are directed to texts written down at some earlier time. Intertextuality is the major factor in the establishment of TEXT TYPES (cf. VII.1), where expectations are formed for whole classes of language occurrences.

4.11.7 INFORMATIVITY is the factor of the relative UNCERTAINTY about textual occurrences or occurrences within a textual world as opposed to possible alternatives. Informativity is high if the alternatives are numerous and if an improbable alternative is actually selected. However, every text has at least the minimal informativity in which its occurrences are opposed to non-occurrences (cf. IV.1.8). I argue in Chapter IV that a medium degree of informativity is maintained in communication by means of regulating extreme degrees.

4.12 These standards are of course not new, but their treatment hitherto has been sporadic and diffuse. Cohesion and coherence, for example, have often been conflated, due perhaps to the widespread confusion regarding the nature of the sentence (cf. I.3.1ff.) (but cf. Widdowson 1973). The notions of cohesion and coherence can be pursued in such works as Halliday (1964); Crymes (1968); Harweg (1968a); Hasan (1968); Palek (1968); Bellert (1970); van Dijk (1972a); Grimes (1975); Hobbs (1976, 1979); Halliday & Hasan

(1976); Bullwinkle (1977); Jones (1977); Reichman (1978); Webber (1978). On intentionality, compare Wunderlich (1971); Dressler (1972a); Bruce (1975); van Dijk (1977a); Schlesinger (1977); Cohen (1978); Allen (1979) (more literature on plans and goals is given in chapter VI). Concerning acceptability, consult Quirk & Svartvik (1966), and Greenbaum (ed.) (1977). On situationality, the work of Halliday (e.g. 1977) and the ethnography of communication (e.g. Gumperz & Hymes [eds.] 1972) are relevant. For some outlooks on intertextuality, consider Kristeva (1968) and Quirk (1978). Regarding informativity, little is available except on "given" and "new" knowledge in sentences as reviewed in section IV.3; but cf. Shannon (1951); Weltner (1964); Grimes (1975); Groeben (1978); Beaugrande (1978b, 1979e). All seven criteria of textuality are discussed in turn in Beaugrande & Dressler (1980).

4.13 Of these seven criteria, two seem prominently text-oriented (cohesion and coherence), two prominently psychological (intentionality and acceptability), two prominently social (situationality and intertextuality), and the last, computational (informativity). But close investigation shows that none of the criteria can be appreciated without considering all four factors: language, mind, society, and processing. Again, the pressing need for interdisciplinary research stands forth. These criteria of textuality figure as CONSTITUTIVE principles in the sense of Searle (1969: 33ff.): whether or not something can be considered a text depends on whether these criteria are upheld. There must also be REGULATIVE principles in the sense of Searle which distinguish the *quality* of a sample already admitted as a text. I surmise that this regulative function is exercised by the criteria of *design* I shall propose.

4.14 While all texts must possess these standards of textuality, there are differences in the DESIGN of their actualization. We must therefore define and investigate DESIGN CRITERIA such as the following (for discussions and illustrations see III.3.5; IV.1.6; IV.4.12; VII.2.37; VIII.2.19). The EFFICIENCY of a text results from its utilization in communication with the *greatest returns for the least effort,* so that PROCESSING EASE is promoted. The EFFECTIVENESS of the text depends upon its *intensity of impact* on text receivers, promoting PROCESSING DEPTH, and upon its *contribution toward the producer's goal,* constituting the RELEVANCE of text materials to *steps in a plan.* The APPROPRIATENESS of a text depends on the *proportionality between the demands of a communicative situation and the degree to which standards of textuality are upheld.* These design criteria are, I believe, much more vital to language users' "competence" than the famous distinction between sentences and non-sentences, or a parallel distinction between texts and non-texts. Normally, the production of non-texts signals a refusal or inability to communicate at all (cf. I.3.4.4; IV.1.23.2; V.4.12). Thus, the absence of cohesion, coherence, intentionality, informativity, etc. is comparatively rare; but texts may often be inefficient, ineffective, or inappropriate. We must study not only how language structures can be *built* and *analyzed,* but also how they can be *evaluated.*

5. TEXTUAL COMPETENCE

5.1 To deal with manifestations and data of any sort, a science must differentiate between the essential, regular, and relevant aspects and the non-essential, idiosyncratic, or irrelevant ones. For example, phonology studies systems of sounds by discounting such factors as the voice quality, age, sex, or personality of speakers; otherwise, no two sound patterns of the same utterance would ever be exactly identical. To establish a theory of sentence grammar, Chomsky (1965) eliminated such factors as memory limitations, changes of plan while speaking, and errors.

5.2 The distinction of competence and performance along the lines of sentence grammar has come increasingly under fire in recent years. Walter Kintsch (1974: 3) adjudges the distinction as "merely an excuse for both the linguist and the psychologist to justify the neglect of each other's findings." Werner Kummer (1975: 163) discards the distinction as inherently tied to a language model incapable of integration into a theory of action. Other researchers retain the distinction while calling for a new orientation toward COMMUNICATIVE COMPETENCE (cf. Wunderlich 1971; Habermas 1971; Hymes 1972; Schmidt 1973).

5.3 I also hold the distinction to be valuable if not indispensible:

5.3.1 Whether we look at the physical properties of a stream of speech or at the wider constellation of a communicative situation, we are forced to admit that elements we consider *equivalent* in their *systemic functions* are *superficially different* in minor though discoverable ways. To communicate at all, people must distribute their attention and resources selectively toward relevant aspects, while disattending the rest. The linguist is certainly justified in emulating this selectivity without which language could never be subjected to identification, generalization, description, and the other tasks enumerated in I.1.8.

5.3.2 To deal adequately with any representative sampling of texts in a language, we must specify a reasonably *limited* set of strategies and procedures that apply to very *diverse* manifestations. Competence must cover these *shared* abilities even though some manifestations may be impaired by restrictions of time, resources, attention, knowledge, or experience on the part of an *individual* language user.

5.3.3 Language activities are frequently CREATIVE. Many texts convey informativity by virtue of their producer's modifications upon the normal or expected organization of texts (cf. Beaugrande 1979e). If we undertook to incorporate every manifestation of creativity into the same framework as conventional procedures, we would misrepresent many issues. A grammar that could produce every creative configuration would eventually be powerful enough to produce every conceivable configuration, thus attaining zero-organization and accounting for nothing at all.[15]

5.4 I would conclude that manifestations *reflect* competence, but they need not *embody* it (cf. I.4.14). The competence/performance distinction should be retained as the opposition between STRATEGIES (procedures applied and held to be useable most of the time) and APPLICATIONS (the detailed events of communicative situations, including disturbances or failures). We should explore the effects that arise when strategies do not work; speech errors, for example, provide valuable evidence regarding mental operations (cf. Fromkin [ed.] 1973; Goodman & Burke 1973; examples in VII.3.14ff.). But it would seem odd to conflate competence with performance by postulating strategies that are designed to produce errors and failures.

5.5 I would not define competence solely as the ability to distinguish between texts and non-texts.[16] Except in the presence of special signals, people probably make the DEFAULT ASSUMPTION that language presentations are texts. The notion of TEXTUAL COMPETENCE (van Dijk 1972a: 204) might rather be required to subsume the following set of KNOWLEDGE and PROCEDURES:

5.5.1 knowledge of the repertories of OPTIONS in virtual systems of language;

5.5.2 knowledge of systemic CONSTRAINTS on the selection and combination of options;

5.5.3 knowledge of the BELIEFS, KNOWLEDGE, and EXPECTATIONS shared by the communicative group or society about the "real world";[17]

5.5.4 knowledge of TEXT TYPES;

5.5.5. procedures for UTILIZING virtual systems during ACTUALIZATION;

5.5.6 procedures for PRODUCING texts;

5.5.7 procedures for RECEIVING texts;

5.5.8 procedures for maintaining TEXTUALITY;

5.5.9 procedures for regulating INFORMATIVITY;

---

[15]In a system with zero organization, no predictions can be made about any occurrences or regularities.

[16]As Schank and Wilensky (1977: 142) point out, the distinction of "grammatical vs. ungrammatical" is unrealistic, because "people don't go around trying to distinguish English from gibberish."

[17]I view the "real world" not as some irrefutably given set of objects, but rather as the socially accepted model of whatever objects are there (cf. IV.1.21.3).

5.5.10 procedures for optimizing DESIGN CRITERIA (efficiency, effectiveness, and appropriateness);

5.5.11 procedures for re-utilizing text-acquired knowledge from mental storage in tasks like RECALLING, REPORTING, SUMMARIZING, or EVALUATING;

5.5.12 procedures for MONITORING and MANAGING SITUATIONS by using texts;

5.5.13 procedures for building, implementing, and revising PLANS toward GOALS;

5.5.14 procedures for PREDICTING the activities of other participants in communication and REGULATING one's discourse actions accordingly;

5.5.15 procedures for maintaining communication despite DISCREP-ANCIES, DISCONTINUITIES, AMBIGUITIES, or NON-EXPECTED occurrences.

5.6 I would surmise that INTELLIGENCE can be defined as *the decoupling of these skills and processes from any particular task at hand*. It is the capacity to operate on a *higher plane* and to recognize and perform any given task as an *instantiation of a general operation type*; and to treat any given data in terms of a *general data type*. I shall accordingly propose that textual communication functions on a high plane: syntax, meaning, information, and planning are processed in terms of *high-plane typologies of occurrences and relationships* (cf. II.2.15ff.; III.4.3ff.; IV.1.6ff.; IV.3.17ff.; V.1.4ff.; VI.1.1ff.; VI.4.14; VII.1.7; VII.2.8ff.; VII.3.15ff.; VII.3.29ff.; VIII.2.8ff.; VIII.2.21ff.; IX.1.4ff.). I suspect that the continuing failure of linguists to solve or explain many major issues of language communication has been due to adopting an unduly low-level perspective (analyzing the meanings of individual words or the exact surface formats of specific sentences, and so on) (cf. IX.8).

6.   TEXT UTILIZATION AS MODEL-BUILDING

6.1 The activities involved in the production and comprehension of a text can be explored in terms of MODEL-BUILDING. The participants in communication can be said to be BUILDING A TEXT-WORLD MODEL (cf. the notions of "world" or "model" in Petöfi & Rieser 1974; Petöfi 1975a; Schank et al. 1975; Collins, Brown, & Larkin 1977; Fahlman 1977; Goldman, Balzer, & Wile 1977; Reichman 1978; Rubin 1978; Webber 1978; Petöfi 1979). The TEXTUAL WORLD is the cognitive correlate of the knowledge conveyed and activated by a text in use. As such, it is in fact only present in the minds of language users. Hence, we must approach the problem via the MODELS of textual worlds as composed of CONCEPTS and RELATIONS in a KNOWLEDGE SPACE (cf. Ch. III). The text-world model is viewed as embedded in a SITUATION MODEL (cf. Clark & Clark 1977: 72; Grosz 1977: 6). The situation model is kept in alignment with the PLANS and GOALS of the participants (in this sense, a goal is a model of a desired future situation—cf. VI.4.4). The text producer can maintain a model of the text receivers and their knowledge (cf. Bruce 1975: 5; Goldman 1975: 346; Bernstein & Pike 1977: 3; Winograd 1977a: 69; Cohen 1978: 16; McCalla 1978a: 19; Carbonell Jr. 1978b; Rubin 1978b: 136; Allen 1979: 6). We could go on to postulate the receivers' model of the producer's model of them, and the latter's model of their model, and so on (see Clark & Marshall 1978). But there is probably a THRESHOLD OF TERMINATION where people in communication do not bother to run through all these models inside models.

6.2 An integrated approach entitled the TEXT-STRUCTURE/WORLD-STRUCTURE THEORY has been set forth by János S. Petöfi and associates (Petöfi 1975a, 1975b, 1978a, 1978b, 1979; Biasci & Fritsche [eds.] 1978). The basic postulate in the theory is that there are regular correspondences between the structure of a text and the structure of the "world" a text evokes. Petöfi (1978a: 44f.) notes that there are two outlooks on the development of such an integrated theory:

> One can either set out from an existing apparatus (with its limitations but well known scope) and try to modify it to the extent required by the object under investigation; or one can start with what is required for the description of the object and try to devise an apparatus accordingly.

Petöfi has proceeded by working with the "existing apparatus" of formal logics. But he realizes the need for substantial modifications, e.g.: "the rule systems of logical syntaxes in use so far are not suitable for the description of natural languages, because the logical formulae assigned by them to natural language utterances are only capable of representing a part of the syntactic information found in natural language utterances" (Petöfi 1978a: 40). The latest version (Petöfi 1979) foresees an elaborate network of components such as lexicon, canonic language, natural language, description, interpretation, formation, composition, transformation,[18] and representation. The canonic language is made flexible via expansion of the object domain and yet is still translatable into first-order predicate calculus. The model-building function is handled by the interpretation component. An unusual feature not found in conventional logics for natural language is Petöfi's attempt to deal with the apperception and description of language sounds.

6.3 One difficult question concerns the nature of a WORLD, i.e., the totality of data given in some context. In the tradition of Carnap and Kripke,

---

[18]Petöfi's "transformations" are not like those of usual sentence grammars, because they convert structures into structures of *different systemic types* (cf. II.1.6).

the LOGICAL WORLD is ATOMISTIC (Cresswell 1973: 38; cf. Hughes & Cresswell 1968). The atomism arises from the DISCRETENESS of objects and functions as required by the formatting and proof techniques of the logic. Hence, content appears as MODULAR and insensitive to many kinds of context. Max Cresswell (personal communication) tells me that attempts are under way to overcome atomism by plotting logical worlds close together on a CONTINUUM (see also Eikmeyer & Rieser 1978). The work on FUZZY SETS by Lotfi Zadeh and others allows the introduction of indistinct or probabilistic boundaries among entities of meaning. These important advances do not in themselves stipulate what the human processes of utilizing knowledge ought to look like. Hence, I follow the other outlook cited by Petöfi and explore what might be required for representations that could be developed in the future.

6.4 A TEXTUAL WORLD plainly has great potential for CONTI-NUITY. The spaces between text-presented concepts and relations can be filled in or enriched with a wide range of COMMONSENSE KNOWLEDGE about how events, actions, objects, and situations are organized. Three factors should be cited here. SPREADING ACTIVATION occurs when the material activated by a text contacts associated material already stored in the minds of text users (e.g., for building up a scene from a few details mentioned in the text) (cf. III.3.24). INFERENCING is done whenever GAPS are noticed among points in a knowledge space (e.g., for solving a crime in a detective story) (cf. Rieger 1974, 1975, 1976; Clark 1977; Collins, Brown, & Larkin 1977; Warren, Nicholas, & Trabasso 1979; cf. III.4.29ff.)[19] UPDATING changes the textual world regarding what is true at any moment as the course of events affects the situation (cf. Sacerdoti 1977: 15; Winston 1977: 386). The extent to which these three processes are actually carried out may vary among individual languages users; empirical testing will, I believe, show a THRESHOLD OF TERMINATION where continuity is considered satisfactory and these processes stop. In any case, these processes make it unnecessary for a text producer to explicitly state all the material needed for coherence.

6.5 Two well-known approaches to model-building correspond to the two approaches cited in the Petöfi quote in I.6.2. The INDUCTIVE approach works by reacting to and generalizing from observations and experience; the DEDUCTIVE approach entails a prior stipulation of what some domain ought to be like. This distinction applies to building text-world models also, especially from the hearer/reader's standpoint. People notice and classify the incoming presentation as BOTTOM-UP input; on the other hand, they steadily form and test hypotheses about what will occur or be stated, applying

---

[19]I further distinguish between spreading activation vs. inferencing in VII.3.20.

TOP-DOWN input (on top-down vs. bottom-up, see R. Bobrow & Brown 1975; Bobrow & Norman 1975; Brown & Burton 1975; Collins, Brown, & Larkin 1977). In this view, the task of understanding is one of integrating presented knowledge into stored knowledge (Kintsch 1974: 11; cf. Ausubel 1963 on "subsumption").

6.6 To decide what knowledge should be applied, cognitive processing operates by PATTERN-MATCHING (cf. Colby & Parkinson 1974; D. Bobrow 1975; Rieger 1975, 1976; Rumelhart 1975, 1977a; Kuipers 1975; J. Anderson 1976; Kintsch 1977a; Winston 1977; Bobrow & Winograd 1977; Hayes 1977; Pavlidis 1977; Havens 1978). A perfect match is not required, but only a reasonably good fit (cf. Rieger 1975: 277; Woods 1978a: 36). For efficiency, it is desirable to match the largest possible pattern and thus treat the greatest amount of input at once (Rieger 1975: 157).

6.7 The best means for representing the procedures of model-building and pattern matching in textual communication is, in my view, GENERAL PROBLEM SOLVING (cf. Newell & Simon 1972; Winston 1977).[20] A PROBLEM can be defined as a state from which the pathway to the successor state has a noticeable probability for FAILURE: the pathway is not traversed because either the pathway or the successor state is wrong. The PROBLEM-SOLVER is a PLANNER, which has to SEARCH the PROBLEM SPACE in order to connect the current state with the intended successor state. A SERIOUS PROBLEM is present when the probabilities for FAILURE are higher than those for SUCCESS. A BLOCK is present if the planner cannot advance at all; it is then necessary to discard the pathway and go to a point where new progress can be made. As we can see, problem solving depends chiefly on techniques of SEARCH, of which at least three kinds should be mentioned (cf. Lenat 1977: 1099f; Winston 1977: 90ff., 130ff.):

6.7.1 In MEANS-END ANALYSIS, the processor focuses on the major differences between the first point (the INITIAL STATE) and the final point (the GOAL STATE). All operations are directed to reducing the differences between these two states. In forward progression, means-end analysis resembles depth-first search as explained in the following section (Winston 1977: 133). But efficiency is greatly increased if means-end analysis works from both ends, forward and backward, leaving markers to eliminate repetitions of paths that have already been tried (Woods 1978b: 19f.).

---

[20]The term "general" was used to suggest that the first program written by Allen Newell, Herbert Simon, and Cliff Shaw in 1957 was divided into "a task-independent part of the system containing general problem solving mechanisms" and "a part of the system containing knowledge of the task environment" (Newell & Simon 1972: 414; cf. IX.1.7). The use I make of general problem-solving here is rather different from that envisioned by these scholars, though, I hope, in line with their general theory.

6.7.2 In BREADTH-FIRST SEARCH, the processor looks ahead from the initial state only as far as a proximate subgoal and sifts through the range of pathways that would lead to the subgoal. When the subgoal is attained, the same procedure is applied to the next subgoal. Though breadth-first search is careful and conservative, it demands extensive time and processing resources, and may be inefficient if the solution is intuitively obvious.

6.7.3 In DEPTH-FIRST SEARCH, the processor attempts to rush all the way to the goal by a single sequence of pathways. As long as hope remains for attaining the goal, the range of alternative pathways at intermediate points is not explored. If a BLOCK is encountered, the planner backs up a step and then rushes forward again. Depth-first search is risky, but required when there is a scarcity of time or processing energy; and it is efficient if the solution is intuitively obvious.

6.8 The importance of problem-solving in the use of texts emerges in light of the central role of CONNECTIVITY among textual occurrences (cf. I.4.4). As this connectivity is often not manifest (cf. I.4.4), people who communicate via texts must constantly process occurrences by linking them to other occurrences; hence, any non-manifest relation between textual occurrences constitutes a problem in the sense just explained in I.6.7. Highly unexpected or abnormal occurrences constitute serious problems (cf. IV.1.12). A total breakdown in communication, e.g. due to incoherence, would constitute a block. I surmise that problem-solving is precisely the factor which makes the processes of actualization distinct from the principles which organize virtual systems of language (cf. I.4.1ff.). If virtual systems are governed by opposition (Saussure) and structural rules (Chomsky), problems are not likely to appear. Actualization, in contrast, requires language users to continually impose connectivity by building structures of multifarious and diverse nature on the spur of the moment. A striking illustration of this contrast is the distinction between a virtual system of concepts in a LEXICON and the actualization process of INFERENCING cited in I.6.4.

6.9 The questions of how much inferencing people do and when inferencing occurs, are still under debate. Rusty Bobrow and John Seely Brown (1975) identify the groups of "if-added" and "if-needed" inferences. The "if-added" inferences are done whenever knowledge is being integrated into the text world model: the new material requires at least satisfactory linkage in order to be connected on at the appropriate points. For example, to understand actions mentioned in a text, a text receiver might make inferences about plausible reasons for the agent of the action (cf. McDermott 1974; Rieger 1974, 1975). The "if-needed" inferences are not performed until an occasion is created by some later occurrence. For instance, we might infer from the actions of someone in a murder mystery that it is really the detective in disguise and rethink the detective's past actions in retrospect (a favorite

tactic in Conan Doyle stories). Charniak (1976) is surely correct in assuming
that "problem-occasioned" inferences are made as soon as the problem is
noticed, e.g. a DISCONTINUITY where linkage is missing; a GAP where
linkage contains a slot whose content is missing; or a DISCREPANCY where
text-asserted knowledge does not match stored world knowledge (cf.
IV.1.12). Clark and Haviland's (1974) notion of "bridging inferences" is also
interpretable in terms of problem-solving. The question of inferencing is
obviously vital for computer simulation of human understanding processes:
how can the program be prepared for later input without doing an explosive
amount of inferencing (cf. Wilensky 1978: 6ff.)? The question is also acute for
theories of human cognition in psychology (cf. Spiro 1977).

    6.10 A text-world model is composed of PROPOSITIONS, the format in
which some researchers believe that all knowledge is stored and used (cf. J.
Anderson & Bower 1973: Kintsch & Keenan 1973; Kintsch 1974; B. Meyer
1975, 1977; Frederiksen 1975, 1977; J. Anderson 1976; van Dijk 1977a;
Simmons 1978). Without insisting on logical rigor, we can define the
proposition as a relation obtaining between two concepts (e.g., in 'the sky is
blue,' the relation "attribute-of" obtains between the concepts evoked by 'sky'
and 'blue'). The connectivity of a textual world requires that there be at least
one relation linking every concept to the overall knowledge space.

    6.11 This outlook has some correlates in older approaches. The traditional
notion of the sentence as an expression of a "complete thought" (I.3.1) can be
cited. In transformational grammar, selectional restrictions on lexical items
were a partial treatment of the issue. In generative semantics, the sentence was
expressly derived from a "base structure" of propositions. Yet even generative
semantics was "not semantic enough" (van Dijk 1972: 36), because it treated
sentence boundaries as something inherent in the organization of
configurations of underlying meaning.

    6.12 It is more plausible that underlying meaning is entirely organized in
terms of concepts and relations which can be MAPPED into sentences (or
phrases of any kind) in various ways. The "conceptual dependency" theory
developed by Roger Schank (1972; Hays 1973; Schank et al. 1975; Schank &
Abelson 1977) works with underlying representations which are in fact
language-independent. When people build text-world models, they utilize
grammatical dependencies and conceptual dependencies in PARALLEL (cf.
Marslen-Wilson 1975; Burton 1976; Woods 1978c). However, the interaction
between the two dependency types is ASYMMETRICAL: without exact one-
to-one relationships between the two domains (cf. Longacre 1976: 12;
Goldman, Balzer, & Wile 1977: 17; Hayes 1977: 166), the grammatical
repertory of a language like English being far smaller than the conceptual one.
Still, there must be PREFERENCES which state that a given grammatical
dependency is more likely to correspond to a small set of conceptual

dependencies than to any alternatives, and vice versa (cf. III.4.16ff.). The use of preferences is another major aspect of cybernetic regulation that makes actualization efficient (cf. I.4.5.2).[21]

6.13 Due to spreading activation, inferencing, updating, and asymmetry, a text-world model underlying a text may look slightly different to individual language users. But I would not agree that the model is hence "unknowable" (Turner & Greene 1977: 4), or that there would be "an infinite number of models" for a text (Webber 1978: 29). Like most entities in human cognition, the text-world model is PROBABILISTIC in nature. Its exact content may be partly UNDECIDABLE, and its relationship to the surface text not fully DETERMINATE (Kintsch 1974: 153). But communication is normally efficient because participants rely on probable occurrences, and control non-determinacy by well-designed utilization of all kinds of cues. The question of how people know what is going on in a text is a special case of the question of how people know what is going on in the world at all. Sensory apperception allows us to understand the world only because we have at least some reliable strategies that allow us to predict and label input (see section IV.2), e.g. by pattern-matching.

6.14 These issues have been downplayed in the past by a conception of human communication as involving a "sender" who "encodes" a message which is then "decoded" by a "receiver." These terms, borrowed from engineering (cf. Rosenstein, Rathbone, & Schneerer 1964: 21), are either trivial, because language messages are obviously not identical with things in the real world; or downright misleading, because "encoding" suggests a mechanical replacement of things with symbols. Morse code, for instance, entails nothing more than a one-to-one substitution of electrical signals for letters of the alphabet. But producing and understanding texts depends on elaborate processes of decision, selection, planning, design, and problem-solving. The vast dissimilarities between these activities and mechanical interchange of symbols were demonstrated by the monumental failure of early attempts at machine translation.

6.15 We may come to understand the whole nature of language communication better by moving from sentences to texts. Though mechanical rule systems are in themselves businesslike and reliable, they fail to capture many aspects of human knowledge and expression. Language is manifested via sequences of *discrete* symbols, but it serves to describe, monitor, and talk about *continuous* worlds of knowledge and experience (cf. I.6.4).[22] Mathematics and formal logic are useful tools of representation, but

---

[21]My use of the notion of "preferences" is somewhat more general than that used by Wilks, although I was originally inspired by his proposals.

[22]Ortony (1978c) views this disparity as a factor that makes metaphors indispensible to human communication.

they must not dictate the issues that we can address. The trend toward representing continuity in logic (cf. I.6.3) is a major step in restoring human priorities often disregarded for the sake of formalisms. So far, it is not clear how these new proposals would handle knowledge operations *in real time*. Unless there are powerful strategies for PREDICTING what worlds should look like and how they follow each other, the plotting of worlds in the manner of Cresswell (cf. I.6.3) could require an explosive amount of calculating (cf. II.1.2 on explosion). I would stress that the non-determinacy and continuity of textual worlds by no means suggest that studying them is imprecise or unscientific; on the contrary it is the fundamental task of science to explore and systemize all kinds of domains with the highest fidelity to the objects and processes involved.

7. OVERVIEW OF THE DISCUSSION

7.1 To pursue the cognitive interests I have tried to outline in this chapter, the traditional formats for linguistic discussions might not be productive: syntax, then semantics, then pragmatics; or phonemes, then morphemes, then words, then sentences, then texts; and so forth. These formats were suited to the demands of discussing virtual systems, whereas I am more concerned with actualization processes. I shall discuss a range of issues that appear relevant to a science of texts, following up the general criteria set forth so far.

7.2 Chapter II deals with the operations for maintaining SEQUENTIAL CONNECTIVITY by means of building grammatical dependencies. I present a formalism called the AUGMENTED TRANSITION NETWORK which functions by moving from one grammatical occurrence to another via prediction and confirmation of the type of pathway in between. I argue that this formalism can handle the major issues of a procedural syntax of the text at least as well as can other candidates.

7.3 Chapter III turns to the operations for maintaining CONCEPUTAL CONNECTIVITY by means of building text-world models. I review some major issues in the notion of "procedural semantics" in which meaning figures as a PROCESS. I suggest that the coherence of texts is part of the larger consideration of how knowledge is acquired, stored, and utilized. I then demonstrate how a text-world model could be built for a sample from a school reader.

7.4 In Chapter IV, I explore the issue of INFORMATIVITY as the extent to which textual occurrences are expected. I present three "orders" of informativity and argue that communication normally functions along the middle order; extremely low or high informativity is regulated accordingly. I suggest that the issue should be investigated in the framework of a general theory of human apperception and information processing (cf. Rumelhart 1977a). The sample text is a newspaper article.

7.5 Chapter V deals with the best-known area of text linguistics, namely cohesive devices that can operate beyond sentence boundaries. I maintain that these devices have the function of keeping activated knowledge spaces current while additions or modifications are performed. They allow the surface format to be compacted and bound together without having to restate everything. The effect is that knowledge can be signaled without keeping a low level of informativity. However, too much compacting in certain settings would destroy these advantages, because the effort saved would be lost again in trying to keep the remainder coherent.

7.6 Chapter VI is devoted to the large-scale entities which supply GLOBAL PATTERNS to support the organization, orientation, and directionality of understanding processes. I differentiate between FRAMES, SCHEMAS, PLANS, and SCRIPTS as knowledge configurations with distinctive perspectives, and show how they might apply to the processing of various samples. I provide evidence from experiments conducted over the past years.

7.7 Chapter VII moves into some further issues of text production and processing. I offer some proposals as to how a processing model might handle the matter of TEXT TYPES. I look into some issues in the PRODUCTION of texts that might apply to both a simple children's story and a Shakespearean sonnet. Some aspects of INTERTEXTUALITY are explored on the basis of processes in recalling the content of texts.

7.8 Chapter VIII looks at two domains that have received special attention in the study of discourse processing. CONVERSATION is analyzed in regard to how topics flow and how participants decide who has a speaking turn. NARRATION is discussed in terms of strategies for telling and understanding interesting stories, as illustrated by an old English folktale.

7.9 Chapter IX concludes the volume with some outlooks on the APPLICATIONS of text linguistics as presented here. I inquire about the nature of the EDUCATIONAL ENTERPRISE and suggest the key position of training in textual skills. I explore upcoming trends in the teaching of reading and writing. Some motives are set forth as to why disciplines such as translation studies and literary studies might be involved in text linguistics. In this horizon of future prospects, the book ends on an auspicious note.

7.10 I hope to have made it clear why I feel that linguistics should be concerned with human activities. Though often disregarded, this view is rooted in venerable traditions, as attested by the words of Otto Jespersen penned over half a century ago (Jespersen 1924: 17):

> The essence of human language is human activity—activity on the part of one individual to make himself understood by another, and activity on the part of that other to understand what was in the mind of the first. These two individuals [. . .] and their relations to one another should never be lost sight of if we want to understand the nature of language.

II
Sequential Connectivity

1. TRANSFORMATIONAL SENTENCE GRAMMARS

1.1 From the standpoint of operation, conventional sentence grammars are MODULAR (cf. I.2.7). A sentence is first generated as a syntactic pattern; subsequently, a "semantic interpretation" is performed; and finally, in some versions at least, a "pragmatic interpretation" follows (I.2.6). This ordering reflects the relative priorities of modern grammatical theories. If language users processed a real sentence in this fashion, they would be re-enacting in miniature the history of the linguistic discipline since 1950. However, they might consider themselves fortunate if they managed to finish a complete sentence in so modest a time as only thirty years.[1]

1.2 The issue at stake is COMBINATORIAL EXPLOSION: a drastic over-computation of possible structures and readings that soon runs into astronomical operation times (cf. Woods 1970; Winograd 1972: 31). To process a sentence, an autonomous syntax cannot consult the decisive cues of meaning and purpose that real utterances provide; it can only test one structural description after another by trying various ways it could generate the sentence until the right one is found (a form of "analysis by synthesis"). Even for a computer with an extremely high speed, this procedure rapidly gets out of hand. One autonomous phrase-structure grammar was calculated by Stanley Petrick (1965; reported in W. Klein 1974: 179) to require, for the analysis of just one sentence at the rate of one millionth of a second per cycle,

---

[1]The fact that linguists analyze sentences in a few moments is due to their *prior* knowledge of what *contexts* the sentences could occur in (cf. I.1.16).

merely 2,300,000,000,000,000,000,000,000,000,000,000,000,000,000, 000,000,000 years—about six times the life expectancy of the sun.[2]

1.3 The picture is not much brighter for a semantics of independent word-meanings. Every word with n possible meanings multiplies the number of alternative ways to understand the whole sequence by n. Thus, for a seven-word sequence in which each element has only three potential meanings, a processor might have to contend with 2,187 readings. A sequence twice that long, but still with only three meanings per word, would have a total of 4,782,969 readings. Consider what would happen with a word like 'take', for which Steven Small (1978: 2) lists 57 meanings.[3]

1.4 These examples for short sequences give some impression of the truly staggering numbers that could be involved in the processing of entire texts. The modularity of logical and quasi-logical grammars means that one cannot take advantage of the contextual interaction of cues that renders the utilization of texts feasible under everyday conditions. If text processing indeed depends on the maintenance of connectivity (I.6.8), then the computation of structural derivations is a roundabout way to proceed. Human language users would not insist on such rigor anyway, but would jump to conclusions or work with fuzzy configurations where an automatic theorem-prover might well run on forever (cf. Goldman 1975: 328).

1.5 It might be helpful to differentiate again between actual and virtual systems (cf. I.4.1). The abstract grammar of a language cannot be required to state an absolute limit on the number or format of all possible sentences: someone could always add a new sentence or make an old one longer. The notion that a language allows an INFINITE set of sentences rests upon the potential for RECURSION: cyclic repetition of a given operation (e.g. adding more and more relative clauses to a sentence). To make an abstract grammar operational, we need to impose controls on length and complexity obtainable via recursion. In other words, we need to impose actualization constraints upon the virtual syntactic system of the language.

1.6 The two tenets of sentence grammarians to (1) uphold the autonomy of syntax and (2) reduce all complex sentences to a fixed set of simple formats, has created a grave obstacle for theories of language processing. The tenets lead to a model of language in which operations consist of converting

---

[2]Recent claims for transformational parsers being as fast as the augmented transition networks we discuss later (cf. Damerau 1977 and references there) are spurious. Petrick and co-workers are using a much smaller vocabulary and knowledge-world, and a much faster computer than Woods' original test runs. Moreover, what has been programmed is *not* Chomsky's "standard" theory. All transformational parsers—among which the one developed by Mitch Marcus (1977, 1978) stands out as especially attractive—have been substantially amended to make them viable on the computer.

[3]In III.3.5, I introduce the term "senses" for these alternative word meanings, following the trend in computational semantics (e.g. P. Hayes 1977; Rieger 1977b; Small 1978).

structures to other structures *within the same system*.[4] To keep syntax isolated, the standard model foresaw a purely syntactic "deep structure" as the immediate goal of sentence processing. When meaning was included, (Katz & Fodor 1963), it followed suit: nothing could be provided except "yet another algorithmic operation defining structures" (Seuren 1972: 245)— namely the conversion of concepts into minimal semantic units (cf. III.2). Syntax and meaning were thus unable to interact during their respective operations. This difficulty has led to a decline in the acceptance of the original notion of "deep structure"(cf. McCawley 1968a, 1968b; Lakoff 1968a, 1968b, 1971; Maclay 1971; van Dijk 1972a; Liefrink 1973; Kintsch 1974; Osgood & Bock 1977; Stockwell 1977). The movement of "generative semantics," which tried to obtain a more concerted interaction of syntax and meaning was *not* a mere "notational variant" of the standard model (Chomsky 1970, 1971; Katz 1970, 1971), at least not in its intention. Both theories can describe grammatical sentences; but the one with autonomous syntax has severe operational disadvantages.

1.7 Chomsky (1961) himself took pains to warn against the "prevalent and utterly mistaken view that generative grammar itself provides or is related in some obvious way to a model for the speaker." Still, we often encounter such contrary assertions as this: "Transformational grammar has the ambition of subsuming *all essential aspects* of a language system" (Hundsnurscher et al. 1970: 1) (emphasis added). Psycholinguistics certainly lavished its time on attempting to prove the psychological reality of the theory (surveys in Fodor, Bever, & Garrett 1974; Clark & Clark 1977). Experimenters were plagued with the bizarre task of eliciting autonomous syntactic behavior by methods like these: (1) reciting sentences in a flat monotone to preclude the use of intonational cues; (2) presenting isolated sentences in print displays and asking subjects later if a certain sentence had been seen before; (3) keeping the content of the sentences trivial, literal-minded, inane, and irrelevant to people's interests and situations. It was assumed that behavior elicited under these unrealistic conditions could somehow reveal the normal procedures of real language use.

1.8 There might be occasions when people actually perform transformations on sentence structures. The celebrated examples such as 'Flying planes can be dangerous' or 'The shooting of the hunters was tragic' could elicit syntactic reformulation that eliminates the ambiguities. More likely, however, people would be careful to signal by intonation or other cues in context what they intended to convey. The deliberate creating or noticing of

---

[4]János S. Petöfi (personal communication) agrees that for a theory of texts, transformation among structures *in diverse systems* must be allowed. His own model shows how this might be done (see note 18 to Chapter 1).

ambiguities is thus a signal of non-cooperation or of an attempt to be humorous. Many well-known jokes rely on this principle:

(1) On a hot day, a fat man in a crowd takes off his hat and pants.

The utilization of such texts is unproblematic because knowledge of the world mediates strongly against one reading. Jerry Hobbs points out the episode from a Burns and Allen show where Gracie is told by a fire inspector:

(2) There's a pile of inflammable trash next to your car. You'll have to get rid of it.

and undertakes to dispose of the car. In the motion picture *The Wizard of Oz,* an arrogant neighbor lady comes to complain about the family's dog, and the following dialogue ensues:[5]

(3.1) UNCLE HENRY: You say Dorothy bit you?
(3.2) NEIGHBOR LADY: No, her dog.
(3.3) UNCLE HENRY: Oh! She bit her dog!

Uncle Henry's utilization of a wrong, though structurally allowable reading, signals his intention to be uncooperative in the situation. It is clearly not the task of grammar to provide rules that preclude such occurrences. Potential ambiguities alone are a less crucial matter than the strategies people use to resolve ambiguities or even to rule them out in advance.

1.9 Laboratory experiments can be designed to bring out transformational behavior, if the researcher so desires. If a situation is constructed in which sentences such as:

(4a) John bought the book.
(4b) The book was bought by John.

are substituted for each other, test subjects will probably do some mental transforming analogous to the rules that would derive (4b) from (4a). It has not been demonstrated that people do any such thing *routinely* if they want to say or understand (4b) in communication. On the contrary, transformations merely substitute one structural pattern for another of the same systemic type with no great gain in processing (cf. I.6.2; II.1.6).

1.10 The difficulties with standard transformational grammar as a language theory can be summed up as follows:

1.10.1 Transformations bring no processing advantages except in specially constructed situations.

1.10.2 The theory does not explain why people would want to use complex sentences at all, when they would apparently save effort by uttering the "deep structure" to begin with.

---

[5] I number the sample texts continuously throughout the book. Decimal places are used to single out parts of samples; letters are used for alternative versions of the same sample.

1.10.3 Lacking interaction with other language levels, transformational syntax would bring a processing overkill of alternative structural descriptions that could scarcely be computed and disambiguated in reasonable times.

1.10.4 Transformations do not really *explain* a complex sentence; instead, they *get rid* of it in favor of simpler structures whose explanation is a foregone conclusion, since the latter are basic axioms to begin with.

1.11 We are left with a definition of the standard model as a *partial theory of paraphrase* (cf. S. Klein 1965; Ungeheuer 1969). Chomsky (1965: 162f.) remarks that his model can account for the relations between sentences of the type:

(5a) John bought the book from Bill.
(5b) The book was bought from Bill by John.

but it cannot deal with the relationships between:

(6a) John bought the book from Bill.
(6b) Bill sold the book to John.

If our hapless fire inspector were "competent" in Chomsky's sense, he could have averted Gracie's misunderstanding by embedding one sentence into another with the required deletions:

(7) You'll have to get rid of the pile of inflammable trash next to your car.

But he could not have performed a conceptual paraphrase:

(8) That pile of inflammable trash next to your car must be disposed of without delay.

And he certainly could not have chosen a format that leaves Gracie to infer the appropriate action on her own:

(9) That pile of inflammable trash next to your car is in violation of city fire ordinances. Please comply with this warning immediately.

It seems counter-intuitive that a theory explaining "the speaker-hearer's knowledge of his language" (Chomsky 1965: 4) should leave the "competent" language user so helpless in everyday affairs.

1.12 The immense importance attributed to the SENTENCE BOUNDARY also seems incongruous. As Horst Isenberg (1971: 155) remarks, it is odd that such nearly synonymous samples as:[6]

(10a) Peter burned the book. He didn't like it.
(10b) Peter burned the book because it didn't like it.

---

[6]Whenever required, I provide my own translations into English.

must be described by entirely different notions in a grammar, simply because one of them happens to be two sentences. The easily discoverable *conceptual connectivity* between the two configurations of content—the action of 'burning' has the "reason-of" a negative "volition" (on these terms, cf. III.4.7)—obtains whether an explicit junctive such as 'because' is used or not (cf. V.7.6ff.). To study that aspect, we do not need a structural description of the sentence or sentences, but a model of how people decide how much conceptual content to load onto a given sentence format (cf. Quillian 1966; Simmons & Slocum 1971; VII.2.17ff.).[7] The main decision criterion, I suspect, is the *degree of knownness or expectedness in context*. The 'not liking' is predictable in view of the 'burning', so that the combining into a single sentence is plausible (cf. van Dijk 1977a: 86). The expression of known or expected content favors longer, more complex sentences than that of new or unexpected (cf. Grimes 1975: 274; VII.2.19ff.; IX.4.6f.).

1.13 The observation that syntax is OVERRIDDEN must also be considered. Strohner and Nelson (1974) found that children treated the following sentences as expressions of the same content:

(11a) The cat chased the mouse.
(11b) The cat was chased by the mouse.

The children were more inclined to rely on world knowledge than on grammar and syntax (cf. also Turner & Rommetveit 1968).[8] David Olson (1974) found that children perform better on the identification of active vs. passive sentences if the agents of the action are given a clear identity. Carol Chomsky (1969) noticed that children acted out both the statements:

(12a) Donald tells Bozo to hop across the table.
(12b) Donald promises Bozo to hop across the table.

by making the Bozo toy hop. Evidently, the close proximity of the expressions for agent and action overruled the grammatical structure, which could not happen if a syntactic "deep structure" were the primary goal of understanding.

1.14 I do not deny that surface structure is often misleading with regard to underlying dependencies. I merely want to justify my preference for a syntactic model unlike the standard transformational one. The syntactic component in a theory of *processing* has two major functions: (1) the LINEARIZATION of elements in production, or their DELINEARIZATION in comprehension; and (2) building the GRAMMATICAL DEPEN-DENCIES among the surface elements *as they are presented in real time*. The

---

[7]The proposal to treat texts as super-long sentences (cf. Katz & Fodor 1963) clouds the issue altogether. The interesting question is why texts are usually *not* super-long sentences.

[8]Dressler (personal communication) observes here that children tend to treat the initial noun phrase of utterances as the agent in all cases.

component is therefore addressed to *connectivity* rather than to *segmentation;* and it is formulated such that syntax, meaning, and actions can be given an analogous representation.

2. SEQUENCING OPERATIONS

2.1 By "sequencing" I wish to designate all activities and procedures whose role is to arrange language elements into a working order, such that speaking, writing, hearing, or reading can be accomplished in a temporal progression. From a very detailed standpoint, we see combined sequences of tiny units of sound or form corresponding to those which have been systemized as phonemes or morphemes, respectively. Obviously, the main activity of adult language use is not that of gluing these tiny units together. The acquisition and use of words and phrases automatically entails the production and identification of their constituent parts. However, speech errors show that word parts do become displaced upon occasion, as in the famous "Spoonerisms" (cf. Clark & Clark 1977; 274). Many of these errors suggest a conceputal ambivalence when the displacement creates a strikingly contrasting statement to the intended one. Imagine the grim satisfaction some churchgoer with a troublesome life might derive when hearing the Reverend Spooner produce this historically attested utterance:

(13) The Lord is a shoving leopard to all his flock.

2.2 For a linguistics of actualization, the organization of phonemes and morphemes in a useable format is no trivial issue. Terry Winograd (1972) demonstrates how morpheme systems of English can be managed as a PROGRAM: a procedural statement of actions to be performed when ENTRY CONDITIONS activate the operations on the data (cf. also Berry 1977). To utilize inflected forms, the program matches the input pattern to an ordered set of hypotheses (cf. Woods 1978b: 30ff.). If the match is satisfactory, a "yes" is returned, and the program advances to the identification of later elements. If a "no" is returned, the program tries out the next hypothesis on the same element (see for example the control diagram for English endings in Winograd 1972: 74).

2.3 These considerations apply to the *syntagmatic* aspect of language, but they have important implications for the *paradigmatic* aspect as well (cf. I.2.2). Paradigms such as noun declensions or verb conjugations cannot be simple listings of forms: there must be some provision for efficient utilization and application. The better organized those provisions become, the less need there is for rote storage of exhaustive listings. Grammatical rules should be able to generate the highest feasible number of inflected forms for the largest range of lexical items. Here, the rule can be called a program, or a subprogram in a main program. The rule set for a given domain, such as verb inflections, should itself be internally ordered in such a way that the most probable, simple, and generally applicable rules are routinely tried first (cf. the notion of "core grammar" in Haber 1975). I have designated a program of this kind with fifteen systemic rules for the complex domain of German stem-changing verbs (Beaugrande 1979c). I undertook to show that some 80% of the extant verbs are rule-governed, and that the rest are mostly explainable via rule conflation. I believe that a computational approach to phonology and morphology deserves further attention.

2.4 When psycholinguistics began to emerge as a discipline, its central task was first construed to be investigating the mental reality of linguistic theories (surveys in Hörmann 1974, 1976). The natural consequence was that the analysis linguists perform on sentences was taken as a model of what language users do in understanding discourse. Emphasis accordingly fell on the extraction of structural descriptions for the various levels of language. The popular "syntactic approach" to language understanding has been summed up by Clark & Clark (1977: 58):

> Listeners have at their command a battery of mental strategies by which they segment sentences into constituents, classify the constituents, and construct semantic representations from them [. . .] As listeners identify constituents, they must not only locate them, but also implicitly classify them—as noun phrases, verb phrases, determiners, and the like. They must do this *before* they can build underlying propositions. [emphasis added]

For English, this approach is embodied, according to Clark and Clark (1977: 59-68), in STRATEGIES like these:

Strategy 1. Whenever you find a function word, begin a new constituent larger than one word.

Strategy 2. After identifying the beginning of a constituent, look for content words appropriate to that type of constituent.

Strategy 3. Use inflections to help decide whether a content word is a noun, verb, adjective, or adverb.

Strategy 4. After encountering a verb, look for the number and kind of arguments appropriate to that verb.

Strategy 5. Try to attach each new word to the constituent that came just before.[9]

Strategy 6. Use the first word (or major constituent) of a clause to identity the function of that clause in the current sentence.

---

[9]I cannot quite grasp the point of this strategy as stated by the Clarks. Surely the direction in which one looks for a constituent varies constantly.

Strategy 7. Assume the first clause to be a main clause unless it is marked at or prior to the main verb as something other than a main clause.

2.5 Despite the avowed importance of SEGMENTATION in the first quote, all of these strategies except numbers 3 and 7 are instead oriented toward CONNECTION. As such, they would be unobjectionable except for the stipulation that they must be run *before* meaning ("underlying propositions") can be recovered. That requirement entails the following practical difficulties:

2.5.1 As the computer simulations described in II.1.2 suggest, there would be a monstrous overcomputation of structural alternatives. In actual practice, even linguists who assert the autonomy of syntax are implicitly consulting meaning in order to decide what structures are present.

2.5.2 The function words (i.e. determiners, prepositions, and conjunctions) and inflections that people are asserted to utilize so decisively in Strategies 1 and 3 are often so slurred in actual speaking that they could scarcely be identified out of context (cf. Pollack & Pickett 1964; Woods & Makhoul 1973). For example, Dressler, Leodolter, and Chromec (1976) collected samples of the speech of Viennese students in which these elements are reduced to the merest outlines.

2.5.3 As Clark and Clark comment (1977: 72), "actual speech is so full of incomplete words, repeats, stutters, and outright errors" that the strategies "should often be stymied from the very start." Striking demonstrations that structural inconsistencies do not impede communication are discussed by Schegloff, Jefferson, and Sacks (1977) on the basis of video-taped conversations of California residents—evidence at least as hard as laboratory experiments.

2.5.4 The strategies seem to presuppose complete, grammatical sentences as the substance of every text. The high number of actually occurring incomplete sentences in everyday communication should make understanding hover constantly on the verge of a break-down. The fact that sentence boundaries are also hard to identify in heard speech (Broen 1971) is another obstacle.

2.5.5 Like much work on syntax, the strategies are Anglo-centric, for example, in regard to the role of "function words." In inflected languages with highly variable word order (e.g. Czech), the notion of autonomous syntax would have appeared far more counter-intuitive from the very beginning than was the case for English.

2.5.6 Due to emphasis upon discovery and analysis, these strategies do not seem to be applicable to speech production. Studies of speech production are in fact very rare (cf. VII.2.1). Fodor, Bever and Garrett (1974: 434) remark that "practically anything one can say about speech production must be

considered speculative, even by the standards current in psycholinguistics";
perhaps they should have said "because of" rather than "even by."

2.5.7 The heavy utilization of syntax does not accord with the findings on
storage and recall of language. Harry Kay (1955) used whole text passages in
tests and found that semantic recall ran about 70% and syntactic recall only
about 30%. It appears that syntactic formatting is not a prominent object of
cognitive resources.[10]

2.6 In recent discussions, support has accrued for the outlook of
RELATIONAL GRAMMAR (cf. Cole & Sadock [eds.] 1977; Johnson &
Postal 1980). Perlmutter and Postal (1978: 1) stress the theoretical opposition
of DERIVATIONAL versus RELATIONAL conceptions of grammar. The
derivational approach deals with structures in terms of constituency and
linear precedence, but it places little emphasis on the connectivity of
grammatical occurrences in surface structure. Yet because text perception
must evolve in real time, people could not afford to wait for sentence
completion and build a derivational tree; instead, they want to start
connecting perceived elements together as soon as possible. This tactic could
be represented by a syntax that constructs links between pairs of related
elements (cf. the "arc pair grammar" of Johnson & Postal 1980). This outlook
frees us from reliance on complete sentences: nothing more than a
GRAMMATICAL DEPENDENCY between two elements is needed for
operation. Indistinct or missing elements would cause at most local
discontinuities that could be overcome by the general PROBLEM-
SOLVING techniques outlined in I.6.7f.

2.7 A fragment from a school reader can illustrate the relational approach:

(14) A great black and yellow rocket stood in a desert.

Anyone hearing or reading the sentence notices at once that only some of the
elements which are directly adjacent in the surface structure are also
grammatically dependent on each other. In 'yellow rocket', the modifier is
adjacent to its head, but the other modifers 'great' and 'black' are at some
distance. The determiner 'a' is also remote. These obvious facts have an
important consequence for processing: the linear sequence is a poor basis for
the production and comprehension of texts. The crucial structure is instead
one in which the dependencies are signaled with explicit links. Figure 1 shows
how direct linkage could be imposed on the sample.

2.8 The proportions of Figure 1 are somewhat misleading. The modifiers
placed at a greater distance are not inherently more remote from their head

---

[10]The notion that surface syntax is stored in "short-term" memory and meaning in "long-
term" memory (cf. discussion in Loftus & Loftus 1976) is too simple (Kintsch, personal
communication). There is probably only a gradation in the storage times and quantities along
these lines.

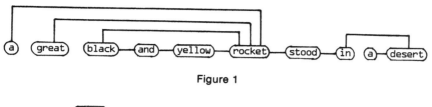

Figure 1

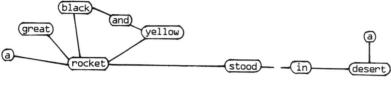

Figure 2

than the adjacent 'yellow.' If we shorten the links to uniform length, the grammatical dependencies yield a NETWORK, as shown in Figure 2 (cf. Perlmutter and Postal 1978). We can designate this configuration as an ACTUALIZED SYSTEMIC NETWORK of GRAMMAR STATES. The processor traverses the LINKS to access the NODES, making the data at the nodes ACTIVE and CURRENT. The action of traversing the link corresponds to PROBLEM-SOLVING: testing a hypothesis about the dependency between the nodes (a simple kind of means-end analysis in the sense of I.6.7.1). The word-class of a current state should be treated as an INSTRUCTION about the PREFERENTIAL or PROBABLE links that should be tested next (cf. I.3.4.6; Winston 1977: 343).

2.9 The structure in Figure 2 differs from the surface structure only in regard to its DELINEARIZATION. It would thus not qualify as a "deep structure" in the standard sentence models, not being a basic format incapable of further reduction. We might term it a "shallow structure" operationally sufficient to represent the connectivity of grammatical occurrences during actualization. Figure 3 suggests the idealized sequence of

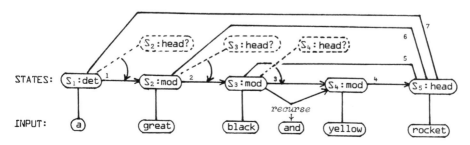

Figure 3

operations when the systemic processor advances from state to state. As soon as the first MICRO-STATE, in this case the determiner 'a', is registered, the processor is able to identify the MACRO-STATE of NOUN PHRASE. Each macro-state constrains the hypotheses about a whole group of occurrences, so that operations are efficient (cf. Rumelhart 1977a: 120; Winston 1977: 169). The macro-state will have a CONTROL CENTER (the noun in a noun phrase, the verb in a verb phrase, etc.), which has the heaviest linkage to other states. Hence, when the processor enters the noun-phrase macro-state, its highest priority will be to discover the head.[10a] The hypothesis is accordingly advanced that the successor state to S_1 (determiner) will be S_2 as head (see Figure 3). This preferred hypothesis fails, so that the next hypothesis on the preference list, namely "modifier," is tested and succeeds. I show the failed hypothesis with dotted lines. The processor again postulates a "head" state and must revise in favor of "modifier" to connect S_3. On encountering the conjunctive 'and,' the processor is alerted that the next state will probably be of the same type as the predecessor (modifier); and this next state will probably be the last of its type in the sequence. A simple RECURSION of the micro-state "modifier" is performed, whereupon the hypothesis "head" is finally successful (S_5). The fulfillment of the top priority establishes the head 'rocket' as the CONTROL CENTER of this macro-state, so that the proper links between all micro-states can be set up as shown in Figure 3 (cf. the procedure in Riesbeck 1975: 112). The numberings on the links suggest the ideal order in which the links would be constructed.

2.10 To understand the procedural ordering of operations, we can view processing in terms of STACKING. Each element is picked up and placed on the top of a HOLD STACK (see Rumelhart 1977a: 131): the active list of working elements to be integrated into a connected structure. If we have a PUSHDOWN STACK, each entry goes on top and pushes the others down a notch. Thus, the determiner and the modifiers in our sample would be entered in the order they occur, but removed in the reverse order. Figure 4 illustrates the stacking of the sample noun phrase. When the head turns up at the top of the stack, the stack is cleared by building a NETWORK of the grammatical dependencies of the macro-state noun phrase. Again, the numbers on the arrows suggest the sequence of building operations as derived from the arrangement of the stack.

2.11 The foregoing demonstration should suggest how the procedural approach to syntax might function. The processor needs an ordered list of preference hypotheses to match against current input, so that the operational

---

[10a]For purposes of demonstration, I do not distinguish between production and reception operations. In either case, the macro-sttate asserts itself as a pattern to be filled with accessed elements (micro-states). The *hypothesis* factor would of course be more dominant in reception, and *search* more dominant in production.

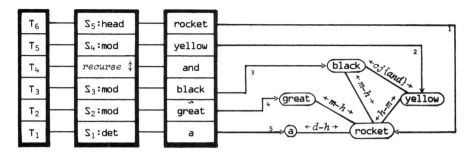

Key: *cj*: conjunction; *d*: determiner; *h*: head; *m*:modifier; S: state; T: time

Figure 4

sequence is efficiently controlled. Nothing more than a grammatical dependency, e.g. a noun phrase, is required as input; incomplete sentences present no such difficulties as they would for a tree-derivational approach in a phrase-structure grammar. The time sequence I have shown in Figures 3 and 4 is probably too strict. I surmise that there might be more than one control center active at a time—in the sample, both noun-phrase head 'rocket' and verb-phrase head 'stood.' And there might be some variations in the order in which the dependent states (e.g. modifiers) are attached. Such matters as the ordering of operations in real time and of hypotheses on a preference list will have to be explored by empirical study. The procedural approach promises to capture the EXPECTATIONS language users would have about what occurrences are PROBABLE at a given time (Rumelhart 1977a: 122). The most important factor is that *the rules of the grammar are simultaneously procedures for utilizing the grammar in real time*—a stipulation I cited as crucial for text linguistics in I.3.5.9 (see also Rumelhart 1977a: 122). At the moment of processing, the relations are ACTUAL, not VIRTUAL, and there is no gap between competence and performance to be overcome. The very notion of "word class" is removed from the domain of abstract taxonomies and made operational for utilizing elements in real input (cf. Rumelhart & Norman 1975a: 64).[11]

2.12 The formalism I have shown is the AUGMENTED TRANSITION NETWORK, a technique of data formatting developed as an alternative to transformational grammar for computer processing of English (Thorne, Bratley, & Dewar 1968; D. Bobrow & Fraser 1969; Woods 1970; Simmons & Slocum 1971). The network is built up in real time by making "transitions"

---

[11]This factor is especially decisive (cf. II.2.16), as it makes possible a flexible processing of word class shifts (e.g. Shakespeare's phrase 'Her art *sisters* the natural roses', *Pericles,* V, chorus, 7).

from one node to the next; this operation requires specifying or discovering the relation between the current node and its successor. The transitions can be "augmented" with any search or recognition procedures considered relevant at the time (Winston 1977: 344). Instead of using a highly detailed set of node types, we could rely on a very general set (with members like "determiner," "modifier," etc.) and attain any desired degree of specificity (e.g., "definite article," "indefinite article," "adjective," "participle," etc.) by augmenting link labels (Winston 1977: 172). Such a design might be the most human-like as well as the most economical: processing routinely picks up only essentials, but can become more thorough if there is any need (cf. III.4.15). Note that the augmented transition network does not have to be built in a single direction (though our demonstration is kept purely linear for the sake of simplicity). There could easily be a CONTROL CENTER such as a "head" with transitions being tested to several dependent elements ("determiners," "modifiers") at once. In III.14ff., I argue that grammatical networks should be set up in *parallel* with conceptual ones.

2.13 The formal potential of augmented transition networks is undeniably attractive. They are able to duplicate the behavior of virtually all kinds of grammars (cf. Woods, 1970; Winograd 1972; Kintsch 1974: 70; Hendrix 1978): context-free grammars, phrase-structure grammars, transformational grammars, and Turing machines. Still greater advantages can be obtained by such generalizations as those proposed by William Woods (1978c). He has built a parsing system from a "cascade" of augmented transition networks such that computations common to various language levels can be merged in operation (cf. III.4.14). He also lifts the restriction that input must be a sequence of symbols, so that he can also analyze apperceptual "fields," e.g. scenes, acoustic substance of speech, medical diagnosis, and data-base monitoring, from various perspectives. He concludes (Woods 1978b: 24):

> Generalized transition networks thus lift the notion of "grammar" away from the limited conception of a set of rules characterizing well-formed sequences of words in sentences. Rather, they are capable of characterizing arbitrary classes of structured entities.

2.14 I find the psychological plausibility of network grammars appealing as well. I suggested in I.4.3f. that if a virtual system is to be actualized, the stability of the system depends crucially on a regulative continuity of occurrences. That continuity emerges clearly in the network format. Psychological testing offers further support. When subjects were interrupted during the perception of sequences and asked to predict the next syntactic occurrence, they were in 75% agreement with each other (Stevens & Rumelhart 1975). Moreover, 80% of the reading *errors* recorded in the same tests were in accordance with the most probable paths as determined from the prediction experiment. Ronald Kaplan (1974) has shown that the notion of the hold stack accounts for the comparative difficulties in processing relative clauses just as well as does transformational grammar.

2.15 A repertory of grammatical states and dependencies can be defined according to the requirements established by investigations such as these. A HEAD would be a grammatical state of noun or verb capable of either appearing alone as a phrase, or acting as the control center of a phrase. Because nouns and verbs might be created on the spot from other word classes (e.g. in usage like 'The yellow rocketed skyward'), we might want to use terms like "noun-entity" and "verb-entity" for whatever elements are *used* as nouns or verbs in current input (as opposed to the virtual lexicon of the language). The MODIFIERS will be the adjectives, adverbs, and prepositional phrases that depend on the heads. The DETERMINERS would be articles, deictics, and numericals. Thus we have modifiers as QUALITATIVE signals about the head, and determiners as QUANTITATIVE signals (number, definiteness, etc.—see V.3). The VERBS differ from the nouns in regard to their complements: SUBJECT, DIRECT OBJECT, INDIRECT OBJECT, AUXILIARY, and DUMMY can all appear as well as MODIFIER. In compounded expressions, where two or more elements of the same class appear as a unit, we would have COMPONENTS. In sequences of phrases and clauses, we could have JUNCTION. The following list of link types seems to be useable for labeling the state transitions in actualized networks of grammatical dependencies. The abbreviations in square brackets will be used in diagramming to save space. In each link type, the control center is named first ("verb" or "head"). In the diagrams, however, I reverse the abbreviated labels where needed so the node label is next to the arrow pointing to the appropriate state.

2.15.1 VERB-TO-SUBJECT [v-s] is the minimal requirement for a clause or sentence, though not for a *discourse action* (cf. sample (26) in II.2.36).

2.15.2 VERB-TO-DIRECT OBJECT [v-o] obtains between a transitive verb (or verb-entity) and a noun (or noun-entity) capable of being affected directly by the event or action expressed via the verb.

2.15.3 VERB-TO-INDIRECT OBJECT [v-i] obtains between a verb and a noun capable of receiving indirect effects of the event or action, e.g. the entity to or for which some action is done or some object is given.

2.15.4 VERB-TO-MODIFIER [v-m] applies when a non-transitive verb (e.g. 'be') links a subject to an expression of a state, attribute, time, location, etc.

2.15.5 VERB-TO-AUXILIARY [v-a] is the link between a member of the open set of verbs (open because of potential word-class shifts in actualization) and a member of the closed set of verbal auxiliaries used to signal tense (e.g. 'have,' 'had,' 'will') or modality (e.g. 'must', 'might', 'should').

2.15.6 VERB-TO-DUMMY [v-d] is the link between a verb and a place-holder that merely fills a structural slot (e.g. 'it' in 'it's a good thing,' or 'there' in 'there's a unicorn in my garden').

2.15.7 HEAD-TO-MODIFIER [h-m] covers the dependency between one element and an expression which modifies it: adjective-to-noun entity, and adverbial-to-verb entity. This dependency is distinct from "verb-to-modifier" in not having the intermediary linking verb present.

2.15.8 MODIFIER-TO-MODIFIER [m-m] obtains when modifiers depend on each other (e.g. adverbial-to-adjective).

2.15.9 HEAD-TO-DETERMINER [h-d] is the link between an article, deictic, or numerical, and its head.

2.15.10 COMPONENT-TO-COMPONENT [c-c] covers the dependencies between elements of the same class, e.g. two nouns ('computer science') or two verbs ('trick or treat').

2.15.11 JUNCTION subsumes the dependencies of: (1) CONJUNCTION [cj] between at least two elements whose relationship in regard to their environment is *additively* the same or similar (tagged with 'and', 'also', 'too', 'moreover', 'in addition', etc.); (2) DISJUNCTION [dj] between at least two elements whose relationship in regard to their environment is *alternatively* the same or similar (tagged with 'or', 'or else', 'either–or'); (3) CONTRA-JUNCTION [oj] between elements whose relationship in regard to their environment is *antagonistically* the same or similar (tagged with 'but', 'however', 'yet', 'nonetheless', etc.); (4) SUBORDINATION [sb] between elements where one is *hierarchically dependent* on the other and cannot constitute a sentence by itself (tagged with 'if', 'because', 'since', 'that', 'which', etc.). Because these dependencies entail coherence and informativity as well as sequencing, I reserve their treatment until section V.7. I note here that conjunction, disjunction, and contrajunction more often link configurations of comparable surface structure than does subordination (cf. V.7.1.4).

2.16 Although my list is not intended to be definitive, it does offer the means for identifying the transitions within grammatical networks. One might argue for a more detailed list, depending on the thoroughness of syntactic processing one wishes to postulate (e.g. subdividing "modifiers" into "adjectives, adverbs, propositional phrases," and the like, cf. II.2.17). Pending detailed empirical tests, we cannot decide on any one degree of thoroughness. I surmise that people may not be too thorough under ordinary conditions (cf. III.4.15). In any case, the list should serve to label the *current use* of elements rather than their status in the lexicon. The use of hypotheses would reduce the enormous searching and combining that would be required if each element were looked up in the lexicon as it came along; the importance of this factor was pointed out by the failure of machine translating years ago.

2.17 The rest of our sample sentence (14) is processed in the same manner as the opening noun phrase. Having parsed the noun-phrase macro-state, the

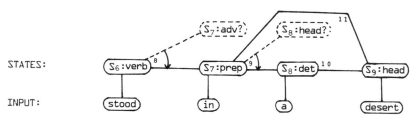

Figure 5

processor postulates the macro-state VERB PHRASE. Note that for a language other than English, the procedures might well be different. In French, for instance, the modifiers often come after the head, so that the end of the noun-phrase would be harder to predict exactly. Even in English we could easily have something else here besides a verb-phrase (e.g. a modifying prepositional phrase). The processor of course needs a backlog of alternative hypotheses to try out. In our sample, however, the occurrence of 'stood' allows immediate entry into the verb-phrase macro-state. The identification of the successor state would require AUGMENTING the transition (in the sense of II.2.12) by a specialized modifier search to distinguish between the sub-classes "adverb" and "prepositional phrase." Presumably, the successor state would preferentially be an "adverb" modifier, with the actually occurring "prepositional phrase" tried after that. The prepositional phrase would be a macro-state inside the verb-phrase macro-state, and would have as its top priority the discovery of the head. I show the transition network for this part of the sentence in Figure 5, again using dotted lines to indicate failed hypotheses.

2.18 The results for the entire sequence yield a fully labeled grammar network as shown in Figure 6. Because the "function words"'and' and 'in' are purely relational signals, I show them as TAGS on links rather than as independent grammar states. Although useful, these signals need not be distinctly apperceivable. In tests with students at the University of Florida, the sentence was uttered with the elements 'and' and 'in' both replaced by a nasalized schwa sound [ə̃]. The students had no difficulty filling in the

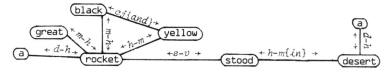

Key: *cj*: conjunction; *d*: determiner; *h*: head; *m*:modifier; *s*: subject; *v*: verb

Figure 6

indistinguishable words. In terms of problem-solving, they were able to connect the available points together with probable pathways via means-end analysis (cf. I.6.7.1; II.2.6).

2.19 I return to the 'rocket' sample in detail in Chapter III, where I am more concerned with conceptual than sequential processing. The important aspect here is to notice how the grammatical sequence interacts as bottom-up input with the top-down predictions of a language processor. Efficiency results from preferential ordering of the hypotheses to be tested first. The attention to probabilities enables the orientation of hypotheses toward the most probable occurrences at a given stage of operation. In effect, the procedures of the language user are adapted to fit the exact structure of the real objects being encountered: a technique I shall call PROCEDURAL ATTACHMENT (cf. D. Bobrow & Winograd 1977). If the objects are highly non-expected and idiosyncratic after all, language users will presumably not spend time running through a lot of syntactic predictions; at the first sign of difficulties, attention will be focused on other cues besides syntax. For example, our test subjects who could not hear 'in' could easily infer the relation "location-of" between 'rocket stood' and 'a desert' by consulting world-knowledge.

2.20 A syntactic model for a theory of actual texts might reasonably be asked to deal with issues like these:

2.20.1 recognizing major structures as familiar patterns;

2.20.2 distinguishing between main and subsidiary classes of elements, such as between "function words" and "content words";

2.20.3 conjunction, disjunction, and contrajunction;

2.20.4 subordination;

2.20.5 recursion and embedding;

2.20.6 dispensable elements;

2.20.7 discontinuous elements;

2.20.8 ambiguous structures;

2.20.9 incomplete, elliptical, or damaged structures;

2.20.10 mapping between surface expression and deeper levels in processing;

2.20.11 decision-making and selection procedures;

2.20.12 applicability to both the production and the reception of texts.

2.21 The first eight issues listed above have been extensively explored in sentence-based linguistics. But headway on the last four has been much more modest, due to a narrow interpretation of "competence." Incomplete or damaged structures would have been an eminent "performance" issue. The mapping from surface to depth never progressed beyond algorithms in which abstract structures were substituted for each other (whereas the decision-making and selection procedures of language users extend far beyond considerations internal to the sentence: contexts, motivations, goals, and situations). I conclude this chapter with an outline of how a network system handles some of these issues; others will be treated later on.

2.22 The *recognition of major structures* is a task for PATTERN-MATCHING (cf. I.6.6; Winograd 1972; Rumelhart 1977a). The BASIC CLAUSES and PHRASES (see Perlmutter & Postal 1978: 1ff.) are treated as macro-state patterns for building or recognizing actual structures in the utilization of a text. These patterns become active when their INITIAL STATES are actualized, such as the determiner beginning a noun phrase in our sample. When a FINAL STATE appears, a phrase or clause boundary is predicted. If pattern-based predictions are overturned, the use of other cues, especially conceptual relations, helps keep processing under reasonable control.

2.23 The *distinction between main and subsidiary categories of elements* is required for the organization of the grammar network. My convention is to place main categories in network nodes—the "content words" being nouns, verbs, adjectives, and adverbials—and the subsidiary ones, such as the "function words" of prepositions and conjunctions, as tags on links (on "content" vs. "function" words, cf. Bolinger 1975). The further function-word classes of articles and pronouns appear as nodes only in the grammatical networks, while their functions are taken over by positioning, linkage, and superpositioning operations in text-world models. Numericals (except for articles used as numerical signals) appear as nodes throughout. The psychological distinction between these main and subsidiary categories should correspond to the comparative indistinctness of the latter in speech as pointed up by my test with slurred sounds. Clark and Clark (1977: 275) suggest that in speaking, the content words are selected first and the function words are subsequently filled in. The order might be the same during comprehension. This is in agreement with the treatment of content words as control centers for problem-solving as outlined in this chapter.[12]

2.24 *Junction,* including *conjunction, disjunction, contrajunction,* and *subordination* can occur between components of very different sizes. The DEFAULT junction would be conjunction, since the relationship among elements in a text is usually additive. In a sample such as Kipling's famous phrase:

(15) The great, gray-green, greasy Limpopo River

the modifiers are taken as added to each other even though no 'and' is present; mere juxtaposition is sufficient. If the junction were disjunction i.e., the river had only one of these attributes, an explicit signal like 'or' would have to be

---

[12]Dressler (personal communication) remarks that aphasiacs with a telegram-like speech often retain content words and omit the function words.

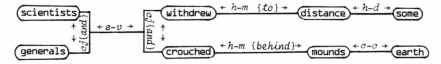

Key: *c*: component; *cj*: conjunction; *d*: determiner; *h*: head; *m*: modifier; *s*: subject; *v*: verb

Figure 7

used. Contrajunction, such as with 'but', 'however', etc., is also likely to be signaled on the surface, though not obligatorily. I adopt the convention of suppressing the signals of conjunction in diagramming text-worlds, but preserving the signals of disjunction, contrajunction, and subordination as link tags. I reserve the further treatment of these relations for V.7.

2.25 Junction of subjects or predicates can be represented by multiple sharing of links among nodes. For example, another fragment from the 'rocket' text runs like this:

(16) Scientists and generals withdrew to some distance and crouched behind earth mounds.

Figure 7 shows how this fragment appears as a grammatical dependency network. The operation of RECURSION upon encountering 'and' was already illustrated in Figures 3 and 4. The processor simply assumes that the next micro-state or macro-state is of the same class as the current one. In diagramming, I adopt the convention of placing earlier occurrences above later ones as far as spatial organization permits.

2.26 *Subordination* of clauses can be treated largely as subordination of the verbal elements; for example, another 'rocket' fragment like:

(17) Radar tracked it as it sped upward.

has the signal 'as' to indicate a temporal proximity between the events expressed by the verbs. In accordance with II.2.23, I show a link between the verb nodes with the junctive element as a tag, giving us Figure 8. Subordination is discussed further in section V.7.6ff.

2.27 *Recursion* is an essential property of context-free grammars (Kasher 1973:63), and is the mainstay of the infinite generative power of sentence systems (II.1.5). Actualization always imposes a THRESHOLD OF

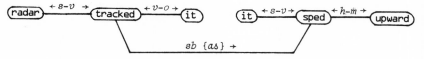

Key: *h*: head; *m*: modifier; *s*: subject; *sb*: subordination; *v*: verb

Figure 8

TERMINATION upon recursion, e.g. upon the length of strings of modifiers or upon embeddings inside embeddings. These constraints arise from processing resources like span of active memory and scope of attention. The popularity of multiple embeddings as test objects in psychological experiments (e.g. Miller & Isard 1963; Blumenthal 1966; Fodor & Garrett 1967; Stolz 1967; Freedle & Craun 1970; Hakes & Foss 1970; and so on) suggests a confusion of virtual and actual systems. Whatever people may do with sentences like:

(18) The pen the author the editor liked used was new.

cannot tell us very much about normal processing strategies, because such sentences are drastically improbable occurrences, and there is no need for routines to handle them (a model for automatic processing of multiple embeddings is offered in J. Anderson 1976: 470ff.). When Osgood (1971) designed an experimental situation in hopes of eliciting self-embedded sentences, he reported: "despite my speakers *all being involved in psycholinguistics, and reasonably familiar with transformational linguistics* [a significant choice of text subjects], only a single subject produced center embeddings, and this happened to be *my own research assistant*" (Osgood & Bock 1977: 517, emphasis added). The obliging assistant eloquently demonstrated how strong PRAGMATIC motivations can be in the selection of syntactic options.

2.28 The reliance upon contrasting grammatical sentences with ungrammatical ones (the latter marked with *) in linguistic discussions points up a potential difficulty. While a grammar must take special account of the *central* aspects of a language (the "core" in Haber 1975), these discussions work with *peripheral* occurrences. There is no good reason to suppose that the latter must necessarily reveal the nature of the former. The discrepancy emerges strongly when intricate elicitation techniques are designed to obtain empirical samples of rare syntactic constructions required by abstract grammar. A more realistic grammar would not need to defend its validity with such contortions.

2.29 Augmented transition networks of the kind I have described are easily able to deal with recursion. The processor simply notices the corresponding signals and repeats the structural operations it has just performed. To be humanly plausible, the probabilities assigned to each recursion in a series should steadily sink, so that language users would be increasingly surprised.[13] A theory of text utilization should foresee operational difficulties for cases where humans clearly have trouble. Transformational grammar was in this regard decidedly too powerful to be realistic.

[13]A psychological correlate of this factor might be "gambler's fallacy"; cf. note 2 to Chapter IV.

2.30 *Dispensable elements* are much less difficult for a systemic grammar of actual occurrences than for an abstract derivational grammar. The latter is obliged to rearrange whole tree structures just to get an element in or out of a sequence. In actualization, the element's appearance is a matter of stronger or weaker expectations being fulfilled or not fulfilled, and whatever is apperceived as a gap can be filled in via problem-solving (cf. II.2.8). In pairs like:

(19a) The pilot saw that the rocket descended.
(19b) The pilot saw the rocket descended.

(20a) A rocket stood in a desert in New Mexico.
(20b) A rocket stood in a New Mexico desert.

the dispensable elements 'that' and 'in' are relational link tags whose conceptual labeling can be done without the tags. Increased processing effort may be needed to handle the structures where the elements are absent (cf. Fodor & Garrett 1967; Hakes & Foss 1970; Hakes 1972), but context would easily influence that factor (Clark & Clark 1977: 64f.). Rudolf Flesch (1972) even suggests that these elements should be deleted to make prose more readable by his (admittedly disputable) standards (cf. IX.3.2ff.).

2.31 *Discontinuous elements,* according to our model, would be difficult to manage if they were placed at some distance from each other. The span of active storage (or the hold stack demonstrated in Figure 4) would become very crowded before the final part of the element appeared. This gradation of difficulty seems appropriate, as (21a) is indeed easier for English language users than (21b):

(21a) They took the rocket down.
(21b) They took the rocket at the launching site that was constructed out in the bleak New Mexico desert near White Sands down.

Probably, an understander would not immediately know where to attach the 'down' of (21b), but could do so by a backward search that favored the verb node over other possible points: another illustration of problem-solving. Some languages, especially German, have a strong potential for positioning the particles of verbal elements at the very end of a clause. This usage does not make German harder to use, however. The native speaker merely stores the corresponding probabilities and expectations so that these final particles are immediately connected to the appropriate prior occurrence. The concern for discontinuous elements is intense only for models of "immediate constituent analysis," which proceed by cutting surface segments into halves, quarters, eighths, and so on (hence, elements are hard to treat if they are scattered throughout a sentence).

2.32 *Ambiguous structures* have been widely discussed in linguistics. As Peter Hartmann (personal communication) remarks, the intense structural analysis done by linguists tends to proliferate ambiguities that people in everyday communication might well not notice. Transformational grammar used ambiguities as a favorite means of justifying the notion of "syntactic deep structure" (cf. II.1.6). For a procedural model, we should inquire whether the ambiguity is or is not resolved later on in the sequence. For many years, Robert Simmons (personal communication) has used this example:

> (22) The old man the boats.

Uttered in a flat monotone, this sentence is extraordinarily hard to comprehend. Either no meaning at all is recovered (as Simmons believes), or people must back up and do a completely new processing in which 'man' is identified as a verb rather than a noun (as Rumelhart 1977a: 123 argues for the same example). The dispute cannot be settled to the extent that everyday contexts would hardly occur spontaneously in which there could be a genuine and lasting ambiguity (the state of affairs being of course different for a computer).

2.33 One class of resolvable ambiguities is called "garden path sentences," because they lead an understander down one track and then present a block (Clark & Clark 1977: 80). The understander is believed to notice only one alternative reading and to pursue that hypothesis until trouble arises. Yet experiments show that if people are asked to make continuations for clauses containing structural ambiguities, they show more hesitations and false starts than for non-ambiguous clauses (MacKay 1966). This finding suggests that more than one reading is being recovered. I suspect that the experimental set-up encouraged a non-typical expenditure of processing resources in an attempt to avoid what might be errors. The test subjects had more motivation to expect and be wary of traps than would be the case in everyday discourse.

2.34 At present, it is computationally more expensive for a computer-simulated understander to back up and reprocess a sentence than to calculate the competing alternatives at once (Robert Simmons, personal communication). This situation may well change when the computer has better knowledge of context and world situations, and a sharper grasp of relative probabilities. However, I would point out that economy is a criterion directly applicable to the comparison of derivational vs. network grammar (cf. II.2.6). Consider the processing of a garden-path sentence (Clark & Clark 1977: 67):

> (23) The dealer offered two dollars for the painting refused.

For a grammar that derives sentences from trees, the revisions needed upon finding the element 'offered' left over are more drastic than those needed for a network grammar. When the unexpected element is found by the network grammar (Figure 9a), the structure set up need only be relabeled along one link and the newcomer added on via the discarded link label ("subject-to-verb") (Figure 9b). In contrast, a tree structure set up for the initial wrong

Key: *d*: determiner; *h*: head; *m*: modifier; *o*: object; *s*: subject; *v*: verb

Figure 9a

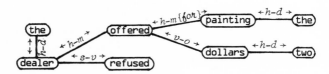

Key: *d*: determiner; *h*: head; *m*: modifier; *o*: object; *s*: subject; *v*: verb

Figure 9b

reading, shown in Figure 10a, would have to be discarded altogether because the topmost branching of noun phrase (NP) and verb phrase (VP) is in error. Of course, much of the structures at the bottom of the tree could be preserved. But since the first rule in grammars of this kind is S → NP + VP, rewriting the sentence as noun phrase plus verb phrase, a strict derivation, if interpreted as a process, would have to begin all over again. Figures 10a and 10b show the contrast involved. We see that this kind of grammar is useful for linguistic analysis of structures after the fact, but hard to envision as a model for human processing in real time.

2.35 The statistics I cited at the beginning of this chapter (II.1.2ff.) were intended to suggest how dangerous a theory without controls upon alternative readings would be in operation. The ambiguities of the kinds just discussed would only be the peak of an endless iceberg. We ought to distinguish carefully between: (1) ambiguities of isolated fragments that

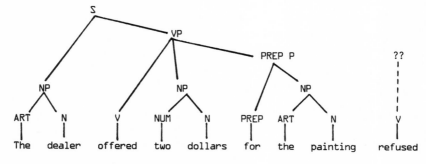

Figure 10a

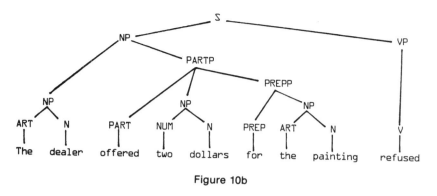

Figure 10b

evaporate in context; (2) ambiguities that are misleading for a time, and then corrected (of the "garden path" variety); and (3) ambiguities that are *intended* to be misleading for special effect. The billboards in London subways with mock headlines about the results of reading the classified ads in the *Times* are of the (3) variety:

(24) Zoo-keeper finds Jaguar queueing for underground ticket.

The text is intentionally devoid of any context, and it would be hard to expand the headline into a story that could maintain the ambiguity very long between the possible agents of the activity 'queueing' (and perhaps also between an automobile and an exotic animal). In contrast, some ambiguities arise from the hearer–reader's intention rather than from the producer's, as in Martin Kay's favorite subway sign:

(25) Bill Stickers Will Be Prosecuted.

where Kay muses over the fate of poor old Bill. These issues regarding ambiguity can be stated, but not settled, in terms of sentence grammars alone. The criteria of TEXTUALITY as enumerated in I.4.11 would normally suffice to disambiguate structures, which, in the abstract, might have several readings. Psychologists influenced by transformational grammar would understandably be inclined to suppose that people actually compute all the structurally possible readings for sentence syntax (cf. Garrett 1970; Lackner & Garrett 1972; Bever, Garrett, & Hurtig 1973). In a model of systemic processing interactions, the matter takes on more modest proportions.

2.36 *Incomplete structures* have conventionally been seen as derived from complete ones. Roger Brown (1973: 209) suggests that "perhaps all utterances are derived from implicit complete sentences." There are good reasons to disbelieve such claims as artifacts of linguistic methodology. Consider the following advertisement from the *Florida Independent Alligator* (October 18, 1978):

(26) PIZZAMAN EXPRESS   WE DELIVER
50¢ OFF ANY PIZZA
plus
2 free cokes

Wednesday only
Open at 11:00 A.M.

I presented this text to a group of University of Florida students and asked
what they thought was missing. Many said they couldn't see that anything at
all was missing. Upon prompting to make sentences out of the text, there were
very few cases where the students could agree on what the full format ought to
be.

2.37 A formal grammar might do no better. If well-formedness of
sentences rather than conceptual-relation coherence were the processing goal,
one could, strictly speaking, only produce dummy structures like this:

(27) WE DELIVER (something). (Somebody) (does) (something)
(about) 50¢ OFF ANY PIZZA plus 2 free cokes. (Something)
(happens) Wednesday only. (Something) (is) open at 11:00 A.M.

This activity seems to be a waste of time and processing resources. People
would surely be more likely to consult the underlying situation and use its
organization to build hypotheses about how these text fragments should fit
together. People will not of course *know* what the missing relations must be,
for example, that the offer is valid 'Wednesday only' while the pizza parlor is
'open at 11:00 A.M.' every day. The juxtaposition of the fragments combined
with commonsense knowledge of the world simply makes these inferences
reasonable, so that processing is satisfactory.

2.38 The same argument applies to *damaged* structures. A person might
walk by the pizza parlor and hear some fragments of the text being announced
over a loudspeaker and partly blotted out by street noises. However,
situational knowledge would again make comprehension unproblematic.
Any spectator at sports events can easily attest that loudspeaker
announcements are very often not couched in complete sentences.[14]

2.39 To attack the remaining issues raised in II.2.20, we need more
groundwork from the following chapters. I rest my case here in support of a
model of syntax as sequencing procedures whose purpose is not segmentation
or derivation, but the maintenance of connectivity. I have adduced the
considerations of procedural order, efficiency, probability, and economy as
desirable traits of realistic models. The imposition of well-formedness criteria
as a standard for real occurrences is shown to be operationally inadequate

---

[14]Dressler (personal communication) notes that the "allegro-styles" of rapid speech offer
further evidence.

and psychologically implausible; indeed, many frequent text types become embarrassments for linguistic theory rather than legitimate objects of inquiry.

2.40 I stress in closing that the connectivity I have looked into here is far too restricted to account for communication. Many possible obstacles to sequential connectivity disappear when processors utilize concepts and relations, or plans and goals. Only in the broad perspective of processing interactions does the vast complexity of successful communication begin to appear manageable.

III

Conceptual Connectivity

1. MEANING AND PHILOSOPHY

1.1 Although often neglected in conventional linguistics, meaning has long been an object of dispute in philosophy. Since antiquity, philosophers have envisioned the construction of a mode of LOGICAL EXPRESSION. The mode was expected to be exact, non-ambiguous, and concise. Strict rules should make it decidable if any statement was true or false, and whether any statement could correctly be proven from another. All statements had obligatory symbolic formats that could be translated into declarative sentences of natural language: the subject/predicate positions corresponded to the symbols or slots for argument/predicate, object/function, etc., depending on the type of logic. To connect statements, JUNCTIVES were defined according to their effects on TRUTH VALUE. If two statements were true by themselves, their conjunction with 'and' was also true; if either was false, the whole conjunction was false. A disjunction with 'or', on the other hand, was true provided only one of the statements was true. (On conjunction and disjunction, cf. II.2.15.11; V.7). The junctives 'if–then' and 'if and only if' (usually written 'iff') were also defined regarding truth value (for further discussion, cf. van Dijk 1977a, 1977b).

1.2 The tendency to identify meaning with truth value has been widespread. Rudolf Carnap (1942: 22), for example, remarks:

> Semantic rules determine truth-conditions for every sentence of the object language [...] *To formulate it another way:* the rules determine the meaning or sense of the sentences. [emphasis added]

60

This conflation has several consequences. First, philosophers have expended great energy on debating unresolvable paradoxes about truth, such as Strawson's (1949: 90) example:

(28) What I am now saying is false

where the statement is true only if it is false. Second, the issue of REFERENCE assumed a disproportionately prominent role in theories of meaning. Third, statements whose truth value cannot be decided are to be considered meaningless; yet undecidable statements are produced and understood constantly in everyday communication (Miller & Johnson–Laird 1976).

1.3 REFERENCE is usually defined as the relationship between expressions and those objects or situations in the world the expressions designate. Among the very diverse and intricate forms of reference, logicians are concerned with very few, notably with "quantificational status." If one unique object is referred to, an "existential quantifier" marks it as an existing object in the real world. The most obvious case is names of persons, as we can see by their frequency in logicians' examples (and inherited over into a linguistics of 'John and Mary' sentences). However, the human activities of using proper names are not at all straightforward, to say nothing of descriptive expressions (cf. J. Anderson & Bower 1973; Ortony & R. Anderson 1977; J. Anderson 1978: Kalverkämper 1978). If a whole set of objects is referred to, a "universal quantifier" signals that any statements must be true of every single object having that name. These two quantifiers allow one to make ASSERTIONS about objects and to construct proofs, which yield values of either true or false (cf. sample (87) in V.3.12).

1.4 Although logics of this kind are in themselves unobjectionable, they create vast confusion if taken as a model for human language communication. The following difficulties must be confronted:

1.4.1 ASSERTION is a HUMAN ACTION of entering a statement into a textual world. Logic misses the important factors of CONTROL (Levesque & Mylopoulos 1978:2) and of the speaker's INTENTION (Cohen 1978: 18). REFERRING is also a human action and not a property of noun phrases (Morgan 1978a: 109).

1.4.2 Human knowledge of the world creates a rich background of defaults, preferences, contingencies, and interactions for any assertion someone might make. Communicative situations are sensorially accessible and related to a wealth of past experience. All of these outside materials are usually allowed no place in logic.

1.4.3 The strict rules of logics render the assertions they permit obvious or even tautological. Human communication thrives on uncertainties, exceptions, variables, and unexpected events—all of which render a statement *interesting,* whether its truth can be determined or not.

1.5 If logics are to be useful in theories of natural language, their flexibility and scope will have to be enormously increased. Methods will have to be found for making logical procedures operational (see Simmons & Bruce 1971; Kowalski 1974; Cercone & Schubert 1975; Warren & Pereira 1977; Levesque & Mylopoulos 1978). The notions of truth and existence could be treated as DEFAULTS assumed in otherwise non-committal contexts. For example, people can be expected to believe in the truth of their statements (Grice 1975) except when signals to the contrary are provided (cf. Weinrich 1966a). This belief would yield not CORRECT ASSERTION (exact correspondence with the world), but JUSTIFIED ASSERTION; in many cases, however, we find MOTIVATED ASSERTION of materials whose truth is undecidable or even known to be false (Beaugrande 1978b: 7).

1.6 Due to an interest in quantification, theories of reference have often made use of SET THEORY. Whereas a CLASS is constituted according to some identifiable characteristic of its members and is thus indispensible for the organization of knowledge (cf. III.3.19), the SET is constituted simply by the fact that some elements belong to it. I have misgivings about the usefulness of set theory in a model of human communication. To claim that by uttering:

(29) Macbeth doth murder sleep, sleep that knits up the ravelled sleeve of care. (*Macbeth,* Act II, scene ii, 36 ff.)

the speaker is intersecting the (single-member) set 'Macbeth' with the set of people who murder sleep, sleep being itself intersected with the set of things that knit the ravelled sleeve of care, certainly doesn't resolve the issue of meaning; it only restates it. Moreover, set intersection is operationally cumbersome,[1] since for a given statement, one often has to look at all members of at least one set, and in the worst case (e.g. disproving false statements about one member of a set) at all members of both sets (but see now Fahlman 1977: 31).

1.7 Future revisions of logic may amend the shortcomings I note here. However, it is difficult to imagine how a logical system could be devised without MODULARITY: independence not only of system components, but also of every statement and expression, from contextual influences (cf. I.2.7). The whole enterprise of formal logic seems to disregard the continuities that people experience through their senses (cf. Shepard & Metzler 1971; Cooper & Shepard 1973; Kosslyn 1975). Perhaps a system for extremely fast computation of discrete symbolic descriptions, as envisioned by Marvin Minsky (1975), may yet approach logical rigor.

---

[1]Smith, Shoben, and Rips (1974) propose a set-theoretical model of meaning in which a concept figures as an ordered set of features. But, as Hollan (1975) contends, their model can, in fact, be formulated as a network model with a gain rather than a loss of representative power. I would add that the ordering of pairs in sets would encourage an atomistic outlook on the task of modeling the meaning of whole texts.

2. MEANING AS FEATURE CLUSTERS

2.1 When meaning entered into American linguistics after a long exile, it was approached with methods similar to those that had been successful in descriptive phonology and morphology. The meaning of all expressions in a language was treated like the sound substance:[2] decomposable into a repertory of minimal units (e.g. Katz & Fodor 1963; Pottier 1963; Prieto 1964; Bierwisch 1966; Greimas 1966; Coseriu 1967; Nida 1975). The minimal units were variously called "semes" or "sememes" (analogy to "phonemes"), or semantic "features" or "markers" (on the last two terms, cf. Hörmann 1976: 78). The status of these constructs was interpreted variously, for example:

2.1.1 as the "linguistic image of properties, relations, and objects in the real world" (Albrecht 1967: 179; compare Pottier 1963);

2.1.2 as distinctive elements arising from the "apperceptive constitution" of "human beings in regard to their environment" (Bierwisch 1966: 98);

2.1.3 as elements for building up a semantic theory (Katz & Fodor 1963);

2.1.4 as conceptual elements into which a "reading" decomposes a "sense" (Katz 1966);

2.1.5 as constituents of a meta-language for discussing meaning (Greimas 1966).

2.2 There are two general perspectives here: (1) psychological reality (Albrecht, Bierwisch, to some extent Katz), versus (2) linguistic theorizing (Katz & Fodor, Greimas). If we adopt the psychological perspective, the substance of meaning becomes an empirical issue (Winograd 1978: 30). In the linguistic perspective, the creation of theories of meaning is entirely the responsibility of introspection and systemization. Whichever approach is adopted, the following questions present inordinate difficulties:

2.2.1 How can the briefest, yet most universally applicable catalogue of units be set up for an entire natural language?

2.2.2 How many minimal units must a human store in order to communicate, and in what format?

2.2.3 How can these units reflect the fact that all domains of meaning cannot look the same (cf. Meehan 1976: 225; III.2.4)?

2.2.4 How can we deal with RESIDUAL MEANING: idiosyncratic meaning in words and expressions that is not covered by usual units? If we convert all residue into units, we explode the system beyond all proportion with elements that might (in the worst case) be needed for only a single word.

2.2.5 Will the set of postulated units also apply to every new expression that could ever be added to the language?

2.2.6 How can the units themselves be expressed without using natural language expressions that could be decomposed in their turn (cf. Wilks 1977a)?

---

[2] I wonder whether this transfer of phonological methods to other levels of language did not undermine, in a meta-perspective, the proclaimed independence of levels from each other.

2.2.7 How can we deal with the adaptation of expressions and their content to contexts: are there different unit configurations here, or the same units with different values (cf. Hörmann 1976: 141)?

2.2.8 Where should decomposition stop without going into INFINITE REGRESS: the continual subdivision into ever smaller components (cf. Winograd 1978: 28)?

2.2.9 How could decomposition operate in real time without a dangerous explosion of content (Wilks 1975a: 22)?

2.2.10 How are word meanings acquired, given that miminal units are not encountered in everyday communication?

2.3 In a processing model, minimal units figure as PRIMITIVES: irreducible units for processing all comparable content in the same terms. Although they would be desirable for procedural considerations such as formatting and storage (cf. Winston 1977: 198), systems of primitives would have to meet formidable requirements: (1) the entire range of language expressions would have to be covered by a finite set of primitives; (2) primitives should not be explained in terms of each other; and (3) primitives should not be capable of further decomposition (Wilks 1977a; Winograd 1978). The question arises whether such thoroughness and completeness is even necessary for everyday comprehension (Rieger 1975: 204). Many utterances would present fearsome intricacies resulting out of unconventionality or vagueness of usage (on dealing with vagueness, cf. Eikmeyer & Rieser 1978).

2.4 There are clear differences in the internal structuredness of knowledge domains. The proponents of minimal units invariably select well-structured domains, such as kinship terminology (e.g. A. Wallace & Atkins 1960; Lounsbury 1964). Here, concepts are almost entirely *relational* themselves and hence perfectly suited for non-residual decomposition: 'male/female', 'parent/child', and so on (Kintsch 1979b: 20). Speakers of English would be hard put to supply the components of concepts like 'intelligence', 'beauty', 'absurdity', 'essence', and so forth with any wide agreement. A model of meaning must make a distinction between concepts whose function is to represent *relations,* and concepts with more diverse and intricate functions of representing *content* (Shapiro 1971).

2.5 There appears to be a TRADE-OFF in the usefulness of minimal units. The larger the store of knowledge becomes and the more diversified the domains, the less we have to gain by reducing everything to minimal units. I would accordingly conclude that decomposition of meaning has the same human psychological status as that assigned to transformations in II.1.9: the operations involved *can* be performed if a task and a domain make it worthwhile, but they are not done *routinely* (see Kintsch 1974: ch. 11 for a survey of tasks). The question will have to be solved empirically rather than by linguists' debate (Kintsch 1974: 242), and the evidence for decomposition is slight so far (J. Anderson 1976: 74).

2.6 The questions involving the featural approach will not be resolved very soon. Perhaps it would be useful to look in the opposite direction: not at *segmentation* but at *continuity*. While there is little evidence yet that humans break meaning into tiny units when they communicate (barring discussions among linguists), there is good evidence that people must build large configurations of meaning in order to utilize whole texts (e.g. when planning, learning, recalling, or summarizing textual content). I shall follow up some PROCESSES which could plausibly contribute to this continuity of meaning in communication via texts.

3. MEANING AS PROCESS

3.1 The identification of meaning with usage was proposed especially by Ludwig Wittgenstein (1953; cf. also Schmidt 1968b). I adopted a similar outlook on Harris's distributional approach (see I.2.3). However, we are hardly likely to ever compile an exhaustive record of all uses of even one word, let alone the whole lexical repertory of a language. We can at best seek to discover processes that operate generally on usage as an activity of building up meanings in context.

3.2 For that undertaking, a PROCEDURAL SEMANTICS would be productive (Miller & Johnson-Laird 1976; Winograd 1976; Bobrow & Winograd 1977; Johnson-Laird 1977; Levesque 1977; Havens 1978; Levesque & Mylopoulos 1978; Schneider 1978). Many approaches that do not expressly call themselves by that term share the outlook that meaning results from actions in an intelligent processor (e.g. Schank et al. 1975; Woods 1975; Fahlman 1977; Hayes 1977; Brachman 1978a; Cohen 1978). The formatting of knowledge for optimal processing has been in debate. DECLARATIVE knowledge is formatted as statements that might be used in many different and possibly unforeseen ways. PROCEDURAL knowledge, in contrast, is formatted as programs designed to run in specifically anticipated ways. Declarative knowledge is thus more versatile in its applications, but its actual uses are less efficient. Debates stressing the opposition of these standpoints (sample in Winston 1977: 390ff.) are misleading, however. The question is one of different PERSPECTIVES taken on what is in essence the same knowledge (cf. discussions in Winograd 1975; Scragg 1976; Bobrow & Winograd 1977; Goldstein & Papert 1977). In a very small knowledge-world, only a few facts are known and the processor is not yet very intelligent, creating a need for explicit programs. But in an extensive and richly interconnected world, the declarative and procedural aspects begin to converge: the structuring of knowledge is simultaneously a statement of how it can be accessed and applied. Only if meaning and use are taken as independent—as "monisms" that deny each other (R. Posner 1979b)—do we have to contend with an antagonism between formats.

3.3 The basic unity for a procedural semantics would be the PROPOSITION as a RELATION obtaining between at least two CONCEPTS (cf. Kintsch 1972, 1974; Rumelhart, Lindsay, & Norman 1972; J. Anderson & Bower 1973; B. Meyer 1975, 1977; Frederiksen 1975, 1977; J. Anderson 1977). These entities depend on the degree of detail required for a processing task. Many concepts can be analyzed into propositions (cf. III.4.4), and in a task like summarizing, propositions might be subsumed into single concepts (cf. Ausubel 1963). Searle (1971: 141) argues that REFERENCE can only be accomplished via propositions, because if someone merely expressed a concept, there would be no way to identify what was meant. Leonard Linsky (1971: 77) supports this view in suggesting that "referring expressions" cannot be treated without their context. It seems to me that referring is in fact accomplished via the entire TEXT-WORLD MODEL as outlined in I.6 and further depicted in the following section. If people do match the content of texts with their notion of the real world, then the completed text-world model should give the clearest indications of what to look for. There is probably a THRESHOLD OF TERMINATION, both for the degree to which concepts are broken into propositions (or propositions subsumed under concepts), and for the extent to which text content is actually matched with whatever is taken to be the "real world."

3.4 A traditional example of a proposition would be something like:

(30) Socrates is Greek.

where 'Socrates' is the ARGUMENT and 'Greek' is the PREDICATE. Since sentences are not propositions, however, many researchers prefer a format such as this:

(31) (GREEK, SOCRATES)

The conventional viewpoint in logic is that predicates are "designations for the properties and relations predicated of individuals" (Carnap 1958: 4). My use of the notion of "proposition" will be kept informal so as to cover a very wide variety of content (cf. III.4.7ff.).

3.5 WORDS or WORD GROUP UNITS are EXPRESSIONS: SURFACE names for UNDERLYING concepts and relations. The use of expressions in communication ACTIVATES these concepts and relations, that is, enters their content into ACTIVE STORAGE in the mind. The transition between expressions and their content is an aspect of MAPPING (cf. I.2.10). A given concept may have alternative names which are SYNONYMS to a greater or lesser extent, depending on how much conceptual/relational substance they activate. Although synonymity is probably rare in the *virtual* system of the LEXICON (cf. I.2.8.2), it is common in the *actual* systems of textual worlds where the interaction of concepts controls the amount of substance being activated. In return, a single expression may be able to activate various concepts according to its use; the expression can then be said to have several SENSES (cf. P. Hayes 1977: Rieger 1977b; Small 1978). The existence of synonyms and multiple senses are evidence of the ASYMMETRY between expressions and their meanings (cf. I.6.12). This asymmetry assumes different proportions in various languages (cf. Wandruszka 1976), so that concepts must be in part language-independent (cf. Schank 1975a: 256, 1975b: 7). The borderline between expressions and concepts is not clear-cut (Wilks 1975a), and is presumably a matter of the DEPTH OF PROCESSING applied to communicative and cognitive operations (cf. S. Bobrow & Bower 1969; Craik & Lockhart 1972; Mistler-Lachman 1974): the degree to which an entity or configuration of entities is removed from the outward surface text. In general, conceptual connectivity is "deeper" than sequential, and planning connectivity deeper than conceptual (cf. I.2.12).

3.6 Concepts have FUZZY BOUNDARIES (Rosch 1973; Hobbs 1976: 44; Kintsch 1977a: 292ff.). They consist of a CONTROL CENTER in a KNOWLEDGE SPACE around which are organized whatever more basic components the concept subsumes (cf. Scragg 1976: 104). The center is the point where activation of the concept's content begins, but not necessarily where knowledge is concentrated (cf. the "superatoms" in Rieger 1975: 166f.). Though often assumed in traditional philosophy (Hartmann 1963b: 104), the unity of a concept is probably not guaranteed by strict identity of substance. Instead, unity emerges from the unifying function of the concept in organizational procedures for managing knowledge. The concept might be described as a block of INSTRUCTIONS for cognitive and communicative operations (cf. Schmidt 1973: 86).

3.7 The constitution of concepts can be explored in regard to three processes: ACQUISITION, STORAGE, and UTILIZATION (Hörmann 1976: 485). A unified representation for all these processes would be desirable. If we assume that CONTINUITY, ACCESS, and ECONOMY are reasonable postulates for processing, the SEMANTIC NETWORK appears attractive (e.g. Quillian 1966, 1968; Collins & Quillian 1969, 1972; Carbonell Sr. 1970; Simmons & Bruce 1971; Simmons & Slocum 1971; Rumelhart, Lindsay, & Norman 1972; Collins & Loftus 1975; Norman & Rumelhart 1975a; Shapiro 1975; Woods 1975; Fahlman 1977; Brachman 1978a, 1978b; Levesque & Mylopoulos 1978; Beaugrande 1979d, 1979e, 1979j; Findler [ed.] 1979).[3] These various networks have a variety of uses, but they all consist of

_____

[3]The term "semantic network" is somewhat misleading, as these nets do not actually analyze the meanings of concepts; hence, I prefer the term "conceptual-relational network" (cf. Hendrix 1978: 1).

NODES and LINKS, similar to the grammatical networks we saw in Chapter II. Whereas those networks were composed of GRAMMATICAL STATES, these are made up of KNOWLEDGE STATES.

3.8 If the network is a valid format for knowledge, it would follow that *the total meaning of a concept is experienced by standing at its control center in a network and looking outward along all of its relational links in that knowledge space* (Havens 1978: 7; cf. Quillian 1966, 1968; Collins & Quillian 1972: 314; Rieger 1975: 169; Fahlman 1977: 12; Brachman 1978a: 44). The interactions among surface words arise from precisely this connectivity: words in contexts (Kintsch 1974: 36), word associations (Deese 1962), the coherence of word senses (P. Hayes 1977; Rieger 1977b), and the preferences for utilizing some word senses over others in context (Wilks 1975b, 1978). Indeed, without this deeper connectivity, the selection and comprehension of words would be explosively unmanageable (see II.1.3). Moreover, conceptual connectivity drastically constrains the utilization of syntactic options (Schank 1975b: 14) (cf. III.4.16ff.).

3.9 The human implications of networks are distinct from those of TAXONOMIES and LISTS. The usual decomposition proposed by linguists results in taxonomies, often with lists for many categories. In more recent research, lists of properties have been proposed for concepts (Collins & Quillian 1972: 313), and lists of propositions for the meaning of texts (Kintsch 1972, 1974; Meyer 1975; Frederiksen 1977; Turner & Greene 1977). For computer simulation of language processing, networks must be put in list format (cf. Simmons & Slocum 1971: 8; Riesbeck 1975: 103f.; Woods 1975: 51; a detailed presentation of the operations involved is given by Simmons & Chester 1979). But this requirement is an artifact of using *serial* processing (single operations in sequences), whereas human cognitive activities presumably function via *parallel* processing (multiple operations upon the same material simultaneously (Collins & Quillian 1972: 314). Scott Fahlman (1977) has shown how parallel processing can be simulated on serial computers.

3.10 The network is suited for an immense variety of representational tasks (cf. Shapiro 1971; Woods 1978b: 24), e.g.: associative memory (Quillian 1966, 1968; J. Anderson & Bower 1973; Collins & Loftus 1975); word disambiguation (P. Hayes 1977); dialogue understanding (Grosz 1977); sensory apperception (Havens 1978); nominal compounds (Brachman 1978a); creativity processes (Beaugrande 1979e); and much more. This diversity strongly recommends the network as a formalism for integrative and interactive models of communication. There may even be purely formal benefits derivable from notions in graph theory, such as "circuit," "separable and non-separable graphs," and so on (cf. Chan 1969: 5ff.). The relevance of graph theory is not obvious (J. Anderson 1976: 147), but could lie in analogies and inspirations for models of communication (cf. Taylor 1974 on abstracting; Dooley 1976 on repartee).[4]

3.11 The spatial organization of the network implies certain EPISTEMOLOGICAL tendencies (cf. Brachman 1979), such as the convictions that:

3.11.1 Entities of knowledge enter into multiple, interlocking, and configurational dependencies rather than sequences or lists.

3.11.2 An active point in a knowledge space can act as a control center from which new impulses can connect on further material as processing continues.

3.11.3 A knowledge space, such as in a textual world, has a characteristic TOPOGRAPHY that people can survey as a gestalt or walk through mentally in performing operations like integrating new knowledge, searching storage, deciding common references, and maintaining coherence. The more complex the topography, the longer the time needed to select the proper point for an addition or modification (cf. Kintsch & Keenan 1973).[5]

3.11.4 The notion of "semantic distance" between concepts might have a graphic correlate: the total number of transition links for moving from one node to another (with caution: see Collins & Quillian 1972).

3.11.5 Cognitive processes work not on words or sentences alone, but more decisively on PATTERNS.

3.11.6 The notion of SPACES can be captured in diagrams in which routes of access are depicted. These spaces might function as CHUNKS, that is, integrated units that fit a great deal of content into ACTIVE STORAGE (cf. Miller 1956; Ortony 1978a) (cf. III.3.16).

3.11.7 A knowledge space could appear in different PERSPECTIVES, depending on the LINK TYPES and UTILIZATIONS being pursued (cf. VI.1.2).

3.11.8 The procedures for acquiring, storing, and utilizing knowledge and meaning can be represented as operations that build, organize, rearrange, develop, simplify, specify, or generalize conceptual-relational structures.

---

[4]Taylor (1974) proposes that automatic summarizing could be done with techniques like these: (1) removing the network nodes with the densest linkage as probable topic nodes (cf. III.3.11.9; III.4.27); and (2) assigning various strengths to the electric signal that each link type can transmit, then doing a signal flow graph analysis. Hollan (1975) suggests that graph theory offers the benefits of: (1) a substantial literature in abstract mathematics (e.g. on traversal and search algorithms; cf. Ahlswede & Wegener 1979); and (2) the ease of implementing graph models as computer programs. I might add that it would be worth considering whether the notion of "circuit" and "separable/non-separable graphs" could be helpful in modeling the coherence of topic flow within textual worlds.

[5]However, this ratio would surely be affected by the *expectedness* of the new material as well (cf. Chapter IV).

3.11.9 The dominant TOPIC or TOPICS of a textual world should be discoverable from the density of linkages around nodes in an interconnected space (cf. III.4.27).

3.11.10 The relationship of a text to alternative versions, such as a paraphrase, summary, or recall protocol, is not a match of words and phrases, but of underlying conceptual-relational patterns (cf. VII.3.31ff.).

3.11.11 Entities of knowledge hardly every occur in actual human experience as isolated elements. Instead, for any entity, there are always *potential contexts* to impose order and efficient recognition on the encounter, especially via SPREADING ACTIVATION (cf. III.3.24). Should the context not be apparent, PROBLEM-SOLVING can be employed (cf. I.6.7).

3.12 The ACQUISITION of concepts has for many years been an object of psychological investigation, though with distinct and disquieting limitations (survey in Kintsch 1977a: ch. 7). The tasks posed were in general designed as classification of "stimulus" items according to some *arbitrary* feature or aspect selected by the experimenter, such as size, color, shape or numerousness. The test subject learns what aspect is relevant by trying out hypotheses (Bruner, Goodnow, & Austin 1956; Restle 1962). The most decisive learning takes place when the subject makes an error and must revise the hypothesis being applied (Bower & Trabasso 1964; Levine 1966).

3.13 Great care was expended on excluding relevant world-knowledge in such studies (Kintsch 1977a: 428). Yet the number of real situations in which people must learn arbitrary distinctions without contexts is surely small in comparison to integrative learning situations. Indeed, an encounter with entities that stand in no recoverable relation to what the experiencer already knows is likely to be profoundly disturbing. It follows that the formation of hypotheses normally draws on previously acquired concepts (Freuder 1978: 234). Even visual apperception depends crucially on what humans expect to see (Neisser 1967, 1976; Kuipers 1975; Minsky 1975; Mackworth 1976; Rumelhart 1977a; Havens 1978).

3.14 Concept acquisition might plausibly be accomplished as follows. A human would first encounter some entity and NOTICE it, i.e. expend processing resources on its presence and characteristics. Attempts would be made to determine what relations obtain between the entity and elements or previously stored knowledge. Let us assume here that it happens to be a new type of entity, so that a new entry must be made for it in storage. As the entity is encountered again or subjected to further mental contemplation, the need to integrate it into knowledge stores becomes more acute. The processor must eventually decide what aspects of the entity should be used to characterize it. The aspect of SALIENCE rests upon the intensity of intrusions upon sensory apperception (cf. Kintsch 1977a: 397ff.). FREQUENCY seems to affect processing also (Ekstrand, W. Wallace, & Underwood 1966), i.e. how often an entity is encountered or a characteristic is noticed. TYPICALITY would concern the number of instances that share some characteristic. Stimulus-response theories of learning might be salvaged in part if we postulate internal cognitive operations that focus discerningly on these different aspects, rather than simple "all-or-none" learning (Hilgard 1951) that reacts mechanically to the environment. Taken in isolation, any single aspect might be irrelevant or misleading. For example, a bright, salient color would be construed as useful for identifying a kind of tropical fruit, but not a kind of automobile (Freuder 1978).

3.15 Since there are staggering numbers of entities and occurrences to conceptualize in order to talk about even that portion of the world that an individual speaker knows about, humans must have powerful techniques for imposing organization upon knowledge to be acquired. CONCEPTUAL-IZATION (conversion of input knowledge into concepts) must entail extracting relevant aspects. The raw input might leave some direct sensory "traces,"[6] but the conceptualization of the input surely involves conversion into a SYMBOLIC format which is *not* a sensory copy (Miller & Johnson-Laird 1976: Ch. 4; Kintsch 1977a: 234). This format is suitable for the PATTERN-MATCHING that so many processes demand (I.6.6). In particular, patterns should be tagged regarding what portions are crucial or probable for most instances. I accordingly use tagging operators for three relative STRENGTHS of conceptual content: (1) DETERMINATE aspects are essential to the identity of any instance in order to belong to the concept (e.g. humans are mortal); (2) TYPICAL aspects are frequent and useful, but not essential to the identity of an instance for its concept (e.g. humans usually live in communities); and (3) ACCIDENTAL aspects concern the inherently unstable or variable traits of particular instances (e.g. some humans are blond).[7] These strengths are probably fuzzy, so that a gradation ("more or less determinate," etc.) should be postulated (Loftus & Loftus 1976: 134). Still, people must agree reasonably well on this gradation if they want to communicate efficiently and informatively.

3.16 The acquisition, storage, and utilization of knowledge require concerted interaction between EPISODIC MEMORY and CONCEPUTAL MEMORY (I prefer the latter term to "semantic memory") (cf. Tulving 1972; Ortony 1975; Abelson 1975: 306f.; Schank 1975a: 225f.; Kintsch 1977a: 283f., 1979b; Rumelhart 1977a: 222–36). Episodic memory contains storage of specific incidents in the person's own experience ("what happened to me"); conceptual memory contains *systemized* knowledge ("what I know about the world at large and how it all fits together"). When the person encounters a

---

[6]We return to the notion of "trace abstraction" later (VI.3.16, VII.3.11, VIII.2.48).

[7]After introducing this design feature, I found out that Hollan (1975: 154) had also proposed to "represent defining and characteristic features within a digraph by labeling the appropriate edges as defining or characteristic."

configuration of input, relevant contents of episodic and/or conceptual memory are brought into ACTIVE STORAGE (III.3.5) to be matched. The dominance of the one or the other type of memory varies according to the familiarity of the input and the person's store of experience and expertise. The acquisition of concepts as sketched in III.3.14 could be described as a gradual feeding of episodic memory into conceptual memory. Of course, many items are lost along the way, since relevant, important aspects must be filtered out of incidental, idiosyncratic ones. If intense processing is not expended because input is familiar, frequent, unimportant, or uninformative, that input would probably decay before it enters the conceptual store. On the other hand, unfamiliar, rare, or highly informative input might be considered beyond the normal organization of the world and hence in opposition to the contents of the conceputal store. I argue in VII.3.29ff. that the interaction of prior storage (and its organization) with current input is substantially affected by the outcome of matching in both active and long-term storage.

3.17 The utilization of texts is a special case in the utilization of knowledge as outlined in III.3.16. The selection of specific lexical and grammatical options tends to remain largely episodic and not enter conceptual storage; the same is true of accidental relations inside the textual world (cf. VII.3.29.5). But these surface options still have a function in concept activation (III.3.5). By applying these activation strategies in the reverse direction, a person might succeed in reconstructing a good deal of the original surface text. This possibility makes it hard to determine experimentally how much seemingly accurate recall is in fact a reproduction rather than a reconstruction (cf. VII.3.1ff.; VII.3.16).

3.18 For a theory dealing with the tremendous volume of knowledge people can handle, ECONOMY of cognitive processing is a major consideration. Stated in extremely strong terms, cognitive economy stipulates that all knowledge is organized in storage as a unified, heavily interconnected, and non-redundant network; in a weaker version, some redundancy would be allowed (cf. Collins & Loftus 1975). Presumably, there could be a compromise: frequently used patterns would constitute fixed entries of stable knowledge; infrequently used ones would have to be assembled by drawing on various storage addresses. There would be a TRADE-OFF between redundant storage consuming much space but allowing rapid search and matching, and non-redundant storage consuming little space but demanding lengthy search to assemble any needed configuration. Here, compactness is balanced against access (cf. Kintsch 1977a: 290). The human mind seems to have vast storage and slow search, while the computer has rapid search but limited, expensive storage (Loftus & Loftus 1976: 128). Economy also suggests that the distinction between linguistic knowledge and world knowledge cannot be very great or clear-cut (cf. Oller 1972: 48; Goldman 1975: 307; Riesbeck 1975: 83; Rieger 1975: 158f., 1978: 44; Wilks 1977b: 390). The issue is rather one of COMPATIBLE MODES of knowledge, such as language versus vision (Minsky 1975; Jackendoff 1978; Waltz 1978). Language ABILITIES should also be analogous to other human abilities (Chomsky 1975: 41ff.; Miller & Johnson-Laird 1976; Winograd 1976: 24; G. Lakoff 1977).

3.19 The INHERITANCE of content among knowledge entries is essential for economy (Falhman 1977; Hayes 1977; Brachman 1978a; Levesque & Mylopoulos 1978). In a hierarchy of classes, each SUBCLASS inherits some knowledge from its SUPERCLASS; and each INSTANCE inherits from its CLASS. For example, if we know that the superclass 'mammals' has the attribute 'warm-blooded', we would not need to store that knowledge again for the subclasses of people and cows; nor for specified groups like Pavlov's dogs, Thorndike's cats, and Skinner's rats; nor for individuals like Clyde the piano-playing elephant and his owner, Scott Fahlman. Depending on the context, inheritance is more or less inclusive. Subclasses inherit from superclasses via SPECIFICATION: a statement in which the traits of the narrower subclass are set forth. For example, people share many traits with mammals, but have atypically inefficient mating practices. INSTANCES inherit all properties of a class unless there are signals to the contrary. Because Napoleon was a human being, he presumably had toes, though we have probably never read such a fact in history books.[8] When a context demands it, any trait can be CANCELLED by an explicit statement that inheritance does not apply to a subclass or instance, e.g.: unlike other elephants, Fahlman's pet was not born, but cloned in a stupendous test tube (Fahlman 1977: 70). We assume in absence of cancellation that inheritance is valid: if Napoleon had not had toes, we would have many historical anecdotes about it (this would be a "lack-of knowledge inference" [cf. Collins 1978; III.3.21]).

3.20 Inheritance could also function via METACLASS inclusion. The classes are "meta-classes" because they are brought together by conscious consideration of their respective natures; class/instance or super-class/subclass relationships are based on subsumption vs. specification. Original metaphoring often entails metaclass assignment, e.g. when Shakespeare's Marullus addresses people as 'blocks', 'stones', and 'worse than senseless things' (sample (134) in V.5.4.1). The people are not, of course, included in those classes; there is at most some overlap of their characteristics with the characteristics that define those classes. The inheritance would thus function via that overlap. As a general principle, inheritance via metaclass inclusion requires more explicit signaling than that via class and superclass inclusion.

---

[8]This has been a long-standing example used by Walter Kintsch.

3.21 The degree of CERTAINTY with which inheritance occurs among classes and instances is variable. Communication entails frequent occasions when people must reason from incomplete knowledge never stored or acquired by direct experience or explicit statement. In the simplest cases, people can reason by ANALOGY of the unknown domain to a known one (cf. D. Bobrow & Norman 1975). For example, experience with Ohio drivers is likely to engender the expectation that any new instance one could encounter is probably incompetent. A variant would be NEGATIVE ANALOGY (Collins 1978): assuming different traits because the unknown domain contrasts with the known. For example, a highly skilled driver encountered in Ohio could be assumed to be a tourist from another state. Certainty also depends upon IMPORTANCE of a trait for a particular context. In industry, Ohio is known for rubber products; in sports, for football players; in politics, for obscure U.S. presidents; and in fashion, for its many Miss Americas. Conversely, people make negative inferences by assuming that they ought to know about important traits if they did apply: here, LACK OF KNOWLEDGE is a significant means of making predictions. For example, it would be generally known if Ohio had high mountains; hence, we are safe in assuming that it does not, even if we have never been there (see also Collins 1978).

3.22 It is disputable whether people use the general classes and superclasses in routine processing of specific instances. If the general class is the actual storage address of the shared knowledge, people might mentally shift up the scale of generality during understanding tasks. In an experiment by Stephen Palmer (reported in Rumelhart 1977a: 234), people were presented with fragments that differed along this dimension, such as:

(32a) The boy noticed the flowers in the park.
(32b) The boy noticed the tulips in the park.

In subsequent recognition tests, people were far more inclined to mistakenly remember seeing the general class after seeing the specific subclass than vice-versa (compare de Villiers 1974).

3.23 The issue of class inclusion is a further demonstration of the TRADE-OFF between compactness of storage and length of access in search (III.3.18). Although non-redundant storing of all detailed classes under the headings of the most general classes would conserve storage space, the activities needed to access a relatively specific class or instance would have to travel much longer, more intricate pathways. Rosch, C. Simpson, and S. Miller (1976) suggest that people normally use a BASIC degree of generality as a compromise between extremely general superclasses and extremely specific subclasses. People would not want to process every object by running up the hierarchy to 'object', 'thing', 'entity', or the like: such computation would be explosive, and these general superclasses are too indeterminate to be of much use. At the other extreme, only experts could be expected to possess detailed knowledge of the most specific subclasses in a domain. Presumably, people would prefer the "basic" degree of generality and would have recourse to other degrees according to the demands of the context for DIFFERENTIATION (cf. IV.2.6.5). Here also, there would be a THRESHOLD OF TERMINATION where processing is sufficiently general or detailed for current needs. In the 'rocket' experiments I discuss in following sections (VI.3; VII.3), our test persons often did not specify a '*V-2* rocket', but they all used 'rocket' as opposed to the more general classes of aircraft' or 'flying object'.

3.24 I cited the UTILIZATION OF CONCEPTS as a third issue besides acquisition and storage (III.3.7). I suggested that concepts are ACTIVATED in the mind and MAPPED onto EXPRESSIONS in text production and mapped back again in text reception (cf. III.3.5). Due to SPREADING ACTIVATION, more material becomes active than just the immediate content covered by the expressions of the text (cf. I.6.4) (Collins & Loftus 1975; Ortony 1978a). The original point from which spreading proceeds would be a special case of the CONTROL CENTERS which I consider essential in text processing (cf. II.2.9; III.3.6; VI.3.5; VII.1.8ff.; VII.3.34). The extent of spreading would be regulated by the THRESHOLD OF TERMINATION that I have also postulated for many processes (cf. I.3.4.3; I.6.1; I.6.4; III.3.3; III.3.23; IV.1.6; VII.2.7; VII.2.10). The controls upon spreading need not be conscious (cf. J. Anderson & Bower 1973; Rieger 1974; M. Posner & Snyder 1975). The spreading would normally proceed from several points at once, so that INTERSECTIONS of activated paths support coherence and engender predictions about how the concepts in a text world fit together (Rieger 1974, 1975; cf. "coincidence detection" in Woods 1978b). Certain types of paths are presumably suited as spreading routes: (1) TYPICAL and DETERMINATE links in CONCEPTUAL memory (cf. III.3.15); and (2) strong associative links of personal experience in EPISODIC memory (cf. III.3.16). However, the activity of daydreaming shows that spreading can on occasion follow paths whose motivation and directionality is not readily evident.

3.25 In an experiment conducted with students of various ages in Gainesville, Florida, I attempted to study some types of activation for familiar concepts.[9] We simply asked our test subjects, ranging from fourth grade to tenth grade, to name the "typical parts of a house, in any order." I observed a small set of strategies at work across most of the population, indicative of a corresponding set of SEARCH TYPES: "part-of," "substance-of," "locationally-proximate-to," and "containment-of" searches. The "part-

---

[9] I am most indebted to Carolyn Cook, Reba Dean, Gail Kanipe, Mamie Kelsey, Mary Morgan, and Mary Sharp of the Gainesville Public Schools for their participation in running these tests.

of" search recovered a listing of major rooms ('living room', 'kitchen', etc.), or of structural components ('roof', 'floor', 'walls', etc.). The "substance-of" search netted building materials ('nails', 'bricks', 'paint', 'glue', etc.). The "locationally-proximate-to" search brought together items that a person could notice by standing at a given location inside a house. Unlike the adults interviewed by Linde and Labov (1975), our subjects did not often perform a continuous mental walk-through of a floor plan, perhaps because in our tests, they were not asked to describe *their own* houses. In one group, 15 out of 28 subjects began with the 'front door', and only 5 made it to the 'back door'. The tendency was rather to switch without mediation from one location to another and begin a new listing of nearby objects.

3.26 The degree of consistency and organization varied according to the children's age. The youngest children did not choose and pursue a given search type with the same concentration as the older ones. Whereas older children preferred a constructivist outlook that stressed parts and substances, the young children took an episodic approach by regarding their own personal homes as typical. They had a corresponding inclination toward "containment-of" searches assembling many objects that houses might well not encompass. They stipulated that houses should have '*three* telephones', a '*walnut* table', and a '*glass what-not* shelf.' They mentioned domestic animals ('bird', 'fish', 'kittens', 'mouse',), items of food ('cake', 'ham', 'coke', 'tea'), and of course 'people'—all considered typical parts of a house. Evidently, even familiar concepts have fuzzy boundaries (cf. III.3.6); indeed, familiar ones might have *especially* fuzzy boundaries because of the richness of personal experience with them (Peter Hartmann, personal communication). The processes of acquiring and stabilizing a concept seem to evolve over considerable time spans, e.g. between the ages of fourth to tenth grade. And the concept looks different within its knowledge space depending upon the PERSPECTIVE of the current utilization (cf. III.3.2; III.3.11.7; VI.1.2).

3.27 Early attempts to systemize the notion of conceptual memory often appealed to "semantic memory" (cf. Collins & Quillian 1969). The main relation in these models was either superclass/subclass (the link type of "specification-of" in III.4.7.25) or class/instance (the link type "instance-of" in III.4.7.24). It was reasoned that the verification of (33a) would take longer than that of (33b) because the processor would have to run through at least one more class layer.

> (33a) A chicken is an animal.
> (33b) A chicken is a bird.

But experiments did not verify this prediction very consistently (Collins & Quillian 1972). Smith, Shoben, and Rips (1974) proposed to account for the distance between concepts in terms of FEATURE OVERLAP (e.g. how many features of a 'bird' a 'chicken' has). High overlap would allow rapid verification of statements about class membership; a low overlap would have the opposite effect (e.g. a 'chicken' is not judged to be a 'bird' as quickly as a 'robin' because the former cannot fly and the latter can). The subclass having the highest overlap with the superclass would be the PROTOTYPE of the latter (cf. Rosch & Mervis 1975; Rosch 1977; V.3.10).

3.28 Principled objections can be raised against such models of human memory. The hierarchical approach is unduly restricted to the relation of class inclusion (cf. Kintsch 1979b). There are doubtless many other relations that hold stored knowledge together (cf. III.4.7ff.). Moreover, in domains less structured than the classification of animals, it might not be clear if a subclass belongs to one or many superclasses, or to no obvious ones at all. A subclass might efficiently be treated via ANALOGY to a superclass that does not in fact include it (e.g. treating a 'whale' as an odd kind of 'fish'). The featural approach is saddled with all of the problems for such theories that I raised in III.2.2. And both the hierarchical and featural approaches leave human memory looking rather static. Perhaps we could reinterpret them both in terms of SPREADING ACTIVATION. In the hierarchical aspect, the intersections of pathways spreading out from the control center of two concepts (e.g. 'chicken', 'bird') occur on "specification-of" links. In the featural approach, the intersections occur on such links as "attribute-of," "form-of," "part-of," "agent-of," and so on. The most rapid and certain judgments about the truth of statements like (33a/b) would arise if these links are DETERMINATE; TYPICAL links would be next best, and ACCIDENTAL links would work the least well.

3.29 In retrospect, the distrust of some researchers (e.g., Schank 1975a; Kintsch 1979b) regarding "semantic memory" certainly seems justified. A more flexible and inclusive model of CONCEPTUAL memory must deal with many more types of relations and with the effects of contexts of utilization upon stored knowledge configurations. In absence of such a model, the differences in times needed to verify the content of isolated sentences may not be telling us much about the organization of memory (Kintsch 1979b). I would submit that the study of textual processing might be a more productive means of gaining insights into knowledge and memory in realistic human situations.

4. BUILDING THE TEXT-WORLD MODEL

4.1 A TEXTUAL WORLD is the cognitive correlate in the mind of a text user for the configuration of concepts activated in regard to a text (I.6.1). Although I occasionally use this term for the configuration of concepts and relations, which I have designed, I am in fact only dealing with TEXT-WORLD MODELS that are idealizations of the actual cognitive entities involved. My models include at least some materials not explicitly signaled in the text as such; but the textual worlds of participants in communication probably include far more. The text functions via the activation of concepts and relations signaled by expressions (III.3.5). Spreading activation, inferencing, and updating perform substantial modifications upon this basic material (I.6.4). The interaction of text-presented knowledge and previously stored knowledge can be depicted in terms of PROCEDURAL ATTACHMENT: the currently active knowledge stores specify and control what is done to build a textual world, so that operations are reasonably efficient (D. Bobrow & Winograd 1977). However, if the text is informative in the sense of I.4.11.7, the textual world will not be a perfect match for stored knowledge. In this section, I explore more conventional aspects of procedural attachment in model-building, and look into questions of informativity in Chapter IV.

4.2 If procedural attachment is to function efficiently for a wide range of occurrences, its categories cannot be unduly diffuse or detailed. I shall propose a TYPOLOGY of concepts and relations, whose task is not to capture the exhaustive meaning of textual occurrences, but only to constrain meanings to the point where the RESIDUE can be picked up as far as the language user desires to do so (cf. I.5.6). Obviously, my typology could hardly contain rare, idiosyncratic concepts like Leskov's (1961) 'left-handed Tula craftsman' or relations like Charniak's (1975a: 21) 'up-to-the-third-floor-of' "which only applies when the action takes the object up to the third floor of a building." My typology will be reasonably small, and designed along comparable lines to that for sequencing: the relational labels for the network links will characterize the concepts in the nodes. Further detail will be obtainable by combining types (cf. III.4.4).[10]

4.3 There are several domains that should be covered by such a semantics, notably: (1) the structures of events, actions, objects, and situations (e.g. attributes, states, times, locations, parts, substances, etc.); (2) general logical notions like class inclusion, quantity, modality, causality, etc.; (3) human experience (apperception, emotion, cognition, etc.); and (4) contingencies of language communication via a symbolic intersystem (e.g. significance, value, equivalence, opposition, etc.). I make no claims that my typology is definitive or exhaustive. It has been sufficient for the text-world models of numerous samples I have studied. And by means of type combining, it is able to handle nearly all of the one hundred primitives developed by Yorick Wilks (1977a) over a ten-year period. Those familiar with Roget's (1947) famous *Thesaurus* may perceive some resemblance to that classification also. Nonetheless, there are concepts whose residual content (III.2.2.4) does not—and indeed, should

---

[10]Upon occasion, I provide labels with arrows for secondary concepts at both ends of a link. As yet, I have no hypothesis about the directionality of control flow in such cases.

not—be captured by such a typology. Residual content is a matter of what is stored in the conceptual LEXICON. My typology merely constrains concepts to the extent needed for intelligent utilization (cf. I.5.6).

4.4 Table 1 shows the typology of concepts I am proposing. It is divided into PRIMARY and SECONDARY concepts. The PRIMARY concepts include: (1) OBJECTS (conceptual entities with a stable constitution or identity); (2) SITUATIONS (configurations of objects present and their current states); (3) EVENTS (occurrences that change a situation or a state within a situation); and (4) ACTIONS (events intentionally brought about by an agent).[11] These primary concepts are the usual CONTROL CENTERS for building textual worlds, i.e. the points of orientation from which a processor sets up the relationships to the secondary concepts. For example, spreading activation tends to work outward from the primary concepts (unless one had a task like 'think of all the yellow objects you know', etc.). In my models, I do not label the primary concepts (though it might be expedient to do so), but only the relations connecting them to secondary ones. The detailedness of secondary concepts utilized in text processing depends in part on the concept names (expressions) selected by the text producer; and in part upon the demands of the context. By combining concepts, we can derive many more specific ones: 'quantity of substance' could yield 'weight' or 'size', 'quantity of motion' could yield 'speed', 'initiation of cognition' could yield 'ideation', and so forth (some highly complex combinations are found in VI.4.33).[11a] As I noted in III.3.3, concepts can often be restated as propositions on a plane of greater detail.

4.5 It might be argued that concepts are themselves not unitary, but possess internal structuration or limits.[12] Leonard Talmy (1978) cites several such considerations: (1) PLEXITY, being the capacity for having discernible component parts (e.g. uniplex vs. multiplex); (2) BOUNDEDNESS, being the presence or absence of defined limits; (3) DIVIDEDNESS, being a lack of internal continuity; and (4) DISTRIBUTION, being the pattern of matter arranged in space or of action arranged in time. Michael Halliday (1967a) calls attention to such distinctions as "action vs. ascription" and "directed action vs. non-directed action." Both Talmy and Halliday appear to suppose that these issues are grammatical in nature. I would view them rather as an interaction between the grammatical, lexical, and conceptual aspects of language. The question then concerns the extent to which grammatical and

---

[11]One might argue that STATE and AGENT should also be included as primary concepts; but these two types seem to be derivative from objects/situations and actions, respectively. I note in VI.3.13 that states do not seem to receive processing focus as much as events.

[11a]I use the division sign "÷" to combine labels in the diagrams.

[12]I noted in III.3.3 that concepts may in principle be decomposable—possibly, Frederiksen's (1977) application of "rank-shifting" would be useful here, provided that the "ranks" are treated as relative, not absolute.

TABLE 1

I. Primary Concepts

EVENTS
ACTIONS
OBJECTS
SITUATIONS

II. Secondary concepts

A. Defining events, actions, objects, and situations

STATE
AGENT
AFFECTED ENTITY
RELATION
ATTRIBUTE
LOCATION
TIME
MOTION
INSTRUMENT
FORM
PART
SUBSTANCE
CONTAINMENT
CAUSE
ENABLEMENT
QUANTITY

B. Defining human experience

REASON
PURPOSE
APPERCEPTION
COGNITION
EMOTION
VOLITION
COMMUNICATION
POSSESSION
MODALITY

C. Defining class inclusion

INSTANCE
SPECIFICATION
SUPERCLASS
METACLASS

D. Defining relations

INITIATION
TERMINATION
ENTRY
EXIT
PROXIMITY
PROJECTION

E. Defining contingencies of symbolic communication

SIGNIFICANCE
VALUE
EQUIVALENCE
OPPOSITION
CO-REFERENTIALITY
RECURRENCE

---

lexical options create PREFERENCES for activating certain aspects of a conceptual-relational space (cf. Fillmore 1977). One can distinguish between expressions such as 'he sighed' (uniplex) and 'he kept sighing' (multiplex), or 'the prisoners marched' (non-directed action) and 'they marched the prisoners' (directed); but surely the structures appealed to by these terms belong to the events, not just to surface grammar. The same might be said for such categories as "count nouns" (e.g., 'bottles') and "mass nouns" (e.g. 'water') (cf. Leech & Svartvik 1975: 49ff.)[13]

4.6 The primitives developed by Roger Schank, on the other hand, show less detail than the concept types I am using. Schank focuses on human ACTIONS, and his set of "primitive acts," though more detailed than in his early work since 1970, are still very global, such as "physical transportation," "mental transportation," and the like (cf. Schank et al. 1975; Schank & Abelson 1977). The focus on actions is justified by their status as OCCURRENCES ON MULTIPLE LEVELS: they are control centers which often have linkage to numerous secondary concepts; they map onto grammatical nodes which are control centers on the level of sequential connectivity (cf. III.4.14); they appear prominently in chainings of cause, reason, enablement, and purpose; they update the situation in a textual world; they update their agents' outlook on the situation in the textual world; they correspond to steps in a plan and are relevant to a goal; and they direct the flow of a narrative. If the maintenance of connectivity and continuity is as crucial for cognitive operations as I claim, it follows that more processing resources are required for actions than for any other concept type. Schank's

---

[13]Christian Rohrer (1979) suggests a correlation in French between count nouns and the simple past, and mass nouns and the imperfect. The boundedness and dividedness of events appear to affect the perspectives adopted on the objects involved.

treatment of other concepts is in fact much closer to the surface, as the appearance of entries like 'cheese', 'mushrooms', 'saliva', 'money', 'fist', 'bullet', or 'poison' in his networks (Schank 1975c: 49-66) attests.

4.7 My typology of relations is designed especially for labeling connections between the secondary concepts and the primary concepts (cf. Table 1; III.4.4). The traversal of any link in the direction indicated by the arrow will thus arrive at a node characterized by the link label. This DIRECTION-ALITY is intended to suggest the flow of control in a manner comparable to the operations of the AUGMENTED TRANSITION NETWORKS described in II.2.12ff. (cf. III.4.16). The relation types are as follows (the mnemonic labels are the first two letters of the word except where avoidance of duplication leads to using the first and third letters):

4.7.1 STATE-OF [st] signals the current condition of some entity, rather than its characteristic one (e.g., 'sea-stormy').[14]

4.7.2 AGENT-OF [ag] is the force-possessing entity that performs an action and brings about a change in the situation that would not have occurred otherwise (cf. von Wright 1967) (e.g. 'general-attack').

4.7.3 AFFECTED ENTITY [ae] is that entity whose situation is changed by an event or action in which it figures neither as agent or instrument. In demonstration sentences, 'Mary' usually gets stuck with this role, e.g. 'John shot Mary' (Schank 1975c: 52).

4.7.4 RELATION-OF [rl] subsumes a range of detailed relations not worth assigning to a separate link, e.g. 'father-of', 'husband-of', 'boss-of' etc.[15]

4.7.5 ATTRIBUTE-OF [at] signals the characteristic or inherent condition of some entity (e.g. 'sea-saline').

4.7.6. LOCATION-OF [lo] links an entity with concepts of spatial position, and is often tagged with prepositions (e.g. 'at', 'in'). Entry (e.g. 'into', 'onto'), exit ('out of', 'off of'), and proximity operators ('next to', 'near', 'above') are very common for this link (cf. III.4.12; VII.3.22).

4.7.7 TIME-OF [ti] links all specifications of time, such as absolute (e.g. dates) or relative ('soon', 'then'), often with proximity ('before', 'after').

4.7.8 MOTION-OF [mo] is used when entities change their location, whether or not the places of origin and destination are given (e.g., 'run', 'rise'). Entry ('arrive') and exit ('leave') are common operators.

4.7.9 INSTRUMENT-OF [it] applies when a non-intentional object provides the means for some event or action (e.g. 'fuel-propulsion', 'scissors-cut'). Instruments thus differ from agents in lacking intention; and from causes and enablements in that instruments are objects, while causes and enablements are events.

---

[14]It follows that there would be no *determinate* state-of linkages.

[15]This label was overused in many early networks, at least in practice (cf. survey in Brachman 1978a). I have not had to use it myself so far.

4.7.10 FORM-OF [fo] connects entities to concepts of form, shape, and contour (e.g. 'block-lumpy').

4.7.11 PART-OF [pa] connects an entity with a component or segment (e.g. 'automobile-engine', or 'Fred-Fred's arm') (cf. Hayes 1977).

4.7.12 SUBSTANCE-OF [su] signals relations between an entity and the materials of which it is composed (cf. "source" and "stuff" in Wilks 1977a) (e.g. 'automobile-metal' or 'Fred-tissue').

4.7.13 CONTAINMENT-OF [co] signals relations between entities of which one contains the other (cf. Wilks 1977a) (e.g. 'automobile-Fred', 'Fred-beer').

4.7.14 CAUSE-OF [ca]: an event E_1 is the cause of an event E_2 if E_1 creates the necessary conditions for E_2 (e.g., 'injury-pain', 'theft-loss').

4.7.15 ENABLEMENT-OF [en]: an event E_1 is the enablement of an event E_2 if E_1 creates the sufficient, but not necessary conditions for E_2 (e.g. 'negligence-injury', 'owner's absence-theft').

4.7.16 REASON-OF [re]: an event E_1 is the reason for an event E_2 if the agent or initiator of E_2 is reacting rationally to E_1 (on cause vs. reason, cf. Rieger 1975; Schank 1975a; Wilks 1977c) (e.g. 'injury-anxiety', 'luck-happiness').

4.7.17 PURPOSE-OF [pu]: an event E_2 is the purpose of E_1 if the agent of E_1 has a plan in which E_1 is expected to enable E_2 (cf. "goal" and "purpose" in Wilks 1977a) (e.g. 'warning-escape', 'theft-being rich'). Whereas cause, enablement, and reason look forward in time from an earlier event to a later one, purpose looks backward from the later to the earlier event (Beaugrande & B. N. Colby 1979; Beaugrande & G. Miller 1980).

4.7.18 APPERCEPTION-OF [ap] relates sensorially endowed entities with the operations whereby knowledge is integrated directly via sensory organs (e.g. 'scientist-observe'). Simulations can fall under this heading as well (e.g. 'radar-track').

4.7.19 COGNITION-OF [cg] links sensorially endowed entities with cognitive operations (e.g. 'Einstein-imagine', 'Schank-think'). Simulation would be possible here also (e.g. 'Shrdlu the robot-compute').

4.7.20 EMOTION-OF [em] links sensorially endowed entities with experientially or evaluatively non-neutral states of excitation or depression (e.g. 'Fred-ticked off', 'Mary-enraptured'). Simulation has been undertaken here also, as in K. Colby & Parkinson's (1974) paranoid computer PARRY.

4.7.21 VOLITION-OF [vo] links sensorially endowed entities with activities of will or desire (e.g. 'population-want', 'Carter-hope').

4.7.22 COMMUNICATION-OF [cm] links sensorially endowed entities with activities of expressing or transmitting cognitions (e.g. 'Fred-say', 'Noam-proclaim').

4.7.23 POSSESSION-OF [po] signals relations where a sensorially endowed entity is believed to own any entity (e.g. 'Fred-have'). Initiation (e.g.

'give'), entry (e.g. 'buy'), termination (e.g. 'take away'), and exit (e.g. 'sell') are all common operators.

4.7.24 INSTANCE-OF [in] obtains between a class and one of its members (e.g. 'automobiles-Fred's automobile'). A member inherits all of the traits of the class that are not cancelled (cf. III.3.19).

4.7.25 SPECIFICATION-OF [sp] obtains between the superclass and its subclass (e.g. 'automobiles-convertibles'). Inheritance is restricted according to the distinguishing traits of the classes (cf. III.3.19).

4.7.26 QUANTITY-OF [qu] labels all links between an entity and a concept of number, extent, scale, or measurement (e.g. in the multiple series 'Clyde-weight-kilograms-3000' in Fahlman 1977: 102). One might want to subdivide quantity into groupings like "measurements" (e.g. 'kilograms') and "numericals" (e.g. '3,000'). Because *empirical tests* do show some differences in processing such groupings (cf. VII.3.29.5), I shall introduce such a scheme in the future. But I do not mark logical quantification (cf. III.1.3), assuming existence as a default (III.1.5), and set inclusion as relevant only if enumerated (cf. III.1.6).

4.7.27 MODALITY-OF [md] labels relations between an entity and a concept of modality (probability, possibility, etc.) (e.g. 'departure-impossible'). Modality subsumes negation, and is often conveyed via modal auxiliary verbs (e.g. 'should', 'can't', 'must').

4.7.28 SIGNIFICANCE-OF [si] applies when two concepts are expressly stated to stand in a symbolic relation (e.g. 'gesture-mean').[16]

4.7.29 VALUE-OF [va] applies to relations between a concept and some assignment of value (e.g. 'diamond-precious'). Value relations can also be comparative (e.g. 'brand X—better than—brand Y').

4.7.30 EQUIVALENT-TO [eq] applies to relations of equality, similarity, correspondence, and so on (e.g. 'high-lofty', 'dark-somber'). These relations, which are crucial to the internal organization of knowledge in texts, frequently involve proximity (e.g. 'dark-grey', 'kiss-caress').

4.7.31 OPPOSED-TO [op] is the converse relation to equivalence, and also figures strongly in knowledge organization (e.g. 'high-low', 'dark-light').

4.7.32 CO-REFERENTIAL-WITH [cr] is the relation between concepts whose inherent content is different, but which happen to be used to refer to the same entity in a textual world (e.g. 'morning star–evening star'). Co-reference often entails the use of pro-forms (cf. V.4).

4.7.33 RECURRENCE-OF [rc] is the relation between two occurrences of the same concept in a textual world, but without necessarily having reference to the same entity (as in 'it fell to the earth near mounds of earth').[17]

---

[16]This label would be frequent in "meta-language" used to assign or explain the meaning of symbolic expressions.

[17]It is not always decidable whether or not recurrence converges with co-reference. Where I feel that such convergence is given, I map the recurrences onto the same node (e.g. 'rocket' in

4.8 Many of these relations are familiar from various attempts to explicate the uses of grammatical structures in terms of conceptual ones. The verb-centered grammars such as the so-called "valence theory" (cf. Tesnière 1959; Brinkmann 1962; Erben 1964; Helbig [ed.] 1971) sought to classify verbs according to the number of elements that were conventionally dependent on them in a sentence. All of these attempts failed to the extent that the grammatical environment of verbs is in part a matter of the conceptual environments of the concepts which verbs can be used to activate. A listing of verbs with "valences" of 1, 2, 3, etc. (i.e. according to connected surface elements) fails to capture these variable and diverse factors.

4.9 In the grammars of some languages, the roles of elements respective to the verb are marked by surface inflections often termed "cases," for example, in Latin. Charles Fillmore's (1968) "case grammar" (proposed in order to introduce some aspects of meaning into transformational grammar) was inspired by this tradition. He naturally tended to focus on the cases that were explicit in languages like Latin. Fillmore's framework of orientation encouraged the assumption that cases are building blocks of abstract sentences, rather than of conceptual dependencies. In recent work (Fillmore 1977), he has migrated away from his original position by taking the structure of cognitive "scenes" into account.

4.10 The notion of "case" has had a profound effect on theory of language. Cases are now generally viewed as conceptual, not grammatical, with a range of compromises and intermediary positions (compare and contrast Chafe 1970; Bruce 1974; Kintsch 1974; Charniak 1975a; Grimes 1975; Nilsen & Nilsen 1975; Schank et al. 1975; Longacre 1976; Minsky 1977; Turner & Greene 1977). Conceptual cases must be MAPPED onto grammatical structures via relevant decisions and controls. Some constraints apply to structures that can be connected to individual verbs, but constraints on situations, events, and actions are more basic (cf. Goldman 1975: 317; Grimes 1975: 52; Schank 1975c: 82). The PREFERENCES for selecting a certain verb arise from the preferences regarding how to connect concepts and relations (cf. Wilks 1978). Although these preference types are not symmetrical, they impose major controls on use of verbs and verb complements (cf. Fillmore 1977).

4.11 There is no clear justification for insisting on the sentence as the framework of conceptual "cases." Language processing ought to be more concerned with the similarities between (34a) and (34b) than with the sentence boundaries (suggested by Robert F. Simmons, personal communication):

(34a) There was a knock at the door. It was John. He was using his cane.
(34b) John knocked at the door with his cane.

---

sample (35)). But the positioning of the recurrences may have psychological consequences that should be explored. It may prove expedient to subdivide recurrence and co-reference into a more detailed typology, such as that outlined in Chapter V.

The "conceptual dependency" understander at Yale, for example, would pick up the relations for (34a) just as if it had been presented with (34b) (Roger Schank, personal communication). Efficient processing obviously needs to extend its predictions about the organization of events and situations beyond the boundaries of single sentences; otherwise, the production and reception of texts would lack continuity. Indeed, Bransford & Franks (1971) found that test persons who saw chopped-up sentences like (34a) were later quite confident in believing they had seen the fluent versions like (34b).

4.12 I complete my set of link labels with the OPERATORS which specify the status of relations as needed. These operators are concerned with: (1) beginnings and endings; (2) fuzziness; (3) counterfactuality; and (4) strength of linkage. To make the operators visually distinctive in the diagrams, I use Greek letters, for example "$\pi \div ti$" would be "proximity of time," "$ca \div \epsilon \div lo$" would be "cause of entry into location," and so on. The operators are:[18]

4.12.1 The INITIATION operator [ι] signals that the relation is just being brought about by some applied force or agency (e.g. 'take-off' is an initiated motion, while 'fly' is not).

4.12.2 The TERMINATION operator [†] signals that the relation is ended by some force or agency (e.g. 'land' as compared to 'descend').

4.12.3 The ENTRY operator [ϵ] signals that an entity is entering into a relation rather than bringing it about (e.g. 'sicken' as entry into state, in comparison to 'sick' as state).

4.12.4 The EXIT operator [χ] signals that an entity is leaving a relation (e.g. 'recover from illness' as exit from state, as opposed to 'healthy' as the new state).

4.12.5 The PROXIMITY operator [π] signals some mediation or distance in a relation (e.g. 'nearby' as proximity of location, 'soon' as proximity of time).

4.12.6 The PROJECTION operator [ρ] signals that a relation is possible and under consideration, but not yet realized in the textual world (e.g. 'if he arrives' as projected entry into location).

4.12.7 The DETERMINATENESS operator [δ] is used in world-knowledge for relations required by the identity of a concept (III.3.15) (e.g. 'house-walls' as a determinate "part-of" link).

4.12.8 The TYPICALNESS operator [τ] applies to world-knowledge relations that are usual, but not obligatory, among representatives of a concept (e.g. 'house-wood' as a typical "substance-of" link). The operators for determinateness and typicality are used only in the configuration I term the "world-knowledge correlate" (cf. III.4.36), as they are not aspects of the text-world itself (unless we had a text-world which was a whole microcosm, e.g., in an extensive novel).

[18]I mark the distinction between "τ" for "typicality" and "†" for "termination"; and between "π" for "proximity" and "ρ" for "projection."

4.13 Here also, one could argue in favor of additional classifications, such as a "cancellation operator" for links that cease to obtain when a textual world is UPDATED by events and actions.[19] However, this operator would make sense only if one wished to take the status of the textual world phase by phase. Eventually, all links would be cancelled by updating, except perhaps conventional stabilizations like 'they lived happily ever after'. Also, one might want to introduce operators to signal the issues raised by Halliday (1967a) and Talmy (1978) (see III.4.5).

4.14 In chapter II, I demonstrated how a grammatical dependency network could be constructed for a sentence-length fragment. I stressed that such a network can serve as a useful indicator of the CONTROL CENTERS for a given stretch of text (cf. II.2.9). The preference strategy would be to postulate that *the heads of grammatical macro-states* (nouns in noun phrases or prepositional phrases, verbs in verb phrases or participial phrases) *are expressions of primary concepts* (cf. III.4.4). The operational consequences of this strategy might work at least two ways. In a *serial* procedure, an understander would run the syntactic analysis forward through a phrase until the head is found; then the conceptual analysis backtracks and incorporates elements into a semantic network (e.g., if the syntactic analysis found a noun head, it could backtrack and pick up the adjectives as attributes or whatever). This is essentially the approach of Rusty Bobrow's RUS system (R. Bobrow 1978). In a *parallel* procedure, an understander runs various kinds of analysis simultaneously and combines all structure-building operations that have the same configurations as an outcome (e.g., a hypothesis about a noun head with adjectives can be tested along with a hypothesis about an object with attributes). This is essentially the approach of William Woods' cascading network system (Woods & Brachman 1978b; cf. II.2.13). In both procedures, the sharing of structural configurations is an important contributor to accuracy and efficiency, especially with regard to refining probabilities. Woods's system, however, is better equipped to deal with missing or indistinct elements, since disconnectivity in one cascading network could be overcome by the connectivity of the others (see Woods, Brown, Bruce, Cook, Klovstad, Makhoul, Nash-Webber, Schwartz, Wolf, & Zue 1976).

4.15 It is conceivable that under certain conditions humans might BYPASS surface syntax during text comprehension. This question has not been pursued in linguistics very far; a sentence linguist who suggested such a thing would have risked being banned in Boston as a threat to public decency. Yet the "key word" systems which pick up particular words here and there (e.g. Weizenbaum 1966) and the "conceptual parsers" such as Riesbeck (1974) did in fact make only limited use of surface syntax. Perhaps humans perform something more like "fuzzy parsing" (Burton 1976), that is, classifying word categories, inflections, and grammatical dependencies only as far as is needed

---

[19]On "cancel links" see III.3.19; VI.3.4. On updating, see I.6.4.

to uncover the conceptual/relational constitution of the textual world. When the hypotheses about the text-world structure are numerous or evenly matched, syntactic parsing would be more thorough—a question of degree of informativity (cf. IV.1.10). In one respect at least, syntax is always relevant to text processes: it determines the *temporal order* of occurrences. That factor may be peripheral in an abstract theory of well-formed sentences, but it is central for a realistic theory of actual texts.

4.16 There ought to be preferences not only between phrase heads and primary concepts, but also between grammatical dependencies and conceptual links. Possibly, a network could be built up by AUGMENTING the TRANSITIONS between nodes with a combined grammatical and conceptual search (cf. II.2.12ff.; III.4.7). The results of the one aspect of the search could thus be applied to aid the other (cf. Burton 1976; Woods 1978c)—bearing in mind, however, that grammatical units and structures are not always of the same size as conceptual ones. All the detailed cues provided by the actual material at hand would be handled by augmenting transitions still further. The following are some reasonable (though certainly not verified) candidates for preferential correlations between the grammatical and the conceptual level (the three dots indicate that other hypotheses would be tested if these fail):

4.16.1 For "subject-to-verb," prefer "agent-to-action," "object-to-state"...

4.16.2 For "verb-to-object," prefer "action-to-affected entity"...

4.16.3 For "verb-to-indirect object," prefer "action-to-affected entity-entering into-state, "action-to-affected entity-entering into-possession"...

4.16.4 For "verb-to-modifier," prefer "state-to-state," "state-to-attribute," "state-to-location"...

4.16.5 For "verb-to-auxiliary," prefer "action-to-time," "action-to-modality"...

4.16.6 For "verb-to-dummy," withhold predictions and continue.

4.16.7 For "modifier-to-head," prefer: (1) for adjectives, "state-to-object," "attribute-to-object," "attribute-to-agent," "attribute-to-affected entity"... (2) for adverbials with verb heads, "attribute-to-action" (cf. "manner"), "location-to-action," "time-to-action," "instrument-to-action"...

4.16.8 For "modifier-to-modifier," prefer "attribute-to-attribute," "attribute-to-location"...

4.16.9 For "determiner-to-head," prefer "quantity-to-object" or test hypotheses about knownness and definiteness (cf. V.3).

4.16.10 For "component-to-component," prefer "possessor-to-object," "superclass-to-subclass," "class-to-instance," "object-to-part," "substance-to-object," "form-to-object"...

4.16.11 For "conjunction," "disjunction," and "contrajunction," try to reapply to the second of the joined configurations those hypotheses that were successful for the first.

4.16.12 For "subordination," prefer "cause-of," "reason-of," "enablement-of," "proximate-in-time-to"....(cf. V.7.6ff.).

4.17 The real ordering of such preferences will have to be discovered by empirical investigation. For the time being, I only suggest some plausible candidates. The preferences would be a major support in the PROBLEM-SOLVING activities of maintaining both sequential and conceptual connectivity: in essence, problems in the one subsystem are solved via hypotheses drawn out of the other. The immediate application of the preferences to actual texts would require considerable PROCEDURAL ATTACHMENT (II.2.19). Many surface expressions, such as classes of nouns, verbs, prepositions, and junctives, would tip the balance toward specific hypotheses. For example, individual prepositions would narrow down the range of conceptual links: 'in' would suggest "location-of," "time-of," "containment-of"...; 'of' would indicate "possession-of," "part-of," "substance-of"...; and so on. Individual conjunctions would have the same effect: 'because' for "cause-of," "reason-of"...; 'when' for "proximate-in-time-to"...; 'beside' for "proximate-in-location-to"...; and so on. Procedural attachment would be maximally efficient if it focused on the most reliable indicators and tested the most constraining hypotheses first (cf. P. Hayes 1977: 8).

4.18 Although the matter is far from worked out, I suspect that tense, voice, and mood can also be utilized as cues for building hypotheses about the arrangement of textual worlds. Tense is responsible both for the time organization of a textual world and for the relationship of the communicative situation to that world. Mood indicators signal the modality of text-world events and situations, e.g. as projected or counterfactual (cf. Goldman 1975: 360). Voice helps to distribute focus on the participants in events and actions (e.g. agent, affected entity, instrument, etc.) (cf. Beaugrande 1977a, 1977b).

4.19 The preferences I have proposed would operate in the other direction during the PRODUCTION of texts. Here, the organization of concepts and relations would give rise to preferences about mapping onto surface structure. There would of course be ASYMMETRY in production just as much as in comprehension, but the problem-solving for sequential continuity of the surface text would still be greatly simplified. The partial non-determinacy that arises from asymmetry would affect production in the form of occasionally competing strategies of expression, i.e. several ways of saying the same thing are trying to assert themselves at the same time—a major source of errors or inconsistencies in speaking and writing (cf. IX.4.3). I shall postpone a more developed treatment of text production for section VII.2.

4.20 Equipped with the typologies of concepts, relations, and operators presented so far, we can observe how a text world model could be built for the 'rocket' sample that has already supplied some fragments for discussion. I use this text, especially because it has been investigated before (e.g. McCall &

Crabbs 1961;[19a] Miller & Coleman 1967; Aquino 1969; Kintsch & Vipond 1979). The text runs like this:

(35.1.1) A great black and yellow V-2 rocket 46 feet long stood in a New Mexico desert. (35.1.2) Empty, it weighed five tons. (35.1.3) For fuel it carried eight tons of alcohol and liquid oxygen.

(35.2.1) Everything was ready. (35.2.2) Scientists and generals withdrew to some distance and crouched behind earth mounds. (35.2.3) Two red flares rose as a signal to fire the rocket.

(35.3.1) With a great roar and burst of flame the giant rocket rose slowly and then faster and faster. (35.3.2) Behind it trailed sixty feet of yellow flame. (35.3.3) Soon the flame looked like a yellow star. (35.3.4) In a few seconds it was too high to be seen, (35.3.5) but radar tracked it as it sped upward to 3,000 mph.

(35.4.1) A few minutes after it was fired, (35.4.2) the pilot of a watching plane saw it (35.4.3) return at a speed of 2,400 mph and plunge into earth forty miles from the starting point.

4.21 In chapter II, we worked through a fragment of the opening stretch of this text, ending up with a labeled grammatical dependency network shown as Figure 6 in II.2.18. If the preference strategy cited in III.4.14 were applied, the nodes of 'rocket' and 'stood' would be taken as the control centers: the primary concepts from which the processor can work outwards to identify the other nodes. The 'rocket' is thus an "object" node, and the connected nodes are not difficult to characterize: 'great', 'black', 'yellow', and 'long' are all "attributes"; 'V-2' is a "specification" of 'rocket', being a subclass; and '46' and 'feet' are both "quantities" hanging on 'long'. In moving from 'rocket' to 'stood', the preference that "subject-to-verb" should correspond to "agent-to-action" (III.4.16.1) is not tested, because 'rocket' was already taken as an "object" concept; the second preference for "object-to-state" is tested and confirmed. The preposition 'in' and the two place names 'New Mexico' and 'desert' offer sufficient evidence that "locations" should be connected to the "state."

4.22 The outcome of this processing is the labeled conceptual/relational network shown in Figure 11. The arrows show the DIRECTIONALITY of the control flow outward from the central points. The arrows are aimed toward the concept node whose type the label describes, e.g., 'great $\xrightarrow{at}$ rocket'

[19a]Reprinted by permission of the publisher from *McCall-Crabbs Standard Test Lessons in Reading,* Book C, p. 8. (New York: Teachers College Press, © 1926, 1950, 1961, by Teachers College, Columbia University.) The original does not have a paragraph break after 'fire the rocket', as I found out after the tests were run; and 'miles per hour' was used rather than 'mph'. Aquino (1969: 353) notes that this text received relatively low scores on cloze tests—a finding which may be related to the inexact match with the schema (cf. VI.3).

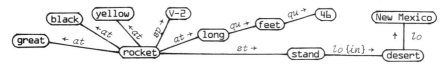

Key: *at*: attribute of; *lo*: location of; *qu* quantity of; *sp*: specification of; *st*: state of

Figure 11

can be read off as "great is an attribute of rocket."[20] I use the English words of the text not as words per se but as *concept names privileged by their actual occurrence*. The creation of such a network is not intended to explicate the meaning of the individual concepts (e.g., what 'yellow' means), but only to show how the concepts are interconnected. This task is a simple case of problem-solving as depicted in I.6.7ff. Notice that the configuration could still be recovered if the surface structure were not fully perceived, as my tests with indistinctly pronounced function words proved (II.2.18). Even a disjointed fragment like 'rocket...desert' would not be hard to label as "object-to-location."

4.23 As we can see, the determiner 'a' was suppressed in the conceptual/relational network as a non-concept; it is, however, a useful signal that a new node should be created for its head, since the indefinite article usually precedes items just being introduced (cf. V.3.13). As processing continues to the next sentence-stretch, the pronoun 'it' is also suppressed as soon as it can be identified with a concept already introduced. From the standpoint of grammar alone, this 'it' might be applicable to 'rocket', 'desert', or even 'New Mexico'. If the criterion of greatest proximity in surface structure were used, the proper referent would not be found. If processing consisted of looking up words in a mental lexicon, there would still be no resolution. No lexicon stipulates what a rocket, a desert, or the state of New Mexico ought to weigh. A lexicon of "markers" in the syle of Katz and Fodor (1963) wouldn't be helpful either, since all three candidates are (+ physical object) and (+ mass), and thus have weight. However, in all of the tests run with this text (see sections VI.3 and VII.3), nobody mistook this referent. People were simply using world knowledge that the weight of flying objects is *relevant* and *problematic* in a world where gravity can cause a flight to fail.[21] In contrast, geographical regions probably won't be moved, so a rational language user would not expect their weight to be relevant, or indeed even calculable. Along the same lines, the referent for 'it' was found in (35.3.4),

[20]On the use of arrows in both directions, see Footnote 10.
[21]I argue that this problematic access also impels readers to recall the 'take-off' especially well (VI.3.11). In VIII.1.11, I further suggest that problematic linkage is favored in continuation utterances in conversation.

(35.4.1), and (35.4.2) to be 'rocket' despite some other candidates in the vicinity ('flame', 'star', 'radar') because of expectations that 'rocket' is the most likely object to be 'fired', to 'return', and to 'plunge'.

4.24 We see that even ostensibly straightforward usage demands inferences from world-knowledge for efficient processing. The knowledge activated when the 'rocket' concept is initially encountered precludes the need for lengthy searching and weighing of common referents throughout the text. The heavy use of 'it' may be a sign of unskilled writing, yet it does not constitute an obstacle to understanding. A linguistic theory which would see syntax and grammar as autonomous of meaning, and linguistic meaning as distinct from world knowledge, would lead to very intricate and possibly unresolvable computations over issues as simple as these.

4.25 In models of language comprehension in both cognitive psychology and artificial intelligence—even models whose creators are quite hostile to conventional linguistics—the SENTENCE is routinely construed as the standard unit of processing. Though I have used a sentence myself in the foregoing demonstration, I have misgivings about such an a priori assumption. Strictly speaking, a sentence is composed of expressions rather than of concepts and relations, so that its use in building networks like mine is somewhat inconsistent. For instance, when I combine all occurrences of a concept onto one node, no matter how many sentences contain the corresponding expression(s), I seem to be moving in a domain in which sentencehood is a disturbing notion.[22]

4.26 The heavy use of sentences in comprehension models keeps us from addressing the question of how long a stretch of text people actually process at one time. The units of surface syntax cannot be the only determining factor for marking off a workable section of material. Other factors might be: (1) the span of active storage for maintaining conceptual connectivity of input; (2) the internal compactness or diffuseness of a knowledge configuration; (3) the number and relative probability of competing hypotheses; (4) noise, i.e. non-useable occurrences in the environment of actualization. The sentence could at most be one convenient and well-structured processing unit alongside others (O'Connell 1977). Other units could be: the PHRASE (a grammatical configuration with a head and at least one dependent element); the CLAUSE (a sentence component with its own subject-verb dependency); the TONE GROUP (a sequence of language items spoken as a unit with an apperceivable beginning and end) (cf. Halliday 1967c); the UTTERANCE (the action of producing spoken language items); the DISCOURSE ACTION (a text-producing action constituting a step in a plan to attain a goal via

---

[22]I suggest in VII.2.18ff. that sentence boundaries arise during text production from the partitioning of conceptual-relational networks according to criteria of motivation, informativity, and focus.

communication) (cf. VI.4.2); and the CONVERSATIONAL TURN (the text that a participant in communication utters before another participant begins to speak) (cf. VIII.1.18). Future research is needed to sort out the role of these units in the utilization of real texts.

4.27 As each stretch of text (of whatever length and nature) is processed and added on to the material already done, a MODEL SPACE within the text-world model is gradually formed (cf. the "activated subgraph" in Ortony 1978a: 57). The model space serves to integrate text-world knowledge into a CHUNK (cf. III.3.11.6) for use in further processing and for both active and long-term storage. I illustrate the model space for the first paragraph of our sample, as viewed in two ways. Figure 12a shows the content in sentence-length fragments; 12b shows the model space fully assembled. The integrating is a straightforward procedure here, because the fragments all share a node

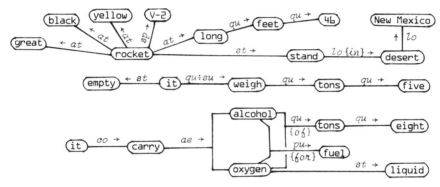

Key: *at*: attribute of; *co*: containment of; *lo*: location of; *pu*: purpose of; *sp*: specification of; *st*: state of; *su*: substance of

Figure 12a

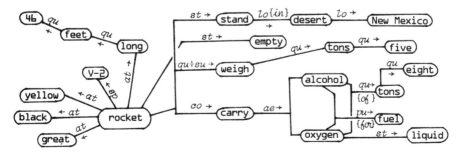

Key: *ae*: affected entity; *at*: attribute of; *co*: containment of; *lo*: location of; *pu*: purpose of; *qu*: quantity of; *su*: substance of; *sp*: specification of

Figure 12b

for 'rocket' in a central position. This node-sharing is a graphic correlate of TOPIC (cf. III.3.11.9). The shared node survives best in storage because of frequent utilization and re-activation during processing. A topic node is thus a privileged CONTROL CENTER attracting material whose status is otherwise vague, e.g. the material introduced with a careless use of 'it' throughout the 'rocket' sample (cf. III.4.23). If only the topic nodes were connected together when the whole text-world model is complete, we would have a MACRO-STRUCTURE (cf. van Dijk 1979b) that could be mapped onto the surface as a SUMMARY (cf. Taylor 1974; van Dijk 1977a: 157). In accordance with this view, model space can be considered a CONCEPTUAL MACRO-STATE analogous to the grammatical macro-states I postulated in II.2.9. The summary rests on linking together the control centers of all macro-states.

4.28 The model space seems a likely correlate of the PARAGRAPH in the surface text. Paragraph boundaries are prone to appear when there is a transition in conceptual material (but cf. IV.4.2). These transitions are not left as gaps, as we shall see, but bridged by inferences as necessary. Our first sample paragraph is conventional in providing a topic node for the entire text (cf. Jones 1977: 32). In traditional school instruction, it was suggested that paragraphs should have "topic sentences." (Of course, it is not the sentence that is topical, but its underlying conceptual content.) The efficacy of beginning with topical content lies in making obvious control centers available right away for the material to be later connected. Yet topic sentences have been found to be less common than is claimed in schools (Braddock 1974). We shall see later that topic *postponement* can also be effective (cf. VII.3.7ff.).

4.29 The model space for the second paragraph is more difficult to build. The three sentence-length fragments appear to activate no shared concepts. We are not told why 'scientists and generals' are on the scene, nor what their motions have to do with 'red flares'. However, INFERENCING readily overcomes these potential discontinuities. The state of 'readiness' can be taken to be the "reason-of" the motions toward shelter, and for the 'rising' of the 'flares' as a 'signal'. Figure 13 shows how this minimal inferencing produces an internally connected model space. More inferencing must be done to connect this space with that for the first paragraph: that 'everything' refers to whatever was required to "enable" the rocket's take-off; and that the 'scientists and generals' were there to observe the rocket. The empirical tests we conducted with this text showed that these inferences were indeed made by a substantial number of readers (cf. VI.3.9; VII.3.26). In Figure 14 we have the merger of the two spaces, with inference nodes in square brackets.

4.30 An individual reader of the text might well do much more inferencing than I have shown here (cf. III.4.1). For example, one might reason that the 'fuel' is about to ignite, so that heat will impel personnel to hide behind non-

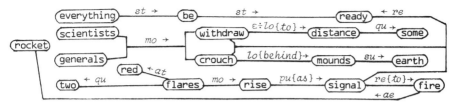

Key: *ae*: affected entity; *at*: attribute of; *ε*: entry; *lo*: location of; *pu*: purpose of; *qu*: quantity of;
re: reason of; *st*: state of; *su*: substance of

Figure 13

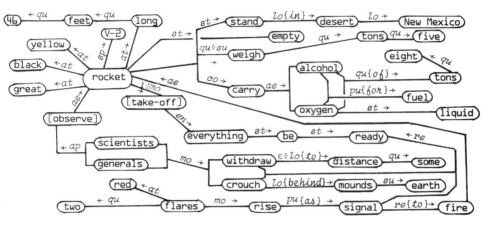

Key: *ae*: affected entity; *ap*: apperception of; *at*: attribute of; *co*: containment of;
en: enablement of; *ε* entry; *ι*: initiation; *lo*: location of; *mo*: motion of; *pu*: purpose of;
qu: quantity of; *re*: reason of; *sp*: specification of; *st*: state of

Figure 14

flammable earth mounds. Later on, I shall illustrate a matching knowledge configuration I call the WORLD-KNOWLEDGE CORRELATE (cf. III.4.36) in which these additional pieces of knowledge are included. As far as the text-world model is concerned, I suggest that inferencing be postulated whenever necessary to establish *at least one* connection between all nodes of the model. In other words, a gap in connectivity is construed as a problem (possibility for failure of transition, cf. I.6.7), and a "problem-occasioned" inference must be done (cf. I.6.9). Empirical research with whole texts will be needed to determine how many additional inferences are made by representative groups of language users.

4.31 In a different perspective, inferencing from world-knowledge could be addressed to the evolution of the textual world. As events are added on, the processor would know that earlier situations have become UPDATED in at least some respects (cf. I.6.4). I pointed out in III.4.13 that this fate overtakes virtually all of the textual world eventually, especially when the events are in past time, as in our sample. Further experiments may show that by interrupting the understanding process at strategic points, we can observe the effects of partial updating along the way. Certainly, computer simulation of understanding has a great updating task to manage, because the knowledge base otherwise stays constant. Roger Schank (1975c: 42) observes that the "true meaning" of an action is the set of inferences and updatings it elicits (cf. III.4.6).

4.32   The model space for the third paragraph resembles that for the first in having a prominent shared 'rocket' node. Figure 15 presents the whole model space with its topic node. Notice the combining of relation types: speed ('slowly') as "quantity of motion," or direction ('upward') as "location of motion." I use a division sign "÷" for combining. We also see some uses of the proximity operator "π", e.g. the "proximity of cause" between the rocket's 'rising' and the 'roar' and 'burst'; or the "proximity of time" between the "apperception" 'tracked' and the "motion" 'sped'. Proximity of cause flows in one direction (hence one arrow); proximity of time could flow in both directions, depending on viewpoint (hence two arrows).

4.33   In order to connect this model space to the previous textual world, we need only merge the topical 'rocket' nodes to attain sufficient connectivity. Figure 16 demonstrates the outcome of the merger. I include the inference that the people who could 'not see' the rocket when it was 'too high' were (or included) the 'scientists and generals'. This inference was also made by our test

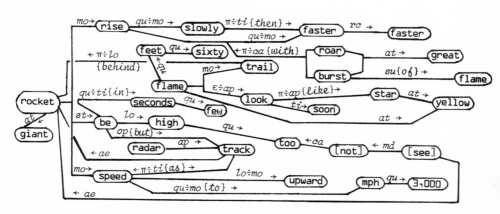

Key: *ae*: affected entity; *ap*: apperception of; *at*: attribute of; *ca*: cause of; *ε*: entry;
lo: location of; *md*: modality of; *mo*: motion of; *op*: opposed to; *π*: proximity; *qu*: quantity of;
su: substance of; *ti*: time of

Figure 15

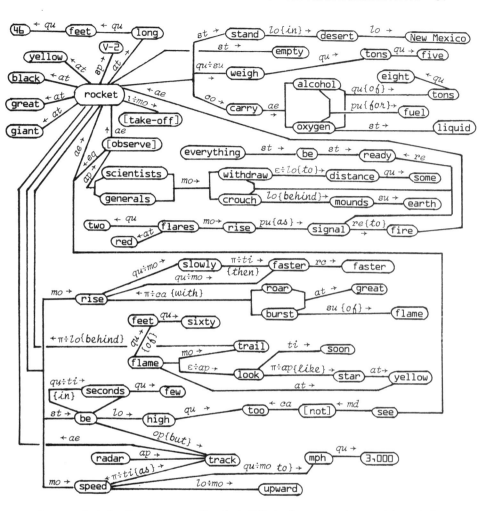

Key: *ae*: affected entity; *ap*: apperception of; *at*: attribute of; *ca*: cause of; *co*: containment of;
ε entry; *en*: enablement of; *ι* initiation; *lo*: location of; *md*: modality of;
mo: motion of; *op*: opposed to; *π*: proximity; *pu*: purpose of; *qu*: quantity of; *re*: reason of;
sp: specification of; *st*: state of; *su*: substance of; *ti*: time of

Figure 16

subjects, and is plausible because it re-uses available material instead of
creating new nodes such as 'everyone on earth' or whatever.

4.34 In the model space for the final paragraph, we have to assign
"quantities" not to nodes, but to links, in order to represent 'a few minutes
after' and 'forty miles from'. I employ pointer links, as in Figure 17. A further
issue is the linkage between 'plane' and 'pilot'. The pilot is in the

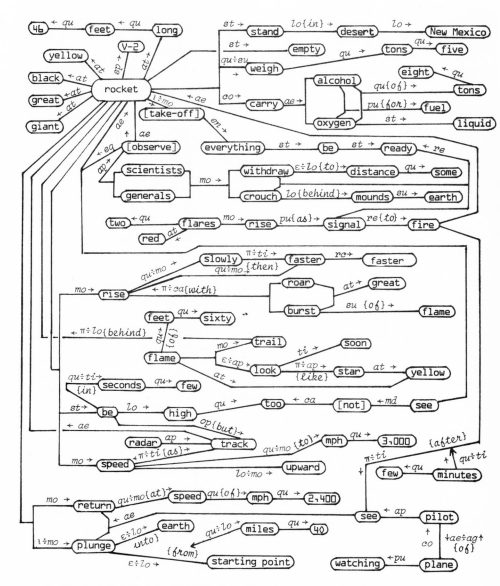

Key: *ae*: affected entity; *ag*: agent of; *ap*: apperception of; *at*: attribute of; *ca*: cause of; *co*: containment of; *en*: enablement of; *ε*: entry; *eq*: equivalent to; *ι*: initiation; *lo*: location of; *md*: modality of; *mo*: motion of; *π*: proximity; *pu*: purpose of; *qu*: quantity of; *rc*: recurrence of; *re*: reason of; *sp*: specification of; *st*: state of; *ti*: time of

Figure 17

"containment-of" the plane, while the plane is the "affected entity-of" the pilot's "agency." I illustrate this double linkage in Figure 17. The extent to which it is advisable to work with multiple linkages throughout the text-world model depends on the detailedness and differentiation one desires to attain. If one breaks a concept down into components and creates links between components—along the lines of "feature overlap" mentioned in III.3.27— multiple links would become the rule rather than the exception. Dedre Gentner (1978) reports evidence that degrees of linkedness among the components of concepts affect ease and frequency of exact recall. I shall content myself here with single links as the *minimum* for coherence.

4.35 The complete text-world model for the 'rocket' sample is diagrammed in Figure 17. The vertical arrangement corresponds to the progression from the initial to the final stage of processing. This model is undeniably an idealization. It suggests complete and accurate recovery of all relations. It shows none of the decay that a human processor would experience in real time (cf. discussions in VII.3). It makes no provision for the time organization in the textual world—I always use the basic form of verbs, irrespective of the tenses in the surface text—but portrays all the relations at once. No attempt is made to capture factors of value, emotion, or mental imagery. Nonetheless, such a text-world model can be a helpful starting point for exploring the processes applied in such tasks as: (1) forming a "gist" of the text; (2) storing the text content and recalling it at a subsequent time; and (3) controlling and compensating for decayed or confused components.

4.36 To suggest how an understander would MATCH the textual content against prior knowledge of the world, I have designed a format I designate the WORLD-KNOWLEDGE CORRELATE. This entity is drawn with the same proportioning as the text-world model. It contains only the nodes that people might reasonably know to be linked before they ever encountered the 'rocket' text. I attempt to distinguish the STRENGTH of linkage with the operators for determinateness and typicalness as expounded in III.4.12, although some cases might be disputed. Figure 18 illustrates the results in a world-knowledge correlate for 'rocket'. For example, it is essential to the identity of the concept 'fuel' that fuel 'burns' and enables some vehicle such as a rocket to move. An object cannot 'rise' except with an 'upward' motion. It is a requisite that 'radar' be able to 'track'. Barring bizzare counter-examples, relations like these can be labeled determinate. Others are merely typical, such as those between 'scientists' and 'explore' or 'generals' and 'attack'; scientists might give up research upon getting tenure, and generals might only march up and down or doze through staff meetings. But the typicalness of exploring and attacking as their respective agencies is the presumed reason they would want to make use of rockets.

4.37 As we can see, these world-knowledge links hold together many elements whose relatedness is not asserted or mentioned in the text itself.

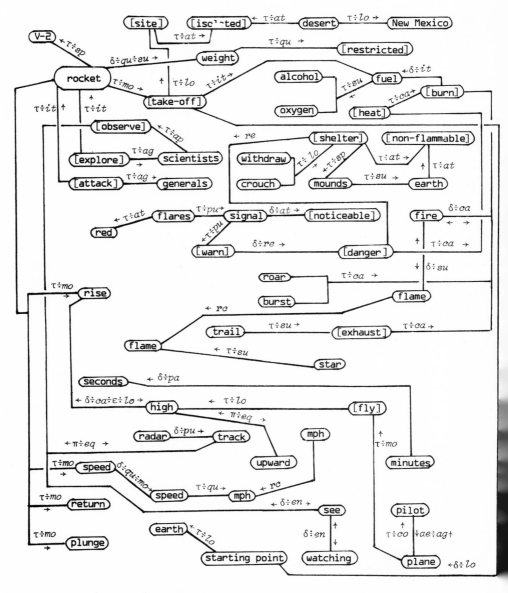

Key: *ae:* affected entity; *ag:* agent of; *ap:* apperception of; *at:* attribute of; *ca:* cause of; *co:* containment of; *δ:* determinate; *en:* enablement of; *ε:* entry; *it:* instrument of; *lo:* location of; *mo:* motion of; *π:* proximity; *pu:* purpose of; *qu:* quantity; *rc:* recurrence of; *re:* reason of; *sp:* specification of; *su:* substance of; *τ:* typical

Figure 18

100

These links would be available by SPREADING ACTIVATION of the pertinent concepts (III.3.24), and would make the recovery of relations that are asserted in the text efficient. This utilization of knowledge is a form of PROCEDURAL ATTACHMENT: modification and specification of stored procedures for an immediate task (cf. III.4.1). The COHERENCE of the text seen in isolation is only partial, since its continuity as a processing object comes from prior knowledge as well as presented knowledge. Without such interaction, processing would be explosive, requiring an unmanageable number of alternatives to be considered (cf. II.1.2f.). A comparable outlook on coherence is suggested in many of the "substitution" types discussed by Roland Harweg (1968a), as well as by notions like "lexical solidarity" used by Eugenio Coseriu (1967; cf. Dressler 1970a: 194) and "preference semantics" used by Yorick Wilks (1975b, 1978).

4.38 The elusive nature of conceptual relations out of context is manifested in some of the linkages in Figure 18. 'Fire' and 'flame' could either one be thought of as the "substance-of" the other, depending on usage; 'seeing' and 'watching' could be each other's "enablements" in appropriate settings. I employ two arrows for such instances. In actualization via a text, however, only one direction would normally be relevant, especially if structural processing is viewed as a directional flow of control.

4.39 The standard for stipulating world knowledge is an admittedly "naive psychology" (Rieger 1975: 187f.). A theory of human activities has no special motives for insisting on an exhaustive, precise, logically perfect base of knowledge. Instead, we want to explore COMMONSENSE REASONING (Wilks 1977c: 236), and COMMONSENSE KNOWLEDGE (Petöfi 1978a: 43) (cf. I.6.4). These domains correspond to what the average person in a given language group of society can plausibly be presumed to know and reason about. The same presumption underlies communicative processes at large, and if it were invalid, people simply could not understand each other much of the time. Moreover, an unduly exact knowledge base would entail very laborious procedures of utilization and matching, rather than the "fuzzy matching" that makes knowledge spaces so versatile and useful (Rieger 1977a: 277).

4.40 Commonsense knowledge easily imposes coherence on the newspaper advertisement cited in II.2.36:

(26) PIZZAMAN EXPRESSES   WE DELIVER
              50¢ OFF ANY PIZZA
                      plus
                2 free cokes
        Wednesday only
        Open at 11:00 A.M.

I argued at the time that such a text is certainly not understood via conversion into complete sentences, but rather via inferencing with concepts and

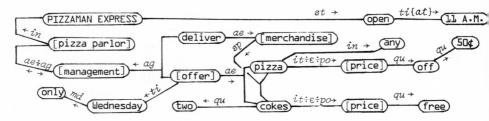

Key: *ae*: affected entity; *ag*: agent of; *ε*: entry; *in*: instance of; *it*: instrument of; *lo*: location of;
md: modality of; *po*: possession of; *qu*: quantity of; *sp*: specification of; *st*: state of; *ti*: time of

Figure 19

relations. Figure 19 demonstrates the resulting text-world model for the ad, again with inferred nodes in square brackets. The 'Pizzaman Express' is an instance of 'pizza parlor' whose 'management' is the agent of the expressed action 'deliver' as well as of the inferrable action 'offer'. The 'pizza' and 'cokes' are "specifications-of" the 'merchandise' that the management 'delivers'. Their 'prices' (the "instrument-of-entry-into-possession") have the "quantities" of being '50¢ less' in the first case and 'free' in the second. Some further nodes are readily attached as "times." The requisite material is supplied from stored knowledge about business dealing and restaurants—a "restaurant script" of the kind cited in VI.1.3 and VI.4.13. The proof that such knowledge is really available is the advertisement itself. Business people do not waste money circulating ineffective or incoherent messages.

4.41 This chapter has been devoted to exploring meaning as a PROCESS, not as a property of grammarians' "sentences." These processes should apply to the acquisition, storage, and utilization of knowledge. The production and comprehension of texts was proposed as a profitable area for studying meaning from the standpoint of maintaining CONCEPTUAL CONNEC-TIVITY as the basis of COHERENCE. These criteria are vital to the stability of systems of meaning in which a CONTINUITY of OCCURRENCES allows a steady directional flow of control (I.4.4). Consequently, text-presented knowledge must interact heavily with previously stored knowledge of the world, so that possible discontinuities are overcome by problem-solving, pattern-matching, spreading activation, inferencing, and class inheritance. I outlined the procedures for building a model of a textual world.

4.42 In the remaining chapters, I explore a number of issues I hold to be vital for a science of texts. These issues offer a rigorous test of the usefulness of the basic theory presented so far, or of any theory which deals with texts in communication.

IV

Informativity

1. MODIFYING INFORMATION THEORY

1.1 Despite some diffuseness in its usage over the years, the term INFORMATION can be taken to designate not the knowlede that provides the content of communication, but rather the aspect of newness or variability that knowledge has in some context (cf. Loftus & Loftus 1976; Groeben 1978). If the actualization of a text system is constituted by a configuration of OCCURRENCES (cf. I.1.3.; I.4.1), then the INFORMATIVITY of a particular occurrence is its relative PROBABILITY (likelihood and predictability) as compared to other ALTERNATIVES. The lower the probability of the occurrence, the higher the informativity (cf. I.4.11.7).

1.2 In classical informational theory (Shannon & Weaver 1949), informativity (information value) was formalized by *statistical* methods. Suppose we had a language with a precisely enumerated set of possible elements (a "finite-state language"). We could select an element, say X, and look at every occurrence of X in any chain. If we had a chain like W-X-Y etc., we could compare all these occurrences and compute the TRANSITION PROBABILITY between W and X, that is, the likelihood of X following W. A chain constituted according to this simple computation of transition probabilities between immediately adjacent elements is called a MARKOV CHAIN. It is questionable, however, whether Markov chains are a useable model for natural language utterances. Natural languages do not have a finite number of states, and the probability of any occurrence does not depend solely on the immediately preceding occurrence.

1.3 I hold a flexible, modified version of information theory to be valuable for theories of human communication via texts. The augmented transition networks I have proposed as operational representations for processes of sequential connectivity (II.2.12) and conceptual connectivity (III.4.7) bear a distant resemblance to the old Markov chains, because the main task is predicting the next link to a new node. Experiments inspired by the model of the augmented transition network did show that language users have fairly uniform expectations about how a sentence sequence will proceed from a given point (cf. II.2.14). A large quantity of learning experiments were based on Markov models, due to their mathematical simplicity (Kintsch 1977a: 82). But purely statistical models in general, and Markov models in particular, would lead to COMBINATORIAL EXPLOSION (II.1.2) for processes as intricate and varied as the utilization of texts: the decision about an impending occurrence rests less upon frequencies between adjacent items than upon the MOTIVATIONS the overall context supplies. Leon Brillouin (1956) suggests that the statistical approach ignores the whole aspect of meaningfulness.

1.4 Psychologically, statistics might be applicable to the aggregate of EPISODES a person has in stored knowledge. Yet as episodic memory gradually feeds over into CONCEPTUAL memory (III.3.16), exact frequencies would tend to become blurred and unreliable for building expectations. To select an option at a given point during the production or prediction of a text sequence, people presumably consult all available CUES (signals for performing a processing action). The availability of cues depends upon the FOCUS of ATTENTION, where "attention" is defined as an expenditure of processing resources that limits the potential for another task at the same time (Keele 1973). Cues would be especially helpful if people were working with the various language systems in PARALLEL and merging shared parts of hypotheses about those systems (cf. Woods 1978b: 11; III.4.14).

1.5 Due to the various exigencies of communication, the occurrence of an element could have quite different probabilities in different systems; it might, for example, be syntactically probable and semantically improbable, or vice versa. If we had PROBABILITY OPERATORS for the links of the grammatical and conceptual/relational networks—a feature I hope to include as soon as sufficient empirical research makes it possible and reliable—the operators on the same link would be opposed in the two networks. I suspect that the PROBLEMATIC transition to the improbable element in one system (cf. I.6.7) is eased by a comparatively unproblematic transition in the other. Probable content in a probable format would be uniformly easy to process and not informative. Improbable content in an improbable format would be uniformly difficult to process and intensely problematic. But improbable content in a probable format, or probable content in an improbable format would be challenging and yet not unreasonably problematic. Literary and poetic texts (cf. VII.1.8.4–5) often manifest these last two combinations (cf. Beaugrande 1978b, 1979e; Koch 1978, 1979). We should bear in mind that the probabilities in *virtual* systems can be overridden by those in *actual* systems (cf. IV.1.23.4). People seem to be quite skillful in adapting their expectations to an intricate pattern of actual episodic occurrences (cf. Friedman, Burke, Cole, Estes, Keller, & Millward 1963). While it was found that, when taken as abstract sentence patterns, the passive is harder to process than the active (Coleman 1964),[1] a text with nothing but passive constructions removes the difficulty (Wright 1968).

1.6 It would be reasonable to distinguish various ranges on a *scale of informativity*. I shall propose three ORDERS, with "order" used in the mathematical sense: a higher-numbered order automatically subsumes the lower-numbered ones. The order results from the extent of PROCESSING RESOURCES that are expended upon input. The lower-order occurrences allow PROCESSING EASE, that is, the linkage of the occurrences to previous ones is non-problematic. The higher-order occurrences call for PROCESSING DEPTH (cf. III.3.5), because the linkage is problematic, often seriously so (cf. I.6.7 on "serious problems"). The THRESHOLD OF TERMINATION where processing is considered satisfactory and discontinued (III.3.24) therefore moves along with the order of informativity.

1.7 The complexity of probabilities suggests that people could rely not only on prediction, but on "postdiction" as well (Kintsch 1979a). The understander would then notice an occurrence and seek some justification after the fact. Reliance on postdiction would increase either (1) if there were a wide spread of equally probable alternatives and a scarcity of determinate cues for selecting any; or (2) if an occurrence seems quite outside the predicted range, so that no cues are readily at hand. The second case doubtless requires a stronger focus of attention, and can be strategically induced for that motive (see note 14 to Chapter I).

1.8 The mere selection of one available option in a context—an option provided by any participating system—results in at least FIRST-ORDER INFORMATIVITY. In the simplest instance (a rare one) where there seems to be only one option, there are still two alternatives: occurrence versus non-occurrence. In a restricted sequence where only two options are possible (as in many learning experiments), there are the trivial alternatives of any

---

[1]The difficulty of passive sentences is exaggerated in many experiments with samples where the roles are *reversible* (i.e. the agent might reasonably also be the affected entity and vice-versa) and no determinate contexts are given. Slobin (1966) demonstrated the importance of reversibility in such measurements.

occurrence being the same as or different from its predecessor[2] (a principle of the "text-score" developed in Weinrich 1972). In more realistic worlds with multiple alternatives, first-order informativity applies when an option in the upper range of probability is selected. In all of these domains, we have a low INTERESTINGNESS value: the degree of cognitive involvement resulting from uncertainty (as well as from such factors as emotivity and salience—see section IV.2).

1.9 Many selections required for the production of any text are of this trivial first order. Given a conceptual configuration and the preferences for mapping it onto surface expression (III.4.16), many decisions regarding surface structure are made *efficiently* (cf. I.4.14). The *effectiveness* of certain formulations, notably in poetry, arises from low probability in mapping. In its attempts to set up a categorical, context-free grammar that stipulates what sentences can and cannot occur, generative grammar implied the postulate that all potential occurrences in a language system are of the first order, because specified by categorical rules (cf. I.3.4.7). People's difficulties with judging unusual sentences (I.1.16) show that the variability of information orders should not be ignored when constructing a grammar for sentences. My proposal to include the notions of DEFAULT and PREFERENCE in a grammar for texts (cf. I.3.4.3) is intended to help resolve this matter.

1.10 A normal reaction to triviality would be to reduce one's ATTENTION, i.e., the concentration of processing resources on one object at the expense of others. In any case, humans in communication are not likely to perform a thorough analysis of all occurrences in all systems, such as a linguist might accomplish. I suggested in III.4.15 that the intense utilization of surface structure would be needed if there were numerous or evenly matched hypotheses about the underlying conceptual/relational structure. If the latter were immediately obvious, on the other hand, people might do only "fuzzy parsing" on the surface. The processor would leave some nodes or links unlabled (cf. Burton 1976: 80), working along via approximative problem-solving. If it later emerges that the unlabeled states are needed after all, but are no longer available in active storage, problem-solving could become more detailed and rigorous to reconstruct the lost material.[3] If this outlook is plausible, then low-order informativity is a reliable signal that fuzzy parsing is adequate in a given context.

1.11 The selection of an option in the middle or lower-middle degrees of probability results in SECOND-ORDER INFORMATIVITY. Here, the

---

[2]Intriguingly, people expect a long series of the same occurrence to be broken for the sake of mere variety, even when probabilities remain constant—a phenomenon called "gambler's fallacy" (cf. Kintsch 1977a: 91f.).

[3]Some successful computer simulation of the processing of indistinct or partial input uses precisely this approach (cf. Woods et al. 1976).

strongest defaults and preferences are noticeably overridden. The presence of at least some second-order occurrences is presumably the usual standard for textual communication, so that first-order occurrences could be UPGRADED (unless they are accorded no further attention) and third-order occurrences could be DOWNGRADED. The demands people make for informativity vary among types of texts and situations. Conversations between married couples appear to function with very low informativity, while contemporary art works strive for very high.

1.12 Occurrences construed as *outside* the range of more or less probable options convey THIRD-ORDER INFORMATIVITY. These are unusual and extremely interesting occurrences, and correspondingly hard to understand and control. A SERIOUS PROBLEM in the sense of I.6.7 is present, because the linkage of the new occurrence to what went before is endangered in an unexpected way, and the probability of FAILURE is great. Major DISCONTINUITIES, GAPS, and DISCREPANCIES as defined in I.6.9 are the usual types of third-order occurrences and activate a MOTIVATION SEARCH to find out a source for the unexpected material. The search returns some pathway which makes the third-order occurrence accessible to its context and hence within the range of probable options after all (cf. Lenat 1977: 1097). This process in effect DOWNGRADES the third-order occurrence into the second order. Downgrading could have different DIRECTIONALITY: (1) if people regress to occurrences of a considerably earlier time to find the motivating pathway, they are doing BACKWARD downgrading; (2) if they wait and look ahead to further occurrences, they are doing FORWARD downgrading; (3) if they go outside the current context, they are doing OUTWARD downgrading. A text producer who deliberately supplies third-order occurrences may anticipate the directionality and results of the downgrading as part of the plan toward a goal (cf. Beaugrande 1978b; VII.2.33). The assumption that downgrading will be done is reliable (Berlyne [1960] suggests that "cognitive conflict" creates "epistemic curiosity" to obtain knowledge).

1.13 The directionality of downgrading suggests the control flow for processing third-order occurrences. In II.2.34, we considered what might ensue if a sentence structure were so misleading that an unaccountable element was left over at the end of parsing. The subsequent relabeling of the structure (Figures 9a and 9b) was an illustration of backward downgrading in the syntactic system. For a structure that cannot be downgraded via syntax alone, such as Simmons' sample of 'The old man the boats' (see (22) in II.2.32), a processor could go outside to consult intonation or conceptual context (outward downgrading); or could leave the structure temporarily unlabeled until the context became more determinate later on (forward downgrading). If the processor interrupted the speaker with a demand for explanation, we would have a convergence of outward and forward downgrading.

1.14 These reasoning procedures doubtless extend far beyond the utilization of texts. If we are arrested with no warning and for no visible motive, we have encountered a third-order experience. We will be prone to react in the following ways: (1) mentally retracing our recent actions to see if any of them could be the "reason-of" the arrest (backward downgrading); (2) waiting to be told the reason by an officer of the law (forward); (3) trying to remember cases where someone was arrested because of mistaken identity (outward). If successful, these activities downgrade the arrest-event, and if not, we will be unable to understand it. Meaninglessness, I would argue, results from the lack of continuity and connectivity, and not from the undecidability of truth values (cf. III.1.2).

1.15 STRENGTH OF LINKAGE (III.3.15) in world-knowledge is relevant to informativity orders. If a textual world asserts relations known to be DETERMINATE already, we have the first order only. The assertion of TYPICAL relations brings more informativity as typicalness decreases. The assertion of ACCIDENTAL relations is by itself neutral for informativity, since accidents may range from the trivial to the unique. The assertion of non-typical relations results in at least second-order, and the contradiction of determinate relations results in third-order informativity. If a tree in a textual world is assigned a trunk, little interest is aroused, that being a stored determinate "part-of" link. If the tree has multiple trunks we are more interested, though not disoriented (non-typical but allowed, hence second-order). If the tree has no trunk at all, its branches hovering in mid-air, we are alarmed by a conflict with a determinate link (third order) and expect an explanation or assume we are dealing with a highly fictional text-world (downgrading).

1.16 The fictional text-world instructs the processor to relax the application of real-world expectations. In *Alice's Adventures in Wonderland* (Carroll 1960), the initial plunge down an impossible rabbit-hole filled with cupboards and bookshelves at once marks the textual world as not governed by the same organization as the reader's. After a series of strange occurrences, the narrator remarks about a normal event (Carroll 1960: 33):

> (36) Alice had got so much into the way of expecting nothing but out-of-the-way things to happen, that it seemed quite dull and stupid for life to go on in the common way.

Yet the Alice-world is by no means devoid of continuity and coherence. Many real-world expectations still apply: gravity makes things fall, water makes things wet, characters speak English, etc. Some domains are understandable via opposition to the real-world: assignment of human roles to animals or playing-cards, violation of politeness conventions, etc. The enduring interestingness of the *Alice* books arises from experiencing a text-world whose third-order occurrences are downgradable by discoverable principles (cf. IV.1.23.1). During the activities of downgrading, readers discover by analogy how the organization of the real-world is arbitrary and amusing (cf. VII.1.8.4).

1.17 Original METAPHORS can constitute third-order occurrences. The fragment of Dylan Thomas' (1971: 196) poem 'In my craft or sullen art' that runs:

(37) In the still night, when only the moon rages

presents a totally non-expected action or emotion of the moon that no reader would have in stored knowledge. To process the fragment, the reader must integrate the problematic element, for example, by reasoning: (1) that the moon's surface resembles the face of a 'raging' person with staring eyes and open mouth; (2) that the moon is traditionally believed to cause lunacy and hence 'raging' in people; (3) that the moon's casting light in all directions resembles a 'raging' person throwing things all around; and so forth. Hence, the original metaphor elicits a resolvable discrepancy between text-presented knowledge and previously stored knowledge. There need be no particular *literal expression* that accomplishes the same thing as the metaphoring (Ortony 1978c). The discrepancy is below surface structure, and its downgrading may be undecidable, as we saw with the Thomas fragment. A literalized restatement could be an impoverishment or even a mis-representation.

1.18 In recent times, literary texts are characterized by more numerous third-order occurrences that are increasingly resistant against downgrading. That trend is conspicuous even in the progression of James Joyce between *Ulysses* and *Finnegan's Wake*. In the earlier novel, the selective principles applied to language options are periodically reorganized, calling forth an adaptation of expectations. In the later novel, the author applies the far more complex principle of *simultaneous partial actualization* of different options, many from other languages besides English, so that no comprehensive expectations about surface structure occurrences can be maintained, and even logical identities are blurred. Experiments of the latter kind (also in the poetry of Hans G. Helms) have an intrinsically limited acceptability as texts, because they run counter to human processing strategies. Constant blocks against downgrading third-order occurrences place an enormous strain on processing energy, which most readers cannot sustain. For some readers, an enriching awareness results about human reliance on expectations in ordinary communication. Yet the processing of a text or situation where continuity is steadily at the break-down point is internally paradoxical and is tolerable only for correspondingly pre-trained readers. It is noteworthy that literary critics have undertaken instead to explicate *Finnegan's Wake* in conventional language: perhaps the most colossal downgrading in history.

1.19 The procedures of UPGRADING are also intriguing. If something is well-known or even determined by standards of logic or science, people should have little reason to assert it by means of a text. Here again, a

MOTIVATION SEARCH (IV.1.12) is likely to take place. Consider the example (in Beaugrande 1978b: 11) of a woman introducing her husband at a party with the utterance:

> (38) My husband is a human being.

She assigns to a person a relation that should be stored already as a determinate "instance-of" link for all people. Hearers will want to discover why the woman makes the effort to say so, because communication is by default presumed to have a reason (cf. Rieger 1975: 160). They could recast the utterance into an expanded format with explicit motivation, such as:

> (38a) My husband is so much like a non-human object that his human status should be asserted when meeting new people.
> (38b) My husband is so nondescript that one can't say much about him except that he is a human being.

(38a) serves to signal that the "instance-of" relation is in fact less probable than might be assumed. (38b) overturns the expectation that one ought to be able to say more than (38). These replacements of (38) with assumed alternative versions illustrate outward upgrading of a first-order occurrence in the conceptual/relational system. A demonstration of forward upgrading in that system—not an uncommon procedure for the beginnings of texts—can be found in this opening passage from a science textbook (quoted in Beaugrande 1978a: 29f.):

> (39) The sea is water only in the sense that water is the dominant substance present. Actually, it is a solution of gases and salts [...]

The first-order informativity of the determinate "substance-of" relation in 'the sea is water' is made upgradable by the subsequent assertion that this piece of common knowledge is 'actually' not accurate and is hence not as probable as it seems. The demands of informativity can even eliminate alternative readings, as is shown by this headline (*Gainesville Sun,* Dec. 20, 1978):

> (40) San Juan Gunfire Kills One

The reading where 'one' is taken as an impersonal pronoun (hence: 'San Juan gunfire kills people') is ruled out as uninformative (unless, of course, gunfire in other cities were not fatal) and hence not newsworthy.

1.20 If a given text allows more than one order of informativity, the second order will presumably have preference over the first. In the final part of Antony's speech (*Julius Caesar,* Act V, Sc. v, 72–75):

> (41) His life was gentle, and the elements
> So mixed in him that Nature might stand up
> And say to all the world, "This was a man!"

the audience will attribute more to the utterance 'this was a man' than a first-order "instance-of" relation. They will rather prefer an understanding in which 'man' is an infrequent class of non-obvious attainment.

1.21 The considerations raised so far suggest an important factor of CYBERNETIC REGULATION in regard to textual communication (cf. I.4.3). The absolute stability of a textual system is guaranteed by a maximum of predictability, because every transition is made rapidly and without effort. Yet this very stability leads to such low informativity that communication lacks all motivation and interest. It follows that textual communication can be envisioned as *the perpetual removal and restoration of stability;* the dynamics of communicative systems arises from an irresolvable antagonism of functional principles. The normal workings of a textual system are therefore kept in the range of second-order occurrences, a degree of moderate but not absolute stability. Upgrading or downgrading of the other orders of informativity are operations of cybernetic regulation in the most basic sense (like the classical example of the thermostat).

1.22 If communication is composed of LEARNING SYSTEMS that adapt to their environment (I.4.3), it follows that the immediate expectations of a context would override those based on general knowledge. Over time, special utilization of systems engenders evolution. For example, highly respected literary texts could serve to expand the possibilities for conventional expression, or to propagate alternative viewpoints about reality via the mode of fictionality (cf. VII.1.8.4f.). Wolfgang Iser (1975: 302) observes that the literary text both stabilizes and interferes with the operations of communicative systems.

1.23 To explore communicative probabilities in more detail, we need to classify expectations into a hierarchy such as the following:

1.23.1 Stored knowledge and episodic experience lead people to see the world in a certain way. The socially dominant model of the human situation and its environment evolves into the notion of the REAL WORLD and is henceforth privileged over all other models. Propositions judged to be true in this world are conventionally called FACTS (cf. Schmidt 1979), and are entered into socially shared BELIEF SYSTEMS (cf. Bruce 1975) as the most fundamental assumptions about the organization of knowledge and experience. Some facts and beliefs are so firmly established that they act as defaults pervading any textual world that might be created: that causes have effects; that time can move in only one direction; that matter cannot be totally destroyed; that entities cannot be both existent and non-existent, present and absent, or possible and impossible at the same time and under the same circumstances; and a great deal more. A textual world in which such basic facts and beliefs are countermanded, e.g. science fiction stories, *must* provide distinct cues in relevant contexts. These cues are instructions that the text receivers should make specified modifications in their expectations lest the textual world become inaccessible and its organization unbearably problematic. On the few occasions where Lewis Carroll does make use of the reversal principle derived from mirror imagery in *Through the Looking-Glass* (Carroll 1960: 205, 249f., 290), he is very emphatic. I suspect that strict adherence to such nonce facts in fictional worlds would soon lose informativity as a corresponding set of expectations is tailored to the occasion (cf. IV.1.5). The continuing interestingness of the *Alice* world is upheld by the variety of its principles for unconventional organization (cf. also IV.1.16).

1.23.2 People also have expectations about LANGUAGE, such as about sequencing (ch. II) and conceptual connectivity (ch. III). People rely on this knowledge to deal with predictable expressions. Users of English do not anticipate unpronounceable clusters of consonants (except in abbreviations), so that when asked to "read aloud" a line on an eye-testing chart, such as:

(42) PDZTLF (Snellen eye chart)[4]

they do not attempt to pronounce the whole line as a unit. Radically disordered syntax, such as:

(43) Mat cat the sat the on.

would not be processable in most contexts (always discounting discussions among linguists). The insistence upon such third-order presentations would more likely be taken as a signal of inability or refusal to communicate, as in Ziff's (1971: 61) example of an "irritable academic" responding to the stupid questions of a military officer with an intentional non-text:

(44) Ugh ugh blugh blugh ugh blug blug.[5]

1.23.3 Expectations also arise from the TEXT TYPE (cf. VII.1.5). The tolerance for violations of expectations is very different for modern poetry than for scientific reports. All fictional text-worlds have some freedom in their organization, though not, as I have pointed out, absolute freedom. Readers would not be disturbed by the appearance of a unicorn in the Alice-world of Lewis Carroll (1960: 283ff.). But a scientific report with a passage such as (Beaugrande 1978b: 6):

(45) The values obtained for white rates (*ratus norvegicus*) were correlated as functions on Vincent curves with those for a control group of unicorns (*equus monoceros*) as shown in Figure 3.

would be deeply disturbing. A scientific-report-world is expected to conform to the organization of the accepted real-world in all aspects. An intriguing

---

[4] I have on occasion read these eye-chart lines as words, only to elicit confusion from the eye-doctor.

[5] Ziff gives no indication of possible phonological distinctions between 'blug' and 'blugh', so that even the tagmemic method for mini-languages (cf. Pike 1967: 210ff.) would fail to extract meaning.

CHAPTER IV INFORMATIVITY **113**

hybrid is 'science fiction', as the name suggests, where the authority and authenticity of science are borrowed to increase the effectiveness of a deliberately impossible reorganized world.

1.23.4 The final type of expectations are those arising in the IMMEDIATE CONTEXT where the text occurs or is utilized. I suggested in IV.1.22 that these expectations can override more general ones in a manner analogous to the adaptation of a learning system to its environment. Hence, the processes of ACTUALIZATION can create a range of expectations which may be quite different from the organization of VIRTUAL systems (cf. I.3.4.3; IV.1.5). An illustration is the phenomenon of STYLE: the characteristic selection and mapping of options among contributing systems of a text (cf. I.2.10). The attempts to characterize styles of a single text, a single text producer, a corpus of texts, a text type, a whole historical period, or even a whole language (cf. survey in Spillner 1974) attest to the ability of language users to create specific expectations for contexts of all sizes. If a text belongs to a highly specialized type, it may by that very token become too predictable and be impelled to break out of the style that it has itself established (cf. Riffaterre 1959, 1960). In such cases, informativity arises from the mapping between systems rather than from the transitions within a single system.

1.24 The divergency of sources for the expectations of text users helps account for the notorious inconsistencies in informants' judgments on the grammaticalness of isolated sentences (cf. I.1.16; IV.1.9). If people were indeed basing their judgments on the availability of imaginable contexts (McCawley 1976), they would naturally need more determinate cues about the uses of an utterance than were provided by the artificial interview situation. If they took the trouble to imagine very detailed contexts, they might accept utterances that would be wholly undesirable for a grammar. Jerry Morgan (1973) notes that an utterance like:

(46) Kissinger conjectures poached.

which should hardly be allowed by a grammar of English, would be a perfectly good reply in a situation where someone had asked:

(47) Anyone know how the president likes his eggs?

Text types can also provide settings where the APPROPRIATENESS (in the sense of I.4.14: mode in which the standards of textuality should be upheld) of structures is clearly given, although the requirements of virtual syntax are not upheld. Milton's lines

(48) Thee, chantress, oft the woods among
     I woo to hear thy evensong. (*Il Penseroso, 63–64*)

are fully acceptable within the poetic diction of his time, and for those familiar with his style, they are not even surprising. Surely the "competence" of language users rests in the ability to fit texts to contexts of many kinds, and not in the ability to mark samples like (46) and (48) with asterisks.

1.25 Expectations also apply to the uses of NEGATION in communication. Experiments prove that people have extra trouble recalling negative sentences (Cornish & Wason 1970) or judging their truth (Fillenbaum 1973; Frederiksen 1975). Usually, there is no motive to negate anything unless people have a reason to believe or expect it (cf. Wason 1965; Osgood 1971; Beaugrande 1978b; Givón 1978). In actualization, a hearer or reader must first activate a knowledge space, and then mark it as non-factual with respect to the textual world (cf. Carpenter & Just 1975). Another account might be that people set up *two* alternative spaces and then discard one. It is, in either case, evident that multiple negations should be increasingly hard to produce or understand:

(49) I never deny that this approach is not otherwise than the opposite of unproductive.

1.26 In this section, I have looked into some issues that reveal the importance of informativity for textual processes. I have suggested that problem-solving techniques for maintaining connectivity of textual occurrences are tied to probabilities for transitions in participating systems. When probable pathways are chosen, efficiency increases, but interest sinks; the reverse is true for improbable pathways. I concluded that there should be at least three orders of informativity: a medium order where efficiency and effectiveness are balanced against against each other, and one order each for the extreme ranges where one heavily outweighs the other. If the medium order is indeed the usual standard for textual communication, then language users must have strategies for upgrading or downgrading the extremes. I identified these factors with the principle of cybernetic regulation, and speculated that textual communication functions by a continual cycle of disturbing and restoring stability.

2. APPERCEPTUAL INFORMATIVITY

2.1 If text utilization interacts with other human abilities and sensory modes (cf. III.3.18), we should investigate the nature of human apperception in general. Humans must distribute attention selectively (IV.1.4) to notice and retain some kinds of episodes and knowledge configurations better than others. The degree of expectedness alone cannot account for all the phenomena involved. At least some effects are due to the inherent nature of the material and some to general processing strategies of apperception.

2.2 Psychologists have devoted considerable study to elementary LEARNING tasks, following several main trends. Some claim that the

FREQUENCY of a presentation decides whether it is learned and utilized (e.g. Ekstrand, Wallace, & Underwood 1966). Others see the basic mechanism as TRANSFER of previously acquired skills to a particular task at hand (e.g. Ferguson 1956). Still others stress the SALIENCE of the concrete cues in a presentation, i.e the force with which cues intrude on sensory apperception (color, brightness, loudness, etc.) (e.g. Goldstein & Scheerer 1941). And some believe that portions of a presentation which are markedly DIFFERENT from the rest are best noticed and recalled (e.g. Hull 1920; Hershberger & Terry 1965; Rundus 1971)—a phenomenon also called the "von Restorff effect" (cf. von Restorff 1933; Wallace 1965).

2.3 In early work, it was hoped that *only one* of these factors could account for *all* kinds of learning behavior—an outlook which immensely simplified the design and interpretation of experiments. More recently, it has become evident that apperception and learning in realistic settings must operate via PROCESSING INTERACTIONS of numerous factors such as those just mentioned. Moreover, these general factors require further specification regarding the situations of apperception and the strategies applied. Several factors ought to receive consideration:

2.3.1 general criteria for ordering and organizing apperceptive material: from higher to lower, from central to peripheral, from mobile to stationary, etc.;

2.3.2 extent of emotional involvement of the apperceiver (cf. Erdelyi 1974);

2.3.3 scales of variables with average versus extreme values;

2.3.4 changing input as opposed to unchanging;

2.3.5 match between current input and stored knowledge (cf. Petöfi 1974);

2.3.6 current need to differentiate among the apperceivable entities, especially those with inherent similarities;

2.3.7 current relevance of input to the apperceiver's own situation, desires, and plans (cf. "ego-seizing" in Ertel 1977).

2.4 The interactions of these factors are unquestionably intricate. Both the apperceiver's state and the organization of a presentation are subject to mutable influences, so that it might be difficult to obtain a consensus. Overreliance upon one factor could be misleading. For example, we would not obtain a very sensible classification of most objects by grouping them according to their salience alone: no one would think of classifying the words of a language according to the loudness with which the current speaker utters them. Moreover, the conflict between stability and informativity noted in I.1.21 may emerge here as well: attention might be focused on the very factors that are interesting because they are extreme and hence not reliable for purposes of classification.

2.5 Within the tradition of "gestalt" psychology (e.g. Koffka 1935), a distinction is drawn between FIGURE and GROUND. The "figure" is the portion of an apperceptual presentation which receives the focus of attention, while the "ground" is the background setting that receives only peripheral attention. For instance, a moving object can appear as the figure, and its stationary environment can appear as the ground (changing vs. unchanging input, cf. IV.2.3.4). To a certain extent, however, the selection of figure and ground depends less on the presentation than on the apperceiver's internal predisposition. It is sometimes hard to tell where the one ends and the other begins; it is safe to say that the two interact in cognition of all kinds (cf. Arnheim 1947; Neisser 1967). The presentation provides the input, but the apperceiver must impose organization if the input is to be utilized as knowledge (cf. Ausubel 1963; Keele 1973; Kintsch 1974).

2.6 There is already some evidence that the factors I have mentioned are also relevant for textual processes. If so, a theory of text processing must be integrated into a general theory of human information processing (Rumelhart 1977a). Such evidence includes the following:

2.6.1 The focus on some part of a scene, such as a mobile object on a stationary background, does affect the format of a linguistic description of the scene (Huttenlocher 1968; Olson 1970; Osgood 1971; Osgood & Bock 1977). The ease of verifying descriptive statements also varies along the same parameter (Olson & Filby 1972; Clark & Chase 1974). Robert E. Longacre (1970) applies the terms of "figure" and "ground" directly to elements in sequences of sentences.

2.6.2 SALIENCE plays a role in speech, where priorities can be signaled by the intensity of intonation in the voice. In general, the greatest stress falls on unexpected elements, such as those contrasting with previously mentioned ones (Bolinger 1972; Brazil 1975; Grimes 1975: 280ff.; Coulthard 1977: 130ff.). Such stress serves to draw attention, and hence to preclude anticipated misunderstandings (Grimes 1975: 282). A rising intonation curve can indicate a lack of belief (Coulthard 1977: 132). Salience also applies to the entities of the textual world. The slaying of a dragon in a children's story will be better noticed than a description of the dragon (cf. Clark & Clark 1977: 238). Salience also affects syntactic choices (Fillmore 1977: 75).

2.6.3 SCALES of VARIABLES can be influential too. Comparisons appear to be recalled better than statements of equivalence (Clark & Card 1969). If a group of objects differ along a scale, the one with the most extreme value serves as a point of orientation in descriptive texts (Flores d'Arcais 1970). There is a considerable literary tradition of text-worlds involving very small and very large objects (Weinrich 1966b).

2.6.4 ORDERING of events and situations correlates with the order in which they are expressed. In describing scenes, speakers were shown to move from the top downward (DeSoto, London, & Handel 1965; Clark & Chase 1974). For event sequences, narration moves from earlier to later (Clark & Clark 1968; E. Clark 1971; Kintsch 1977a: 315). In describing apartments, people expressed major rooms more often in subject positions of sentences; minor rooms emerged more often in predicates (Linde & Labov 1975). Focus on either an agent or an affected entity in a scene depicting an action has been found to correlate with preferences for active versus passive sentence formats (Olson & Filby 1972).

2.6.5 DIFFERENTIATION among the components of a textual world determines the degree of explicitness of descriptive references. The "basic" concepts apparently follow a medium degree of specificity (Rosch, Simpson, & Miller 1976). If there are many similar objects present, speakers use more modifiers in mentioning them (Krauss & Weinheimer 1967; Olson 1970). Some researchers see differentiation as a basic motive in the entire evolution of communicative systems (e.g. Vygotskii 1962; Minsky 1977; cf. the notion of "opposition" in Saussure 1916).

2.6.6 EMOTIONAL INVOLVEMENT of language users exerts controls on deciding what should be expressed, and in what sequence. It has been suggested that entities having the greatest degree of involvement for the speaker are preferentially placed earlier in text production (cf. Osgood 1971), for instance, in the subject slot of a sentence (cf. Ertel 1977). In return, other items outside the involvement focus seem difficult to describe and express (cf. Erdelyi & Appelbaum 1973; Erdelyi 1974).

2.7 These findings are not yet fully reliable, since they were often obtained in simplified situations. Doubtless, the correlations are less straightforward when several factors apply at once, so that competition arises. Nonetheless, just as we cannot successfully divorce language use from world knowledge (III.3.18), we shall have to explore the relationships between the processes of producing or understanding texts and those for utilizing apperceptive material in human experience at large.

2.8 Even the fundamental question of how sounds or printed symbols are recognized must be answered. Acoustic and visual input as raw material could hardly be handled at the requisite speeds without extensive prior conditioning. Hearers adapt to the characteristics of a particular voice (Ladefoged & Broadbent 1957). There appears to be a short-term sensory impression of sounds like an echo of sorts which can be retained long enough to impose organization upon it (cf. Neisser 1967; Crowder & Morton 1969; Darwin, Turvey, & Crowder 1972). A comparable "iconic" impression is seemingly maintained for visual input (Sperling 1960; Neisser 1967). Letters in words figure partly as images and partly as confirmation of predicted patterns (Selfridge & Neisser 1960). The letters that are contained in words are of course recognized better than those which are not (Miller, Bruner, & Postman 1954). If a test word is semantically related to an already identified one, its recognition is quicker (Meyer, Schvaneveldt, & Ruddy 1974)—an effect that would also be explainable as arising from spreading activation of concepts (III.3.24). Not surprisingly, recognition is further aided for predictable words in sentences (Tulving, Mandler, & Baumal 1964). Increasing well-formedness of sentences makes their recognition more resistant against noise disturbance (Miller & Isard 1963).

2.9 The interactions between text utilization and cognitive operations of all kinds demand intensive research. I predict that the complexity of these issues may yet be mastered to the extent that a limited number of efficient and very flexible strategies may underlie a wide range of operations. It would be strange if there should turn out to be a huge number of totally disparate and specialized strategies working independently. The decisive argument in support of interactive processing, as I have argued, is the NON-DETERMINACY of the materials and configurations of textual communication if subdivided into levels of tiny units and steps. As William S. Havens (1978: 2) puts it, cognitive processing "must tolerate non-determinacy by exploiting context and allowing multiple partial interpretations to be hypothesized and their confirmation attempted concurrently."

3. INFORMATIVITY WITHIN THE SENTENCE

3.1 The declarative sentence with its subject and predicate has traditionally been regarded as a statement wherein "the speaker announces a topic and then says something about it" (Hockett 1958: 301). However, this consideration was downplayed in language models where sentences were treated as derived from logical formulas. The sequential format of such formulas is inflexibly and precisely fixed a priori by the construction of the type of logic being used. One cannot arrange things in a special order just because they happen to be expected or unexpected at any particular moment. To the extent that a logical world is composed on discrete and atomistic principles (I.6.3), assertions could influence each other only by certain rules, such as for 'if/then' conclusions. Assertions made in natural language, on the other hand, are often built in a given way because what is already known can be compressed, while what is not yet known or expected can be set into focus via special arrangments.

3.2 There are several options for treating informativity in logic-based linguistics. One can assign the labels of "topic" (already known) and "comment" (new) to fixed elements in a formula, e.g. Chomsky (1965: 221), who defines topic simply as "the leftmost NP immediately dominated by S in the surface structure" and the comment as "the rest of the string." Or one can restructure the logical formulas themselves to obtain the desired correspondence between positioning and knownness (essentially the method of Sgall, Hajičová, & Benešová 1973). And finally, one can adopt the view that underlying logical formulas and the devices for indicating knownness or expectedness are mutually antagonistic, so that surface structure is often misleading; such is the view of Robert P. Stockwell (1977: 168), when he writes:

> But after these focusing and compression devices have *worked their destructive way*, some *restitution* must be made if only to give the hearer *at least a 50–50 chance of reconstructing the meaning* of the sentence, the underlying *Logical Form*. [all emphases added]

Stockwell's indignation at the perverse behavior of language users stands in a venerable tradition among logicians deploring the sloppiness of natural languages.

3.3 Inspired by the work of Vilém Mathesius (1924, 1928, 1929), a group of Czechoslovakian linguists have long been concerned with "functional sentence perspective": how sentence structures can "function" in projecting a specific "perspective" on the content activated by particular elements (survey in Daneš [ed.] 1974; Jones 1977). Their work was brought to the attention of western linguists by Halliday (1967a, 1967b, 1968) and Chafe (1970) in particular. There have been substantial differences in the treatment of the issues, but the central distinction was between "old" or "given" knowledge versus "new" or "focused" knowledge.[6]

3.4 In the multiplicity of terms and proposals (Chafe 1976 and Jones 1977 undertake to sort them out), it has remained unclear precisely what phenomenon we are dealing with:

3.4.1 the grammatical notions of "subject" and "predicate" as structurally defined positions for noun phrase and verb phrase, respectively;

3.4.2 the distinction between what has already been said or mentioned and what has not;

3.4.3 the totality of "presuppositions" entailed by an utterance;

3.4.4 the options for mapping concepts and relations onto sentence positions;

3.4.5 the rate of informativity as a sentence format is presented;

3.4.6 the notions of "psychological subject" as "the idea which appears first in the consciousness of the speaker" and of "psychological predicate" as whatever is added to that idea (von der Gabelenz 1891, cited in Gundel 1977: 19);

3.4.7 the means for signaling alternatives and contrasts;

3.4.8 the relevance of certain sentence formats as answers to specific questions;

3.4.9 the informativity of a textual element seen against the background of probabilities and expectations;

---

[6]If information is defined as extent of unknownness, there could not strictly speaking be any "old information," but only "previous informing actions." See VIII.1.8.

3.4.10 the density of conceptual connectivity around some nodes in a text-world model (e.g. 'rocket' as topic, cf. III.4.27).

3.5 The extent to which linguistic theories can or cannot deal with these phenomenon varies according to the insistence upon a borderline between language and other kinds of knowledge, and between a sentence and the contexts in which sentences are utilized. A compromise has been drawn by many researchers who concern themselves with PRESUPPOSITIONS (cf. Petöfi & Franck [eds.] 1974; Wilson 1975). Following the usual trends in linguistics, these presuppositions are envisioned as sentences that could precede the sentence one wishes to analyze (van Dijk 1972a: 73; Harweg 1974: 98). However, the ability to presuppose something is more a matter of stored knowledge of the world than of an enumeration of preceding sentences. So far, the conventional treatment of presuppositions as sentences has not, in fact, been very successful. I see more hope for a theory of the interaction between stored world knowledge and text-presented knowledge (for some proposals in such a theory, cf. VII.3). At the very least, we should investigate CO-TEXTS (textual environments, cf. I.3.4.5) rather than sentences.

3.6 The need to take some notice of co-text was reflected in the popular "question test" (cf. Daneš 1970; Sgall, Hajičová, & Benešová 1973). For example, a statement such as this (*Tampa Tribune,* Oct. 8, 1978):

(50) The Syrian command in Lebanon ordered a cease-fire Saturday.

seems a better answer to (51a) than to either (51b) or (51c):

(51a) What did the Syrian command in Lebanon do?
(51b) Who ordered a cease-fire?
(51c) Which Syrian command ordered a cease-fire Saturday?

The difficulty here is that (50) would not normally be given as an answer to any of (51); the latter questions would—embarrassingly—not be answered with complete sentences at all, but rather like this:

(52a) Ordered a cease-fire Saturday.
(52b) The Syrian command in Lebanon.
(52c) The one in Lebanon.

A further difficulty is that (50) could be an answer to questions that do not suggest any detailed presuppositions about content, such as:

(53) What's new in the world? [to someone seen reading a newspaper]

3.7 If we start out from the questions rather than the answers, we still can't settle the matter. It is true that there are heavy constraints upon the RELEVANCE (VII.2.8) of question-answer pairs, depending on context. If the person giving the answer picks out some detail not in the questioner's focus of attention, the answer is irrelevant, e.g. in these exchanges:

(54.1) CLAUDIO: Benedick, didst thou *note* the daughter of Signior Leonato?

(54.2) BENEDICK: I *noted* her not, but I *look'd* on her.
(*Much Ado about Nothing,* I, i)[7]

(55.1) JACK: How you can sit there, *calmly* eating muffins when we are in this horrible trouble, I can't make out. [...]

(55.2) ALGERNON: Well, I can't eat muffins *in an agitated manner*. The butter would probably get on my cuffs.
(*The Importance of Being Earnest,* II [Wilde 1940: 446])

Our realization of inappropriateness rests not on sentence structure, but on our knowledge of purposes and motives in human interaction. The same can be said of Labov's (1970) example:

(56.1) A: I feel hot today.

(56.2) B. No.

People should be allowed to know for themselves if they are cold or hot. Yet this is not always the case:

(57.1) LADY CAROLINE: I think you had better come over here, John. It is more sheltered.

(57.2) SIR JOHN: I am quite comfortable, Caroline.

(57.3) LADY CAROLINE: I think not, John. You had better sit beside me. (*A Woman of No Importance,* I [Wilde 1940: 311f.])

Lady Caroline may not know if her husband is cold, but she does know that she wants to watch over him all the time.

3.8 Another technique for identifying topic/comment formats is to construct follow-up statements that might be fitting responses ("commentations") to the sample (R. Posner 1972). The witness's response to (58.1) and (59.1) is precisely the same, yet it protests against different content (Posner 1973: 129f.):

(58.1) DISTRICT ATTORNEY: Before the defendant emptied the safe, he shot down the watchman.

(58.2) WITNESS: That's not true!

(59.1) DISTRICT ATTORNEY: After the defendant shot down the watchman, he emptied the safe.

(59.2) WITNESS: That's not true!

Posner observes that the *truth* of the content expressed in the subordinate clauses is neither asserted nor denied. He concludes that formatting thus signals a GRADATION of RELEVANCE (here, *relevant* to the *task* of

---

[7]I italicize the elements I wish to point out within the samples.

denial, cf. VII.2.8). The informativity of more highly relevant material would be more readily noticed.

3.9 The issues raised here should perhaps be better treated within a model of conversational interaction such as I outline in Chapter VIII. In general, the mechanics of topic and comment seem to be based on the ways in which a world-model from a previously produced text can be expanded into a jointly developed DISCOURSE MODEL. The TOPIC is that portion of the on-going discourse model to which the next speaker adds on material such that density of linkage results (cf. III.4.27). In an exchange like this:

> (60.1) LEONATO: Don Pedro hath bestowed much honour on a young Florentine named Claudio.
> (60.2) MESSENGER: Much deserved on his part.
> (*Much Ado about Nothing*, I,i)

the "comment" of the first utterance becomes the "topic" for the next—the most neutral sort of topic/comment flow (cf. Firbas 1966). The messenger's text picks upon a "reason-of" relation for connecting 'deserve' to 'bestow'. World knowledge makes it unnecessary to specify the co-referent for 'his' (cf. V.4.11), there being only one person in the topic the messenger is commenting upon.

3.10 For efficient communication, it is sensible to present material already established before making additions or modifications. It follows that the early portion of a sentence would be preferentially used for mapping what is previously known. In English, the subject slot betrays a preference for containing old knowledge, but as pointed out by Firbas (1966), by no means obligatorily. By the same token, new or focused knowedge would be strategically well positioned in the predicate (cf. Chafe 1970: ch. 15). For special focus, marked sentence structures can be employed. The "cleft" sentence (Quirk, Greenbaum, Leech, & Svartvik 1972: 951; Leech & Svartvik 1975: 180f.), in which a dummy 'it' and a form of 'be' are followed by a focused element and then a relative clause whose content is known or expected, can exert focus on practically any material, while the usual declarative sentence format is better for focusing the verb phrase or a noun phrase after the verb. If focus were needed for attribute, location, or time (e.g., because of possible confusion with alternatives), then (61a), (61b), or (61c) respectively, could be used:

> (61a) It was the *Syrian* command that ordered a cease-fire Saturday (not the Lebanese).
> (61b) It was *in Lebanon* that the Syrian command ordered a cease-fire (not in Syria).
> (61c) It was *on Saturday* that the Syrian command ordered a cease-fire (not on Friday).

In terms of processing, the cleft sentence is effective because of the way it distributes attention. The first part is a mere dummy subject and verb whose sole function is to create a predicate slot where the intended material can have maximal focus. In exchange, the rest of the material falls into a dependent clause, which, as we saw from (58–59), tends to have reduced focus. Hence, the formats of (61) would only be fitting if the material following 'that' in each case were presumed already known and not in dispute.

3.11 Another focusing device is the so-called "pseudo-cleft" construction (Quirk et al. 1972: 954f.). This one entails beginning with a relative pro-form of the 'wh-' sort, as in:

(62a) What the Syrian command did was order a cease-fire.
(62b) What the Syrian command ordered was a cease-fire.

The opening can also contain a pro-form like 'one' or a very general expression such as 'thing':

(63a) The one who ordered the cease-fire was the Syrian command.
(63b) The thing the Syrian command did was to order a cease-fire.

Like the cleft construction, the pseudo-cleft can be used when most of the material is presumed known or expected. The pseudo-cleft withholds the focused element until the very end of the sentence, creating particular suspense; the appearance of the 'wh-' items even conveys a distant impression of a question being posed and then answered. Notice that the arrangement of the pseudo-cleft construction renders it useful if some context is to be supplied. For instance, following a lecture at the University of Florida, this utterance was heard:

(64) What bothered me was how you used that first example.

This statement uses the opening stretch to pick out certain content from a large framework and to establish that the speaker wishes to protest. The cleft version:

(65) It was your use of the first example that bothered me.

would work better if some indication of protest had already been given.

3.12 The volume and variety of potential expectations sometimes make it expedient to deny things that might be assumed. REPUDIATION—the explicit rejection of stated or implied content (cf. Halliday & Hasan 1976)—is available to handle such cases. In the remark cited below, the follow-up sentence suggests a repudiation of 'family' via a construction that looks like a cleft with the relative clause left unexpressed:

(66) I was in hopes he would have married Lady Kelso. But I believe he said her family was too large. Or *was it* her feet?
(*A Woman of No Importance,* I [Wilde 1940: 310])

A deictic (i.e. pointing) expression like 'that' can be used to indicate what content is repudiated (*MAD Magazine*, Jan. 1979, 42):

(67.1) Suddenly a strange metamorphosis took place.

(67.2) Well, not *that* strange. After all, I could've changed into Wonder Woman!

The speaker can preface his or her remarks with a repudiation of conclusions that a hearer might draw:

(68) Lady Bracknell, *I hate to seem inquisitive,* but would you kindly inform me who I am?

(69) *I am known for the gentleness of my disposition, and the extraordinary sweetness of my nature,* but I warn you, Miss Cardew, you may go too far. (both from *The Importance of Being Earnest* [Wilde 1940: 456 and 444])

These uses might be called FORWARD repudiation, as opposed to the BACKWARD repudiation in (66) and (67). We could also have OUTWARD repudiation, if people want to deny material that is not part of the discourse model, but is probably assumed, as in the common American saying:

(70) It's not the money, it's the principle of the thing!

used especially when it *is* the money that annoys the speaker. Many of our examples show negation, which is by and large employed for repudiation in natural communication (cf. IV.1.25), whatever its uses in formal logic.

3.13 The relationships between degrees of informativity and sentence structure appear from these examples to be highly sensitive to context. "Functional sentence perspective" might very well be termed "functional text perspective" as a control upon the formatting of sentences along with many other factors (cf. Dressler 1974a; Jones 1977; Palková & Palek 1978). We need not expect every sentence to have its own "topic" as distinct from a "comment"—unless we decide to define these notions in terms of sentence positions to begin with (e.g. Chomsky 1965; Halliday 1967a); in that case, we are no longer dealing with informativity. At most, we could explore "local topics" and "global topics" (cf. Grimes 1975: 103), without explicit commitment to sentence-length fragments (cf. VIII.1.9).

3.14 If spreading activation applies to sequences of utterances, very little of what people say is likely to be truly "new." Francis Bacon (1869: 268f.) even denies that we can invent anything new when we speak:

The invention of speech or argument is not properly an invention: for to invent is to discover that we know not, and not to recover or resummon that which we already know; and the use of this invention is no other but out of the knowledge whereof our mind is already possessed, to draw forth or call before us that which may be pertinent to the purpose which we take into our consideration.

It might not be too fanciful to see in Bacon's sixteenth-century outlook an anticipation of the modern theory of problem-solving. The elements of knowledge are considered already present in the mind, and the task is to decide how to connect them together to suit a plan and a topic. As textual communication proceeds, more and more material becomes active, and much of it may not be "pertinent." The task of communicating is then not to *fill* other people's minds wtih content, but to instruct them how to *limit* and *select among* the content they already have in their minds. That task is aided by the surface formats of sentences that signal focus vs. background (cf. "figure and ground" in IV.2.5). There may be mapping preferences here also (cf. III.4.16) between the surface and the underlying organization. The greater ease of the cleft construction for focusing modifiers and nouns makes it more suitable for drawing attention to objects, attributes, times, locations, and the like, as in (61a–61c); the pseudo-cleft construction handles verb and verb phrases better, and so is more expedient for drawing attention to actions and events, as in (62a), (62b), (63b), and (64) (cf. Quirk et al. 1972: 951ff.). But such preferences can be circumvented if need be, for instance, by mapping an event or action onto a noun, as in (65).

3.15 The construction of sentences must presumably have some relationship to the relative PROBABILITIES within a context. The notion of "communicative dynamism" advanced by Firbas (1971) is one of the few reflections of that fact in sentence linguistics. Third-order informativity of occurrences like discrepancies or discontinuities (IV.1.12) would correspond to the highest "communicative dynamism." For normal occurrences in languages with fairly free word sequencing, the progression of a sentence should reflect much of this scale (Sgall et al. 1973: 237). In English, however, constraints on sequencing are forthcoming from many other factors, the more so as there are few inflections within the individual words to signal grammatical dependencies (contrasted with, say, Czech).

3.16 The conclusion is that we will not clarify these matters by working from inside the sentence as a bounded unit. In doing that, we would be taking as given something we ought to explain: how people decide how much knowledge forms a unit and how much to load onto a surface format (cf. II.1.12). Question-answer pairs, or statement-commentation sequences, are composed of utterances whose nature is fully textual and only partly sentential. As Jerry Morgan (1975: 434) notes, topics are not noun phrases in sentences, but items of knowledge used by people.

3.17 If we move to deeper levels than sentences, we may eventually hit upon the UNIVERSALS of language after all, though not much like the ones linguists usually look for (cf. Greenberg [ed.] 1963). Instead, they may be along these lines (cf. the list of skills in IX.1.4):

3.17.1 PROBLEM-SOLVING capacities;

3.17.2 PLANNING capacities;

3.17.3 capacities for INFERRING the problem-solving and planning activities of other people;

3.17.4 capacities for GENERATING, TESTING, and REVISING HYPOTHESES about current input and its relevance to larger contexts;

3.17.5 processing EASE for expected or probable output and input;

3.17.6 processing DEPTH for non-expected or improbable output and input;

3.17.7 processing LIMITATIONS regarding COMPLEXITY (cf. VIII.2.15);

3.17.8 capacities for REDUCING COMPLEXITY;

3.17.9 capacities for selective FOCUS of ATTENTION;

3.17.10 capacities for maintaining CONTINUITY of EXPERIENCE.

3.18 As already suggested in I.5.6, I believe that INTELLIGENCE arises from the independence of these capacities from the details of using them in specific instances. The most powerful and flexible application of these capacities will thus lead to the highest intelligence. It follows that research on textual communication may reach far beyond establishing the inter-disciplinary nature of a science of texts; there will be significant implications for the development of human intelligence at large (cf. IX.1.5).

4.   A NEWSPAPER ARTICLE

4.1 The task of the journalist is an intriguing one: to find an interesting and informative format for presenting content which may range from events affecting the world situation all the way down to the most trivial and irrelevant episodes. Accordingly, journalistic texts ought to show highly developed techniques for controlling the focus of attention and upholding interest and effectiveness. The following sample demonstrates, the techniques involved (*Gainesville Sun,* Oct. 8, 1978):

(71.1) It was three years ago when Dr. Tony Pfeiffer first met Larry.

(71.2.1) Larry, a native of Sierra Leone, Africa, was an adolescent big for his age. (71.2.2) He didn't know how to run. (71.2.3) He couldn't bear to be touched. (71.2.4) He opened and closed his hands and rocked back and forth in the characteristic fashion of a psychotic.

(71.3.1) Dr. Pfeiffer is an anthropologist. (71.3.2) Larry is a chimpanzee driven more or less crazy by years of confinement in dark, antiseptic cages of medical laboratories.

The article concludes by noting that experimentation has placed chimpanzees on the list of endangered species, so that Dr. Pfeiffer was given funds to rehabilitate these animals on a small island in Florida.

4.2 The mere appearance of the text on the page is revealing. The short paragraphs allow reading with a short span of active storage. The content of the first and second paragraphs is so closely related that no division is actually necessary. Yet the division elicits expectations of newness and informativity that accord well with other tendencies in the same text.

4.3 The text begins with a cleft construction (cf. IV.3.10). Although a non-cleft version could contain the same material:

(71.1a) Dr. Pfeiffer first met Tony three years ago.

it does not create comparable focus. Actually, this time designation is not important knowledge. But it launches the reader into the article with increased attention and serves the writer's plan of withholding more crucial knowledge for strategic motives.

4.4 Like many text beginnings, (71.1) has no given knowledge as its background. It announces as new both 'three years ago' and 'first met Larry' in the two predicate slots. The second piece of knowledge becomes topical for the entire following paragraph (71.2).[8] Its sentence subjects are all co-referent with Larry, and no confusion of the pronoun 'he' is likely, since the TOPIC acts as a control center to attract otherwise undecidable material (cf. III.4.27). A pattern is established in these sentences, especially in the PARALLELISM between (71.2.2) and (71.2.3). The effectiveness of grammatical parallelism lies in freeing attention away from parsing surface structures, so that conceptual-relational content can receive greater concentration. The cognitive principle is the contrast of changing input being more intensively processed than unchanging (IV.2.3.4). The concluding sentence (71.2.4) breaks the pattern with a junctive predicate whose extended second constituent leads up to the focused final element 'psychotic'. An arrangement which ran like this:

(71.2.4a) In the characteristic fashion of a psychotic, Larry opened and closed his hands

would draw much less attention to that same element.

4.5 We see that the entire second paragraph is built according to the preference strategy of placing established knowledge early in each sentence format (grammatical subject) and leading up to new material toward the sentence conclusion. In each case, the new material is most specific and crucial at the very end: 'big for his age' (71.2.1); 'run' (71.2.2), 'touched' (71.2.3), and 'psychotic' (71.2.4). The sentence formatting of the third paragraph follows the same pattern: subjects are again expressions for

---

[8]The positioning of this knowledge in the cleft construction suggests it should have been previously mentioned—another overturning of conventional usage to draw the reader into the text-world.

previously activated conceptual entities, while the predicates provide new characterizations (assignment of instances to classes). Such similarities of structuring could be utilized via TEXT-INTERNAL PATTERN-MATCHING (cf. V.7.1; VII.2.36).

4.6 Superposed on these recurrent sequencing techniques is a calculated activating and subsequent overturning of reader expectations on the conceptual level. The proper names in the opening sentence (71.1) are revealing. 'Dr. Pfeiffer' will be taken as a member of the class of 'doctors' and via spreading activation, 'Larry' as a member of the class of 'patients'. This subtle class assignment encourages putting Larry into the superclass of 'human beings' at the same time. That assignment can be upheld throughout the second paragraph with terms like 'native', 'adolescent', 'hands', and 'psychotic' that all apply preferentially to humans, not animals. (It would be easy to eliminate this ambiguity with expressions like 'paws' rather than 'hands', or 'imported from' rather than 'a native of'. Larry's actual 'age', if given, could also show non-human status, since the chimpanzee matures much more rapidly than the human.) Following this preparation, some occurrences of the third paragraph convey third-order informativity that is easily subjected to backward downgrading: the reader will regress and discover that the hypothesis 'Larry—instance of—human beings' was founded on *typical* but not *determinate* concepts and relations.

4.7 The flow of informativity inside the second paragraph is itself noteworthy. After learning that Larry 'was an adolescent big for his age', the reader does not expect to find that Larry still doesn't 'know how to run'—a description that should fit only small children. But the discrepancy can be integrated by the inference that 'meeting' a doctor would have the "reason-of" Larry's being abnormal (backward plus outward downgrading). The hypothesized "state-of" 'abnormal' is carried forward and strengthened by the content underlying the next sentence, whose surface structure is moreover parallel—a mapping of expectedness on two levels. In the final sentence (71.2.4), the actions/motions of opening and closing the hands and rocking back and forth, in themselves not necessarily ominous, are brought into line with the 'abnormal'-hypothesis when the key concept 'psychotic' arrives to subsume what has been communicated so far. We have an instantiation of a FRAME of knowledge (see Chapter VI) which could be labeled 'actions and states of the psychotic'. Via spreading activation, Dr. Pfeiffer is assigned via "specification" to the class 'psychotherapist' rather than 'doctor'.

4.8 It is clear how the material of the second paragraph is so arranged and presented that the material of the third one hits the reader quite unprepared. I tested the effects on a group of 20 University of Florida undergraduates. Using a technique developed especially by Rumelhart (1978), I interrupted their reading at various points and asked them to describe how they envisioned Larry and Dr. Pfeiffer. All 20 said after the first one-sentence paragraph that they were thinking of a doctor and patient. The first-name

designation led 14 to assume that Larry was substantially younger than the
doctor. The latter assumption was of course strengthened by the appearance
of 'adolescent' in (71.2.1). After (71.2.2), all 20 assumed that Larry was an
abnormal youngster, and that Pfeiffer was called in to treat him for that
reason. This view remained stable for the rest of the second paragraph.

4.9 After reading (71.3.1), the students became disoriented, wondering
why an anthropologist would be doing what seemed to be the work of a
psychotherapist. When pressed for an explanation, 11 reasoned that an
anthropologist might have discovered a new method of treating mental
disorders, and that this discovery would be the point of the article; five more
said that in a remote part of the world like Sierra Leone, and anthropologist
might be doing the work of other specialists; and the rest ventured no opinion.
When the final sentence (71.3.2) of this excerpt was read, all 20 subjects said
they had been fooled, and several had trouble believing that they hadn't
actually read the material they had supposed. Four mentioned that the
'anthropologist' made better sense then. One said she "had been kinda
wondering about that 'anthropologist' but didn't worry too much about it at
the time."

4.10 The comprehension process had clearly been guided by inferences
based on what is TYPICAL, e.g. that 'hands' are more typical of humans than
animals. The writer has carefully avoided stating DETERMINATE material
that would have precluded the ambiguity. The author has another goal
besides the usual journalistic one of making presentations interesting and
surprising. By forcing the readers to confuse humans and chimpanzees, the
author leads us to a dramatic realization of how similar these two classes are.
In that perspective, the motivation for rehabilitating animals driven insane by
humans seems much greater. This technique of introducing disturbances into
communication and yet providing strong motivation for them can contribute
much to intensifying writer-reader interaction (cf. Beaugrande 1979e; Kintsch
1979a), and thus to impelling the reader to accept the writer's outlook. In
extreme cases, the reader must adopt that outlook just to process the text at
all; such is the case for literary texts like Rilke's *Duineser Elegien*
(Beaugrande 1978a: 74).

4.11 For samples such as our article, it is necessary to envision a text-world
model undergoing REVISION during the construction processes. We would
have a fairly consistent model for the knowledge spaces underlying the first
and second paragraphs, as shown in Figure 20. I include the inferred material
(in square brackets) that subsequently proves to be erroneous: the classes
'psychotherapist' and 'human.' On encountering the third paragraph, this
model space undergoes a "clash" (cf. Fahlman 1977: 33). The inferred nodes
must be tossed out to make room for the explicitly activated 'anthropologist'
and 'chimpanzee' nodes. The operations involved are actually rather small,
yielding a configuration such as shown in Figure 21. As was observed in the
case of sequencing in II.2.34, the network modeling is quite suitable for

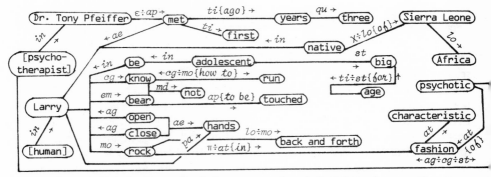

Key: *ae*: affected entity; *ag*: agent of; *ap*: apperception of; *at*: attribute of; *cg*: cognition of; *ε*: entry; *lo*: location of; *md*: modality of; *mo*: motion of; *pa*: part of; *π*: proximity; *qu*: quantity of; *st*: state of; *ti*: time of

Figure 20

changes due to subsequent discoveries (cf. Burton 1976: 44f.). In a model where concepts have to be derived from a branching hierarchy of features (e.g. Katz & Fodor 1963), extensive rearrangement would be demanded on finding that the most general class concept 'human' had been mistakenly utilized. Networks are pledged to connectivity only, and context-dependent revisions can thus be more economically represented.

4.12 This demonstration text points up the eminent role of *text-activated expectations* for processing (cf. IV.1.23.4). EFFICIENCY is upheld by a DESIGN presenting old knowledge before new in short stretches, and surface structuring is analogous from stretch to stretch. A carefully planned-out mapping of options among levels controls the flow of informativity, such that this efficiency can be reconciled with the EFFECTIVENESS of sudden, non-expected occurrences at strategic points. This design is effective in the sense of I.4.14 in furthering the text producer's plan toward a goal (empathy with chimpanzees and a concern for their fate). The design is APPROPRIATE because it is cohesive, coherent, and plan-oriented in precisely the mode established for communication via newspaper reporting. Hence, the three criteria advocated for the evaluation of structural design (I.4.14) all assign a favorable rating to our text. Small wonder if we find such a design elsewhere; I close with a strikingly analogous text which you may wish to analyze and compare with (71) (*TIME*, January 22, 1979) (cf. discussion in Beaugrande & Dressler 1980, Ch. VII):

> (72) Twenty-year old Willie B. is a diehard TV addict. He hates news and talk shows, but he loves football and gets so excited over food commercials that he sometimes charges at the set, waving a fist. Says a friend: "He's like a little child."
>
> Willie B. is a 450-lb. gorilla at the Atlanta Zoo. In December a Tennessee TV dealer heard about Willie B's lonely life as the zoo's only gorilla and gave him a TV set.

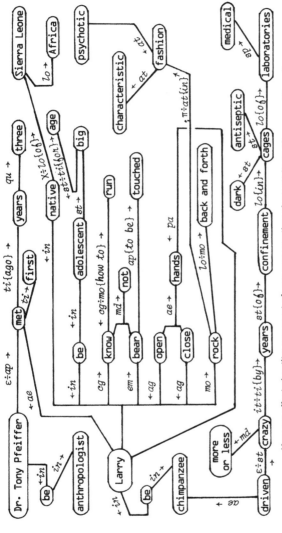

Key: *ae*: affected entity; *ag*: agent of; *ap*: apperception of; *at*: attribute of; *cg*: cognition of;
ε: entry; *em*: emotion of; *in*: instance of; *it*: instrument of; *lo*: location of; *md*: modality of;
mo: motion of; *pa*: part of; *π*: proximity; *qu*: quantity of; *sp*: specification of; *st*: state of;
ti: time of

Figure 21

V
Textual Efficiency

1. MOTIVES FOR EFFICIENCY

1.1 I have argued throughout that the utilization of texts in communication entails constant management of blocks of knowledge, only some of which are relevant at a given moment. The sheer volume of this knowledge usually precludes making even a majority of it explicit in an individual statement. It follows that a language should provide numerous options for compacting surface expression without damaging the connectivity of underlying knowledge. In effect, these sets of options point the participants in communication toward that portion of active knowledge which is to be currently expanded or modified. The options are clearly an important contribution to the EFFICIENCY of textuality: processing the largest amounts with the smallest expenditure of resources. In terms of CYBERNETICS, the use of formats for restatement responds to the CURRENT CONTROLS on communication (cf. I.3.4.7), regulating the flow of knowledge up to the surface.

1.2 The notion of "cohesion" has been used by some researchers for devices such as pronominalization, substitution, and ellipsis (see especially Halliday 1964; Hasan 1968; Halliday & Hasan 1976). Often, no special consideration is given to the underlying connectivity of text-knowledge and world-knowledge that makes these devices possible and useful (except in the discussion of "lexical cohesion" in Halliday & Hasan 1976: ch. 6). Many factors in linguistic outlooks were responsible for this omission: limitations to sentences, exclusion of world-knowledge, lack of interest in real communication, and a general discomfort regarding semantics. The primacy of syntax in linguistics is revealed by the very terms that were proposed for the devices we are considering: "hypersyntax" (Palek 1968), "macrosyntax" (Gülich 1970), or "suprasyntax" (Dressler 1970a). Evidently, the notion of "syntax" here is not that of syntax proper, but a hybrid of "semantics of syntax" and "syntax of semantics" as envisioned by the scheme set forth in I.2.8. Bonnie Webber (1980) remarks on the tendency to treat the cohesive devices as if they served to refer to *surface words* rather than to the conceptual-relational content underlying words. Jerry Morgan (1978a: 109f.) notices that tendency even in the writings of Halliday and Hasan (1976: 2), "who probably know better." But Morgan may be too severe: surely we may say metaphorically that words "refer" to other words, and mean that words refer to the same referents as other words, provided we do not go on to claim that we are dealing with nothing but words.

1.3 An exception to general trends is the very broad outlook of Roland Harweg (1968a). His notion of "substitution" subsumes not only the usual devices such as pronouns and articles, but a diverse range of conceptual relations like inclusions among classes, superclasses, or metaclasses, part/whole, causality, and proximity. He is one of the few linguists to make free use of world-knowledge in defining textuality. In the main, "substitution" is any connection between two components of a text or textual world that allows the second to activate a configuration of knowledge shared with the first. Hence, a good portion of his examples would be in line with the spreading activation model of knowledge use (cf. III.3.24).

1.4 I will undertake to outline some of the most important devices of cohesion. My criteria will be their contributions to the processing efficiency. These devices are:

1.4.1 RECURRENCE is the actual repetition of expressions. The repeated elements may have the same, different, or overlapping reference, and the extent of conceptual content they can be used to activate varies accordingly.

1.4.2 DEFINITENESS is the extent to which the text-world entity for an expression at a given point is assumed to be identifiable and recoverable, as opposed to being introduced just then.

1.4.3 CO-REFERENCE is the application of different surface expressions to the same entity in a textual world.

1.4.4 ANAPHORA is the type of co-reference where a lexical expression is later *followed* by a PRO-FORM (e.g. pronoun) in the surface text.

1.4.5 CATAPHORA is the type of co-reference in which the pro-form *precedes* its lexical expression in the surface text.

1.4.6 EXOPHORA is the application of a pro-form to an entity not expressed in the text at all, but identifiable in the situational context.

1.4.7 ELLIPSIS is the omission of surface expressions whose conceptual content is nonetheless carried forward and expanded or modified by means of noticeably incomplete expressions.

1.4.8 JUNCTION subsumes the devices for connecting surface sequences together in such a way that the relations between blocks of conceptual text-world knowledge are signaled, such as: addition, alternativity, contrast, and causality. Subtypes of junction are CONJUNCTION, DISJUNCTION, CONTRAJUNCTION, and SUBORDINATION (see II.2.24ff.).

1.5 These devices offer a number of contributions to efficiency: (1) the *compacting* of surface expression; (2) the *omission* of surface elements; (3) the *carrying forward* of materials to be *expanded, developed, modified,* or *repudiated;* (4) the signaling of *knownness, uniqueness,* or *identity;* and (5) a workable balance between *repetition* and *variation* in surface structure as required by the considerations of *informativity.*

1.6 The dependence of these devices on context emerges from this list of advantages. At any particular moment during the production and comprehension of a text, people need cues about what ALTERNATIVES among possible continuations are more or less probable (cf. IV.1.1). At the same time, it is necessary to keep the intended alternatives CURRENT without cluttering up the surface text by lengthy restatement or repudiation.

1.7 The STABILITY PRINCIPLE was proposed in I.4.4 as a major factor of systemic regulation of the kind I envision in the actualization of texts. Such a principle assigns a high priority to strategies for co-ordinating surface expressions that share common or contiguous conceptual content. The ECONOMY PRINCIPLE stipulates that, wherever expedient or doubtful, preference should be given to re-using already activated content, rather than activating new content. It follows that cohesive devices like those enumerated in V.1.4 do not *make* the text coherent; the *prior assumption* that the text is coherent makes these devices useful (cf. Morgan 1978a: 110).

2.   RECURRENCE

2.1 The recurrence of surface expressions with the same conceptual content and reference is especially common in spontaneous speaking, as opposed to formal situations. The eyewitness report of a distraught county supervisor after a flood in Arizona contained these statements (*Gainesville Sun,* Dec. 20, 1978):

>   (73) There's *water* through many homes—I would say almost all of them have *water* in them. It's just completely under *water.*[1]

---

[1]Throughout this chapter, I use the convention of placing the elements I wish to address in italics.

The accumulated effect of this usage has something of the disastrous, disordered copiousness of the water, an entity normally in short supply in Arizona.

2.2 According to the principles of stability and economy, recurrence would entail sameness of reference. But this could lead to conflicts in texts where there seem to be no alternative expressions for different referents (*Gainseville Sun*, Dec. 20, 1978):

(74.1) Weapons and projectile toys have a built-in threat to *eyes* and cannot be made child-proof.

(74.2) Consumer safety groups have also warned about stuffed animals with loose *eyes* and poorly sewn-on accessories. Small children can pull them off and swallow them.

(74.3) "We find *eyes* all over the place," one toy store clerk said.

We assume that the clerk was finding toy eyes, not children's eyes, 'all over the place' because in the latter case, the press treatment would be much more explicit (lack of knowledge inference, III.3.21). Ambiguity is similarly overcome for this passage of the *Ohio Drivers Handbook:*

(75) A restricted *license* may be issued to any person otherwise qualified who is subject to episodic impairment of consciousness upon a statement from a *licensed* physician.

None of my Ohio informants interpreted the passage such that the physician is required to have a *driver's license* (though some wondered how 'episodic impairment of consciousness' differs from the usual state of Ohio drivers).

2.3 Deliberate violations of the stability and economy principles might increase informativity and interest. For example, a poem allegedly written by the 18-year-old conspirator Chidiock Tichborne just before his execution in 1586 contains the line (Simpson [ed.] 1967: 85f.):

(76) My *glass* is full, and now my *glass* is run.

A discrepancy (I.6.9) arises when the second 'glass' cannot be taken as a drinking vessel and must be processed as 'hourglass' instead, reverting to knowledge about the writer's personal situation of impending execution.

2.4 Psychologically, recurrences should distribute attention away from their components, except in cases like (76). If the frequency principle of learning (IV.2.2) applies, the recurrent elements should be impressed on memory. Processing should be easy, as the point of connection in the ongoing text-world model should be obvious (cf. Kintsch 1974: 86). Whatever factors may apply, there must be a difference between the TRIVIAL recurrences required by the limited repertories of language options and MOTIVATED recurrences where repetition has some deeper justification (cf. Werth 1976; Beaugrande 1978b, 1979e, 1979g).

2.5 Consider for instance the Biblical proverb:[2]

(77) As in water *face reflects face,*
So the heart of *man reflects man.*

The two lines are very similar in surface structure, and each contains an element repeated on either side of the element 'reflects'. This organization of expression enacts the content of the textual world: images 'reflected' in a mirror. Less striking is the use of recurrence for signaling repetitious events, as in Steinbeck's passage:

(78) They *work at it* and *work at it.*

This use is similar to that of the county supervisor preoccupied with an overabundance of water in (73). Speaker outlook can be signaled with recurrences such as this one from Jeannie Morris:

(79) There are *no distractions*—and I mean *no distractions.*

This time, the surface format enacts the insistence of the speaker on an attitude as unchanging as the expressions themselves. Possible objections are accordingly discouraged (cf. Beaugrande & Dressler 1980).

2.6 Recurrence can be employed with a shift in the syntactic function of an expression (Dressler 1979). The recurring element is adapted to its environments, yet the identity of reference is still obvious. In the American *Declaration of Independence,* we find these stretches of text:

(80.1) to assume among the powers of the earth, the *separate* and equal station [. . .] (80.2) they should declare the causes which impel them to the *separation*

The shift from adjective for an attribute to noun for an action neatly signals the overall coherence while avoiding the monotony of an exact repetition. Dressler (1979) notes that this recurrence type offers the text producer the potential to create new language items, since one occurrence can provide for the comprehension of the other. Such is the case when Erich Fried entitles a story '*Turtle-Turning*' and includes this passage (Fried 1975):

(81) Everywhere he finds a helpless *turtle* fallen on its back, he *turns* it over

The title would be highly non-determinate without this recurrence via word-class shifting.

2.7 Recurrences of lengthy expressions or whole passages can be disadvantageous, because they depress informativity unless strong motivation is present. It is strategically sound to vary expression with

---

[2]These examples are taken from a textbook entitled *Rhetoric: From Athens to Auburn,* edited by Richard Graves (Auburn: Auburn University Press, 1976, pp. 33, 32, and 19 respectively).

paraphrases or synonyms. Yet as in the case of 'water' (73), there may be only one readily available name for the desired concept. In scientific reports, the use of specially defined terms must be consistent, despite the repetitiousness entailed. Hearers and readers presumably adapt their expectations in response to these factors.

3.   DEFINITENESS

3.1 The issue of definiteness takes on various dimensions, depending upon whether one's outlook is logical or psychological. If meaning is identified directly with "truth value" (III.1.2), definiteness becomes a property of objects asserted in a logical world. If meaning is viewed as mental processes, then definite entities are those that are "uniquely identifiable" to participants in communication (Clark & Clark 1977: 249f.). Whether the entities are logical or real, both criteria are too strong. Definiteness applies to many entities that need not be identified at all with specific objects. Ortony and Anderson (1977) distinguish the identifiable reference as "extensional representation" and the reference to entities needed only for conceptual content as "intensional representation" (cf. I.2.8.2).

3.2 The utilization of ARTICLES is revealing, as the terms "definite and indefinite article" suggest. Usually, the definite article is claimed to precede the expression of entities already mentioned, and the indefinite that of newly introduced ones (cf. Firbas 1966). But the following fragment of a Thurber story (in Thurber 1948: 34)[2a] suggests that the matter is more intricate:

(82.1)   Once upon a time, there lived *a* king whose daughter was *the* prettiest princess in the whole world. (82.2) On the day *the* princess was eighteen, *the* king sent a royal ambassador to the courts of *the* five neighboring kingdoms to announce that he would give his daughter's hand in marriage to *the* prince whose gift she liked most. (82.3) *The* first prince to arrive at the palace [...]

The classical distinction of new = indefinite vs. previously mentioned = definite applies here only to 'a king' (82.1) and 'the king' (82.2). The beginnings of texts are, of course, likely places for indefinite articles (Weinrich 1976: 172). Yet the first occurrence of 'princess' has the definite article, being a superlative. The usage in 'the five neighboring kingdoms' rests on the postulate of continuity in a textual world (I.6.4): a geographical region can be expected to have neighbors. 'The prince' in (82.2) is a projected entity not yet having any referent: any prince who meets that description (an

---

[2a]Copr. © 1948 James Thurber. Copr. 1976 Helen W. Thurber and Rosemary Thurber Sauers. From *The Princess and the Tin Box*, in THE BEAST IN ME—AND OTHER ANIMALS, published by Harcourt Brace Jovanovich. Reprinted by permission.

"intensional representation" in the sense of Ortony & R. Anderson 1977); and 'the first prince' in (82.3) is a member of the candidate class in which there can be only one for each number in a series. Such varied uses of articles are essential for the connectivity of the story. De Villiers (1974) found that if the definite articles in a story text are replaced by indefinite, readers don't take the component sentences as parts of a story at all. Loftus and Zanni (1975) found that eyewitness reports could be influenced by inserting definite articles in front of strategic items: the articles impelled the eyewitnesses to accept as factual some items they hadn't really seen to begin with. Here, the text surface actually *created* background knowledge while pretending to keep it active.

3.3   At least the following entities would seem to be eligible for the status of definiteness:

3.3.1   MENTIONED entities as established in a textual world (e.g. 'the king');

3.3.2   SPECIFIC entities established by constraining description or definition (e.g. 'the day the princess was eighteen');

3.3.3   EPISODIC entities stored in the shared knowledge of language users personally acquainted with each other (e.g. 'the movie' in Clark & Marshall 1978: 57; cf. also Goldman 1975: 347);

3.3.4   UNIQUE entities which every sensorially endowed member of a communicative group is assumed to know about (e.g. 'the sun', 'the earth');

3.3.5   INSTITUTIONALIZED entities that social organization is presumed to require ('the president', 'the fire department', 'the police');

3.3.6   DEFAULT entities created on demand for the continuity of a textual world (e.g. 'the five neighboring kingdoms' in [82.2]);

3.3.7   PROTOTYPICAL entities that function as the representative of a class (e.g. 'the man on the street', 'the ugly American') (cf. III.3.27);

3.3.8   SUPERLATIVE entities that occupy the extreme position on some scale of variables (e.g. 'the prettiest princess in the whole world');

3.3.9   RELATIONAL ENTITIES accessible via TYPICAL and DETERMINATE links from already definite entities.

3.4   The criterion of being "uniquely identifiable" fails to cover these various uses. Often, definite entities have no more identity than is required for the particular context wherein they appear (Rieger 1975: 204). We can talk about 'the police', 'the ugly American', or 'the prettiest princess in the whole world' without any commitment to an object, or even to a complete entity: we are addressing a conceptual configuration whose content may be no more than the properties we need at the moment. The 'police' are people only in their official capacity, not as private individuals. An 'ugly American' need by no means possess a repellant outward appearance. We can easily envision the 'man on the street' not being on any street at all. And 'the prettiest princess' may be decidable in a children's tale, but hardly in a reality where beauty is a matter of opinion.

3.5 Definiteness might be explicated as the status of entities in a textual world whose FUNCTION in their respective context is non-controversial. To fix the status, e.g. with proper names or definite descriptions, is to instruct the hearer/reader that the appropriate conceptual content should be easily suppliable on the basis of already activated knowledge spaces. INDEFINITE entities, on the other hand, require the activation of further knowledge spaces. Hence, de Villier's (1974) test subjects thought that the version with indefinite articles could not constitute a unified story world. They took the indefinite articles as instructions to activate new spaces rather than use already active ones.

3.6 No one would have trouble with entities like 'the sun' and 'the moon'. These entities are not in fact unique, as the exploration of astronomers attests. But in lack of any wider setting such as a science fiction story, preference is at once given to the usual referents. Since a textual world is not committed to exact correspondence with the accepted real world, conventionally unique entities can be recontextualized into non-unique. In this view, uniqueness begins to converge with default. Consider this excerpt from a news article on prostitution (*Gainesville Sun,* Oct. 8, 1978):

(83) Now that *the* adult bookstores, formerly *the* vice squad's primary target, have been closed down, *the* agents are able to devote more time to busting hookers.

The definiteness of 'bookstores', 'vice squad', and 'agents' rests on their typical or institutionalized status in American social organization. They can be assumed as defaults without any clear notion of where or who they might be in this particular town. If occasion arises, their uniqueness can be established. Yet communication would operate very slowly if we had to establish uniqueness merely in order to talk about these entities.

3.7 The spreading activation model of knowledge use, as frequently cited in this book, is relevant to definiteness. Although it is not decided whether spreading is consciously controlled or not (cf. M. Posner & Snyder 1975), definiteness can be one means for channeling it. The appearance of a definite entity not previously mentioned would then have the effect of singling out a point in knowledge space to which activation is assumed to have spread. DETERMINATE and TYPICAL links clearly provide the soundest basis for that assumption. Consider this news item (*Florida Independent Alligator,* Oct. 9, 1979):

(84) A seat belt saved a UF student when he fell asleep at *the* wheel of his 1977 Subaru and turned off into *the* path of a train.

The definiteness of 'wheel' arises as a determinate "part-of" a 'Subaru', and that of 'path' as a typical "location-of-motion-of" a 'train'.

3.8 Perhaps the following definition deserves consideration: *definiteness can spread to any text-world entity standing in a determinate or typical linkage* (cf. III.3.15) *to an entity whose definiteness is already established in the textual world.* To see how this principle would work, imagine that (85.1) were a text beginning; any of the continuations in (85.2) should then be acceptable via the link types (from III.4.7) cited in square brackets:

(85.1) Never before had we seen such a house.

(85.2a) *The* plot of land was quite deserted. [location-of]
(85.2b) *The* rectangular outline looked oddly lopsided. [form-of]
(85.2c) *The* walls were leaning inward. [part-of]
(85.2d) *The* plaster was peeling off. [substance-of]
(85.2e) *The* furniture was awfully rickety. [containment-of]
(85.2f) *The* edifice seemed doomed to collapse. [specification-of]

In all of these continuations, the 'house' is taken as a topic node and thus as a control center to which new material is preferentially connected (cf. III.4.27). This configuration is shown graphically in Figure 22, with all continuations included. However, if the linkage were *accidental*, definiteness would not be so likely to spread, e.g. (85.2g) is an odd continuation:

(85.2g) *The* canary seemed depressed. [containment-of]

The oddness of some of my school children's "parts of a house" (III.3.26) is due to accidentalness. Definiteness also seems reluctant to spread down

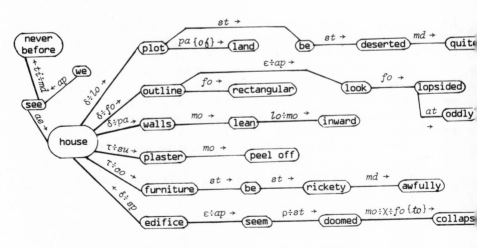

Key: *ae*: affected entity; *ap*: apperception of; *at*: attribute of; *co*: containment of; *fo*: form of; *lo*: location of; *md*: modality of; *mo*: motion of; *pa*: part of; *sp*: specification of; *st*: state of; *su*: substance of; *ti*: time of; *δ*: determinate; *ε*: entry; *χ*: exit; *ρ*: projection; *τ*: typical

Figure 22

longer pathways, so that (85.2h) is an odd continuation if the house's owner is meant:

(85.2h) *The* face was ugly. [part-of-agent-of-possession-of?]

If a single accidental instance is taken from an otherwise accessible class, we are adding an "instance-of" link. Again, definiteness is not clear in such continuations as:

(85.2i) *The* nail was rusty. [instance-of-part-of]
(85.2j) *The* brick hurt our elbows. [instance-of-part-of]

We can improve upon these continuations by providing some intermediary entities not included in numerous classes:[3]

(85.2k) *The* nail in *the* name-plate on *the* front door was rusty. [location-of-location-of-part-of]
(85.2l) *The* brick in *the* doorway hurt our elbows. [part-of-part-of]

3.9 Linkages to an *event* can function like these linkages to an *object*. If a text begins with (86.1), then the continuations in (86.2a–c) connect up to the whole event:

(86.1) The sun was just emerging from behind a cloud.

(86.2a) *The* day was not yet over. [time-of]
(86.2b) *The* sudden brightness hurt our eyes. [cause-of]
(86.2c) *The* improvement in our spirits was remarkable. [reason-of]

We could also link back to 'sun' as object:

(86.2d) *The* golden color was impressive. [attribute-of]
(86.2e) *The* orb blazed down on us. [form-of]

3.10 Inclusion in classes, superclasses, and metaclasses (III.3.19f.) renders these matters quite intricate. One entity which usually has no unique or identifiable referent is the PROTOTYPE (cf. P. Hayes 1977; Fahlman 1977; Rosch 1977; Brachman 1978a; Webber 1978). The prototypical member has a determinate "instance-of" link to its class, to the extent that the class has a discoverable identity. In a conversation like the following from *The Importance of Being Earnest* (Wilde 1940: 420):

(87.1) ALGERNON: In married life, three is company and two is none.
(87.2) JACK: That is the theory that *the* corrupt French Drama has been propounding for the last fifty years.
(87.3) ALGERNON: Yes, and that *the* happy English home has proved in half the time.

---

[3]There may be a constraint that definiteness cannot spread to an accidental instance of an unordered class unless the class itself is first evoked.

it matters little if speakers have any particular French drama or English home in mind. The context demands no more than a FUZZY concept which supplies the needed content.

3.11 A class combined with scales of values can yield a SUPERLATIVE as the class member situated at the extreme end of a scale. Because value scales are in the main imprecise, superlatives share the fuzziness of prototypes. The usage of 'the prince whose gift she liked most' in (82.2) is straightforward enough, since the princess's decision will automatically define the referent. But when Leroy Brown is asserted in the popular American song to have been:

(88) *the* baddest man in the whole damn town[4]

no one would seriously suppose a precise value determination. Leroy is simply being characterized as an extreme representative of the already extreme class of 'bad men in south Chicago'. Where competition is so keen, expirical verification would be absurd (and dangerous). In this one textual world, Leroy is the superlative, at least until his sudden demise.

3.12 As I mentioned in III.1.3, logicians have traditionally been concerned with at least certain aspects of classes and class inclusions, namely those that fall under the heading of QUANTIFICATION (cf. Stegmüller 1969: 15f.). As I observed at a philosophical symposium at the University of Bielefeld in June 1979, logicians generally suppose that definiteness and the use of definite articles depends on the types of quantification described in III.1.3. My own impression was that quantification has been introduced not so much for matters of this kind, but for the special requirements of logic in constructing valid proofs. In the following famous example, we have a universally characterized class of 'men' in (89.1) and the unique member 'Socrates' in (89.2):

(89.1) All men are mortal. (89.2) Socrates is a man. (89.3) Therefore, Socrates is mortal.

Although the proof is clearly valid, I do not see why it should depend particularly on definiteness of existence or uniqueness. We might replace 'men' and 'Socrates' with 'unicorns' and 'the King of France's pet' without making the line of reasoning faulty. The questions of existence and definiteness, I submit, hinge upon *context of occurrence*. The demands of formal logics for precise quantification far exceed the conditions of many contexts of everyday communication. Whereas logicians have for years debated the status of the donkey in the (incidentally false) assertion:

(90) Every man who owns a donkey beats it.

---

[4]In some contemporary American dialects (e.g. in southern Californian), 'baddest' is the superlative rather than 'worst' for 'bad in character'.

the language user need merely create a default donkey with whatever further traits (besides being beaten) are required for the textual world. The demands exerted by logical quantification are far too strict for natural language communication. For the text psychologist, the interesting questions are rather how people *recognize* objects, and under what conditions they are more or less disposed to *believe* statements. People concern themselves with existence and abstract truth only in special contexts.

3.13 INDEFINITENESS, I suggested in V.3.5, is the property of entities for which no knowledge space is currently active. The beginning of our rocket text:

> (35.1.1) *A* great black and yellow V-2 rocket 46 feet long stood in *a* New Mexico desert.

accordingly instructs the reader to create active nodes for 'rocket' and 'desert' and to hang the supplied attributes, locations, etc. onto them. However, the text could also have begun with ' *The* great black and yellow V-2 rocket [...]' and still have been perfectly coherent. The effect would be the writer's commitment to make further use of the node beyond that one statement. For example *Through the Looking Glass* (Carroll 1960: 175) starts right out with the statement:

> (91) One thing was certain, that *the* white kitten had had nothing to do with it.

The reader justly expects to hear at least enough about the white kitten to make the statement believable. Such usage is very widespread in texts whose format requires engaging the reader's interest, because a knowledge deficit is created. In one collection of short essays (G. Levin [ed.] 1977), definite articles for not yet established entities at the beginning of texts is clearly the rule, not the exception (cf. Harweg 1968b):

> (92) Each year I watched *the* field across from *the* Store turn caterpillar green. (Maya Angelo, p. 13)
> (93) *The* judging formally begins with *the* Saturday luncheon at *the* Heart of Wilson Motel. (Frank Deford, p. 115)
> (94) *The* train, its metal wheels squealing as they spin along the silvery tracks, rolls slower now. (Robert Ramirez, p. 127)
> (95) Before you even get *the* cone, you have to do a lot of planning. (L. Rust Hills, p. 182)

3.14 The introduction of entities as definite right at the beginning of the text does not disprove or undermine the status of the definite/indefinite distinction. We do see that, given a regularity of natural language communication, people freely do just the opposite for special effect. It is pointless to argue whether the essays just cited are "well-formed." In a linguistics of actual texts, a rule such as "Use the indefinite article for the first mention, and the definite for later mention" can be no more than a DEFAULT or PREFERENCE (cf. I.3.4.3). Communication takes place against a backdrop of defaults and preferences, but text users will go their own ways when it is expedient to do so (cf. I.3.4.8).

3.15 The treatment of PROTOTYPES illustrates another facet of the definite/indefinite distinction. Either of the following utterances could be produced in a situation of receiving unqualified advice:

> (96a) *A* layman shouldn't give advice to *an* expert.
> (96b) *The* layman shouldn't give advice to *the* expert.

If one utters (96a), hearers are instructed to look immediately into the situational context for referents, so that the indefiniteness is removed. One can use (97b) with a less obvious directness, because the tendency is to envision prototypes for the class of laymen and experts. Once more, the question of "well-formedness" would miss the main point.

3.16 Indefiniteness could also be applied unconventionally. If we had the utterance (traditional saying):[5]

> (97) A man who never loses his head doesn't have *a* head to lose.

the usage 'a head' presents as indefinite something that is a determinate "part-of" 'man'. The effect is to weaken the determinateness of that link by suggesting that there could be men without heads after all.

3.17 The definiteness of text-world entities, as we can see, is complex. The usual criteria (cf. V.3.1f.) for exploring the issues are too narrow. If people could assign definiteness only to uniquely identifiable objects in the world, or objects whose existence (either singly or as a class) has been explicitly asserted, communication as we now find it would scarcely be feasible. We might make better headway by treating definiteness as something that arises out of the connectivity of stored knowledge being used in a real situation, where efficiency is more crucial than exactness, and where concepts are utilized only as far as necessary at that moment.

4.   CO-REFERENCE VIA PRO-FORMS

4.1 If REFERENCE is the relationship between expressions and the objects, events, and situations in a world those expressions designate (III.1.3), the use of alternative expressions in a text for the same text-world entity could be termed CO-REFERENCE. Although there are many types of co-reference (e.g. synonyms, paraphrase), I shall explore only co-reference via PRO-FORMS. Pro-forms are derivative in their actualized content from their co-

---

[5]A similar saying in German goes back to Gotthold Lessing.

referring expressions. As such, pro-forms differ from their co-referring expressions in systematic ways (cf. Paduǎeva 1970; Dressler 1972a: 26f.):

4.1.1 Pro-forms have a *wider range* of potential application.

4.1.2 Pro-forms are *comparatively empty* of inherent content.

4.1.3 Pro-forms are usually *shorter*—a fact which Dressler (1972a: 26f.) sees in agreement with Zipf's (1935) "law": the more frequently a word is used, the shorter it tends to be or become.

4.1.4 Pro-forms obey *constraints* upon their occurrences, such that comprehension is not rendered unduly problematic.

4.1.5 Pro-forms need a *distinctive* surface appearance. In English, PRONOUNS are the only word class in the nominal system that maintains different forms for gender (masculine, feminine, neuter) and case (subject vs. object)—nouns distinguish at most possessive, singular, and plural. DEICTICS (pointing words) generally begin with 'th-' and are the only word class in which initial 'th' is voiced in pronunciation (except the article 'the' and the pro-forms 'they/their/them').

4.2 PRONOUNS are the best known type of pro-forms. In general, they have as co-referent expressions nouns appearing in the text (cf. Postal 1969). Yet some uses of pronouns do not have this application, for instance, in the popular American imperatives:

(98) Stop *it!*

(99) Hold *it!*

(100) Forget *it!*

(101) Shove *it!*

Inferencing may be required to recover some referents, as in the well-known slogan of the Bell Telephone Company:

(102) Calling long distance is the next best thing to being *there.*

where 'there' must be co-referent with an inferrable location. Pronouns may apply to entities whose previous introduction did not occur via nouns, as in a recent statement by a U.S. newscaster:

(103) The Congressional privilege of giving consent to treaties is one *they* seem unwilling to sacrifice.

where the co-referent must be derived from the adjective 'Congressional'.

4.3 If other expressions sharing referents are used together with pronouns, the natural order would seem to be from most specific to least. Lakoff (1968a) foresees an order of: (1) proper name; (2) specific description; (3) a general class name; and (4) pronoun. An example might be:

(104.1) *Napoleon* entered the room. (104.2) *The famous general* made some announcement. (104.3) *The man* was very excited. (104.4) *He* spoke at top speed.

Yet this order is not obligatory. A text producer might use just the reverse in order to create a knowledge deficit (like the deficit evoked by introducing new entities as definite, cf. V. 3.13). We find that tactic used for suspense in this passage by the Russian story-teller Nikolai Leskov (1961: 55). The door to the cell of the Archbishop mysteriously opens:

> (105) *Who* should walk in but a venerable old *man* in whom his Grace immediately recognized one of *the saints of the church,* no other than *the Right Reverend Sergius.*

The order of 'who'-'man'-'saint'-'Sergius' is a complete reversal of that foreseen by Lakoff,[6] and the gradual emergence of the mysterious figure's identity is perfectly matched to the gradual increase of specificity in the co-referring expressions. The usage is both effective and appropriate (cf. I.4.14).

4.4 The replacement of surface expressions also brings up the problem of class inclusions such as we saw in V.3.10ff. The pro-forms can refer to the same set of entities as their co-referent expressions (examples here from Webber 1978: 45):

> (106a) Several linguists attended the masquerade. *They* were dressed up as cyclic transformations.

But distinctions can be found between a COLLECTIVE inclusion, as in (106b), and a DISTRIBUTIVE inclusion, as in (106c):

> (106b) Several linguists attended the masquerade. *They all* came as parse trees.
> (106c) Several linguists attended the Yorktown Strutters' Ball. *They each* came dressed as a different transderivational constraint.

This distinction has important effects upon the text-world model, as these examples (from Webber 1978: 44) reveal:

> (107a) The three men who tried to lift a piano dropped *it.*
> (107b) The three men who tried to lift a piano dropped *them.*

The pronoun 'it' creates a textual world with the men lifting one piano together, while 'them' leaves us with the three lifting one piano each.

4.5 The efficiency of pro-forms is especially evident when they apply to large stretches of discourse that activate sizeable knowledge spaces:

> (108) "Give your evidence," said the King, "and don't be nervous, or I'll have you executed on the spot." *This* did not encourage the witness at all. (Carroll 1960: 148)

---

[6]This example is not meant as a refutation of Lakoff, who was dealing with sequels where each element was in a separate sentence. At most, it illustrates how flexible language regularities are in general (cf. note 10 to Chapter I).

In (108), 'this' stands for the content of what the King has said, and places the entirety in a "reason-of" relation to the state of the 'witness'. A pro-form can even stand for a block of content whose limits are left open by remaining unexpressed:

(109) "My father and mother were honest, though poor—"
"Skip *all that!*" cried the Bellman in haste. [...]
"I skip forty years," said the Baker [...]
(*The Hunting of the Snark,* [Carroll 1973: 63])

The depiction of forty years would have constituted a vast expanse of content.

4.6 Pro-forms also serve in the REPUDIATION of some portion of previously expressed content (cf. IV.3.12), as in (Belloc 1940: 177f.):

(110) I shoot the hippopotamus
With bullets made of platinum
Because if I use leaden *ones*
His hide is sure to flatten 'em.

The class of 'bullets' is divided into the subclass of 'platinum' versus 'leaden', and the expectation that the latter subclass should be used is repudiated. In the following remark of the White King, 'one' designates a currently present member of the class of 'pencils', while a still indefinite 'thinner' member is envisioned:

(111) My dear, I must get a thinner pencil. I can't manage this *one* a bit. (Carroll 1960: 190).

Different referents in a textual world can be similar in every respect but one, and the pro-form need only attach that respect to keep them distinct, as in the case of Tweedledee and Tweedledum (Carroll 1960: 229, e.a.):

(112) She was just going around to see if the word "TWEEDLE" was written on the back of each collar, when she was startled by a voice coming from the *one* marked "DUM."

The pro-form 'one' is useful also if the entity in question is to be kept indefinite (Carroll 1960: 100):

(113) The March Hare said: "I vote the young lady tells us a story."
"I'm afraid I don't know *one*," said Alice.

4.7 For reusing event-based knowledge, PRO-VERBS can be employed, such as 'do' (Carroll 1960: 47):

(114) "I don't know the meaning of half those long words, and what's more, I don't believe you *do,* either."

The pro-form 'so' can be added on to 'do' in order to cover material attached to the original verb:

> (115) To this day I am ashamed that I did not spring up and pinion him then and there. Had I possessed one ounce of physical courage, I should have *done so*. (Beerbohm 1958: 57).

This 'do so' carries forward the content of an entire phrase of two actions with direction and time. Alternately, 'do it' can perform such a function:

> (116) "Smoothe her hair—lend her your nightcap—and sing her a soothing lullaby."
> "I haven't got a nightcap with me," said Alice, as she tried to obey the first direction; "and I don't know any soothing lullabies."
> "I must *do it* myself then," said the Red Queen.
> (Carroll 1960: 326)

The pro-forms pick up the content of two out of three mentioned actions.

4.8 By selecting pro-forms of various word-classes, speakers can allow hearers to re-utilize their mapping strategies between grammatical and conceptual dependencies. For 'spring up/ pinion [...] then and there', the 'do so' repeats the "head-to-modifier" dependency (II.2.15.7). For 'lend [...] nightcap/sing [...] lullaby', the 'do it' repeats the "verb-to-direct object" dependency (II.2.15.2). One might want to set up a scheme with designations like "pro-modifier," "pro-direct object," etc. However, pro-forms can have diverse applications in the same occurrence. In:

> (117) Yond Cassius has a lean and hungry look.
> He thinks too much. *Such* men are dangerous.
> (*Julius Caesar*, II. ii, 194–95)

the pro-modifier 'such' carries forward both the modifiers 'lean and hungry' and the "cognition"-verb 'think too much'. In the following sample, the text receiver is left to infer, as co-referent for 'such', an attribute not expressed in a surface modifier at all: (Carroll 1960: 279):

> (118) "I see nobody on the road," said Alice. "I only wish I had *such* eyes," the King remarked in a fretful tone. "To be able to see Nobody! And at that distance too!"

The King's remarks suggest that the implied modifier might be 'good' or 'sharp'.

4.9 Pro-forms are more likely to occur ANAPHORICALLY, i.e. after their co-referring expressions, than CATAPHORICALLY, i.e. before them. The anaphoric use would provide a control center to which the material attached to the pro-form can be readily added on (cf. III.4.27). It is harder to envision how cataphoric use can be managed. The pro-form might be placed on a HOLD STACK until its co-referring expression occurs (cf. II.2.10); or it might be left as an unlabeled state in FUZZY PARSING until labeling becomes feasible (cf. IV.1.10). In either case, it would not be advisable to create substantial distance between the pro-form and its co-referring expression. Cataphora is most common inside the single sentence, e.g. in this student paper from the University of Florida:

> (119) I don't know if *he*'s serious, but my roommate wants to walk a tightrope over Niagra Falls.

Cataphora can also announce a large block of content that spans a series of utterances:

> (120) That you have wronged me doth appear in *this*:
> You have condemned and noted Lucius Pella [...]
> For taking bribes here of the Sardians,
> Wherein my letters, praying on his side
> Because I knew the man, were slighted off.
> (*Julius Caesar,* IV, iii, 1–5)

Like definiteness, cataphora can be used to create a knowledge deficit that will be later filled (cf. V.3.13). Warwick Deeping (1930: 720) deliberately begins a story with a cataphoric pro-noun for which the co-referring expression is postponed to the end of a long sentence:

> (121) *Her* father was a snuffy little man, who, after living for fifteen years as a widower in the white house at the end of Prospect Terrace, had developed mannerisms and peculiarities that were neither criticized nor questioned by his *daughter*.

4.10 The constraints upon cataphora are part of the conditions of language processing at large. It is hard to maintain connectivity between elements which are either placed far apart or whose identity is uncertain because of alternative candidates. Our 'rocket' sample (35) in III.4.20, however, shows that these difficulties can be offset, for example, by attaching co-references across wide spaces to a TOPIC node; or by considering what concepts are preferentially compatible in the sense of Wilks (1978) (e.g. 'rocket-plunge').

4.11 Ambiguous pro-forms have received considerable attention in linguistics, such as the classic example:

> (122) I love my wife. *So* does Harry.

where the social implications of the possible textual worlds are intriguing. If English differentiated reflexivity in the way that Russian does, this kind of ambiguity would be precluded (Dressler 1972a: 24). All the same, such ambiguities are seldom really unresolvable. Wallace Chafe (1976: 47) suggests that in:

> (123) Ted saw Harry yesterday. *He* told *him* about the meeting.

the co-referents might be sorted by keeping the subject and direct object slots constant, hence 'Ted = he', and 'Harry = him'. That account would agree with the principle of STABILITY (V.1.7), though it may be agents rather than subjects that are decisive here. But world-knowledge is surely an overriding factor. For a sample such as:

(124) Billy told Johnny's mother that *he* hit *him*.

we might not rely on stability of subject or agent (making 'Billy' do the 'hitting') so much as on the knowledge that children tell parents about others' misdeeds more often than about their own (hence 'Billy' was 'hit'). Still more constraining is this passage about the death of a solicitor (*Ipswich Journal,* Jan. 12, 1878):

(125) He was going to the Court, when he staggered as if in a fit, and fell against the wall close to the watchman's room in the central hall. The watchman and a policeman, running to his assistance, took him into a room. Some brandy was administered to no effect, and Mr. Bond, the surgeon of Parliament Street, arriving, *he* pronounced *him* dead.

A language user with "autonomous syntax" would spend a long time computing alternatives about who pronounced whom dead (solicitor? watchman? policeman? surgeon?), getting 12 readings in all; most real readers notice only one possibility. Indeed, world-knowledge will find referents even where a wrong pro-form is used (headline from the *Midnight Globe,* July 4, 1978):

(126) Sophia Loren reveals love scandals that haunt *my* marriage.[7]

4.12 With so many supporting factors to use, the recovery of a wrong co-referent is unlikely and might signal a refusal or inability to communicate. Gracie's mistake in applying 'it' to her 'car' rather than the 'pile of trash' in (2) (II.1.8) would not be made by any reasonable person. To create a non-text without 'an atom of meaning in it', Lewis Carroll (1960: 158) needs merely to provide no co-referents for pro-forms:

(127) *They* told *me you* had been to *her,*
And mentioned *me* to *him* [...]

Throughout this poem, no cues regarding identity are forthcoming. A language model using world-knowledge is justly stumped here, though a reader with a strong enough attitude on acceptability can wring some meaning even from these verses, as the King of Hearts demonstrates.

---

[7]The effect is one of "erlebte Rede"—Ms. Loren seems to be speaking herself, though the predicate has a third-person verb.

4.13 The TRADE-OFF between compactness and rapid access already mentioned in regard to the storage of knowledge in memory (III.3.18) is also applicable to the use of co-reference via pro-forms. The pro-forms allow an enormous savings in the creation and utilization of surface structure. But the gain would be lost again if there were problematic ambiguities in the identification of the co-referring expressions. I have argued above that people use all kinds of cues to preclude ambiguities which the pro-forms themselves, due to their inherent indeterminacy, might allow. The fact that actual misunderstandings are so seldom in human communication is an impressive indicator of the co-operative nature of textuality (especially intentionality and acceptability), and of the regulatory controls upon systemic actualization (cf. I.4.5.1).

5.   EXOPHORIC REFERENCE

5.1 In exophoric reference, the pro-forms apply directly to entities recoverable in the situation, rather than via co-referent expressions in the same text or discourse. Such a device argues against a division between language and its settings (cf. III.3.18). Exophora is particularly efficient in that it bypasss the intermediary step of concept-naming. Like anaphora and cataphora, exophora depends crucially on context. If a concept's meaning is its place in a textual world, the meaning of an exophoric expression's referent is its place in a text-world with focus on the situational world of communicating. For example, (128) was used as the very first utterance of a conversation by someone opening a door and finding a familiar person outside:

(128) *She*'s not here.

The speaker was aware of the visitor's usual intention to pay a call on a certain person, and the visitor in turn knew about that awareness.

5.2 In some situations, the pro-form can be applied to entities that may not be given conceptual classification:

(129) What on earth is *that?*
(130) I can't believe *this!*

These uses can also signal that the speaker's expectations—provided they are presupposed to be known to the hearer—are being disappointed, so that an explanation or change is in order.

5.3 Exophora is handy for SITUATION MANAGING, where participants might have conflicting views about what is going on. Some robbers recently confronted the drivers of an armored car with (*Gainesville Sun,* Dec. 20, 1978):

(131) *This* is a holdup. We're not kidding.

Their description of the situation was, as might be expected, reinforced with the authority of firearms (cf. Goffman 1974: 447). When an engineer said about the Arizona floods (*Gainesville Sun,* Dec. 20, 1978):

(132) *It*'s going to get worse before *it* gets better.

there was no clear definition of what the 'it' designated; presumably the entire situation brought about by the events being depicted in previous utterances.

5.4 Halliday and Hasan (1976: 53) cite several types of "institutionalized exophoric reference" in which pro-forms are conventionally used without commitment to specific conceptual content:

5.4.1 First and second person pronouns are inherently exophoric, and their use presupposes the mutual identifiability of the communicative participants, though more directly for speaking than for writing. Conceptual content enters prominently when the referents are assigned to METACLASSES (III.3.20):

(133) O, what a rogue and peasant slave am *I!* (*Hamlet,* II, ii, 576)
(134) *You* blocks, *you* stones, *you* worse than senseless things! (*Julius Caesar,* I, i, 40)

5.4.2 A conceptually empty dummy (II.2.15.6) is employed in subject slots for describing the state of the weather:

(135) *It*'s raining/snowing/hailing/etc.

The preferences for mapping continuous events onto verbs and for having at least one subject and verb in a clause (III.4.26) creates a need for a dummy subject lacking content, agency or instrumentality. This usage is often designated by the French term "servitude grammaticale."

5.4.3 A frequently unspecified 'they' points toward anonymous agents whose status is not currently relevant, let alone "uniquely identifiable" (V.3.1), as in this opening from a student's paper:

(136) *They* told me when I came here I would have to work hard.

These vague agents are DEFAULT entities created for the connectivity of events (cf. V.3.3.6), and they are processed no further than they need to be.

5.4.4 A partly non-determinate 'we' permits the speaker to include himself or herself into a broad class of undetermined size, e.g. in another fragment from that student's paper:

(137) In Florida, *we* don't see things like other Southerners.

The writer probably had no intention of including the entire class of Florida inhabitants, but only a group of PROTOTYPES (V.3.3.7). Another vague use of 'we' is enlisted to "identify the writer and reader as involved in a joint enterprise" (Quirk et al. 1972: 208), as in this passage from the Atomic Energy Commission (cited and discussed in Beaugrande 1977b: 329):

(138) Now *we* are hearing more and more about another kind of radiation [...]

Here, the expert writer and the lay readers are hardly 'hearing about' atomic energy in any comparable way. But the hope of obtaining readers' support for atomic power plants makes it desirable to evoke solidarity.

5.4.5 In general, 'you' serves as agent for actions that are considered typical, whoever may be doing them. We find this element also in students' papers, for example:

(139) *You* never know what the teacher wants on these assignments.

Advertisers are fond of suggesting a personal address with 'you', even though they are talking to an anonymous group (cf. Marcuse 1964: 92). One brand of car, for instance, claims to be (*TIME,* Nov. 13, 1978):

(140) The difference between a car *you* like and a car *you* love.

This 'you' is a cross between an impersonal pro-form and the kind of direct address we see in this ad (*TIME,* Nov. 13, 1978):

(141) Could the car *you*'re driving pass this test?

5.5 A tendency to rely on exophora without clear conceptualization is noted by Halliday and Hasan (1976: 34), who supply this dialogue between Hasan and their three-year old son (stressed words double-spaced):

(142)   CHILD: Why does *t h a t one* come out?
        HASAN: *That what?*
        CHILD: *T h a t one!*
        HASAN: *That what?*
        CHILD: *That o n e!*
        HASAN: *That one what?*
        CHILD: *That* lever *there* that *you* push to let the water out.

The child was reluctant to provide a conceptual description, assuming that the adult must have the same focus of attention as he himself. The shifting of stress among pro-forms indicates his hope that more emphatic pointing will do the job. The 'you' in his final remark is that cited in V.5.4.5.

5.6 In a highly publicized study, Peter Hawkins (1969) noted exophora in descriptions of pictured scenes to be more prevalent in the speech of working-class children than in that of middle-class. His illustrations were like this:

(143a) Three boys are playing football and one kicks the ball and it goes through the window [...]

(143b) *They*'re playing football and *he* kicks *it* and *it* goes through *there*
[...]

Influenced by Basil Bernstein (cf. Bernstein 1964), Hawkins took this material as a demonstration of the divergence between the "elaborated code" of the middle class (i.e., having many options) and the "restricted code" of the working class (i.e., having few options). Aside from the dubiousness of these notions (cf. Oevermann 1970), they seem to miss the point here. The working-class children probably saw no reason for conceptual naming of events and objects which they could see and point out in front of them. In contrast, the middle-class children probably had much richer experience with the WRITTEN code, whose "elaborateness" is due to its frequent removedness from an apperceivable situation. Also, the middle-class children would identify an interview with a school situation where the written code is favored. Still, (142) shows that even a child of university professors tends naturally to rely on exophora in relaxed situations. Perhaps Hawkins would have us view Shakespeare as a user of the "restricted code" because of exophora in this famous scene from *Hamlet* (III, iv, 131–34)?

(144)   QUEEN: To whom do you speak *this*?
HAMLET: Do you see nothing *there*?
QUEEN: Nothing at all; yet *all* that is I see.
HAMLET: Nor did you nothing hear?
QUEEN: No thing but ourselves.
HAMLET: Why, look you *there*! Look how *it* steals away![8]

5.7 Halliday and Hasan (1976: 36) point out the influence of PEER GROUPS on exophoric reference. They quote Bernstein's listing of "close-knit social groups" compiled without apparent realization of the biting sarcasm in this juxtaposition: "prison inmates, combat units of the armed forces, criminal subcultures, the peer group of children and adolescents, and married couples of long standing." The close-knitness of working-class children, as suggested by the Hawkins data, might have to do with their limited social mobility.

5.8 Conceivably, the superfluous pronouns taken as social markers in phrases like:

(145) My sister *she* plays the piano.

are quasi-exophoric. Due to predominant experience with the spoken mode, text producers might use a two-stage means of referring: (1) present a concept name; and (2) co-refer to the concept via a pro-form. Significantly, this

[8]For an Elizabethan audience, the ghostly referent might have been real enough.

construction appears, as far as I can judge, virtually always in subject slots—we would not, for instance, encounter:

(146) They gave my sister *her* a piano *it*.

If this account is justified, the initial naming of the concept ('my sister') in (145) would function as an announcement of TOPIC that is not deemed a part of the subject-verb dependency. Apparently, the creation of a control center for the conceptual-relational network is detached from that for the grammatical dependency network—a departure from a standard preference (cf. III.4.14).

5.9 In principle, exophora can be applied to whatever is evident in the communicative situation. Entering a room where food was spilled on the floor, a Florida mother was recently heard to say to her child:

(147) You did that?

where the entire utterance consists of pro-forms. However, as Adrian Akmajian (personal communication) notes, there are constraints upon the compacting of utterances. The mother could have said (148a), but hardly (148b), and almost certainly not (148c) or (148d):

(148a) You?
(148b) That?
(148c) Did?
(148d) You that?

5.10 Exophora demonstrates the reciprocity of the interaction between language use and situation. The situation strongly effects the actualization of strategies, but certain conventions will nonetheless be upheld. In the samples (148a–d), the terseness of exophora is constrained by the sequencing operations of English. We shall note further illustrations of the limits upon terseness of expression in the next section on *ellipsis*.

6. ELLIPSIS

6.1 Discussions of ellipsis, sometimes called "substitution by zero," have been marked by controversy (compare Karlsen 1959; Gunter 1963; Isačenko 1965; Crymes 1968; Dressler 1970b; Halliday & Hasan 1976; Grosz 1977). The dispute can be stated as follows. The surface structures in texts are often not so complete as they *might* be in the judgment of the investigator. Language theories with clearly drawn boundaries of grammatical or logical well-formedness necessarily proliferate the treatment of utterances as elliptical, according to the explicitness of the well-formed idealizations. A rather extreme view is suggested by Clark and Clark (1977: 16) when they assert that (149a) is really an elliptical version of (149b):

(149a) Napoleon conquered Italy, Prussia, and Austria.

(149b) Napoleon conquered Italy, Napoleon conquered Prussia, and Napoleon conquered Austria.

It is hard to see the psychological justification for such a claim. It would seem either to exhume the old notion that people have to work with kernel sentences in communication; or to imply an overly literal interpretation of the notion of the PROPOSITION LIST (cf. VII.3.6). A processor would scarcely create three separate entries for 'Napoleon' and 'conquered' for either (149a) or (149b).

6.2 The standpoint apparently advanced by the Clarks would make it necessary to view most utterances as elliptical, and to bloat procedures enormously with redundant entries requiring subsequent removal. Even less extreme examples seem difficult to classify as elliptical. In the following samples from an essay (Jim Brown, in Levin [ed.] 1977: 42ff.), I have added in square brackets items that might conceivably be considered elided:

(150) Manhasset was going to be just as playful as St. Simons Island [was].

(151) She was, no doubt, a good woman, but [she was] quite [a] stern [woman].

(152) I loved my mother as much as any son would [love his mother].

It is still questionable whether the production and comprehension of these fragments as they stand would be improved or impeded by filling in the bracketed additions. I argued in II.2.36f. and III.4.40 that people could not plausibly be converting everything they say or understand into complete sentences. If they did that, they ought to prefer talking in complete sentences much more than they do. Grammatical completing turns out many pointless, undecidable structures. Similar dilemmas attend upon such a literal interpretation of the notion of proposition lists as the Clarks seem to accept. Walter Kintsch (1977a: 312) reports that (153a) is indeed *easier* to perceive than (153b):

(153a) Fred runs faster than the girl.

(153b) Fred runs faster than the girl runs.

A model of completion-then-deletion predicts the opposite findings. A model using conceptual-relational networks, on the other hand, is in agreement, since (153b) requires testing to see if a second node is needed in addition to an earlier one, as opposed to direct reutilization of one node in (153a).

6.3 If the surface unity is taken to be the GRAMMATICAL DEPENDENCY between two elements, one of which at least cannot stand alone, then ellipsis ought to be identifiable via a dangling structural component. We can use empirical tests to probe people's judgments on missing components, analogous to the studies of grammatical expectations (e.g. Stevens & Rumelhart 1975), although bearing in mind their expectations about text types (cf. my findings given in II.2.36). We would be able to settle the dispute on the basis of what language users, rather than abstract sentence grammarians, consider to be elliptical.

6.4 The phenomenon of GAPPING (Ross 1970b) can safely qualify as ellipsis: a follow-up utterance without a verb, but with a structure otherwise similar to its predecessor's, as in this synopsis of a Brecht play (*Ohio State Lantern,* Sept. 30, 1970):

(154) It is the story of someone trying to achieve something (Mother Courage survival).

The sequence 'Mother Courage survival' is noticeably discontinuous, even by Ohio standards, and must be given connectivity via transfer from the preceding structure to yield 'Mother Courage trying to achieve survival'. The transfer is eased by the fact that the preceding structure contains placeholders ('someone', 'something'), so that a reader would be on the lookout for integrating further knowledge. A preceding structure can supply various quantities of material to fill a gap. In:

(155) PASTOR: Do you promise to have, hold, love, cherish, and respect this man?
BRIDE: Me him!?

the whole series of verbs supplies content addressed by the bride's response. In a series with diverse direct objects, only applicable ones could be addressed, e.g.:

(156) PASTOR: Do you promise to have a fit, hold your tongue, love your neighbor, cherish this ring, and respect this man?
BRIDE: Me him!?

This time, only 'respect' carries over into the "gap."

6.5 The term SLUICING (Dressler 1972a: 35) signifies a device in which the verb in a subordinate clause is elided:

(157) John is busy staring at the girls. I think at the blondes.

Again, a sequence like 'think at the blondes' is noticeably discontinuous as it stands, and the content of 'John is staring' must be carried over.

6.6 Ellipsis is most noticeable for verbs, because English clauses can dispense with other elements more readily. For example, utterances without subjects are more common than those without verbs. However, as Leech and Svartvik (1975: 168) remark, the ellipsis of subjects in subordinate clauses is not usual; we would not be likely to encounter such an utterance as:

(158) He was so tired that went to sleep.

This constraint is similar to the requirement of dummy subjects for verbs, even where no agency is to be conceived (cf. V.5.4.2).

6.7 Ellipsis, like co-reference, is helpful for REPUDIATING content that hearers might expect (cf. V.4.6):

(159) And tell them that I will not come to-day.
Cannot, is false; and that I dare not, falser.
(*Julius Caesar,* II, ii, 62–63)

In quarrels, ellipsis can be used, with proper intonation, to signal a repudiation of content expressed by someone else (cf. Brazil 1975):

(160) BRUTUS: Let me tell you, Cassius, you yourself
Are much condemned to have an itching palm [...]
CASSIUS: I an itching palm?
(*Julius Caesar,* IV, iii, 9–10, 13)

6.8 Under normal conditions, people tolerate substantial ellipsis, depending on the extent to which SITUATIONALITY is mediated (cf. I.4.11.5). SPREADING ACTIVATION alone would allow for ellipsis of determinate and typical linkage, and INFERENCING could be applied where needed. Even the notoriously disjointed texts of Dickens' (1899: 25) Alfred Jingle are quite intelligible:

(161) Negus too strong here—liberal landlord—very foolish—very—lemonade much better—hot rooms—elderly gentlemen—suffer for it in the morning—cruel.

Whatever is taken to be missing can be supplied by inferencing as PROBLEM-SOLVING (cf 1.6.4ff.). However, ellipsis as extensive as Mr. Jingle's is not convenient to hearers who have to perform inferencing in many directions at once in limited time. Having the text preserved in print makes matters easier.

6.9 Unco-operative hearers might, of course, impede communication by supplying inappropriate content for elliptical utterances. Uncle Henry's response (3.3) cited in II.1.8 makes it plain that he does not wish to be sociable. For ellipsis to be unresolvably ambiguous, we would have to find very unusual settings. Imagine the still greater confusion that would make (162) ambiguous, as opposed to (120) with pro-form:

(162) I love my wife. Harry too.

6.10 Ellipsis is a further illustration of the TRADE-OFF between compactness and rapid access (cf. III.3.18). Heavy ellipsis, while cutting drastically back on surface structure, would demand increased effort for connecting the underlying text-world model. The presence of ellipsis in varying degrees, each APPROPRIATE to a type of text and situation (cf. I.4.14), is another demonstration of the regulatory controls on actualization.

7. JUNCTION

7.1 Whereas recurrence, co-reference, and ellipsis keep knowledge spaces current, junction serves to signal the relations between spaces or between entities within spaces. The configurations joined via conjunction, disjunction, and contrajunction are preferentially taken as possessing an analogous surface organization. Previously successful model-building strategies can accordingly be applied to the mapping phase for the following structures (cf. III.4.16.11). This constitutes PATTERN-MATCHING *between occurrences of the same text,* so that one stretch of input acts as a model for another (cf. IV.4.5; VII.2.36). Junction also signals the compatability and relatedness of elements and configurations in the textual world (cf. VIII.1.24). I shall look into four types of junction:

7.1.1 CONJUNCTION links two or more knowledge configurations which, in regard to their environment, are *additively* the same or similar.

7.1.2 DISJUNCTION links two or more knowledge configurations which, in regard to their environment, are *alternatively* the same or similar. While in conjunction, *all* content is taken as valid for the textual world, only *one* configuration in disjunction need be valid.

7.1.3 CONTRAJUNCTION links two knowledge configurations which, in regard to their environment, are *antagonistically* the same or similar, i.e. that deal with related topics, but via combinations not foreseen in spreading activation. Both configurations may be true for the textual world, but their inherent relatedness is not obvious.

7.1.4 SUBORDINATION signals that the relationship between two knowledge configurations is *hierarchical,* i.e., that the determinacy of the one is contingent upon access to the other. Roland Posner (1972) observes that the subordinated material has a lower position on a gradation of relevance (cf. IV.3.8). Unlike other kinds of junction, subordination need not signal any analogous organization of surface structure; indeed, in many languages (e.g. German), subordinate clauses have a markedly dissimilar structure from that of main clauses.

7.2 These various relationships among knowledge configurations can often obtain without the explicit use of junction, simply because people have predictable ways of organizing knowledge. It seems reasonable to use the term "junction" only where there are junctive expressions ('and', 'or', 'but', 'because', and so on). The behavior of natural language junctives is in many ways different and much more diversified than that of logical connectives (van Dijk 1977a, 1977b) whose main function is to decide the truth values of complex statements (cf. III.1.1).

7.3 The stories extracted by Hawkins (1969) from children's protocols illustrate an extreme of conjunction:

(163) Three boys are playing football *and* one boy kicks the ball *and* it goes through the window *and* the ball breaks the window *and* the boys are looking at it *and* a man comes out [etc.].

The joined configurations are similar to each other: actions, motions, and apperceptions; and their surface structuring is comparable. The conjunction signals simple addition of events in a temporal and causal sequence. Because those relations are recoverable from content, the junctive expression 'and' is dispensable, or replaceable with subordinatives:

(164a) Three boys are playing football. One boy kicks the ball. It goes through the window. [etc.]

(164b) Three boys are playing football *when* one boy kicks the ball *so that* it goes through the window. [etc.]

This non-committal nature of conjunction makes it the default junction (II.2.24). Children might use 'and' as a signal of incompleteness (VII.1.18) so as not to lose their speaking turn. It might also be used as a filler during whose utterance a continuation of the discourse can be planned out.

7.4 Disjunction, in contrast, requires express signaling and cannot be replaced by subordinative junctives (cf. Leech & Svartvik 1975: 160). Perhaps the processing of disjunctive configurations is difficult, because the exclusivity between alternatives is a threat to connectivity and continuity. To keep a text-world integrated, a processor would want to select the valid alternative and attach it, discarding the others. Disjunction thus functions as an even stronger opposition than contrajunction. Consider the watchman's refrain from Gilbert and Sullivan's *Iolanthe:*

(165) Every man that's born into this world alive is *either* a little bit Liberal *or else* a little Conservative.

There is no room here for compromise between alternatives. In logic, disjunction also figures as the "law of the excluded middle" ('either the sun is shining *or else* it isn't', etc.).

7.5 Contrajunction is usually thought of in terms of opposition; but it is, I have suggested, weaker than disjunction in that dimension. Two situations, events, or whatever are treated as inherently not compatible, yet nonetheless co-existing in a textual world. Accordingly, spreading activation would not be expected to connect the two, and hearers must be alerted. A football player commented on an infamous incident during a game (*Gainesville Sun,* Dec. 31, 1978):

(166) I was on the field, *but* I didn't see what happened.

One normally expects that people at a location notice the events there. Many contrajunctions link longer stretches of material (van Dijk 1977a: 87), and the opposition is accordingly more elaborate. Paragraph 7.4 begins with a phrase containing 'in contrast' to announce the differences between conjunction and disjunction regarding replaceability by subordination. The reader may have entertained no particular expectations on the matter. Yet if systemic actualization depends on continuity (I.4.4), contrajunction eases transitions between antagonistic knowledge blocks and hence supports stability.

7.6 Subordination signals more detailed and diffuse dependencies than do conjunction, disjunction, and contrajunction. Subordinative junctives can be treated as TAGS on conceptual relations of the types propsed in III.4.7. Their distribution is strikingly unequal across the set of relations, with causal and temporal linkage being favored over others. The tags for cause, enablement, and reason overlap somewhat: 'because', 'since', 'as', 'so', 'accordingly', 'hence', 'thus', etc. Time relations indicate order, such as previous ('before'), subsequent ('after', 'next'), and concurrent ('as', 'while'); proximity is often entailed. Many relations have junctives made from preposition plus relative pronoun, such as location ('near which', 'under which'), and so forth. The density of tags for causality and time shows the prominence of those relations for organizing textual worlds, at least for the English-speaking cultures, especially in narratives (VIII.2). The one-word junctives for these relations and the several-word junctives for others would illustrate Zipf's (1935) law of correlation between frequency of use and shortness.[9]

7.7 If causality and time relations are indeed so prominent for coherence, they should naturally be favored in spreading activation and inferencing, whether there are surface junctives used or not. The junctives might increase processing ease and yet be dispensable. Consider the old nursery rhyme:

(167) The king was in his counting house, counting all his money;
      The queen was in the parlor, eating bread and honey;
      The maid was in the garden, hanging out the clothes;
      Along came a blackbird and pecked off her nose.

There are no subordinating junctives here; the surface text consists of main-clause sentences. Yet the mere juxtaposition of the statements, reinforced by their parallel structure, gives rise to strong inferences: that the 'counting-house', 'parlor', and 'garden' are proximate in their location; that the actions expressed in the first three lines are proximate in time, while that of the last line interrupts the others; and that it was the maid's nose, not the queen's, that was 'pecked off', because the location of 'garden' would enable the bird's action more readily than 'parlor'. This inferrability of relations which can dispense with junction is a significant difference between the junctives of natural languages and those employed in logic.

---

[9]Indeed, in many dialects of spoken English, 'because' has been shortened down to 'cause', as we see in sample (230.2) in VIII.1.14.

7.8 A text producer might deliberately omit a statement of causality relations, lowering processing ease but increasing depth (cf. IV.1.6). The Bell Telephone Company issues this warning to people doing excavations:

(168) Call us before you dig. You may not be able to afterwards.

leaving the reader to recover the disenablement relation. People also can infer the *reason* or *purpose* of utterances on their own. The following sign reputed to be displayed in Swedish youth hostels offers only the advice which the management of the hostel has reason to believe important for the respective groups of addressees:

(169) Germans: don't get up before 6 A.M. Americans: don't come home after 2 A.M. Italians: don't sing after 10 P.M. Swedes: don't bring girls into the hostel.

7.9 Hearers might even infer causality relations that the text producer presumably did not intend. This classified advertisement (*Gainesville Sun,* Sept. 24, 1978):

(170) For sale: office safe. Owner out of town. Call after 6 P.M.

is probably not calculated to encourage the inference that the owner's absence enables the safe to be stolen after business hours. And a psychologist discussing and evaluating the work of Neal E. Miller on motor learning of rats, where curare is used as a local anaesthetic to eliminate any intentional physical interference,[10] was surely not envisioning a causality based on the use of curare by certain South American tribes to manufacture deadly poisonous darts when he said:

(171) Over the years, Miller's use of curare has silenced many critics.

7.10 I have argued here that explicit subordination provides surface signaling of underlying conceptual relations that might, in some cases, be inferrable via world knowledge. The subordinative junctives contribute to the efficiency of processing as long as their use does not become unduly frequent; one would certainly not want to signal *every* relation with a junctive. The preference strategy is probably to use junctives for relations that cannot be readily inferred because they are variable or non-expected. We saw, however, in (168) that effectiveness can be increased by not employing junction. I would conclude that the use of natural language junctives in communication—quite in contrast to that of logical junctives in proofs—should be accounted for in terms of such design criteria as I proposed in I.4.14.

---

[10]On the experiments involved and the role of curare, see Gerald Jonas, "Visceral Learning," *New Yorker,* Aug. 26, 1972, pp. 49ff. The use of curare would 'silence critics' who claimed that Miller's animals were intentionally producing such effects as altered rate of heartbeat by some trick of the muscles.

VI

Frames, Schemas, Plans, and Scripts

1. GLOBAL PERSPECTIVES ON KNOWLEDGE

1.1 Efficient processing of texts cannot afford to operate on a LOCAL scale. Procedures which could handle only single items or small groups of items would lack the requisite DIRECTIONALITY and CONTROL that keep tabs on predictions and probabilities in such a diverse intersystem as communication. I noted in II.2.9, for example, that syntactic processing should treat single items as MICRO-STATES inside MACRO-STATES, so that the building of structures would have orderly priorities. In III.4.27, I argued that the SPACES in text-world models can be viewed as conceptual macro-states. However, these structures originate largely *from within* the text, i.e., they are BOTTOM-UP macro-states; there must also be TOP-DOWN macro-states coming *from outside* the text and supplying GLOBAL hypotheses about what is going on in the textual world (on top-down versus bottom-up, cf. I.6.5). In this chapter, I shall explore recent work concerning these large-scale stored organizers for knowledge.

1.2 Whether in memory storage or in actual utilization, configurations of knowledge can have at least four PERSPECTIVES (III.4.11.7). First, knowledge can be viewed as an ARRAY in which elements are ARRANGED such that access of potentially relevant elements is provided. This perspective is called a FRAME[1] (cf. Minsky 1975; Charniak 1975c; Winograd 1975;

---

[1] Some researchers seem to treat "frame" and "schema" as synonymous, but the distinction is both crucial in theory and borne out by the major sources I cite. Of course, still other ways could be found to contrast them (cf. Tannen 1979).

Scragg 1976; Petöfi 1976; Metzing[ed.] 1979). For example, a 'house'-frame would be a network of entries such as parts, substances, uses, etc. that houses have (cf. III.3.25). The format is one of links fanning out from a conceptual control center (III.3.8), with no single commitment to a sequence of actualization. Second, knowledge can be viewed as a PROGRESSION in which elements OCCUR during actualization. This perspective is called a SCHEMA (cf. Bartlett 1932; Rumelhart 1975, 1977a, 1977b; Rumelhart & Ortony 1977; Spiro 1977; Kintsch 1977a; Mandler & Johnson 1977; Thorndyke 1977; Kintsch & van Dijk 1978a, 1978b; Adams & Collins 1979; Freedle & Hale 1979). For example, a 'house'-schema could describe the order in which houses are assembled, or in which people can walk through them. The schema is thus much more committed to an ordered sequence of actualization than is the frame.

1.3 Third, knowledge can be viewed as relevant to a person's PLAN in which elements advance the planner toward a GOAL (cf. Sussman 1973; Abelson 1975; Sacerdoti 1977; Schank & Abelson 1977; Allen & Perrault 1978; Carbonell Jr. 1978a; Cohen 1978; McCalla 1978a; Wilensky 1978; Beaugrande 1979a, 1979b). For example, someone who wants a house or is told that somebody else wants one would summon up plans for building or buying a house. The 'house-getting'-plan will look very different depending on the method selected. A plan to buy a house will also differ from a plan to burgle one—a factor affecting priorities of processing (R. Anderson & Pichert 1978). Fourth, knowledge can be viewed as a SCRIPT in which elements are INSTRUCTIONS to PARTICIPANTS about what they should say or do in their respective ROLES (Schank & Abelson 1977; Cullingford 1978; McCalla 1978a, 1978b). For example, a 'restaurant'-script has instructions for the customer, the waiter, and the cashier, to be enacted in an established pattern.

1.4 These four perspectives yield a gradation from general access toward operational directionality and order. Frames and schemas are more oriented toward the internal arrangement of knowledge, while plans and scripts reflect human needs to get things done in everyday interaction. One could argue that schemas are frames put in serial order, that plans are goal-directed schemas, and scripts socially stabilized plans (on the latter cf. Schank & Abelson 1977: 72f.). In this progression, the pattern becomes more selective, and expectations more definite at any given time of application; consequently, the EPISODIC aspect dominates over the purely CONCEPTUAL-RELA-TIONAL one more and more. However, considerations of economy (III.3.18) lead me to suppose that much knowledge is shared by these perspectives. For example, the 'house'-frame could be selectively activated to produce a 'house-building'-schema by following "part-of" and "substance-of" links and then putting the results in an order dictated by knowledge about gravity and construction. The frame would be useful for a descriptive text about existing houses, and the schema helps in telling or understanding a story about houses being built. If people were then called upon to actually build a house themselves, they could convert the schema into a plan via further knowledge about how to buy or obtain materials, how to select a site, and how to procure the co-operation of other people. A professional contractor doubtless has a complete, detailed, and routinely applied 'house-building'-script that other people do not possess.

1.5 These large-scale knowledge configurations supply top-down input for a wide range of communicative and interactive tasks. Their utilization is a form of PROCEDURAL ATTACHMENT, where operations are adapted and specified to fit a current requirement (Bobrow & Winograd 1977; cf. II.2.19; III.4.1). This attachment requires more processing as the task at hand becomes more detailed. For instance, a schema or plan for 'house-building' undergoes more development for a large, luxurious edifice than for a small, modest one. Still, the availability of global patterns of knowledge cuts down on non-determinacy enough to offset idiosyncratic bottom-up input that might otherwise be confusing (cf. IV.2.9).

1.6 Depending on context and co-text, the selection of the appropriate global pattern may be difficult (cf. Wilks 1975a: 47, 1977b: 389; Collins, Brown, & Larkin 1977; Schank & Abelson 1977: 58; Charniak 1978; Rumelhart 1978; Woods 1978b: 9ff.). The consensus is that an understander must watch for cues and their "intersections" (Charniak) or "coincidences" (Woods). Obviously, the understander can not afford to wait and gather large numbers of cues, or the pattern won't be selected in time to do much good. Hypotheses should be formed early and used until a major snag is encountered (cf. Kuipers 1975). This procedure is not without drawbacks: the early hypothesis might be wrong and bias understanding such that contradictory cues would be overlooked for a long time (cf. Bruner & Potter 1964). The understander should be able to adjust by treating the first hypothesis, now rejected, as a "near miss" (Winston 1975) that is useful for reasoning by ANALOGY (cf. III.3.21).

1.7 The occurrence of DETERMINATE cues is plainly more reliable than that of TYPICAL ones, and typical in turn more reliable than ACCIDENTAL. If a text starts right out with (Charniak 1978: 187):

(172) The woman waved as the man on stage sawed her in half.

a 'magician'-frame or 'magic-trick'-schema can be confidently applied, even without having these domains named in the surface text. However, if the text beginning were less determinate:

(173) John walked thoughtfully down the aisle.

too many candidate frames (supermarket, church, airplane) or schemas (shopping, getting married, getting on a plane) could fit. The understander would have to wait for a continuation, such as:

(174a) He swiped a can of caviar from the display shelf.

(174b) He swiped a Bible from a pew.

(174c) He swiped a bottle of tequila from the stewardess's cart.

1.8 Bransford and M. Johnson (1973) deliberately constructed non-determinate texts for people to read. They found that the following sample was treated as nearly incomprehensible and was poorly recalled (1973: 392f.):

(175) If the balloons popped the sound wouldn't be able to carry since everything would be too far away from the correct floor. A closed window would also prevent the sound from carrying, since most buildings tend to be well insulated. Since the whole operation depends on a steady flow of electricity, a break in the middle of the wire would also cause problems. Of course, the fellow could shout, but the human voice is not strong enough to carry that far. An additional problem is that a string could break on the instrument. Then there could be no accompaniment to the message. It is clear that the best situation would involve less distance. Then there would be fewer potential problems. With face to face contact, the least number of things could go wrong.

They supplied some subjects with a picture showing a young man presenting a serenade with guitar accompaniment to his girlfriend; she was positioned at the window of her sixth-floor apartment, obliging the man to transmit the song via a microphone whose loudspeaker was supported outside her window by six lighter-than-air balloons.[2] The subjects with the picture understood the text right away and recalled more than twice as much as the others. This text describes a rare and improbable situation, but Bransford and Johnson (1973: 400) also prepared an unresolvably non-determinate text about the everyday activity of washing clothes, and the results were the same.

1.9 Normally, texts are not constructed with the intention to be irreducibly non-determinate. This tactic is not uncommon in literary texts, however, especially those produced in settings of political censorship. Wolf Biermann's song about 'China behind the wall' ostensibly comments on conditions in the People's Republic of China; but it can (and, given Biermann's situation, probably should) be taken as applying to conditions in East Germany. Religious texts avail themselves of non-determinacy, so that some metaphysical mode of existence can be portrayed in terms of everyday existence; such is the case with the allegories in the New Testament. An intriguing but still open question is whether these alternative textual worlds

---

[2]The picture provides the background knowledge which the definite articles presuppose; the articles become exophoric (cf. V.5).

are built up in parallel, or whether processing has to treat them sequentially (the latter view taken in Schmidt 1979).

1.10 Non-determinacy can be introduced from the side of the receiver as well. One can take many texts and apply to them knowledge patterns that their producers may not have even considered. For example, managers of a recent seminar on "Marketing Warfare" proclaimed that "what works best in warfare also works best in marketing." They distributed posters with quotations from Carl von Clausewitz's 1832 book 'On War', each quote being translated into the frames, schemas, and plans of American business, e.g.:

(176.1) Napoleon's objective was not to merely outmaneuver but to annihilate the opposing force.

(176.2) Translation: Keep pushing till you hear from the feds [federal government agencies controlling business practices].

(177.1) Moral effects are greater on the side of the conquered rather than the conqueror.

(177.2) Translation: God is on the side of General Motors.

In support of their metaphoric outlook, the managers circulated a statement of a female business executive:

(178) In presenting my ideas to an all-male board, I've found I'm understood better when I use the military or football terminology of offensive-defensive.

1.11 Frames, schemas, plans, and scripts should be capable of INHERITANCE (cf. III.3.19). Inheritance would apply for relations of classes to superclasses and metaclasses. A 'sun'-frame could inherit from a 'star'-frame, a 'folktale'-schema from a 'story'-schema, a 'bank-robbing'-plan from a 'steal'-plan, and a 'pizza-parlor'-script from a 'restaurant'-script. The storage address of knowledge would depend upon what patterns were more likely and efficient in use (see especially Fahlman 1977). A statement of CANCELLATIONS (cf. III.3.19; VI.3.4) could apply, e.g. changing the 'visible at night' of the 'star'-frame to 'visible during the day' for the 'sun'-frame. Undoubtedly, text processing often requires several frames, schemas, etc. to interact with each other, leading to further modifications in context (cf. D. Bobrow & Norman 1975; Adams & Collins 1979).

1.12 The nature of INFORMATIVITY requires that understanding cannot involve perfect matching of input to a frame or schema; instead, there must be at least minor variables or discrepancies to uphold interestingness. Thus, an understander can't afford to discard a frame or schema at the slightest difficulty. Other recourses could be: (1) check to see if the mismatching element is connected by determinate, typical, or accidental linkage to its environment in the frame or schema; (2) if accidental, continue as before; (3) if typical or determinate, check to see if the text is fictional. We saw in IV.4 that a newspaper writer constructed an article so that a 'psychoanalyst-patient'-frame worked for the opening stretch of text, but had to be discarded in favor of an 'anthropologist-chimpanzee'-frame later on. The discarding does not vitiate the usefulness of the original frame for understanding the context where it did apply.

1.13 When the text fails to match receivers' frames, an operation of FRAME DEFENSE may ensue: the text is rejected or simply not understood in order to preserve the validity of the frame (Beaugrande 1978b: 9f.). A striking demonstration was provided by an editorial board's comments on a paper I submitted to a prominent journal in educational research. One reviewer was a professor of English Education and another of Linguistics. The paper was rather critical of conventional linguistics and proposed to deal with the issues from a quite different direction. While the English professor remarked that "the untempered rejection of sentence grammars (context-free) [...] as avenues of understanding reading is important (and, I believe, correct) and in need of restatement," the Linguist decried the paper as "polemical about linguistics, unnecessarily." The intriguing point was that due to frames, the two reviewers reached totally opposite judgments of the *readability* and *style* of the paper. The English professor's remarks on these headings are in (179) and the Linguist's in (180):

(179) Appropriate to this purpose, objective. Lucid. The subject matter is necessarily complex, including multiple, systemic inter-relationships. The writing style clarifies and exemplifies relationships as simply and directly as necessary.

(180) If I didn't have to review this article I would have stopped reading it shortly after I began. His/her main points are buried in a writing style that surely tested my patience, to be utterly frank. Diffuse, tiring, not to the point.

In this fashion, evidence in support of frames can be garnered even among scholars who are reluctant to admit the existence of such mental constructs.

1.14 So far, it is not settled how global knowledge organizers should be constituted. To conduct empirical studies, we need at least some indication of the nature, extent, and construction of mental patterns. Although we cannot observe the patterns themselves, we can observe their influence upon human utilization of knowledge. I shall illustrate this approach in regard to frames, schemas, and plans in the course of this chapter; I do not treat scripts because they have received thorough attention already (see especially Schank & Abelson 1977; Cullingford 1978). My explorations are all oriented toward the use of texts. It would be desirable to find some text-independent means of studying global organizers, but I have not yet worked out any convincing experiments to do so.

2. FRAME ATTACHMENT

2.1 A text whose topic is not familiar should make people uncertain about finding a frame. An experiment I conducted with the help of Richard Hersh at the University of Florida pursued this prediction by presenting the following brief text:

> (181.1) Sunspots are believed to be caused by magnetic fields inside the sun. (181.2) These fields slow down the energy flowing up from inside the sun, (181.3) so that the gases above them are cooler and seem darker in color.

Two groups of subjects heard the text read aloud and were asked to write down as much as they could remember of it. The second group, however, was required to wait five minutes before writing, during which time no activities were imposed. I felt that direct reproduction from short-term sensory storage would certainly become impossible in that interval.

2.2 If the text were perfectly understood as is, the result might be a configuration such as that in Figure 23. The entire content is encased in a BELIEF SPACE, evoked by 'are believed' (cf. Hendrix 1975, 1978).[3] In addition to 'sunspots', the main nodes are 'magnetic fields', and 'gases', as indicated by their multiple linkage. The explanation for sunspots is a causal chain: (1) magnetic fields slow down energy; (2) gases above become cooler; (3) cooler places are darker; (4) darkness yields spots.

2.3 I did not anticipate that our test subjects, all first-year college students, would have prior expertise about sunspots. In fact, only 3 out of 35 rendered intact the causal chain just stated. The rest omitted or altered the textual world in ways suggestive of attempts to subsume the material under some non-specialized frame-like concept.

2.4 The most striking instance was the student who declared the text to be dealing with an '*eclipse* of the sun',[4] cued apparently by 'sun' plus 'darker'. In contrast, the addition of 'scientists' as holders of the 'belief' was a fully reasonable inference for the type of material. We tabulated our protocols to find the concepts that fared the best, with these results: 'magnetic fields' won out with 25 out of 35; 'dark' then followed with 21, 'gases' and 'cool' with 18 each, and 'slow' had only 6 recalls. The tendency to utilize 'magnetic fields' as a subsuming frame over others is very manifest in the amount of associated

---

[3] I include the inference that the 'belief' is held by 'scientists', as verified by our test results (VI.2.4). We also have an instance of an underlying relation—"cause-of"—being mapped onto a surface expression. I use the convention of simply passing the link label "*ca*" along to the next node.

[4] In this chapter, I italicize the changes our test subjects made on the text or text-world when composing their protocols.

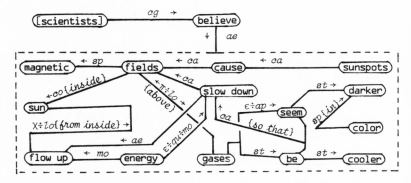

Key: *ae*: affected entity; *ap*: apperception of; *at*: attribute of; *ca*: cause of; *cg*: cognition of;
ε: entry; *lo*: location of; *mo*: motion of; *π*: proximity; *qu*: quantity of; *sp*: specification of;
st: state of; *χ*: exit

Figure 23

entries readers added to that node. Consider for instance these protocol fragments:

(182) Sunspots are believed to be caused by lines of magnetic force which radiate outward from the center of the sun.

(183) Sunspots are caused by magnetic fields around the sun that build up the heated particles in one area.

Clearly, this content is derived from knowledge about magnetism rather than from the presentation. The same source must have supplied their statements about 'electricity' (1 subject), 'force' (5), 'radiation' (3), and 'disturbance' (1); and three subjects relocated the fields '*around* the sun', following a 'lines of force' notion like that in (182). On the other hand, the students had a hard time envisioning magnetism slowing down gases. One converted the 'fields' to '*shields*' to make this effect more acceptable.

2.5 The causality between cooling and darkening was better recalled (18 subjects). The notion of 'spot' depends determinately on the attribute 'dark' or at least 'darker than surrounding area'. One subject mentioned 'blotches,' one 'patches', and one even made the spots 'black'. The subject who recalled only:

(184) Sunspots in the sun are always dark in color.

and another whose protocol was almost the same (both on the no-delay condition!) may have understood or recalled almost none of the text, but knew of course what 'spots' should be. One subject drew the concepts of 'cool' and 'dark' even closer together by eliminating the need for causality:

(185) The temperature of the gases on the sun *varies in color,* resulting in dark spots.

2.6 The candidate frame of 'sun', however, was not heavily used, perhaps because it doesn't provide much help for this particular text world. This frame may have been used by the subjects who mentioned 'molten gases', 'hotter gases', and 'extra heat at the surface of the sun', where an "attribute" was inferred; and the recall of the 'spots' as 'circles', evidently by conflation with the "form" of the sun. Experts on astronomy would doubtless have made better use of the 'sun'-frame—a sketch is provided in Beaugrande (1979j)— and might have had a 'sunspot-formation'-schema stored.

2.7 These results only begin to suggest the intricacies of frame attachment. However, they already show that even a straightforward, short (37-word) text is processed via general knowledge patterns akin to the "advance organizers" envisioned by David Ausubel (1960). In the following section on schema attachment, I suggest that global knowledge patterns have their own priorities regarding what materials are important.

3.   SCHEMA ATTACHMENT

3.1 To explore schema attachment, I return to the 'rocket' sample (35) given in full in III.4.20. That text is better treated by a schema than a frame, since it deals with a sequence of events rather than with a description of a rocket as such. Of course, a 'rocket'-frame could apply to some portions, and we should probably designate processing as DOMINATED by the schema, not as exclusively and exhaustively attached by it.

3.2 A schema can also be represented as a NETWORK, although with a fixed ordering: its nodes appear as a progression of EVENTS and STATES in a time continuum. Our surface text is conventional in that it follows the underlying time order consistently, although, as we shall see, the surface signaling of the various events and states is uneven.

3.3 The 'flight'-schema is regular and balanced, as is graphically evident from Figure 24. The internal patterning of "location" state exited via a "motion" event that leads to entry into a new "location" state runs recursively throughout. The initiation operator 'ι' applies to the initial 'take-off' event, and the termination operator '$\dagger$' to the 'land' event. The minimal components of 'flight' would be an object in the class of 'flying objects' (or a subclass of it) that 'takes off', 'ascends' to a 'peak', then 'descends' 'near the ground', and 'lands' finally 'on the ground'. The actual text does not make all these events and states explicit. It follows that if people nonetheless recall them, the existence of the schema as a mental pattern is proven (more evidence cited in VIII.2.2).

3.4 The superclass of 'flying objects' could have various subclasses, such as 'aircraft', 'birds', 'bats', 'cannon balls', 'stewardesses', and so on. Our 'rocket' belongs to a further subclass of 'aircraft', and its SPECIFICATION could

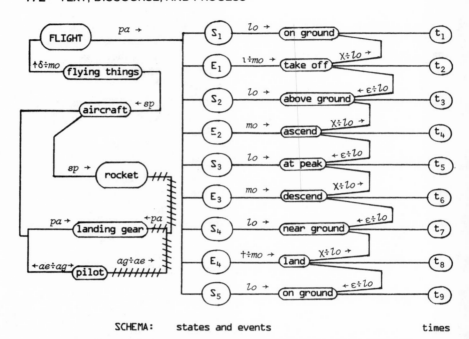

SCHEMA: states and events   times

Key: *ae*: affected entity; *ag*: agent of; *δ*: determinate; *E*: event; *ε*: entry; *ι*: initiation ;
lo: location of; *mo*: motion of; *pa*: part of; *S*: state; *sp*: specification of; *t*: time of; *†*: termination;
χ exit; *//////*: cancel links

Figure 24

CANCEL (III.3.19) some expectations about 'aircraft' that would otherwise be INHERITED (cf. Fahlman 1977: 94): rockets do not usually have pilots and landing gear, for example. These cancel links are shown in Figure 24.

3.5 If this schema were applied as top-down input to the reading of the 'rocket' text, its nodes would be inserted as CONTROL CENTERS into the text-world model, and text-world entries confirming each node would be hooked on, yielding a configuration such as we see in Figure 25. The various densities reflect the different degrees of node confirmation. The cues that the rocket begins down 'on the ground' are reliable: 'stood' indicates a stationary location that is at once asserted to be a known geographical region in the southwestern United States. At the moment of being 'empty', it could certainly not be in motion yet. Note that despite the lack of tense distinction ('had weighed' would be clearer), readers would infer the 'empty' state to be earlier than the 'carry' of the next assertion. The presence of the entire fuel supply also indicates the rocket still being on the ground, because none has been burned up.

3.6 As was suggested in III.4.29, the proposition 'everything was ready' can be taken as subsuming whatever was needed to "enable" the 'take-off' event.

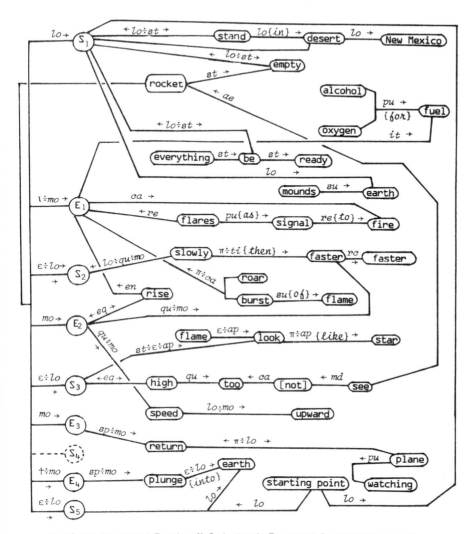

Key: S₁: on the ground; E₁: take-off; S₂: in the air; E₂: ascend; S₃: at peak; E₃: descend; S₄: near the ground; E₄: land; S₅: on the ground; *ae*: affected entity; *ap*: apperception of; *ca*: cause of; *en*: enablement of; *ε*: entry; *eq*: equivalent to; *ι*: initiation; *it*: instrument of; *lo*: location of; *md*: modality of; *mo*: motion of; *π*: proximity; *pu*: purpose of; *qu*: quantity of; *re*: reason of; *sp*: specification of; *st*: state of; *su*: substance of; †: termination

Figure 25

173

That event is shown to be imminent by the 'flares' serving 'as a signal to fire the rocket'. The 'take-off' is expressed only by means of 'rise', though the "causal proximity" to 'roar' and 'burst of flame' points to the initial motion rather than to simply 'ascending'. The following state of being 'near the ground' is only inferentially represented by the first 'slow' rate of rising, since at low altitudes, propulsion must work hardest against gravity and inertia. The entry 'rise' also represents the 'ascend' event, along with 'sped upward' and the increase in velocity ('faster and faster').

3.7 The peak height of this particular flight is never mentioned at all, and must be inferred to have been reached somewhere between 'sped upward' and 'return'. The notion of extreme altitude is at most suggested by the flame's resembling 'a yellow star' and the rocket's being 'too high to be seen'— reasoning by analogy in the first instance, and by disenablement in the second. The 'descend' event easily attaches 'return', and by a further inference, the 'watching plane' whose altitude would be lower than the rocket's.[5] The state of 'near the ground' doesn't attach anything, not being relevant to a rocket without landing gear (hence, it is not problematic). The 'land' event attaches 'plunge into earth', and the final state 'on the ground' emerges from the mention of the 'starting point'. It is significant that the producer of our sample text saw no reason to say anything more as soon as the final schema event and state had been expressed. The mapping of text boundaries onto schema boundaries is an efficient strategy for signaling beginnings and endings of texts.

3.8 To investigate the role of the schema in comprehension and recall, we turn to the findings on this text obtained by Walter Kintsch and Althea Turner at the University of Colorado and later replicated by Richard Hersh and Roger Drury at the University of Florida. College students (mostly first-year) read the text either aloud or silently and were asked to write in their own words whatever they could remember. If a 'flight'-schema had indeed been used, people should recall materials connected to schema nodes the best; or, if material had been overlooked or subjected to decay, the schema could guide a PROBLEM-SOLVING search to restore connectivity (cf. I.6.7). Both of these predictions were confirmed by the data.

3.9 The inference that the 'ready' state should be associated with the take-off was often expressed in protocols. In one group of 36 readers, 9 wrote 'ready for blast-off' or words to that effect. The treatment of the 'take-off' and 'ascend' events was still more revealing. They are represented in the sample text by the same expression 'rise'. But our subjects frequently split their recall into an expression with an initiation component, and an expression without one—precisely the distinction at stake here. The expression 'take-off'

---

[5] This inference was well documented in our empirical data (e.g. in the sample protocol shown in VII.3.35).

appeared verbatim in no less than 29 out of the 72 protocols for this text version. Counting alternative expressions with initiation (e.g. 'lift off', 'launch', 'shoot off' etc.), there was a striking total of 71 occurrences. Surely such a result could not come from any source other than a 'flight'-schema. The expression 'ascend' was used by 6 subjects, and, added to alternative expressions without initiation (e.g. 'go up'), reached 21 occurrences; the original 'rise' turned up in only 4 protocols. This dominance of initiation expressions reflects their higher relevance for introducing the initial schema event, without which nothing more can happen.

3.10 The text makes no mention of the point where the rocket attained its maximum height. Thus, two subjects who mentioned the rocket being 'at its peak' must also have been using the schema. Of course, an 'ascend' followed by a 'descend' obviates the peak to a large extent, as the original text attests. Many subjects might have inferred this content but not bothered to mention it.

3.11 Subjects were less insistent on getting the rocket back down than they had been on getting it up. This finding might arise from the focus on the more PROBLEMATIC aspects: propulsion and gravity make FAILURE more imminent (cf. I.6.7).[6] The expression 'descend' (used by 7 subjects), together with alternatives (e.g. 'come down'), yielded 27 recalls. The expressions with a termination component (especially 'land', 16 subjects) totalled 33 occurrences. The original expressions fared better than 'rise', whose disfavoring might be due to its representing two schema nodes at once (cf. VII.3.6). With 14 uses, 'return' survived better than any schema-node expression, and 'plunge' was reasonably preserved with 8.

3.12 A question arises here of fundamental import for language experiments. We have seen that certain concepts are well recalled independently of the language material originally employed to express them. My data suggest that expressions failing to correspond to the schema pattern, such as 'rise' for two nodes, will be replaced more often than those which fit better, such as 'return' and 'plunge'. However, what looks like *verbatim* recall might also be *reconstruction via the schema,* or a mixture of both factors. The question is especially hard to settle because of domain-specific effects, such as the high relevance of 'take-off' in this particular event sequence.

3.13 The material connected to schema *states* was retained much less well than that for *events* (note here that I did not include states among primary concepts, cf. III.4.4). The trend was to build an event-centered perspective into the recall of states. The original text starts off with the rocket merely 'standing' in a desert, with no indication that flight is impending. Yet our subjects incorporated flight into their openings. They had the rocket 'on the launch pad', 'pointing toward the sky', 'waiting for blast-off', and so on (cf.

---

[6]Compare with footnote of 21 Chapter III on p. 91.

the treatment of 'ready' cited in 3.9). Nothing like 'on the ground' appeared in any protocols. Similarly, no expressions like 'in the air' were found, but only the event-oriented '*into* the air'. No one recalled 'high', but 3 wrote '*higher*' and one ' *further* into the air', again showing focus on motion, not location. All protocols emulated the original in making no reference to a location 'near the ground'. Description of the final state 'on the ground' was often attuned to the initial event: the rocket was recalled reaching 'the launch site' or the place 'where it took off' etc., in no less than 49 cases out of 72. Some original state expressions in the text were well preserved, however. The locations of 'desert' (36 uses) and 'earth' (30) were doubtless supported by world-knowledge about rockets and by the lack of equally available alternative expressions. 'Stood' came up 7 times, and 'starting point' only 3.

3.14 The clear dominance of event-based over state-based recall confirms my premise that processing was dominated by a schema rather than a frame (VI.3.1). Like actions, events are multiple occurrences for processing (cf. III.4.6). They update the textual world by definition and hence make the progression from the initial to the final state possible. The 'flight'-schema is eminently suited for evoking concentrated focus on events, because the motion between take-off and landing is continuous, during which locations can be only momentary. Moreover, a moving object will attract attention over a stationary background (IV.2.5). Given a situation where people have to do their best with the content of a textual world, they justly focus their processing resources on events and actions. If restrictions are placed on the extent of their protocols, for instance, if a SUMMARY is requested, events and actions will survive more often than other material.

3.15 Event representation in recall might accordingly correlate with the intuitive notion of "good understanding" for narrative texts, and for stories in particular. If we simply count the total number of propositions recalled, we might give higher ratings to someone who recovered a flurry of incoherent details, e.g. attributes, than to someone who remembered a small number of main events. When a tabulation method with higher numerical values for events was tested by Walter Kintsch and myself, the resulting scores did appear to correspond to our intuitive impression that one protocol attested better understanding than another. But we have no basis yet for deciding how large the scale of numerical differences ought to be.

3.16 If processing involves spreading activation (III.3.24), tabulation should perhaps take into account the number of propositions that some conceptual node might cause to arise through activation alone. I present in Chapter VII some intriguing evidence that our test subjects were indeed supplying material in this fashion. Again, the problem of direct remembering versus reconstructing becomes acute. The conventional assumption that people are simply creating "traces" of input (cf. Gomulicki 1956) obviously makes experimentation convenient, and theoretical models simple, but fails to account for the data I present. There is no doubt some abstraction of "traces" going on, but it interacts heavily with patterns of expectations such as schemas (Beaugrande & Miller 1980). Future research will shed more light on the matter.

4.   PLAN ATTACHMENT

4.1 For the orthodox behaviorist, human activities are exemplified by jerking a knee struck with a rubber hammer or a hand burnt on a hot stove. The faculties for building and implementing complex plans whose individual actions may not be explainable via outward stimuli simply did not enter the picture. Carried to its conclusion, behaviorism seems to end in either of two severe dilemmas. If every response must be paired with exactly one stimulus, people would never know what to do when encountering new stimuli. If stimuli and responses can be generalized over whole types and classes, operations would bog down in combinatorial explosion while searching for a means to characterize each stimulus coming along (cf. II.1.2). These dilemmas only appear escapable if human actions are *plan-directed,* so that stimuli from the environment can be judged regarding their relevance and appropriate response.

4.2 The need for human interaction emerges from the complex organization of social reality. DISCOURSE is a mode of SYMBOLIC interaction demand especially when a situation is too intricate or diffuse, or resources too limited, or contingencies too dependent on personal motives, to allow successful management by physical intervention. Discourse functions as ACTION and INTERACTION that controls the course of events (cf. van Dijk 1977a; Morgan 1978b: 265); and as META-ACTION and META-INTERACTION that provides a verbal monitoring and evaluating of the course of events (cf. Winston 1977: 72). The "performative utterances" of "speech-act" theory (Austin 1962: 4ff.), e.g. those used to perform a marriage or open a meeting, are situations where this dual status of discourse converges: the monitoring utterance *is* the event. The more general case is only partial convergence: the discourse action is relevant to the speaker's plan, but not in ways openly and explicitly proclaimed. People hardly ever say things like (cf. Bruce 1975: 35):

(186) I am now describing the situation in accord with my personal interests.

(187) I hereby get you to see this my way.

A theory of language that treats all utterances as performative by inserting 'I assert' in front of them and then deleting it to get the utterances back to their original form (cf. Ross 1970a; Sadock 1970; Ballmer 1976) is, I think, missing the point. The important differences of context are levelled, as if speech-acts need not be adapted to their environments of occurrence (cf. Cohen 1978: 26). I cannot see how pragmatics can make headway unless we are willing to explore the empirical realities of language use.

4.3 To be relevant to a GOAL, discourse actions should be relevant to steps in a PLAN. There are PRECONDITIONS to be met (Sacerdoti 1977; Schank & Abelson 1977; Cohen 1978; cf. "prerequisites" in Charniak 1975b). Preconditions include both MATERIAL RESOURCES, e.g. objects providing instrumental support for actions and events;[7] and PROCESSING RESOURCES, e.g. mental capacities providing attention, understanding, and problem-solving (cf. IX.1.4 for a more extensive list). The standards of textuality as set forth in I.4.11 are pervasive and fundamental preconditions for using discourse in plans. For that reason, the violation of the standards is usually taken as a signal of a plan to block communication.

4.4 A plan can be formally represented as composed of PATHWAYS leading from one situation or event to another, or on occasion, looping back to a previous one. The plan begins with an INITIAL STATE and runs to the FINAL STATE via a progression of INTERMEDIATE STATES—the "states" being defined from the planner's standpoint. A plan is successful if the FINAL state matches the planner's GOAL state. The goal state is thus a situation expected to be true in the world when the requisite actions and events have modified the current state of the world (cf. Cohen 1978: 26).

4.5 Under the simplest circumstances, the planner needs only to test its current state in the situation and to decide what action should be performed, continued, or terminated—the familiar "test-operate-test-end" ("TOTE") model of Miller, Galanter, and Pribram (1960, 1968). But Miller et al.'s (1968) example of someone pounding a nail into a board is far too simplistic as a model of human interaction. In real situations, there are often many ALTERNATIVE actions to consider, and the resulting future states are much harder to predict. For one thing, long-range goal attainment demands the co-ordination and protection of subgoals (Rieger & London 1977; Sacerdoti 1977). If a block or even outright failure is encountered (cf. I.6.7), the planner should not just back up and try again, but analyze the failure to improve the plan (Sussman 1973; Davis & Chien 1977; Sacerdoti 1977; Wilensky 1978).

4.6 The study of how people select actions has been hampered in the past by a simplistic "trial-and-error" outlook on learning as inherited from Thorndike's (1911) heavily biased experiments. Thorndike's puzzle-cage was equipped with levers, only one of which opened the door. Placed in the cage, the cat could only try one lever after another and with repeated trials, the cat was able to open the door right away. Such planless actions are in reality the

---

[7]Cf. Wilensky (1978) on "objects" in story-worlds as compared with my notion of "material resources" (also in VIII.2.39, VIII.2.41).

only way to handle such a situation—as Walter Kintsch (1977a: 441) comments, even a Gestalt psychologist couldn't have escaped from the cage except by trial-and-error. The objection to this mechanism as a means of normal behavior is the same that applies to all stimulus-response theories: unworkability in complex settings because of combinatorial explosion (cf. VI.4.1). If people communicated by trying out this word or phrase, then that, then yet another, to see if discourse would result, language interaction would look quite different from the way it does.

4.7 One could go to the other extreme and argue for the traditional criterion of *maximal utility:* choosing the most gainful alternative (cf. Stegmüller 1969: 391). But the game-theoretical situations used in philosophical discussions do not bear much resemblance to human situations of communicative interaction. In the latter, participants seldom know the exact gains that a given discourse action brings. I would suggest that we should therefore envision the selection of discourse actions in a model of PROBLEM-SOLVING where trial-and-error, as well as maximal utility, have only approximate application. To find a path from the initial state to the goal state is a matter of SEARCH (cf. I.6.7ff on search types). Before a "trial" is made, the planner estimates the probabilities of bringing the goal nearer. The next state can thus be identified within a plan sequence in the same kind of operation described for AUGMENTED TRANSITION NETWORKS (cf. II.2.12ff.; III.4.7): the processor tries to predict and define the linkage to successor states. The pathway to a goal or subgoal is a MACRO-STATE in which each action is a MICRO-STATE (cf. II.2.9; VI.1.1). Whatever contextual knowledge the planner may possess about the situation serves to predict and define links. If the situation is complex or unfamiliar, the planner must use general knowledge about causalities (cause, reason, enablement, purpose) and try to infer the goals of other participants on that basis. A trial-and-error setting emerges only in the rare case where the planner has neither contextual nor general knowledge of what to do. A maximal utility setting emerges only in the rare case where every result of every action is foreseeable and calculable on a unified scale of values.

4.8 If the notions just cited can indeed be generalized, we might be able to apply the standards of textuality to action sequences as well as to texts. We can, for example, describe PLAN COHERENCE as guaranteed by the RELEVANCE of its component actions to the states leading toward a goal (on "relevance" as task-oriented, cf. VII.2.8). PLAN COHESION results from the manifest connectivity between one action and the next in the sequence. INTENTIONALITY and ACCEPTABILITY covers the attitudes of the planner and the co-participants of interaction, respectively. The highest priority is the maintenance of stability via connectivity and continuity. A PLANBLOCK—an occurrence which prevents the further pursuit of a goal—figures as a SERIOUS PROBLEM (I.6.7) and elicits corrective action at that stage. There could be several ACTIVE CONTROL CENTERS: the current state, the goal state, and important intermediate states expected to occur. FORWARD PLANNING is done best with the current state as control center, and BACKWARD PLANNING with the goal state or with an intermediate state between the current one and the goal (cf. Schank & Abelson 1977: 82; Cohen 1978: 124).[8] MEANS-END ANALYSIS (I.6.7.1) allows both forward and backward planning at once (Woods 1978b: 19f.). Quite possibly, planning may be going on simultaneously in various directions from several control centers (cf. Fikes & Nilsson 1971).

4.9 A workable planner apparently requires *multiple models of future worlds,* only some of which show the goal state successfully attained. The criteria for choosing one path over another would depend upon the expected probabilities of attaining the goal and upon the relative undesirability of alternative final states. Shortness, ease, and directness would be inherently attractive traits for a pathway; and past experience would be influential. These considerations might be in conflict. A bank robbery would be a short, direct pathway to the common goal 'have money', but it carries a high probability of entry into intensely undesirable states ('in jail', 'shot', etc.). A successful bank robber might disregard the risks and try again, even though the overall probabilities are much the same.

4.10 Multiple goals are another factor to explore, ranging from momentary desires to long-range undertakings. I propose the DEFAULT or PREFERENCE assumption that a goal should at least qualify as a DESIRABLE state. One may dispute about what people's desires are, and whether they are all secondary to the desire for mere survival (cf. Pugh 1977). Yet it seems safe to suggest that desires are both personally and socially defined. Table 2 offers what I take to be a plausible listing of desirability traits and their negative counterparts, such as might act as defaults and preferences (after Beaugrande 1979a: 475) (for an assortment of mysteriously elaborate formalisms for desirability, see Kummer 1975: 58ff.). As with a typology of concepts, the degree of detail depends on the applications we want to make (cf. III.4.2ff.). One might want to introduce goals like 'have money' or 'outlive your enemies' as primitives, to say nothing of the many whims that beset our everyday consciousness. I think it useful, however, to seek a general set of features whose interaction and combination should make these goals generally describable. For example, 'have money' could figure as "possession of instrument" for such state types as health, satisfaction, comfort, enjoyment, attractiveness, acceptance, independence, control, and so on. Another possible outlook is to rate desirable states on scales of intensity, as undertaken by Schank (1975c: 45ff.).

---

[8]The process of UPDATING (I.6.4) probably has a correlate of BACKDATING whereby a processor reasons from a given state about antecedent states. The same linkages of causality would apply as those for updating.

TABLE 2

TYPE OF STATE	DESIRABLE		UNDESIRABLE	
PHYSICAL STATE	PH1a	health	PH1b	illness
	PH2a	comfort	PH2b	discomfort
	PH3a	satisfaction	PH3b	need
EMOTIONAL STATE	EM1a	happiness	EM1b	unhappiness
	EM2a	enjoyment	EM2b	suffering
	EM3a	stimulation	EM3b	depression
CHARACTER STATE	CH1a	kindness	CH1b	unkindness
	CH2a	modesty	CH2b	vanity
	CH3a	honesty	CH3b	dishonesty
KNOWLEDGE STATE	KN1a	order	KN1b	disorder
	KN2a	completeness	KN2b	incompleteness
	KN3a	knownness	KN3b	unknownness
	KN4a	believability	KN4b	unbelievability
	KN5a	interest	KN5b	boredom
SOCIAL STATE	SO1a	attractiveness	SO1b	repulsiveness
	SO2a	acceptance	SO2b	rejection
	SO3a	independence	SO3b	domination
	SO4a	solidarity	SO4b	confrontation
ENVIRONMENTAL STATE	EN1a	manageability	EN1b	unmanageability
	EN2a	supportiveness	EN2b	contrariness
	EN3a	identifiability	EN3b	non-identifiability
	EN4a	pleasantness	EN4b	unpleasantness
STATE TRANSITIONS	TR1a	achievement	TR1b	failure
	TR2a	control	TR2b	lack of control
	TR3a	directness	TR3b	circuitousness
	TR4a	economy	TR4b	expenditure
	TR5a	ease	TR5b	difficulty

4.11 The default character of desires arises from the fact that people often don't make open declarations of what they want (cf. Schank & Abelson 1977: 108). To discover other people's plans, a planner must make extensive INFERENCES based on this aspect of knowledge. The planner relies on the general postulate of NORMALITY: that a given person has the usual desires unless evidence is provided to the contrary (cf. Rieger 1975: 234). Defaults can be overridden by such evidence, or simply because desires CONFLICT with each other. A TRADE-OFF ensues in which one desire is sacrificed for the sake of another. Limitations upon resources (VI.4.3) mean that expenditure in current states must be balanced against plans for expenditure later. Short-range planning may attain desirable states with such speed or intensity that highly undesirable states become ineluctable afterwards.[9] Undesirable states can also result merely from incomplete, contradictory, or erroneous knowledge among agents.

4.12 Everyday situations might seem replete with counter-examples where people are seeking undesirable states. But the instances brought to my attention so far all indicate a trade-off. Good health could be undesirable for people seeking sympathy (trade-off: health for solidarity) or trying to escape school, military service, or heavy labor (example of the last in Goffman 1974: 116) (trade-off: small portion of health for comfort). To avoid work, people might desire to not understand requests and instructions (trade-off: knowness for comfort). Altruistic people might sacrifice their own comfort for that of others (trade-off: comfort for kindness). The masochist seeking pain trades comfort for stimulation. We might also include here the antagonism between knowness and interestingness that is inherent in the nature of informativity in communication (cf. IV.1.21).

4.13 The complexities of desirability can be brought readily under control by SCRIPTS. A participant can enter a ROLE, i.e. assume the identity resulting from a characteristic constellation of attributes and actions in conventional situations. It is then a straightforward matter to predict what a participant in a given role desires, at least as far as the role is being represented. A person entering the 'customer'-role in a 'restaurant'-script can be assumed by default to be in the state of 'hunger', a subtype of 'need' (PH3b), and to desire 'satisfaction' (PH3a). Someone not desiring to move from this one state to the other should not enter the role. The other roles in the script exert similar controls on the respective participants (waiter, cashier, etc).

4.14 I shall use a common situation type to illustrate how discourse actions figure in building and carrying out a plan. The sample is the situation of desiring possession of an object belonging to another agent. Schank and Abelson (1977) propose a set of plans for this eventuality, being—in the order from the least radical and emphatic to the most—ASK, INVOKE THEME, INFORM REASON, BARGAIN FAVOR, BARGAIN OBJECT, THREATEN, STEAL, and OVERPOWER.[10] The stronger the opposition

---

[9]We see some disadvantages of such short-sighted planning and resulting goal conflicts in the stage-play discussed later in this section.

[10]This is my own ordering. Schank and Abelson (1977) usually put STEAL after OVERPOWER (depending, I suppose, on what one considers the last resort). Notice that for all cases, these ACTIONS provide the current owner a *reason* for transferring possession of the object; the exceptions are STEAL (which *enables* the transfer without the owner's agency), and OVERPOWER (where *cause* is applied to the owner). Looking backward in time, the transfer of possession is the *purpose* of all these actions. The progression from milder to more extreme plans is described in terms of *planbox escalation* in Beaugrande & Dressler (1980).

from the current possessor, the further the planner would move down the list. Good friends might give you the object if you simply ASK. You might INVOKE some known THEME, i.e. recurrent content in your life, such as your tastes or your long-standing friendship with the possessor. You might go on to INFORM the possessor of a REASON to give up the object (strictly speaking, if the reason is already known, it is INVOKED; cf. VIII.1.8). You might BARGAIN to do some FAVOR for the possessor in return, or to exchange some OBJECT you possess yourself. If all these failed you might THREATEN the possessor or STEAL the object when no one is present. If the possessor remains adamant and stays at the scene, the last resort is OVERPOWER. Although effective, threatening, stealing, and overpowering are usually subject to institutionalized means of retribution intended to serve as deterrents.

4.15 All of these plans except steal and overpower require DISCOURSE ACTIONS to control the course of events. In our sample text, the owner of the object has no notion of the object's monetary value, being attached to the object for sentimental reasons. This state of 'unknownness' (KN3b) puts the owner at a disadvantage, but also places uncomfortable constraints on the discourse content of the other agents. In effect, the latter must conceal the intensity of their desire for the object in intricate and often amusing ways.

4.16 The text is a scene from a realistic comedy by the American playwright Sidney Howard (1891–1939) entitled *The Late Christopher Bean* (completed 1932). A rural New England doctor and his family, scraping along in a village near Boston during the depression, suddenly learn that the works of Christopher Bean, an impoverished, fatally ill painter they once befriended, are now fetching vast sums of money in the art world. Besieged by lucrative offers from galleries and dealers, they search their home for canvases Bean might have left at his death. In our scene, they recall that the painter left with Abby, their housemaid, a large portrait of her. The family hits on the plan of restoring themselves to social acceptance and affluence with the money they would obtain by selling the portrait. But they decide they must not allow the maid to infer the painting's real value.

4.17 We observe Dr. Haggett, his wife, and their daughter Ada in the dining room of their home. The maid is at present out in her quarters, where the family kitchen is also located, preparing the midday meal. The maid is acting on the default assumption that the family is hungry (cf. VIII.2.24), whereas their real goal is quite different. The text of the scene, given here with small omissions, is as follows (Warnock [ed.] 1952: 160ff.):[11]

[11]The reprint rights for this passage were leased from Samuel French, Inc., of New York. Copyright, 1932 (under the title "Muse of All Work") by Sidney Howard. Copyright, 1933, by Sidney Howard. Copyright, 1959, 1960 (in renewal) by Dolly Damrosch Howard. Reprinted by permission of Samuel French, Inc.

(188)

DR. HAGGETT: (1) Chris Bean did paint one portrait while he was here!

ADA: (2) Who did he paint it of?

DR. HAGGETT: (3) Of Abby! (4) What's become of it?

MRS. HAGGETT: (5) She's had it hanging in her room ever since he died!

DR. HAGGETT: (6) Ada, go in and see if it's still there.

ADA: (7) But Pa, if it is, it must belong to Abby!

DR. HAGGETT: (8) I ain't going to do nothing that ain't fair and square. (9) And don't talk so loud! (10) You want Abby to hear?

MRS. HAGGETT: (11) Never mind her, Milton! (12) We got one thing, and one thing only, to do now! (13) And that is to find out if Abby's planning to take that portrait to Chicago with her.

DR. HAGGETT: (14) Call her in and ask her.

ADA: (15) She'd get on to you!

MRS. HAGGETT: (16) If it was me I wouldn't hesitate. (17) I'd walk right into Abby's room and take that picture like it wasn't no account.

DR. HAGGETT: (18) There's a point of conscience here. (19) One way of looking at it, the portrait's our property. (20) Abby's no artist's model. (21) She's our help. (22) We was paying her thirty dollars a month and keep....

MRS. HAGGETT: (23) We only paid her fifteen in those days.

DR. HAGGETT: (24) The principle's the same. (25) And the question is: did she have the right to let him paint her portrait on the time we paid for?

MRS. HAGGETT: (26) Your conscience is clear, Milton. (27) There ain't no doubt but that portrait belongs to us. (28) Ada, go into Abby's room and get it.

ADA: (29) But what will Abby say?

MRS. HAGGETT: (30) Wreck the room! (31) Tear down the window curtains! (32) Then your Pa can tell her a burglar must have got it!

DR. HAGGETT: (33) I'm only a simple country doctor. (34) I don't care for money. (35) It's only for my loved ones I got to have it.

MRS. HAGGETT: (36) Go along, Ada. (37) Take it out the back way and upstairs. [*Then to* DR. HAGGETT *as* (38) ADA *goes out into the kitchen.*] (39) Once we get it we'll hide it under your bed.

DR. HAGGETT: (40) If Abby feels bad I can give her a little something.

[(41) ADA *returns.*]

ADA: (42) Abby's out there!

MRS. HAGGETT: (43) How about the picture?

ADA: (44) That's there too!

MRS. HAGGETT: (45) What's it like?

ADA: (46) You know! Terrible!

DR. HAGGETT: (47) Well, it's some comfort to know that it's still all right.

MRS. HAGGETT: (48) What's Abby doing?

ADA: (49) Packing her trunk.

MRS. HAGGETT: (50) Tell her she ought to be getting dinner ready.

ADA: (51) But if she stays out there in the kitchen!

MRS. HAGGETT: (52) Call her to come in and set the table.

ADA: (53) You call her!

MRS. HAGGETT: [*in her sweetest tones*] (54) Abby! Abby!

[(55) *They watch the kitchen door.* (56) ABBY *enters.*]

DR. HAGGETT: [*a heroic effort at play-acting*] (57) I'm sorry I spoke so rough to you just now.

ABBY: [*eyeing him askance*] (58) Oh, that's all right.

MRS. HAGGETT: [*she drops a folded cloth on the table*] (59) You can go ahead and set the table for dinner.

ABBY: (60) Yeah. [*She proceeds to spread the cloth.*]

[(61) MRS. HAGGETT *nods to* ADA *who slips into the kitchen.* (62) MRS. HAGGETT *moves over to the kitchen door and blocks it.*]

DR. HAGGETT: [*as before*] (63) It's nice of you to wait on us your last day, Abby.

ABBY: [*busy about the table*] (64) It's nothing.

[(65) ADA *returns.*]

ADA: [*a whisper*] (66) Ma! The new maid's there![12]

MRS. HAGGETT: (67) Tell her to go out and take a walk around the village.

[(68) ADA *retires.* (69) ABBY *starts for the kitchen.*]

MRS. HAGGETT: (70) Where're you going, Abby?

ABBY: (71) Just out to the kitchen to get the mustard pickles.

MRS. HAGGETT: (72) Oh, I don't think we need mustard pickles for dinner. (73) Do you think we do, Milton?

DR. HAGGETT: (74) I'll be frank with you, Abby. (75) Them mustard pickles don't seem to set good with me.

[(76) ABBY *starts again for the kitchen.*]

DR. HAGGET: (77) Abby! [(78) *She turns back again.*] (79) Didn't you hear us, Abby? (80) We said we didn't care for mustard pickles.

ABBY: (81) I was going to get some watermelon preserves. (82) You always liked my watermelon preserves.

MRS. HAGGETT: [*stumped*] (83) That's so, Milton! You have always liked them particular!

DR. HAGGETT: [*likewise stumped*] (84) I know I have. (85) And I can't think of a thing against them now!

MRS. HAGGETT: [*still blocking the way to the kitchen*] (86) I thought you wanted to talk to Abby, Milton?

DR. HAGGETT: (87) That's right, Hannah, I did!

ABBY: (88) What was it you wanted to talk to me about?

DR. HAGGETT: [*at a total loss*] (89) Well, about several things. (90) Let me see now. (91) To begin with, I. . . .

[(92) ADA *returns.*]

ADA: [*a whisper*] (93) Ma! She says she don't want to take a walk!

---

[12]A new maid has been engaged to replace Abby on her departure for Chicago.

MRS. HAGGETT: (94) Tell her either she takes a walk or she goes back to Boston!

[(95) ADA *goes.*]

DR. HAGGETT: [*quickly*] (96) I know what it was I wanted to talk to you about, Abby! (97) It was about that new maid. (98) What do you think of her?

ABBY: (99) Oh, she's a nice girl.

DR. HAGGETT: (100) Of course she's a very nice girl. (101) Mrs. Haggett wouldn't have chosen anything else. [(102) *He becomes confidential.*] (103) But Abby . . . think carefully. (104) Will she give the same satisfaction you've given us?

ABBY: [*really touched*] (105) Now, that's real kind of you to say that, Dr. Haggett. (106) Of course, in fairness, you got to remember I had fifteen years to study your manners and ways. (107) But she's a nice girl, and if she finds she likes the place enough . . .

MRS. HAGGETT: (108) Do you think she will, Abby?

ABBY: (109) Well, maybe she will and maybe she won't. (110) I'll get dinner on the table first and talk afterwards. [(111) *Once more she starts for the kitchen door.* (112) Dr. HAGGETT *takes a step after her, helplessly.*]

MRS. HAGGETT: (113) But Abby, you ain't even got the table set!

ABBY: [*brushing her aside*] (114) I know, but I can't stand here talking with my biscuits burning! [(115) *She is gone into the kitchen.* (116) *Sensation.*]

MRS. HAGGETT: (117) Why didn't you stop her?

DR. HAGGETT: (118) How could I? (119) Why didn't you?

MRS. HAGGETT: (120) You seen me try, didn't you? (121) Now you'll just have to face it!

DR. HAGGETT: (122) It was your idea. (123) I never would have done it.

MRS. HAGGETT: (124) Keep quiet! [(125) *She is listening at the kitchen door.*] (126) Not a sound!

DR. HAGGETT: (127) Ada must be in Abby's room now.

[(128) ADA *returns, tottering.*]

MRS. HAGGETT: (129) Did you get it?

ADA: [*gasping, her hand on her heart*] (130) No!

MRS. HAGGETT: (131) She didn't catch you?

ADA: (132) If the biscuits hadn't been burning she would have!

MRS. HAGGETT: (133) We'll just have to try again. (134) We'll eat dinner quiet as if nothing happened. (135) Then I'll send her out on an errand.

[(136) ABBY *enters from the kitchen, carrying a soup tureen.*]

ABBY: (137) I never seen you in such a state, Dr. Haggett. (138) It's all them New York folks coming here![13]

DR. HAGGETT: [*deep self-pity*] (139) And they're all coming back any minute, too!

ABBY: (140) Why do you bother with them, Dr. Haggett?

DR. HAGGETT: (141) Can't avoid responsibilities in this life, Abby. [*Then with unaccountable intention he adds*] (142) Wouldn't mind so much if this

---

13These 'folks' are the art collectors wanting to buy the portrait.

room looked right. (143) It's that patch over the fireplace where Ada's picture was.

ABBY: (144) You could hang up one of Warren Creamer's pictures.

DR. HAGGETT: (145) Warren's pictures ain't big enough for that. (146) We need something to cover up the whole place.

ABBY: (147) Well, I got nothing to suggest.

DR. HAGGETT: [*as though a thought struck him suddenly*] (148) Abby, ain't you got a picture Chris Bean painted of you before he died?

ABBY: (149) I got my portrait.

DR. HAGGETT: (150) Well, if that isn't just the thing! (151) We'll hang that there! (152) Just till you go!

ABBY: [*She is covered with embarrassment*] (153) Why, I couldn't have my portrait in here! (154) What'd people say if they come into your dining room and seen a picture of me hanging there, scraping carrots?

DR. HAGGETT: (155) Ain't this a democracy? (156) I'd rather have you there scraping carrots than half of these society women who can't do nothing!

ABBY: (157) I never could say no to Dr. Haggett! [(158) *She goes.*]

DR. HAGGETT: (159) A much better way than stealing it would have been. (160) This has got to be done, but it's got to be done legitimate!

MRS. HAGGETT: (161) She ain't give it up to you yet.

DR. HAGGETT: (162) You can't take more than one step at a time! (163) I got it all thought out.

[(164) ABBY *returns, carrying the portrait.*]

ABBY: (165) Well, here it is.

DR. HAGGETT: (166) That's very nice of you, Abby (167) We're fond of you! (168) Look, we got two Abbies in here now. (169) One of them standing here in flesh and blood and the other in an oil painting. (170) Seems a pity to let both of them leave us, don't it?

ABBY: (171) Oh Doctor Haggett! I don't know how to thank you!

DR. HAGGETT: (172) If seeing the both don't give me an idea! (173) I'll let you have it just as it come to me. (174) Since you're going away after all these years, it'd be awful nice for you to leave the portrait behind you here with us.

ABBY: (175) Leave it here for good!

DR. HAGGETT: (176) Oh, I wouldn't ask you to make such a sacrifice without giving you something in return.

ABBY: (177) How could you give me anything in return?

DR. HAGGETT: (178) Oh, I don't say I could give you anything equal to what the portrait would mean to us. (179) But I guess twenty-five dollars would come in handy in Chicago!

[(180) ABBY *shakes her head.*]

ADA: (181) Make it fifty, Pa!

DR. HAGGETT: (182) All right! I will make it fifty! (183) It comes pretty hard to be handing out presents that size these days, but I'll make it fifty! (184) I guess you ain't got much to say against that!

ABBY: (185) Oh, but I could never see my way to giving up my portrait.

DR. HAGGETT: (186) Abby, you amaze me!

ADA: (187) How'd it be, Abby, if we had a nice photograph made of it and gave you that to keep with you in Chicago?

ABBY: (188) I'll tell you! I'll get the photograph for you and send it back!

MRS. HAGGETT: (189) No photograph'd ever give us the comforting feeling that we still had you with us!

ABBY: (190) Would it really mean so much to all of you to have me hanging there in an oil painting?

MRS. HAGGET: (191) Would we want anyone we didn't love in our dining-room?

ABBY: (192) But it ain't me. (193) It's the time when I was young! (194) It's all how things used to be in the old days!

4.18 I argued in Chapter IV that the uncertainty or unexpectedness of occurrences enhances their INTERESTINGNESS, because informativity is higher. In a planning space, interest increases along with the probability of FAILURE to attain the goal. Hence, a SERIOUS PROBLEM (failure chances outweigh those of success, I.6.7) can make the planning space interesting: the goal must not be immediate, obvious, or inevitable. The scene just quoted is a good illustration. The various planning pathways meet repeated plan-blocks, and at times failure seems almost assured. Indeed, when the play ends, the painting has still not been relinquished.

4.19 In earlier scenes of the play, the family is shown in need of money. Due to the economic depression, it has become hard to collect doctor bills. To marry off Ada, it is deemed requisite to spend the winter in Florida, where she can be exhibited in a bathing suit. The New England setting was doubtless selected by the playwright because of its reputation as the home of thrifty people. All of these factors reinforce the global goal 'have money' that could be readily assumed for people at large. We are concerned in the scene above with the local goal 'have painting'. In terms of means-end analysis (I.6.7.1), this local goal would decisively reduce the difference between the family's current impoverished state and the affluent goal state.

4.20 However, the PROBLEM SPACE for attaining the 'have-painting'-goal is filled with alternative pathways. Since the maid presumably wants to keep her portrait for sentimental reasons, a simple ASK would not do. The preference is given instead to a STEAL plan, which is essentially DEPTH-FIRST search rushing as directly and blindly toward the goal as possible (I.6.7.3). The audience is able to follow the interaction from (16) to (135) only by recourse to knowledge about stealing. For example, Ada's utterances (42), (51), and (66) are relevant to the situation because an absence of owner and witness is a precondition for successful stealing. Also, a STEAL plan is the sole member of the plan repertory cited in VI.4.14 with a *secrecy precondition,* i.e. the stealer's desire for the object must remain unknown to the possessor. The secrecy that would be desirable regarding the painting's high value is prone to removal, yielding the *serious problem* cited in VI.4.18.

4.21 As soon as the existence of the portrait is remembered (1–5), the family desires knowledge about its location and about its owner's plans concerning its possible change of location (6, 13). The immediately obvious solution of ASKing the maid (14) is blocked by the secrecy precondition: 'she'd get on to you' (15). The mother's reaction is the immediate invoking of STEAL as 'taking that picture like it wasn't no account' (17). One way in which a steal action updates the world is changing the agent's character state to 'dishonest', a value marked undesirable in Table 2. The doctor's mention of a 'point of conscience' (18) is understandable in that light. He solves this sub-problem with an INFORM REASON that the family is the painting's owner by having paid for the time spent producing it (19–25). The mother immediately accepts the doctor's reason as sufficient (26–27), though we notice that it is not presented directly to the maid. The reason fails to transform the steal plan into anything like a rightful 'possession' state: the undesirable 'dishonesty' state is still impending, as attested by the many attempts to shift actions to other agents: 'go into Abby's room and get it' (28); 'call her to come in' (52); 'you call her' (53); 'I thought you wanted to talk to Abby' (86); 'why didn't you stop her' (117); 'why didn't you' (119); 'it was your idea' (122). At one point, a 'burglar' is suggested as a fictitious agent (32).

4.22 Despite its directness of action, STEAL is clearly a high-risk plan. The doctor, still disturbed by its implications, falls back on another INFORM REASON: needing the money for his 'loved ones'—a bizarrely motivated expression for accomplices in a theft (35). While Mrs. Haggett calmly fills in the detailed steps of the plan, namely a route to carry off and a place to hide the stolen object (37, 39), the doctor tacks on an intention of BARGAIN OBJECT: 'a little something' for the picture (40).

4.23 Ada's announcing the maid's presence (42) is at once recognizable as a planblock. To remove the owner from the scene, Abby's role as housemaid is invoked by ASKing her to 'set the table' (52, 59). Because the maid was yelled at in an earlier part of the play, the doctor greets her with a "performative" discourse action (VI.4.2) of apologizing. Moreover, because the maid is intending to leave for Chicago, he feels it wise to INVOKE the THEME of her loyal service 'on her last day' (63). Her replies to both ventures are non-committal (58, 64).

4.24 The sub-problem arises of keeping the maid from returning to the location of the painting. Her role as housemaid conflicts with that requirement, because the kitchen is in the same vicinity. Her intention to fetch 'mustard pickles' is blocked by the assertion that no such item is needed, and the doctor gives an explicit INFORM REASON: indigestibility (71–75). The maid's updated intention to fetch 'watermelon preserves' offers a new problem: the doctor cannot convincingly disavow his favorite food (81–85). This situation demonstrates the trade-off principle among desires (VI.4.11). A usual desire is overridden by a non-expected one, creating the incongruous goal of trying to escape being given what one likes.

4.25 The solution is to detain the maid by means of conversation (86–87). Here, ASK becomes a goal of its own, rather than a means of obtaining knowledge. Indeed, the ASK plan is run even before the doctor has thought of anything to ask about (89–91). He is saved by an outside planblock, the presence of a new maid just arriving to replace Abby (93–94). The mother's seemingly unreasonable command to 'take a walk' (67) has been rejected, and is reinforced now with THREATEN (94). This tactic succeeds (as we find out in a different scene, the new maid returns to Boston in a rage). At the same time, the new maid is seized upon as topic material for the doctor's ASK (96–98)—an illustration of the dual function of discourse as action and meta-action (VI.4.2). The request to 'think carefully' is motivated by the special plan of wasting time (103). The doctor skillfully blends in an INVOKE THEME of Abby's satisfactory service through the years (104), eliciting in her apperception a desirable character state of 'kindness' (CH1a in Table 2).

4.26 This new solution to the sub-problem of how to detain the maid in the dining room fails, again due to her scripted role as housekeeper preparing dinner. She rushes off to the kitchen to rescue her burning biscuits (114), leaving the family to expect discovery of the steal. They accordingly hasten to shift agency back and forth, each hoping to evade the consequences (117–123). However, discovery is avoided after all. Discouraged by repeated planblocks, the family abandons STEAL for the time being (133–135), and later for good (159).

4.27 The depth-first rush of a STEAL plan, though holding forth hopes of quick success, is subject to too many uncontrollable planblocks which endanger its preconditions and enablements. The result is a gradual shifting to BREADTH-FIRST search (I.6.7.2), where many alternative paths are considered. For example, STEAL is supplemented in the passage I have discussed with ASK, INVOKE THEME, INFORM REASON, and THREATEN. The outright adoption of breadth-first problem-solving is manifested in the rest of the scene. The global problem space of how to get possession of the painting is broken down into sub-problem spaces: (1) how to get the painting moved to the dining room (142–165); and (2) how to persuade the maid to leave it there (166–194). The shift to breadth-first search is in fact announced by the doctor: 'it's got to be done legitimate' (160) (abandonment of STEAL), and 'you can't take more than one step at a time' (162) (look ahead only to a proximate subgoal by breaking problem space down). The new approach again involves some variety: ASK, INVOKE THEME, INFORM REASON, BARGAIN FAVOR, and BARGAIN OBJECT.

4.28 The plan of moving the painting is initiated with an INFORM REASON: an unsightly patch of wall needs to be covered (142–143). When the maid suggests some paintings brought by a village tradesman in a previous scene, the REASON for rejection is: 'not big enough' (144–146). When she protests at the incongruity of her portrait in its intended setting, yet another REASON is INFORMED: the doctor values working women over 'society women who can't do nothing' (153–156)—the latter being, as was shown in earlier scenes, just what the mother and daughter would like to be.

4.29 The special precondition for this planning phase is not *secrecy,* but *spontaneity.* The desire to move and later to keep the painting must appear to arise on the spur of the moment, i.e. with no other motivation than the situation. The family carefully distributes signals in strategic places: 'as though a thought struck him suddenly' (148); 'well, if that isn't just the thing' (150); 'if seeing the both don't give me an idea' (172); 'I'll let you have it just as it come to me' (173). These signals are clustered around the actual requests to move and leave behind the desired object. Notice that the absence of "sincerity conditions" (Searle 1969) by no means renders the utterances meaningless or inappropriate ("unhappy"), let alone ill-formed—quite the opposite.

4.30 When the subgoal 'move painting' is finally attained, the superior goal 'have painting' is still remote. As Mrs. Haggett says, matching the current state against the goal state, 'she ain't gave it up to you yet' (161). The doctor, who has learned something about problem-solving ('you can't take more than one step at a time', 162), answers that he has the further steps 'all thought out' (163). He plans to extend the attained subgoal by a combination of ASKing the maid to leave her painting to the family, INVOKing the THEME of her long service and their fondness for her, and INFORMing the REASON that the painting would be a fitting souvenir. When this combination of ASK fails, he switches to BARGAIN OBJECT: money for the painting. As is customary, a bargaining refusal is countered by increasing the amount offered (180–184). A renewed refusal (185) leads to a shift over to BARGAIN FAVOR: making a photograph of the painting (187). Abby simply reverses this BARGAIN by offering to make and send the photograph to the family (188). The INVOKE THEME of fondness is renewed as grounds for preferring the painting itself to the photograph (191). At this point, Abby's true motives for refusing all tactics emerge when she INVOKES the 'old days' which the painting represents to her (192–194). This block is decisive, and the play ends later on with her still in possession of her portrait.

4.31 I provide planning networks of the structure of the scene. In Figure 26, we have the DEPTH-FIRST plan for STEAL, in which all actions are subordinated to the rush toward the goal 'painting stolen'. There are repeated planblocks intruding (lower section of Figure 26) and eliciting new discourse actions from the family F. Most of the blocks come from the action track of Abby A, but the new maid NM also contributes. When the family's counter-actions (shown by arrows pointed toward blocks) are effective, the main STEAL path can advance until the next block. The track ends with goal unattained, due to the block of the owner's presence (cf. VI.4.20) (Abby's running out to save her biscuits).

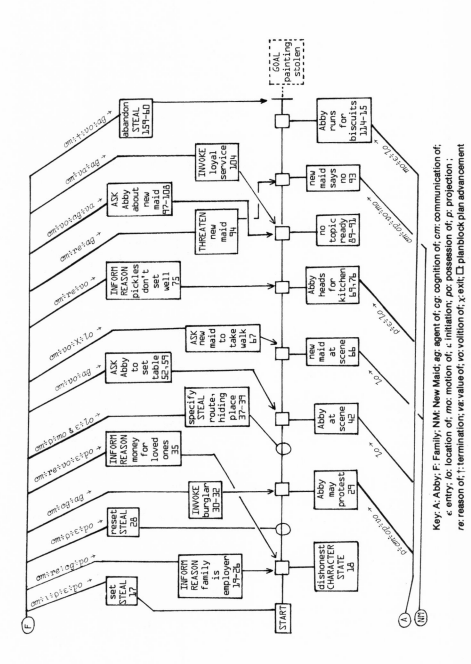

Figure 26

Key: A: Abby; F: Family; NM: New Maid; ag: agent of; cg: cognition of; cm: communication of; ε: entry; lo: location of; mo: motion of; ι: initiation; po: possession of; p: projection ; re: reason of; †: termination; va: value of; vo: volition of; x: exit; ◻ planblock plan advancement

192

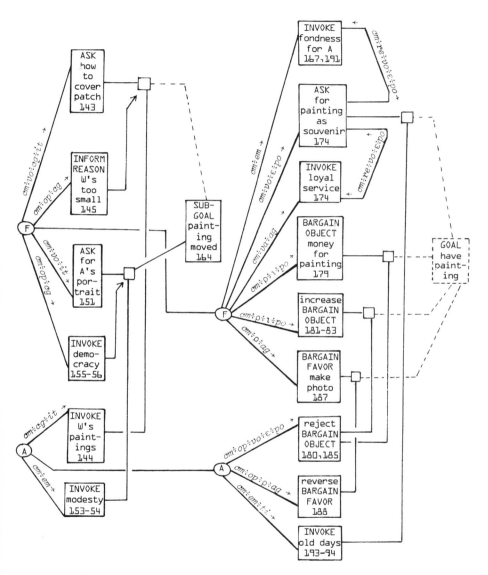

Key: A: Abby; *ag*: agent of; *cg*: cognition of; *cm*: communication of; *em*: emotion of; *ε*: entry;
F: family; *ι*: initiation; *it*: instrument of; *op*: opposed to; *po*: possession of; *p*: projection;
re: reason of; *ti*: time of; *va*: value of; *vo*: volition of; □: planblock

Figure 27

193

4.32 In Figure 27, we see the BREADTH-FIRST planning of the later scene. The organization of actions in this planning space is mainly *alternative* (disjunctive), while that of actions in the previous space was mainly *additive* (conjunctive).[14] This time, actions are directed to the simpler SUBGOAL of 'painting moved' in hopes of an extension toward the GOAL 'have painting'.[15] Abby again provides continual blocks for each pathway. She is apparently persuaded by the INVOKing of 'democracy' (155–156) and allows the SUBGOAL to be realized, but her INVOKing the 'old days' (193–194) reveals her unalterable conviction.

4.33 The linkages for these networks require the representation of discourse actions in my repertory of types. For example, the declaration of intention to steal becomes "communication of-projection of-entry into-possession" ("$cm \div \rho \div \epsilon \div po$") with initiation at the first mention and termination at the abandonment; giving the reason why the doctor needs money ('for loved ones') becomes "communication of-reason of-volition of-entry into-possession" ("$cm \div re \div vo \div \epsilon \div po$"); asking about the new maid is "communication of-volition of-cognition of-value" ("$cm \div vo \div id \div va$"); and so forth. Although more cumbersome than the Schankian primitives (VI.4.14), these representations allow us to sort out the components of discourse actions in greater detail.

4.34 We have seen how plan attachment correlates discourse actions with a continuity of motivation and purpose. If we had looked only at conditions for truth or sincerity as discussed in philosophy (e.g. Searle 1969), many utterances would appear invalid or "unhappy." Yet if we look at the *context,* the design of the component texts receives a good rating for efficiency and effectiveness in advancing goals and overcoming planblocks. Plan attachment is also a model for the understanding processes of the *theatre audience.* The traits of being "realistic" and "well-made" as a play rest on the connectivity of actions and the plan-relevance of the discourse. Interest and humour arise from the uncertainties, planblocks, and failure probabilities in the planning space. Thus, plan attachment guarantees global comprehension and integration of both predictable and surprising occurrences into a connected text-world model for participants in communicative interaction as well as for observers.

---

[14]Here again is a parallel between textual aspects (cf. V.7 on disjunction vs. conjunction) and the organization of actions (cf. VI.4.8).

[15]'Painting moved' is an *unstable goal* of the type noted in VIII.2.11.2.

VII
Further Issues in Text Processes

1. TEXT TYPES

1.1 To progress from a study of abstract structures in possible sentences to the study of texts as communicative occurrences, we must confront a new challenge in the domain of linguistic TYPOLOGY. In descriptive linguistics, typology centered on minimal units, i.e., on repertories for distinctive features, phonemes, morphemes, etc. In transformational grammar, typology centered on a set of basic sentence patterns and classes of rules for building other patterns. Alternative typologies for sentences used categories like "declarative/interrogative/imperative/exclamatory" (traditional grammar); or "process/action/judgment/identification" (Brinkman); or "process/action/feature/classification" ("functional" grammar) (see Helbig 1974: 159, 186). These latter typologies suggest a fundamental confusion about the nature of the sentence. It is *people,* not sentences, who "declare," "interrogate," and "exclaim." It is *concepts* and *relations* that are the basis of "processes," "classifications," and the like, not grammatical formats. Hence, the usual typologies of sentences cannot offer a means of classsifying texts as occurrences in communicative interaction (cf. Morgan 1975).

1.2 If sentence typologies are simple but sterile, text typologies are forbiddingly vast and subjective. Early attempts to press conventional linguistic methods into service for text typologies were discouraging. We may count up word classes or measure sentence length and complexity (Mistrík 1973) with no certainty of distilling out crucial distinctions. Being told that advertising texts have an abundance of adjectives, and news reports have lots of verbs (Grosse 1976a), provides us a statement of symptoms for deeper-lying tendencies, but doesn't explain the types themselves.

1.3 The landmark colloquium at the Center for Interdisciplinary Research at the University of Bielefeld in January 1972 (proceedings in Gülich & Raible [eds.] 1972) brought new issues to light. The proliferation of binary oppositions so well known in phonology was proposed, yielding such questionable and diverse constructions as "± spontaneous" (Sandig) or "± figurative" (Stempel). The plus-or-minus sign, placed in front of any convenient expression as if it could transform an intuitive notion into a scientific one, was denounced as indicating the absence of all formalisms (Kummer) and hindering the development of theory altogether (van Dijk) (remarks in Gülich & Raible [eds.] 1972: 136, 181). In effect, such features don't account for a phenomenon, but simply mark it with one of a large, totally unsystematic set of arbitrary labels.

1.4 It might be more productive to study text types from the standpoint of evolution and usage. The INTERTEXTUALITY I suggested as indispensible for utilizing texts (I.4.11.6) evolves from social as well as linguistic factors:

1.4.1 A differentiation of social settings and participant roles leads to a differentiation of situation types.

1.4.2 The differentiation of situation types engenders reliance upon those text types held to have greater *appropriateness* (cf. I.4.14).

1.4.3 The accrual of episodic knowledge about situations and texts fosters expectations about what is *acceptable* and *effective* in a given context.

1.4.4 People build strategies to fit those expectations and to control textual occurrences accordingly.

1.4.5 The priorities of control result in the relative dominances of surface features, e.g. word class proportions and syntactic complexity.

1.4.6 These surface dominances gain the status of heuristic patterns against which new texts can be matched.

1.4.7 The patterns may exert influence back on the control strategies applied to *situation management* (I.3.4.6).

1.5 In this view, text types cannot be defined independently of pragmatics (Dressler 1972: 95; Kummer 1972a; Schmidt 1972; notwithstanding Grosse 1976b: 119). People use text types as fuzzy classifications to decide what sorts of occurrences are *probable* among the totality of the *possible* (cf. IV.1.23.3). As such, the text type can be defined only as strictly as considerations of efficient applicability allow. Unduly stringent criteria, like the rigorous borderline between sentences and non-sentences, can either (1) open up endless disputes over the admissability of unusual or creative texts to a type, or (2) lead to so many detailed types that any gains in heuristic usefulness are lost. It has often happened that preconceived notions about a text type have led people to reject a particular text which later became an acclaimed and classic representative. The history of literature is filled with examples.

1.6 Two approaches to the typology of texts are readily evident (Schmidt 1978: 55). First, one could begin with the traditionally accepted text types, e.g. narrative, descriptive, literary, etc., and seek to define distinctive traits of each one; second, one could undertake to define a theory of texts independently, and then observe whether one obtains a workable typology. The issue may have to be resolved by a compromise: in the development of a text theory, the applicability to text typology should be envisioned such that traditional types become definable. I shall adopt this approach here.

1.7 Perhaps the following definition of the notion might prove useful for further research. *A text type is a distinctive configuration of relational dominances obtaining between or among elements of: (1) the surface text; (2) the textual world; (3) stored knowledge patterns; and (4) a situation of occurrence.* The relevant dominances can apply to elements of any size, according to the circumstances. Without stipulating exactly what a text must look like for a given type, these dominances powerfully influence the preferences for selecting, arranging, and mapping options during the production and processing of the text. We can at most obtain FUZZY sets of texts among which there will be mutual overlap. Some textual traits will be DOMAIN-SPECIFIC, i.e. peculiar to the situation, topic, and knowledge being addressed.

1.8 Some conventional categories of texts in our own culture (on some very different cultures, cf. Grimes 1975) could be explicated along these lines:

1.8.1 In DESCRIPTIVE texts, the CONTROL CENTERS in the textual world are in the main *object* and *situation* concepts whose environments are to be enriched with a *multiple directionality* of linkage. The link types of *state, attribute, instance,* and *specification* will be frequent. The surface text will reflect a corresponding density of *modifier* dependencies. The most commonly applied global knowledge pattern will be the *frame.*

1.8.2 In NARRATIVE texts, the control centers in the textual world are in the main *event* and *action* concepts which will be arranged in an *ordered directionality* of linkage. The link types of *cause, reason, enablement, purpose,* and *time proximity* will be frequent (cf. VIII.2.13). The surface text will reflect a corresponding density of *subordinative* dependencies.[1] The most commonly applied global knowledge pattern will be the *schema.*[1a]

1.8.3 In ARGUMENTATIVE texts, the control centers in the textual world will be *entire propositions* which will be assigned values of truthfulness and reasons for belief as facts (cf. IV.1.23.1); often there will be an opposition between propositions with conflicting value and truth assignment. The link

---

[1]Accordingly, the version (164b) of the Hawkins protocols seems to be a more fitting narrative than version (163) with 'and' used throughout (cf. V.7.3).

[1a]Freedle and Hale (1979) show that a narrative schema, once learned, can easily be transferred to the processing of a descriptive text on the same topic.

types of *value, significance, cognition, volition,* and *reason* will be frequent. The surface text will contain a density of evaluative expressions. The most commonly applied global knowledge pattern will be the *plan* whose goal state is the inducement of shared beliefs.

1.8.4 In LITERARY texts, the textual world stands in a principled *alternativity* relationship to matchable patterns of knowledge about the accepted real world. The intention is to motivate, via contrasts and rearrangements, some new insights into the organization of the real world. From the standpoint of processing, the linkages within real-world events and situations is PROBLEMATIZED, that is, made subject to potential failure (cf. I.6.7), because the text-world events and situations may (though they need not) be organized with different linkages. The effects would be an increased *motivation* for linkage on the side of the text producer, and increased *focus* for linkage on the side of the receiver. This problematized focus sets even "realistic" literature (reaching extremes in "documentary" art) apart from a simple report of the situations or events involved: the producer intends to portray events and situations as *exemplary* elements in a framework of possible *alternatives.*

1.8.5 In POETIC texts, the alternativity principle of literary texts is extended to the *interlevel mapping of options,* e.g. sounds, syntax, concepts/relations, plans, and so on. In this fashion, both the organization of the real world and the organization of discourse about that world are problematized in the sense of VII.1.8.4, and the resulting insights can be correspondingly richer. The increase of producer motivation and receiver focus will also be more intense, so that text elements will be assignable *multiple functions* (cf. Schmidt 1971a).

1.8.6 In SCIENTIFIC texts, the textual world is expected to provide an optimal match with the accepted real world unless there are explicit signals to the contrary (e.g., a disproven theory). Rather than alternative organization of the world, a more exact and detailed insight into the established organization of the real world is intended. In effect, the linkages of events and situations are eventually *de-problematized* via statements of causal necessity and order.

1.8.7 In DIDACTIC texts, the textual world must be presented via a process of gradual integration, because the text receiver is not assumed to already have the matchable knowledge spaces that a scientific text would require. Therefore, the linkages of established facts are problematized and eventually de-problematized.

1.8.8 In CONVERSATIONAL texts, there is an especially episodic and diverse range of sources for admissable knowledge (cf. VIII.1.4ff.). The priorities for expanding current knowledge of the participants are less pronounced than for the text types depicted in VII.1.8.4-7. The surface organization assumes a characteristic mode because of the changes of *speaking turn* (cf. VIII.1.2ff.; VIII.1.18).

1.9 Even within this modest typology, we can see that types cannot all be explicated along the same dimensions. Whereas there may well be dominances of concept and relation types for descriptive, narrative, and argumentative texts, the concept and relation types in the other text types are probably domain-specific in the sense of VII.1.7. Moreover, description, narration, and argumentation will be found in various combinations in the other text types. And finally, if text types are dependent upon situational settings (cf. VII.1.4ff.), the basic question is how people use CUES to assign texts of various formats to a given type.

1.10 People can seek cues outside the text itself. Some situation types are institutionally defined regarding the text types to be used, e.g. a church service (cf. Pike 1967). Explicit announcements may establish the situation type, e.g. a political gathering. Appearances of particular speakers or of a writer's name in print can activate expectations about the forthcoming text type. A printed format, as in poems or newspapers, or a characteristic title, such as dime novels have, may be influential. Even a specific topic, such as those in many technical reports, can act as a cue. In accordance with what I hold to be a general principle of human processing (cf. III.4.15; IV.1.10; IV.2.9), the less evidence there is in the immediately apperceived text, the more the text receivers will gather and utilize all kinds of cues.

1.11 A single text can indeed be shifted from type to type by altering its situation of presentation. For example, it has become fashionable to "find" poems by removing texts from their original environments (Porter 1972), such as cooking recipes (Nöth 1978: 29f.) or classified advertisements (Kloepfer 1975: 88). Conversely, poems are converted into advertisements (Reiss 1976: 70). Although the text remains stable, the audience's processing procedures are placed under different controls and priorities. A non-poem presented as a poem is subjected to the intensified assignment of multiple communicative functions to language options (Schmidt 1971a, 1971b; Beaugrande 1978b). Presented as an advertisement, a poem undergoes an impoverishment of the functions of its elements.

1.12 For a linguistics of texts as communicative occurrences, the issue of text types is one of global processing controls. People are probably able to utilize texts without identifying the type, but efficiency suffers, and the mode of interaction of speaker/writer and hearer/reader remains vague. It seems unlikely that we can throw away the traditional text types; after all, they have a function in language users' heuristics. Here as in many other areas, we may instead have to throw away the hopes for air-tight, exhaustive, and mechanical sorting techniques that consult only formal features without regard for human activities.

2.   THE PRODUCTION OF TEXTS

2.1 In comparison to comprehension, the production of texts has been left unexplored (Fodor, Bever, & Garrett 1974: 434; Goldman 1975: 289; Osgood & Bock 1977: 89; Rosenberg 1977: xi; Levin & Goldman 1978: 14; Simmons 1978: 26). The reason is that linguists' analysis can be taken as a model for language understanding much more readily than for language production (II.2.4). If we take linguistics too literally, the production of utterances seems like a miracle of computation (cf. II.1.2f.). R. Jacobs and Rosenbaum (1968: 286) criticize traditional grammar for conveying the impression that "human language is a fragile cultural invention, only with difficulty maintained in good working order." But the transformational grammar advocated by Jacobs and Rosenbaum is infinitely more fragile with its endless lists of rules that can barely be kept under control and, to this day, have never been assembled into a complete grammar for any language (cf. Achtenhagen & Wienold 1975: 9f.).

2.2 It would be desirable to have a language model that uses the same procedures for both the reception and the production of texts (cf. Klein 1965; Harris 1972; Simmons 1973; Simmons & Chester 1979). The mapping between the surface text and the underlying text-world would then be SYMMETRICAL in either direction (Simmons & Chester 1979). However, this procedurally advantageous approach would not be entirely plausible for humans. Mapping is, in some ways at least, clearly asymmetrical in textual communication (cf. I.6.12; III.3.5)—even people with good memories will report what they have heard and understood in words differing slightly from the original presentation. However, there is probably considerable symmetry among the *operations* of mapping from one level to another and back again (cf. VII.2.11). In practice, generating has usually been performed with what Goldman (1975: 290) calls "canned output": a small repertory of expressions that forces everything into the same format. An alternative with more varied options selected by weighting probabilities has been developed by Sheldon Klein and co-workers (1973) (cf. the "weighted filters" for paraphrasing advocated by Mel'čuk & Žolkovskij 1970). But a more detailed, circumspect model of the *motivations* for selecting a particular option (some of these will be outlined below) is still needed.

2.3 Procedurally, reversals of operations would cover some differences between production and reception of texts, but by no means all.[2] A text producer has to map a plan onto conceptual/relational content, and the content onto a surface format; the receiver maps the surface back to the content, and the content back to the plan. But it is surely an idealization to

---

[2]The processing via a transition network would foresee parallel control in prediction of occurrences, but reversed control in stacking and building the network (cf. II.2.7ff.).

claim that the receiver arrives at the same material which the producer started out with. In some cases, the producer would prefer keeping the plan secret or creating the impression of a quite different plan. The receiver may also adopt an unexpected personal outlook on the presentation. Reversability is furthermore not applicable to the textual operations in which production and reception are running *in parallel:* the producer monitoring the reception, and the receiver predicting the production. And the production involves much more active selection and decision processes which consume more resources and attention than does reception.

2.4. These considerations suggest that text production can only be treated by a linguistics of *actualization.* The older linguistic methods oriented toward identification, generalization, and description (cf. I.1.10f.) were purely *analytic,* whereas a linguistics for explanation, reconstruction, and management, such as is needed to study text production, must also have a *synthetic* outlook.

2.5 Consider the issue of *misfunctions.* We can recognize fairly clearly cases where our own texts have been *misunderstood,* and we can discover the causes in factors like surface ambiguities or misleading expectations. But it is vastly more difficult to recognize when a text has been *misproduced,* i.e. when operations have been *wrong* rather than merely *inefficient, ineffective,* or *inappropriate* (I.4.14). If we count ambiguities as mistakes, we end up with vastly fuzzy borderlines, because language options are systematically ambiguous in their potential, and their usages possess variable degrees of determinacy. If we count ungrammatical surface formats, we include occurrences such as Milton's famous passage:

(189) Him who disobeys, me disobeys. (*Paradise Lost,* V, 611–12)

To deal with misfunctions, we evidently need a language model which does not simply discover and analyze structures, but also relates structures to processes operating with greater or lesser satisfactoriness.

2.6 In *face-to-face communication,* decisions and selections often have a provisional character. The speaker may reconsider and introduce revisions when difficulties ensue—"self-initiated repair," according to Schegloff, Jefferson, and Sacks (1977). Due to numerous factors competing for limited time and processing resources, the operational load for spontaneous speaking may become unduly heavy. People expect, on the other hand, much more controlled organization in *written* texts, where the producer has time to discover and develop an efficient and effective arrangement. If processing is overloaded during the initial phase of expression, the producer has opportunity of going back and reviewing results with a specially distributed focus. Hence, merely writing down the same utterances one might produce in conversation—a frequent practice of untrained writers—should not be expected to result in satisfactory texts. Writing demands that situational factors, such as intonation, gestures, facial expression, and immediately available feedback, be given compensation via a more thoroughgoing text-internal organization. The aspects of participant roles, time, and location seem unproblematic in face-to-face communication, where people are immediately present. In writing, they too must be accounted for by the organization of the text world and its expression.

2.7 Like reception, production must involve a satisfaction THRESHOLD where operations are TERMINATED (cf. I.6.4). Just as a receiver might go on and on with inferences and spreading activation, a producer might keep revising a text over and over. At some point, a decision to cease must be made, based on the intended effects of the text on its audience; taken by itself, production appears to be an open-ended operation. I shall attempt to sketch out the various phases of this operation before going on to actual samples. I shall be concerned in particular with the production of *written* texts (for a more thorough treatment, see Beaugrande, in preparation).

2.8 The production process can be seen to consist of PHASES.[3] The phases are presumably not separate operations in a time sequence, but rather stages of PROCESSING DOMINANCE during which some operations are accorded more resources and attention than others. I distinguish at least four phases: PLANNING, IDEATION, DEVELOPMENT, and EXPRESSION. During the PLANNING phase, a text producer focuses on the PURPOSE of the text as a step toward a personal, social, or cognitive GOAL, and on the intended AUDIENCE of text receivers. A TEXT TYPE is selected, and correlations set up between the various component steps of the plan and the general criteria of the production process. I use the term RELEVANCE to designate these correlations: knowledge or discourse is thus not inherently relevant, but relevant only with respect to a task at hand (cf. I.4.14).

2.9 The IDEATION phase places processing dominance upon the discovery of CONTROL CENTERS for cognitive content. An IDEA is the internally activated configuration of concepts and relations, which lies at the foundation of meaning-creating behavior, including text production. It is extremely difficult to judge how ideas originate, because the operations involved are in part at least beyond the reach of conscious control. As a comparison, we could envision the focus of attention as a beam of light sweeping across an enormously elaborate network of knowledge; whatever the beam hits becomes active and can be inspected with regard to its RELEVANCE. To write a friendly letter, the ideation phase could cast about for material bearing the traits of INTERESTING (i.e., not obvious as a matter of course) and EPISODICALLY RECENT (i.e., experiences in one's personal environment that the text receiver would not already know). To

---

[3]I note a different, simpler phase model proposed by Milic (1971) in VII.2.38.

write a scientific text, ideation could focus on a pre-decided knowledge space with its own dense internal connectivity. To write a news report, ideation would be directed toward the episodic storage of a situation or event sequence. To write a novel, the ideation of situations and events would be substantially less controlled by episodic storage of the producer.

2.10 These early production phases of planning and ideation need not be dependent upon language. The raw materials feeding into production are essentially points and pathways of knowledge: concepts, relations, mental images, states of the world (past, present, projected), emotions, desires, and so on. The correlation of all of these entities among themselves and with natural language expressions is, I suspect, accomplished via PROBLEM-SOLVING: search, testing, and traversing of access routes. To attain COHERENCE, the access routes are established among knowledge points; to attain EXPRESSION, access routes are established between knowledge points and language expressions; to attain COHESION, access routes are established among expressions within a surface format (cf. I.4.4); and to attain RELEVANCE, access routes must be established between knowledge points or expressions (or whole configurations of these) and the steps and conditions of the producer's plan in the current setting.

2.11 Although there is surely considerable ASYMMETRY among these various accessing operations (cf. I.6.12), I would view the operations themselves as comparable; while the materials to be managed differ, the SYSTEMATICITY of their management is unified by a common commitment to search, access, and connectivity. The operations all require CONTROL CENTERS that determine the DIRECTIONALITY of search and access (cf. II.2.9; III.3.6; VI.3.5; VII.1.8.1.ff.; etc.). They all vary according to *degree of detail* from LOCAL to GLOBAL (cf. VI.1.1, etc.) and from MICRO-elements to MACRO-elements (cf. II.2.9; III.4.27; VI.4.7; etc.). They all work toward a THRESHOLD OF TERMINATION where processing is deemed satisfactory for the task at hand (cf. I.6.4; III.3.3; III.3.23f.; IV.1.6; VII.2.7; etc.) These common factors only emerge in the *synthetic* outlook I advocated for a linguistics of textual communication in VII.2.4, where structures and rules are interpreted as processes and procedures (cf. I.3.5.8).

2.12 The DEVELOPMENT phase receives the results of planning and ideation, whether or not language expressions are already in sight at this moment. This phase is responsible for the detailed internal organization of concepts and relations. To the extent that this organization is not stored as determinate or typical linkage, ORIGINALITY results. Originality may even lead to the creation of new concepts. However, I suspect that if we go into sufficient detail, we may find even new concepts to be composed of established materials put together in new ways (cf. IV.3.14). As the development phase goes forward, the control centers passed on from ideation continue to spread and intersect. If the conceptual-relational configuration were mapped into expression at an early stage, we would have a terse text that would appear as an OUTLINE (not fully cohesive) or a SUMMARY (fully cohesive) of the text that would be mapped out at a later stage;[4] at a still later stage, the summary relationship would be reiterated, and so on indefinitely. The oppositions of local/global or micro/macro are thus relative to the scope of the perspective we adopt.

2.13 Some typical operations of development could be carried out via linkages of *specification* and *instance,* e.g. 'people—young people—my friends—my best friend'. *Time* and *location* can be subdivided into steadily smaller components, e.g. 'what I did this year—what I did this summer—what I did on a weekend at the seashore'; or 'life in the south—life in Florida—life in Miami'. The priorities of development, including link types, are strongly controlled by the *text type,* e.g. descriptive, narrative, or argumentative (cf. VII.1.8ff.). A further factor influencing development is the use of the global knowledge patterns we explored in chapter VI: frames, schemas, plans, and scripts. These patterns act as channels for spreading activation, alerting the writer about what components require specification in a relevant context. For such a pattern to become active, TOPIC configurations need to emerge from densities of linkage in the ongoing textual world (cf. III.4.11.9). The type of linkage will affect the type of pattern, e.g. states, attributes, parts, etc, for frames; event or action progressions for schemas; pathways of goal-attainment for plans and scripts. The variables in the pattern will be filled in with applicable individuals. Some modifications might also be required to make the intended content fit. Nonetheless, the PROCEDURAL ATTACHMENT of the pattern to the planned output makes decision and selection much more efficient (VI.1.5).

2.14 Global patterns, though channelling the development of the text-world model, do not necessarily determine the format of the surface text. The most supportive pattern is the schema, which provides an ordered progression of underlying events and actions. The writer is free to express those events and actions in some other order than their temporal and/or causal sequence, provided signals are given; but the pattern offers guidance even then. The frame, in the sense I use the term here, is less obvious in its ordering. To describe a scene or a room, a writer has some typical strategies, such as moving from higher to lower, central to peripheral, mobile to stationary (cf. IV.2.3ff). Yet these strategies could compete with each other, and they might fail to respect the nature of the scene components per se, i.e. relative importance from a human perspective such as a plan. As a result, the normal ordering strategies for text world content are usually applied

---

[4]The difference between outline and summary would be that the outline possesses a fragmentary surface structure, and the summary a regular one (e.g. more complete sentences).

EPISODICALLY, in response to the demands of context and interest. Consider, for example, Dickens (1899: 35f.) depicting a newly introduced character:

(190) It was a careworn-looking man, whose sallow face and deeply sunken eyes were rendered still more striking than nature had made them, by the straight black hair which hung in matted disorder half-way down his face. His eyes were almost unnaturally bright and piercing; and his jaws were so long and lank, that an observer would have supposed that he was drawing the flesh of his face in, for a moment, by some contraction of the muscles, if his half-opened mouth and immovable expression had not announced that it was his ordinary appearance. Round his neck he wore a green shawl, with the large ends straggling over his chest, and making their appearance occasionally beneath the worn button-holes of his old waistcoat. His upper garment was a long black surtout; and below it he wore wide drab trousers and large boots, running rapidly to seed.

We can observe here a number of strategies for describing a person. The general direction is to begin with the face and move from there to the clothes, working gradually from highest (shawl) to lowest (boots). Superposed on this conventional design is a focus on unusual features: eyes that are 'deeply sunken' and 'piercing', and jaws that are 'long and lank'. An episodic comparison to a man contracting his facial muscles follows for emphasis. As the writer passes on to describe the clothes, focus is directed to all cues indicating poverty and neglect. The spatial ordering is generally preserved: 'neck–shawl–chest–beneath [...] waistcoat–surtout–trousers–boots'. The writer's selection is motivated by his plan to introduce shortly afterwards a remarkably dismal tale of 'want and sickness' narrated by this ominous-looking character.

2.15 This illustration suggests how the EPISODIC tendencies of organizing text-worlds can be controlled by DIRECTIONALITY. No writer would want to describe every aspect of someone's appearance, and Dickens' careful depictions are more detailed than the average. The writer must distribute attention only to those portions of the available material which are INTERESTING (i.e. not predictable), and RELEVANT (i.e. fitting to the plan for guiding the presentation of the textual world along a given course). The untrained writer is hard-pressed to make a selection and shifts about in a maze of episodic pursuits, assembling a mass of discontinuous or superfluous details. Notice the unity of the Dickens' passage despite the divergent descriptive strategies. The features he mentions are relevant not merely by belonging to the same character, but by suggesting a consistent impression of the 'striking' (interest) and 'careworn' (writer's plan) aspects.

2.16 Like the development phase, the EXPRESSION phase during which the actual surface text emerges is subject to a range of control factors. I would propose at least three CONTROL LEVELS that are important for the mapping operations in the expression phase:

2.16.1 The ORGANIZATION of EVENTS, ACTIONS, SITUATIONS, and OBJECTS in the textual world exerts certain influences upon the organization of the surface text. I reviewed in IV.2.6ff. the experimental literature regarding this issue, such as the strategies of moving from higher to lower, central to peripheral, changing to unchanging, mobile to stationary, earlier to later, and so on. I cited in III.4.18 some correspondences between text-world organization and the use of tense, voice, and mood. Harald Weinrich (1977) shows how tenses in French convey either a *descriptive* or a *narrative* perspective on the textual world. Halliday and Hasan (1976: 40) suggest that the characteristics of objects are cited in a certain order when modifiers are linearized in a noun phrase such as:

(191) two high stone walls along the roadside

where number is followed by size and substance (on modifier positioning, see also Vendler 1968; Martin 1969; Danks & Glucksberg 1971).

2.16.2 The STANDARD SEQUENCING OPERATIONS for imposing a linear format on English texts must be respected. I suggested in section II.2 that the basic phrases, clauses, and sentences of English act as frameworks for judging what surface occurrences are probable. These frameworks are not obligatory, but they must be kept in mind when departing from them, because they still act as a means of orientation. The correlations between sequencing operations and text-world organization can be arbitrary on occasion. In English, it is customary to place expressions of location before those of time, while in German, the reverse order is preferred; yet the event or situation may be the same. Such formatting standards reduce the decision-making load, not so much concerning *what* to say as *when* to say it. Sometimes, sequencing operations require conceptually empty placeholders without justification in the text world, e.g. the dummy 'it' used for expressions of the weather (cf. V.5.4.2). And the LINEARIZATION PROGRAMS often fail to reflect grammatical dependencies via direct adjacencies (II.2.7ff.).

2.16.3 The INFORMATIVITY of text-world entries can also affect the order in which they are expressed in surface formatting (cf. IV.3). The general trend is to mention new or focussed material after known or marginal material. For expressing configurations of familiar content, sentences will generally be longer and more complex than for expressing unfamiliar (cf. IX.4.6); perhaps the *more problematic coherence* of the unfamiliar content is compensated via a *less problematic cohesion*. The distribution of focus depends not only on the internal linkage of knowledge (whether pathways are predictable vs. problematic), but also on the RELEVANCE of knowledge organization to the producer's plan (cf. VII.2.8): the arrangement of materials

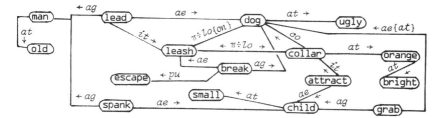

Key: *ae*: affected entity; *ag*: agent of; *at*: attribute of; *co*: containment of;*it*: instrument of;
lo: location of; *pu*: purpose of; *π*: proximity

Figure 28

is co-ordinated with the ordering of steps in a plan (see for instance Dr. Haggett's utterances [96–104] in the stage play of VI.4.17). This control level thus applies not only to *what* to say and *when* to say it, but also to *why*. A striking illustration was the arrangement of the chimpanzee text discussed in IV.4.

2.17 Let us pursue the interaction of these control levels by envisioning how a writer might describe a simple event sequence. The writer observes a man leading a dog whose bright-colored collar attracts a child; in order not to be grabbed, the dog breaks its leash to escape. The man spanks the child. If we arrange this much content in a network of concepts and relations, we might obtain Figure 28. The three animate agents: man, dog, and child, appear as object nodes with their respective actions and attributes. I include some descriptive traits, e.g. 'old', 'ugly', 'small', for purposes of demonstration. The writer's task is to find a surface expression, that is, to find a sequential connectivity that captures the conceptual connectivity of the text world. This is a special instance of PROBLEM-SOLVING: mapping out points in problem space according to the already solved and connected points in a problem space on a different level (cf. VII.2.10).[5]

2.18 The easiest solution would be to chop up the network into individual events and parse each event onto a surface structure according to PREFERENCES. The agent of an action (or, for inanimate objects, the instrument) is then mapped onto the grammatical subject, the event/action onto the verb, and the affected entity onto the direct object (cf. Bever 1970).[6] To include the third control level, that of informativity, we stipulate that the agent or instrument be known, and the action or affected entity be new. This could result in the following text:[7]

---

[5]Burton's (1976) "semantic grammar" functions by using these two levels in close correlation; compare also the "cascading networks" (Woods & Brachman 1978b) depicted in III.4.14.

[6]This strategy does not apply to "ergative" languages, in which an "ergative" case for agency is differentiated from a "nominative" (Dressler, personal communication).

[7]For still greater banality (cf. I.1.16), we could start out with "kernel" sentences: 'I saw a man. The man was old. [etc. ad nauseam]'

(192.1) I saw an old man. (192.2) He was leading an ugly dog. (192.3) The dog was wearing a bright orange collar. (192.4) The collar attracted a small child. (192.5) The child grabbed at the dog. (192.6) The dog broke its leash. (192.7) The leash hurt the man's hand. (192.8) The hand spanked the child.

The surface text is perfectly clear and cohesive, and there are no obstacles to coherence and comprehension. The "process-type" actions (in terms of Halliday 1967a) are expressed with the continuous form ('be' + verb + 'ing'); the "uniplex" actions (in terms of Talmy 1978) are expressed via the simple forms (here, simple past). Notwithstanding, the text is objectionable. It is monstrously uninteresting to read, precisely because the continued use of preferences makes such a predictable and repetitious pattern. The mapping is not efficient because each underlying node has to appear so often in surface structure: 'dog' in four sentences, 'man' and 'child' in three each, and 'collar', 'leash', and 'hand' in two. To suggest how our network from Figure 28 has been divided up for the surface text, I partitioned the diagram of Figure 29 with dotted-line spaces for each sentence (small numbers are sentence numbers) (on network partitioning, see Hendrix 1975, 1978).[8] We can observe that REDUNDANCY is graphically visible as partition overlap. It might be a general definition that redundancy can be formalized as the overlap of systemic unity partitioning of an actualization network for the next deeper-level system.

2.19 The writer has good reason to be dissatisfied with this particular mapping. Let us consider how an alternative version can be generated which, being based on the same network, counts as a PARAPHRASE of the first (cf. III.3.11.10). This new version will adopt a more flexible standpoint regarding event boundaries and interestingness, and will cut down on redundancy. This procedure is not comparable to sentence transformations, though the latter are also of paraphrase character (II.1.11): transformations are done by an autonomous syntax in which interestingness or efficiency of communication play no distinct role.

2.20 Let us follow the production of the new version along and observe how decisions are made. The opening sentence is a strategic place to introduce the topic (cf. VII.3.9). Here, the topic is not so much the old man, as (192.1) would imply, but the events involving the dog being on a leash. It is therefore expedient to load this topic material onto the opening sentence, yielding:

(193.1) I saw an old man leading an ugly dog.

The predicate has been expanded with a participial modifier, so that the topic material is effectively located toward the end of the sentence. A gain in

---

[8]Each space encloses its nodes and link labels. The numbers of dots of enclosing lines match the sentence numbers of (192).

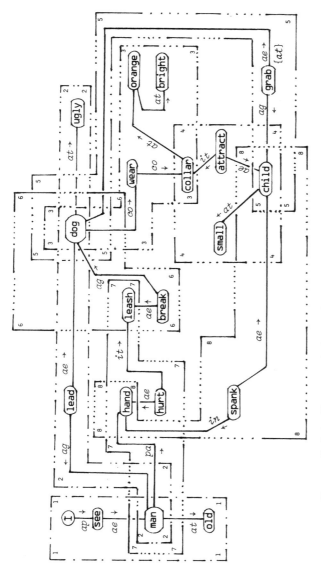

Figure 29

Key: *ae*: affected entity; *ag*: agent of; *at*: attribute of; *co*: containment of; *it*: instrument of; *pa*: part of

209

efficiency is also attained by reducing the number of sentences, and hence the number of focusable predicate slots; moreover, the single occurrence of 'man' in (193.1) supplants the redundant occurrences in (192.1–2) with no loss of clarity.

2.21 The next task is mapping out the events involving the collar. Because a collar is typically in "containment" of a dog, and a determinate "instrument-of" leading a dog, there is no motive to assert the collar's presence in a separate sentence such as (192.3): a predicate slot is wasted on content that is easily predicted. Instead, the predictable relation can be mapped onto a possessive modifier dependency and the predicate slot filled with the unpredictable event in which the collar figures as instrument:

(193.2) The dog's bright orange collar attracted a small child.

Again, this paraphrase saves resources by conserving a predicate slot and cutting out a second expression for 'collar' vis-à-vis (192.3–4).

2.22 The TURNING POINT of this little story (cf. VIII.2.7) is composed of the events of grabbing and leash-breaking, because these deflect the course of things most decisively. As I shall argue in Chapter VIII, the turning point of a story is usually accompanied by MOTIVATIONAL STATEMENTS that justify the central actions (cf. VIII.2.23ff.; VIII.2.32). We might want to state the relation between the 'grabbing' and the 'breaking' that is left implicit (192.5–6). A subordinative junctive preferentially indicative of purpose will do:

(193.3) In order not to be grabbed, the dog broke its leash and ran away.

The 'run away' action can be derived from the original text-world model via inferencing based on knowledge of purposes. This presentation helps to integrate the least predictable event into the reader's ongoing text-world model.

2.23 The final task is mapping out the conclusion. The 'hand' node is linked to one event as 'affected entity' and to another as 'instrument'. If we want to map out the node only once onto surface expression, we need a sentence format that has a passivizing and an activizing constituent. The passivizing construction is preferentially the passive voice, or the past participle. We could then have a choice between:

(193.4a) The man's hand was hurt by the sharp tug and spanked the child.
(193.4b) Hurt by the sharp tug, the man's hand spanked the child.

To decide between them, a writer should consider the knownness or inferrability of the underlying events. The stronger those factors are, the less likely one is to devote a separate subject-predicate construction to the surface expression of the event. Because breaking a leash is very likely to hurt the owner's hand, (193.4b) is the better selection. It has the added advantage of a surface symmetry with 'hand' located between the expressions of the two events in which it was involved, thus enacting the balance where one hurt is the reason for the inflicting of another.

2.24 Following the decision process along as shown, we arrive at this version:

> (193.1) I saw an old man leading an ugly dog. (193.2) The dog's bright orange collar attracted a small child. (193.3) In order not to be grabbed, the dog broke its leash and ran away. (193.4) Hurt by the sharp tug, the man's hand spanked the child.

Although still not great literature, (193) is better reading than (192). The redundancy of (192) has been dramatically cut down: 'dog' in three sentences, not four; 'man' and 'child' in two each, not three; and 'collar', 'leash', and 'hand' in one, not two (cf. VII.2.18). The savings allows the addition of some further material in (193), e.g. 'in order to' and 'ran away', yet the total word count is still less than (192): 43 versus 47. The new version is thus more READABLE then the old, conveying as much with fewer expressions, yet maintaining interest by motivated variety of structuring. The partitioning of the textual world into sentence-length spaces for (193) is illustrated in Figure 30. The lower redundancy appears as reduced overlap.

2.25 Strategic control upon decision and selection is crucial. The mere loading of more material onto more intricate sentence frameworks offer no certainty of producing a worthwhile text. Untrained writers, who want to break out of the monotony resulting from using the same mapping over and over, may fail to retain the necessary control. Consider the following expression of the same text-world model loaded onto a single sentence:

> (194) An old man I saw whose dog's leash, attached to a bright orange collar, attracting a small child who grabbed at the dog that broke its leash, hurt his hand, spanked the child.

The uncontrolled overloading of the sentence structure yields two participial dependencies and four relative clauses. This structuring is in principle allowable by rules of syntax proper. It cannot be the task of a grammar to state at what length or degree of complexity a sentence is no longer allowed for a language (I.3.4.5). Moreover, redundancy has been reduced still lower than in (193): 'dog' mapped only twice and 'man' only once. Still, the text is less readable than (192) or (193). All events except the 'spanking' are packed into modifiers and relatives as if they were already known to the reader. Distinctions between predictable and non-predictable events are flattened. The reader's attention is scattered all around with no cues as to what might be important. For example, the phrase 'the dog that broke its leash' suggests that a previously mentioned dog with this action should be in the reader's active storage.

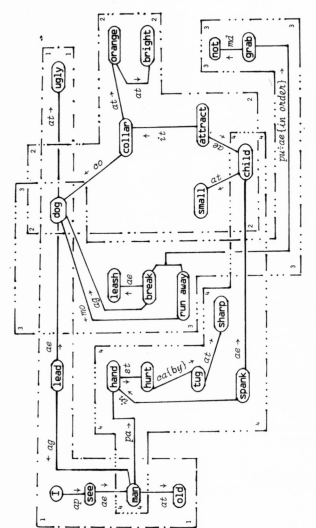

Key: *ae*: affected entity; *ag*: agent of; *at*: attribute of; *ca*: cause of; *co*: containment of; *in*: instrument of; *md*: modality of; *mo*: motion of; *pa*: part of; *pu*: purpose of

Figure 30

2.26 These samples illustrate how writers must correlate the strategies used on the three control levels depicted in VII.2.16. After noticing and developing the internal structure of the events, the writer has to utilize the sequencing operations of English in accordance with reasonable rates of informativity. The arrangement of expressions for knowedge depends decisively on what the reader is expected to know and to find interesting. The writer cannot fill in every detail, nor make every underlying relation explicit. The writing and revising process is terminated with a reasonable balance between what is said and what is known, between what is said and what can be supplied by spreading activation or inferencing, and between what is informative and what is dispensible.

2.27 To produce a text of enduring quality, substantially more extensive processing is demanded. Both the original search for knowledge and the subsequent mapping must be carried on with great circumspection. I shall attempt to follow the processes that might create the following Shakespearean sonnet (number 33) (discussed also in Beaugrande 1979e, 1979i):[9]

(195)
1   Full many a glorious morning have I seen
2   Flatter the mountain-tops with sovereign eye,
3   Kissing with golden face the meadows green,
4   Gilding pale streams with heavenly alchemy;
5   Anon permit the basest clouds to ride
6   With ugly rack on his celestial face,
7   And from the forlorn world his visage hide,
8   Stealing unseen to west with this disgrace:
9   Even so my sun one early morn did shine
10 With all-triumphant splendour on my brow;
11 But, out, alack! he was but one hour mine,
12 The region cloud hath masked him from me now.
13   Yet him for this my love no whit disdaineth;
14 Suns of the world may stain where heaven's sun staineth.

2.28 The writer's problem for this text is especially delicate: to present the poetic expression of a complaint to a particular addressee in such a way that reconciliation is not precluded. The PLANNING phase decides to characterize some of the addressee's actions negatively, yet without direct confrontation. The underlying macro-structure of events for this communicative situation is built along these lines: (1) addressee treats speaker as friend; (2) addressee changes to unfriendly treatment; (3) speaker enters a negative emotional state; and (4) speaker complains, the text itself being the instrument.

---

[9]Here, as in all other Shakespeare quotations in this volume, I follow the Kittredge edition (Shakespeare 1936).

2.29 The avoidance of confrontation can be navigated by strategies of role division and content selection. The SPEAKER of the text (here 'I') is kept distinct from the PRODUCER, and the ADDRESSEE (here 'he') from the audience of RECEIVERS. The outcome is that the personal message fades into the background—a common principle in literary and poetic communication. The content is selected via ANALOGY. The actual event sequence is displaced by a sequence from another topic domain and yet kept recoverable via strategic placement of cues.

2.30 The planning phase sets up a pathway toward the goal: create a linkage among entities of knowledge that will make the underlying event series discoverable via PATTERN-MATCHING. The IDEATION phase accordingly searches knowledge stores for a TOPIC IDEA that will be a CONTROL CENTER for a textual world entailing a contrast of positive and negative events. The topic idea is readily accessed from the UNIVERSE OF DISCOURSE (I.1.3) for Shakespeare's cultural setting: the workings of nature as the background of human activities. This general knowledge frame offers some obvious contrasts; for example, day versus night comes to mind, but is too unreconcilable and determinate, whereas an accidental contrast would be more relevant to the writer's plan. Accidental contrasts are available in the unstable domain of 'weather' (especially in England). If the TOPIC IDEA were 'change in the weather', the DEVELOPMENT phase can easily attach the contents of a 'weather'-frame, e.g. 'sun', 'sky', 'clouds', and so on, along with their attributes, locations, motions, etc. To suggest what a typical person's 'weather'-frame might look like, linked onto a 'landscape'-frame, I provide a network diagram in Figure 31. It seems safe to assume at least this much commonsense knowledge as well established.

2.31 As the development phase continues, the positive state called for by the plan can attach a favorable state of the weather; that state should also have an early time indicator to match the early stage of the personal relationship between speaker and addressee. It follows that the morning sunrise is a natural selection, allowing the plan-relevant attribute 'glorious'. We notice that the underlying element 'sun' in the 'weather'-frame is not explicitly attached yet, but introduced via a further analogy: a 'person'-frame. The "parts-of" a person that correspond to the sun include those sharing the same "form," such as 'eye' and 'face'. The 'person'-frame is exploited by the mention of humanlike actions: 'flatter', 'kiss', and 'gild'. The first two of these suggest the subclass 'friend', pointing back to the underlying macro-structure of events (cf. VII.2.28).

2.32 In this fashion, several commonsense frames are attached concurrently to build a text-world model. The opening stretch (lines 1–4) describes the morning light and its effects on some typical elements of the landscape. But the selection of expressions is so designed as to point the reader away from that domain toward 'actions of a friend'; otherwise, entries

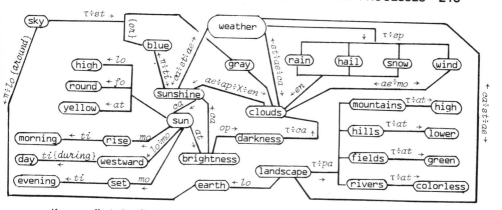

Key: *ae*: affected entity; *ap*: apperception of; *at*: attribute of; *ca*: cause of; *en*: enablement of;
ε entry; *fo*: form of; *lo*: location of; *mo*: motion of; *pa*: part of; *π*: proximity; *sp*: specification of;
st: state of; *ti*: time of, *τ*: typical; *χ*: exit

Figure 31

like 'flatter' and 'kiss', being incompatible with the 'weather'-frame, cannot be integrated into the textual world. The phase of conceptual-relational development (VII.2.11) has recovered some incidental knowledge from these frames, such as attributes, locations, and parts. The cognitive outcome of this multiple attachment is to force the reader to recognize the analogy required by the writer's plan: events of the weather versus events in a personal relationship.

2.33 This design process becomes a pattern to be repeated in the next set of four lines (5–8). The sunny morning is set in opposition to the 'clouds' which block out the light. The opposition spreads outward into the attributes and motions of clouds, rendering them uniformly negative: 'basest', 'ugly', 'forlorn', 'steal', 'disgrace'. A series of elements is presented, the integration of which requires the interface of the 'weather'-frame and the 'person'-frame: 'face', 'forlorn', 'visage', 'steal', 'disgrace'. The analogies for asserting that 'clouds' can 'ride on' and 'hide' the 'face' of the sun that moves 'to west' are derivable from the 'weather'-frame-based knowledge about locations and motions. The outcome is the complex structure of concepts and relations, many shared among frames, represented in Figure 32. The concepts of 'morning' and 'cloud' appear as topic nodes with the material from the first four and second four lines, respectively, being connected on. We see the further connectivity between the two knowledge spaces that result, including both equivalences and oppositions. The mastery of Shakespeare as a text designer is attested in the multiple justification he had for all of the selections and arrangements. He implements his global plan of complaining via a textual world with an inherent apperceptual power of its own. He presents high-informational occurrences as discrepancies and discontinuities between

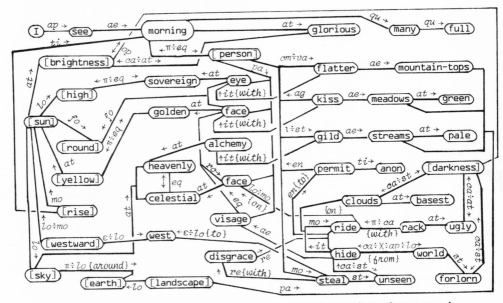

Key: *ae*: affected entity; *ag*: agent of; *ap*: apperception of; *at*: attribute of; *ca*: cause of;
co: communication of; *en*: enablement of; *ε*: entry; *eq*: equivalent to; *fo*: form of; *ι*: initiation;
it: instrument of; *lo*: location of; *mo*: motion of; *pa*: part of; *π*: proximity; *qu*: quantity of;
rc: recurrence of; *re*: reason of; *st*: state of

Figure 32

elements of frame-based knowledge; in downgrading the occurrences, the reader is irresistably impelled to recover the planned underlying message.

2.34 The mapping of the textual world onto surface expression must also conform to the formatting demands of the text type 'sonnet'. This requirement creates a special problem setting where cohesion must be managed such that a closely patterned arrangement is obtained: (1) syntactic arrangement; (2) line arrangement; (3) sound arrangement; and (4) lexical arrangement. Shakespeare's constitutive principle for all of these levels is above all EQUIVALENCE (cf. Jakobson & Jones 1970). In regard to syntax, six lines contain the configuration "preposition-modifier-head," the preposition being 'with' in all cases (2, 3, 4, 6, 8, 10) (in line 8, there is a determiner rather than a modifier). Three of those lines (3, 4, 8) also begin with a present participle expressing an action belonging to the 'person'-frame. The syntax also interacts with the line divisions. The first two groups of four lines, and the last three groups of two have a clear internal cohesion. The first eight lines form a single sentence; lines 9 and 10 form another sentence; 11 and 12 are a run-on sentence, easing perhaps the transition to the marked separation of sentences in 13 and 14. These divisions accord well with the flow of content: (1) positive early events (1–4); (2) negative events as a change

(4–8); (3) comparison of these events to the speaker's own experience (9–12); and (4) withdrawal of the complaint (13–14).

2.35 These divisions are characteristic of the 'sonnet' text type as employed by Shakespeare (the term 'Shakespearean sonnet' is still in use today). The couplet at the end is often opposed to the rest in content and format. Here, in effect, it deflects the whole impact of the statement so far; and it breaks the alternating rime patterns with consecutive rime. The internal organization is also reflected in the rhythm pattern. The first four lines have a syllable distribution of 12–10–10–11; the second have 10–10–10–10; the third group has 11–10–11–10; and the couplet is 11–12. The four-line groups are thus all distinctive, and the 12-syllable pattern of the first line returns in the last—just as the speaker hopes that the harmonious early stage of the personal relationship may return.

2.36 The careful interlocking of mapping options is, as we shall note, essential to the writer's plan. The lines (9–12) begin with the junctive 'even so' to signal that knowledge from the first eight lines should be kept active and re-applied. That signal is reinforced by lexical recurrences and equivalences: 'morn' (9) looking back to 'morning' (1), 'splendour' (10) to 'glorious' (1), 'but one hour' (11) to 'anon', 'region' (12) to 'heavenly' (4), 'cloud' (12) to 'clouds' (5), and 'masked' (11) to 'hide' (7). Such extensive correlation supports the transfer of knowledge from an already constructed model space to an ongoing one—an example of TEXT-INTERNAL INHERITANCE via pattern-matching (cf. IV.4.5: V.7.1). The intriguing aspect here is that the negative terms of lines (1–8) have no correlates in (9–12). The characterization of the addressee's actions regarding the speaker's situation in (9–12) is accomplished entirely by inheritance from (1–8). Moreover, the writer is careful not to personify the 'sun' in (9–12). As a result, the complaint is delivered with the greatest mediation and indirectness. Whatever negative comments are made about the addressee are filtered through an ennobling analogy in which the latter figures as nothing less than the 'sun'; the 'sun' is not at fault if 'clouds' intrude; and the message is even so arranged as to keep some surface distance between the 'sun' and those negative terms that do appear. To conclude, the final couplet withdraws the complaint as inappropriate to a being of such grandeur. The contrajunctive 'yet' in line (13) signals a surface reversal, but the trend of content organization has been conciliatory all along.

2.37 The total text-world model for the sonnet is diagrammed in Figure 33. I have drawn in the various recurrences, equivalences, or class inclusions that render the text-world model so uniquely motivated in its DESIGN (cf. I.4.14). The exceptional density of linkage holding so many entities in place is indicative of the extraordinarily skillful selection and decision processes of the writer. The surface text is so designed as to elicit spreading activation within several frames at once. The intersections, as such, are unforeseeable and hence interesting, and yet convincing by virtue of their dense

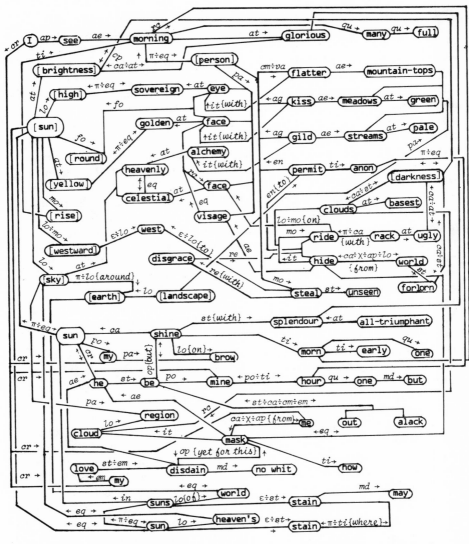

Key: *ae*: affected entity; *ag*: agent of; *ap*: apperception of; *at*: attribute of; *ca*: cause of;
cm: communication of; *cr*: co-referential with; *em*: emotion of; *en*: enablement of; *ε*: entry;
eq: equivalent to; *fo*: form of; *in*: instance of; *it*: instrument of; *lo*: location of; *md*: modality of;
mo: motion of; *pa*: part of; *po*: possession of; *π*: proximity; *qu*: quantity of; *rc*: recurrence of;
re: reason of; *st*: state of; *ti*: time of; *va*: value of; *χ*: exit

Figure 33

218

connectivity. The processing that recovers such a configuration underneath the already intensely structured surface expression is the foundation of AESTHETIC EXPERIENCE: discovering a multiplicity of functions among elements of the message (cf. VII.1.8.5), and overcoming problematic linkages by finding their motivations.

2.38 No one would deny the staggering difference between the Shakespeare sonnet and the 'ugly dog' story. But I would surmise that the production processes for both are analogous: a macro-structure of events is selected and developed according to content-internal standards and criteria of informativity; the result is mapped onto a surface structure under interactive controls. The effectivity of the results varies because of the differences in expenditure of processing resources. Louis T. Milic (1971) was led by such differences to postulate two phases of text production: (1) the selection of "stylistic options" needed to produce any surface structure at all; and (2) the making of "rhetorical choices" by evaluating and improving upon what has been generated. Milic concedes that these two phases cannot be separate in real time—a point I have stressed for my own model with four phases. But I wonder if Milic might be drawing a line along the inappropriate dimensions. A good share of Shakespeare's rhetorical power is antecedent to anything like the selection of stylistic options: it originates in his ideation and development phases, e.g. the interfacing of frames for 'weather' and 'person'. Milic's scheme appears to imply the notion I rejected in IV.1.17 that all metaphors have commonplace, literal equivalents.

2.39 My experiments regarding the production and reception of creative texts have been inconclusive so far, due to empirical obstacles of obtaining creative behavior under reliable conditions. In one set of tests run by Walter Kintsch and co-workers, subjects who recalled a Shakespeare solioquy did undertake to rephrase the content in everyday language. Those subjects who did not only recovered a few bits of the original. Until conclusive evidence to the contrary is obtained, I claim that creativity is an intensification of normal production processes rather than something altogether different. The question of whether all *content* can be accorded creative treatment remains in debate. Given sufficient motivation, one could wring a poem even out of the 'ugly-dog' story:

(196)
Not many a dotard gentleman I spy
Lead distasteful dog on lanky leash,
Drawing with collar orange a child nigh,
Breaking forth from its rapacious reach;
 With stinging hand the man requites the prank,
Belaboring the infant nether flank—
Even so did God His new-made beasts display
Before our childish fancy in parade;

But we who snatch and seize in wanton way
Must harrow hence the habitants He made.
Yet thus we deem ourselves creation's dears
And blight the earth till heaven interferes.

3.   RECALLING TEXTUAL CONTENT

3.1 Many years ago, Sir Frederick Bartlett (1932) obtained experimental evidence that recall is not merely a REPRODUCTION of what people experience, but also a RECONSTRUCTION.[9a] Since then, a series of experiments showing pervasively accurate recall (e.g. Gomulicki 1956; R. Johnson 1970; B. Meyer & McConkie 1973) apparently challenge Bartlett's viewpoint. However, these new results are no genuine refutation of Bartlett. Conventional psychological tests are routinely designed so that people have little motivation to integrate the content of texts into their store of useable knowledge, because the tests lack relevance to everyday life. Also, our educational system stresses rote memory work so heavily that, placed in a formal test situation, people may strain to the utmost in order to render every detail as exactly as possible. I shall explore some new data and suggest ways in which reproduction and reconstruction interact.

3.2 It is essential to bear in mind that a person's recall protocol is a text in its own right (Kintsch & van Dijk 1978a: 374). The production of the protocol, at least under natural conditions, ought to entail the developmental and selective processes I outlined in the foregoing section. The recently processed original would of course be an important source. But if people are building their own cognitive models of a textual world, their recall should naturally include material they supplied themselves by spreading activation, inferencing, and updating (cf. I.6.4). They should be especially prone to add material if their protocols would otherwise lack cohesion in expression or coherence in the textual world.

3.3 At first glance, VERBATIM recall ought to be straightforward beyond dispute. Output looks exactly like input, so that we feel comfortable about considering memory a mechanism of "trace abstraction" (Gomulicki 1956) like a tape recorder or photographic plate. And yet the possibility cannot be eliminated that seemingly verbatim recall could result from reconstructive processes (cf. VI.3.12; VII.3.16). Suppose someone understands a surface expression by recovering the appropriate concept. If that concept had only the original expression as a plausible name, recall would probably be verbatim. But we cannot conclude that the person abstracted a trace of the surface structure and simply reproduced it. From this consideration, it would

---

[9a]Royer (1977) sees three positions, with "construction" being more moderate use of the text user's own disposition. A possible means of reconciling these positions is discussed in Beaugrande (1980c).

follow that verbatim recall may be telling us more about the availability of alternative names for the concept in a particular text-world than about the general memory strategies of people at large (cf. VI.3.12).

3.4 To pursue the interactive roles of surface expression and text-world coherence in processing, I designed a reading experiment for the Computer Laboratory of Psychological Research of Walter Kintsch and co-workers at the University of Colorado. My test was one of varying text versions (cf. Bower 1976; Jones 1977; Thorndyke 1977), although the parameters of variation were, as far as I know, rather unusual. I created five alternative versions of the 'rocket' text cited in III.4.20 to be presented to separate groups of readers, mostly first-year college students venturesome enough to enroll in an elementary psychology course. No test subject saw more than one version. The five alternatives read as follows:[10]

(197) [INVERTED]

(1.1) Empty, it weighed five tons. (1.2) For fuel it carried eight tons of alcohol and liquid oxygen. (1.3) There it stood in a New Mexico desert: a great black and yellow V–2 rocket 46 feet long.

(2.1) Scientists and generals withdrew to some distance and crouched behind earth mounds. (2.2) Two red flares rose as a signal to fire the rocket. (2.3) Everything was ready.

(3.1) Trailing behind it sixty feet of yellow flame that soon came to look like a yellow star, the giant rocket rose slowly and then faster and faster amid a great roar and burst of flame. (3.2) Radar tracked it at 3,000 mph when it soon became too high to be seen.

(4.1) As the rocket returned at 2,400 mph and plunged into earth a few minutes after it was fired, the pilot of a watching plane saw it return to a point 40 miles from the starting point.

(198) [ORNAMENTAL]

(1.1) In a bleak New Mexico desert, a vast black and yellow rocket towered 46 feet into the sky. (1.2) In order to lift this five-ton colossus into space, eight tons of alcohol and liquid oxygen were stored in the fuel chambers.

(2.1) Scientists and generals scrambled for cover behind mounds of earth as the signal for launching blazed forth: two bright red flares. (2.2) Amid a deafening roar and a blinding burst of fire, the giant ascended with mounting speed. (2.3) Its trail of yellow flame became a distant star poised on the outer verge of human vision. (2.4) The eyes of radar alone could follow the traveler's flight at 3,000 mph.

(3.1) High above the earth, a pilot watched from an observation plane as the rocket retraced its path, slowing to 2,400 mph. (3.2) Only forty miles from the place of departure, the huge aircraft came to rest. (3.3) The giant was home again.

---

[10]Tests have revealed some weaknesses in the design of these samples. I have made improved versions and run them, including one in German for a group of German natives. The outcome is discussed in Beaugrande (1979d)

(199) [CONDENSED]

(1.1) With eight tons of alcohol and liquid oxygen as fuel to carry its five-ton frame, a 46-foot black and yellow rocket stood ready in a New Mexico desert. (1.2) Upon a signal of two red flares, scientists and generals withdrew to crouch behind earth mounds. (1.3) With a trail of yellow flame that soon resembled a star, the rocket ascended with increasing speed. (1.4) Radar clocked it at 3,000 mph after it had passed out of sight. (1.5) Within minutes an observation plane recorded the return at 2,400 mph and plunge to earth 40 miles from the launching site.

(200) [DISORGANIZED]

(1.1) It was in a desert in New Mexico where, forty-six feet of black and yellow, a great rocket stood. (1.2) Of its thirteen tons of total weight, five tons of empty weight were added to eight tons of fuel, this being alcohol and liquid oxygen.

(2.1) Behind mounds of earth scientists and generals, when everything was ready, withdrew, crouching. (2.2) To fire the rocket, two red flares were given as a signal.

(3.1) With behind it sixty feet of yellow flame, the giant rocket rose with a great roar and a burst of flame faster and faster after starting slowly. (3.2) Before it became too high to be seen, the flame soon looked like a yellow star would look. (3.3) But radar tracked it upward, speeding to 3,000 miles in an hour.

(4.1) A few minutes after it was fired, the pilot of a watching plane saw its return to be at a speed of 2,400 mph and plunge to earth 40 miles from the place where it all started. (4.2) What goes up must come down.

(201) [MISLEADING]

(1.1) In a New Mexico desert, a yellow and bleakly isolated rocket stood already waiting for take-off. (1.2) When empty, it had weighed five tons. (1.3) Now, when fuel, being alcohol and liquid oxygen, was added, it weighed thirteen tons. (1.4) Ready to fly as a wild blue wonder, it stood there motionless, waiting for the signal station to start the take-off.

(2.1) When everything was red as the station, two warning flares sent scientist and general alike to shelter areas provided at a distance pointed out by large signs.

(3.1) With a roar and a burst of flares, the giant rocked on its pad and then rose colored fire traced its flight into the sky's open space. (3.2) Behind it trails its yellow path that soon comes to look just lightly distinct from a star. (3.3) When it was too high to be a scene of human observation, it was tracked by the reader of radar screens. (3.4) Its speed was clocked as 3,000 mph.

(4.1) A few minutes after, it returned, observation planes clocking it at 2,400 miles. (4.2) The rocket, descent aimed toward the starting point, plunged down to the earth's surface 40 miles from the launching padded by landing gear.

3.5 Version (197) was produced by inverting stretches of text, so that the order of presentation was turned around. To create version (198), ornamental expressions were deployed, including apperceptually salient imagery and metaphors. The compacting of the original yielded version (199). Version (200) was brought forth by deliberate use of poor planning, such as we find in hasty rough drafts. Version (201) was designed to mislead readers in eliciting expectations that are overturned by bizarre occurrences.

3.6 Half of the subjects were taped reading aloud; the other half read silently. The texts were then removed, and subjects wrote down "everything they could remember in their own words." The total numbers of propositions in each version were calculated according to the usual Kintsch methods (cf. Kintsch 1974; A. Turner & Greene 1977), and the protocols were scored according to the amount of propositions recovered.[11] Kintsch and I both expected that the variations in the text would make important differences in ease of reading and recall. To our amazement, *quantitative* recall varied across all six versions only to a statistically insignificant extent! There was a rise up to 54% for version (198), and a drop to 41% for (200), but the original (35), and (197), (199), and (201) were all recalled with a ratio between 43% and 47%. This finding suggests the powerful role of prior storage and processing strategies in imposing cohesion and coherence, even when deliberate obstacles are presented. Procedural attachment was evidently able to offset the oddly arranged surface formats of (200) and (201), for example by attaching the 'flight'-schema I discussed in VI.3. There were, however, some intriguing *qualitative* differences in recall, which I shall review.

3.7 Because of the inversion of the opening paragraph, version (197) entails a postponement of announcing the topic (compare the original in III.4.20). The text opens with cataphoric pronouns ('it') for which the co-referent is not supplied until after a delay (cf. V.4.9). The effect was a strikingly different distribution of attention for this version than for the original. On version (197), 8 out of 10 readers correctly recalled both of the fuels, whereas only 3 out of 10 who saw the original did as much. The topic postponement apparently forced readers to utilize the opening stretch of material heavily in order to identify a subsuming frame or schema; subsequently, the material was better organized and more available for recall. Interestingly enough, a replication of the test by Richard Hersh and Roger Drury at the University of Florida found that a five-minute pause of non-

[11]This count follows a list of propositions formatted like (31) in III.3.4: close to the surface text (the text expressions are usually used as concept names). But there are problems of formatting expressions such as 'not particularly different from' (how many propositions?). My network format allows me to place only concepts with their own substance onto nodes, and to load all relational signals onto the links.

activity before the writing of protocols reduced this difference in availability down to slight dimensions.

3.8 According to the mechanics of the "von Restorff effect" (cf. IV.2.2), unusual items in a presentation draw attention to themselves, but in exchange, other items are learned less well (Posner & Rossman 1965; Waugh 1969). We found here that total recall for original and inverted versions was about the same. Whereas readers of the inverted one did well with fuels, they did badly with the colors ('black' and 'yellow'). Only 3 out of 10 recalled them, whereas 8 out of 10 readers of the original remembered—exactly turning around the proportions for fuels. We attribute this difference also to a noticeable favoring of initial and final text elements across all six versions (compare Garrod & Trabasso 1973). This finding calls to mind the superior learning of initial and final entries in word-list testing (Murdock 1962). But we have also to consider that the final entries of several versions (original, 197, and 199) are confirmations of the final schema nodes (cf. VI.3.7); and the ending of (200) is a well-chunked cliché.

3.9 The topic postponement in (197) elicited another noteworthy effect. The tendency to present topic material in the opening statement of texts (cf. van Dijk 1977a: 150) is violated. In creating their protocols, our subjects should regularly move the mention of 'rocket' into that position. On the no-pause tests, 3 out of 10 subjects preserved the beginning as 'Empty, it weighed five tons', and 5 said 'The rocket weighed five tons'. On the pause condition, not a single subject began with the pronoun version; 7 out of 18 opened with 'the rocket weighed [. . .]'. The rest of the subjects in both groups had different openings, but all subjects, other than the three using pronouns, opened their protocols with a mention of the topical 'rocket'.

3.10 We were fascinated to observe that our test subjects varied the style of their protocols according to the version each group happened to read. Version (198) demonstrated this phenomenon with special clarity. Half of our subjects toned the ornamental style down to commonplace expressions, such that the dramatic opening was recalled as 'a rocket waits for lift-off' or 'a 46ft. rocket was launched' (probable reliance on 'flight'-schema). The other half used stylistically marked expressions, even adding to those offered in the text: 'the giant colossus *spewed forth* a huge yellow flame'; 'the burst of *explosive* noise is deafening and the *explosive* fire is blinding as the rocket *zooms* away'. Whereas the first half prosaically remembered a 'radar transmitter' following the rocket 'in the atmosphere', the second spoke of 'the eyes of radar' directed toward a rocket 'on the verge of human sight'.

3.11 The condensed expression of version (199) also inspired imitation in protocols. The subjects expressed their recall in lengthy, complex sentences like this one: 'the rocket filled with tons of fuel and oxygen took off after two flares were shown and the scientists had hidden behind mounds of dirt.' One subject made his entire protocol a single unbroken sentence, splicing phrase and clause boundaries together with 'and' or with commas:

(202) With 8 tons of alcohol and liquid oxygen for the 5 ton rocket, the rocket is signaled by 2 red lights and the scientists and generals crouch down behind an earth mound, the rocket takes off with a trail of yellow light, and the radar clocked the rocket at 3,000 mph as soon as it got out of sight, and a plane clocked the rocket at 2,400 mph when it was returning back to earth, and it landed 4 miles from the launching site.

Nothing like this remarkable protocol was elicited by any other version. People are manifestly able to remember style even when they cannot reproduce the exact expressions they read. When the impression is strong enough, people even intensify stylistic tendencies. It is difficult to say what kind of "trace" style may impart—probably not like the notion in Gomulicki's (1956) "trace abstraction." There is evidently a storage for selectional controls similar to those applied when people are producing a given text type for a specific audience (cf. VII.1.4ff.).

3.12 Readers did surprisingly well understanding and remembering the poorly written version (200). It would seem plausible that lower readability would make reading slower and more difficult; but we did not even observe any slowness in reading aloud (for a discussion of that issue, see also Coke 1976). We attributed this lack of effect to the efficiency of schema attachment. For instance, the text suggests a number of misleading relations: that rockets begin with 'fuel' and 'add' on 'empty weight' (200.1.2); that the 'scientists and generals' were already 'behind earth mounds' when they 'withdrew' (200.2.1); that the 'flares' somehow 'fired the rocket' (200.2.2); that the rocket's 'faster' speed was reached before the 'slow' one (200.3.1); and that the 'radar' was 'speeding upward' rather than the rocket (200.3.3). In their protocols, subjects showed little confusion, rearranging things into a more reasonable coherence. The oddly inverted 'faster and faster after starting slowly' was put back in normal order by 4 out of 10 subjects. All the same, the bad style did interfere with the organization of expression in protocols, as we can see here:

(203) What goes up must come down. A rocket standing tall yellow and black took off. Which was part oxygen and part water, the fuel. 3,000 miles. Before it went out of sight, it looked like a yellow star should look. A big yellow flame. At the end it came falling back to earth. Scientists and soldiers huddled behind a barrier. Then crept out.

We see confusion about when to mention recalled items, especially in the displacement of the 'scientists and soldiers' to a later time. The high incidence of sentence fragments (4 out of 10 units), of which there are none in the original, indicates a disoriented control of text production as a side-effect of the original's poor style.

3.13 Subjects used various methods for dealing with the misleading version (201). Some noticed and recalled the discrepant expressions exactly, having apparently expended increased energy on them, e.g. 'radar reader', 'the giant rocked on its pad', and 'nearby shelters pointed out'. Others recalled instead more probable expressions than those in the text; 'launching, padded' (201.4.2), for example, elicited 'launching pad' in 8 of 10 protocols. 3 subjects reacted to the mysterious phrase 'when everything was red as the station, two warning flares [. . .]' (201.2.1) by moving 'red' in front of 'flares' where it had been in the original. One replaced 'red' with 'ready'. Other solutions included: 'everything was *red and ready* at the control tower'; and 'As the *instrument panel* became *as red as the rocket officials*'. These results testify to the importance of PROBLEM-SOLVING in composing a textual world in the face of discrepancies and discontinuities. Compromises were drawn between what had been presented and what made sense. We see some ambivalence between these two loyalties, as in 'red and ready'; similarly, the odd expression 'be a scene' (201.3.3) where 'be seen' could fit, caused one subject to write: 'the rocket could no longer be *sceen*'.

3.14 Badly or misleadingly organized surface structures should cause people to make errors, because their predictions do not match the text. These discrepancies between printed text and reading aloud are termed MISCUES by Kenneth S. Goodman (Goodman & Burke 1973; Allen & Watson [eds.] 1976). Goodman shows that miscues are normal in all kinds of reading and favor substitutions of visually similar material, just as speech errors favor acoustically similar replacement (Fromkin [ed.] 1973). Colorado tests with 'rocket' were taped to pursue the source of miscues. Some errors arose from simple botching of hard words and replacing rare expressions with more common ones (examples in Beaugrande 1979d). Others, however, clearly arose from people's intention to make their protocols cohesive and their text-worlds coherent.

3.14.1 Miscues due to COHESION concern sequential connectivity in areas such as surface fluency, definiteness, and co-reference. Taped versions showed how readers were planning ahead: 'the flame soon . . .' (200.3.2) was changed to 'the flame *was* soon'; '[. . .] flares. Amid a [. . .]' (198.2.1–2) to 'flares *aimed at*'; 'ascended with' (198.2.2) to 'ascended *into*'. Definiteness was signaled by the addition of articles: 'signal for launching' (198.2.1) became 'signal for *the* launching', with the schema being supportive of expectations; 'to earth' (199.1.5) became 'to *the* earth', where 'earth' is a unique entity (cf. V.3.3.4). Parallelism was introduced, evincing a tendency to re-use already apperceived structures (cf. IV.4.4): 'a great roar and burst' (35.3.1) was altered to 'a great roar and *a* burst', while 'rose as a signal' (197.2.2) was altered to 'rose as a signal *rose*' (with a shift from "purpose" to "proximity of time" for the junctive 'as').

3.14.2 Miscues due to COHERENCE occur when spreading activation of already processed concepts provides material interpolated at other points. After reading about a rocket 'fired' in the presence of 'generals', a reader said '*war*' for 'roar' (35.3.1). In the co-text 'a pilot watched from an observation plane as the rocket retraced its path, slowing' (198.3.1), the major relation is "apperception"; and one subject read '*showing*' for 'slowing'. Expectations were influential again when 'aircraft' (198.3.2) was read as '*air force*'. The 'flight'-schema was probably the culprit when readers said '*landing*' for 'launching' at the conclusion (199.1.5). A test series with a different sample brought one finding worth mentioning here. One version of a Whitman text contained the co-text 'from the hills the cannon were thinning them [the soldiers]'. No fewer than 7 out of 10 subjects read the passage as 'from the hills the *canyon*', the canyon being the place one arrives when going 'from hills', as our Colorado students well know. Another version with the co-text 'cannon from the hills', with 'cannon' being activated before 'hills', elicited no miscues at all.

3.14.3. Our subjects made many of the miscues designed into version (201). Thus, 'distance, pointed' was read as 'distant *point*', 'be a scene' as 'be *seen*', 'reader of radar' as just 'radar', 'launching, padded' as 'launching *pad*', and 'giant rocked' as 'giant *rocket*'. One young lady struggled valiantly but vainly with 'giant rocked', saying instead 'giant rocket' three times in succession in a state of some duress. She must have experienced a conflict of control between concept activation and local impulses of articulation.

3.15 These data suggest that surface sequencing has an important influence on text processing, even though quantitative recall was not severely affected. I now review the data concerning the interaction between a text world and the processing strategies based on prior knowledge of text receivers. I deal mostly with the data for the original (35) and the inversion (197) containing roughly the same expressions. The processes to be explored are:

3.15.1 CONCEPT RECOVERY, during which expressions make conceptual content active in working memory, can be documented when readers recall other expressions than the ones they actually encountered (cf. III.3.5).

3.15.2 SUPERCLASS INCLUSION is shown when readers recall more general class names than were used in the text (cf. III.3.22f.; Ausubel 1963).

3.15.3 INFERENCING is observable when readers undertake to bridge apparent DISCONTINUITIES (missing linkage) or GAPS (empty nodes) in the textual world which they set up in their minds (cf. I.6.9; III.4.29f).

3.15.4 SPREADING ACTIVATION is manifested when readers report additional material which they associated with the text-world materials in their minds (cf. I.6.4; III.3.24).

3.16 CONCEPT RECOVERY is evident in all protocols. I cited in VI.3.9ff. some examples of how the concepts in the 'flight'-schema were expressed quite differently in protocols than in the original. For example, our subjects did not usually say that the rocket 'rose'; instead, they used other expressions such as the following: 'went up', 'shot up', 'was launched', 'ascended', 'lifted off', 'took off', 'climbed', 'moved', 'soared skyward', 'took to the sky', 'fired', 'set off', 'was released', 'blasted off', and 'started out'. Some of these expressions include an "initiation" component, while others do not—perhaps because of the structure of the 'flight'-schema (VI.3.9). I could have paraphrased the text to deploy the more popular expressions, e.g. 'take off' (used by 29 out of 72 subjects). Yet we would be on shaky grounds in claiming that we were getting verbatim recall (cf. VII.3.3) We might simply be getting back a more probable concept name.

3.17 SUPERCLASS INCLUSION was at work where our subjects recalled 'plane' as 'aircraft' (cf. VI.3.4), and 'radar' as 'machine'. 'Scientists and generals' were subsumed under 'men' and 'the people that control the rocket'—in the latter case, the overly general 'people' is narrowed down again with the ascribed agency. The selection of superclasses influenced the recoverability of the subclasses and instances. A subject who mentioned 'something composed of two chemicals' went on to guess 'hydrogen' and 'oxygen', because 'alcohol' is less typical in schoolroom chemistry. A subject who mention 'propellants', on the other hand, remembered 'alcohol' but substituted 'gasoline' for 'oxygen'. Four subjects apparently leaning toward 'chemicals' recalled as a fuel 'nitrogen', which does not even burn.

3.18 INFERENCING as found in protocols confirms the bridges I postulated in III.4.29. The inference that 'scientists and generals' were present in order to observe the rocket was made so often that 24 subjects recalled it as part of the original. 17 subjects made the relation between 'ready' and the 'take-off' a part of their protocols. Inferencing filled not only these gaps in the presented version, but also gaps due to decay in storage. Having forgotten the 'scientists', a subject mentioned 'generals and soldiers', the latter being supplied as people for the generals to order around. Another subject who forgot the landing concluded that the 'rocket', being a subclass of 'spacecraft', went 'into orbit'.

3.19 Our subjects were evidently aware of GAPS, which they did not attempt to fill. Instead, they created placeholders: '*somewhere* in New Mexico'; 'alcohol and *something else*'; '*something* composed of two chemicals'; 'generals and *others*'; and 'scientists and *something else* were behind earth dunes'. There are two plausible accounts for this phenomenon. Either there is some psychological reality to the notion of "model space," such that people walking through mental storage could notice indistinct or empty areas. Or else people retain some traces of input, but not enough to recover entire elements.

3.20 Although the two processes doubtless interact, it is useful to distinguish between SPREADING ACTIVATION and INFERENCING. Spreading activation is based on ASSOCIATION and results naturally from concept activation in ideation or comprehension without specially directed impulses. Inferencing is based on express PROBLEM-SOLVING and is directed to overcoming discontinuities and gaps. Spreading activation runs via the organization of prior knowledge in episodic and conceptual memory (cf. III.3.16); inferencing runs via the particular organization of the textual world at hand. When sufficient empirical results are available, I expect to represent spreading activation in the WORLD-KNOWLEDGE CORRE-LATE, and inferencing in the TEXT-WORLD MODEL. These differences suggest that we might make a consistent distinction in the processes of knowledge management and recovery. UPDATING (I.6.4) and INHERI-TANCE (III.3.19) during comprehension, and RECONSTRUCTION and REPRODUCTION during recall (VII.3.1), could each have an associative function running on spreading activation and a problem-solving function running on inferencing. So far, it has been difficult to get an empirical handle on questions such as: (1) how much material is added right away during comprehension, and how much is added later for recall; and (2) what language users consider as a discontinuity or gap. I shall review the changes our test subjects made according to LINK TYPES, rather than according to the processes responsible.

3.21 LOCATION was by far the most popular addition, probably because it is so crucial to the understanding of 'flight'. The opening scene was described with new details. The 'desert' became 'desert *plains*', where launching 'took place *under a bright sun*'. Reasoning that rockets are shot off far from population centers, subjects recalled events '*in the middle of* a desert' where the rocket 'lay *alone*', or even '*far out* on a *Moroccan* desert'. The rocket's attribute of 'great' led people to remember how the 'rocket *towered over* the many scientists and technicians *below*'. The expected flight was no doubt responsible for mentioning the rocket 'on a *launch pad pointing toward the sky*'. When time came for take-off, one subject wrote: 'the rocket blasted *off, up,* and *away from the launch pad*'. Later events were described like this: '*at its peak* it reversed and plummeted *downward on its journey back to earth*'.

3.22 Locational proximity is, of course, useful for continuity. Subjects recalled the opening scene with the scientists and generals '*gathered all around* the rocket'; and 'land mounds were *surrounding* the lift-off'. Proximity served to compensate for changes. The readers who converted the 'mounds' into a 'mountain' had to fit the larger item in somewhere: 'a rocket is *in front of a mountain* in *Arizona*'; or 'a rocket is *in front of a mountain* where the people that control it are' (with a new function supplied). The pilot was introduced in a '*nearby* plane' or '*aboard* an airplane'. One subject who ended his protocol with the rocket '*hovering over*' used proximity to compensate for having forgotten the landing.

3.23 TIME was the next most frequent type of addition, in accordance with the importance of time in a 'flight'-schema. Because time is a steady flow during 'flight', the addition of proximities is natural. For instance, the content of the second paragraph was drawn together in that fashion. The events took place '*when the time came* for the rocket to be launched'; and 'scientists crouched behind mounds *as* the rocket was launched'. Later, '*while* it was ascending, radar tracked' the rocket. The missile was seen from a 'plane flying *at the same time* the rocket was'. On the other hand, the time expressions in the original ('soon', 'in a few seconds', 'a few minutes after') were among the expressions reproduced least frequently by our subjects. People seem to create their own time cues as needed for organizing textual worlds.

3.24 CAUSE and ENABLEMENT were contributed occasionally. Some readers sensed a discrepancy between the rocket's great distance and its continued visibility, and they inferred: 'being very big in size, the rocket could be seen by the naked eye for quite a distance'; 'the bright yellow flame could be seen from very far, a pilot in a plane was even able to see it'. Other readers inferred the final fate of the rocket: 'a *huge explosion* followed the rocket's impact'; 'going approximately 2,400 mph, it *must have made quite a recess in the earth's crust*'.

3.25 The frequency with which APPERCEPTION was contributed may be due to the emphasis on that relation in the original, or else to readers' reliance on mental imagery (cf. Paivio 1971). The latter source indicates the need to explore compatible modes for language and vision (see III.3.18). One subject introduced a new instrument for observing the rocket and still felt that visibility must fail eventually: 'we can *see* it by *satellite,* but it speeds up and we *lose track* of it'. Another subject was especially insistent on continuity of apperception:

(204) They *watched* the take off and *paid attention* to the flames that followed the rocket until they could not be *seen* anymore and then they *looked into* a radar *detector* to *find* the distance of the rocket. A pilot in a plane *watched* the rocket, he *saw* it go up and return down to earth.

3.26 AGENCY is not too important for the 'flight'-schema, because propulsion and gravity do most of the work. However, some readers thought that the 'scientists and generals' at the site ought to be doing more than just 'lurking behind mounds' (as one subject put it). Four readers recalled them as agents of setting off the flares, and three others had them actually fire the rocket. The preferential treatment was via apperception: 24 subjects had their scientists observing the rocket (cf. III.4.29)—a typical activity for scientists (III.4.36).

3.27 ATTRIBUTES were filled in when motivation arose. To explain visibility, the rocket's 'trail' was made 'huge' and the 'star' it resembled 'bright'. On the other hand, four readers supposed that, because of the distance, the star should be 'tiny'. Three made the pilot's plane 'small', perhaps to contrast better with the 'great' rocket.

3.28 We obtained a scattering of further link types. MOTION was transferred to the 'star' which the rocket 'looked like': 'a star *rising* in the sky' and a '*shooting* star'. PURPOSE was assigned to the whole text-world: 'an *experiment* had taken place'. SUBSTANCES were envisioned for the rocket's trail which figured as 'a tail of *burnt gases*', 'a stream of *exhaust*', and a yellow stream of fire which turned into *smoke*' (note the similarity of these inferences to some content in the world-knowledge correlate in III.4.36). PARTS were added when a subject remembered 'a flame from the *rear* of the *last stage* of the rocket'. COMMUNICATION was assigned to the 'pilot' who '*reported*' the rocket's return (four protocols).

3.29 This evidence confirms the postulate that meaning can be viewed as a process (cf. III.3). However diverse individual concepts and expressions may be in themselves, there appears to be a limited set of strategies for putting them together in texts and textual worlds. These strategies apply both to the immediate needs of cohesion and coherence in reception (e.g. reading) and production (e.g. protocol-writing) of texts, and to the organization of knowledge in the mind. Decay can thus be offset, though the results will lead to modification of the original material; decay appears to proceed even in such a short time space as the five-minute pause we used in our testing. I now propose six theses about the interaction of text-presented knowledge with prior stored knowledge. Although I arrived at these theses independently they bear striking resemblances to the notions of David Ausubel (1960, 1963; Ausubel & Fitzgerald 1962) working in the tradition of Bartlett (1932).

3.29.1 *Text-presented elements are privileged in storage and recall if they match stored world-knowledge patterns.* Following the widely publicized space program, it is not surprising that our readers made sense out of the rocket text, even on the badly expressed versions. News coverage favored the scientific over the military aspect for political motives; and our readers remembered the scientists in 42 out of 72 cases, but the generals in only 14. 10 of those 14 were on the no-pause condition, suggesting that the 'military'-frame withstood decay less well than the 'science'-frame. Because rockets are known to be powered by combustion, the recall of 'flame' by 48 subjects was not surprising. 32 remembered the presence of 'fuel'. The 'yellow' color of the flame was mentioned by 30. The location of 'desert' is natural enough because an abandoned area is needed, and was indeed recalled by 36 subjects. The use of radar was retained by 26. These figures are quite substantial for free recall without pressure to perform, and would have been much higher for cued recall or recognition tests. In contrast, readers are much less likely to know about sunspots than rockets, and the recall protocols for the much shorter 'sunspot' text—presumably a smaller memory load in itself—show much poorer retention of events and causes (cf. VI.2).

3.29.2 *Text-presented elements are privileged if they are attachable to major nodes and links of a global stored knowledge pattern, such as a frame or schema.* I reviewed the evidence for the 'flight'-schema in VI.3, and cited the fact that schema-related elements were recalled with the highest absolute frequency. I looked at the influence of frames on the understanding and remembering of the 'sunspot' text in VI.2, where 'magnetic field' was most often taken as the subsuming pattern. I explored the support that knowledge about plans provides for deciding what to say and for understanding actions and utterances of a stage play in VI.4. I shall further investigate the use of schemas for stories in VIII.2.

3.29.3 *Text-presented elements are altered to produce a better match with world-knowledge.* At first glance, the 'rocket' text contains little disturbing material. Yet the "chunking" together of knowledge might lead to improving linkages still further. One subject converted the colors 'black and yellow' to '*silver*', the color of metal. The location 'desert' impelled people to transform the 'earth mounds' into '*sand dunes*' and '*rock formations*'. Evidently reflecting on the "purpose" of these mounds to shelter scientists, one reader made them into '*concrete bunkers*'. The comparison of the 'rocket' to a 'star' was also smoothed over by making the star into a '*glow*', a '*blur*', and a '*dot*'. Particularly striking was the compensation of a reader who must have seen V–2 rockets only in World War II stories; he recalled the 'launching of a *captured German* V–2 rocket'. Alterations were also required when readers had rearranged other portions of the textual world. A reader who had recalled the rocket's trail as 'red' by conflation with the 'flares' had to say later: '*red streaks* in back of the rocket at the beginning *turned yellow*'. After stepping up the length of the rocket from 46 to *1,000* feet, a subject depicted a '*massive*' rocket that '*erupted*' like a volcano with its trail becoming a '*brilliant display* of fire'. By inferring that the rocket passed out of sight because of speed, not distance, another subject had to match things up again: 'it is *only* going 3,000 mph, but it *speeds up* and we lose track of it and it comes back at *20,000*'. These text-internal rematchings are indicative of the cybernetic regulation outlined in I.4.5.4.

3.29.4 *Text-presented elements become conflated or confused because they are closely related in world-knowledge.* Readers occasionally expressed concepts that combined the content of those in the original. 'Withdraw' plus 'crouch' added up to '*hide*'; 'roar' and 'burst' to '*explosion*'; and 'return' and 'plunge' to '*descend back*', '*turn back down*', and '*come crashing back down*'. The 'flares' were conflated with the rocket's 'flame': 'the rocket went off in a burst of flares'; 'when the rocket was launched it *looked like a red flare*'; 'the rocket was followed by a long fiery *flare*'. Two subjects moved the 'red' color from the flares to the rocket's (yellow) trail, and one compromised upon *'orange'*. The star suffered a like fate to the flares when a subject declared: 'as the rocket leaves it trails bright yellow *and red* flames like a burst of *stars'*.

3.29.5 *Text-presented elements decay and become unrecoverable if they are neutral or accidental in world-knowledge.* The prime illustration here was the treatment our subjects gave to quantities.[12] They reversed the respective weights of frame versus fuel, or calculated 5 and 8 tons as 5,000 and 8,000 pounds. The rocket's length telescoped from 26 to 1,000 feet, and its speeds ranged from 300 feet per minute (a mere 3.13 mph) to 300,000 mph. The distance between take-off and landing accordioned between 60 feet and 164 miles. Speeds were converted to altitudes, e.g. '2,400 *feet in the air'*. A quantity with no use was supplied: 'there was *something* about '2,400'. Many subjects hedged their recall with *'about'* or *'approximately'*, or claimed that radar merely *'estimated'* the speed. Others contented themselves with *'very fast'*, 'a *certain* speed', and *'lots of* fuel'. The rocket's colors went by the same route. About one half of the subjects recalled no colors. One fourth recalled both 'black and yellow', and the rest vacillated between these two and *'red'* *'green'*, *'white'*, *'silver'*, and *'blue'*.

3.29.6 *Text-presented entries become indistinguishable from inferences and spreading activations on the text receiver's part.* I have already surveyed considerable evidence here in VII.3, and further evidence is given in VI.2, VI.3, and VIII.2 (cf. also Beaugrande 1979d; Beaugrande & Miller 1979). The longer the times are which elapse between text reception and the producing of a protocol, the harder it should become to uphold such a distinction, unless the receiver assigns special importance to it. Harry Kay (1955) noted a striking effect in this regard. His subjects not only made important changes upon the material they read; the renewed presentation of the text was not employed to return toward the original! Instead, the subjects kept their own versions time after time, consistently preferring the latter to the version in the text itself.

3.30 These six postulates are not without some correlates in conventional psychology, even though the work of Bartlett, Ausubel, and their followers was often ignored. The privileged status of entries which match stored patterns agrees with the finding that prior frameworks aid retention on associative learning tasks (cf. Jenkins & Russell 1952; Bousfield 1953; G. Mandler & Pearlstone 1966; Bugelski, Kidd, & Segman 1968). Alteration for the sake of a better match has been observed in tests where people changed anomalous sentences to make better sense (Herriot 1969; Fillenbaum 1971, 1974; Strohner & Nelson 1974). Conflation of associated elements agrees with the interference of similar "stimuli" (Gibson 1942; Anisfeld & Knapp 1968;

---

[12]Possible implications of the treatment of numerical vs. measurement expressions were noted in III.4.7.26.

Underwood & Freund 1968). The loss of distinctions between presented and inferred elements was impressively documented by Bransford, Barclay,and Franks (1972) and Johnson, Bransford, and Solomon (1973). Bransford's work is already beyond the mainstream of these established traditions, looking instead to the approach of psychologists like Bartlett and Ausubel who admitted the factor of world knowledge. The labor expended to *circumvent* world knowledge would have been more wisely invested in seeking to *systemize* world knowledge—at least commonsense knowledge (cf. III.4.39). Perhaps the study of texts instead of nonsense syllables and word lists may be vital in exploring this admittedly vast domain.

3.31 One promising direction I am pursuing is to observe how cognitive processing creates the individual text-world models of particular readers through the interactions of text knowledge and world knowledge. I design these models and then compare and contrast them with the model for the original text. Eventually, this proceeding may provide a dynamic notion of "text meaning" as *the core operations of content processing performed by a representative group of text receivers.* In that case, the vital importance of INTERTEXTUALITY (cf. I.4.11.6) for defining textuality would be established. After designing a large number of protocol models, I am convinced that the strategies used by text receivers can be systemized along the lines I have undertaken to sketch out in this section. A graphic representation for the coherence of whole texts can show regularities of STORING and FORGETTING, which might not be visible via other means. I shall briefly portray this approach as applied to our 'rocket' sample.

3.32 The following protocol was written by a subject who read the original version on the no-pause condition:

(205) In a New Mexico desert, a V–2 rocket waited to be launched: it was 60 feet tall and weighed 5 tons empty. The generals and technicians stepped back behind dirt mounds and launched two red flares signaling the launch of the rocket.

The rocket sped upward at increasing velocity, leaving a 60 ft. exhaust flame behind it. It reached a velocity of 3,000 mph on the way up and later an airplane pilot clocked it at 2,400 mph on the way down.

This subject divided his attention between the preparations for launching and the actual flight. His first paragraph subsumes what had remained of the first two original paragraphs, and his second the surviving content of the original third and fourth. The suppression of paragraph transitions has noticeable effects: '*the* generals' suggests that their identity should be clear from the situation; and the junctive 'and' before 'later an airplane pilot' downplays any discontinuity between the 'way up' and the 'way down'. I show this compacted text-world model for (205) in Figure 34. I adopt the following conventions: as

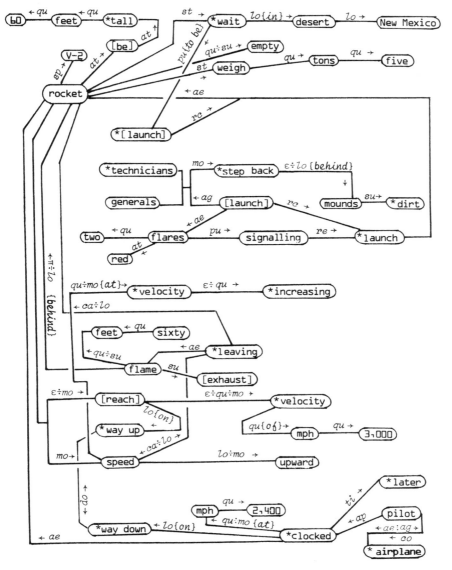

Key: *ae*: affected entity; *ag*: agent of; *ap*: apperception of; *at*: attribute of; *ca*: cause of; *co*: containment of; *ε*: entry; *lo*: location of; *mo*: motion of; *π*: proximity; *pu*: purpose of; *qu*: quantity of; *re*: reason of; *sp*: specification of; *st*: state of; *su*: substance of; *ti*: time of; *χ*: exit

Figure 34

235

far as possible, reproduced materials appear in positions corresponding to those in the original text world model; *identical expressions* appear as they are; *alternative expressions* for the same concepts are marked with '*', and *placeholders* or *hedges* with '§'; and concepts added by inferencing and/or spreading activation are in square brackets (cf. III.4.29).

3.33 As a result of compacting, the representation of schema elements is simplified over the original. The 'take-off' event is represented by 'launch' and 'sped upward', the former being in the old position of 'fire' and the latter moved up from a later mention in regard to speed (cf. 35.3.5). This displacement creates a need for a signal of the 'ascend' event which is provided with 'on the way up' to accompany the specification of 'velocity'. That same expression was simply varied to take care of 'descend': 'on the way down', preserving the balance of the 'flight'-schema (VI.3.3) in miniature. The subject's focus on 'velocity' throughout the second model space drew attention away from the 'land' event that is hardly definable in terms of speed. The subject probably knew that the rocket landed, but focus was directed elsewhere.

3.34 The modifications and additions performed by this test subject agree with my remarks so far, e.g. that the 'rocket *waited to be launched*' (having the opening state look forward to the first schema event, cf. VI.3.13). '*Exhaust*' was supplied as a "substance-of" of the flame (cf. VII.3.28). To offset decay and change, PROBLEM-SOLVING techniques were evidently used to create new linkage among surviving material. After 'crouch' was lost, '*stepped back*' (synonym of 'withdraw') was linked directly to 'dirt mounds' (rather than to 'some distance'). The agents 'technicians and generals' were linked to a new action of '*launching*' the 'flares', so that their presence is motivated (cf. VII.3.26). The general tendency was to lose *whole spaces* of the text-world model rather than *random isolated nodes*. For instance, the knowledge of fuels, the noises at the take-off, the use of radar, the resemblance of the rocket to a star, the landing—all of these spaces disappeared. It seems reasonable to suppose that if a CONTROL CENTER is removed, whatever is hanging on it will be hard to recover or integrate. Of course, this tendency reflects not a rule, but at most a proclivity.

3.35 We can contrast (205) with a rendering that shows somewhat different results, also from the no-pause condition:

(206) A big black and yellow rocket, 46 feet long and 200 tons, was in the Arizona desert.

Everyone was waiting for this missile to be fired into the sky. Everything was ready.

All of a sudden it fired into the sky. As the general and others watched, they saw the rocket and a long trail of flame following it into the sky, until they could not see it any more.

Radar picked it up and estimated its speed at 3,000 miles.

> A plane down below saw the rocket coming back down to earth
> in a ball of flame at approximately 2,400 mph, and then crash right
> into the earth.

This subject arranged the material into shorter paragraphs than those in (205). Evidently noticing a loss of material, she filled out her textual world by copying repeatedly off the same concepts and concept configurations. We have here a special use of CONTROL CENTERS to produce REDUN-DANCY rather than ASSOCIATIONS.[13] 'Everything was ready' was expressed redundantly as *'everyone was waiting'*—notice again the inference linking up to the 'firing'. The location *'into the sky'* was mapped three times onto the surface text. The observation by the 'generals', also mentioned three times, incorporated the inference that they were the ones who lost sight of the rocket at a certain height (cf. III.4.33). The 'tracked' of the original radar was subdivided into *'picked up'* (with initiation) and *'estimated'* (with proximity).

3.36 Decay made a number of inferences necessary to keep things connected. Due to the loss of knowledge about preparations for take-off (flares, shelter), the subject reasoned that the rocket must have taken off *'all of a sudden'*. Having forgotten the 'scientists' (though 'others' shows awareness of the gap) and retained one 'general', the subject chose the superclass 'missile' as suitable for military purposes. The subject transferred her own uncertainty about speeds into the text-world via *'approximately'* and *'estimated'* (cf. VII.3.29.5). The 'plane' was inferred to be *'down below'* the rocket, and the landing was envisioned as a *'crash'*. The 'trail of flame' encouraged the wrong inference that the rocket would 'come back down *in a ball of fire'* (more likely, the fuel would have been exhausted). The model for this textual world is presented in Figure 35.

3.37 The representation of SCHEMA elements also indicates the interaction of text knowledge and world knowledge. The concept 'fire' was transferred from the original context of the flare signal to the representation of the 'take-off' event. The 'ascend' event appears to have been satisfactorily covered by the three uses of *'into the sky'*. The 'descend' event was expressed as *'come back down'*, which captures both the 'return' and the 'plunge' in the original. Having stepped up the rocket's weight from 5 to 200 tons, the subject readily concluded with a *'crash'* landing of added impact.

3.38 Figure 36 shows the text-world for a recall protocol with the five-minute pause. The state of decay is more advanced than in the samples we have seen so far, but coherence is nonetheless maintained with similar strategies. The text reads as follows:

(207) Far out on a Moroccan desert, a V–2 rocket was prepared for its blast-off. It was 26 feet long and was silver in color. Once the

---

[13] I draw these redundancies as links of equivalence or recurrence in Figure 35.

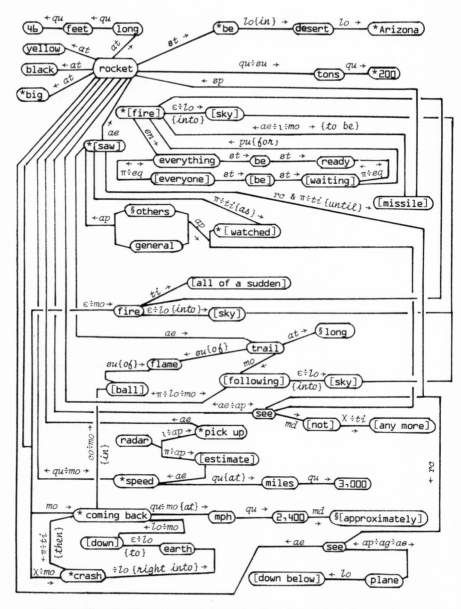

Key: *ae*: affected entity; *ag*: agent of; *ap*: apperception of; *at*: attribute of; *co*: containment of; *ε*: entry; *eq*: equivalent to; *ɩ*: initiation of; *lo*: location of; *md*: modality of; *mo*: motion of; *π*: proximity; *pu*: purpose of; *qu*: quantity of; *st*: state of; *su*: substance of; †: termination; *ti*: time of; *χ* exit

Figure 35

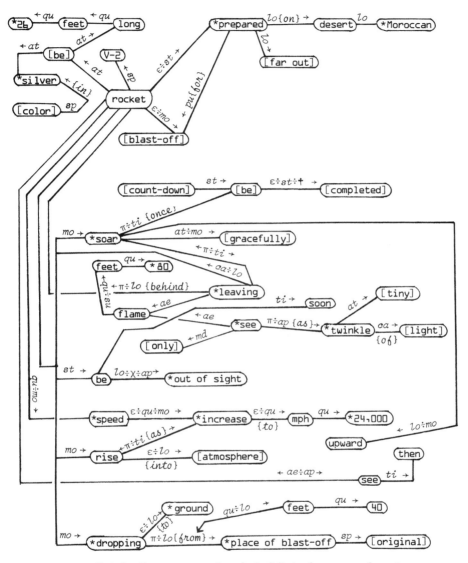

Key: *ae*: affected entity; *ap*: apperception of; *at*: attribute of; *ca*: cause of; ε entry;
lo: location of; *mo*: motion of; *pu*: purpose of; π: proximity; *qu*: quantity of; *sp*: specification of;
su: substance of; *ti*: time of; χ: exit

Figure 36

239

count-down was completed, the rocket gracefully soared upward, leaving an 80 ft. flame behind. Soon the rocket was out of sight, and the flame was only seen as a tiny twinkle of light. The speed increased to 24,000 mph as it rose into the atmosphere. Then it was seen dropping to the ground 40 feet from its original place of blast-off.

3.39 The schema events are all represented. Having lost the knowledge spaces involving the personnel and the flares—the rocket being *'prepared for its blast-off'* may have made them superfluous—the subject filled in his prior knowledge that a *'count-down'* would be *'completed'*. The 'take-off' and 'ascend' concepts are subsumed in *'soared'*, analogous to the 'rose' of the original. Indeed, the expression 'rose' was itself still available, and was deployed to introduce a further stage of flight *'into the atmosphere'*, so that the displaced original verb 'sped' became the noun *'speed'*. The inferred *'increase'* of the speed may have been due to the intensity indicated by *'soared'* or to the further inference that, on entering the *'atmosphere'*, the rocket would have to overcome the gravitational pull of the earth. The 'descend' and 'land' events are expressed via 'dropping to the ground'. The final *'place of blast-off'* follows the original, and harks back to the expression introduced by inferencing into the opening sentence.

3.40 The treatment of non-schema-based entries relied on inferencing. A metal rocket could be *'silver'*, and a 'desert' is known to exist in *'Morocco'* doubtless deemed a remote, unpopulated area (cf, VII.3.21). The attribute *'gracefully'* is suggested by *'soared'*, and the *'twinkle'* of light ('twinkle' probably being spreading activation from 'star') should be *'tiny'* at a great distance. The specification of *'atmosphere'* as the highest location of the flight could be attributable to prior knowledge about space exploration.

3.41 By viewing these three protocols as textual systems, rather than as only sequences of sentences or propositions, we can notice some aspects of quasi-cybernetic controls on knowledge utilization. The decay of system components leads to regulative compacting and inferencing. If the compacted or inferred elements are not fully compatible to their environents, compensations are made along the lines of problem solving: finding pathways to connect points in spaces. Schema-related materials survive with the greatest endurance. Decay favors accidental elements, and tends to suppress whole spaces rather than leaving space fragments floating unattached.

3.42 Hierarchical trees for text worlds (e.g. Bower 1976; Mandler & Johnson 1977; Meyer 1977) suggest that only unimportant details ought to be lost. But we have seen here that important elements are also subject to various kinds of modification. We can illustrate the difference between human processing and ideal hierarchical processing by contrasting (205) through (207) with the summaries generated by a computer from the same text. Robert F. Simmons designed a LISP representation of the content in Horn clauses of successor arithmetic using a generalized production system interpreter (cf. Simmons & Correira 1978). The program and its summary protocols are given in the appendix at the end of the book.

3.43 What I have been able to offer here is no more than a modest beginning toward a psychological theory of text processing. Because I am still in the first stages of exploration, I cannot claim to make statistical predictions capable of verification or falsification. Instead, I am searching for plausible accounts after the fact. Perhaps this approach has the advantage of not being committed a priori to ignoring certain issues that a ready-made theory might find unaccountable. In closing, I must stress that what I take to be indeed the central issues must be pursued through interdisciplinary co-operation of the sciences. The hopes of finding a small, powerful, and unified set of processing strategies lies in the readily observable fact that people do use and retain textual meaning in all kinds of communicative activities.

VIII
Conversation and Narration

1. CONVERSATION

1.1 According to Peter Hartmann (1970: 91), every text essentially functions as a contribution to a dialogue (see also Coulthard 1977: 100). For various text types, the dialogue between producer and receiver is carried out with a greater or lesser MEDIATION in regard to SITUATIONALITY (I.4.11.5; cf. Beaugrande & Dressler 1970: Ch. VIII). In conversation, mediation is not extensive, due to mutual awareness of participants, usually (except via telephone or the like) supported by physical presence. The immediacy of the communicative situation leads to heavy reliance on INTERTEXTUALITY (I.4.11.6; Beaugrande & Dressler 1978: Ch. IX), the principle whereby the textuality of any one text arises from interaction with other texts. What is cohesive, coherent, and acceptable in conversation may be quite different from what meets those standards in other modes of communication.

1.2 In VI.4.2 I noted the dual status of texts in discourse as both *action* and *meta-action,* i.e. verbal monitoring of actions and situations. These two outlooks can lead to different research methods for the study of conversation:

1.2.1 The action-oriented perspective began with the behaviorist definition of conversation as a pairing of stimulus and response (Ruesch 1957: 189). This narrow approach was replaced by the investigation of TURN-TAKING, in which a discourse action and reaction are seen as constituents of a "speech exchange system" (Sacks, Schegloff, & Jefferson 1974: 696). Here, sociologists have undertaken to define the ways people select or delegate speaking turns in a conversation. Most recently, conversational actions have been probed from the standpoint of how people plan to attain goals

242

(Winograd 1977a; Allen & Perrault 1978; Cohen 1978; McCalla 1978a, 1978b; Allen 1979; cf. VI.4).

1.2.2 The meta-action-oriented perspective is obliged to deal with content and topic, issues pursued at first with hesitation (Sacks 1968, cited in Coulthard 1977: 75) in absence of general methods to deal with meaning. Little can be gained by the common linguistic procedure of assigning structural descriptions to abstract sentences. However, advances have been forthcoming from disciplines besides linguistics: sociology (Sacks, Schlegloff), discourse analysis (Sinclair, Coulthard),[1] and artificial intelligence (Grosz 1977; Schank 1977; Lehnert 1978), so that topic and content are gradually becoming more thoroughly explored.

1.3 Earlier work on conversation understandably preferred to address relatively restricted domains. The study of comparatively stabilized communicative situations, such as rituals (Salmond 1974), verbal duels (Dundes, Leach, & Özkök 1972; Labov 1972a, 1972c), litigation (Frake 1972; Leodolter 1975), and chanting (Scherzer 1974), is concerned with a limited range of conventional topics and actions. The study of "registers" (characteristic styles of text production in typical situations or among certain groups, e.g. dialect options, (cf. Blom & Gumperz 1972; Ervin-Tripp 1972), focuses more on the variations within the virtual systems of sound and grammar/syntax than on topic or action.

1.4 Harvey Sacks (cited in Coulthard 1977: 75) states as a "general rule about conversation that it is your business not to tell people what you can suppose they know." It might be more accurate to state that a great deal of conversational material is indeed already known to all participants, but that the *particular configuration of text-world models in discourse* is not known as such, because there are new combinations, limitations, modifications, or directions present (see IV.3.14). We could say that the DISCOURSE MODEL which conversational participants co-operate in building (cf. Reichman 1978; Rubin 1978b; Webber 1978) often fails to provide a complete or exact match with the stored knowledge of those who enter the receiver role. This partial match is especially attributable to a diversity of sources for conversational materials, such as the following:

1.4.1 *Typical and determinate concepts and relations in world knowledge* can safely be taken to be accessible to conversational participants at large, e.g. that the sky is blue, water boils and freezes, humans live in houses, and so on. Such knowledge is therefore reliable material for conversing with strangers.

1.4.2 *Cultural and social attitudes,* such as conventions of politeness or standards of desirability and value (cf. VI.4.10), can be presupposed to apply in most situations, unless signals are given to the contrary.

---

[1]Many of the papers on conversational analysis have circulated as mimeographs and are difficult to obtain. The situation has worsened since the sudden death of Harvey Sacks in an automobile accident in 1975.

1.4.3 *Conventional scripts and goals* serve to alert conversationalists to what people are expected to say, and why, in familiar situations. In the enactment of scripts, e.g. going to a restaurant, participants need not provide explanation of why they are speaking, as long as they are conforming to expectations.

1.4.4 *Apperceivable traits of the current situation* are presumably known to all participants present or can be pointed out with little difficulty. The countless conversations about weather fall under this heading, aided by the social convention that weather is a universally acceptable topic.

1.4.5 *Episodic knowledge of shared experiences* among participants applies when some past situation involved the presence of people in the current conversation. This knowledge contributes to the speaker's internal model of the hearer (cf. I.6.1), and extends the store of shared situations (cf. Clark & Marshall 1978). The speaker may assign as defaults and preferences the components of his or her own self-model to the hearer-model (Cohen 1978: 93; cf. VIII.1.14).

1.5 Conversation differs from other text types especially in its greater reliance on SITUATIONALITY (VIII.1.1), whether current or shared in the past. This factor allows rich UPDATING of expectations and steady FEEDBACK about the effects of utterances (cf. Rubin 1978b). The participants' plans and goals will be more directly evident or firmly established in prior knowledge (cf. the notion of "life themes" in Schank & Abelson 1977).

1.6 This immediacy of situationality lends conversation an enormous range and flexibility. Paul Grice (1975, 1978) has undertaken to systemize conversation somewhat by formulating some "conversational maxims" with the status of preferences or defaults. In comparing his maxims to my own model, I noticed what seemed to be some unclearness and overlap in his definitions. I accordingly asked Grice himself about the disputed points, and my discussion below incorporates the explanations he kindly afforded (for a more detailed treatment, cf. Beaugrande & Dressler 1980: Ch. VI).

1.6.1 The principle of CO-OPERATION is cited as: "Make your conversational contribution such as is required, at the state at which it occurs, by the accepted purpose or direction of the talk exchange in which you are engaged" (Grice 1975: 45; cf. Clark & Clark 1977: 122ff.). My own criteria of INTENTIONALITY and ACCEPTABILITY (I.4.11.3f.) seem applicable here in regard to participant attitudes, and that of SITUATIONALITY in regard to "direction and purpose." I cited some examples of deliberately unco-operative utterances in II.1.8 and IV.3.7.

1.6.2 The principle of QUANTITY is cited as: "Make your contribution as informative as (but not more informative than) is required" (Grice 1975: 45). This principle concerns the amount of content presented, and seems related to my notion of RELEVANCE to communicative plans (cf. I.4.14; VII.2.8). I would not equate the principle with my own notion of informativity as expounded in Chapter IV, because I am concerned more with knownness and expectedness than with volume. A text which is "more informative than is required" would, in my model, be too discontinuous or discrepant (cf. IV.1.12); for Grice, such a text could be merely too extensive.

1.6.3 The principle of QUALITY is concerned with truthfulness: "Do not say what you believe to be false, or that for which you lack adequate evidence" (Grice 1975: 46). The expectation that a textual world ought to match at least the determinate elements and configurations of a corresponding world-knowledge pattern is, I suspect, stronger for text types other than conversation (e.g. science texts, cf. VII.1.8.6). Indeed, conversation often demands false assertions for the sake of social conventions, e.g. insincere praise of other people's appearance or possessions. Also, the pursuit of a plan may require false assertions for motives such as we saw in the stage play in VI.4. Still, these usages are probably parasitic on a principle such as Grice has proposed, or else they would not be effective.

1.6.4 The principle of RELATION is cited simply as "be relevant" (Grice 1975: 46). Grice's notion subsumes at least some factors of my notions of relevance (oriented toward a plan or goal) and knowledge access (what kind of contents are in principle related to each other). One could devise cases where these two notions of mine come into conflict, for example, when someone's plan calls for a sudden change of content to a topic not accessible from the previous one (e.g. Mrs. Haggett's attempt to stall in (86) of sample (188); or the mother's change of song in (15) of sample (247)). But these cases could plausibly be seen as violations of normal conversation.

1.6.5 The principle of MANNER is rather diverse: (1) "be perspicuous"; (2) "avoid obscurity of expression"; (3) "avoid ambiguity"; (4) "be brief"; and (5) "be orderly" (Grice 1975: 46). In a recent presentation at the University of Bielefeld Symposium on Theories of Language Use (June 1979), Grice also proposed to state this maxim as "Frame whatever you say such as to be appropriate to a reply." These notions can be clarified as follows (I rely here again on Grice's explanations). *Be perspicuous* would yield this maxim: "Be such that the intentions you have for what you say are plainly served." *Avoid obscurity* could be stated as: "Do not be difficult to understand." *Avoid ambiguity* can be rephrased as: "Do not express yourself such that your audience will take meanings other than what you intend." *Be brief* could be: "Do not use more time than necessary to make your contribution"; hence, "quantity" concerns how much you say, and "brevity" concerns how much you take to say it. *Be orderly* could be restated as: "Present your materials in the order in which they are required." Grice's illustration of *appropriateness to a reply* was the use of formats suitable for a denial.

1.6.6 Grice also has introduced the notion of IMPLICATURE (not a "maxim") for utterances whose intended utilization is recoverable from their conceptual content only via social conventions (cf. also McCawley 1978; Sadock 1978). A well-known illustration is the utterance:

(208) Can you pass the salt?

where a request is presented as an inquiry about someone's abilities. The need for implicature arises from the ASYMMETRY between the connectivities of concepts/relations and those of planning. My notion of RELEVANCE would account for how implicatures are created and recovered.

1.7 The principles suggested by Grice and others exert powerful controls on expectations, defaults, and preferences in conversation. Their violation is likely to elicit regulative utterances such as:

(209) So what? [violation: co-operation]
(210) Big deal! [violation: quantity]
(211) Why are you telling me this? [violation: perspicuity]
(212) I don't know what you're talking about! [violation: obscurity]

These signals cannot be used freely on participants with pronounced social dominance over the speaker. Also, some social situations require people to converse in absence of materials needed to live up to Grice's principles. Many discussions of the weather arise, and (209) through (212) would not be usable responses.

1.8 We can distinguish between the DICOURSE ACTIONS of INVOKING: calling up material presumed to be known to participants; and INFORMING: modifying known material or presenting new material (cf. VI.4.14). The distinction is one of degree rather than opposition, and exists not in the material as such, but in the participants' outlook on material and on each other. Invoking is a good means for maintaining the desirable social states of acceptance and solidarity (VI.4.10), and thus accounts for many conversations of low informativity. Invoking can serve for exploring the attitudes of certain other people whose co-operation is needed for the speaker's plans.

1.9 I have proposed to define TOPIC with reference to the density of conceptual-relational configurations in text-world models (e.g. in III.4.27). A single utterance in conversation might not have its own topic, but might rather present material which would become topical if developed in follow-up utterances (Schank 1977: 424). Hence, topic is a dynamic aspect of the flow and shift of knowledge drawn from the various sources enumerated in VIII.1.4ff. Topic shifts are especially pronounced among participants with rich knowledge stores regarding each other's personal histories. An illustration would be this dialogue I overheard on the University of Florida campus:

(213.1) Hey, what's happening?
(213.2) Keeping busy. You going to the game Saturday?

(213.3) If I get the physics paper done. Your brother back yet?
(213.4) Sometime next week. Got hung up somehow.
(213.5) Sounds just like him.

Without a context of shared experience, these utterances would hardly occur together. Conversely, unco-operative speakers can deflect interaction by deliberately discontinuous shifts, as in this recent campus exchange:

(214.1) BIBLE EVANGELIST: It's a fearful thing to meet with God the King!
(214.2) STUDENT: Like when Godzilla meets King Kong?

The student used superficial similarities among expressions to move the topic from religion to a monster movie made some years ago.

1.10 If one participant has the initiative, others can restrict their contributions to simple feedback—"commentation" in the sense of Roland Posner (1972) (cf. IV.3.8). Consider this exchange between Sam Weller and another servant in the *Pickwick Papers* (Dickens 1899: 547):[2]

(215.1) I'm afraid I've been dissipating.
(215.2) That's a very bad complaint that.
(215.3) And yet the temptation, you see, Mr. Weller.
(215.4) Ah, to be sure.
(215.5) Plunged into the very vortex of society, you know, Mr. Weller.
(215.6) Dreadful indeed.

Sam's contributions display his solidarity without affecting topic flow. This type of response can extend back further than to a previous utterance, though clarification may be needed (Dickens 1899: 552):

(216.1) What a lucky fellow you are!
(216.2) How do you mean?
(216.3) That there young lady. She knows what's what, she does.
(216.4) I'm afraid you're a cunning fellow, Mr. Weller.

Sam's first remark looks back to a topic raised some time before, so that its motivation is not at once obvious. The final remark (216.4) takes Sam's feedback as grounds for inferring his mental abilities.

1.11 It should be possible to state some strategies for generating feedback. Like many other issues, topic flow depends on how knowledge is acquired, stored, and utilized (cf. III.3.7). First, participants must know what elements of knowledge are connected to each other, for example, by appealing to global patterns like frames, schemas, plans, and scripts. Second, participants must distinguish what elements are INTERESTING because they involve

---

[2]For the sake of illustration, I omit the cues such as 'said Sam' in these passages, unless—as in (237)—they are relevant to the discussion. I have normalized a few dialect spellings.

possible PROBLEMS, that is, uncertainty of access or variability of node content in either real-world events and situations, or internal knowledge stores, e.g. how something is to be obtained or achieved, or how improbable or infrequent something is. By focusing on such problems, one can respond to many conversational contributions with follow-up questions via the LINK TYPES proposed in III.4.7ff.:

(217) Why did you do that? [reason-of]
(218) What happened then? [proximity in time-to]
(219) How did you manage that? [enablement-of, instrument-of]
(220) What was your purpose in doing that? [purpose-of]
(221) When did that happen? [time-of]
(222) Where did that happen? [location-of]
(223) What's it made of? [substance-of]
(224) What brought that on? [reason-of]
(225) How did you find out? [apperception-of]
(226) How did you think that up? [cognition-of]
(227) Where did you get it from? [entry-into-possession-of]

1.12 To use these questions, participants would search the applicable knowledge pattern for problematic entries (cf. examples in Schank 1977). The acceptability of a question rises with the uncertainty of the elements in its focus, and with their relevance to an event, action, object, or situation involved. A statement like:

(228) I fell in love last night.

could be responded to with (218), (219), (221), or (222), while (217), (220), (223), and (227) would be less likely: falling in love is not supposed to be guided by reason or purpose, nor to have substance, nor to change possession. A good test for problematic and interesting aspects of some assertion is to try the effects of these various follow-up questions upon it. Put into a quasi-Gricean maxim, but with my terms, we obtain: "Select an active node of the discourse world and pursue from it a pathway whose linkage or goal node is problematic or variable."

1.13 The relevance of such linkages directs the course of conversation in many ways. Consider this exchange between Mr. Pickwick and Sam Weller who is telling one of his memorable stories (Dickens 1899: 651):

(229.1) Next morning he gets up, has a fire lit, orders in three shillings worth of crumpets, toasts them all, eats them all, and blows his brains out.
(229.2) What did he do that for?

Although the pro-form 'that' is itself non-determinate, there is no doubt that Mr. Pickwick's follow-up question (229.2) is directed toward the final action mentioned by Sam: 'blowing one's brains out' is an action whose access is extremely problematic, requiring an unusually powerful "reason-of" linkage. People 'get up', 'light fires', 'eat crumpets', etc. in the normal course of life.

1.14 Actions of some participant that appear unique or without reason are likely topics for the conversation (Dickens 1899: 651):

> (230.1) Will you allow me to inquire why you make up your bed under that there deal table?
>
> (230.2) Cause I was always used to a four-poster afore I came here, and I find the legs of the table answer as well.

A speaker can elicit conversation by withholding some problematic knowledge and allowing others to make guesses. A cobbler Sam meets in debtors' prison turns out to have a very unusual cause for his arrest (Dickens 1899: 653):

> (231.1) What do you suppose ruined me now?
>
> (231.2) Why, I suppose the beginning was that you got into debt.
>
> (231.3) Never owed a farthing. Try again.
>
> (231.4) You didn't go to law, I hope?
>
> (231.5) Never in my life. The fact is, I was ruined by having money left me.

This cause is so non-expected that a regulatory interchange concerning believability ensues:

> (231.6) Come, come, that won't do.
>
> (231.7) Oh I daresay you don't believe it. I wouldn't if I was you; but it's true all the same.

The final remark (231.7) clearly shows how participants project their own knowledge and beliefs onto others in conversation (VIII.1.4.5).

1.15 Topic flow can also move along links of *class inclusion*. The conversation may be directed toward a class or superclass from which an instance or subclass has been mentioned. In the following exchange between Sam Weller and his father, the discussion of the situation drifts onto a SUPERTOPIC (cf. Schank 1977) about a prototype of the class of 'prophets' (Dickens 1899: 641):[3]

> (232.1) Well now, you've been a-prophesying away very fine, like a red-faced Nixon as the sixpenny books gives pictures on.
>
> (232.2) Who was he, Sammy?

---

[3]To the extent that Mr. Weller is himself included under the heading 'prophet' by METACLASS INCLUSION (cf. III.3.20), we might have here an example of a METATOPIC (cf. Schank 1977).

(232.3) This here gentleman was a prophet.

(232.4) What's a prophet?

(232.5) Why, a man as tells what's a-going to happen.

(232.6) I wish I'd known him, Sammy. Perhaps he might have throwed a small light on that there liver complaint as we was a-speaking on just now. Howsoever, if he's dead and ain't left the business to nobody, there's an end on it. Go on, Sammy.

The elder Mr. Weller steers the topic back to an earlier one ('liver complaint') and then signals a return to the previous point of (232.1), where the digression occurred, with 'go on' (232.6).

1.16 The flow of topic can also be guided by traits of the current situation (VIII.1.4.4). When Mr. Pickwick is driven by the elder Weller to 'the turnpike at Mile-End', this dialogue begins (Dickens 1899: 318):

(233.1) Very queer life is a pike-keeper's, sir.

(233.2) Yes; very curious life—very uncomfortable.

(233.3) There all on 'em men as has met with some disappointment in life.

(233.4) Ay, ay?

(233.5) Yes. Consequence of which they retires from the world and shuts themselves up in pikes; partly with the view of being solitary, and partly to revenge themselves on mankind by taking tolls.

1.17 These examples illustrate conversations whose components are less goal-directed than those we looked at in the stage play in VI.4. They are typical of situations where people are motivated by social factors to uphold a continuity of communication. That continuity requires a corresponding continuity of topic, but shifts may pursue a wide variety of links. Situational settings and participants' episodic apperception and knowledge can readily be used, since they rest upon experiential continuity.

1.18 The question of how SPEAKING TURNS are allotted is correlated both with topic flow and with participant roles. Sacks, Schegloff, and Jefferson (1974) distinguish two groups of conventions: (1) the current speaker selects the next one, for instance, by direct address; and (2) the next speaker "self-selects" by beginning to speak at an available utterance boundary. Conversations contain remarkably few long silences, and little overlap among utterances. Participants must have powerful and efficient strategies for introducing their contributions at the opportune instant. Sacks et al. (1974: 709) note the heuristic role of the sentence as an indicator of completing utterances (cf. III.4.26), though sentences provide options for continuation in many cases (cf. Coulthard 1977: 59). To retain the turn and discourage interruptions, people can insert cues of incompleteness, such as 'however', 'and then too', so that the intention to continue is evident (cf.

Sacks' notion of "utterance incompletor" cited in Coulthard 1977: 57). The speaker can also announce a forthcoming series of contributions, e.g. these utterances at a recent university meeting:

(234) I'd like to say three things about that.
(235) There are several points we're overlooking here.

The speaker hopes that no reply will come except at most an encouragement to continue. Anything else would be considered as clear an interruption as breaking into the midst of a half-uttered sentence.

1.19 The assignment of turns can also depend on the distribution of knowledge among participants. Someone reputed to be very knowledgeable on a topic has a right to be heard if the topic comes up in conversation. Such is the case with Mr.Pickwick's remark made 'hoping to start a subject which all the company could take a part in discussing' (Dickens 1899: 293):

(236.1) Curious little nooks in a great place like London these old inns are.
(236.2) By Jove, you have hit upon something that one of us at least would talk upon forever. You'll draw old Jack Bamber out.

And Jack Bamber was indeed 'the figure that now started forward and burst into an animated torrent of words'. Similarly, people encourage conversation by searching memory for a special topic that a given participant, especially a socially important personage, should know about (Dickens 1899: 530):

(237.1) "Have you seen his lordship's mail cart, Bantam?" inquired the Honourable Mr. Crushton after a short pause, during which [...] Mr. Crushton had been reflecting upon what subject his lordship could talk about best.
(237.2) "Dear me, no," replied the M.C.; "a mail-cart! What an excellent idea! Remarkable!"
(237.3) "Gwacious heavens!" said his lordship, "I though evewebody had seen the new mail cart; it's the neatest, pwettiest, gwacefullest thing that ever wan upon wheels. Painted wed, with cweam piebald. [etc.]"[4]

This 'gwacious' conversationalist was 'the richest young man in Bath'.

1.20 Prior knowledge among participants also plays a part in QUESTION ANSWERING. Truthful answers that fail to account for the questioner's purpose may not be appropriate, as in Lehnert's (1978: 5) samples:

(238.1) Do you drink?
(238.2) Of course. All humans drink.

---

[4]His lordship has an infantile speech habit of replacing [r] with [w].

(239.1) Who wasn't in class today?
(239.2) George Washington and Moby Dick.

(240.1) Would you like to dance?
(240.2) Sure. You know anyone who wants to?

The questioner of (238.1) and (240.1) presumably wants to offer drinking and dancing to the addressee, and the answer violates the principle of co-operation (VIII.1.6.1). The questioner of (239.1) doubtless wishes to learn the identity of those members of the class who should have been present, but weren't, so that the answer violates the principle of quantity (VIII.1.6.2).

1.21 Shared procedures for maintaining coherence allow considerable economy in exchanges like this (Ortony 1978b):

(241.1) Would like a piece of cake?
(241.2) I'm on a diet.

Ortony argues that the coherence of the answer rests on an underlying chain of inferences such as the following:

(241.2a) People on diets ought not to eat fattening things.
(241.2b) Cake is fattening.
(241.2c) I ought not to eat any cake.
(241.2d) I will not eat any cake.

He points out (1978b: 76) that any of these steps in the chain of reasoning could also be mapped onto a surface utterance instead of (241.2). These steps must all be available anyway for the discourse action of (241.2) to take effect.

1.22 Participants may be under a social obligation to correct inferrable prior knowledge. In an exchange like the following (J. Kaplan 1978: 204):

(242.1) Which students got a grade of F in CIS 500 in Spring 1977?
(242.2a) None.
(242.2b) CIS 500 was not given in Spring 1977.

the response (242.2a) is literally true if the computer science course was not given, but it is misleading, whereas (242.2b) is helpful in correcting a wrong presupposition. Answerers might, of course, have reasons for encouraging wrong presuppositions, as in the soldiers' reply (Carroll 1960: 110):

(243.1) "You shan't be beheaded!" said Alice, and she put them [the gardeners] into a large flower-pot that stood near. The three soldiers wandered about for a minute or two, looking for them, and then quietly marched off after the others.
(243.2) "Are their heads off?" shouted the Queen.
(243.3) "Their heads are gone, if it please your majesty!" the soldiers shouted in reply.

1.23 By the same token, questioners can influence the answerer's state by deploying strategic phrasing. Since the question action indicates that reason for doubt exists, positives encourage negative responses and vice-versa:

(244a) Do you think you ought to go?
(244b) Don't you think you ought to go?

From (244a), the hearer could infer the speaker's belief that 'going' is inadvisable, and from (244b) just the opposite (cf. Fillenbaum 1968). The question format interacts with the conventions for negation. If negation is typically used for material that might otherwise be believed (cf. IV.1.25), the question countermands that setting by implying that the addressee has doubtful grounds for disbelief. Elizabeth Loftus (1975) explores a number of ways in which question formats set up expectations in eliciting eye witness reports. When test subjects were asked (246) after (245a), 53% said yes, but only 35% said yes after (245b):

(245a) How fast was Car A going when it ran the stop sign?
(245b) How fast was Car A going when it turned right?
(246) Did you see a stop sign?

and yet there was no stop sign shown in the film of the accident!

1.24 Rachael Reichman (1978) has undertaken to describe the mechanisms of topic flow and shift across the various turns of entire conversations. Using actually recorded sample conversations, she argues that coherence relations can obtain between chunks of discourse in which topic appears to change over considerable distance. She proposes a distinction between *issues spaces* ("a general issue of concern" plus the agents, affected entities, and times, etc. involved) and *event spaces* ("a particular episode and the events that occurred therein" plus agents, affected entities, times, locations, etc. involved) (Reichman 1978: 291f.). The coherence of conversation depends on how these space types are related. An *illustrative* or *restatement* relation obtains when an event space is adduced to demonstrate or clarify what has been asserted in an issue space. Conversely, a *generalization* relation obtains if an event space is followed up with a discussion of the "general activity" to which the event belongs. If an issue space or event space is temporarily abandoned in favor of an unrelated one and then resumed, we have *interruption* and *return* relations. If an event space is used to show that two issue spaces are contingent upon each other (e.g., via causality), we have a *subissue* relation; if the two issue spaces are merged into "one composite issue," we have a *joining* relation. A *respecification* relation obtains if an event or issue already fully discussed is rediscussed in a different perspective. A *total shift* relation obtains if the new discourse chunk is not at all related to its predecessor. Reichman shows that these various discourse relations are frequently accompanied by surface signals such as 'like' and 'like when' (illustrative), 'by the way' (interruption), 'anyway' (return), and so forth.

1.25 The mechanisms of conversation are undeniably complex. Nonetheless, the work I have reviewed in this section promises to reveal at least some of the major factors worthy of exploration. There is a pronounced interaction among sources of knowledge, organization of topics, participant roles, and criteria for considering what is interesting and worth talking about. An entire discourse must have textuality, even when the textuality of its component texts is not obvious in isolation (cf. VIII.1.1; Beaugrande & Dressler 1980). Clearly, the study of conversation must be carried out with co-operation among the various disciplines—linguistics, psychology, sociology, anthropology, computation—that will profit from insights into this versatile and vital domain.

2. NARRATION

2.1 The investigation of stories prefigures the general trend to which this book also belongs. Early methods inspired by linguistic structuralism sought to isolate standard units in chains (cf. Propp 1928; Dundes 1962; Bremond 1964). Later on, transformational grammar became the source of inspiration (e.g. Greimas 1967; Žolkovskij & Ščeglov 1967). Recently, however, attention has been directed away from *abstract units* and *forms* toward *cognitive processes* in the *comprehension* of stories (e.g. Charniak 1972; Kintsch 1974, 1977b, 1979a; Rumelhart 1975, 1977b, 1978; Mandler & Johnson 1977; Schank & Abelson 1977; Thorndyke 1977; Cullingford 1978; Rieger 1978; Wilensky 1978; Beaugrande & Colby 1979; Beaugrande & Miller 1980). The trend is thus away from abstractions upon surface artifacts and their features toward human activities of utilizing texts. Whereas the former are often specific to a language, a topic, or a cultural and historical domain, the latter may be UNIVERSAL (cf IV.3.17ff.).

2.2 One major consequence has been the realization of how much prior knowledge is deployed by the understander. The effects of SCHEMAS as global knowledge patterns applied to stories have been irrefutably demonstrated. Readers can put scrambled stories back into the proper order (Kintsch 1977b; Kintsch, Mandel, & Kozminsky 1977; Stein & Nezworski 1978). The removal of material needed to match important schema elements interferes with comprehension and recall (Thorndyke 1977). Stories in which events of different sequences are so interlaced that concurrent schemas must be maintained for each sequence are rearranged so as to separate the schemas (J. Mandler 1978).

2.3 Despite its recognized importance, the schema appears in very diverse formats in research. Some investigators envision a set of REWRITE RULES of the familiar transformational type, in which large story components are "rewritten" as smaller ones (e.g. Rumelhart 1975; Mandler & Johnson 1977; Simmons 1978). Others make use of TREES in which story constituents are arranged in a hierarchy of size, containment, or importance (cf. Bower 1976; Rumelhart 1977b; Thorndyke 1977). These two formats are essentially equivalent, because the rewriting, in effect, acts as a parent node descending to offspring nodes (hence Mandler & Johnson use both formats). However, the cognitive implications of formatting have often been glossed over. Where do the story components actually come from? Are they (1) segments of supersegments, (2) instances of a class, (3) elements of an unordered set, or (4) products of transformational derivation? These relationships would have significantly different impacts on actual processing.

2.4 Ideally, hierarchical structuring ought to reflect cognitive priorities. The higher-up components should be noticed and recalled better than the lower-down ones (Meyer 1975, 1977). However, the data I reviewed for the 'rocket' text suggest that recall is more diffuse and topographical in nature— as documented by the contrast between our protocols in VII.3.32ff. and the idealized hierarchical summaries generated by Simmons' computer simulation in the appendix. People apparently retain quite a lot of material that would figure as lower-down components in a hierarchy. Their recall manifests the priority of connectivity and continuity more than that of height in tree structures.

2.5 To clarify issues of topography vs. hierarchy, we should explore the effects of BOTTOM-UP input on the TOP-DOWN input during story comprehension (cf. I.6.5). During the PROCEDURAL ATTACHMENT of a story schema to an actual story text, the schema is evidently specified and modified as occasion arises (Beaugrande & Miller 1980). The enduring qualities of great folktales must depend upon the processing of their inherent structures in interaction with schemas. By the standards of informativity and interestingness proposed in chapter IV, it follows that these famous tales cannot be a perfect match for the stored schema pattern: some uncertainties, alternatives, and surprises are, I suspect, virtually obligatory for the actualization of interesting and enduring stories. Indeed, one might want to insert such a requirement into the story schemas themselves (cf. Beaugrande & Colby 1979).

2.6 A minimal STORY-WORLD must contain at least a pair of states linked by an action or event. But to be interesting, the story-world needs a structure in which the progression from the INITIAL to the FINAL state is not so obvious that it would happen on its own in the normal course of things. For a story-world fraught with alternative pathways, the narrator and the readers engage in joint PROBLEM-SOLVING in which the narrator's solution eludes that of the readers at least some of the time.

2.7 Narrators can create uncertainty by using CHARACTERS (story-world persons) with opposing PERSPECTIVES. A given character is assigned a particular goal to seek in the course of events (cf. the notions of "objective" and "achievement" in Bremond 1973). If the reader audience sees that goal with positive values, the character will be a PROTAGONIST; for negatively valued goals, the role is that of ANTAGONIST.[5] The interaction of characters appears as a pursuit and mutual blocking of goals (cf. Wilensky 1978; compare the notion of "polemics" in Greimas 1970). Goal-blocking readily upholds uncertainty, especially when the narrator creates a powerful and resourceful antagonist. The event or action which makes a main goal decisively attainable or non-attainable is a TURNING POINT. In terms of the drama, a positive turning point for the protagonist is the conventional mark of "comedy," and a negative one the mark of "tragedy."

2.8 These considerations might be used to formulate some STORY-TELLING STRATEGIES (rather than abstract rewrite rules) such as the following (cf. Beaugrande & Colby 1979: 45f.):

2.8.1 Create a STORY-WORLD with at least one CHARACTER.

2.8.2 Identify an INITIAL STATE, a PROBLEM, and a GOAL STATE for the character.

2.8.3 Initiate a pathway that attempts to resolve the problem and attain the goal state.

2.8.4 Block or postpone the attainment of the goal state.

2.8.5 Mark one event or action as a TURNING POINT.

2.8.6 Create a FINAL STATE identified as matching or not matching the goal state.

2.9 These strategies can be applied recursively, generating STORY EPISODES of varying complexity or number. My own definition of "episode" is that of a space in a story-world with an initial state, a problem, a turning point, and a goal state (but compare the definitions in Rumelhart 1975, 1977b; Kintsch 1977b; Simmons 1978). A frequent demand for recursion arises from having a story-world with multiple main characters, each of them assigned actions and goals. The story-world with PROTAGONIST and ANTAGONIST could be governed by a rule set like this (cf. Beaugrande & Colby 1979: 46):

2.9.1 Create a story-world with two characters, the PROTAGONIST P and the ANTAGONIST A.

2.9.2 Create a PROBLEM for P that is caused or desired by A, and a goal state desired by P and opposed by A.

2.9.3 Initiate a pathway that attempts to resolve P's problem and attain P's goal state.

---

[5]Like language regularities in general (cf. note 14 to Chapter I), this one can be turned around for special effect, e.g. in the "picaresque" narrative where the protagonist's goals violate the official standards of conduct, though readers may still find them positive in context. A completely goalless neutral protagonist such as that in Camus' *L'Etranger* is both hard to present and not especially convincing.

2.9.4 Create actions of A to block P's solution and goal.

2.9.5 Mark one action or event as a turning point in which either P's or A's plans and values win out.

2.9.6 Create a final state identifiable as matching or being relevant to either P's or A's goal state.

2.10 If the narrator makes the antagonist extremely powerful, a compensatory strategy may be required:

2.10.1 Introduce one or more HELPING CHARACTERS to create ENABLEMENTS or to block DISENABLEMENTS of P's actions and goal.

2.11 The traditional categories of the narrative (cited in Kintsch 1977b) could be viewed as clusterings of realizations for these various strategies. The EXPOSITION would include 2.8.1 through 2.8.3; the COMPLICATION would be in 2.8.4; and the RESOLUTION in 2.8.5 and 2.8.6. The realization of the strategies is flexible in many ways. By adding more characters, the narrator has the options of making their goals in COMPETITION or in CONCORD (Wilensky 1978). For competition, Wilensky (1978) discusses various means of "anti-planning" including sabotage, concealment, distraction, removing enablements, and overpowering. Also, a single character may have different goals in conflict with each other (cf. VI.4.11; Wilensky 1978: ch. 6). Even just one goal may raise formidable problems if its attainment is difficult enough. Wilensky (1978: 253) cites typical circumstances of difficult plans:

2.11.1 if the plan requires exceptionally great RESOURCES, such as are probably not available;

2.11.2 if the plan leads to UNSTABLE GOALS (cf. VIII.2.22).

2.12 All of the participants in narrating—narrator, audience, and the story-world characters—are engaged in activities of planning and predicting. The narrator must: (1) plan out coherent tracks of states and actions for each character; (2) relate narrated actions to recoverable plans of the agent character; and (3) anticipate and monitor how the audience recovers or reconstructs characters' plans and predicts upcoming actions and events. The narrator needs to outplan the audience at least sometimes to keep the story interesting. The narrator can achieve this effect in several ways:

2.12.1 by selecting a rather improbable pathway to follow in the story line, e.g. by having characters make bad or unreasonable selections and decisions;

2.12.2 by introducing unforeseeable interactions among events, e.g. by having independent characters suddenly happen to come into contact or conflict;

2.12.3 by purposefully withholding knowledge that would otherwise render upcoming events predictable, e.g. by failing to identify someone's true goals;

2.12.4 by introducing apparently impossible events, e.g. magical occurrences that cause or enable states which could never be attained in the normal organization of the real world.

2.13 The narrator must be careful not to destroy connectivity with such tactics. Events and actions should be linked with cause, enablement, reason, or purpose (cf. Stein & Glenn 1979). This linkage may often be concealed or unexpected, but it must be there. For instance, a story-world governed by magic would appear to make anything possible. Yet there is nearly always some kind of modified but stable causality after all. A magic spell does not have random effects, even if its user may not be able to predict them. We see once again the regulatory nature of text-worlds as systems. Modifications are always allowable, but under control and subject to compensation. If new connections of causality are introduced, they are explicitly stated and stand in analogy to accepted causality. Consider, for instance, how many folktales contain passages in which some helper-figure explains magical causalities to the protagonist (e.g. *Jack and the Beanstalk* or *Childe Rowland* in Jacobs [ed.] 1891). Another tactic is to use recursions, such that the first event sequence serves as a model of the special causalities for the others (e.g. the many folktales where the same task is undertaken by one brother or sister after another, such as *Three Heads in a Well* in Jacobs [ed.] 1891)—text-internal pattern-matching (cf. IV.4.5; V.7.1; VII.2.36; VIII.2.29).

2.14 The narrator's tactics outlined above are grounds for looking at the narrating and understanding of stories as problem-solving (VIII.2.6). The harder a narrator strives to make the problem solution difficult and unexpected, the deeper the audience's processing will be (cf. IV.1.6). The users of Meehan's (1976) story-telling program have the unusual opportunity of deciding how hard the problems should be in the stories they are given; significantly, they "make the problem *very* hard; they find the resulting 'Trials and Tribulations' story more 'interesting' (their word)" (Meehan 1977: 96). For the murder mystery story, the narrator is expressly expected to mislead the audience about the solution until just before the final state, for example, by creating a complex world of characters with diverse and competing desires and goals (cf. S. Klein et al. 1973).

2.15 It might be objected that people enjoy hearing the same story over again even though they know the solution and thus cannot be outplanned. Beaugrande and Colby (1979:49f.) propose two accounts for this phenomenon. According to the first, knowledge of global structures (VI.1.1ff.) or macro-structures (II.2.9; III.4.27) might not be at the same processing depth as that of local or micro-structures. Interest is upheld during repeated narrations because the audience recovers only global knowledge and rediscovers local knowledge each time. Enduring narratives—and perhaps enduring human artifacts at large—would then have to manifest inherent structural complexities whose demands upon processing, despite repeated encounters, remain above the capabilities for total storage, and yet below the threshold where processing simply breaks down. The notions of processing limitations expounded by Norman and Bobrow (1975) would apply here. On the one hand, the storage of both global and local knowledge could be too much for the mind to manage because of the diverse elements and linkages needed to hold everything in place, resulting in "data limitations" which practising cannot overcome. On the other hand, the allotment of attention during story comprehension to the global signals that match the schema draws attention away from the local data, so that the latter is discovered rather than predicted; this effect is due to cognitive "resource limitations."

2.16 The other account might well be interactive with the first. If people process story-worlds in terms of state-event pathways with branching alternatives, then each repeated narration obliges them to compute the series of possible events all over again. Especially at turning points, audiences keep envisioning the alternatives that the pathways inherently suggest, even though it is known which alternatives will not be used. A highly probable disaster can awaken anxiety over and over in the same way as remembering narrow escapes in real life. The story-reader's experience is detached from the expenditure of material resources.

2.17 The combination of the two accounts suggests that the distinction between STORED KNOWLEDGE and EXPERIENTIAL IMMEDIACY may be extremely important. The actualization of knowledge in producing and understanding texts may always exert higher demands on processing than even highly detailed storage can record and match. Hence, the experience of a story being told at a given moment exceeds the mere matching of the most accurate patterns acquired in the past. Hearers may record and reuse the story as knowledge; but the ongoing actualization is dynamic to a degree that cannot become stabilized in storage.

2.18 In this regard, the activities of narrating may come to be a model for textual processing (and even information processing) overall. At this time, it is certainly the most thoroughly explored aspect of utilizing texts. The candidates suggested in IV.3.17 as possible UNIVERSALS do appear to be emerging from the experiments with stories. Future research will reveal how far-reaching those "universals" are and whether they can be applied to natural-language communication of all kinds (cf. IX.1.4ff.).

2.19 Each specific story ought to manifest an organization and surface format that allow general (or universal) strategies to be applied via PROCEDURAL ATTACHMENT. I shall investigate a sample folktale from that standpoint, noting how the narrator actualizes the general story-telling strategies in such a way as to create an interesting and effective text. Due to the age and wide geographical distribution of this tale and its variants, we presumably have a collective narrator rather than an individual one. If so, repeated retellings tend to tighten up the structure to a high degree of internal order, economy, and impact (cf. Mandler & Johnson 1977). The ratings for the design criteria of *efficiency, effectiveness,* and *appropriateness* are therefore high.

2.20 The sample is "an old Suffolk Folk-tale" that appeared in the *Ipswich Journal* on January 12, 1878 and was included as the opening piece in the collection of tales gathered by Joseph Jacobs (1891). This version is a compromise between the strong dialect of the 1878 version and the standardized 1891 version. I adhere to the 1878 grammar and vocabulary, but use conventional spellings for the convenience of the reader. The same story has been discussed before by Beaugrande and Colby (1979), whose commentary I follow.[6]

(247)
TOM TIT TOT

(1) Well, once upon a time there were a woman and she baked five pies. And when they come out of the oven, they was that overbaked, the crust were too hard to eat. So she says to her darter:

(2) "Darter," says she, "put you them there pies on the shelf an' leave 'em there a little, an' they'll come agin"—she meant, you know, the crust'd get soft.

(3) But the gal, she[7] says to herself, "Well, if they'll come agin, I'll ate 'em now." And she set to work and ate 'em all, first and last.

(4) Well, come supper time the woman she said: "Go you and git one o' them there pies. I dare say they've came agin now."

(5) The gal she went an' she looked, and there weren't nothin' but the dishes. So back she come and says she, "Noo, they ain't come agin."

(6) "Not none on 'em?" says the mother.

(7) "Not none on 'em," says she.

(8) "Well, come agin or not come agin," says the woman, "I'll have one for supper."

(9) "But you can't, if they ain't come," says the gal.

(10) "But I can," says she,[8] "Go you and bring the best of 'em."

(11) "Best or worst," says the gal, "I've ate 'em all, and you can't have one till that's come agin."

(12) Well, the woman she were wholly famished, and she took her spinnin' to the door to spin and as she span she sang:

"My darter ha' ate five, five pies today.
My darter ha' ate five, five pies today."

(13) The king he were a-comin' down the street an' he heard her sing, but what she sang he couldn't hear, so he stopped and said:

---

[6] I am most grateful to G. P. Putnam's Sons of New York for the generous permission to reprint this story. Prof. Robert Thomson points out to me that this tale was much studied by 19th-century British folklorists; see e.g. Edward Clodd, *Tom Tit Tot: An Essay on Savage Philosophy* (London: Duckworth, 1898).

[7] These redundant subjects, as I mentioned in V.5.8, are socially marked, but not, I think, without function in topic announcement. The original text is inconsistent as to whether a comma should be placed before the pronoun.

[8] Notice that the MODEL of the NARRATIVE SITUATION precludes any problem in sorting out the co-referring expressions for these various uses of 'she'.

(14) "What were that you was a-singin' of, mum?"

(15) The woman, she were ashamed to let him hear what her darter had been a-doin',' so she sang, 'stead o' that:

"My darter ha' spun five, five skeins today.

My darter ha' spun five, five skeins today."

(16) "Stars o' mine!" said the king, "I never heerd tell of anyone as could do that!"

(17) Then he said: "Look you here, I want a wife and I'll marry your darter. But look you here," says he, "eleven months out o' the year she shall have all the vittles she likes to eat, and all the gowns she likes to git, and all the company she likes to have; but the last month o' the year she'll have to spin five skeins every day, an' if she doon't, I shall kill her."

(18) "All right," says the woman: for she thought what a grand marriage that was. And as for them five skeins, when th' time come to it, there'd be plenty o' ways o' gettin' out of it, and likeliest, he'd have forgot about it.

(19) Well, so they was married. An' for eleven months the gal had all the vittles she liked to eat and all the gowns she liked to git, an' all the company she liked to have.

(20) But when the time was gettin' over, she began to think about them there skeins an' to wonder if he had 'em in mind. But not one word did he say about 'em an' she wholly thought he'd forgot 'em.

(21) Howsoever, the last day o' the last month, he takes her to a room she'd never set eyes on afore. There weren't nothin' in it but a spinnin' wheel and a stool. An' says he, "Now me dear, here you'll be shut in to-morrow with some vittles and some flax, and if you ain't spun five skeins by the night, your head'll go off."

(22) An' away he went about his business.

(23) Well, she were that frightened. She'd always been such a gatless gal, that she didn't so much as know how to spin, and what were she to do tomorrow, with no one to come nigh her to help her? She sat down on a stool in the kitchen, and lork! how she did cry!

(24) Howsoever, all on a sudden she heerd a sort of knockin' low down on the door. She upped and oped it, an' what should she see but a small little black thing with a long tail. That[9] looked up at her right curious, an' that said:

(25) "What are you a-cryin' for?"

(26) "What's that to you?" says she.

(27) "Never you mind," that said, "but tell me what you're a-cryin' for."

(28) "That woon't do me noo good if I do," says she.

(29) "You doon't know that," that said an' twirled that's tail round.

(30) "Well," says she, "that woon't do me noo harm, if that doon't do me noo good," and she upped and told about the pies an' the skeins an' everything.

(31) "This is what I'll do," says the little black thing, "I'll come to your window every mornin' an' take the flax an' bring it spun at night."

(32) "What's your pay?" says she.

---

[9]The form 'that' as a pronoun is typical of the dialect; perhaps it also stresses the unknown status of the 'little black thing'.

(33) That looked out o' the corners o' that's eyes an' that said: "I'll give you three guesses every night to guess my name, an' if you ain't guessed it afore the month's up, you shall be mine."

(34) Well, she thought she'd be sure to guess that's name afore the month was up. "All right," says she, "I agree."

(35) "All right," that says, an' lork! how that twirled that's tail.

(36) Well, the next day her husband he took her into the room an' there was the flax an' the day's vittles.

(37) "Now there's the flax," says he, "an' if that ain't spun up this night, off goes your head." An' then he went out an' locked the door.

(38) He'd hardly gone, when there was a knockin' agin the window.

(39) She upped and she oped it, an' there sure enough was the little old thing a-settin' on the ledge.

(40) "Where's the flax?" says he.

(41) "Here it be," says she. And she gave it to him.

(42) Well, come the evenin', a knockin' come agin to the window. She upped and she oped it and there were the little old thing, with the five skeins of flax on his arm.

(43) "Here it be," says she, an' he gave it to her.

(44) "Now, what's my name?" says he.

(45) "What, is that Bill?" says she.

(46) "Noo, that ain't," says he. An' he twirled his tail.

(47) "Is that Ned?" says she.

(48) "Noo, that ain't," says he. An' he twirled his tail.

(49) "Well, is that Mark?" says she.

(50) "Noo, that ain't," says he, and he twirled his tail harder, and away he flew.

(51) Well, when her husband he come in: there was the five skeins ready for him. "I see I shan't have for to kill you tonight, me dear," says he. "You'll have your vittles and your flax in the mornin'," says he, an' away he goes.

(52) Well, every day the flax an' the vittles, they was brought, an' every day that there little black impet used for to come mornings an' evenings. An' all the day the gal she set a-trying' for to think of names to say to it when it came at night. But she never hit on the right one. An' as it got toward the end of the month, the impet began to look so maliceful, and that twirled that's tail faster and faster each time she gave a guess.

(53) At last it come to the last day but one. The impet that come at night along of the five skeins, an' that said:

(54) "What, ain't you got my name yet?"

(55) "Is that Nicodemus?" says she.

(56) "Noo, t'ain't," that says.

(57) "Is that Sammle?" says she.

(58) "No, t'ain't," that says.

(59) "A-well, is that Methusalem?" says she.

(60) "Noo, t'ain't that neither," that says.

(61) Then that looks at her with that's eyes like a coal o' fire, and that says:

"Woman, there's only to-morrow night, and then you'll be mine!" An' away it flew.

(62) Well, she felt that horrid. Howsoever, she heerd the king a-comin' along the passage. In he came, an' when he see the five skeins he says, says he:

(63) "Well, my dear," says he, "I don't see but what you'll have your skeins ready to-morrow night as well, an' as I reckon I shan't have to kill you, I'll have supper in here to-night." So they brought supper, and another stool for him, an' down the two they set.

(64) Well, he hadn't eat but a mouthful or so, when he stops and begins to laugh.

(65) "What is it?" says she.

(66) "A-why," says he, "I was out a-huntin' to-day, an' I got away to a place in the wood I'd never seen afore. An' there was an old chalk-pit. An' I heerd a sort of a humming, kind of. So I got off my hobby an' I went right quiet to the pit, an' I looked down. Well, what should there be but the funniest little black thing you ever set eyes on. An' what was that a-doin' on, but that had a little spinnin' wheel an' that were a-spinnin' wonderful fast, an' a-twirling that's tail. An' as that span that sang:

'Nimmy nimmy not
My name's Tom Tit Tot.'"

(67) Well, when the gal heerd this, she fared as if she could have jumped outer her skin for joy, but she didn't say a word.

(68) Next day, that there little black thing looked so maliceful when he come for the flax. An' when night come she heerd that a-knockin' agin the window panes.

(69) She oped the window, an' that come right in on the ledge. That were grinnin' from ear to ear an' Oo! that's tail were twirlin' round so fast.

(70) "What's my name?" that says, as that gave her the skeins.

(71) "Is that Solomon?" she says, pretendin' to be afeared.

(72) "Noo, t'ain't," that says, an' that come further into the room.

(73) "Well, is that Zebedee?" says she agin.

(74) "Noo, t'ain't," says the impet. An' then that laughed and twirled that's tail till you couldn't hardly see it.

(75) "Take time, woman," that says; "next guess, an' you're mine." An' that stretched out that's black hands at her.

(76) Well, she backed a step or two, an' she looked at it, and then she laughed out, an' says she, a-pointin' of her finger at it:

"'Nimmy nimmy not
Your name's Tom Tit Tot.'"

(77) Well, when that heerd her, that shrieked awful an' away that flew into the dark, an' she never saw it no more.

2.21 To parallel the story-telling strategies suggested in VIII.2.8f., we could envision story-understanding strategies intended to recover the structure of events and situations and build a model of the story-world. I shall expand upon the story-telling outlook somewhat by extracting some further aspects from our sample. The understanding strategies include (cf. Beaugrande & Colby 1979: 54f.):

2.21.1 Notice the MAIN CHARACTERS, and their PROBLEMS and GOALS.

2.21.2 Relate the characters' ACTIONS to PLANS for SOLVING PROBLEMS and ATTAINING GOALS.

2.21.3 Recover the CONNECTIVITY of SITUATIONS and EVENTS with linkages of CAUSE, ENABLEMENT, REASON, and PURPOSE.

2.21.4 Notice MOTIVATIONAL STATEMENTS.

2.21.5 Notice VALUE ASSIGNMENTS.

2.21.6 Notice indicators of TIME, LOCATION, and MATERIAL RESOURCES.

2.21.7 Notice TURNING POINTS.

2.21.8 Match the FINAL STATE against the characters' GOAL STATES.

2.22 The highest priority presumably goes to identifying the various STORY EPISODES by noticing when a cycle of story-telling rules has been traversed. The essential components are the problem, the turning point, and a final state related to characters' goals (VIII.2.9). Our sample has three episodes: (1) an opening span running from the initial baking to the royal marriage (paragraphs 1–19); (2) a problem-to-goal sequence with a spinning task (20–34); and (3) a problem-to-goal sequence with a name-guessing task (33–77). The goal for the spinning task, i.e. the delegation of agency to someone else, is UNSTABLE, because it creates a new problem (cf. VIII.2.11.2). The goal for the name-guessing task, on the other hand, is a stable one, and the narrator in fact ends the story at that point without further elaboration. The potential problem of the same spinning task being demanded again in eleven months is not even raised.[10]

2.23 To get the story moving, the narrator faces the problem of leading from a commonplace situation of housekeeping and a trivial event of baking up to a momentous marriage with a sinister BARGAIN FAVOR (VI.4.14) involved (unless one is concerned with the exchange: vittles/gowns/company for skeins of spun flax, in which viewpoint we have BARGAIN OBJECT). In one variant of this tale, the well-known German version about 'Rumpelstiltskin',[11] the daughter is precipitated into her disastrous bargain by her father's incautious boasting. Our narrator uses a different pathway with a

---

[10]One of our test subjects for this story who heard the normal version (cf. VIII.2.42ff.) remarked that 'the story had one thing wrong with it', namely that it didn't say what would happen after another eleven months; the daughter had 'exploited the black guy and couldn't use him again'.

[11]The German name is descriptive: 'little person with long, crooked legs'.

greater number of small steps. To assist coherence and connectivity, the narrator supplies numerous MOTIVATIONAL STATEMENTS: explicit announcements of the reasons, causes, enablements, and purposes that lead to events and actions. The pies are not eaten right away because 'they was that overbaked, the crust were too hard to eat' (1). The state of the pies in turn motivates the mother's ambiguously formulated request (2). Notice that the narrator stops to explain to the audience what 'she meant, you know' (2)—an illustration of how an instability in the systemic text-world is regulated by explicit signaling. The ambiguity is instrumental in the daughter's reason for overeating, as her utterances reveal (3, 5, 7, 9, 11). To spread the knowledge of the daughter's action within the textual world, the narrator sends the mother 'to the door' to spin and sing (12), and then has the king 'a-comin' down the street' (13). The king's inquiry is motivated because 'what she sang he couldn't hear' (13), and the mother's change of the song by her being 'ashamed to let him hear what her darter had been a-doin' (15). The king's reaction follows because he 'never heerd tell of anyone as could do that' (16) and because he 'wants a wife' (17). The mother accepts his offer because she 'thought what a grand marriage that was' (18).

2.24 This care in providing motivational statements is undoubtedly encouraged by the large mismatch between the initial and final states/events of the opening episode. The narrator adopts a strategy of bridging the gap with local dependencies of small events that gradually add up to the total outcome. Accordingly, there is a diversity of small problems rather than one main one in this episode: hunger—a default problem arising automatically in the course of time (Meehan 1976)—an ambiguous instruction, no supper, a partially inaudible song, and the mother's embarrassment. The solutions adopted at each phase happen to direct the progression of the story in a way that the mother and daughter could not have foreseen. The king applies a literal understanding to the altered song text, and as a ruler, his mistakes have "the force of legal authority" (Charniak 1975b: 10).[12] I draw two conclusions from these considerations:

2.24.1 First, we can distill out another story-telling strategy: for episodes with a large mismatch between initial and final states, build a pathway of LOCAL actions and supply frequent MOTIVATIONAL STATEMENTS.

2.24.2 Second, the STORY-TREE of the usual format fails to capture some important factors (cf. VIII.2.3). I propose instead an ACTION-STATE NETWORK with a track for each character. To capture MOTIVATIONS, I show alternative paths as branchings (dotted lines) that lead the agent to

[12]Perhaps in some earlier cultural setting, the song had the function of an incantation that makes true what it says. The spinning song used to defeat Tom certainly acts like an exorcism; his recitation of it while spinning might conceivably have served as a spell to make the spinning faster. Due to the perspective from which our story is told, such matters cannot be clarified.

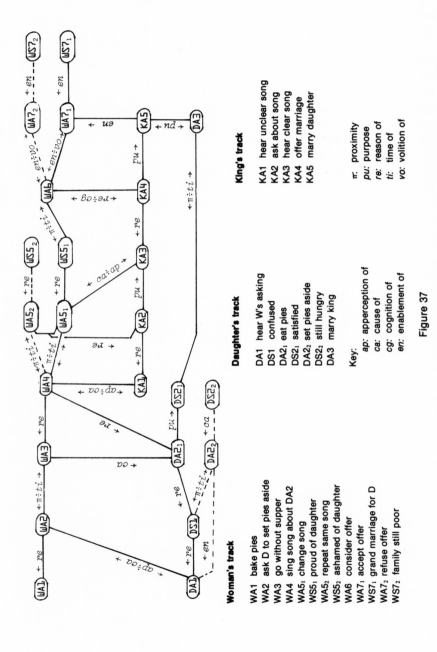

Woman's track

WA1 bake pies
WA2 ask D to set pies aside
WA3 go without supper
WA4 sing song about DA2
WA5₁ change song
WS5₁ proud of daughter
WA5₂ repeat same song
WS5₂ ashamed of daughter
WA6 consider offer
WA7₁ accept offer
WS7₁ grand marriage for D
WA7₂ refuse offer
WS7₂ family still poor

Daughter's track

DA1 hear W's asking
DS1 confused
DA2₁ eat pies
DS2₁ satisfied
DA2₂ set pies aside
DS2₂ still hungry
DA3 marry king

King's track

KA1 hear unclear song
KA2 ask about song
KA3 hear clear song
KA4 offer marriage
KA5 marry daughter

Key:

ap: apperception of
ca: cause of
cg: cognition of
en: enablement of

π: proximity
pu: purpose
re: reason of
ti: time of
vo: volition of

Figure 37

UNDESIRABLE STATES (cf. VI.4.10). Figure 37 shows the results for the opening span of our story. All links are labeled: cause, enablement, reason, purpose, or proximity in time (the last being the weakest link and not to be overused in story-telling). We obtain a visual MACRO-STRUCTURE whose elements provide the MINIMAL CONNECTIVITY needed to render the story-world coherent.

2.25 The ominous BARGAIN FAVOR and the conditions upon failure (17) allow the understander to recognize a new initial state (eleven months of marriage) followed by a problem (spin an impossible amount) and a goal (stay alive—the most desirable goal, according to Pugh 1977). This configuration triggers a recognition of a new episode with high probability of a negative ending. The only chance for a positive outcome appears to be the shared expectation of mother and daughter that the king will 'forget about' the five skeins (18, 20). This hope is blocked when the king rehearses the bargain at the stipulated time (21). The element of ANTAGONISM enters the story with its first real strength at this point: the king blocks the daughter's plan and endangers her positively valued goal of staying alive (cf. VIII.2.9.4); his later action of locking her in furthers the antagonist role by precluding obvious solutions like escape or outside help. Accordingly, the understander should assign the ANTAGONIST role to the king for this episode by noticing the realizations of strategy 2.9.4. The PROTAGONIST is the daughter, since the audience will accept her stay-alive goal over the king's have-flax-spun goal. Her problem is intensified by her own state of not even knowing how to spin. Against the combined odds, strategy 2.9.3 (initiate a pathway to solve the problem) cannot be realized for the daughter's action track, and she can only cry over the final state she must expect (23). We note here an illustration of how actualization affects the attachment of a basic story schema (cf. VIII.2.5).

2.26 The story line is suspended here with all probabilities pointing to disaster. However, strategy 2.10.1 should become active upon noticing the overbalance of the antagonist's power over that of the protagonist. The understander should react to the 'knockin' on the door (24) by predicting a HELPER CHARACTER and classifying the 'small little black thing' (24) accordingly in that role. To enable the helping action, the narrator first navigates the problem of making knowledge accessible (cf. VIII.2.23): there is a brief exchange of Tom's ASK and the daughter's INFORM REASON that telling him 'woon't do noo harm' (30). When Tom's offer (31) opens a pathway to the daughter-protagonist's goal, the understander should recognize a TURNING POINT as defined in VIII.2.7. The daughter's decision is therefore crucial, and the narrator justifies it with the motivational statement: 'she thought she'd be sure to guess that's name afore the month was up' (34).

2.27 Tom's BARGAIN FAVOR matches the pattern established previously by the king's. The attainment of one goal entails a new problem, whose solution becomes a new goal. This time, the protagonist's problem is to find missing knowledge in a limited number of trials (we see the dismal inefficiency of trial-and error as a model of action, cf. VI.4.6). Because this new problem involves a goal conflict also, the antagonist role must be shifted from the king to Tom. This particular role transfer is a delicate matter, as the king's dangerous bargain must be kept in force to motivate the new bargain and maintain suspense. The narrator adopts the expedient of restricting the realization of the antagonist strategies. The king does not set up the daughter's beheading as a planned goal, nor would his plans be defeated if she succeeded. This weakening of strategies 2.9.2 and 2.9.5–6 leaves the king in an ambivalent role of mixed intentions, so that he can become a helper character himself later on (66). We might distill from these considerations a further story-telling strategy:

2.27.1 If the antagonist character for one episode is to enter a helper role for a later episode, restrict the realization of the antagonist strategies for that earlier episode.

2.28 This strategy again illustrates the attachment of global procedures in response to local requirements. By the same token, Tom's role evolves from helper into antagonist. He appears in the story-world as an agent who enables the daughter's stay-alive goal, but a conflict of his own goals with hers becomes steadily more distinct. The narrator pursues this evolution by negative value assignments as well, suggesting a complementary story-telling strategy to 2.27.1:

2.28.1 If the helper character is to enter an antagonist role later, develop a conflict of goals with the protagonist and assign negative values to the helper at suitable points.

2.29 Just before proposing what he knows to be an imbalanced bargain, Tom 'looks out o' the corners o' that's eyes' (33)—a culturally determined signal of the intention to deceive. The fairly neutral, though not flattering expression 'thing' for Tom (24, 31, 39, 42) is soon replaced by the clearly negative 'impet' (small demon) (52, 53, 74). Tom's facial characterization is at first 'right curious' (24), but later changes to 'so maliceful' (52, 68). The daughter goes from being 'that frightened' (23) over the king's demands to feeling relieved at the prospect of help; yet she evolves again into feeling 'that horrid'—a recurring state that shows how the antagonist role has been reassigned via TEXT-INTERNAL PATTERN-MATCHING (cf. VIII.2.13). Her state changes only when a new pathway of solution is opened by the revelation of the name, whereupon she 'fared as if she could have jumped outer her skin for joy'. Recalling that the king-helper was a former antagonist, she cannot share her relief and doesn't 'say a word' (67).

2.30 The negative tendencies in describing Tom are reinforced by the narrator's attention to details. Tom's 'long tail' signals his semi-human status, the other half being animal or devil (cf. VIII.2.29). The cue for recognizing actions and events that advance Tom's plan to gain control of the daughter is the arbitrary, but contextually determined action of tail-twirling. Hardly has the bargain been concluded when 'lork! how that twirled that's tail' (35). Wrong guesses elicit steadily faster twirling (46, 48, 50, 52). The final situation, in which cues are very densely clustered, introduces Tom with 'oo! that's tail were a-twirlin' round so fast' (69). The penultimate guess brings Tom the closest he ever comes to his goal, and we are accordingly cued with: he 'twirled that's tail till you couldn't hardly see it' (74). The narrator has modified the systems for social interaction by creating a totally new action; as a regulatory compensation, its contextual position is made clearly determinate and recurrent. The activity serves to mark both goal pursuit and Tom's semi-human status that invites us to reject his goal of obtaining the daughter (a nobly depicted, marriageable young man in his role would make the story disturbingly ambivalent).

2.31 We can conclude that a major portion of story understanding is the noticing of cues that render the underlying story schema discoverable for procedural attachment. *Value assignments* are clustered around turning points (cf. Labov & Waletzky 1967). The initial episode is neutral about the actions until need arises to motivate the mother's alteration of the song, whereupon she is 'ashamed' (15). To motivate her acceptance of the king's offer, the narrator terms the resulting marriage 'grand' (18). The second episode demands an explanation why the daughter does not try herself to solve the problem, and only then are we told she is 'gatless' (lazy). The turning point of the final episode shows Tom 'grinning from ear to ear', which hardly renders his goals attractive. At the second wrong guess, he 'laughs' at his opponent's misfortune (74), foreshadowing her echoing laugh at his defeat, accompanied by her echoing his song (76). The almost triumphant Tom 'stretches out that's black hands at her' (75) (compare the expression of the same action as 'he held out his hand to her'), and she 'backs a step or two' in revulsion (76). Her delivery of the name chant is introduced with the socially stigmatizing action of 'pointin' of her finger at it' (76). Even pronouns are pressed into service to reify Tom: 'it' and 'that' are used throughout the final scene as opposed to 'he' in the first round of guesses (43–50).

2.32 The later episodes also contain *motivational statements*. The daughter's distress and fright arise from not knowing how to spin and having 'no one to come nigh to help her' (23). Before accepting the bargain, she reasons that 'she'd be sure to guess that's name' (34). To intensify her danger later, we are told how Tom delivers his prediction 'with eyes like a coal o' fire' (61). The king's presence in the room, where he will inadvertently solve the daughter's problem, is motivated by his statement: 'as I reckon I shan't have to kill you, I'll have supper in here to-night' (63). To lead up to the story, the king's dinner must be interrupted by a laugh and a request for explanation (64–66).

2.33 The interaction between motivation and value assignment is manifest. The story-world should appear plausible to the audience even when the course of events takes unexpected or disadvantageous pathways. At major or minor turning points, the narrator guides the audience's outlook with the two kinds of signals just illustrated. We could distill out another story-telling strategy:

2.33.1 When a character makes a decision that leads to a new problem state, give material that suggests why the selected path is better than it seems, and the discarded path(s) not so good.

2.34 The narrator weights the probabilities for outcomes in such a way that no one pathway can be distinctly superior. The mother and the daughter concluded their disastrous bargains in hoping to 'get out of' them (18, 34). Failing that, chances of spinning an impossible amount or guessing a unique name in 30×3 tries are dishearteningly slight. The event progression is therefore informative and interesting by the standard of problematic access.

2.35 I have diagrammed the second and the final episodes of the story as a network in Figure 38. Whereas the mother had the densest track in the opening span (cf. Figure 37), the daughter's track is the richest here. Her actions, however, are largely re-actions to the impulses from the tracks for the king K and Tom T. As in Figure 37, I show the alternative paths for events which might have but did not occur at turning points. These alternatives form the context for fully understanding the actually selected pathways.[13] This additional knowledge is unfortunately suppressed by the usual story trees which include only actualized events. Yet some occurrences make very little sense unless the audience knows what might happen otherwise.

2.36 The interactive tracks show a characteristic looping in the latter part of the story. Each day, Tom fetches the flax (TA3), spins it (TA4), and brings it back (TA5). The daughter gets the flax (DA8), and guesses wrong names (DA9₁). Tom gleefully loops back. The king comes in (KA7), finds the flax (KA8₁), and reprieves the daughter (KA9₁), whereupon both loop back. The looping contingency, in effect, requires the daughter to guess wrong every day but the last: a right guess before then would deprive Tom of a reason to continue spinning, and the king's bargain would bring her downfall. Significantly, the narrator passes over all guessing rounds but the first (44–50), next to last (54–60), and the last (70–76). There is actually no freedom of alternatives for the rest, and to recount any more would destroy interest

---

[13]This format reflects the *disjunction* of *alternative events,* which I noted as a parallel between textuality and interaction (note 14 to Chapter VI).

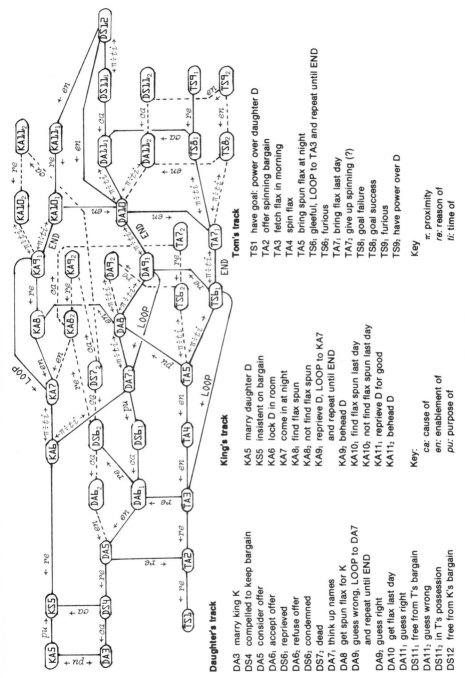

Daughter's track

DA3 marry king K
DS4 compelled to keep bargain
DA5 consider offer
DA6₁ accept offer
DS6₁ reprieved
DA6₂ refuse offer
DS6₂ condemned
DS7₂ dead
DA7₁ think up names
DA8 get spun flax for K
DA9₁ guess wrong, LOOP to DA7
and repeat until END
DA9₂ guess right
DA10 get flax last day
DA11₁ guess right
DS11₁ free from T's bargain
DA11₂ guess wrong
DS11₂ in T's possession
DS12 free from K's bargain

King's track

KA5 marry daughter D
KS5 insistent on bargain
KA6 lock D in room
KA7 come in at night
KA8₁ find flax spun
KA8₂ not find flax spun
KA9₁ reprieve D, LOOP to KA7
and repeat until END
KA9₂ behead D
KA10₁ find flax spun last day
KA10₂ not find flax spun last day
KA11₁ reprieve D for good
KA11₂ behead D

Key:

ca: cause of
en: enablement of
pu: purpose of

Tom's track

TS1 have goal: power over daughter D
TA2 offer spinning bargain
TA3 fetch flax in morning
TA4 spin flax
TA5 bring spun flax at night
TS6₁ gleeful, LOOP to TA3 and repeat until END
TS6₂ furious
TA7₁ bring flax last day
TA7₂ give up spinning (?)
TS8₁ goal failure
TS8₂ goal success
TS9₁ furious
TS9₂ have power over D

Key

π: proximity
re: reason of
ti: time of

Figure 38

271

through predictability. The narrator simply suggests the continued guessing by moving from the common names of the opening round to the uncommon ones of the last two.

2.37 It might escape notice that the event-action-state progressions are subtly marked in the surface text by junctives. When events follow closely on each other, 'and' (or 'an") is regularly inserted, even where it is otherwise dispensable (e.g. in 12 and 66). The inclusion of the 'baking' action in the opening sentence via 'and'-conjunction signals that a topic element is being introduced (van Dijk 1977a: 150). If causality (cause, reason, etc.) is in focus, 'so' is used (e.g. 1, 5, 13, 15). If there are small discrepancies or discontinuities, we find 'but' (e.g. 3, 13, 20). A larger discrepancy/ discontinuity is marked by 'howsoever' (e.g. 21, 24, 62), when a new direction of the event sequence begins. If there is relative consistency, but a lapse of time or an indirect causality, 'well' is inserted (4, 12, 19, 23, 36, 42, 51). On three occasions, 'well' marks the transition from an external event to a mental reaction (34, 62, 67). The function of 'well' in dialogue is similarly to signal that the speaker will express an inner reaction to an event (8, 30, 63). In the guessing dialogue, 'well' precedes the final guess in the first two rounds (49, 59); but in the last round, where the pattern will be broken, 'well' is moved up to the second guess (73).

2.38 When Tom and the king want to direct attention to their bargains with the daughter, they begin their utterances with 'now' (21, 37, 44). The bargains themselves are stated in the format of negated 'if'-clauses followed by a statement of what happens (17, 21, 33, 37). When Tom is feeling confident, he shifts to 'and', the usual marker of close junction: 'there's only to-morrow night, and you'll be mine' (61); 'next guess, and you're mine' (75). These consistent uses of junctives are an economic support for the tightly organized story-world.

2.39 The ECONOMY of the story-world regarding LOCATION, TIME, and MATERIAL RESOURCES is an important contributor to the text's EFFICIENCY (greatest amount of knowledge transmitted with the least means). These aspects are stipulated only as required directly for continuity of events. For instance, the only mention of location concerns: the whereabouts of the pies, which come 'out of the oven' (1) and never arrive 'on the shelf' (2); the motion of the mother 'to the door' (12), so the king can 'come down the street' and enter the action; the 'kitchen' to cry in (23); an unused 'room' for the ordeal (21, 36), equipped with a 'door' (24) for the king and daughter, and a 'window' plus 'ledge' (38, 42, 68, 69) to get Tom in and out; and 'an old chalk pit' away 'in the wood' (66) as a location for the discovery of the name. All other possible locations, such as where the mother and daughter live or what other rooms the king's palace has, are not mentioned.

2.40 Time figures chiefly (aside from the default of folktales, 'once upon a time') in the daily rhythm of spinning and guessing. The greater density of pointers to 'evening' or 'night' (31, 33, 42, 51, 52, 61, 63, 68) in comparison to 'morning' (31, 51, 52) reflects the distribution of potential turning points— guessing and possible beheading.

2.41 Material resources (cf. Wilensky 1978: ch. 11 on "functional and consumable objects") are sparse as well: one 'spinning wheel' each for the daughter and Tom (21, 66); three 'stools' as the only furniture (21, 23, 63); a 'hobby' (horse) to get the king to the scene for learning the name (66); 'pies' whose 'tough crusts' get the whole story going (1–2); an unlimited quantity of 'vittles' and 'gowns' for the 'eleven months' (19), and whatever 'vittles' and 'flax' are needed for the daughter's spinning ordeal. It is noteworthy that 'flax' and 'vittles' are topically intertwined throughout. The actions are chained so that overconsumption of food leads to spinning; a song about eating becomes a song about spinning; the king's offer provides immense food in return for immense spinning; and the spinning ordeal is resolved by knowledge imparted over a dinner. This powerful balance has apparently inspired the surface expression as a pattern of reversals: 'some vittles and some flax' (21), 'the flax an' the day's vittles' (36), 'your vittles and your flax' (51), and 'the flax an' the vittles' (52).

2.42 Such tight organization as I have pointed out is surely the result of skillful and repeated narrating. In experimenting with story recall, we must bear in mind that our test subjects might not command the skills needed to render a story in its original design. To point up this difficulty, our sample story (247) was used in recall tests with University of Florida students. On the first run, we accidentally obtained an intriguing set of responses to a DISCREPANT story: the experimenter, Nathan Robinson, pronounced 'skeins' as 'skins' due to dialect, and did not explain the object to the test persons. Consequently, a second run taken by Patsy Lynn was prefaced by some elucidation of this unfamiliar word. We were interested to see evidence of intense disorientation on the first run, but not on the second. Among the 10 subjects on the first, 3 simply left the 'spinning of skins' as such. One changed it into 'sewing skins' (e.g. animal skins?), and another into 'collecting skins'. More remote rearrangements involved 'spinning five skills', 'spinning five spuns of spin', and even 'spinning pies'. The other two subjects eliminated the trouble altogether by recounting a story only about baking, for example:

(248) This story reflects how a woman started off baking five pies. Then she ate them all. She was then told by a man to bake five more or it would mean her death. I believe that the baker's problem was that every time pies were baked, she would eat them.

This protocol suggests how a macro-structure can still be used in procedural attachment, even when a substantial amount of the originally presented content is missing. The other baking-world story introduces a woman whose failure at baking is cured by the intervention of a mysterious lady arriving to give lessons in cookery; the results are so miraculous that 'in the last part of the story [...] all the woman wanted to do was bake pies'.

2.43 The story protocols support the storage and recall processes I postulated in VII.3.29 concerning the interaction of text knowledge with stored knowledge. When the spinning was explained in the second test run, the corresponding entries in the textual world were brought into focus, and recall of the spinning task was extremely accurate—evidence that material matching prior knowledge is indeed privileged (VII.3.29.1). The subjects who reported recognizing the story as a variant of the 'Rumpelstiltskin' tale recalled the name-guessing contest distinctly.

2.44 The alterations to produce a better match with stored knowledge (VII.3.29.3) arose noticeably from differences between a contemporary American audience and a nineteenth-century Suffolk one. The unfamiliar 'flax' was often replaced with better-known materials: 'wool', 'yarn', and 'cloth'. Subjects recalled that the marriage was proposed to and accepted by the daughter herself; that the pies were for dessert, not supper; and that the king arrived at the woman's residence on a horse rather than walking (6 protocols)—rich Americans wouldn't walk. Instances of conflation via world-knowledge (VII.3.29.4) included remembering both mother and daughter baking together; having the daughter spinning at the door; and confusing Tom's spinning with his tail-twirling, e.g.:

(249) a little black creature that helped her simply by spinning his tail
(250) Each time that he came to visit he would spin faster and faster

this conflation occurring in the group who heard the discrepant version. Decay of accidental knowledge (VII.3.29.5) was documented by the treatment of Tom's name. 3 students remembered it accurately; 16 recovered no name at all. The new versions among the remainder included: Tom Thompkin, Dit Dot, Tom Tick Tock, and this heroic attempt to reconstruct the whole song:

(251) Ippity oppity dot,
My name is Tiny Tim the Snot.

Tom's unclear status led people to recall him as an 'animal', a 'black nymph', a 'lady' (cf. VIII.2.42) and a 'black cat' (this last because of color plus tail?).

2.45 Due to the ECONOMY noted in VIII.2.39, subjects were prone to enrich the textual world with *inferencing* and *spreading activation*. Two subjects remembered the mother and daughter inhabiting a 'little village house' ("location-of" spreading). The dispute over the pies was given a "time", e.g. 'later in the afternoon' or 'later that night'. The mother was repeatedly described as 'mad' or 'beside herself' over the loss of pies ("emotion-of").

2.46 The importance of *story-world characters solving their problems* (VIII.2.14) is well known (cf. Meehan 1976; Rumelhart & Ortony 1977; Wilensky 1978). Even the confused subject who wrote a story on baking (248) mentioned the protagonist's 'problem'. We obtained some evidence of subjects' thinking in terms of characters' PLANS, such as:

(252) She sang low so the king wouldn't hear her.
(253) The lady was embarrassed and covered up for her daughter's immaturity.
(254) When the black thing came back with the skeins of flax, he was ready to take the daughter with him.

On the other hand, much less investigation has been concerned with *how narrators solve the problems of story-world connectivity*. In the 'Tom-Tit-Tot'-world, the narrator confronts the problem of getting the opening episode from a trivial baking event to a momentous royal marriage (VIII.2.23). If subjects have forgotten how the original narrator proceeded, they use their own methods. For instance, the word-play with 'come again' as 'get soft' was lost, so that our students reasoned about the daughter's motives for overeating in these ways:

(255) The girl couldn't wait so she ate the five pies.
(256) The daughter decided that the crusts would never become soft so she sat and ate all five pies.

Fourteen subjects simply had the daughter eat the pies out of hand; sometimes she was recalled as a 'little girl' to make her action more plausible.

2.47 The subjects who forgot the circumstances of the king's entry deployed considerable ingenuity in solving the problem of how to introduce him. One had him just 'drop in'; another had the mother address the passing 'king and his troop' with a deliberate 'boasting'; four sent the mother out on a walk through the village, singing to herself; two had the furious mother 'yell' her daughter's misdeed out the door. The following protocol excerpts illustrate how people strive for continuity despite very incomplete recall:

(257) Being irate and upset, she spun [!] to the doorway and yelled, "My daughter has eaten all five pies!" It was quite a coincidence, because as she yelled the king was passing by and asked her to repeat it.
(258) The mother got screaming mad and yelled out the door. While she looked out the front door, she heard a man singing along in the street and joined in.
(259) After she had eaten the pies, she began to sing a strange song. The mother sought help for her daughter by asking the king to marry her and take care of her. He agreed to do so if she would collect five skins for him each day.

2.48 The conclusion to be drawn from the assembled evidence on the recall of stories is clear. Like all texts, stories are not just sequences of sentences or propositions, but also cohesive systems of expression and coherent systems of knowledge. However much or however little of the originally presented material is processed, stored, and recovered, story receivers will make sense out of what is available by working for sequential, conceptual, and planning connectivity. To tabulate accuracy of recall is to look at only a fraction of the total picture. The abstraction of traces or the analysis of surface features cannot be the highest priority for communicative activities such as narration. All participants—story tellers, story receivers, characters in story worlds— utilize whatever is necessary and accessible to solve their problems and attain their goals in a co-operative enterprise whose texts, though highly varied and flexible, are suitably designed for those tasks.

IX

Applications for a Science of Texts

1. THE EDUCATIONAL ENTERPRISE

1.1 The complaints voiced by educators, students, and society at large suggest grave disillusionment with the efficacy of public education in contemporary America: what is being taught is not retained, not useful, and not relevant to the tasks learners will face in later life. In this environment, learner motivation is generally low. The ominous failure quota dooms a substantial portion of American youth to an existence permanently devoid of professional and social opportunities. The bizarre Darwinian notion of the "grade curve"—a statistical construct that demands a balance of superior grades against failures or near-failures, with a broad mass of learners in the middle—suggests that failure is not viewed as a personal tragedy, but as a normal condition of schooling. Educators who undertake to encourage superior performance for all learners can become the target of committees against "grade inflation"—a purported "overbalance" of favorable grading.

1.2 When public schooling became generally available in the eighteenth and nineteenth centuries, the traditional curriculum was upheld—a curriculum which by and large goes back to the schools of Ancient Greece. The question of whether such a curriculum is relevant to the needs of modern children has seldom been officially raised. Educators "assumed a cultural trust, a vast body of unspoken but shared routines that freed them from the need to explain what they were up to" (Shaughnessy 1976: 153). A methodology that is not openly expounded and discussed can hardly be revised.

1.3 My investigations of American schooling have left me with the impression that the main orientation is *behavioristic,* despite the dramatic downfall of behaviorism as an account of human knowledge and abilities. Altogether too much energy is expended on rote acquisition and recitation of isolated facts. Testing and evaluation inhabit a disquieting world where everything is either "correct" or "incorrect." The consequences of forcing HUMANISTIC domains into such a methodology are disastrous. Language skills must then be measured by "grammar quizzes," and writing exercises graded via mechanical tabulation of surface errors or deviations from prestigious usage. Literature is demeaned and impoverished into a contest of identifying quotations or authors' names and biographies. In short, CREATIVITY is routinely discouraged because it eludes the distinction of "correct and incorrect responses." Getzels and Jackson (1962) found that standard measurements of intelligence ("IQ tests") scarcely measure creativity at all. The result is doubtless a loss of motivation among learners who justly feel that their individual talents and skills are welcome and approved only for a restricted range of pre-decided tasks of questionable value and relevance. Typically, the failure to learn in such an environment is blamed on the child (cf. criticism in Dittmar 1976: 95).

1.4 In cognitive terms, education is on the wrong track as long as it stresses EPISODIC KNOWLEDGE over CONCEPTUAL-RELATIONAL (cf. Kintsch 1977a: 284; Groeben 1978: 15). The learner's mind is cluttered with an array of incidental facts which elude integration into a coherent functioning system of world-knowledge. Each batch of poorly digested facts is promptly forgotten after testing, because the systemic organization needed for application is not provided. I submit that this dreary situation can be vastly improved if we shift the whole emphasis of schooling away from the *memorization of facts* toward the development of a *powerful and flexible set of strategies for acquiring, organizing, and applying knowledge* irrespective of the specific content in a task or textbook (cf. I.5.6; IV.3.18). These strategies should become the openly proclaimed theme of *all* curricular subjects from the first to the last year of schooling. A fully co-ordinated corpus of learning materials reflecting this priority should be provided for each and every classroom. The judgment of performance should be done not for the sake of discrimination and retribution against the individual child, but for the sake of diagnosis and arranging of training priorities. The strategies I envision include the following (cf. the list of processing strategies in IV.3.17ff.):

1.4.1 general problem-solving capacities in the sense of I.6.7ff.;

1.4.2 flexibility in task management;

1.4.3 ability to decompose large, difficult tasks into small, simple ones;

1.4.4 ability to focus and distribute attention wisely;

1.4.5 ability to judge efficiency, effectiveness, and appropriateness of available options (cf. I.4.14);

1.4.6 ability to build, implement, and revise goal-directed plans;

1.4.7 ability to weigh competing goals and decide among them;

1.4.8 ability to analyze and learn from failure;

1.4.9 reasoning by causality (cause, reason, enablement, purpose);

1.4.10 reasoning by generalization from examples;

1.4.11 hierarchical reasoning (e.g. superclass inclusion, cf. III.3.19);

1.4.12 analogical reasoning (e.g. metaclass inclusion, cf. III.3.20);

1.4.13 differential reasoning (e.g. class definition and determination);

1.4.14 reasoning from incomplete knowledge;

1.4.15 computation of relative probabilities and success chances;

1.4.16 strategies of adapting to improbable or non-expected occurrences;

1.4.17 strategies for modifying available systems in response to a reasonable motivation;

1.4.18 strategies for organizing, integrating, and storing content;

1.4.19 strategies for judging and maintaining interestingness and informativity;

1.4.20 strategies for arguing in support of views and beliefs;

1.4.21 self-reliance in intellectual undertakings of all kinds.

1.5 Though this list of abilities is not necessarily novel (cf. Newell & Simon 1972; Collins 1977, 1978; Resnick 1977), its implications for the development of the human intellect have not been fully appreciated. The raising of human INTELLIGENCE can be achieved *by training learners to decouple these abilities from the performance of individual tasks in the classroom* (cf. I.5.6; IV.3.18). Only then can learners operate on the high plane of *types of knowledge and operations,* rather than on the low plane of daily "facts" and "assignments." Rote memorization and mechanical activities would sink down to reasonable proportions. The teacher would act as a diagnostician or specialized consultant, and not as a relentless inspector of exact details. We would no longer equate rapid, accurate storage and recall with intelligence at large—a misconception which educators seem to share with many psychologists. We should rather undertake to explore and manage the rate at which individual children can discover and apply cognitive strategies to the broadest possible range of tasks and knowledge. Every school activity must be supportive of this general objective. Children must realize that the different subjects and topics in the various classes are all intended to cultivate a common repertory of intellectual abilities. Learning materials must not be viewed as incontrovertible artifacts to be swallowed and disgorged under stressful conditions, but only as sample tools for rehearsing the cognitive skills that learners will need for successful thought and action in later life.

1.6 I view activities of utilizing texts as the center of such an educational enterprise. *The production and reception of efficient, effective, and appropriate texts demands all of the twenty-one cognitive abilities I have cited.* Hence, the language-based disciplines offer a unique pivotal domain from which cognitive development across the whole curriculum can be co-ordinated. Although my plans for the re-organization of schooling along these lines are still in the primary stage of development, I shall suggest in this chapter at least some aspects worthy of consideration.

1.7 The shift of emphasis and methodology will consume considerable time and resources at first, but in the long run, an enormous increase in the power and successfulness of schooling will be attainable. A major source of support for the already overworked teacher will be a new approach to *computer-assisted instruction*. The notion of GENERAL PROBLEM-SOLVING (mentioned in I.6.7) evolved from the realization that *general strategies of reasoning and procedure can and should be recognized as independent of the demands of any particular task domain* (cf. Ernst & Newell 1969; Newell & Simon 1972: 414).[1] Powerful computer programs have already been developed for training precisely such skills as I have listed above over a wide range of curricular subjects; geography, chemistry, mathematics, medicine, and machine assembly (cf. Carbonell Sr. 1970; Papert 1973; Collins, Warnock, & Passafiume 1974; Collins & Grignetti 1975; Collins, Warnock, Aiello, & Miller 1975; Brown & Burton 1975, 1977; Davis, Buchanan, & Shortliffe 1977; Collins 1977, 1978; Brown, Collins, & Harris 1978). These programs differ fundamentally from the conventional computer-assisted instruction in which there is a rigid sequence of specific, material-dependent question-answer routines. In these new programs, knowledge is stored not as rote facts, but as NETWORKS that allow the automatic tutor to use facts in many ways, to ask flexible, mutually relevant questions, and to deal perspicaciously with a variety of student replies and inquiries. Hence, the tutor does not simply *drill facts*; it impels the student to *acquire and apply general reasoning strategies* such as Socratic logic, generalization from examples, analogical reasoning, and even reasoning in absence of knowledge (cf. Collins 1977, 1978). Errors are taken as opportunities to show how the correlation of strategies can be optimized.

1.8 There is a further interdependency between education and a science of texts. The acquisition of both humanistic and scientific knowledge cannot occur without well-organized discourse. Indeed, a good portion of the work in mastering a discipline lies in mastering its established mode of discourse (cf. for instance, Bross 1973). The science of texts must provide clear, workable standards for the production of all texts employed in learning. Norbert Groeben (1978: 83) asserts that the success of learning strategies depends heavily on the READABILITY of instructional texts—a factor all too often passed over hitherto.

1.9 No one would deny that the educational enterprise is a vast and complex field whose reorganization will be an enormous undertaking. Yet I

[1] See footnote 20 to Chapter 1.

hold that complexity will diminish dramatically via the emphasis upon a common base of cognitive training throughout the curriculum. Just as old-style linguistics was unduly concerned with isolated aspects of language, so that a clear picture of communication overall never emerged; in the same way, preoccupation with scattered bits and pieces of knowledge in education renders learning unnecessarily laborious, and solutions to individual problems arbitrarily intricate. A science of texts with open borders toward all language-related disciplines (cf. I.1.2) and with emphasis upon the deeper processes of human cognition can become the paradigm of a new outlook in both science and the humanities, so that educational concerns of whatever kind can be integrated within a forceful continuity and relevance.

2. TRADITIONAL GRAMMAR VERSUS APPLIED LINGUISTICS

2.1 For thousands of years, the socialization and education of children has involved some kind of language training. That training seldom became institutionalized at the outset of language acquisition: actual schooling usually began at an age where extensive prior ability and experience could be safely presupposed. Schooling focused less on the language as a complete intersystem, than on certain PROBLEMATIC aspects deemed to require MANAGEMENT. Unfortunately, management is difficult to achieve without a workable description or explanation of language (I.1.9).

2.2 Traditional grammar drew on a diversity of sources that can not always be reconciled with each other. Logic, philosophy, rhetoric, literature, public attitudes, personal views of grammarians, and even grammars of entirely different languages (notably Latin) served as inspiration. The outcome was a wide diversity of principles that worked sporadically or at cross-purposes. The "rules" of English usage are a striking demonstration. The "rule" forbidding double negation came from logic, where two negatives yield an affirmative; in normal speaking, they often yield an emphatic negative.[2] The "rules" that proscribe split infinitives and sentence-final prepositions were derived from the structure of Latin. And many "rules" were introduced to discredit the speech habits of non-prestigious social groups. Not surprisingly, a system of "rules" like these is not very helpful to the learner, because: (1) the principles at work are vague and inconsistent; (2) the emphasis is mostly on what *not* to say or write; and (3) there is a divergence between the official version of the language and the usage people can find all around the culture.

---

[2]See, for instance, (6) and (7) in the 'Tom Tit Tot' story (VIII.2.20). I suspect that the extra negatives are used to direct focus to precisely those elements in which expectations are being overturned (cf. IV.1.25), i.e., where a non-negative state of affairs is desirable or normal.

2.3 Weaknesses like these were seized upon by modern linguistics as grounds for rejecting the whole undertaking of traditional grammar. Paul Roberts (1958) announced "the grammarian's funeral" and extolled the precision and objectivity of linguistic methods. The linguist undertook to describe languages as they *are,* not as they *should be* in the opinion of small, prestigious groups. Each language was investigated in its own terms, not in terms of Latin. Despite these important improvements, early optimism about the application of linguistics to language training soon waned. Linguistics was addressing essentially different issues from traditional grammar, and was not suitable for language management in any direct way. The analysis of utterances into structures of minimal units offers no obvious means for discovering how language options should be selected and utilized in communication. Linguistics *presupposes* communication just as traditional grammar often had done.

2.4 In retrospect, the limitations upon "applied linguistics" for language training seem obvious. Educators failed to appreciate the high cost of the division of language into "langue vs. parole," or "competence vs. performance." If taken in an extremely narrow sense—as in the recent polemic of Dresher and Hornstein quoted in I.1.17.3—the idealized version of language is far removed from the practical concerns of the teacher. Similarly, the mysterious "language acquisition device" postulated as an innate mechanism for building transformational grammars in the human brain—the rules are too numerous and intricate to be learned in any other way—has not materialized so far.

2.5 I believe the notion of "applied linguistics" will make a valuable contribution only for a *linguistics of actualization.*[3] The study of *virtual* systems of phonemes, morphemes, lexical items, and sentence patterns can offer only an incomplete insight into the operations of language *in use.* While there are many options in such virtual repertories, only some options are EFFICIENT to use, EFFECTIVE in getting things achieved, and APPROPRIATE to the demands of textuality in a particular setting (cf. I.4.14). By discarding altogether the *evaluative* component of traditional grammar, linguistics cannot advance much beyond the task of *description;* even *explanation* will eventually have to account for the value judgments that underlie language users' motives for selecting language options. The errors of old-style evaluation evolved from the belief that one can state once and for all what language options are "correct" or "incorrect" under all circumstances.

2.6 The monumental *Grammar of Contemporary English* (Quirk, Greenbaum, Leech, & Svartvik 1972) demonstrates that a traditional grammar can both reflect the realities of current usage and provide helpful

---

[3]See for example the contributions in Kohonen & Enkvist (eds.) 1978.

criteria for selecting options in common situations. The grammar is based not on the opinions of a few grammarians, but on an exhaustive survey of English usage directed by Randolph Quirk. Socially and regionally marked options are described as such rather than proscribed as "incorrect." Current methods of linguistics are deployed without dogmatic allegiance to a single approach. The scope of the survey approximates completeness as far as any educational purpose is likely to demand. Thus, the work vindicates the undertaking of traditional grammar and opens the way to a reasonable integration of grammar into developmental education.

2.7 One can continue to debate the question of whether linguistics has a commitment to language training or not. I hold the task of language management to be among the most pressing issues in the whole educational enterprise; what right have we to talk about "competence" if our language theories cannot be used to develop competence? To insist any longer on carefully screened abstractions as the only "scientific" object for the study of languages is to incur the onus of evaded responsibility toward the intellectual development and self-expression of our children.

3.   THE TEACHING OF READING

3.1 In the absence of a useable account of language actualization, traditional reading instruction has laid undue emphasis upon the recognition of single words and sentences. Occurrences in which the reader's "response" did not fit the "stimulus" on the page were dismissed as "errors" to be eradicated at all costs. Ernst Z. Rothkopf (1976: 109) surveys reading education and concludes: "human theories during the last three decades treated learning as if it were the passive consequence of bombardment by environmental particles." I have devoted considerable space in this volume to supporting the view that, on the contrary, knowledge acquisition requires circumspect prediction and matching operations that integrate new material into systems. Changes of the surface presentation are normal and natural for experienced readers. "Miscues" in reading aloud (cf. VII.3.14) happen routinely among all reader groups and provide important evidence of the cognitive strategies at work (cf. Goodman & Burke 1973). Indeed, I would view miscues as a signal of a fluent reader who is not chained slavishly to the printed page.

3.2 The study of READABILITY concerns the *proportionality between processing effort and obtainable knowledge during the activity of reading* (cf. VII.2.24). Klare (1963) cites some thirty readability "formulas," many of them derivative to some extent from the work of Rudolf Flesch (1949). In most cases, reliance is placed on the superficial standards of length and complexity of words or sentences. Rothkopf (1976: 108) criticizes such standards:

The lexical characteristic chiefly tapped is familiarity. Vividness and concreteness are neglected. Exposition and organization are disregarded completely. Content factors are ignored.

3.3 As far as I can judge, the usual measurements of readability reveal some severe misunderstanding of the nature of texts and textuality. For one thing, I cannot see how the options of *virtual* systems of language can be assigned a degree of difficulty for all possible contexts of occurrence. One can, for example, conduct experiments to find out what sentence patterns are easy to read (cf. Groeben 1978: 18ff.); but it is surely an error to demand that the easiest patterns must always be used in order to make the text optimally readable. On the contrary: the constant use of easy patterns was shown in VII.2.18ff. to yield an egregiously *un*readable story. I consider the principle of the "least effort" wholly misconceived as a standard of human activities at large and of the reading of texts in particular. Readers will gladly expend more effort, *provided that the text awakens interest and rewards the effort with informative insights.* The "least-effort" principle has bequeathed us an armory of inane, boring readers for children (called "Dick-and-Jane" books in America) because of the view that we should pursue only processing *ease* and ignore processing *depth* (cf. I.4.14; IV.1.6).

3.4 A sensible measurement of readability cannot be content with looking at the surface text or at virtual systems alone. We need to consider all of the operations that map the surface text onto an underlying representation and utilize that representation as relevant to a task. Cunningham (1978) found children who performed quite well at recognizing and defining words (virtual system: lexicon), but quite poorly at understanding and remembering the content of whole passages (actual system: text). He attained some improvement by having the children make up titles or endings for stories—tasks in which large blocks of knowledge must be organized and tested for relevance. The restoration of scrambled stories (cf. Kintsch, Mandel, & Kozminsky 1977) encourages children to use schemas actively.

3.5 It seems clear that we can hardly measure the effort demanded for reading if we have no model of the processes being used by readers. My own model leads me to suppose that readability depends on the kind of *problems* which a text presents—e.g. discontinuities in the surface or in the text-world model—and the goals to be achieved by solving those problems. Literary and poetic texts are frequently problematic because of their reorganization of the world and of discourse about the world (cf. VII.1.8.4f.); but their readability is such that they often outlive all other texts of their time and continue to be read widely even now. I suspect that the use of creative texts will do much to engage children in learning to read.

3.6 The role of a science of texts in this area is readily evident. We must set up integrated models of the reading processes and test the variables that could affect operations, e.g.: (1) extent of *discontinuities* within texts or textual worlds; (2) extent of *discrepancies* between texts or textual worlds and prior knowledge or expectations; (3) extent of *redundancy* among textual levels (cf. VII.2.18); (4) extent of individual *reading experience;* (5) the outlook of reader groups on *orders of informativity;* (6) distribution of *attention;* (7) extent of *recall.* All of these variables must be considered before we can decide how readable a given text should be for a given audience: we will be able to measure readability as *relative,* not *absolute* (cf. Hirsch 1977), and in terms of *cognitive procedures* rather than of *surface texts.*

4. THE TEACHING OF WRITING

4.1 In the wake of an alarming decline in writing skills, the demand for a full-scale theory of the writing processes has become acute. Following the priorities of conventional linguistics, research has dwelt chiefly on structural analysis, as Richard L. Larson (1976: 71) remarks:

> We have, in studies of form, largely a record of search for formulas and patterns in discourse, and a record of advice on the properties that well-ordered discourse ought, in the a priori judgement of theorists, to exhibit. But the reasons for the effectiveness of different patterns, the ways in which their parts interact, the most useful techniques of deciding upon particular sequences of steps in composing [...] have been dealt with slightly, hesitantly, or not at all.

4.2 Perhaps we should inquire not what applied linguistics can offer, but rather what applied linguistics should become if it is to have something worth offering.[4] The following contributions appear desirable (cf. Beaugrande 1978c):

4.2.1 a realistic account of the cognitive activities in writing;

4.2.2 a statement and classification of the options and categories of the WRITTEN mode as opposed to the SPOKEN;

4.2.3 an account of the relative efficiency, effectiveness, and appropriateness of written options in recognizable contexts;

4.2.4 a statement of the procedures for applying the options of writing that are relevant to a plan toward a goal;

4.2.5 a model of orderly decision and selection based on all of the above;

---

[4]One direct offshoot of linguistics for composition is the method of "sentence combining" introduced by Bateman and Zidonis (1964) and popularized by Mellon (1969) and O'Hare (1971). I have argued, however, that sentence combining is of little value until we have a workable account of the *motives* for combining sentences in a given context (Beaugrande 1979h) (cf. IX.4.5f.). Here again, the distinction between virtual and actual is crucial.

4.2.6 a corresponding methodology for presenting and training the skills involved.

4.3 I expect that such an approach to writing—I am currently engaged in its development myself (Beaugrande, in preparation)—will make it possible to diagnose writing problems which hitherto have simply been viewed as a chaotic array of surface "errors." The strangely disordered texts many untrained writers produce arise, I think, from PLAN COMPETITION: a collision of functions in the two divergent systems: face-to-face communication vs. public written discourse (cf. VII.2.6).

4.4 Consider the well-known error of the "comma splice," in which a writer fuses two otherwise independent sentences together with only a comma. The traditional treatment in composition classes was to advocate simply replacing the comma with a period or a semicolon. However, we might inquire how these comma splices evolve. In my view, this usage is intended to signal a close relatedness of content that makes the writer hesitate to use a period. It would thus be sensible to connect the sentences into a single sentence with a subordinating junctive (V.7.6ff). My experiments show that beginning writers can use this sort of approach to attain considerable improvement.

4.5 The focus of a theoretically well-founded methodology of writing should be upon MOTIVATION and DECISION. Learners who acquire workable standards for evaluating their own prose as *a protocol of decision-making* need not rely constantly on the teacher's feedback. Instead, they can compare their text to their current motivations and goals, and revise inadequate decisions accordingly. In this fashion, untrained writers can distribute their attention selectively during several phases rather than trying to manage all writing operations successfully in the first run. Presumably, this latter proceeding simply overloads processing resources. We must therefore break the writing task down into sufficiently small subtasks which any learners can manage, irrespective of their prior experience and social background. As training progresses, the ability to co-ordinate more and more subtasks at once should rise in the same fashion that active storage can hold more material when larger, better integrated "chunks" are formed (cf. III.3.11.6).

4.6 A research group I direct at the University of Florida, including Richard Hersh, Patsy Lynn, Genevieve Miller, Nathan Robinson, and Patty Street, is initiating experiments along the lines I have sketched so far. A brief demonstration can be found in these four alternative text fragments:

(260.1a) Many people are thrifty these days. (260.2a) My husband is thrifty. (260.3a) He saves used toothpicks for firewood.

(260.1b) Many people are thrifty these days. (260.2b) My thrifty husband saves used toothpicks for firewood.

(260.1c) Many people are extravagant these days. (260.2c) My husband is thrifty. (260.3c) He saves used toothpicks for firewood.

(260.1d) Many people are extravagant these days. (260.2d) My thrifty husband saves used toothpicks for firewood.

The decision in focus here is whether to place the modifier 'thrifty' of the follow-up sentences (260.2a–d) in the "attributive" position (before the head 'husband') or the "predicate" position (after a linking verb). In a textual world where thriftiness is usual and hence expected (samples a and b), the attributive positioning (260.2b) is a better choice than the predicate (260.2a). In a textual world where extravagance is the norm, the focus-creating predicate positioning (260.2c) is superior to the attributive (260.2d). We can notice these differences just by reading the samples aloud and listening for the stressed items. Of course, the samples are artificial in several respects: (1) the normal state of things is not usually expressed in an immediately preceding sentence; (2) a contrajunctive expression like 'however' would probably be used in cases such as (260.2c); and (3) the opposition of 'thrifty' vs. 'extravagant' is more pronounced than would often be found in spontaneous texts. Nonetheless, I hold such samples to be useful precisely because they make their point so obviously and insistently.

4.7 In systemic terms, the point of such an exercise is to temporarily (and artificially) STABILIZE the greater part of acualization operations in order to direct focus toward a single variable factor. This channeling of focus might be compared to the intensified apperception of a moving "figure" against a stationary "ground" (cf. IV.2.5). Further decisions we have rehearsed with this tactic include; main clause vs. relative clause or verbal participle for expressing events and actions; active vs. passive; and two sentences vs. one subordinative sentence (cf. Beaugrande, in preparation, for more details). In all cases, the crucial factor is the degree of expectedness vs. informativity within the underlying content (cf. VII.2.20ff.).

4.8 Notice that such training is not at all centered upon ERRORS, i.e. upon *negative* instructions about what *not* to write. All samples like (260a) through (260d) are well-formed according to the grammar of English. What I am trying to instill is an awareness of differences in efficiency, effectiveness, and appropriateness of options which are all in themselves allowable. Only in this way do I see some hopes for a *positive* approach that lends an understanding of what good writing *is* rather than only what it *is not*. Learning to write well is learning to navigate between the extreme poles of the known and the unknown, the expected and the unexpected, between contentionality and uniqueness, between economy and expenditure, and between processing ease and processing depth (cf. VII.2.26).

4.9 Future research on composition depends in particular upon contributions such as these:

4.9.1 *Perspicacious fact-finding techniques* are needed to probe the prior discourse systems of beginning writers. As I indicated in IX.4.3f., surface errors are probably symptomatic of conflicts on the deeper levels of planning.

The exclusive reliance on face-to-face communication can leave a learner quite unfamiliar with the different organization of the written mode (cf. IX.4.3; Rubin 1978a). In general, the access to the text receiver is subject to greater mediation in writing, so that a higher degree of structural designing is required to compensate (cf. Iser 1976: 114).

4.9.2 *Empirical studies* can discover how representative learner groups react in a writing situation with stabilized content, such as narrating the course of events in a silent film. Research on READABILITY as outlined in IX.3.5 will provide a firm basis for our claims that certain textual organizations deserve a higher rating than others.

4.9.3 *Integrated theoretical models of the writing processes* must be developed in co-ordination with the considerations of fact-finding techniques and empirical studies. Each model must have HUMAN ACTIVITIES as the goal of its cognitive interests (cf. I.1.5).

4.9.4 *Operational training materials* must be developed that mediate between the insights of the theoretical models and the exigencies of language management. This mediation is especially important when aspects of a theory are too complex to be capable of direct implementation as exercises.

4.10 My inclination is to look toward PROBLEM-SOLVING as the most general and flexible model for writing activities of all kinds. I have suggested throughout this volume that problem-solving as search for connectivity of points in a space can serve to model all major aspects of textuality. John Richard Hayes and Linda Flower (1978) have observed intriguing analogies between writing activities and the solving of arithmetic and algebra problems. I take this evidence as supportive of my claim that the utilization of texts taps all central cognitive operations that are performed in intellectual acts of every kind (cf. IX.1.4ff.). If so, a theory of writing must be an integral part of a theory of cognition at large (cf. Bruce, Collins, Rubin, & Gentner 1978; Collins & Gentner 1978).

5. THE TEACHING OF FOREIGN LANGUAGES

5.1 For many people in American universities, the term "applied linguistics" is taken to denote only linguistically oriented approaches to instruction of foreign languages. The rise of this application came during and after World War II when there arose an acute need for extreme fluency in strategic languages such as German, Japanese, and Russian. The aid of such linguists as Leonard Bloomfield and Charles Carpenter Fries was enlisted to develop special intensive programs on the basis of current linguistic methods. For example, speaking and hearing were declared pre-eminent over writing and reading. Exact descriptions of sound systems were prepared. Care was expended to describe languages as used by the average native speaker.

5.2 These improvements have, in the long run, failed to advance the state of the discipline materially. In no other educational domain, as far as I know, is the disproportion between expenditure of time or effort and successful learning so dismally manifest as in foreign language instruction. Behaviorism has become firmly entrenched in a stimulus-response methodology of endless repetition and imitation—the so-called "audio-lingual" method. Any materials that appealed to the cognitive abilities of the learner, such as the presentation of language systems and regularities, were taboo. The use of the native language was banned from the classroom under the illusion that it would equally disappear from the learners' awareness (no stimulus, hence no response). Tedious "pattern drills" in which inane, prefabricated sentences were varied by word replacements bore little resemblance to natural communication. An "acoustic grammar" was even proposed in which learners were trained to respond to foreign language stimuli without knowing at all what they were saying (R. Morton 1966).

5.3 Under conditions like these, the failure rate is hardly astonishing. The audio-lingual method is degrading if not openly wasteful of human resources in its denial of any more sophisticated learning strategies than a "classical conditioning" in the tradition of Ivan Pavlov (1927), aided by desirable grades as a kind of "reinforcement" (cf. Thorndike 1931). The method is horribly inefficient, covering as it does such a tiny and unrealistic range of situations, and leaving the learner helpless in actual communication. Only the surface aspects of sounds, morphemes, and syntax are treated with any thoroughness, and only for pointless sentences devoid of context. As a result, the strategies of DISCOURSE PLANNING are left untouched, along with most factors of situationality.

5.4 To be sure, the complexities of teaching a foreign language in a classroom setting are alarmingly vast. Perhaps a reorganization of our methods, however, would bring substantial improvements. First, it is clear that the teaching situation can under no conditions suffice to impart the *entire* language. Hence, I would propose the design of an *artificially restricted intersystem functioning with maximally powerful rules and options*. The POWER of rules and options is their ability to handle a wide range of cases with simple operations. In grammar, power would be a trait of rules which generate the highest number of paradigm members or syntactic patterns from the least numerous steps (cf. Beaugrande 1979c). In vocabulary, power would obtain for items used to express, explain, or circumscribe the largest amount of concepts (cf. the "basic English" of Ogden 1932). These criteria would discourage the inclusion of rare vocabulary or rules that belong to an unrealistically elevated style of speaking (e.g. many subjunctives and anterior tenses in French).

5.5 Another crucial consideration is that we have been teaching VIRTUAL systems without an account of ACTUALIZATION strategies. If actualization can indeed override virtual systems, as I claim (cf. I.3.4.3), then not even basic language instruction can afford to dispense with communicative CONTEXTS (cf. Wienold 1973). Casual conversations, for instance, often fail to exhibit the formation rules upon which so much effort is expended in the classroom. I propose that textbooks be replaced, at least in part, with film media capable of showing integrated communicative situations (including the vital gestures and facial expressions used in the foreign culture). Super-8 projectors that are simultaneously tone recorders offer a convenient and inexpensive means for learners to fit their own utterances into dynamic contexts. The "drilling" of empty forms should be removed as much as possible from the class to the terminals for computer-assisted instruction.

5.6 An important obstacle to the acquisition of a foreign language can be called INTERFERENCE: the influence of the native language on the use of the foreign one. Interference studies have mostly been concerned with the divergencies in organization of the grammar (e.g. different categories) or the lexicon (e.g. different distribution of expressions for a conceptual domain). My own experiments suggest that *discourse planning* and *actualization strategies* are also major sources of interference. I accordingly developed adjunct strategies which the learners can superpose upon their native-language strategies to combat interference. This tactic enabled several test classes I taught to attain a marked improvement in a period of about five to seven weeks.

5.7 The question of strategies indicates that an operational account of native language *in use* is antecedent to a really workable methodology for acquiring a foreign language. The hopes that transformational grammar would fill this requirement (e.g. in Achtenhagen 1969) naturally led to disillusionment. I would not view the poor results of applied linguistics in the past, however, as proof that linguistics is inherently inapplicable. Considerably more may become possible if we can agree to establish a linguistics which assumes its proper role in a comprehensive account of meaningful human activities.

6.   TRANSLATION STUDIES

6.1 Text linguistics can offer a substantial contribution to translation studies (see especially Dressler 1970b, 1972b, 1974b). Old-style linguistics of virtual systems had comparatively little to offer, because translating is always a matter of actualization (cf. Beaugrande 1978a: ch. 1). The celebrated disaster of machine translation shows that a processor with only a grammar and a dictionary can be constantly misled or entangled in alternative readings. The processor simply couldn't perform the *problem-solving* which discovers or imposes *connectivities* upon language occurrences (cf. I.6.8). Considerable knowledge about how events and situations in the world are preferentially organized and combined is needed here (cf. Wilks 1972). The Yale Artificial Intelligence project directed by Roger Schank applies programmed knowledge of events and situations to the understanding of reports coming directly from the wires of news services; it then uses language-independent representations to paraphrase, summarize, or answer questions about the reports in Chinese, Russian, Dutch, and Spanish (cf. Schank & Abelson 1977; Cullingford 1978 has many Spanish examples).

6.2 A central domain of translation studies is CONTRASTIVE LINGUISTICS (cf. surveys in Nickel [ed.] 1971, 1972). Early trends using the descriptive approach contrasted only *virtual* systems: phonemes, morphemes, grammatical paradigms, and syntax in particular (Catford 1964; Ellis 1966). This outlook emphasizes formal differences of the surface so strongly that translating seems incapable of having a sound theoretical basis. Georges Mounin (1963) devotes an elaborate treatise to the refutation of this conclusion, noting along the way that linguistic models of the time were too myopic. Later appeals to transformational grammar (e.g. Nida 1964) brought no great headway, because here also, we are dealing with a purely virtual system.

6.3 Translating is possible only because human beings share an experiential world and perhaps also universal processing strategies (cf. IV.3.17; IX.1.4). Those factors stand in ASYMMETRICAL relationships to the surface options of individual languages (cf. I.6.12). These relationships have such complexity that they are unlikely to be inferred by working from the surface alone. At most, we could search for surface tendencies that reflect processing universals, e.g. the placement of known/expected material before unknown/unexpected (cf. IV.3), or the structural differentiation of co-referring pro-forms (cf. V.4). Yet similar principles of sequencing and differentiation are no guarantee that the resulting forms will be similar in various languages.

6.4 For a linguistics of actualization processes, the EQUIVALENCE between a text and its translation can be neither in form nor lexical meanings, but only in *the experience of text receivers* (Beaugrande 1978a, 1979l). Translating is then an issue of INTERTEXTUALITY (I.4.11.6) in which mediation works across different language intersystems. The danger is that the translator will interpose his or her own receiver experience as the only possible one for the text. For example, the translator might bridge or fill in all discontinuities and discrepancies such that the goal language receiver finds the text wholly devoid of informativity and interest. This tactic is applied with lamentable frequency in translating LITERARY and POETIC texts, and the multiplicity of functions and meanings is often destroyed (cf. Beaugrande 1978a). Instead of arguing over "free" versus "literal" translating, we might find the true opposition in "receiver-based" and "translator-based" translating: only the former can claim communicative equivalence. The question of how and whether forms or meanings are preserved can only be settled in such a framework.

7.   LITERARY STUDIES

7.1 For many years, literary studies was the main discipline for the investigation of whole texts. In absence of the necessary groundwork, discussions had to be carried on without consistent or explicit theoretical models of texts and text processing. The nature of literary and poetic texts as vehicles for alternative organizations of the world and of discourse about the world (VII.1.8.4f.) renders the construction of such models particularly intricate. While it was often recognized that these texts represent deviations from some norm (cf. Riffaterre 1959, 1960; Mukařovský 1964; Thorne 1969; Enkvist 1973), no integrated language theories were available to describe what norms should be consulted to begin with.

7.2 These matters were demonstrated by the attempt to postulate a "generative grammar of literary texts" (cf. Bierwisch 1965b; van Dijk 1972b; Ihwe 1972). It was reasoned that a set of subsidiary transformational rules could be added onto the standard grammar of the language, such that literary and poetic texts could be generated. Two objections seem readily evident. First, a grammar expanded in this fashion would gain such ominous power that every conceivable structure would be produceable, so that the grammar would in the end have explained nothing at all. Second, the effectiveness of literary and poetic texts arises from the MODIFICATIONS performed on language systems *for that particular occasion.* If the modifications were rule-governed, they would lose quite a bit of their informativity and interestingness.

7.3 Perhaps we could envision literariness and poeticalness as arising from CREATIVITY, modeled as the *motivated modification of systems* (Beaugrande 1979e). The strategies at work might be as simple as this: (1) insert a highly *non-systemic pathway* into some actualized text system (e.g. bizarre combinations of concepts or expressions); (2) test the *interestingness* of the resulting configuration; and (3) test the *relevance* of the configuration for the task of mediating insights into *alternative organizations* of the world and of discourse about the world. Whether a given text is effective and acceptable or not depends on the *proportionality* between the effort expended on systems modification and the enriching insights thus mediated. Many highly deviant texts (e.g. Baroque, Gongorism) seem to us disproportionate along this dimension.

7.4 Possibly, the notion of STYLE as a literary issue might also be approached along the lines I propose. I suggested in I.2.10 that style arises from the characteristic mapping procedures among the various levels of participating language systems. Some of these mappings affect the distribution of phonemes and morphemes (cf. Jakobson & Jones 1970) and the formatting of sentences (cf. Ohmann 1964). Yet to depict style fully, we must consult all the mapping from the phases of PLANNING and IDEATION all the way to the LINEARIZATION of the surface text (cf. VII.2.8ff.). We must note the particular *modifications* performed in or between these phases as an additional non-obligatory contributor to style. Finally, we must confront the observed processes with the EXPECTATIONS of potential text receivers about the respective domains (cf. IV.1.23ff.).

7.5 It would also be worth investigating how literary and poetic modifications can be integrated into existing systems and thus create an impetus for further modifications (cf. Mukařovský 1964). This evolution can even occur in miniature within a single text where modifications in one part of a text can be overthrown by others in a later part (cf. Riffaterre 1959, 1960). Of course, the epochs of the past and their communicative systems are removed from our empirical investigation as such. However, we can ascertain many things via the *self-contextualizing* nature of texts (I.4.7). If system users must orient themselves toward the functions of the systems themselves (whether or not modifications are performed), then we can reconstruct a substantial portion of the systems via the procedural analysis of sample texts. Eventually, the key role of literary discourse within the total universe of discourse in historically evolving societies may become clear.

7.6 I have conducted experimental classes in which the *teaching* of literature was carried on along the lines I advocate. After a short introductory demonstration, I turn the class over to the students. They each present a poem which, for whatever reason, they find appealing. Then they ask and answer these questions: (1) what is the overall topic; (2) what steps and goals does the writer's plan contain; (3) what elements seem unusual, out of place, or surprising; and (4) what motivations can be found for the use of those elements. I have observed a dramatic increase in the abilities of understanding and appreciating poetry. Indeed, many insights which my (largely first-year) college students articulated are worthy of dissemination in scholarly journals. I plan a book-length presentation of the method and its results shortly.

8. A FINAL WORD

8.1 Following this brief overview of interdisciplinary applications, I must rest my case in favor of a science of texts—a fitting conclusion for a method whose very substance is so highly interdisciplinary. I have undertaken to marshal a broad spectrum of support for my thesis that linguistics can and should explore texts and textuality from the standpoint of human activities in actual utilization. Such an approach can be useful both for traditional linguistic issues such as phrase structures or grammar and for new issues emerging from the investigation of cognitive processes.

8.2 I am not at all convinced that a broader scope must lead to an alarming increase in the complexity of our theories and models. The complexity problem in linguistics is of course important, and was handled in the past via severe reductions of the domain of study (Weinrich 1976: 74ff.). But I believe that the development of INTERACTIVE theories and models in which operations are closely interconnected from system to system will show that the separation of language systems in fact increases rather than reduces complexity. A case in point is the explosion of arbitrary rules for an autonomous syntax.

8.3 I would draw an analogy to the famous "Waltz effect." Although there are staggering numbers of *abstractly possible* ways to label vertices in analyzing visual scenes, David Waltz (1975) found that the *interaction of physical constraints* reduces the number of *actually occurring* labelings down from billions to a few thousand. I foresee the same trend in a "linguistic Waltz effect": the infinity of sentences, the vast multitudes of natural language expressions and their senses, the variety of communicative situations, the huge expanse of human knowledge and experience—all these do not simply complicate the picture of communication; they also impose mutual control, determinacy, and relevance upon each other. The principle of continuity as the regulative stability of all participating systems drastically limits the decisions and selections that are *probable* among the total range of the abstractly *possible*.

8.4 I am therefore confident that the kind of science of texts which I have tried to present will advance much more rapidly than the perspectives of old-style linguistics could lead one to believe. The new perspectives will encompass wider, more diverse, and more vital issues, and, at the same time, move closer to an understanding of the powerful processes of human cognition and expression.

Appendix

The following is a program written by Robert F. Simmons in UT LISP 1.5 for the University of Texas computer. The first portion represents the 'rocket' text in terms of Horn clauses in successor arithmetic (Simmons & Correira 1978). The bracketing shows hierarchical depths, as usual in LISP implementation. The symbol "<" is for antecedent-consequent theorems, meaning: "is true, if...". The letters "TF" followed by a number designate "transformations" for ordering the clauses. "R" of course stands for 'rocket'.[1]

```
(GENPRINT RULES)
((V2 ROCKET) < (SETTING R) (EPI R) (TF (2 3) (A 1 WAS FLOWN)))
((SETTING R) < (TOPIC R) (STATES R) (TF (2 3) (THERE WAS A R)))
((TOPIC R) < (R ISA ROCKET) (STOOD IN A NEW MEXICO DESERT) (SPEC R) (TF
    (4 3) (A R 3)))
((SPEC R) < (A GREAT) (BLACK AND YELLOW) (V2) (FORTY-SIX FEET LONG) (TF
    (2 3 4 R 5)))
((STATES R) < (EMPTY IT WEIGHED 5 TONS) (STATE 1 R) (TF (2 3) (2)))
((STATE1 R) < (IT CARRIED 8 TONS OF FUEL) (KIND R) (TF (2 3) (2)))
((KIND R) < (—ALCOHOL AND LIQUID OXYGEN) (TF (2)))
((EPI R) < (EVERYTHING WAS READY) (ACT R) (TF (2 3) (2 AND IT FLEW OFF)))
((ACT R) < (PREACT R) (FLIGHT R) (TF (2 3) (AFTER TAKEOFF IT FLEW)))
((PREACT R) < (PREACT1 R) (PREACT2 R) (TF (2 3) (SIGNALS WERE GIVEN)))
```

---

[1] A detailed rationale for the treatment of this particular text in terms of clausal logic is now available in Simmons and Chester (1979). An extensive rule formalism is provided for automatic extraction of the network from the text and generation from the network back to the text.

((PREACT1 R) < (SCIENTISTS AND GENERALS WITHDREW) (PURPOSE1) (TF (2 3)
    (2)))
((PURPOSE1) < (SOME DISTANCE TO CROUCH BEHIND EARTH MOUNDS) (TF
    (2)))
((PREACT2 R) < (TWO RED FLARES ROSE) (PURPOSE2) (TF (2 3) (2)))
((PURPOSE2) < (AS A SIGNAL TO FIRE THE ROCKET) (TF (2)))
((FLIGHT R) < (ASCEND R) (CRUISE R) (DESCEND R) (TF (2 3 4) (THE R ASCENDED
    AND LATER PLUNGED TO EARTH)))
((ASCEND R) < (THE GIANT R ROSE) (HOWROSE R) (TF (2 3) (2)))
((HOWROSE R) < (WITH A GREAT ROAR AND A BURST OF FLAME) (HOW1) (TF
    (2 3) (2)))
((HOW1) < (THE ROCKET ROSE SLOWLY THEN FASTER AND FASTER (DISPLAY1)
    (TF (2 3) (2)))
((DISPLAY1) < (BEHIND THE ROCKET TRAILED 60 FEET OF YELLOW FLAME)
    (SOON THE FLAME LOOKED LIKE A YELLOW STAR (TF (2 3)))
((CRUISE R) < (IN A FEW SECONDS THE R WAS TOO HIGH TO BE SEEN)
    (CRUISE2) (TF (2 3) (2)))
((CRUISE2) < (BUT RADAR TRACKED IT AS THE ROCKET SPED UP TO 3000 MPH)
    (TF (2)))
((DESCEND R) < (TIME1) (IT PLUNGED INTO EARTH 40 MILES FROM THE
    STARTING POINT) (TF (2 3) (3)))
((TIME1) < (A FEW MINUTES LATER) (OBSERVER1) (TF (2 3) (2)))
(OBSERVER1) < (THE PILOT OF A WATCHING PLANE SAW THAT) (TF (2)))
((X ISA X))

Below are some summaries generated by truncating the hierarchy at various
depths of nesting. Each "say proof" is more detailed than its predecessor.

*VALUE: *T*

(SAY PROOF 1)
*VALUE: (A (V2 ROCKET) WAS FLOWN)

(SAY PROOF 2)
*VALUE: (THERE WAS A ROCKET (EVERYTHING WAS READY (AFTER TAKEOFF IT
FLEW)))

(SAY PROOF 3)
*VALUE: (THERE WAS A ROCKET (EVERYTHING WAS READY (SIGNALS WERE
GIVEN (THE ROCKET ASCENDED AND LATER PLUNGED TO EARTH))))

(SAY PROOF 4)
*VALUE: (A ROCKET (STOOD IN A NEW MEXICO DESERT) (EMPTY IT WEIGHED 5
TONS) (EVERYTHING WAS READY (SIGNALS WERE GIVEN (THE ROCKET
ASCENDED AND LATER PLUNGED TO EARTH))))

(SAY PROOF 5)
*VALUE: (A GREAT (BLACK AND YELLOW) V2 ROCKET (FORTY-SIX FEET LONG)
(STOOD IN A NEW MEXICO DESERT) (EMPTY IT WEIGHED 5 TONS (IT CARRIED 8
TONS OF FUEL)) (EVERYTHING WAS READY (SCIENTISTS AND GENERALS

WITHDREW (TWO RED FLARES ROSE) (THE GIANT ROCKET ROSE (IN A FEW
SECONDS THE ROCKET WAS TOO HIGH TO BE SEEN) (IT PLUNGED INTO EARTH
40 MILES FROM THE STARTING POINT)))))

(SAY PROOF 6)

*VALUE: (A GREAT (BLACK AND YELLOW) V2 ROCKET (FORTY-SIX FEET LONG)
(STOOD IN A NEW MEXICO DESERT) (EMPTY IT WEIGHED 5 TONS (IT CARRIED 8
TONS OF FUEL (—ALCOHOL AND LIQUID OXYGEN))) (EVERYTHING WAS READY
(SCIENTISTS AND GENERALS WITHDREW (SOME DISTANCE TO CROUCH
BEHIND EARTH MOUNDS) (TWO RED FLARES ROSE (AS A SIGNAL TO FIRE THE
ROCKET)) (THE GIANT ROCKET ROSE (WITH A GREAT ROAR AND A BURST OF
FLAME) (IN A FEW SECONDS THE ROCKET WAS TOO HIGH TO BE SEEN (BUT
RADAR TRACKED IT AS THE ROCKET SPED UP TO 3000 MPH)) (A FEW MINUTES
LATER (IT PLUNGED INTO EARTH 40 MILES FROM THE STARTING POINT))))))

(SAY PROOF 7)

*VALUE: (A GREAT (BLACK AND YELLOW) V2 ROCKET (FORTY-SIX FEET LONG)
(STOOD IN A NEW MEXICO DESERT) (EMPTY IT WEIGHED 5 TONS (IT CARRIED 8
TONS OF FUEL (—ALCOHOL AND LIQUID OXYGEN))) (EVERYTHING WAS READY
(SCIENTISTS AND GENERALS WITHDREW (SOME DISTANCE TO CROUCH
BEHIND EARTH MOUNDS) (TWO RED FLARES ROSE (AS A SIGNAL TO FIRE THE
ROCKET)) (THE GIANT ROCKET ROSE (WITH A GREAT ROAR AND A BURST OF
FLAME (THE ROCKET ROSE SLOWLY THEN FASTER AND FASTER)) (IN A FEW
SECONDS THE ROCKET WAS TOO HIGH TO BE SEEN (BUT RADAR TRACKED IT AS
THE ROCKET SPED UP TO 3000 MPH)) (A FEW MINUTES LATER (THE PILOT OF A
WATCHING PLANE SAW THAT) (IT PLUNGED INTO EARTH 40 MILES FROM THE
STARTING POINT)))))))

References

For the convenience of readers in all disciplines, I provide the first names of authors cited. Journal abbreviations are explained in a table on pp. 327–328.

Abelson, Robert. 1975. Concepts for representing mundane reality in plans. In Bobrow & Collins (Eds.), 273–309.

Achtenhagen, Frank. 1969. *Didaktik des fremdsprachlichen Unterrichts*. Weinheim: Beltz.

Achtenhagen, Frank, & Weinold, Götz. 1975. *Lehren und Lernen im Fremdsprachenunterricht*. Munich: Kösel.

Adams, Marilyn & Collins, Allan. 1979. A schema-theoretical view of reading. In Freedle (Ed.), 1–22.

Albrecht, Erhard. 1967. *Sprache und Erkenntnis*. Berlin: Deutscher Verlag der Wissenschaften.

Allen, James. 1979. *A plan-based approach to speech act recognition*. Toronto: University of Toronto dissertation (CS-TR 131/79).

Allen, James, & Perrault, Raymond. 1978. Participating in dialogues: understanding via plan deduction. *2nd CSCSI*, 214–223.

Allen, Paul, & Watson, Dorothy (Eds.). 1976. *Findings of research in miscue analysis*. Urbana: National Council of Teachers of English.

Anderson, John. 1978. The processing of referring expressions within a semantic network. *TINLAP-2*, 51–56.

Anderson, John. 1976. *Language, memory, and thought*. Hillsdale: Lawrence Erlbaum Associates.

Anderson, John, & Bower, Gordon. 1973. *Human associative memory*. Washington, D.C.: Winston.

Anderson, Richard. 1977. The notion of schemata and the educational enterprise. In Anderson, Spiro, & Montague (Eds.), 415–431.

Anderson, Richard, & Pichert, James. 1978. Recall of previously unrecallable information following a shift in perspective. *JVLVB*, 17, 1–12.

Anderson, Richard, Spiro, Rand, & Montague, William (Eds.). 1977. *Schooling and the acquisition of knowledge*. Hillsdale: Lawrence Erlbaum Associates.

Anisfeld, Moshe, & Knapp, Margaret. 1968. Association, synonymity, and directionality in false recognition. *JExP*, 77, 171–179.

Apostel, Leo. 1961. Toward the formal study of models in the non-formal sciences. In Hans Freudenthal (Ed.), *The concept and role of the model in mathematics and natural and social sciences*. Dordrecht: Reidel, 1–37.

298

Aquino, Milagros. 1969. The validity of the Miller-Coleman readability scale. *Reading Research Quarterly,* 4, 342–357.

Arnheim, Rudolf. 1947. Perceptual abstraction and art. *PR,* 54, 66–82.

Austin, John. 1962. *How to do things with words.* Cambridge: Harvard.

Ausubel, David. 1963. *The psychology of meaningful verbal learning.* New York: Grune & Stratton.

Ausubel, David. 1960. The use of advance organizers in the learning and retention of meaningful verbal material. *JEdP,* 51, 267–272.

Ausubel, David, & Fitzgerald, Donald. 1962. The role of discriminability in meaningful verbal learning and retention. *JEdP,* 53, 243–249.

Bacon, Francis. 1869. *The works of Francis Bacon.* New York: Hurd & Houghton.

Ballmer, Thomas. 1976. Macrostructures. In van Dijk (Ed.), 1–22.

Ballmer, Thomas. 1975. *Sprachrekonstruktionssysteme.* Kronberg: Scriptor.

Bartlett, Frederick. 1932. *Remembering.* Cambridge, England: Cambridge University Press.

Bateman, Donald, & Zidonis, Frank. 1964. *The effect of a knowledge of generative grammar upon the growth of language complexity.* Columbus: Ohio State University.

Beaugrande, Robert de. In preparation. *The Science of Composition.*

Beaugrande, Robert de. 1980a. The role of linguistics in a science of texts. *Text,* 1.

Beaugrande, Robert de. 1980b. Theory and process in the teaching of writing. *IRAL,* 18.

Beaugrande, Robert de. 1980c. The status of texts in reading research. In Robert Tierney, Patrica Anders, & Judy Nichols Mitchell (Eds.), *Understanding a Reader's Understanding.* Hillsdale: Erlbaum.

Beaugrande, Robert de. 1979a. Text and sentence in discourse planning. In Petöfi (Ed.), 467–494.

Beaugrande, Robert de. 1979b. The pragmatics of discourse planning. *JPrag,* 3/6.

Beaugrande, Robert de. 1979c. Generative phonology in paradigmatic formation. *Linguistics,* Special issue (dated 1978), 73–99.

Beaugrande, Robert de. 1979d. Modeling cognitive processes for research on texts. Technical report to appear in *Discourse Processes.*

Beaugrande, Robert de. 1979e. Toward a general theory of creativity. *Poetics,* 8/3, 269–306.

Beaugrande, Robert de. 1979f. Psychology and composition. *CCC,* 30/1, 50–57.

Beaugrande, Robert de. 1979g. A rhetorical theory of audience response. In Robert Brown & Martin Steinman (Eds.), *Rhetoric 78. Proceedings of theory of rhetoric: An interdisciplinary conference.* Minneapolis: University of Minnesota, 9–20.

Beaugrande, Robert de. 1979h. Moving from product toward process. *CCC,* 30/4, 357–363.

Beaugrande, Robert de. 1979i. The process of invention: Association and recombination. *CCC,* 30/3, 260–267.

Beaugrande, Robert de. 1979j. Theoretical foundations for the automatic production and processing of technical reports. *JTWC,* 9/3, 239–268.

Beaugrande, Robert de. 1979k. Transformational grammar and cognitive science as paradigms for a science of language. Bielefeld: University of Bielefeld (TR LiLi-42).

Beaugrande, Robert de. 1979l. Towards a semiotics of literary translating. In Wolfram Wilss (Ed.), *Semiotik und Übersetzen.* Tübingen: Narr, 23–42.

Beaugrande, Robert de. 1978a. *Factors in a theory of poetic translating.* Assen: van Gorcum.

Beaugrande, Robert de. 1978b. Information, expectation, and processing. *Poetics,* 7/2, 3–44.

Beaugrande, Robert de. 1978c. Linguistic theory and composition. *CCC,* 29/2, 134–140.

Beaugrande, Robert de. 1978d. Semantic evaluation in grammar in poetry. *PTL,* 3/2, 315–325.

Beaugrande, Robert de. 1977a. Generative stylistics: Between grammar and rhetoric. *CCC,* 28/3, 240–246.

Beaugrande, Robert de. 1977b. Information and grammar in technical writing. *CCC,* 28/4, 325–332.

Beaugrande, Robert de, & Colby, Benjamin. 1979. Narrative models of action and interaction. *Cognitive Science,* 3, 43–66.

Beaugrande, Robert de, & Dressler, Wolfgang. 1980. *Introduction to text linguistics.* London: Longman.

Beaugrande, Robert de, & Miller, Genevieve. 1980. Processing models of children's story comprehension. *Poetics,* 9.

Beerbohm, Max. 1958. *Selected essays.* London: Heinemann.

Bellert, Irene. 1970. On a condition of the coherence of texts. *Semiotica,* 2, 335–363.

Belloc, Hilaire. 1940. *Cautionary verses.* London: Duckworth.

Berlyne, Daniel. 1960. *Conflict, arousal, and curiosity.* New York: McGraw-Hill.

Bernstein, Basil. 1964. Elaborated and restricted codes: Their social origins and some consequences. In John Gumperz & Dell Hymes (Eds.), *The ethnography of communication. American Anthropologist,* special issue, 66/2, 55–69.

Bernstein, Jared, & Pike, Kenneth. 1977. The emic structure of individuals in relation to dialogue. In van Dijk & Petöfi (Eds.), 1–10.

Berry, Margaret. 1977. *Introduction to systemic linguistics.* London: Batsford.

Bertalanffy, Ludwig von. 1962. *General systems theory.* New York: Braziller.

Bever, Thomas, 1970. The cognitive basis for linguistic structures. In John Richard Hayes (Ed.), *Cognition and the development of language.* New York: Wiley, 279–352.

Bever, Thomas, Garrett, Merrill, & Hurtig, Richard. 1973. The interaction of perceptual processes and ambiguous sentences. *MemCog,* 1, 277–286.

Biasci, Claudia, & Fritsche, Johannes (Eds.). 1978. *Texttheorie— Textrepräsentation: Theoretische Grundlagen der kanonischen sinnsemantischen Repräsentation von Texten.* Hamburg: Buske.

Bierwisch, Manfred. 1966. Strukturalismus: Geschichte, Probleme, Methoden. *Kursbuch,* 5, 77–152.

Bierwisch, Manfred. 1965a. Rezension zu Z. S. Harris, "Discourse Analysis." *Linguistics,* 13, 61–73.

Bierwisch, Manfred, 1965b. Poetik und Linguistik. In Helmut Kreuzer & Rul Gunzenhäuser (Eds.), *Mathematik und Dichtung.* Munich: Nymphenburger, 46–66.

Blom, Jan-Petter, & Gumperz, John. 1972. Social meaning in linguistic structures. Code-switching in Norway. In Gumperz & Hymes (Eds.), 407–434.

Blumenthal, Arthur. 1966. Observations with self-embedded sentences. *PsySci,* 6, 453–454.

Bobrow, Daniel. 1975. Dimensions of representation. In Bobrow & Collins (Eds.), 1–34.

Bobrow, Daniel, & Collins, Allan (Eds.). 1975. *Representation and understanding: Studies in cognitive science.* New York: Academic Press.

Bobrow, Daniel, & Fraser, Bruce. 1969. An augmented state transition network analysis procedure. *1st IJCAI.*

Bobrow, Daniel, & Norman, Donald, 1975. Some principles of memory schemata. In Bobrow & Collins (Eds.) 131–149.

Bobrow, Daniel, & Winograd, Terry. 1977. An overview of KRL: A knowledge representation language. *Cognitive Science,* 1, 3–46.

Bobrow, Robert. 1978. The RUS System. In Bonnie Webber & Robert Bobrow, *Research in natural language understanding.* Cambridge: Bolt, Beranek, & Newman, Inc. (TR 3878).

Bobrow, Robert, & Brown, John Seely. 1975. Systematic understanding: Synthesis, analysis, and contingent knowledge in specialized understanding systems. In Bobrow & Collins (Eds.), 103–129.

Bobrow, Samuel, & Bower, Gordon. 1969. Comprehension and recall of sentences. *JExP,* 80, 455–461.

Bolinger, Dwight. 1975. *Aspects of language.* New York: Harcourt, Brace, & Jovanovich.

Bolinger, Dwight. 1972. Accent is predictable (if you're a mind reader). *Language,* 48, 633–644.

Bormuth, John. 1969. *Development of readability analyses.* Chicago: University of Chicago Press.

Boulding, Kenneth. 1956. General systems theory: the skeleton of science. *Management Science,* 2, 197–208.

Bousfield, Weston. 1953. The occurrence of clustering in the recall of randomly arranged associates. *JGenP,* 49, 229–240.

Bower, Gordon. 1976. Experiments on story understanding and recall. *QJExP,* 28, 511–534.

Bower, Gordon, & Trabasso, Tom. 1964. Concept identification. In Richard Atkinson (Ed.), *Studies in mathematical psychology.* Stanford: Stanford University Press, 32–94.

Brachman, Ronald. 1978a. *A structural paradigm for representing knowledge.* Cambridge: Bolt, Beranek, & Newman (TR 3605).

Brachman, Ronald. 1979. On the epistemological status of semantic networks. In Findler (Ed.), 3–50.

Braddock, Richard. 1974. The frequency and placement of topic sentences. *Research on the Teaching of English,* 8, 287–302.

Bransford, John, Barclay, Richard, & Franks, Jeffrey. 1972. Sentence memory: A constructive versus interpretative approach. *CogP,* 3, 193–209.

Bransford, John, & Franks, Jeffrey. 1971. Abstraction of linguistic ideas. *CogP,* 2, 331–350.

Bransford, John, & Johnson, Marcia. 1973. Considerations of some problems of comprehension. In William Chase (Ed.), *Visual information processing.* New York: Academic Press, 383–438.

Brazil, David. 1975. *Discourse intonation.* Birmingham: English Language Research.

Bremond, Claude. 1973. *Logique du récit.* Paris: Seuil.

Bremond, Claude. 1964. Le message narratif. *Communications,* 4, 4–32.

Breuer, Dieter. 1974. *Einführung in die pragmatische Texttheorie.* Munich: Fink.

Brillouin, Leon. 1956. *Science and information theory.* New York: Academic Press.

Brinkmann, Hennig. 1962. *Die deutsche Sprache: Gestalt und Leistung.* Düsseldorf: Schwann.

Broen, Patricia. 1971. A discussion of the linguistic environment of the young language-learning child. Paper at the American Speech and Hearing Convention, Chicago.

Bross, Irwin. 1973. Languages in cancer research. In Gerald Murphy, David Pressman, & Edwin Mirand (Eds.), *Perspectives in cancer research.* New York: Liss, 213–221.

Brown, John Seely, & Burton, Richard. 1977. A paradigmatic example of an artificially intelligent instructional system. In *Proceedings of the First International Conference on Applied General Systems Research: Recent developments and trends.* New York: Binghamton.

Brown, John Seely, & Burton, Richard. 1975. Multiple representations of knowledge for tutorial reasoning. In Bobrow & Collins (Eds.), 311–349.

Brown, John Seely, Collins, Allan, & Harris, Gregory. 1978. Artificial intelligence and learning strategies. In Harry O'Neill (Ed.), *Learning strategies.* New York: Academic, 107–139.

Brown, Roger. 1973. *A first language; The early stages.* Cambridge: Harvard.

Bruce, Bertram. 1975. *Belief systems and language understanding.* Cambridge: Bolt, Beranek, & Newman (TR 2973).

Bruce, Bertram. 1974. *Case systems for natural language.* Rutgers: Rutgers University (CS–TR 32).

Bruce, Bertram, Collins, Allan, Rubin, Andee, & Gentner, Dedre, 1978. *A cognitive science approach to writing.* Urbana: ERIC Report (EC 157038).

Bruner, Jerome, Goodnow, Jacqueline, & Austin, George. 1956. *A study of thinking.* New York: Wiley.

Bruner, Jerome, & Potter, Mary. 1964. Visual recognition. *Science,* 144, 424–425.

Buckley, Walter (Ed.). 1968. *Modern systems research for the behavioral scientist.* Chicago: Aldine.

Bugelski, Bergen, Kidd, Edward, & Segman, John. 1968. The image as a mediator in one-trial paired associate learning. *JExP,* 76, 69–73.

Bühler, Karl. 1934. *Sprachtheorie: Die Darstellungsfunktion der Sprache.* Jena: G. Fischer.

Bullwinkle, Candace. 1977. Levels of complexity in discourse for anaphora disambiguation and speech act interpretation. *5th IJCAI,* 43–49.

Burton, Richard. 1976. *Semantic grammar: An engineering technique for constructing natural language understanding systems.* Cambridge: Bolt, Beranek, & Newman (TR 3453).

Carbonell, Jaime, Jr. 1978a. POLITICS: Automated ideological reasoning. *Cognitive Science,* 2, 27–51.

Carbonell, Jaime, Jr. 1978b. Intentionality and human conversations. *TINLAP-2,* 141–148.

Carbonell, Jaime, Sr. 1970. AI in CAI: An artificial intelligence approach to computer-aided instruction. *IEEE Transactions on Man-Machine Interaction,* 11/4, 190–202.

Carden, Guy. 1970. A note on conflicting idiolects. *LingInq,* 1, 281–290.

Carnap, Rudolf. 1958. *Introduction to symbolic logic.* New York: Dover.

Carnap, Rudolf. 1942. *Introduction to semantics.* Cambridge: Harvard University Press.

Carpenter, Patricia, & Just, Marcel. 1975. Sentence comprehension: A psycholinguistic processing model of verification. *PR,* 82, 45–73.

Carroll, Lewis. 1960. *The annotated Alice; Alice's adventures in Wonderland & Through the looking-glass.* New York: Potter.

Carroll, Lewis. 1973. *The annotated Snark: The hunting of the snark.* Harmondsworth: Penguin.

Catford, John. 1964. *A linguistic theory of translation.* London: Oxford.

Cercone, Nick, & Schubert, Len. 1975. Toward a state-based conceptual representation. *4th IJCAI,* 83–90.

Chafe, Wallace. 1976. Givenness, contrastiveness, definiteness, subjects, topics, and point of view. In Li (Ed.), 27–55.

Chafe, Wallace. 1970. *Meaning and the structure of language.* Chicago: University of Chicago Press.

Chan, Shu-Park. 1969. *Introductory topological analysis of electrical networks.* New York: Holt, Rinehart, & Winston.

Charniak, Eugene. 1978. With spoon in hand, this must be the eating frame. *TINLAP-2,* 187–193.

Charniak, Eugene. 1976. Inference and knowledge. In Charniak & Wilks (Eds.), 1–21 and 129–154.

Charniak, Eugene. 1975a. *A brief on case.* Castagnola: Institute for Semantic and Cognitive Studies (TR 22).

Charniak, Eugene. 1975b. *A partial taxonomy of knowledge about actions.* Castagnola: Institute for Semantic and Cognitive Studies (TR 13).

Charniak, Eugene. 1975c. *Organization and inference in a frame-like system of common-sense knowledge.* Castagnola: Institute for Semantic and Cognitive Studies.

Charniak, Eugene. 1972. *Toward a model of children's story comprehension.* Cambridge: MIT dissertation (AI–TR 51).

Charniak, Eugene, & Wilks, Yorick (Eds.). 1976. *Computational semantics: An introduction to artificial intelligence and natural language communication.* Amsterdam: North Holland.

Chomsky, Carol. 1969. *The acquisition of syntax in children from 5 to 10.* Cambridge: MIT Press.

Chomsky, Noam. 1975. *Reflections on language.* New York: Pantheon.

Chomsky, Noam. 1972. *Studies on semantics in generative grammar.* The Hague: Mouton.

Chomsky, Noam. 1971. Deep structure, surface structure, and semantic interpretation. In Steinberg & Jakobovits (Eds.), 183–216.

Chomsky, Noam. 1970. *Some empirical issues of the theory of transformational grammar.* Bloomington: Indiana University Linguistics Club.

Chomsky, Noam. 1965. *Aspects of the theory of syntax.* Cambridge: MIT Press.

Chomsky, Noam. 1961. On the notion "rule of grammar." In *Proceedings of Symposia in Applied Mathematics XII*, 6–24.

Chomsky, Noam. 1957. *Syntactic structures*. The Hague: Mouton.

Clark, Eve. 1971. On the acquisition of the meaning of 'before' and 'after'. *JVLVB*, 10, 266–275.

Clark, Herbert. 1977. Inferences in comprehension. In LaBerge & Samuels (Eds.), 243–263.

Clark, Herbert, & Card, Stuart. 1969. The role of semantics in remembering comparative sentences. *JExP*, 82, 545–552.

Clark, Herbert, & Chase, William. 1974. Perceptual coding strategies in the formation and verification of descriptions. *MemCog*, 2, 101–111.

Clark, Herbert, & Clark, Eve. 1977. *Language and psychology*. New York: Harcourt, Brace & Jovanovich.

Clark, Herbert, & Clark, Eve. 1968. Semantic distinctions and memory for complex sentences. *QJExP*, 20, 129–138.

Clark, Herbert, & Haviland, Susan. 1974. Psychological processes as linguistic explanation. In David Cohen (Ed.), *Explaining linguistic phenomena*. Washington, D.C.: Hemisphere, 91–124.

Clark, Herbert, & Marshall, Catherine. 1978. Reference diaries. *TINLAP-2*, 57–63.

Clippinger, John. 1977. *Meaning and discourse: A computer model of psychoanalytic speech and cognition*. Baltimore: Johns Hopkins University Press.

Cohen, Philip. 1978. *On knowing what to say: Planning speech acts*. Toronto: University of Toronto dissertation (CS–TR 118).

Coke, Esther. 1976. Reading rate, readability, and variations in task-induced processing. *JEdP*, 68/2, 167–173.

Colby, Kenneth, & Parkinson, Richard. 1974. Pattern-matching rules for the recognition of natural language dialogue expressions. *AJCL*, 1, 1–70.

Cole, Peter (Ed.). 1978. *Syntax and semantics IX: Pragmatics*. New York: Academic Press.

Cole, Peter, & Morgan, Jerry (Eds.). 1975. *Syntax and semantics III: Speech Acts*. New York: Academic Press.

Cole, Peter, & Sadock, Jerrold. 1977. *Syntax and semantics VIII: Grammatical relations*. New York: Academic Press.

Coleman, Edmund. 1964. The comprehensibility of several grammatical transformations. *JApP*, 48, 186–190.

Collins, Allan. 1978. Fragments of a theory of human plausible reasoning. *TINLAP-2*, 194–201.

Collins, Allan. 1977. Processes in acquiring knowledge. In Anderson, Spiro, & Montague (Eds.), 339–363.

Collins, Allan, Brown, John Seely, & Larkin, Kathy. 1977. *Inference in text understanding*. Cambridge: Bolt, Beranek, & Newman (TR 3684) (also in Spiro, Bruce, & Brewer [Eds.], 1980).

Collins, Allan, & Gentner, Dedre. 1978. *A framework for a cognitive theory of writing*. Cambridge: Bolt, Beranek, & Newman.

Collins, Allan, & Grignetti, Mario. 1975. *Intelligent CAI*. Cambridge: Bolt, Beranek, & Newman (TR 3181).

Collins, Allan, & Loftus, Elizabeth. 1975. A spreading-activation theory of semantic processing. *PR*, 82, 407–428.

Collins, Allan, & Quillian, Ross, 1972. How to make a language user. In Tulving & Donaldson (Eds.), 309–351.

Collins, Allan, & Quillian, Ross. 1969. Retrieval from semantic memory. *JVLVB*, 8, 240–247.

Collins, Allan, Warnock, Eleanor, Aiello, Nelleke, & Miller, Mark. 1975. Reasoning from incomplete knowledge. In Bobrow & Collins (Eds.), 383–415.

Collins, Allan, Warnock, Eleanor, & Passafiume, Joseph. 1974. *Analysis and synthesis of tutorial dialogues*. Cambridge: Bolt, Beranek, & Newman (TR 2789).

Cooper, Lynn, & Shepard, Roger. 1973. Chronometric studies of the rotation of mental images. In Chase, William (Ed.), *Visual information processing*. New York: Academic Press, 75–176.

Cornish, Elizabeth, and Wason, Peter. 1970. The recall of affirmative and negative sentences in an incidental learning task. *QJExP*, 22, 109–114.

Coseriu, Eugenio. 1971. Thesen zum Thema "Sprache und Dichtung". In Stempel (Ed.), 183–188.

Coseriu, Eugenio. 1967. Lexikalische Solidaritäten. *Poetica*, 1, 293–303.

Coseriu, Eugenio. 1955–56. Determinación y entorno. *Romanistisches Jahrbuch*, 7, 29–54.

Coulthard, Malcolm. 1977. *An introduction to discourse analysis*. London: Longman.

Craik, Fergus, & Lockhart, Richard. 1972. A framework for memory research. *JVLVB*, 11, 671–684.

Cresswell, Max. 1973. *Logics and languages*. London: Methuen.

Crowder, Robert, & Morton, John. 1969. Precategorical acoustic storage. *PerPsy*, 5, 365–373.

Crymes, Ruth. 1968. *Some systems of substitution correlations in modern American English*. The Hague: Mouton.

Cullingford, Richard. 1978. *Script application: Computer understanding of newspaper stories*. New Haven: Yale dissertation (CS-TR 116).

Cunningham, James. 1978. Toward understanding readers' understanding. Paper at the Pacific Reading Research Symposium, Tucson.

Damerau, Fred. 1977. Advantages of transformational grammar for question answering. *5th IJCAI*, 192.

Daneš, František. 1970. Zur linguistischen Analyse der Textstruktur. *Folia Linguistica*. 4/1–2, 72–78.

Daneš, František (Ed.). 1974. *Papers on functional sentence perspective*. Prague: Academia.

Daneš, František, & Viehweger, Dieter (Eds.). 1976. *Probleme der Textgrammatik*. Berlin: Akademieverlag.

Danks, Joseph, & Glucksberg, Sam. 1971. Psychological scaling of adjective orders. *JVLVB*, 10, 63–67.

Darwin, Christopher, Turvey, Michael, & Crowder, Robert. 1972. An auditory analogue of the Sperling partial report procedure: Evidence for a brief auditory storage. *CogP*, 3, 255–267.

Davis, Paul, & Chien, Robert. 1977. Using and re-using partial plans. *5th IJCAI*, 494.

Davis, Randall, Buchanan, Bruce, & Shortliffe, Edward. 1977. Production rules as a representation for a knowledge-based consultation system. *AI*, 8, 15–45.

Deeping, Warwick. 1930. *The short stories of Warwick Deeping*. London: Cassell.

Deese, James. 1962. On the structure of associative meaning. *PR*, 69, 161–175.

Derrida, Jacques. 1974. *Glas*. Paris: Galilée.

Derrida, Jacques. 1972. *La dissemination*. Paris: Seuil.

Derrida, Jacques. 1967a. *De la grammatologie*. Paris: Editions de minuit.

Derrida, Jacques. 1967b. *L'ecriture et la différance*. Paris: Seuil.

DeSoto, Clinton, London, Marvin, & Handel, Stephen. 1965. Social reasoning and spatial paralogic. *JPersSP*, 2, 513–521.

Dickens, Charles. 1899. *The posthumous papers of the Pickwick Club*. London: Nelson & Sons.

Dijk, Teun van. 1979a. *The structures and functions of discourse*. Lectures at the University of Puerto Rico, Rio Piedras.

Dijk, Teun van. 1979b. *Macro-structures*. Hillsdale: Lawrence Erlbaum Associates.

Dijk, Teun van. 1977a. *Text and context*. London: Longman.

Dijk, Teun van. 1977b. Connectives in text grammar and text logic. In van Dijk & Petöfi (Eds.), 11–63.

Dijk, Teun van. 1977c. Acceptability in context. In Greenbaum (Ed.), 39–61.

Dijk, Teun van. 1972a. *Some aspects of text grammars*. The Hague: Mouton.

Dijk, Teun van. 1972b. On the foundations of poetics: Methodological prolegomena to a generative grammar of literary texts. *Poetics*, 1, 89–123.

Dijk, Teun van, Ihwe, Jens, Petöfi, János, & Rieser, Hannes. 1972. *Zur Bestimmung narrativer Strukturen auf der Grundlage von Textgrammatiken*. Hamburg: Buske.

Dijk, Teun van (Ed.). 1976. *Pragmatics of language and literature*. Amsterdam: North Holland.

Dijk, Teun van, & Petöfi, János (Eds.). 1977. *Grammars and descriptions: Studies in text theory and text analysis*. Berlin: de Gruyter.

Dik, Simon. 1978. *Functional grammar*. Amsterdam: North Holland.

Dik, Simon. 1968. *Coordination*. Amsterdam: North Holland.

Dik, Simon. 1967. Some critical remarks on the treatment of morphological structure in transformational generative grammar. *Lingua*, 18, 352–383.

Dingwall, William. 1971. Linguistics as psychology: A definition and some initial tasks. In William Dingwall (Ed.), *A survey of linguistic science*. College Park: University of Maryland Press, 758–797.

Dittmar, Norbert. 1976. *A critical survey of sociolinguistics*. New York: St. Martin's Press.

Dooley, Richard. 1976. Repartee as a graph. In Longacre 1976, 348–358.

Dresher, Elan, & Hornstein, Norbert. 1976. On some supposed contributions of artificial intelligence to the scientific study of language. *Cognition*, 4, 321–398.

Dressler, Wolfgang. 1979. Zum Verhältnis von Wortbildung und Textlinguistik. In Petöfi (Ed.).

Dressler, Wolfgang. 1977. Elements of a polycentristic theory of word formation. *Wiener linguistische Gazette*, 15, 13–32.

Dressler, Wolfgang. 1974a. Funktionelle Satzperspektive und Texttheorie. In Daneš (Ed.), 87–105.

Dressler, Wolfgang. 1974b. Der Beitrag der Textlinguistik zur Übersetzungswissenschaft. In Volker Kapp (Ed.), *Übersetzer und Dolmetscher*. Heidelberg: Quelle & Meyer, 61–71.

Dressler, Wolfgang. 1972a. *Einführung in die Textlinguistik*. Tübingen: Niemeyer.

Dressler, Wolfgang. 1972b. Textgrammatische Invarianz in Übersetzungen? In Gülich & Raible (Eds.), 98–106.

Dressler, Wolfgang. 1970a. Textsyntax. *Lingua e stile*, 5, 191–213.

Dressler, Wolfgang. 1970b. Textsyntax und Übersetzung. In Peter Hartmann & Henri Vernay (Eds.), *Sprachwissenschaft und Übersetzen*. Munich: Hueber, 64–71.

Dressler, Wolfgang, Leodolter, Ruth, & Chromec, Eva. 1976. Phonologische Schnell-sprechregeln in der Wiener Umgangssprache. In Viereck (Ed.), 71–92.

Dressler, Wolfgang (Ed.). 1978. *Current trends in text linguistics*. Berlin: de Gruyter.

Dressler, Wolfgang, & Schmidt, Siegfried (Eds.). 1973. *Textlinguistik: Kommentierte Bibliographie*. Munich: Fink.

Dundes, Alan. 1962. From etic to emic units in the structural study of folktales. *Journal of American Folklore*, 75, 95–105.

Dundes, Alan, Leach, Jerry, & Özkök, Bora. 1972. The strategy of Turkish boys' verbal dueling rhymes. In Gumperz & Hymes (Eds.), 130–160.

Eikmeyer, Hans-Jürgen, & Rieser, Hannes. 1978. *Vagheitstheorie*. Bielefeld: University of Bielefeld.

Ekstrand, Bruce, Wallace, William, & Underwood, Benton. 1966. A frequency theory of verbal discrimination learning. *PR*, 73, 566–578.

Ellis, Jeffrey. 1966. *Toward a general comparative linguistics*. The Hague: Mouton.

Enkvist, Nils-Erik. 1973. *Linguistic stylistics*. The Hague: Mouton.

Erben, Johannes. 1964. *Abriss der deutschen Grammatik*. Berlin: Akademie der Wissenschaften.

Erdelyi, Matthew. 1974. A new look at the new look: Perceptual defense and vigilance. *PR*. 81, 1–25.

Erdelyi, Matthew, & Appelbaum, Anat. 1973. Cognitive masking. BulPsyS, 1, 59–61.

Ernst, George, & Newell, Allen. 1969. *GPS: A case study in generality and problem solving.* New York: Academic Press.

Ertel, Suitbert. 1977. Where do the subjects of sentences come from? In Rosenberg (Ed.), 141–167.

Ervin-Tripp, Susan. 1972. On sociolinguistic rules: Alternation and co-occurrence. In Gumperz & Hymes (Ed.), 213–250.

Fahlman, Scott. 1977. *A system for representing and using real-world knowledge.* Cambridge: MIT dissertation (AI–TR 450) (to appear in the MIT Press).

Ferguson, George. 1956. On transfer and the abilities of man. *CanJP,* 10, 121–131.

Fikes, Richard, & Nilsson, Nils. 1971. STRIPS: A new approach to problem solving. *AI,* 2/3–4, 189–208.

Fillenbaum, Samuel. 1974. Pragmatic normalization: Further results for some conjunctive and disjunctive sentences. *JExP,* 87, 93–98.

Fillenbaum, Samuel. 1973. *Syntactic factors in memory.* The Hague: Mouton.

Fillenbaum, Samuel. 1971. On coping with ordered and unordered conjunctive sentences. *JExP,* 87, 93–98.

Fillenbaum, Samuel. 1968. Recall for answers to "conducive" questions. *Language and Speech,* 11, 46–53.

Fillmore, Charles. 1977. The case for case reopened. In Cole & Sadock (Eds.), 59–81.

Fillmore, Charles. 1968. The case for case. In Emmon Bach & Robert Harms (Eds.), *Universals in linguistic theory.* New York: Holt, Rinehart, & Winston, 1–88.

Findler, Nicholas (Ed.). 1979. *Associative networks: The representation and use of knowledge in computers.* New York: Academic Press.

Firbas, Jan. 1971. On the concept of communicative dynamism in the theory of functional sentence perspective. *Sborník prací Filosofické Fakulty Brněnské University,* A 19, 135–144.

Firbas, Jan. 1966. Non-thematic subjects in contemporary English. *Travaux linguistiques de Prague,* 2, 239–256.

Firth, John. 1957. A synopsis of linguistic theory. In *Studies in linguistic analysis.* Oxford: Blackwell, 1–32.

Flesch, Rudolf. 1972. *Say what you mean.* New York: Harper & Row.

Flesch, Rudolf. 1949. *The art of readable writing.* New York: Harper & Row.

Flores d'Arcais, Giovanni. 1970. Linguistic structure and focus of comparison in processing of comparative sentences. In Flores d'Arcais & Levelt (Eds.), 307–321.

Flores d'Arcais, Giovanni, & Levelt, Willem (Eds.). 1970. *Advances in psycholinguistics.* Amsterdam: North Holland.

Fodor, Jerry, Bever, Thomas, & Garrett, Merrill. 1974. *The psychology of language.* New York: McGraw-Hill.

Fodor, Jerry, & Garrett, Merrill. 1967. Some syntactic determinants of sentential complexity. *PerPsy,* 2, 289–296.

Fowler, Roger. 1977. Cohesive, progressing, and localizing aspects of text structure. In van Dijk & Petöfi (Eds.), 64–84.

Frake, Charles. 1972. "Struck by speech": The Yakan concept of litigation. In Gumperz & Hymes (Eds.), 106–129.

Frederiksen, Carl. 1977. Semantic processing units in understanding text. In Freedle (Ed.), 57–88.

Frederiksen, Carl. 1975. Effects of context-induced processing operations on semantic information acquired from discourse. *CogP,* 7, 136–166.

Freedle, Roy (Ed.). 1979. *New directions in discourse processing.* Norwood: Ablex Publishing Co.

Freedle, Roy (Ed.). 1977. *Discourse production and comprehension.* Norwood: Ablex Publishing Co.

Freedle, Roy, & Craun, Marlys. 1970. Observations with self-embedded sentences using written aids. *PerPsy*, 7, 247–249.

Freedle, Roy, & Hale, Gordon. 1970. Acquisition of new comprehension schemata for expository prose by a transfer of a narrative schema. In Freedle (Ed.), 121–136.

Freuder, Eugene. 1978. Hypothesis-guided induction: Jumping to conclusions. *2nd CSCSI*, 233–235.

Fried, Erich. 1975. *Fast alles Mögliche*. Berlin: Wagenbach.

Friedman, Morton, Burke, Cletus, Cole, Michael, Estes, William, Keller, Leo, & Millward, Richard. 1963. Two-choice behavior under extended training with probabilities of reinforcement. In Richard Atkinson (Ed.), *Studies in mathematical psychology*. Stanford: Stanford University Press, 250–291.

Fries, Charles. 1952. *The structure of English*. New York: Harcourt, Brace, & Co.

Fries, Udo. 1975. *Studien zur Textlinguistik. Frage- und Antwortsätze: Eine Analyse an neuenglischen Dramentexten*. Vienna: Braumüller.

Fries, Udo. 1972. Textlinguistik. *Linguistik und Didaktik*, 7, 219–234.

Fromkin, Victoria (Ed.). 1973. *Speech errors as linguistic evidence*. The Hague: Mouton.

Gabelenz, Georg von der. 1891. *Die Sprachwissenschaft: Ihre Aufgaben, Methoden, und bisherigen Ergebnisse*. Leipzig: Weigl Nachfolger.

Gardiner, Alan. 1932. *The theory of speech and language*. Oxford: Clarendon.

Garrett, Merrill. 1970. Does ambiguity complicate the perception of sentences? In Flores d'Arcais & Levelt (Eds.), 48–60.

Garrod, Simon, & Trabasso, Tom. 1973. A dual-memory information processing interpretation of sentence comprehension. *JVLVB*, 12, 155–167.

Gentner, Dedre. 1978. Testing the psychological reality of a representational model. *TINLAP-2*, 1–7.

Getzels, Jacob, & Jackson, Philip. 1962. *Creativity and intelligence*. New York: Wiley.

Gibson, Eleanor. 1942. Intralist generalization as a factor in verbal learning. *JExP*, 30, 185–200.

Gindin, Sergei. 1978. Contributions to textlinguistics in the Soviet Union. In Dressler (Ed.), 261–274.

Gindin, Sergei. 1972. *Vnutrennjaja semantika ritma i ee matematičeskoe modelirovanie*. Moscow: University of Moscow dissertation.

Givón, Talmy. 1978. Negation in language: pragamtics, function, ontology. In Cole (Ed.), 69–112.

Glinz, Hans. 1979. Text, Satz, Proposition. In Petöfi (Ed.), 43–47.

Glinz, Hans. 1973. *Textanalyse und Verstehenstheorie I*. Wiesbaden: Athenaion.

Glinz. Hans. 1952. *Die innere Form des Deutschen*. Bern: Francke.

Goffman, Erving. 1974. *Frame analysis*. New York: Harper & Row.

Goldman, Neil. 1975. Conceptual generation. In Schank et al., 289–371.

Goldman, Neil, Balzer, Robert, & Wile, David. 1977. *The inference of domain structure from informal process descriptions*. Marina del Rey: University of Southern California Information Sciences Institute (RR 77–64.)

Goldman-Eisler, Frieda, 1972. Pauses, clauses, sentences. *Language and Speech*, 15, 103–113.

Goldstein, Ira, & Papert, Seymour. 1977. Artificial intelligence, language, and the study of knowledge. *Cognitive Science*, 1, 84–123.

Goldstein, Kurt, & Scheerer, Martin. 1941. Abstract and concrete behavior: An experimental study with special tests. *Psychological Monographs*, 53/239.

Gomulicki, Bronislaw, 1956. Recall as an abstractive process. *Acta Psychologica*, 12, 77–94.

Goodman, Kenneth, & Burke, Carolyne. 1973. *Theoretically based studies of patterns of miscues in oral reading performance*. Washington, D.C.: U.S. Department of Health, Education, & Welfare.

Graves, Richard, 1976. *Rhetoric: From Athens to Auburn*. Auburn: Auburn University Press.

Greenbaum, Sidney (Ed.). 1977. *Language and acceptability*. The Hague: Mouton.

Greenberg, Joseph (Ed.). 1963. *Universals of language.* Cambridge: MIT Press.
Greimas, Algirdas. 1970. *Du sens: Essais sémiotiques.* Paris: Seuil.
Greimas, Algirdas. 1967. La structure des actants du récit: Essai d'approche générative. *Word,* 23, 221–238.
Greimas, Algirdas. 1966. *Sémantique structurale: Recherches de méthode.* Paris: Larousse.
Grewendorf, Günther, & Meggle, Georg (Eds.). 1974. *Linguistik und Philosophie.* Frankfurt: Athenäum.
Grice, Paul. 1978. Further notes on logic and conversation. In Cole (Ed.), 113–127.
Grice, Paul. 1975. Logic and conversation. In Cole & Morgan (Eds.), 41–58.
Grimes, Joseph. 1975. *The thread of discourse.* The Hague: Mouton.
Grimes, Joseph (Ed.). 1978. *Papers on discourse.* Dallas: Summer Institute of Linguistics.
Groeben, Norbert. 1978. *Die Verständlichkeit von Unterrichtstexten.* Münster: Aschendorff.
Grosse, Ernst-Ulrich. 1978. French structuralist views on narrative grammar. In Dressler (ed.), 155–173.
Grosse, Ernst-Ulrich. 1976a. *Texttypen: Linguistik nichtliterarischer Kommunikation.* Freiburg: University of Freiburg habilitation dissertation.
Grosse, Ernst-Ulrich. 1976b. *Text und Kommunkation.* Stuttgart: Kohlhammer.
Grosz, Barbara. 1977. *The representation and use of focus in dialogue understanding.* Menlo Park: Stanford Research Insitute (AI–TR 151).
Gülich, Elisabeth. 1970. *Makrosyntax der Gliederungssignale im gesprochenen Franzosisch.* Munich: Fink.
Gülich, Elisabeth, & Raible, Wolfgang. 1977. *Linguistische Textmodelle.* Munich: Fink.
Gülich, Elisabeth, & Raibel, Wolfgang (Eds.). 1972. *Textsorten: Differenzierungskriterien aus linguistischer Sicht.* Frankfurt: Athenäum.
Gumperz, John, & Hymes, Dell (Eds.). 1972. *Directions in sociolinguistics: The ethnography of communication.* New York: Holt, Rinehart, & Winston.
Gundel, Jeannette. 1977. *Role of topic and comment in linguistic theory.* Bloomington: Indiana University Linguistics Club.
Gunter, Richard. 1963. Elliptical sentences in American English. *Lingua,* 12, 137–150.
Haber, Lynn. 1975. The muzzy theory. In *Papers from the Eleventh Regional Meeting, Chicago Linguistic Society.* Chicago: CLS, 240–256.
Habermas, Jürgen. 1971. Vorbereitende Bemerkungen zu einer Theorie der kommunikativen Kompetenz. In Jürgen Habermas & Niklas Luhmann, *Theorie der Gesellschaft oder Sozialtechnologie.* Frankfurt: Suhrkamp, 101–141.
Hakes, David. 1972. Effects of reducing complement constructions on sentence comprehension, *JVLVB,* 11, 278–286.
Hakes, David, & Foss, Donald. 1970. Decision processes during sentence comprehension: Effects of surface structure reconsidered. *PerPsy,* 8, 413–416.
Halliday, Michael. 1977. Text as semantic choice in social contexts. In van Dijk & Petöfi (Eds.). 176–225.
Halliday, Michael. 1969. Some notes on "deep grammar". *JLing,* 5, 57–67.
Halliday, Michael. 1967a, 1967b, 1968. Notes on transitivity and theme in English. *JLing,* 3, 37–81; 3, 199–244; 4, 179–215.
Halliday, Michael. 1967c. *Intonation and grammar in British English.* The Hague: Mouton.
Halliday, Michael. 1964. The linguistic study of literary texts. In Horace Lunt (Ed.), *Proceedings of the 9th International Congress of Linguists.* The Hague: Mouton, 302–307.
Halliday, Michael, & Hasan, Ruqaiya. 1976. *Cohesion in English.* London: Longman.
Halliday, Michael, McIntosh, Angus, & Strevens, Peter. 1965. *The linguistic sciences and language teaching.* London: Longman.
Harper, Kenneth. 1965. *Studies in inter-sentence connection.* Santa Monica: Rand Corporation (Memorandum 4828–PR).

Harper, Kenneth, & Su, Stanley. 1969. *A directed random paragraph generator.* Santa Monica: Rand Corporation (Memorandum 6053-PR).

Harris, Larry, 1972. *A model for adaptive problem-solving applied to natural language acquisition.* Ithaca: Cornell (CS-TR 72-133).

Harris, Zellig. 1952. Discourse analysis. *Language,* 28, 1-30 and 474-494.

Harris, Zellig. 1951. *Methods in structural linguistics.* Chicago: University of Chicago.

Hartmann, Peter. 1979. Text und Satz. In Petöfi (Ed.).

Hartmann, Peter. 1975. Textlinguistische Tendenzen in der Sprachwissenschaft. *Folia Linguistica,* 8/14, 1-49.

Hartmann, Peter. 1972. *Zur Lage der Linguistik in der BRD.* Frankfurt: Athenäum.

Hartmann, Peter. 1970. *Aufgaben und Perspektiven der Linguistik.* Konstanz: University of Konstanz.

Hartmann, Peter. 1965. Modellbildung in der Sprachwissenschaft. *Studium Generale,* 18, 364-379.

Hartmann, Peter. 1964. Text, Texte, Klassen von Texten. *Bogawus,* 2, 15-25.

Hartmann, Peter. 1963a. *Theorie der Grammatik.* The Hague: Mouton.

Hartmann, Peter. 1963b. *Theorie der Sprachwissenschaft.* Assen: van Gorcum.

Harweg, Roland. 1978. Substitutional text linguistics. In Dressler (Ed.), 247-260.

Harweg, Roland. 1974. Textlinguistik. In Koch (Ed.) 1973/74, II, 88-116.

Harweg, Roland. 1968a. *Pronomina und Textkonstitution.* Munich: Fink.

Harweg, Roland. 1968b. Textanfänge in geschriebener und gesprochener Sprache. *Orbis,* 17/2, 343-388.

Hasan, Ruqaiya. 1978. Text in the systemic-functional model. In Dressler (Ed.), 228-246.

Hasan, Ruqaiya. 1968. *Grammatical cohesion in spoken English.* London: Longman.

Havens, William. 1978. *A procedural model of recognition for machine perception.* Vancouver: University of British Columbia dissertation.

Hawkins, Peter. 1969. Social class, the nominal group, and reference. *Language and Speech,* 12/2, 125-135.

Hayes, John Richard, & Flower, Linda. 1978. Protocol analysis of writing processes. Paper at the AERA Meeting, Toronto.

Hayes, Phillip. 1977. *Some association-based techniques for lexical disambiguation by machine.* Rochester: University of Rochester (CS-TR 25).

Hays, David, 1973. Types of processes on cognitive networks. Paper at the International Conference on Computational Linguistics, Pisa.

Heger, Klaus. 1976. *Monem, Wort, Satz und Text.* Tübingen: Niemeyer.

Heger, Klaus. 1971. *Monem, Wort und Satz.* Tübingen: Niemeyer.

Heidolph, Karl-Erich. 1966. Kontextbeziehungen zwischen Sätzen in einer generativen Grammatik. *Kybernetika,* 2, 274-281.

Helbig, Gerhard. 1974. *Geschichte der neueren Sprachwissenschaft.* Hamburg: Rowohlt.

Helbig, Gerhard (Ed.). 1971. *Beiträge zur Valenztheorie.* The Hague: Mouton.

Hempel, Carl. 1966. *Philosophy of natural science.* Englewood Cliffs: Prentice-Hall.

Hempfer, Klaus. 1976. *Poststrukturale Texttheorie und narrative Praxis.* Munich: Fink.

Hendrix, Gary. 1978. *Encoding knowledge in partitioned networks.* Menlo Park: Stanford Research Institute (AI-TR 164) (also in Findler [Ed.], 51-92).

Hendrix, Gary. 1975. *Partitioned networks for the mathematical modeling of natural language semantics.* Austin: University of Texas (CS-TR NL-28).

Heringer, James. 1970. Research on quantifier-negative idiolects. In *Papers from the Sixth Regional Meeting, Chicago Linguistic Society.* Chicago: CLS, 287-296.

Herriot, Peter. 1969. The comprehension of active and passive sentences as a function of pragmatic expectation. *JVLVB,* 8, 166-169.

Hershberger, Wayne, & Terry, Donald. 1965. Typographical cuing in conventional and programmed texts. *JExP,* 49, 55-60.

Hilgard, Ernest. 1951. Methods and procedures in the study of learning. In Stanley Stevens (Ed.), *Handbook of experimental psychology.* New York: Wiley, 517–567.

Hirsch, Eric Donald. 1977. *The philosophy of composition.* Chicago: University of Chicago.

Hjelmslev, Louis. 1943. *Omkring sprogteoriens grundlæggelse.* Copenhagen: Lunos.

Hobbs, Jerry. 1979. Coherence and coreference. *Cognitive Science,* 3/1, 67–90.

Hobbs, Jerry. 1978. *Why is discourse coherent?* Menlo Park: Stanford Research Institute (AI–TR 176).

Hobbs, Jerry. 1976. *A computational approach to discourse analysis.* New York: City University of New York dissertation (CS–TR 76–2).

Hockett, Charles. 1958. *A course in modern linguistics.* New York: Macmillan.

Hollan, James. 1975. Features and semantic memory: Set-theoretic or network model? *PR,* 82, 154–155.

Hörmann, Hans. 1977. *Psychologie der Sprache.* Berlin: Springer.

Hörmann, Hans. 1976. *Meinen und Verstehen.* Frankfurt: Suhrkamp.

Hörmann, Hans. 1974. Psycholinguistik. In Koch (Ed.) 1973–74, II, 138–155.

Householder, Fred. 1960. Opening statement. In Sebeok (Ed.), 339–349.

Hughes, George, & Cresswell, Max. 1968. *An introduction to modal logic.* London: Methuen.

Hull, Clark. 1920. Quantitative aspects of the evolution of concepts. *Psychological Monographs,* 28/123.

Hundsnurscher, Franz. 1970. *TSG: Transformationelle Schulgrammatik.* Göppingen: Kümmerle.

Huttenlocher, Janellen. 1968. Constructing spatial images: A strategy in reasoning. *PR,* 75, 550–560.

Hymes, Dell. 1972. On communicative competence. In John Pride and Janet Holmes (Eds.), *Sociolinguistics.* Hammondsworth: Penguin, 269–285.

Hymes, Dell. 1962. The ethnography of speaking. In Thomas Gladwin and William Sturtevant (Eds.), *Anthropology and human behavior.* Washington, D. C.: Anthropological Society of Washington, 13–53.

Ihwe, Jens. 1972. *Linguistik in der Literaturwissenschaft.* Munich: Bayrischer Schulbuchverlag.

Ihwe, Jens (Ed.). 1971. *Literaturwissenschaft und Linguistik: Ergebnisse und Perspektiven.* Frankfurt: Athenäum.

Ihwe, Jens, & Rieser, Hannes. 1972. Versuch einer Exploration des "Versuchs einer Exploration der neuentdeckten Formelwälder von der Insel Mainau" von Werner Kummer. *Linguistische Berichte,* 18, 56–58.

Ingarden, Roman. 1931. *Das literarische Kunstwerk.* Halle: M. Niemeyer.

Isačenko, Alexander. 1965. Kontextbedingte Ellipse und Pronominalisierung im Deutschen. In *Beiträge zur Sprachwissenschaft, Volkskunde und Literaturforschung,* 163–173.

Isenberg, Horst. 1971. Überlegungen zur Texttheorie. In Ihwe (Ed.), 150–173.

Iser, Wolfgang. 1978. *The act of reading: A theory of aesthetic response.* London: Routledge & Kegan Paul.

Iser, Wolfgang. 1976. *Der Akt des Lesens.* Munich: Fink.

Iser, Wolfgang. 1975. Die Wirklichkeit der Fiktion: Elemente eines funktions-geschichtlichen Textmodells. In Warning (Ed.), 277–324.

Ivić, Milka. 1965. *Trends in Linguistics.* The Hague: Mouton.

Jackendoff, Ray. 1978. An argument on the composition of conceptual structure. *TINLA P-2,* 162–166.

Jacobs, Joseph (Ed.). 1891. *English fairy tales.* New York: G. P. Putnam.

Jacobs, Roderick, & Rosenbaum, Peter. 1968. *English transformational grammar.* Waltham: Blaisdell.

Jakobson, Roman. 1973. *Main trends in the science of language.* New York: Harper.

Jakobson, Roman, & Jones, Lawrence. 1970. *Shakespeare's verbal art in 'Th'expence of spirit'.* The Hague: Mouton.

Jenkins, James, & Russell, Wallace. 1952. Associative clustering during recall. *JAbSocP*, 47, 818–821.

Jespersen, Otto. 1924. *Philosophy of grammar*. London: Allen & Unwin.

Johnson, David, & Postal, Paul. 1980. *Arc-pair grammar*. Princeton: Princeton University Press.

Johnson, Marcia, Bransford, John, & Solomon, Susan. 1973. Memory for tacit implications of sentences. *JExP*, 98/1, 203–205.

Johnson, Ronald. 1970. Recall of prose as a function of the structural importance of linguistic units. *JVLVB*, 9, 12–20.

Johnson-Laird, Philip. 1977. Procedural semantics. *Cognition*, 5, 189–214.

Jones, Linda. 1977. *Theme in English expository discourse*. Lake Bluff, Ill.: Jupiter.

Kallmeyer, Werner, Klein, Wolfgang, Meyer-Hermann, Reinhard, Netzer, Klaus, & Siebert, Jürgen. 1974. *Lektürenkolleg zur Textlinguistik*. Frankfurt: Athenäum-Fischer.

Kalverkämper, Hartwig. 1978. *Textlinguistik der Eigennamen*. Stuttgart: Klett.

Kaplan, Jerrold. 1978. Indirect responses to loaded questions. *TINLAP-2*, 202–209.

Kaplan, Ronald. 1974. *Transient processing load in relative clauses*. Cambridge: Harvard dissertation.

Karlsen, Rolf. 1959. *Studies in the connection of clauses in current English: Zero, ellipsis, and explicit form*. Bergen: Eides Boktrykkeri.

Kasher, Asa. 1973. Linguistik und Mathematik. In Renate Bartsch & Theo Vennemann (Eds.), *Linguistik und Nachbarwissenschaften*. Kronberg: Scriptor, 59–74.

Katz, Jerrold. 1971. Generative semantics is interpretative semantics. *LingInq*, 2, 313–330.

Katz, Jerrold. 1970. Interpretative semantics vs. generative semantics. *FoundLang*, 6, 220–259.

Katz, Jerrold. 1966. *The philosophy of language*. New York: Harper & Row.

Katz, Jerrold, & Fodor, Jerry. 1963. The structure of semantic theory. *Language*, 39, 170–210.

Kay, Harry. 1955. Learning and retaining verbal material. *BritJP*, 46/2, 81–100.

Keele, Steven. 1973. *Attention and human performance*. Pacific Palisades: Goodyear.

Kintsch, Walter. 1979a. Learning from text, levels of comprehension, or: Why anyone would read a story anyway. *Poetics*, 9.

Kintsch, Walter. 1979b. Semantic memory: A tutorial. In Raymond Nickerson (Ed.), *Attention and performance VIII*. Hillsdale: Lawrence Erlbaum Associates.

Kintsch, Walter. 1977a. *Memory and cognition*. New York: Wiley.

Kintsch, Walter. 1977b. On comprehending stories. In Marcel Just & Patricia Carpenter (Eds.), *Cognitive processes in comprehension*. Hillsdale: Lawrence Erlbaum Associates, 33–62.

Kintsch, Walter. 1974. *The representation of meaning in memory*. Hillsdale: Lawrence Erlbaum Associates.

Kintsch, Walter. 1972. Notes on the structure of semantic memory. In Tulving & Donaldson (Eds.), 247–308.

Kintsch, Walter, & Dijk, Teun van. 1978a. Toward a model of text comprehension and production. *PR*, 85, 363–394.

Kintsch, Walter, & Dijk, Teun van. 1978b. Cognitive psychology and discourse: recalling and summarizing stories. In Dressler (Ed.), 61–80.

Kintsch, Walter, & Keenan, Janice. 1973. Reading rate and retention as a function of the number of propositions in the base structure of sentences. *CogP*, 5, 257–274.

Kintsch, Walter, Mandel, Theodore, & Kozminsky, Ely. 1977. Summarizing scrambled stories. *MemCog*, 5, 547–552.

Kintsch, Walter, & Vipond, Douglas. 1979. Reading comprehension and readability in educational practice. In Lars-Göran Nilsson (Ed.), *Perspectives on memory research*. Hillsdale: Lawrence Erlbaum Associates, 329–365.

Klare, George. 1963. *The measurement of readability*. Ames: Iowa State University.

Klaus, Georg. 1972. *Kybernetik und Erkenntnistheorie*. Berlin: Verlag der Wissenschaften.

Klaus, Georg. 1963. *Kybernetik in philosophischer Sicht*. Berlin: Dietz.

312 TEXT, DISCOURSE, AND PROCESS

Klein, Sheldon. 1965. Automatic paraphrasing in essay format. *MechTrans,* 8/2–3.
Klein, Sheldon, Aeschlimann, John, Balsiger, David, Converse, Stephen, Court, Claudine, Foster, Mark, Lao, Robin, Oakley, John, & Smith, Joel. 1973. *Automatic novel-writing: A status report.* Madison: University of Wisconsin.
Klein, Wolfgang. 1974. *Computerlinguistik.* Stuttgart: Kohlhammer.
Kloepfer, Rolf. 1975. *Poetik und Linguistik.* Munich: Fink.
Koch, Walter. 1979. *Poetry and science.* Bochum: University of Bochum.
Koch, Walter. 1978. Poetizität zwischen Metaphysik und Metasprache. *Poetica,* 10, 285–341.
Koch, Walter. 1976. Ontologiethese und Relativitätsthese für eine Textlinguistik. In Koch (Ed.), 1–37.
Koch, Walter. 1973/74. Einleitung. In Koch (Ed.), xi–lv.
Koch, Walter. 1973. *Das Textem.* Hildesheim: Olms.
Koch, Walter. 1971. *Taxologie des Englischen.* Munich: Fink.
Koch, Walter (Ed.). 1976. *Textsemiotik und strukturelle Rezeptionstheorie.* Hildesheim: Olms.
Koch, Walter (Ed.). 1973/74. *Perspektiven der Linguistik I & II.* Stuttgart: Kröner.
Koch, Walter (Ed.). 1972. *Strukturelle Textanalyse.* Hildesheim: Olms.
Koffka, Kurt. 1935. *Principles of gestalt psychology.* New York: Harcourt, Brace, & Co.
Kohonen, Viljo, & Enkvist, Nils-Erik (Eds.). 1978. *Text linguistics, cognitive learning, and language teaching.* Åbo: Åbo Akademi.
Kosslyn, Stephen. 1975. Information representing visual images. *CogP,* 7, 341–370.
Kowalski, Robert. 1974. *Logic for problem solving.* Edinburgh: University of Edinburgh (CS Memo 75).
Krauss, Robert, & Weinheimer, Sidney. 1967. Effects of referent similarity and communication mode on verbal encoding. *JVLVB,* 6, 359–363.
Kristeva, Julia. 1968. Problèmes de la structuration du texte. *Linguistique et Littérature,* 12, 55–64.
Kuhn, Thomas. 1970. *The structure of scientific revolutions.* Chicago: University of Chicago Press.
Kuipers, Benjamin. 1975. A frame for frames: Representing knowledge for retrieval. In Bobrow & Collins (Eds.), 151–184.
Kummer, Werner. 1975. *Grundlagen der Texttheorie.* Hamburg: Rowohlt.
Kummer, Werner. 1972a. Aspects of a theory of argumentation. In Gülich & Raible (Eds.), 25–49.
Kummer, Werner. 1972b. Versuch einer Exploration der neuentdeckten Formalwälder von der Insel Mainau. *Linguistische Berichte,* 18, 53–55.
Kummer, Werner. 1972c. Zum "Versuch einer Exploration des 'Versuchs einer Exploration der neuentdeckten Formelwälder von der Insel Mainau' von W. Kummer." *Linguistische Berichte,* 19, 78–79.
Kuno, Susumu. 1978. Generative discourse analysis in America. In Dressler (Ed.), 275–294.
Kuno, Susumu. 1972. Functional sentence perspective: A case study from Japanese and English. *LingInq,* 3, 269–320.
LaBerge, David, & Samuels, Jay (Eds.). 1977. *Basic processes in reading: Perception and comprehension.* Hillsdale: Lawrence Erlbaum Associates.
Labov, William. 1972a. *Language in the inner city: Studies in the Black English vernacular.* Philadelphia: University of Pennsylvania Press.
Labov, William. 1972b. *Sociolinguistic patterns.* Philadelphia: University of Pennsylvania Press.
Labov, William. 1972c. Rules for ritual insults. In David Sudnow (Ed.), *Studies in social interaction.* New York: Free Press.
Labov, William. 1971. The notion of "system" in Creole languages. In Dell Hymes (Ed.), *Pidginization and creolization of languages.* London: Cambridge, 447–472.

Labov, William. 1970. The study of language in its social context. *Studium Generale*, 23, 30–87.

Labov, William. 1969. Contraction, deletion, and inherent variability of the English copula. *Language*, 45, 715–762.

Labov, William, 1966. On the grammaticality of everyday speech. Paper at the 41st Annual Meeting of the American Linguistic Society, New York.

Labov, William, & Waletzky, Joshua. 1967. Narrative analysis: Oral versions of personal experience. In June Helm (Ed.), *Essays on the verbal and visual arts*. Seattle: University of Washington Press, 12–44.

Lackner, James, & Garrett, Merrill. 1972. Resolving ambiguity: Effects of biased context in the unattended ear. *Cognition*, 1, 359–372.

Ladefoged, Peter, & Broadbent, Donald. 1957. Information conveyed by vowels. *JAcouSA*, 29, 98–104.

Lakoff, George. 1977. Linguistic gestalts. In *Papers from the Thirteenth Regional Meeting, Chicago Linguistic Society*. Chicago: CLS, 236–287.

Lakoff, George. 1971. On generative semantics. In Steinberg & Jakobovits (Eds.), 232–296.

Lakoff, George. 1969. Presuppositions and relative grammaticality. In William Todd (Ed.), *Studies in philosophical linguistics*. Evanston: Great Expectations, 103–116.

Lakoff, George. 1968a. *Pronouns and reference*. Bloomington: Indiana University Linguistics Club.

Lakoff, George. 1968b. *Counterparts, or the problem of reference in transformational grammar*. Bloomington: Indiana University Linguistics Club.

Lakoff, George. 1968c. *Deep and surface grammar*. Bloomington: Indiana University Linguistics Club.

Lakoff, Robin. 1977. You say what you are: Acceptability and gender-related language. In Greenbaum (Ed.), 73–86.

Larson, Richard. 1976. Structure and form in non-fiction prose. In Tate (Ed.), 47–71.

Leech, Geoffrey, & Svartvik, Jan. 1975. *A communicative grammar of English*. London: Longman.

Lees, Robert. 1960. *The grammar of English nominalizations*. Bloomington: Indiana University Press.

Lehiste, Ilse. 1970. *Suprasegmentals*. Cambridge: MIT Press.

Lehnert, Wendy. 1978. *The process of question answering*. Hillsdale: Lawrence Erlbaum Associates.

Lenat, Douglas. 1977. The ubiquity of discovery. *5th IJCAI*, 1093–1105.

Leodolter, Ruth. 1975. *Das Sprachverhalten von Angeklagten vor Gericht*. Kronberg: Scriptor.

Leskov, Nikolai. 1961. *Selected tales* (trans. David Magarshack). New York: Noonday.

Levesque, Hector. 1977. *A procedural approach to semantic networks*. Toronto: University of Toronto (CS–TR 105).

Levesque. Hector, & Mylopoulos, John. 1978. *A procedural semantics for semantic networks*. Toronto University of Toronto (CS–TR) (also in Findler [Ed.], 93–120).

Levin, Gerald (Ed.). 1977. *Short essays*. New York: Harcourt, Brace, & Jovanovich.

Levin, James, & Goldman, Neil. 1977. *Process models of reference in context*. Marina del Rey: University of Southern California Information Sciences Institute (TR 78–72).

Levin, Samuel. 1962. *Linguistic structures in poetry*. The Hague: Mouton.

Levine, Marvin. 1966. Hypothesis behavior by humans during discrimination learning. *JExP*, 71, 331–338.

Lévi-Strauss, Claude. 1958. *Anthropologie structurale*. Paris: Plon.

Li, Charles (Ed.). 1976. *Subject and topic*. New York: Academic Press.

Liefrink, Frans. 1973. *Semantico-syntax*. London: Longman.

Linde, Charlotte, & Labov, William. 1975. Spatial networks as a site for the study of language and thought. *Language*, 51, 924–939.

Linsky Leonard. 1971. Reference and referents. In Steinberg & Jakobovits (Eds.), 76–85.

Löbner, Sebastian. 1976. *Einführung in die Montague-Grammatik*. Kronberg: Scriptor.

Loftus, Elizabeth. 1975. Leading questions and the eyewitness report. *CogP*, 7, 560–572.

Loftus, Elisabeth, & Zanni, Guido. 1975. Eyewitness testimony: The influence of the wording of a question. *BulPsyS*, 5, 86–88.

Loftus, Geoffrey, & Loftus, Elizabeth. 1976. *Human memory: The processing of information*. Hillsdale: Lawrence Erlbaum Associates.

Longacre, Robert. 1976. *An anatomy of speech notions*. Lisse: de Ridder.

Longacre, Robert. 1970. *Discourse, paragraph, and sentence structure in selected Philippine Languages*. Santa Ana: Summer Institute of Linguistics.

Longacre, Robert. 1964. *Grammar discovery procedures*. The Hague: Mouton.

Lounsbury, Floyd. 1964. The structural analysis of kinship semantics. In Horace Lunt (Ed.), *Proceedings of the 9th International Congress of Linguistics*. The Hague: Mouton, 1073–1093.

Luhmann, Niklas. 1970. *Soziologische Aufklärung: Aufsätze zur Theorie sozialer Systeme*. Cologne: Westdeutscher Verlag.

MacKay, Donald. 1966. On the retrieval and lexical structure of verbs. *JVLVB*, 15, 169–182.

Mackworth, Alan. 1976. Model-driven interpretation in intelligent vision systems. *Perception*, 5, 349–370.

Maclay, Howard. 1971. Overview. In Steinberg & Jakobovits (Eds.), 157–182.

Malinowski, Bronislaw. 1923. The problem of meaning in primitive languages. In Charles Ogden & Ivor Richards, *The meaning of meaning*. London: Oxford, 296–336.

Mandler, George, & Pearlstone, Zena. 1966. Free and constrained concept learning and subsequent recall. *JVLVB*, 5, 126–131.

Mandler, Jean. 1978. A code in the node: The use of a story schema in retrieval. *Discourse Processes*, 1, 14–35.

Mandler, Jean, & Johnson, Nancy. 1977. Remembrance of things parsed: Story structure and recall. *CogP*, 9, 111–151.

Marckwardt, Albert. 1966. *Linguistics and the teaching of English*. Bloomington: Indiana University Press.

Marcus, Mitchell. 1978. Capturing linguistic generalizations in a parser for English. *2nd CSCSI*, 64–73.

Marcus, Mitchell. 1977. *A theory of syntactic recognition for natural languages*. Cambridge: MIT dissertation.

Marcuse, Herbert. 1964. *One-dimensional man*. Boston: Beacon.

Marslen-Wilson, William. 1975. Sentence perception as an interactive parallel process. *Science*, 189, 226–228.

Martin, Judith. 1969. Semantic determinants of preferred adjective order. *JVLVB*, 8, 697–704.

Mathesius, Vilém, 1929. Zur Satzperspektive im modernen Englisch. *Archiv fur das Studium der neueren Sprachen und Literaturen*, 155, 202–210.

Mathesius, Vilém. 1928. On linguistic characterology with illustrations from modern English. In *Actes du Ier Congrès International des Linguistes*, 56–63.

Mathesius, Vilém. 1924. Několik poznamek o funcki podmětu v moderní angličtině. *Časopis pro moderní filologii*, 10, 244–248.

McCall, William, & Crabbs, Lelah. 1961. *Standard test lessons in readability*. New York: Teachers' College Press.

McCalla, Gordon. 1978a. *An approach to the organization of knowledge for the modelling of conversation*. Vancouver: University of British Columbia (CS–TR 78–4).

McCalla, Gordon. 1978b. Analyzing conversation. *2nd CSCSI*, 224–232.

McCawley, James. 1978. Conversational implicature and the lexicon. In Cole (Ed.), 245–259.

McCawley, James. 1976. Some ideas not to live by. *Die neueren Sprachen*, 75, 151–165.

McCawley, James. 1968a. Concerning the base component of a transformational grammar. *FoundLang*, 4, 243–269.

McCawley, James. 1968b. The role of semantics in a grammar. In Emmon Bach & Robert Harms (Eds.), *Universals in linguistic theory*. New York: Holt, Rinehart, & Winston, 125–169.

McDermott, Drew. 1974. *Assimilation of new information by a natural language understanding system*. Cambridge: MIT (AI–TR 291).

Meehan, James. 1977. TALE-SPIN, an interactive program that writes stories. *5th IJCAI*, 91–98.

Meehan, James. 1976. *The metanovel: Writing stories by computer*. New Haven: Yale (CS–TR 74).

Mel'čuk, Igor, & Žolkovskij, Alexander. 1970. Towards a functioning meaning-text model of language. *Linguistics*, 57, 10–47.

Mellon, John. 1969. *Transformational sentence-combining: A method for enhancing syntactic fluency in English composition*. Urbana: National Council of Teachers of English.

Metzing, Dieter (Ed.). 1979. *Frame conceptions and text understanding*. Berlin: de Gruyter.

Meyer, Bonnie. 1977. What is remembered from prose: A function of passage structure. In Freedle (Ed.), 307–336.

Meyer, Bonnie. 1975. *The organization of prose and its effects on memory*. Amsterdam: North Holland.

Meyer, Bonnie, & McConkie, George. 1973. What is recalled after learning a passage? *JEdP*, 65, 109–117.

Meyer, David, Schvaneveldt, Roger, & Ruddy, Margaret. 1974. Functions of phonemic and graphic codes in visual word recognition. *MemCog*, 2, 309–321.

Milic, Louis. 1971. Rhetorical choice and stylistic option. In Seymour Chatman (Ed.), *Literary style: A symposium*. London: Oxford, 77–94.

Miller, George. 1956. The magical number seven, plus or minus two. *PR*, 63, 81–97.

Miller, George, Bruner, Jerome, & Postman, Leo. 1954. Familiarity of letter sequences and tachistoscopic identification. *Journal of Genetic Psychology*, 50, 129–139.

Miller, George, Galanter, Eugene, & Pribram, Karl. 1968. Plans and the structure of behavior. In Buckley (Ed.), 369–381.

Miller, George, Galanter, Eugene, & Pribram, Karl. 1960. *Plans and the structure of behavior*. New York: Holt, Rinehart, & Winston.

Miller, George, & Isard, Stephen. 1963. Some perceptual consequences of linguistic rules. *JVLVB*, 2, 217–228.

Miller, George, & Johnson-Laird, Philip. 1976. *Language and perception*. Cambridge: Harvard University Press.

Miller, Gerald, & Coleman, Edmund. 1967. A set of thirty-six prose passages calibrated for complexity. *JVLVB*, 6, 851–854.

Minsky, Marvin. 1977. Plain talk about neurodevelopmental epistemology. *5th IJCAI*, 1083–1093.

Minsky, Marvin. 1975. A framework for representing knowledge. In Winston (Ed.), 211–277.

Minsky, Marvin, & Papert, Seymour. 1974. *Artificial intelligence: Condon lectures*. Eugene: Oregon State System of Higher Education.

Mistler-Lachman, Janet. 1974. Depth of comprehension and sentence memory. *JVLVB*, 13, 98–106.

Mistrík, Josef. 1973. *Exakte Typologie von Texten*. Munich: Sagner.

Montague, Richard. 1974. *Formal philosophy*. New Haven: Yale University Press.

Morgan, Jerry. 1978a. Toward a rational model of discourse comprehension. *TINLAP-2*, 109–114.

Morgan, Jerry. 1978b. Two types of convention in indirect speech acts. In Cole (Ed.), 261–280.
Morgan, Jerry. 1975. Some remarks on the nature of sentences. In Robin Grossman, James San, & Timothy Vance (Eds.), *Papers from the parasession on functionalism*. Chicago: CLS.
Morgan, Jerry. 1973. Sentence fragments and the notion "sentence". In Braj Kachru (Ed.), *Issues in linguistics*. Urbana: University of Illinois Press, 719–751.
Morton, Rand. 1966. The behavioral analysis of Spanish syntax: Toward an acoustic grammar. *IntJAL*, 32, 170–184.
Mounin, Georges. 1963. *Les problèmes théoriques de la traduction*. Paris: Gallimard.
Mukařovský, Jan. 1967. *Kapitel aus der Poetik* (trans. Walter Schamschula). Frankfurt: Suhrkamp.
Mukařovský, Jan. 1964. Standard language and poetic language. In Paul Garvin (Ed.), *A Prague School reader on aesthetics, literary structure, and style*. Washington, D.C.: Georgetown University Press, 17–30.
Murdock, Bennett. 1962. The serial position effect in free recall. *JExP*, 64, 482–488.
Neisser, Ulric. 1976. *Cognition and reality*. San Francisco: Freeman.
Neisser, Ulric. 1967. *Cognitive psychology*. New York: Appleton-Century-Crofts.
Newell, Allan, & Simon, Herbert. 1972. *Human problem solving*. Englewood Cliffs: Prentice-Hall.
Nickel, Gerhard (Ed.). 1972. *Reader zur kontrastiven Linguistik*. Frankfurt: Athenäum.
Nickel, Gerhard (Ed.). 1971. *Papers in contrastive linguistics*. Cambridge, England: Cambridge University Press.
Nida, Eugene. 1975. *Exploring semantic structures*. Munich: Fink.
Nida, Eugene. 1964. *Toward a science of translating*. Leyden: Brill.
Nilsen, Don, & Nilsen, Alleen. 1975. *Semantic theory: A linguistic perspective*. Rowley: Newbury.
Norman, Donald, & Bobrow, Daniel. 1975. On data-limited and resource-limited processes. *CogP*, 7, 44–64.
Norman, Donald, & Rumelhart, David. 1975a. *Explorations in cognition*. San Francisco: Freeman.
Norman, Donald, & Rumelhart, David. 1975b. Reference and comprehension. In Norman & Rumelhart 1975a, 65–87.
Nöth, Winfried. 1978. The semiotic framework of text linguistics. In Dressler (Ed.), 31–34.
O'Connell, Daniel. 1977. One of many units: The sentence. In Rosenberg (Ed.), 307–313.
Oevermann, Ulrich. 1970. *Sprache und soziale Herkunft*. Frankfurt: Suhrkamp.
Ogden, Charles. 1932. *The ABC of Basic English*. London: Paul, Trench, & Trubner.
O'Hare, Frank. 1971. *Sentence combining: Improving student writing without formal grammar instruction*. Urbana: National Council of Teachers of English.
Ohmann, Richard. 1964. Generative grammars and the concept of literary style. *Word*, 20, 423–439.
Oller, John. 1972. On the relation between syntax, semantics, and pragmatics. *Linguistics*, 83, 43–55.
Oller, John. 1970. Transformational theory and pragmatics. *MLJ*, 54, 504–507.
Olson, David. 1974. Towards a theory of instructional means. Paper at the AERA Meeting, Toronto.
Olson, David. 1970. Language and thought: Aspects of a cognitive theory of semantics. *PR*, 77, 257–273.
Olson, David, & Filby, Nikola. 1972. On the comprehension of active and passive sentences. *CogP*, 3, 161–181.
Ortony, Andrew. 1978a. Remembering, understanding, and representation. *Cognitive Science*, 2, 53–69.

Ortony, Andrew. 1978b. Some psycholinguistic constraints on the construction and interpretation of definite descriptions. *TINLA P-2*, 73–78.

Ortony, Andrew. 1978c. Comprehension of figurative language. Paper at the 28th Annual Meeting, National Reading Association, St. Petersburg Beach.

Ortony, Andrew. 1975. How episodic is episodic memory? In Schank & Nash-Webber (Eds.), 55–59.

Ortony, Andrew, & Anderson, Richard. 1977. Definite descriptions and semantic memory. *Cognitive Science*, 1, 74–83.

Osgood, Charles. 1971. Where do sentences come from? In Steinberg & Jakobovits (Eds.), 497–529.

Osgood, Charles, & Bock, Kathryn. 1977. Salience and sentencing: Some production principles. In Rosenberg (Ed.), 89–140.

Padučeva, Elena. 1970. Anaphoric relations and the manifestations in the text. In *Proceedings of the 10th International Congress of Linguists*, 693–697.

Paivio, Allan. 1971. *Imagery and verbal processes*. New York: Holt, Rinehart, & Winston.

Palek, Bohumil. 1968. *Cross-reference: A study from hyper-syntax*. Prague: Charles University Press.

Palková, Zdena, & Palek, Bohumil. 1978. Functional sentence perspective and text linguistics. In Dressler (Ed.), 212–227.

Papert, Seymour. 1973. *Uses of technology to enhance education*. Cambridge: MIT (AI–TR 298).

Pavlidis, Theodosios. 1977. *Structural pattern recognition*. Berlin: Springer.

Pavlov, Ivan. 1927. *Conditioned reflexes: An investigation of the physiological activity of the cerebral cortex*. London: Oxford.

Perlmutter, David, & Postal, Paul. 1978. *Some proposed laws of basic clause structure*. Yorktown Heights: IBM Thomas J. Watson Research Center.

Petöfi, János. 1979. Die Struktur der TeSWeSt. Aspekte der pragmatisch-semantischen Interpretation von objektsprachlichen Texten. In Fritz Neubauer (Ed.), *Coherence in natural language texts*. Hamburg: Buske.

Petöfi, János. 1978a. A formal semiotic text theory as an integrated theory of natural languages. In Dressler (Ed.), 35–46.

Petöfi, János. 1978b. Wissenschafts theoretische Überlegungen zum Aufbau einer Texttheorie. In Biasci & Fritsche (Eds.), 5–31.

Petöfi, János. 1976. A frame for FRAMES: A few remarks on the methodology of semantically guided text processing. In *Proceedings of the Second Annual Meeting of the Berkeley Linguistic Society*. Berkeley: University of California, 319–329.

Petöfi, János. 1975a. *Vers une théorie partielle du texte*. Hamburg: Buske.

Petöfi, János. 1975b. Beyond the sentence, between linguistics and logic. In Håkan Ringbom et al. (Eds.), *Style and text: Studies presented to Nils-Erik Enkvist*. Stockholm: Skriptor.

Petöfi, János. 1974. Towards an empirically motivated grammatical theory of verbal texts. In Petöfi & Rieser (Eds.), 205–275.

Petöfi, János. 1972. Modell 2: Eine generative Textgrammatik mit einer nichtlinear festgelegten Basis. In van Dijk, Ihwe, Petöfi, & Rieser, 77–129.

Petöfi, János. 1971a. *Transformationsgrammatiken und eine ko-textuelle Texttheorie*. Frankfurt: Athenäum.

Petöfi, János. 1971b. Probleme der ko-textuellen Analyse von Texten. In Ihwe (Ed.), 173–212.

Petöfi, János. (Ed.). 1979. *Text vs. sentence: Basic questions of text linguistics*. Hamburg: Buske.

Petöfi, János, & Franck, Dorothea (Eds.). 1974. *Presuppositions in philosophy and linguistics*. Frankfurt: Athenäum.

TEXT, DISCOURSE, AND PROCESS

Petöfi, János, & Rieser, Hannes. 1974. *Probleme der modelltheoretischen Interpretation von Texten.* Hamburg: Buske.

Petöfi, János, & Rieser, Hannes (Eds.). 1974. *Studies in text grammar.* Dordrecht: Reidel.

Petrick, Stanely. 1965. *A recognition procedure for transformational grammar.* Cambridge: MIT dissertation.

Piaget, Jean. 1966. La psychologie, les relations interdisciplinaires, et le système des sciences. Paper at the 18th International Congress of Psychologists, Moscow.

Pike, Kenneth. 1967. *Language in relation to a unified theory of the structure of human behavior.* The Hague: Mouton.

Pollack, Irwin, & Pickett, James. 1964. Intelligibility of excerpts from fluent speech: Auditory vs. structural content. *JVLVB, 3,* 79–84.

Porter, Bern. 1972. *Found poems.* New York: Something Else.

Posner, Michael, & Rossman, Ellen. 1965. Effect of size and location of information transforms on short-term retention. *JExP, 70,* 496–505.

Posner, Michael, & Snyder, Charles. 1975. Attention and cognitive control. In Solso (Ed.), 55–86.

Posner, Roland. 1979a. Bedeutungen und Gebrauch der Satzverknüpfer in den natürlichen Sprachen. In Günther Grewendorf (Ed.), *Sprechakttheorie und Semantik.* Frankfurt: Suhrkamp, 345–385.

Posner, Roland. 1979b. Semantics and pragmatics of sentence connectives in natural languages. In Manfred Bierwisch, Ferenc Kiefer, & John Searle (Eds.), *Speech act theory and pragmatics.* Amsterdam: North Holland.

Posner, Roland. 1973. Redekommentierung. In *Funk-Kolleg Sprache 2: eine Einführung in die moderne Linguistik.* Frankfurt: Fischer, 124–133.

Posner, Roland. 1972. *Theorie des Kommentierens.* Frankfurt: Athenäum.

Postal, Paul. 1969. Anaphoric islands. In *Papers from the Fifth Regional Meeting, Chicago Linguistic Society.* Chicago: CLS, 205–239.

Postal, Paul. 1968. Cross-over phenomena: A study in the grammar of co-reference. In Warren Plath (Ed.), *Specification and utilization of a transformational grammar.* Yorktown Heights: Thomas J. Watson Research Center.

Pottier, Bernard. 1963. *Recherches sur l'analyse sémantique en linguistique et en traduction méchanique.* Nancy: University of Nancy.

Prieto, Luis. 1964. *Principes de noologie.* The Hague: Mouton.

Propp, Vladimir. 1928. *Morfologija skazki.* Leningrad: Akademia.

Pugh, George. 1977. *The biological origins of human values.* New York: Basic Books.

Quillian, Ross. 1968. Semantic memory. In Marvin Minsky (Ed.), *Semantic information processing.* Cambridge: MIT Press, 227–270.

Quillian, Ross. 1966. *Semantic memory.* Cambridge: Bolt, Beranek, & Newman (TR–AFCRL–66–189).

Quirk, Randolph. 1978. Focus, scope, and lyrical beginnings. *LangSty,* 11/1, 30–39.

Quirk, Randolph, Greenbaum, Sidney, Leech, Geoffrey, & Svartvik, Jan. 1972. *A grammar of contemporary English.* London: Longman.

Quirk, Randolph, & Svartvik, Jan. 1966. *Investigating linguistic acceptability.* The Hague: Mouton.

Reichman, Rachael. 1978. Conversational coherency. *CogSci, 2,* 283–327.

Reiss, Katharina. 1976. *Texttyp und Übersetzungsmethode.* Kronberg: Scriptor.

Resnick, Lauren. 1977. Holding an instructional conversation. In Anderson, Spiro, & Montague (Eds.), 365–372.

Restle, Frank. 1962. The selection of categories in cue learning. *PR, 69,* 329–343.

Restorff, Hedwig von. 1933. Über die Wirkung von Bereichsbildungen im Spurenfeld. *Psychologische Forschungen,* 18, 199–342.

Rieger, Charles. 1978. GRIND-1: First report on the magic grinder story comprehension project. *DisPro,* 1, 267–304.

Rieger, Charles. 1977a. Spontaneous computation in cognitive models. *CogSci,* 1, 315–344.

Rieger, Charles. 1977b. *Viewing parsing as word sense discrimination.* College Park: University of Maryland (CS–TR 511).

Rieger, Charles. 1976. *Spontaneous computation in cognitive models.* College Park: University of Maryland (CS–TR 459).

Rieger, Charles. 1975. Conceptual memory and inference. In Schank et al., 157–288.

Rieger, Charles. 1974. *Conceptual memory.* Palo Alto: Stanford University dissertation.

Rieger, Charles, & London, Phil. 1977. Subgoal protection and unravelling during plan synthesis. *5th IJCAI,* 487–493.

Riesbeck, Christopher. 1975. Conceptual analysis. In Schank et al., 83–156.

Riesbeck, Christopher. 1974. *Computational understanding: Analysis of sentences and context.* Palo Alto: Stanford University dissertation.

Rieser, Hannes. 1978. On the development of text grammar. In Dressler (Ed.), 6–20.

Rieser, Hannes. 1976. *Aspekte einer partiellen Texttheorie.* Bielefeld: University of Bielefeld habilitation dissertation.

Riffaterre, Michael. 1960. Stylistic context. *Word,* 16, 207–218.

Riffaterre, Michael. 1959. Criteria for style analysis. *Word,* 15, 154–174.

Ringen, Jon. 1975. Linguistic facts: A study of the empirical scientific status of transformational generative grammars. In David Cohen & Jessica Wirth (Eds.), *Testing linguistic hypotheses.* New York: Wiley, 1–41.

Roberts, Paul. 1958. *Understanding English.* New York: Harper.

Robinson, Ian. 1975. *The new grammarian's funeral.* London: Cambridge.

Roget, Peter. 1947. *Thesaurus of words and phrases.* New York: Grosset & Dunlap.

Rohrer, Christian. 1979. The mass/count distinction applied to French tenses. Paper at the Bielefeld Symposium on Theories of Language Use, June 1979.

Rosch, Eleanor. 1977. Human categorization. In Neil Warren (Ed.), *Advances in cross-cultural psychology.* London: Academic Press, 3–49.

Rosch, Eleanor. 1973. Natural categories. *CogP,* 328–350.

Rosch, Eleanor, & Mervis, Carolyn. 1975. Family resemblances: Studies in the internal structure of categories. *CogP,* 7, 573–605.

Rosch, Eleanor, Simpson, Carol, & Miller, Scott. 1976. Structural bases of typicality effects. *JExP: Human Perception and Performance,* 2, 491–502.

Rosenberg, Sheldon (Ed.). 1977. *Sentence production: Developments in research and theory.* Hillsdale: Lawrence Erlbaum Associates.

Rosenstein, Allen, Rathbone, Robert, & Schneerer, William. 1964. *Engineering communications.* Englewood Cliffs: Prentice-Hall.

Ross, John. 1970a. On declarative sentences. In Roderick Jacobs & Peter Rosenbaum (Eds.), *Readings in English transformational grammar.* Waltham: Ginn, 222–272.

Ross, John. 1970b. Gapping and the order of constituents. In *Proceedings of the 10th International Congress of Linguists,* 841–852.

Rothkopf, Ernst. 1976. Writing to teach and reading to learn: A perspective on the psychology of written instruction. *Yearbook of the National Society for the Study of Education,* 75, 91–129.

Royer, James. 1977. Remembering: constructive or reconstructive? In Anderson, Spiro, & Montague (Eds.), 167–173.

Rubin, Andee. 1978a. A theoretical taxonomy of the differences between oral and written language. Cambridge: Bolt, Beranek, & Newman (TR 3731) (also in Spiro, Bruce, & Brewer [Eds.]).

Rubin, Andee. 1978b. A framework for comparing language experiences, with particular emphasis on the effect of audience on discourse models. *TINLAP-2*, 133–140.

Ruesch, Jürgen. 1957. *Disturbed communication*. New York: Norton.

Rumelhart, David. 1978. Comprehension of stories. Paper at the 28th Annual Meeting, National Reading Association, St. Petersburg Beach.

Rumelhart, David. 1977a. *Introduction to human information processing*. New York: Wiley.

Rumelhart, David. 1977b. Understanding and summarizing brief stories. In LaBerge & Samuels (Eds.), 265–303.

Rumelhart, David. 1975. Notes on a schema for stories. In Bobrow & Collins (Eds.), 211–236.

Rumelhart, David, Lindsay, Peter, & Norman, Donald. 1972. A process model for long-term memory. In Tulving & Donaldson (Eds.), 197–246.

Rumelhart, David, & Norman, Donald. 1975a. The active structural network. In Norman & Rumelhart 1975a, 35–64.

Rumelhart, David, & Norman, Donald. 1975b. The computer implementation. In Norman & Rumelhart, 1975a, 159–178.

Rumelhart, David, & Ortony, Andrew. 1977. The representation of knowledge in memory. In Anderson, Spiro, & Montague (Eds.), 99–135.

Rundus, Dewey. 1971. Analysis of rehearsal processes in free recall. *JExP*, 89, 63–77.

Rüttenauer, Martin (Ed.). 1974. *Textlinguistik und Pragmatik*. Hamburg: Buske.

Sacerdoti, Earl. 1977. *A structure for plans and behavior*. New York: Elsevier.

Sacks, Harvey, Schegloff, Emmanuel, & Jefferson, Gail. 1974. A simplest systematics for the organization of turn-taking for conversation. *Language*, 50, 696–735.

Sadock, Jerrold. 1978. On testing for conversational implicature. In Cole (Ed.), 281–297.

Sadock, Jerrold. 1970. Super-hypersentences. *Papers in Linguistics*, 1, 1–15.

Salmond, Anne. 1974. Rituals of encounter among the Maori: Sociolinguistic study of a scene. In Richard Bauman & Joel Scherzer (Eds.), *Explorations in the ethnography of speaking*. London: Cambridge, 192–212.

Saussure, Ferdinand de. 1916. *Cours de linguistique générale*. Lausanne: Payot.

Schank, Roger. 1978. What makes something "ad hoc". *TINLAP-2*, 8–13.

Schank, Roger. 1977. Rules and topics in conversation. *CogSci*, 1, 421–441.

Schank, Roger. 1975a. The structure of episodes in memory. In Bobrow & Collins (Eds.), 237–272.

Schank, Roger. 1975b. The conceptual approach to language processing. In Schank et al., 5–21.

Schank, Roger. 1975c. Conceptual dependency theory. In Schank et al., 22–82.

Schank, Roger. 1972. Conceptual dependency: A theory of natural language understanding. *CogP*, 3, 552–631.

Schank, Roger, & Abelson, Robert. 1977. *Scripts, plans, goals, and understanding*. Hillsdale: Lawrence Erlbaum Associates.

Schank, Roger, & Colby, Kenneth (Eds.). 1973. *Computer models of thought and language*. San Francisco: Freeman.

Schank, Roger, Goldman, Neil, Rieger, Charles, & Riesbeck, Christopher. 1975. *Conceptual information processing*. Amsterdam: North Holland.

Schank, Roger, & Nash-Webber, Bonnie (Eds.). 1975. *Theoretical issues in natural language processing: An interdisciplinary workshop*. Cambridge: Bolt, Beranek, & Newman.

Schank, Roger, & Wilensky, Robert. 1977. Response to Dresher & Hornstein. *Cognition*, 5, 133–145.

Schegloff, Emmanuel. 1978. On some questions and ambiguities in conversation. In Dressler (Ed.), 81–102.

Schegloff, Emmanuel, Jefferson, Gail, & Sacks, Harvey. 1977. The preference for self-correction in the organization of repair in conversation. *Language*, 53, 361–382.

Scherzer, Joel. 1974. "Naummakke, summake, kormakke": Three types of Cuna speech event. In Richard Bauman & Joel Scherzer (Eds.), *Explorations in the ethnography of speaking*. London: Cambridge, 262–282.

Schlesinger, Izhak. 1977. *Production and comprehension of utterances.* Hillsdale: Lawrence Erlbaum Associates.

Schmidt, Siegfried. 1979. *Grundzüge der empirischen Literaturwissenschaft.* Braunschweig: Vieweg.

Schmidt, Siegfried. 1978. Some problems of communicative text theories. In Dressler (Ed.), 47–60.

Schmidt, Siegfried. 1975. *Literaturwissenschaft als argumentierende Wissenschaft.* Munich: Fink.

Schmidt, Siegfried. 1973. *Texttheorie.* Munich: Fink.

Schmidt, Siegfried. 1972. Ist "Fiktionalität" eine linguistische oder eine text-theoretische Kategorie? In Gülich & Raible (Eds.), 59–71.

Schmidt, Siegfried. 1971a. *Ästhetizität.* Munich: Bayrischer Schulbuchverlag.

Schmidt, Siegfried. 1971b. *Ästhetische Prozesse.* Berlin: Kiepenheuer & Witsch.

Schmidt, Siegfried. 1971c. Text und Bedeutung: Sprachphilosophische Prolegomena zu einer textsemantischen Literaturwissenschaft. In Siegfried Schmidt (Ed.), *Text, Bedeutung, Ästhetik.* Munich: Bayrischer Schulbuchverlag, 43–79.

Schmidt, Siegfried. 1971d. Allgemeine Textwissenschaft: Ein Programm zur Erforschung ästhetischer Texte. *Linguistische Berichte.* 12, 10–21.

Schmidt, Siegfried. 1968a. Alltagssprache und Gedichtsprache. *Poetica,* 2, 285–303.

Schmidt, Siegfried. 1968b. *Bedeutung und Begriff.* Braunschweig: Vieweg.

Schneider, Peter. 1978. *Organization of knowledge in a procedural semantic network.* Toronto: University of Toronto (CS-TR 115).

Scragg, Greg. 1976. Semantic nets as memory models. In Charniak & Wilks (Eds.), 101–128.

Sebeok, Thomas (Ed.). 1960. *Style in language.* Cambridge: MIT Press.

Searle, John. 1975. Indirect speech acts. In Cole & Morgan (Eds.), 59–82.

Searle, John. 1971. The problem of proper names. In Steinberg & Jakobovits (Eds.), 134–141.

Searle, John. 1969. *Speech acts.* London: Cambridge.

Selfridge, Oliver, & Neisser, Ulrich. 1960. Pattern recognition by machine. *Scientific American,* 203, 60–68.

Seuren, Pieter. 1977. *Zwischen Sprache und Denken.* Wiesbaden: Athenaion.

Seuren, Pieter. 1972. Autonomous versus semantic syntax. *FoundLang,* 8, 237–265.

Sgall, Petr, Hajičová, Eva, & Benešová, Eva. 1973. *Topic, focus, and generative semantics.* Kronberg: Scriptor.

Shakespeare, William. 1936. *The complete works of Shakespeare* (Ed. George Lyman Kittredge). Boston: Ginn & Co.

Shannon, Claude. 1951. Prediction and entropy of printed English. *Bell System Technical Journal,* 30, 50–64.

Shannon, Claude, & Weaver, Warren. 1949. *The mathematical theory of communication.* Urbana: University of Illinois Press.

Shapiro, Stuart. 1975. Generation as parsing from a network into a linear string. *AJCL,* 33, 45–62.

Shapiro, Stuart. 1971. A net structure for semantic information storage, deduction, and retrieval. *2nd IJACI,* 512–523.

Shaughnessy, Mina. 1976. Basic writing. In Tate (Ed.), 137–167.

Shepard, Roger, & Metzler, Jacqueline. 1971. Mental rotation of three-dimensional objects. *Science,* 171, 701–703.

Silman, Tamara. 1974. *Probleme der Textlinguistik.* Heidelberg: Quelle & Meyer.

Simmons, Robert. 1978. *Towards a computational theory of discourse.* Austin: University of Texas (CS-TR NL-37).

Simmons, Robert. 1977. *Rule-based computations on English.* Austin: University of Texas (CS-TR NL-31).

Simmons, Robert. 1973. Semantic networks: Their computation and use for understanding sentences. In Schank & Colby (Eds.), 63–113.

Simmons, Robert, & Bruce, Bertram. 1971. Some relations between predicate calculus and semantic net representations of discourse. *2nd IJCAI*, 524–529.

Simmons, Robert, & Chester, Daniel. 1979. *Relating sentences and semantic networks with clausal logic.* Austin: University of Texas (CS–TR 39).

Simmons, Robert, & Correira, Alfred. 1978. *Rule forms for verse, sentences, and story trees.* Austin: University of Texas (CS–TR NL–35). Also in Findler (Ed.), 1979, 363–392.

Simmons, Robert, & Slocum, Jonathan. 1971. *Generating English discourse from semantic networks.* Austin: University of Texas (CS–TR NL–3).

Simpson, Louis (Ed.). 1967. *An introduction to poetry.* New York: St. Martin's Press.

Sinclair, John, & Coulthard, Malcolm. 1975. *Towards an analysis of discourse.* London: Oxford.

Sitta, Horst, & Brinker, Klaus (Eds.). 1973. *Studien zur Texttheorie und zur deutschen Grammatik.* Düsseldorf: Schwann.

Slama-Cazaca, Tatiana. 1961. *Langage et contexte.* The Hague: Mouton.

Slobin, Dan. 1966. Grammatical transformations and sentence comprehension in childhood and adulthood. *JVLVB*, 5, 219–227.

Small, Stephen. 1978. *Conceptual language analysis for story comprehension.* College Park: University of Maryland (CS–TR 663).

Smith, Edward, Shoben, Edward, & Rips, Lance. 1974. Structure and process in semantic memory: A featural model for semantic decisions. *PR*, 81, 214–241.

Smith, Raoul. 1973. *Probabilistic performance models of language.* The Hague: Mouton.

Snow, Catharine, & Meijer, Guus. 1977. On the secondary nature of syntactic intutions. In Greenbaum (Ed.), 163–177.

Solso, Robert (Ed.). 1975. *Information processing and cognition.* Hillsdale: Lawrence Erlbaum Associates.

Sperling, George. 1960. The information available in brief visual presentations. *Psychological Monographs*, 74, 1–29.

Spillner, Bernd. 1974. *Linguistik und Literaturwissenschaft: Stilforschung, Rhetorik, Textlinguistik.* Stuttgart: Kohlhammer.

Spiro, Rand. 1977. Remembering information from text: The "state of schema" approach. In Anderson, Spiro, & Montague (Eds.), 137–177.

Spiro, Rand, Bruce, Bertram, & Brewer, William (Eds.). 1980. *Theoretical issues in reading comprehension.* Hillsdale: Lawrence Erlbaum Associates.

Stegmüller, Wolfgang. 1969. *Probleme und Resultate der Wissenschaftstheorie und analytischen Philosophie. I: Wissenschaftliche Erklärung und Begründung. II: Theorie und Erfahrung.* Berlin: Springer.

Stein, Nancy, & Glenn, Christine. 1979. An analysis of story comprehension in elementary school children. In Freedle (Ed.), 53–120.

Stein, Nancy, & Nezworski, Teresa. 1978. The effects of organization and instructional set on story memory. *DisPro*, 1, 177–193.

Steinberg, Danny, & Jakobovits, Leon (Eds.). 1971. *Semantics.* London: Cambridge.

Stempel, Wolf-Dieter (Ed.). 1971. *Beiträge zur Textlinguistik.* Munich: Fink.

Stevens, Albert, & Rumelhart, David. 1975. Errors in reading: Analysis using an augmented transition network model of grammar. In Norman & Rumelhart 1975a, 136–155.

Stockwell, Robert. 1977. *Foundations of syntactic theory.* Englewood Cliffs: Prentice-Hall.

Stoltz, Walter. 1967. A study of the ability to decode grammatically novel sentences. *JVLVB*, 6, 867–873.

Strawson, Peter. 1949. Truth. *Analysis*, 9/6, 83–97.

Strohner, Hans, & Nelson, Keith. 1974. The young child's development of sentence comprehension: Influence of event probability, nonverbal context, syntactic form, and strategies. *Child Development*, 45, 567–576.

Sussman, Gerald. 1973. *A computer model of skill acquisition.* Cambridge: MIT dissertation (AI-TR 297).

Takefuta, Yukio. 1975. Analysis of intonational signals by computer simulation of pitch-perception behavior in human listeners. *SIGLASH Newsletter,* 8/1, 1–8.

Talmy, Leonard. 1978. The relation of grammar to cognition: A synopsis. *TINLAP-2,* 14–24.

Tannen, Deborah. 1979. What's in a frame? Surface evidence for underlying expectations. In Freedle (Ed.), 137–182.

Tate, Gary (Ed.). 1976. *Teaching composition.* Fort Worth: Texas Christian University Press.

Taylor, Stephen. 1974. *Automatic abstracting by applying graphical techniques to semantic networks.* Evanston: Northwestern University dissertation.

Tesnière, Lucien. 1959. *Elements de syntaxe structurale.* Paris: Klincksieck.

Thomas, Dylan. 1971. *The poems of Dylan Thomas.* New York: New Directions.

Thorndike, Edward. 1931. *Human learning.* New York: Appleton-Century-Crofts.

Thorndike, Edward. 1911. *Animal intelligence.* New York: Macmillan.

Thorndyke, Perry. 1977. Cognitive structures in comprehension and memory of narrative discourse. *CogP,* 9, 77–110.

Thorne, James. 1969. Poetry, stylistics, and imaginary grammars. *JLing,* 5, 147–150.

Thorne, James, Bratley, Paul, & Dewar, Hamish. 1968. The syntactic analysis of English by machine. In Donald Michie (Ed.), *Machine intelligence 3.* Edinburgh: Univ. of Edinburgh Press, 281–309.

Thurber, James. 1948. *The beast in me—and other animals.* New York: Harcourt, Brace, & Co.

Trager, George. 1950. Review of K. L. Pike, *Phonemics. Language,* 26, 152–158.

Tulving, Endel. 1972. Episodic and semantic memory. In Tulving & Donaldson (Eds.), 382–404.

Tulving, Endel, & Donaldson, Wayne (Eds.). 1972. *The organization of memory.* New York: Academic Press.

Tulving, Endel, Mandler, George, & Baumal, Ruth. 1964. Interaction of two sources of information in tachistoscopic word recognition. *CanJP,* 18, 62–71.

Turner, Althea, & Greene, Edith. 1977. *The construction and use of a propositional text base.* Boulder: University of Colorado Institute for the Study of Intellectual Behavior (TR 63).

Turner, Elizabeth, & Rommetveit, Ragnar. 1968. The effects of focus of attention on storing and retrieving of active and passive voice sentences. *JVLVB,* 7, 543–548.

Uhlenbeck, Eugene. 1973. *Critical comments on transformational generative grammar 1962-1972.* The Hague: Smits.

Uldall, Hans Jörgen. 1957. *Outline of glossematics.* Copenhagen: Nordisk Sprog- og Kulturforlag.

Underwood, Benton, & Freund, Joel. 1968. Errors in recognition, learning, and retention. *JExP,* 78, 55–63.

Ungeheuer, Gerold. 1969. Paraphrase und syntaktische Tiefenstruktur. *Folia Linguistica,* 3/3–4, 178–227.

Vendler, Zeno. 1968. *Adjectives and nominalizations.* The Hague: Mouton.

Viereck, Wolfgang (Ed.). 1976. *Sprachliches Handeln—Soziales Verhalten.* Munich: Fink.

Villiers, Peter de. 1974. Imagery and theme in recall of connected discourse. *JExP,* 103, 263–268.

Vygotskii, Lev. 1962. *Thought and language.* Cambridge: MIT Press.

Wagner, Carl. 1974. *Methoden der naturwissenschaftlichen und technischen Forschung.* Mannheim: Bibliographisches Institut.

Walker, Donald (Ed.). 1978. *Understanding spoken language.* Amsterdam: North Holland.

Wallace, Anthony, & Atkins, John. 1960. The meaning of kinship terms. *American Anthropologist,* 62, 58–60.

Wallace, William. 1965. Review of the historical, empirical, & theoretical status of the von Restorff phenomenon. *Psychological Bulletin,* 63, 410–424.

Waltz, David. 1978. On the interdependence of language and perception. *TINLAP-2*, 149–156.
Waltz, David. 1975. Understanding line drawings of scenes with shadows. In Winston (Ed.), 19–91.
Wandruszka, Mario. 1976. *Interlinguistik: Umrisse einer neuen Sprachwissenschaft*. Munich: Piper.
Warning, Rainer (Ed.). 1975. *Rezeptionsästhetik*. Munich: Fink.
Warnock, Robert (Ed.). 1952. *Representative modern plays: American*. Glenview: Scott, Foresman, & Co.
Warren, David, & Pereira, Luis. 1977. PROLOG: The language and its implementation compared with LISP. *SIGPLAN Notices*, 12/8, 109–115.
Warren, William, Nicholas, David, & Trabasso, Tom. 1979. Event chains and inferences in understanding narratives. In Freedle (Ed.), 23–52.
Wason, Peter. 1965. The contexts of plausible denial. *JVLVB*, 4, 7–11.
Waterhouse, Viola. 1963. Independent and dependent sentences. *IntJAL*, 29, 45–54.
Waugh, Nancy. 1969. Free recall of conspicuous items. *JVLVB*, 8, 448–456.
Webber, Bonnie. 1980. Syntax beyond the sentence: Anaphora. In Spiro, Bruce, & Brewer (Eds.).
Webber, Bonnie. 1978. *A formal approach to discourse anaphora*. Cambridge: Bolt, Beranek, & Newman (TR 3761).
Wedge, George, & Ingemann, Frances. 1970. Tag questions, syntactic variables, and grammaticality. In Frances Ingemann (Ed.), *Papers from the 5th Kansas Linguistics Conference*. Lawrence: Univ. of Kansas, 166–203.
Weinreich, Uriel. 1966. *Explorations in semantic theory*. The Hague: Mouton.
Weinreich, Uriel. 1954. *Languages in contact*. New York: Linguistic Circle.
Weinrich, Harald. Forthcoming. *Textgrammatik der französischen Sprache*.
Weinrich, Harald. 1977. *Tempus: Besprochene und erzählte Welt*. Stuttgart: Kohlhammer.
Weinrich, Harald. 1976. *Sprache in Texten*. Stuttgart: Klett.
Weinrich, Harald. 1972. Thesen zur Textsortenlinguistik. In Gülich & Raible (Eds.), 161–169.
Weinrich, Harald. 1966a. *Linguistik der Lüge*. Heidelberg: Schneider.
Weinrich, Harald. 1966b. Das Zeichen des Jonas: Über das sehr Große und das sehr Kleine in der Literatur. *Merkur*, 20, 737–747.
Weizenbaum, Joseph. 1966. ELIZA: A computer program for the study of natural language communication between man and machine. *CACM*, 9, 36–43.
Weltner, Klaus. 1964. Zur empirischen Bestimmung subjektiver Informationswerte von Lehrbuchtexten mit dem Ratetest von Shannon. *Grundlagenstudien aus Kybernetik und Geisteswissenschaft*, 5, 3–11.
Werth, Paul. 1976. Roman Jakobson's verbal analysis of poetry. *JLing*, 12, 21–73.
Wheeler, Alva. 1967. Grammatical structure in Siona discourse. *Lingua*, 19, 60–77.
Widdowson, Henry. 1973. *An applied linguistic approach to discourse analysis*. Edinburgh: University of Edinburgh dissertation.
Wienold, Götz. 1973. *Die Erlernbarkeit der Sprachen*. Munich: Kösel.
Wienold, Götz. 1972. *Semiotik der Literatur*. Frankfurt: Athenäum.
Wilde, Oscar. 1940. *The best-known works of Oscar Wilde*. New York: Blue Ribbon.
Wilensky, Robert. 1978. *Understanding goal-based stories*. New Haven: Yale (CS-TR 140).
Wilks, Yorick. 1978. Making preferences more active. *AI*, 10, 197–223.
Wilks, Yorick. 1977a. *Good and bad arguments about semantic primitives*. Edinburgh: University of Edinburgh (AI-TR 42). Also in *Communication and Cognition*, 10, 1977, 181–221.
Wilks, Yorick. 1977b. Natural language understanding systems within the AI paradigm: A survey and some comparisons. In Antonio Zampolli (Ed.), *Linguistic structures processing*. Amsterdam: North Holland, 341–398.
Wilks, Yorick. 1977c. What sort of a taxonomy of causation do we need? *CogSci*, 1, 235–264.

Wilks, Yorick. 1976. Parsing English. In Charniak & Wilks (Eds.), 89–100 and 155–184.

Wilks, Yorick. 1975a. *Seven theses on artificial intelligence.* Castagnola: Institute for Semantic and Cognitive Studies.

Wilks, Yorick. 1975b. Preference semantics. In Edward Keenan (Ed.), *The formal semantics of natural languages.* London: Cambridge, 329–350.

Wilks, Yorick. 1972. *Grammar, meaning, and the machine analysis of language.* London: Routledge.

Wilson, Deirdre. 1975. *Presuppositions and non-truth-conditional semantics.* New York: Academic Press.

Winograd, Terry. 1978. On primitive prototypes, and other semantic anomalies. *TINLAP-2,* 25–32.

Winograd, Terry. 1977a. A framework for the understanding of discourse. In Marcel Just & Patricia Carpenter (Eds.), *Cognitive processes in comprehension.* Hillsdale: Lawrence Erlbaum Associates, 63–88.

Winograd, Terry. 1977b. On some contested suppositions of generative linguistics about the scientific study of language. *Cognition,* 5, 151–179.

Winograd, Terry. 1976. *Towards a procedural analysis of semantics.* Palo Alto: Stanford (AI-TR 292).

Winograd, Terry. 1975. Frame representations and the declarative-procedural controversy. In Bobrow & Collins (Eds.), 185–210.

Winograd, Terry. 1975. Frame representations and the declarative-procedural controversy. In Bobrow & Collins (Eds.), 185–210.

Winograd, Terry. 1972. *Understanding natural languages.* New York: Academic Press.

Winston, Patrick. 1977. *Artificial intelligence.* Rowley, Mass.: Addison-Wesley.

Winston, Patrick. 1975. Learning structural descriptions from examples. In Winston (Ed.), 157–209.

Winston, Patrick (Ed.). 1975. *The psychology of computer vision.* New York: McGraw-Hill.

Wittgenstein, Ludwig. 1953. *Philosophical investigations.* New York: Macmillan.

Woods, William. 1978a. Taxonomic lattice structures for situation recognition. *TINLAP-2,* 33–41.

Woods, William. 1978b. Knowledge-based natural language understanding. In Woods & Brachman 1978a, 4–35.

Woods, William. 1978c. Generalizations of ATN grammars. In Woods & Brachman 1978b, 21–77.

Woods, William. 1975. What's in a link: Foundations for semantic networks. In Bobrow & Collins (Eds.), 35–82.

Woods, William. 1970. Transition network grammars for natural language analysis. *CACM,* 13, 591–606.

Woods, William, & Brachman, Ronald. 1978a. *Research in natural language understanding.* Cambridge: Bolt, Beranek, & Newman (Quarterly Progress TR 1, 3742).

Woods, William, & Brachman, Ronald. 1978b. *Research in natural language understanding.* Cambridge: Bolt, Beranek, & Newman (Quarterly Progress TR 4, 3963).

Woods, William, & Makhoul, John. 1973. Mechanical inference problems in continuous speech understanding. *3rd IJCAI,* 200–207.

Woods, William, Brown, Geoffrey, Bruce, Bertram, Cook, Craig, Klovstad, John, Makhoul, John, Nash-Webber, Bonnie, Schwartz, Richard, Wolf, Jared, & Zue, Victor. 1976. *Speech understanding systems: Final report.* Cambridge: Bolt, Beranek, & Newman (TR 3438).

Wright, Georg von. 1967. The logic of action. In Nicholas Rescher (Ed.), *The logic of decision and action.* Pittsburg: University of Pittsburgh Press, 121–136.

Wright, Patricia. 1968. Sentence retention and transformation theory. *QJExP,* 20, 265–272.

Wunderlich, Dieter. 1971. Pragmatik, Sprechsituation, Deixis. *Literaturwissenschaft und Linguistik,* 1, 153–190.

Yngve, Victor. 1969. On achieving agreement in linguistics. In *Papers from the Fifth Regional Meeting, Chicago Linguistic Society*. Chicago: CLS, 445–462.

Ziff, Paul. 1971. On H. P. Grice's account of meaning. In Steinberg & Jakobovits (Eds.), 60–65.

Zipf, George Kingsley. 1935. *The psycho-biology of language*. Boston: Houghton-Mifflin.

Žolkovskij, Alexandr, & Ščeglov, Jurij. 1967. Strukturnaja poëtika—poraždajuščaja poëtika! *Voprosy Literatury*, 11, 74–89.

Table of Abbreviations

AERA: American Educational Research Association
AI: Laboratory or program in artificial intelligence
AI: Artificial Intelligence
AJCL: American Journal of Computational Linguistics
BritJP: British Journal of Psychology
BulPsyS: Bulletin of the Psychonomic Society
CACM: Communications of the Association for Computing Machinery
CanJP: Canadian Journal of Psychology
CCC: College Composition and Communication
CLS: Chicago Linguistic Society Press
CogP: Cognitive Psychology
CogSci: Cognitive Science
CS: Department of computer science(s)
*CSCSI: Proceedings of the National Conference of the Canadian Society for
    Computational Studies of Intelligence*
CS–TR: Department of computer science(s) technical report
DisPro: Discourse Processes
FoundLang: Foundations of Language
IJCAI: International Joint Conference on Artificial Intelligence
IntJAL: International Journal of American Linguistics
IRAL: International Review of Applied Linguistics
JAbSocP: Journal of Abnormal and Social Psychology
JAcouSA: Journal of the Acoustic Society of America
JAppP: Journal of Applied Psychology
JEdP: Journal of Educational Psychology

JExP: Journal of Experimental Psychology
JGenP: Journal of General Psychology
JLing: Journal of Linguistics
JPersSP: Journal of Personality and Social Psychology
JPrag: Journal of Pragmatics
JTWC: Journal of Technical Writing and Communication
JVLVB: Journal of Verbal Learning and Verbal Behavior
LangSty: Language and Style
LingInq: Linguistic Inquiry
MechTrans: Mechanical Translation
MemCog: Memory and Cognition
MLJ: Modern Language Journal
PerPsy: Perception and Psychophysics
PR: Psychological Review
PsySci: Psychonomic Science
PTL: Journal of Descriptive Poetics and Theory of Literature
QJExP: Quarterly Journal of Experimental Psychology
TINLAP: Theoretical Issues in Natural Language Processing
TR: Technical report (in-house publication of an institution)

Index of Names

All numbers refer to paragraphs except the small raised numbers for chapter footnotes.

Abelson, Robert I.6.12, III.3.16, III.4.6,
  VI.1.3, VI.1.6, VI.1.14, VI.4.3, VI.4.6,
  VI.4.11, VI[9], VIII.1.5, VIII.2.1, IX.6.1
Achtenhagen, Frank VII.2.1, IX.5.7
Adams, Marilyn VI.1.2
Ahlswede, Rudolf III[4]
Akmajian, Adrian V.5.9
Albrecht, Erhard III.2.1.1
Allen, Gracie II.1.8, II.1.11, V.4.12
Allen, James I.4.12, I.6.1, VI.1.3, VIII.1.2.1,
  VIII.1.6.4
Allen, Paul VII.3.14
Anaxogoras I.1.12
Anderson, John I.1.17.2, I.1.18, I.2.12,
  I.3.5.8, I.6.6, I.6.10, II.2.27, III.1.3,
  III.2.5, III.3.3, III.3.10, III.3.24
Anderson, Richard I.4.7, III.1.3, V.3.1,
  V.3.2, VI.1.3
Angelo, Maya V.3.13
Anisfeld, Moshe VII.3.30
Apostel, Leo I.1.6, I.1.12
Appelbaum, Anat IV.2.6.6
Aquino, Milagros III.4.20, III[19a]
Arnheim, Rudolf IV.2.5
Atkins, John III.2.4
Austin, George III.3.12
Austin, John VI.4.2
Ausubel, David I.6.5, III.3.3, IV.2.5, VI.2.7,
  VII.3.29, VII.3.30

Bacon, Francis IV.3.14
Ballmer, Thomas I.4.10, VI.4.2
Balzer, Robert I.2.10, I.6.1, I.6.12
Barclay, Richard VII.3.30
Bartlett, Frederick VI.1.2, VI[1], VII.3.1,
  VII.3.29, VII.3.30
Bateman, Don IX[4]
Baumal, Ruth IV.2.8
Beaugrande, Robert de 0.1, 0.3, I.2.12,
  I.4.12, I.5.3.3, II.2.3, III.1.5, III.3.7,
  III.3.10, III.4.7.17, III.4.18ff., IV.1.5,
  V.2.4, VI.1.2f., VI.1.3, VI.4.10, VII.1.11,
  VII.2.7, VII.2.27, VIII.2.8f., VIII.2.20f.,
  IX.6.4
Beerbohm, Max. V.4.7
Bellert, Irene I.4.12
Belloc, Hilaire V.4.6
Berlyne, Daniel IV.1.12
Bernstein, Basil V.5.6, V.5.7
Bernstein, Jared I.6.1
Berry, Margaret I.1.7, I.2.11, II.2.2
Bertalanffy, Ludwig von I.1.7
Bever, Thomas I.3.5.7, I[8], II.1.7, II.2.5.6,
  II.2.35, VII.2.1, VII.2.18
Biasci, Claudia I.6.2
Biermann, Wolf VI.1.9
Bierwisch, Manfred III.2.1, III.2.1.2, IX.7.2
Blom, Jan-Petter VII.1.3
Bloomfield, Leonard IX.5.1

Blumenthal, Arthur II.2.27
Bobrow, Daniel 0.7, I.6.5, I.6.6, II.2.12,
  III.3.2, III.4.1, VI.1.5, VI.1.11,
  VIII.2.15
Bobrow, Robert I.6.5, I.6.9, III.4.14
Bobrow, Samuel III.3.5
Bock, Kathryn II.1.6, II.2.27, IV.2.6.1,
  VII.2.1
Bolinger, Dwight II.2.23, IV.2.6.2
Boulding, Kenneth I.1.7
Bousfield, Weston VII.3.30
Bower, Gordon III.1.4, III.3.3, III.3.5,
  III.3.12, VII.3.4, VII.3.42, VIII.2.3
Brachman, Ronald III.3.2, III.3.7, III.3.8,
  III.3.10, III.3.11, III.3.19, III.4.14, III[15],
  V.3.10, VII[5]
Braddock, Richard III.4.28
Bransford, John I.3.4.9, VI.1.8, VII.3.30
Bratley, Paul II.2.12
Brazil, David 0.9, IV.2.6.2, V.6.7
Brecht, Bertolt I.4.10, V.6.4
Bremond, Claude VIII.2.1, VIII.2.7
Breuer, Dieter I.4.3
Brillouin, Leon IV.1.3
Brinkmann, Hennig III.4.8, VII.1.1
Broadbent, Donald IV.2.8
Broen, Patricia I.3.1, II.2.5.4
Bross, Irwin IX.1.8
Brown, Jim V.6.2
Brown, John Seely I.3.4.3, I.6.1, I.6.4, I.6.5,
  I.6.9, VI.1.6, IX.1.7
Brown, Roger II.2.36
Bruce, Bertram I.4.12, I.6.1, III.1.5, III.3.7,
  III.4.10, IV.1.23.1, VI.4.2, IX.4.10
Bruner, Jerome III.3.12, IV.2.8, VI.1.6
Buchanan, Bruce IX.1.7
Buckley, Walter I.1.7
Bugelski, Bergen VII.3.30
Bühler, Karl 0.3, I.1.5
Bullwinkle, Candace I.4.12
Burke, Carolyn I.5.4, VII.3.14, IX.3.1
Burke, Cletus IV.1.5
Burns, George II.1.8
Burton, Richard I.6.5, I.6.12, III.4.15,
  IV.1.10, IV.4.11, VII[5], IX.1.7

Camus, Albert VIII[5]
Carbonell, Jaime Jr. I.6.1, VI.1.3
Carbonell, Jaime Sr. III.3.7, IX.1.7
Card, Stuart IV.2.6.3
Carden, Guy I.1.16

Carnap, Rudolf I.6.3, III.1.2, III.3.4
Carpenter, Patricia IV.1.25
Carroll, Lewis IV.1.16, IV.1.23.1, IV.1.23.3,
  V.3.13, V.4.5, V.4.6, V.4.7, V.4.8,
  V.4.12, VIII.1.22
Catford, John IX.6.2
Cercone, Nick III.1.5
Chafe, Wallace 0.9, I.3.4.7, III.4.10, IV.3.3,
  IV.3.4, IV.3.10, V.4.11
Chan, Shu-Park III.3.10
Charniak, Eugene 0.6, 0.7, I.6.9, III.4.2,
  III.4.7.5, III.4.10, VI.1.2, VI.1.6, VI.1.7,
  VI.4.3, VIII.2.1, VIII.2.24
Chase, William IV.2.6.1, IV.2.6.4
Chester, Dan III.3.9, VII.2.2
Chien, Robert VI.4.5
Chomsky, Carol II.1.13
Chomsky, Noam 0.5, I.1.1, I.1.14, I.1.16,
  I.2.3, I.2.5, I.3.1, I.3.4.9, I.4.2, I.4.8,
  I.5.1, I.6.8, II.1.6, II.1.7, II.1.11, II[2],
  III.3.18, IV.3.2, IV.3.13
Chromec, Eva II.2.5.2
Clark, Eve 0.7, I.1.1, I.1.7, I.6.1, II.1.7,
  II.2.1, II.2.4, II.2.5.3, II.2.23, II.2.3O,
  II.2.33, II.2.34, IV.2.6.2, IV.2.6.4, V.3.1,
  V.6.1, VIII.1.6.1
Clark, Herbert 0.7, I.1.1, I.1.7, I.6.1, II.1.7,
  II.2.1, II.2.4, II.2.5.3, II.2.23, II.2.30,
  II.2.33, II.2.34, IV.2.6.2, V.3.1, V.6.1,
  V.6.2, VIII.1.6.1
Clausewitz, Carl von VI.1.10
Clippinger, John I.4.3
Cohen, Phillip I.4.12, I.6.1, III.1.4.1, III.3.2,
  VI.1.3, VI.4.2, VI.4.3, VI.4.4, VI.4.8,
  VIII.1.2.1, VIII.1.4.5
Coke, Esther VII.3.12
Colby, Benjamin III.4.7.17, VI.1 2, VIII.2.1,
  VIII.2.5, VIII.2.8, VIII.2.9, VIII.2.15,
  VIII.2.20, VIII.2.21
Colby, Kenneth 0.6, 0.7, I.6.6, III.4.7.20
Cole, Michael IV.1.5
Coleman, Edmund III.4.20, IV.1.5
Collins, Allan 0.6, 0.7, I.3.4.3, I.6.1, I.6.4,
  I.6.5, III.3.7, III.3.8, III.3.9, III.3.10,
  III.3.11.4, III.3.18, III.3.21, III.3.24,
  III.3.27, V.1.3, VI.1.2, VI.1.6, IX.1.5,
  IX.1.7, IX.4.10
Cook, Carolyn III[9]
Cooper, Lynn III.1.7
Cornish, Elizabeth IV.1.25
Correira, Alfred VII.3.42

Coseriu, Eugenio 0.3, III.2.1, III.4.37
Coulthard, Malcolm 0.7, I[2], IV.2.6.2,
    VIII.1.1, VIII.1.2.2, VIII.1.4, VIII.1.18
Crabbs, Lelah III.4.20, III[19a]
Craik, Fergus III.3.5
Craun, Marlys II.2.27
Cresswell, Max 0.7, I.6.3, I.6.15
Crowder, Robert IV.2.8
Crymes, Ruth 0.4, I.4.12, V.6.1
Cullingford, Richard VI.1.4, VI.1.14,
    VIII.2.1, IX.6.1
Cunningham, James IX.4.3

Damerau, Fred II[2]
Daneš, František IV.3.3, IV.3.6
Danks, Joseph VII.2.16.1
Darwin, Christopher IV.2.7
Davis, Paul VI.4.5
Davis, Randall IX.1.7
Dean, Reba III[9]
Deeping, Warwick V.4.9
Deford, Frank V.3.13
Derrida, Jacques 0.8
DeSoto, Clinton IV.2.6.4
Dewar, Hamish I.2.12
Dickens, Charles V.6.9, VI.6.8, VII.2.14,
    VII.2.15, VIII.1.9, VIII.1.10, VIII.1.13,
    VIII.1.14, VIII.1.15, VIII.1.16
Dijk, Teun van 0.4, 0.6, 0.7, I.1.3, I.1.7,
    I.1.17.3, I.3.4.4, I.3.4.7, I.3.4.9, I.3.5.10,
    I.4.10, I.4.12, I.5.5, I.6.10, I.6.11, II.1.6,
    II.1.12, III.1.1, III.4.27, V.7.2. V.7.5,
    VI.1.2, VI.4.2, VII.1.3, VII.3.2, VII.3.9,
    VIII.2.15, VIII.2.37, IX.7.2
Dik, Simon 0.4, I.1.17.1, I.1.17.2
Dingwall, William I.1.11
Dittmar, Norbert 0.7, IX.1.3
Donaldson, Wayne 0.6
Dooley, Richard III.3.10
Dresher, Elan I.1.17.3, IX.2.7
Dressler, Wolfgang 0.1, 0.3, 0.7, I.2.11,
    I.4.12, II.2.5.2, II[7], II[11], II[13], III.4.37,
    IV.3.13, V.1.2, V.2.6, V.4.1, V.4.1.3,
    V.4.11, V.6.1, VII.1.5, VII[6], IX.6.1
Drury, Roger VI.3.8, VII.3.7
Dundes, Alan I.1.2, VIII.1.3, VIII.2.1

Eikmeyer, Hans-Jürgen I.6.3, III.2.3
Ekstrand, Bruce III.3.14, IV.2.2
Ellis, Jeffrey IX.6.2
Enkvist, Nils-Erik IX.7.1, IX[3]

Erben, Johannes III.4.8
Erdelyi, Matthew IV.2.6.6
Ernst, George IX.1.7
Ertel, Suitbert IV.2.3.7, IV.2.6.6
Ervin-Tripp, Susan VIII.1.3
Estes, William IV.1.5

Fahlman, Scott I.6.1, III.1.6, III.3.2, III.3.7,
    III.3.8, III.3.9, III.3.19, III.4.7.26,
    IV.4.11, V.3.10, VI.1.11, VI.3.4
Ferguson, George IV.2.2
Fikes, Richard VI.4.8
Filby, Nikola IV.2.6.1, IV.2.6.4
Fillenbaum, Samuel IV.1.25, VII.3.30,
    VIII.1.23
Fillmore, Charles 0.5, III.4.5, III.4.9f,
    IV.2.6.2
Findler, Nicholas 0.7, III.3.7
Firbas, Jan IV.3.9, IV.3.10, IV.3.15, V.3.2
Firth, John I.1.7
Fitzgerald, Donald VII.3.29
Flesch, Rudolf II.2.30, IX.3.2
Flores d'Arcais, Giovanni IV.2.6.3
Flower, Linda IX.4.10
Fodor, Jerry I.3.5.7, II.1.7, III.2.5.6, II.2.27,
    II.2.30, III.2.1, III.2.1.3, III.2.2,
    III.4.23, IV.4.11, VII.2.1
Foss, Donald II.2.27, II.2.30
Fowler, Roger I.3.4.7, I.4.1
Frake, Charles VIII.1.3
Franck, Dorothea IV.3.5
Franks, Jeffrey I.3.4.9, III.4.11, VII.3.30
Fraser, Bruce II.2.12
Frederiksen, Carl 0.6, I.6.10, III.3.3, III.3.9,
    III[12], IV.1.25
Freedle, Roy 0.7, II.2.27, VI.1.2, VII[1a]
Freuder, Eugene III.3.13, III.3.14
Freund, Joel VII.3.30
Fried, Erich V.2.6
Friedman, Morton IV.1.5
Fries, Charles I.3.1, IX.5.1
Fries, Udo 0.7
Fritsche, Johannes I.6.2
Fromkin, Victoria I.5.4, VII.3.14

Gabelenz, Georg von der IV.3.4.6
Galanter, Eugene VI.4.5
Gardiner, Alan I.3.1
Garrett, Merrill I.3.5.7, II.1.7, II.2.5.6,
    II.2.27, II.2.30, II.2.35, VII.2.1
Garrod, Simon VII.3.8
Gentner, Dedre III.4.34, IX.4.10

Getzels, Jacob IX.1.4
Gibson, Eleanor VII.3.30
Gilbert, William V.4.7
Gindin, Sergei 0.6, 0.7
Givón, Talmy IV.1.25
Glenn, Christine VIII.2.13
Glinz, Hans 0.8, I.3.1
Glucksberg, Sam VII.2.16.1
Goffman, Erving V.5.3, VI.4.12
Goldman, Neil I.2.10, I.6.1, I.6.12, II.1.4,
    III.4.18, III.4.10, III.4.18, V.3.3.3,
    VII.2.1, VII.2.2, VII.2.3
Goldman-Eisler, Frieda I.3.1
Goldstein, Ira 0.7, III.3.2
Goldstein, Kurt IV.2.2
Gomulicki, Bronislaw VI.3.16, VII.3.1,
    VII.3.3, VII.3.11
Goodman, Kenneth I.5.4, VII.3.14, IX.3.1
Goodnow, Jacqueline III.3.12
Graves, Richard V[2]
Greenbaum, Sidney I.4.12, IX.2.6
Greenberg, Joseph IV.3.17
Greene, Edith I.6.13, III.3.9, III.4.10,
    VII.3.6
Greimas, Algirdas III.2.1, III.2.1.5, III.2.2,
    VIII.2.1, VIII.2.7
Grewendorf, Günther 0.7
Grice, Paul III.1.6, VIII.1.6ff., VIII.1.7,
    VIII.1.12
Grignetti, Mario IX.1.7
Grimes, Joseph 0.9, 0.10, I.1.4, I.4.9, I.4.12,
    II.1.12, III.4.10, III.4.26, IV.2.6.2,
    IV.3.13, VII.1.8, VII.3.35
Groeben, Norbert I.4.12, VII.1.8, IX.1.4,
    IX.1.8, IX.3.3
Grosse, Ernst-Ulrich 0.7, VII.1.2, VII.1.5
Grosz, Barbara I.6.1, III.3.10, V.6.1,
    VIII.1.2.2
Gülich, Elisabeth 0.3, 0.7, I.1.6, I.1.12, I.4.1,
    V.1.2, VII.1.3
Gumperz, John 0.6, 0.7, VIII.1.3
Gundel, Jeanette IV.3.4.6
Gunter, Richard V.6.1

Haber, Lynn II.2.3, II.2.28
Habermas, Jürgen I.5.2
Hajičová, Eva IV.3.2, IV.3.6
Hakes, David II.2.27, II.2.30
Hale, Gordon VI.1.2, VII[1a]
Halliday, Michael I.1.7, I.2.11, I.4.7, I.4.12,
    III.4.5, III.4.13, III.4.26, IV.3.3,
    IV.3.12, IV.3.13, V.1.2, V.5.4, V.5.7,
    V.6.1, VII.2.16.1

Handel, Stephen IV.2.6.4
Harper, Kenneth 0.4, 0.5
Harris, Gregory IX.1.7
Harris, Larry VII.2.2
Harris, Zellig 0.3, I.2.3, I.2.4, I.2.5, I.3.1,
    I.4.10, I[2], III.3.1
Hartmann, Peter 0.3, 0.7, I.1.2, I.1.3, I.1.4,
    I.1.6, I.1.7, I.2.2, I.1.4, I[4], III.3.6,
    III.3.26, VIII.1.1
Harweg, Roland 0.3, 0.4, 0.7, I.3.4.7, I.4.12,
    III.4.37, IV.3.5, V.1.3
Hasan, Ruqaiya 0.4, I.4.1, I.4.12, IV.3.12,
    V.1.2, V.5.4, V.5.5, V.5.7, V.6.1,
    VII.2.16.1
Havens, William III.3.2, III.3.8, III.3.10,
    III.3.13, IV.2.9
Hawkins, Peter V.5.6, V.7.3, VII[1]
Hayes, John IX.4.10
Hayes, Philip I.6.6, I.6.12, II[3], III.3.2,
    III.3.5, III.3.8, III.3.10, III.3.19,
    III.4.17, V.3.10
Hays, David I.6.12
Heger, Klaus I.1.7, I.4.1
Heidolph, Karl-Erich 0.4
Helbig, Gerhard III.4.8, VII.1.1
Helms, Hans IV.1.8
Hempel, Carl I.1.6
Hempfer, Klaus 0.8
Hendrix, Gary II.2.13, III[3], VII.2.18
Heringer, James I.1.16
Herriot, Peter VII.3.30
Hersh, Richard VI.2.1, VI.2.2, VI.3.8,
    VII.3.7, IX.4.6
Hershberger, Wayne IV.2.2
Hilgard, Ernest III.3.14
Hills, Rust V.3.13
Hirsch, Don I.4.8, IX.3.6
Hjelmslev, Louis 0.3, I.1.11
Hobbs, Jerry I.4.12, II.1.8, III.3.6
Hockett, Charles IV.3.1
Hollan, James III[1], III[4], III[7]
Hörmann, Hans 0.7, I.1.1, I.3.1, I.3.5.8, I[6],
    II.2.4, III.2.1, III.2.2.7
Hornstein, Norbert I.1.17.3, IX.2.4
Householder, Fred I.1.16
Howard, Sidney VI.4.16
Hughes, George I.6.3
Hull, Clark IV.2.2
Hundsnurscher, Franz II.1.6, IX.2.6
Hurtig, Richard II.2.35
Huttenlocher, Janellen IV.2.6.1
Hymes, Dell 0.6, 0.7, I.1.2, I.4.12,
    I.5.2

Ihwe, Jens I.2.10, I.4.10, IX.7.2
Ingemann, Frances I.1.16
Isačenko, Alexander V.6.1
Isard, Stephen II.2.27, IV.2.8
Isenberg, Horst 0.4, 0³, II.1.12
Iser, Wolfgang IV.1.22, IX.4.9.1
Ivić, Milka I.3.1

Jackendoff, Ray III.3.18
Jackson, Philip IX.1.3
Jacobs, Joseph VIII.2.13, VIII.2.20
Jacobs, Roderick VII.2.1
Jakobson, Roman 0.11, I.1.2, VII.2.34,
    IX.7.4
Jefferson, Gail II.2.5.3, VII.2.6, VII.1.2.1,
    VIII.1.18
Jenkins, James VII.3.30
Jesperson, Otto I.7.9
Johnson, David II.2.6
Johnson, Marcia VI.1.8, VII.3.30
Johnson, Nancy VI.1.2, VII.3.42, VIII.2.1,
    VIII.2.3, VIII.2.19
Johnson, Ronald VII.3.1
Johnson-Laird, Philip III.1.2, III.3.2,
    III.3.15, III.3.18
Jones, Lawrence VII.2.34, IX.7.4
Jones, Linda 0.7, I.4.1, I.4.12, III.4.28,
    IV.3.3, IV.3.4, IV.3.13, VII.3.4, IX.7.3
Joyce, James IV.1.18
Just, Marcel IV.1.25

Kallmeyer, Werner 0.3, 0.7
Kalverkämper, Hartwig III.1.3
Kanipe, Gail III⁹
Kaplan, Jerrold VIII.1.22
Kaplan, Ronald II.2.14
Karlsen, Rolf 0.3, V.6.1
Kasher, Asa II.2.27
Katz, Jerrold II.1.6, II⁶, III.2.1, III.2.1.3,
    III.2.1.4, III.2.2, III.4.23, IV.4.11
Kay, Harry II.2.5.7, VII.3.29.6
Kay, Martin II.2.35
Keele, Steven IV.1.4, IV.2.5
Keenan, Janice 0.6, III.3.11.3
Keller, Leo IV.1.5
Kelsey, Mamie III⁹
Kidd, Edward VII.3.30
Kintsch, Walter 0.4, 0.6, I.5.2, I.6.5, I.6.6,
    I.6.10, I.6.13, I⁸, II.1.6, II.2.13, III.2.5,
    II.2.9, III.3.11.3, III.3.12, III.3.13,
    II.3.14, III.3.15, III.3.16, III.3.18,
    III.3.28, III.3.29, III.4.20, III⁸, IV.1.3,
    IV.1.7, IV.2.5, IV.2.6.4, IV.4.10, IV²,

V.2.4, V.6.2, VI.1.2, VI.3.8, VI.3.15,
    VII.3.2, VII.3.6, VIII.2.1, VIII.2.2,
    VIII.2.9, VIII.2.11, IX.1.4, IX.3.4
Kipling, Rudyard II.2.24
Klare, George IX.3.2
Klaus, George I.4.3
Klein, Sheldon II.1.11, VII.2.2
Klein, Wolfgang II.1.2
Kloepfer, Rolf VII.1.11
Knapp, Margaret VII.3.30
Koch, Walter 0.4, 0³, I.1.2, I.2.12, IV.1.5
Koffa, Kurt IV.2.5
Kohonen, Viljo IX³
Kosslyn, Stephen III.1.7
Kowalski, Robert III.1.5
Kozminsky, Ely VIII.2.2, IX.3.4
Krauss, Robert IV.2.6.5
Kripke, Saul I.6.3
Kuhn, Thomas I.1.1, I.1.5
Kuipers, Benjamin I.6.6, III.3.13, VI.1.6
Kummer, Werner I.3.4.6, I.4.10, I.5.2,
    VI.4.10, VII.1.3, VII.1.5
Kuno, Susumu 0.6, 0.7, VI.4.6

Labov, William 0.6, I.1.7, I.1.16, I.3.4.8,
    III.3.25, IV.2.6.4, IV.3.7, VIII.1.3,
    VIII.2.31
Lackner, James II.2.35
Ladefoged, Peter IV.2.8
Lakoff, George 0.5, I.1.16, II.1.6, III.3.18,
    V.4.3
Lakoff, Robin I.3.4.4
Larkin, Kathy I.3.4.3, I.6.1, I.6.4, VI.1.6
Larson, Richard IX.4.1
Leach, Jerry VIII.1.3
Leech, Geoffrey III.4.5, IV.3.10, V.6.6,
    V.7.4, IX.2.6
Lees, Robert I.3.2
Lehiste, Ilse 0.9
Lehnert, Wendy VIII.1.2.2, VIII.1.20
Lenat, Douglas I.6.7, IV.1.12
Leodolter, Ruth II.2.5.2
Leskov, Nikolai III.4.2, V.4.3
Lessing, Gotthold V⁵
Levesque, Hector I.2.7, III.1.4.1, III.1.5,
    III.2, III.3.7, III.3.19
Levin, Gerald V.3.2, V.3.13, V.6.2
Levin, James VII.2.1
Levin, Samuel I.3.4.4, I.4.2
Levine, Marvin III.3.12
Lévi-Strauss, Claude I.1.2
Li, Charles 0.9
Liefrink, Frans I.1.11, I.3.5.8, II.1.6

Linde, Charlotte III.3.25, IV.2.6.4
Lindsay, Peter III.3.3, III.3.7
Linsky, Leonard III.3.3
Löbner, Sebastian 0.8
Lockhart, Richard III.3.5
Loftus, Elizabeth 0.7, I.3.5.8, II[9], III.3.7,
   III.3.10, III.3.15, III.3.18, III.3.24,
   IV.1.1, V.3.2, VIII.1.23
Loftus, Geoffrey 0.7, I.3.5.8, II[9], III.3.5.8,
   III.3.15, III.3.18, IV.1.1
London, Marvin IV.2.6.4
London, Phil VI.4.5
Longacre, Robert 0.9, I.1.10, I.6.12,
   III.4.10, IV.2.6.1
Loren, Sophia V.4.11, V[7]
Lounsbury, Floyd III.2.4
Luhmann, Niklas I[7]
Lynn, Patsy VIII.2.42, IX.4.6

MacKay, Donald II.2.33
Maclay, Howard 0.5, I.1.2, II.1.6
Mackworth, Alan III.3.13, IV.2.8
Makhoul, John II.2.5.2
Malinowski, Bronislaw I.1.5
Mandel, Theodore VIII.2.2, IX.3.4
Mandler, George IV.2.8, VII.3.30
Mandler, Jean VI.1.2, VII.3.42, VIII.2.1,
   VIII.2.2, VIII.2.3
Marcus, Mitch II[2]
Marcuse, Herbert V.5.4.5
Marslen-Wilson, William I.6.12
Markov, Andrei IV.1.2, IV.1.3
Marshall, Catherine I.6.1, V.3.3.3, VIII.1.4.5
Martin, Judith VII.2.16.1
Mathesius, Vilém IV.3.3
McCall, William III.4.20, III[19a]
McCalla, Gordon I.6.1, VI.1.3, VIII.1.2.1
McCawley, James 0.5, I.1.16, II.1.6,
   IV.1.24, VIII.1.6.6
McConkie, George VII.3.1
McDermott, Drew I.6.9
McIntosh, Angus I.4.7
Meehan, James III.2.2.3, VIII.2.14,
   VIII.2.24, VIII.2.46
Meggle, Georg 0.7
Meijer, Guus I.1.16
Mel'čuk, Igor VII.2.2
Mellon, John IX[4]
Mervis, Carolyn III.3.23
Metzing, Dieter VI.1.2
Metzler, Jacqueline III.1.7
Meyer, Bonnie 0.6, I.6.10, III.3.3, III.3.9,
   VII.3.1, VII.3.42, VIII.2.4

Meyer, David IV.2.8
Milic, Louis VII.2.38, VII[1]
Miller, Genevieve III.4.7.17, VI.3.16,
   VII.3.29.6, VIII.2.1, VIII.2.5, IX.4.6
Miller, George II.2.27, III.1.2, III.3.11.6,
   III.3.15, III.3.18, IV.2.8, V.7.9, VI.4.5
Miller, Gerald III.4.20
Miller, Mark IX.1.7
Miller, Scott III.3.23
Millward, Richard IV.1.5
Milton, John IV.1.24, VII.2.5
Minsky, Marvin 0.7, III.1.7, III.3.13,
   III.4.10, IV.2.6.5, VI.1.2, VI[1]
Mistler-Lachman, Janet III.3.5
Mistrík, Jozef VII.1.2
Montague, Richard 0.8, I.1.13.2, I.3.5.8
Morgan, Jerry III.1.4.1, IV.1.24, IV.3.16,
   V.1.2, V.1.7, VI.4.2
Morgan, Mary III[9]
Morris, Jeannie V.2.5
Morton, John IV.2.8
Morton, Rand IX.5.2
Mounin, Georges IX.6.2
Mukařovský, Jan I.2.12, I.4.2, IX.7.1,
   IX.7.5
Murdock, Bennett VII.3.8
Mylopoulos, John I.2.7, I.3.5.8, III.1.4.1,
   III.1.5, III.3.2, III.3.7, III.3.19

Neisser, Ulric III.3.13, IV.2.5, IV.2.8
Nelson, Keith II.1.13, VII.3.30
Newell, Allen I.6.7, I[21], IX.1.5
Nezworski, Teresa VIII.2.2
Nicholas, David I.6.4
Nickel, Gerhard IX.6.2
Nida, Eugene III.2.1, IX.6.2
Nilsen, Alleen III.4.10
Nilsen, Don III.4.10
Nilsson, Nils VI.4.8
Norman, Donald I.3.5.8, I.6.5, II.2.11,
   III.3.3, III.3.7, III.4.4, VI.1.11,
   VIII.2.15
Nöth, Winfried 0.7, VII.1.11

O'Connell, Daniel I.3.1, I.3.2, I.3.4.9,
   I.3.4.9, III.4.26
Oevermann, Ulrich V.5.6
Ogden, Charles IX.5.4
O'Hare, Frank IX[4]
Ohmann, Richard IX.7.4
Oller, John III.3.18, IX.4.4

Olson, David I[8], II.1.13, IV.2.6.1, IV.2.6.4, IV.2.6.5
Ortony, Andrew I.3.4.9, I[23], III.1.4, III.3.11.6, III.3.16, III.3.24, III.4.27, III.4.35, IV.1.17, V.3.1, V.3.2, VI.1.2, VIII.1.21
Osgood, Charles II.1.6, II.2.27, IV.1.25, IV.2.6.1, IV.2.6.6, VII.2.1
Özkök, Bora VIII.1.3

Padučeva, Elena V.4.1
Paivio, Allan VII.3.25
Palek, Bohumil 0.4, I.4.12, IV.3.13, V.1.2
Palková, Zdena IV.3.13
Palmer, Stephen III.3.22
Papert, Seymour 0.7, III.3.2, IX.1.7
Parkinson, Richard I.6.6, III.4.7.20
Passafiume, John IV.1.7
Pavlidis, Theodosios I.6.6
Pavlov, Ivan III.3.19, IX.5.3
Pearlstone, Zena VII.3.30
Pereira, Luis III.1.5
Perlmutter, David II.2.6, II.2.8, II.2.22
Perrault, Raymond VI.1.3, VIII.1.2.1, VIII.1.4
Petöfi, János 0.3, 0.6, 0.7, I.2.9, I.3.4.5, I.4.10, I.6.1, I.6.2, I.6.5, I[11], I[18], III.4.39, IV.3.5, VI.1.2
Petrick, Stanley II.1.2, II[2]
Piaget, Jean I.1.2
Pichert, James VI.1.3
Pickett, James II.2.5.2
Pike, Kenneth 0.3, 0.4, 0.9, 0[2], I.1.3, I.1.10, I.2.2, I.4.1, I.6.1, IV[6], VII.1.10
Pollack, Irwin II.2.5.2
Porter, Bern VII.1.11
Posner, Michael III.3.24, V.3.7, VII.3.8
Posner, Roland III.3.2, IV.3.8, V.7.1.4, VIII.1.10
Postal, Paul 0.4, II.2.6, II.2.8, II.2.22, V.4.2
Postman, Leo IV.2.8
Potter, Mary VI.1.6
Pottier, Bernard III.2.1, III.2.1.1
Pribram, Karl VI.4.5
Prieto, Luis III.2.1
Propp, Vladimir VIII.2.1
Pugh, George VI.4.10, VIII.2.25

Quillian, Ross 0.6, II.1.12, III.3.7, III.3.8, III.3.9, III.3.10, III.3.11.4, III.3.27
Quirk, Randolph I.4.12, IV.3.10, IV.3.11, IV.3.14, V.5.4.4, IX.2.6

Raible, Wolfgang 0.3, 0.7, I.1.6, I.1.12, VII.1.2
Ramirez, Robert V.3.13
Rathbone, Robert I.6.14
Reichman, Rachael I.4.12, I.6.1, VIII.1.24
Reiss, Katharina VII.1.11
Resnick, Lauren IX.1.5
Restle, Frank III.3.12
Restorff, Hedwig von IV.2.2, VII.3.8
Rieger, Charles I.6.4, I.6.6, I.6.9, II[3], III.2.3, III.3.5, III.3.6, III.3.8, III.3.18, III.3.24, III.4.39, IV.1.19, V.3.4, VI.4.5, VI.4.11, VIII.2.1
Riesbeck, Christopher II.2.9, III.3.9, III.3.18, III.4.15
Rieser, Hannes 0.3, 0.7, I.1.17.2, I.3.4.5, I.3.5.4, I.4.10, I.6.1, I.6.3, I[11], III.2.3
Riffaterre, Michael IV.1.23.4, IX.7.1, IX.7.5
Rilke, Rilke IV.4.10
Ringen, Jon I.1.16
Rips, Lance III.3.27, III[1]
Roberts, Paul IX.2.3
Robinson, Ian I.1.16
Robinson, Nathan VIII.2.42, IX.4.6
Rohrer, Christian III[13]
Rommetveit, Ragnar II.1.13
Rosch, Eleanor II.3.6, III.3.27, IV.2.6.5, V.3.10
Rosenbaum, Peter VII.2.1
Rosenberg, Sheldon 0.7, VII.2.1
Rosenstein, Allan I.6.14
Ross, John Robert V.6.4, VI.4.2
Rossman, Ellen VII.3.8
Rothkopf, Ernst IX.3.1, IX.3.2
Royer, James VII[9a]
Rubin, Andee I.6.1, VIII.1.5, IX.4.9.1, IX.4.10
Ruddy, Margaret IV.2.8
Ruesch, Jürgen VIII.1.21
Rumelhart, David 0.7, I.3.5.8, I.3.5.9, I.6.6, I.7.4, II.2.9, II.2.10, II.2.11, II.2.22, II.2.32, III.3.3, III.3.7, III.3.13, III.3.16, III.3.22, III.4.4, IV.2.6, IV.4.8, V.6.3, VI.1.2, VI.1.6, VIII.2.1, VIII.2.3, VIII.2.9, VIII.2.46
Rundus, Dewey IV.2.2
Russell, Wallace VII.3.30
Rüttenauer, Martin 0.7

Sacerdoti, Earl I.6.4, VI.1.3, VI.4.3, VI.4.5
Sacks, Harvey II.2.5.3, VII.2.6, VIII.1.2.1, VIII.1.2.2, VIII.1.4, VIII.1.18, VIII[1]
Sadock, Jerrold II.2.6, VI.4.2, VIII.1.6.6

Salmond, Anne VIII.1.3
Sandig, Barbara VII.1.3
Saussure, Ferdinand de I.1.7, I.1.14, I.4.2,
   I.6.8, IV.2.6.5
Ščeglov, Jurii VIII.2.1
Schank, Roger 0.6, 0.7, I.2.10, I.6.1, I.6.12,
   I[16], III.3.2, III.3.5, III.3.8, III.3.16,
   III.3.29, III.4.6, III.4.7.3, III.4.7.16,
   III.4.10, III.4.11, III.4.31, VI.1.3,
   VI.1.6, VI.1.14, VI.4.10, VI.4.11, VI[9],
   VIII.1.2.2, VIII.1.5, VIII.1.9, VIII.1.12,
   VIII.1.15, VIII.2.1, VIII[3], IX.6.1
Scheerer, Martin IV.2.2
Schegloff, Emmanuel II.2.5.3, VII.2.6,
   VIII.1.2.1, VIII.1.18
Scherzer, Joel VIII.1.3
Schlesinger, Izhak I.1.17.2, I.4.12
Schmidt, Siegfried 0.3, 0.7, I.1.5, I.3.4.6,
   I.5.2, III.3.6, IV.1.23.1, VI.1.9, VII.1.5,
   VII.1.6, VII.1.11, IX.7.2
Schneerer, William I.6.14
Scheider, Peter III.3.2
Schubert, Len III.1.5
Schvaneveldt, Roger IV.2.8
Scragg, Greg III.3.2, III.3.6, VI.1.2
Searle, John I.4.13, III.3.3, VI.4.29,
   VI.4.34
Segman, John VIII.3.30
Selfridge, Oliver IV.2.8
Seuren, Pieter II.1.6
Sgall, Petr IV.3.2, IV.3.6, IV.3.15
Shakespeare, William I.7.7, II[10], III.3.20,
   V.5.6, VII.2.27, VII.2.34, VII.2.35,
   VII.2.38, VII[9]
Shannon, Claude I.4.12, IV.1.2
Shapiro, Stuart III.2.12, III.3.7, III.3.10
Sharp, Mary III[9]
Shaughnessy, Mina IX.1.2
Shaw, Cliff I[21]
Shepard, Roger III.1.7
Shoben, Edward III.3.27, III[1]
Shortliffe, Edward IX.1.7
Simmons, Robert 0.6, I.1.18, I.6.1, I.6.10,
   II.1.12, II.2.12, II.2.32, II.2.34, III.1.5,
   III.3.7, III.3.9, III.4.11, VII.2.1, VII.2.2,
   VII.3.42, VIII.2.3, VIII.2.4, VIII.2.9
Simon, Herbert I.6.7, I[21], IX.1.5
Simpson, Carol III.3.23, IV.2.6.5
Simpson, Louis V.2.3
Sinclair, John 0.10, VIII.1.2.2
Skinner, Burrhus III.3.19

Slobin, Dan IV[1]
Slocum, Jonathan 0.6, II.1.12, II.2.12,
   III.3.7
Small, Stephen II.1.3, II[3], III.3.6
Smith, Edward III.3.27, III[1]
Smith, Raoul I.3.5.2
Snyder, Charles III.3.24, V.3.7
Socrates III.3.4, V.3.12, IX.1.9
Solomon, Susan VII.3.30
Snow, Catherine I.1.16
Sperling, George IV.2.8
Spillner, Bernd IV.1.23.4, IX.7.3
Spiro, Rand I.6.9, VI.1.2
Spooner, William II.2.1
Stegmüller, Wolfgang I.1.6, I.1.8, V.3.12
Stein, Nancy VIII.2.2, VIII.2.13
Steinbeck, John V.2.5
Stempel, Wolf-Dieter VII.1.3
Stevens, Albert II.2.14, V.6.3
Stockwell, Robert 0.5, IV.3.2
Stoltz, Walter II.2.27
Strawson, Peter III.1.2
Street, Patty IX.4.6
Strevens, Peter I.4.7, IV.1.3
Strohner, Hans II.1.13, VII.3.30
Sullivan, Arthur V.4.7
Sussman, Gerald I.2.7, VI.1.3, VI.4.5
Svartvik, Jan I.4.12, III.4.5, IV.3.10, V.6.6,
   V.7.4, IX.2.6

Takefuta, Yukio 0.9
Talmy, Leonard III.4.5, III.4.13, VII.2.18
Tannen, Deborah VI[1]
Taylor, Stephen III.3.10, III.4.27, III[4]
Terry, Donald IV.2.2
Tesnière, Lucien III.4.8
Thomas, Dylan IV.1.17
Thomson, Robert VIII[6]
Thorndike, Edward III.3.19, VI.4.6, IX.5.3
Thorndyke, Perry VI.1.2, VII.3.4, VIII.2.1,
   VIII.2.2, VIII.2.3
Thorne, James I.3.4.4, I.4.2, II.2.12, IX.7.1
Thurber, James V.3.2
Tichborne, Chidiock V.2.3
Trabasso, Tom I.6.4, III.3.12, VII.3.8
Trager, George I.2.2
Tulving, Endel 0.6, III.3.16, IV.2.8
Turner, Althea I.6.13, III.3.9, III.4.10,
   VI.3.8, VII.3.6
Turner, Elizabeth II.1.13
Turvey, Michael IV.2.8

Uhlenbeck, Eugene I.1.4, I.1.16, I.1.17.1
Uldall, Hans 0.3
Underwood, Benton III.3.14, IV.2.2,
    VII.3.30
Ungeheuer, Gerold II.1.11

Vendler, Zeno VII.2.16.1
Viereck, Wolfgang VII.2.16.1
Villiers, Peter de III.3.22, V.3.2, V.3.5
Vipond, Douglas III.4.20
Vygotskii, Lev IV.2.6.5

Wagner, Carl I.1.12
Waletzky, Joshua VIII.1.3, VIII.2.31
Walker, Donald 0.7
Wallace, Anthony III.2.4
Wallace, William III.3.14, IV.2.2
Waltz, David 0.7, III.3.18, IX.8.3
Wandruszka, Mario III.3.5
Warning, Rainer I.4.8
Warnock, Eleanor IX.1.7
Warnock, Robert VI.4.17
Warren, David III.1.5
Warren, William I.6.4
Wason, Peter IV.1.25
Waterhouse, Viola 0.4
Watson, Dorothy VII.3.14
Waugh, Nancy VII.3.8
Weaver, Warren IV.4.2
Webber, Bonnie I.4.12, I.6.1, I.6.13, V.1.2,
    V.3.10, V.4.4, VIII.1.4
Wedge, George I.1.16
Wegener, Ingo III[4]
Weinheimer, Sidney IV.2.6.5
Weinreich, Uriel I.1.7
Weinrich, Harald 0.3, 0.4, I.1.3, I.3.4.6,
    III.1.5, IV.1.8, IV.2.6.3, V.3.2,
    VII.2.16.1, IX.8.2
Weizenbaum, Joseph III.4.15
Weltner, Klaus I.4.12
Werth, Paul V.2.4

Wheeler, Alva 0.4
Whitman, Walt VII.3.14.2
Widdowson, Henry I.4.12
Wienold, Götz VII.2.1, IX.5.5
Wilde, Oscar IV.3.7, IV.3.12, V.3.10
Wile, David I.6.1, I.6.12
Wilensky, Robert I.6.9, I[16], VI.1.3, VI[7],
    VIII.2.1, VIII.2.7, VIII.2.11, VIII.2.41,
    VIII.2.46
Wilks, Yorick 0.7, I[10], III.2.2.6, III.2.2.9,
    III.2.3, III.3.5, III.3.8, III.3.18, III.4.3,
    III.4.7.12, III.4.7.13, III.4.10, III.4.37,
    III.4.39, VI.1.6, IX.6.1
Wilson, Deirdre IV.3.5
Winograd, Terry 0.7, I.1.7, I.2.7, I.2.12,
    I.4.7, I.6.1, I.6.6, II.1.2, II.2.2, II.2.13,
    II.2.22, III.2.2, III.2.2.8, III.2.3, III.3.2,
    III.3.18, III.4.1, VI.1.2, VI.1.5,
    VIII.1.2.1
Winston, Patrick 0.7, I.6.4, I.6.6, I.6.7,
    I.6.7.1, II.2.8, II.2.9, II.2.12, III.2.3,
    III.3.2, VI.1.6, VII.4.2
Wittgenstein, Ludwig III.3.1
Woods, William 0.6, I.2.12, I.6.6, I.6.7,
    I.6.12, II.1.2, II.2.2, II.2.5.2, II.2.12,
    II.2.13, II[2], III.3.2, III.3.7, III.3.9,
    III.3.10, III.3.24, III.4.10, III.4.14,
    IV.1.4, IV[3], VI.4.8, VII[5]
Wright, Georg von III.4.7.2
Wright, Patricia IV.1.5
Wunderlich, Dieter I.4.12, I.5.2

Yngve, Victor I.1.2

Zadeh, Lotfi I.6.3
Zanni, Guido V.3.2
Zidonis, Frank IX[4]
Ziff, Paul IV.1.23.2, IV[6]
Zipf, George V.4.1.3, V.7.6
Žolkovskii, Alexander VII.2.2, VIII.2.1

Index of Terms and Concepts

All numbers refer to paragraphs except the small numbers for chapter footnotes. Italicized numbers indicate passages where the terms are explained. I offer further explanation where appropriate. Abbreviations: f/ff: one/more than one following paragraph; pas: passim; s: see; in cross-referring, I abbreviate terms with their first letter.

A

abstraction: s. trace a.

acceptability I.3.4.4,*I.4.11.4*, I.4.12, I[12], VI.4.8, VII.1.4.3, VIII.1.6.1

access: operational means of calling data I.3.5.8, III.3.7

accidentalness *III.3.15*, III.3.28, IV.1.15, V.3.8, VI.1.7, VI.1.12, VII.3.29.5, VII.3.41, VIII.2.44

acquisition III.3.7, III.3.12ff. IX.1.4

action I.3.4.6, I.4.6, *III.4.4*, III.4.6, VI.4.2, VI.4.25, VIII.1.2f.

action-state network VIII.2.24.2

activation: II.2.8, III.3.5, *III.3.24*, V.4.5, *VII.3.15ff.*

active storage II.2.31, III.3.5, III.3.11.6, *III.3.16*, III.4.26

actualization *I.4.1*, I.5.5.5, I.6.8, I[7], III.4.38, VII.2.4, IX.2.5, IX.5.5

actual system I.3.4.1, I.3.4.10, *I.4.1*, II.1.5, II.2.11, III.3.5, IV.1.5

advance organizers VI.2.7

aesthetic experience *VII.2.37*

affected entity *III.4.7.3*

agent-of *III.4.7.2*, III[11], VII.3.26

all-or-none learning III.3.14

alternatives I.4.8, II.1.10.3, II.2.5.1, II.2.17, IV.1.1, IV.3.4.7, V.1.6, V.4.1ff., VI.3.9, VII.3.32, VIII.2.16, VIII.2.35, IX.7.3

ambiguities I.4.5.3, I.4.8, I.5.5.15, II.1.8, II.2.32ff., II.2.35, V.2.2, V.6.9

analogy III.3.21, III.3.28, IV.1.16, VI.1.13, VII.2.29

analysis-by-synthesis *II.1.2*

anaphora *V.1.4.4*, V.4.9

antagonist *VIII.2.7*, VIII.2.9ff., VIII.2.25, VIII.2.27ff.

aphasia II[12]

apperception: direct input via sensory organs I.6.3, I.6.13, II.2.13

apperception-of *III.4.7.18*, VII.3.25

application *I.5.4*

applied linguistics IX.2pas., IX.4.2, IX.5.1

appropriateness *I.4.14*, IV.1.24, IV.4.12, V.4.3, V.6.10, VI.1.4.2, VIII.2.19, IX.2.5

approximation: inexactness between a model and its domain I.1.6, VI.4.7

arbitrariness: correspondence whose
motivation is not immediate III.3.12
argument: entity about which something is
asserted III.3.3
argumentative text *VII.1.8.3*
array: configuration with a characteristic
arrangement VI.1.2
articles V.3pas.; cf. definite or indefinite a.
ask VI.4.14, VI.4.21ff., VI.4.25ff., VI.4.30,
VIII.2.26
assertion III.1.3, *III.1.4.1*, IV.3.1
asymmetry *I.6.12*, III.3.5, III.4.10, VII.2.2,
VII.2.11, VIII.1.6.6
atomism: outlook centered on minimal
components I.6.3, I^{19}, III^1, IV.3.1, V.3.12
attachment VIpas.; s. frame a.; plan a.;
procedural a; schema a
attention I.4.11.5, I.5.3.1f., II.2.27, *IV.1.4*,
IV.1.7, IV.1.10, VII.2.8, VII.2.25, IX.3.6
attribute III.4.14, III.4.16.7, VII.3.27
attribute-of *III.4.7.5*
augmented transition network I.7.2,
II.2.12ff., II^2, III.4.7, III.4.16, IV.1.3,
VI.4.7
autonomous syntax 0.5, I.2.3ff., II.1pas.,
V.4.11, IX.8.2
auxiliary *II.2.15.5*

B

backdating *VI^8*
backup: return to revise a previous data
definition II.2.32, II.2.34
backward downgrading *IV.1.12*
backward planning *VI.4.8*
backward repudiation *IV.3.12*
backward search *I.6.7.1*
banality I.1.16, VII^7
bargain favor VI.4.14, VI.4.27, VI.4.30,
VIII.2.23ff.
bargain object VI.4.14, VI.4.22, VI.4.27,
VIII.2.23
base structure I.6.11
behaviorism: study of exclusively manifest
actions of organisms VI.4.1, IX.1.3,
IX.5.2
belief: cognitive state of holding a
proposition to be true in a world I.5.5.3,
IV.1.23.1, VI.2.2
belief systems IV.1.23.1

binariness: outlook with sets of two
opposed elements I.3.4.4, II.2.31, VII.1.3
block *I.6.7ff.*, II.2.33, VI.4.8, VI.4.31f.
bottom-up: input from outside the
processor's storage I.6.5, VI.1.1, VI.1.5,
VIII.2.5
boundedness *III.4.5*
breadth-first search *I.6.7.2*, VI.4.27, VI.4.32
bridge principles *I.1.6*
bridging inference: insertion of knowledge
to overcome a discontinuity I.6.9
bypassing: non-utilization of a level in an
intersystem III.4.15, IV.1.10

C

cancellation III.3.19, III.4.13
cancel links: pathways that suppress
inheritance III.3.19, III.4.7.24, VI.1.11,
VI.3.4
canonic representation: standardized
format for all data in all contexts I.6.2
cascades: interactive networks doing
parallel operations on different aspects of
the same data II.2.13, III.4.14, VII^5
case: a grammatical role of a noun in a
clause III.4.9
case grammar III.4.9
cataphora *V.1.4.5*, V.4.9f., VII.3.7
categorical rules: operations that always
apply to a language I.3.4.7f., I.4.6, I.4.9,
I^{10}, IV.1.9
category: class of entities postulated for a
theory or model II.2.23
causality *III.4.3*, V.7.6f., VIII.2.13
cause-of *III.4.7.14*, VII.3.24
central vs. peripheral II.2.28
certainty III.3.21
change I.3.4.6f., IV.2.3.4, IV.4.4
chanting VIII.1.3
characters: persons or personified objects in
a story-world VIII.2pas.
chunks *III.3.11.6*, III.4.27
circuit: network configuration with node
access in two directions III.3.10, III^4
circularity: argumentation in which the
conclusion both results from and proves
the premise I.1.17.1
class *III.1.6*, III.3.19, V.3.8, V.3.10, V.4.3ff.,
VI.1.11

classical conditioning: training in which a
stimulus eliciting a natural response is
replaced by an arbitrary stimulus to elicit
the same response IX.5.3

clause II.2.22, *III.4.26*

cleft sentence *IV.3.10*, IV.3.14, IV.4.3, IV[8]

cognition-of *III.4.7.19*

cognitive conflict IV.1.12

cognitive interests *I.1.5*, I.5.6, IX.4.9.3

coherence *I.4.11.2*, I.4.12, I.7.5, III.4.37,
V.1.7, VI.4.8, VII.2.10, VII.3.14.2

cohesion *I.4.11.1*, I.4.12f., Vpas., VI.4.8,
VII.2.10, VII.3.14.1

coincidence detection III.3.24, VI.1.6

collective pro-form: one referring to a
group of entities as one unit V.4.4

combinatorial explosion *II.1.2*, IV.1.2,
V.4.6, VI.4.1

comma splice *IX.4.4*

comment: stretch of a sentence in which
something is presented about the topic
IV.3.2

commentation IV.3.8, VIII.1.10

commonsense: general knowledge and
reasoning shared by a society I.6.4,
II.2.37, III.4.39f., VII.3.30ff.

communication: transfer of knowledge via
meaningful interaction I.1.1ff.

communication-of *III.4.7.22*, VII.3.28

communicative competence I.5.2

communicative dynamism: extent to which
a proposition expands or modifies a
textual world IV.3.15

compatible modes III.3.18, VII.2.12

competence I.4.14f., I.1.17.3, I.3.3, I.3.5.7,
I.4.14, II.1.11, II.2.21, IV.1.24, IX.2.4; s.
textual c.

competition VIII.2.11, IX.4.3

complexity IV.2.9, IV.3.17.7f., IX.8.3

complication VIII.2.11

components II.2.15, II.2.15.10

compound entity with two or more
components of the same class II.2.15,
II.2.25

computer-assisted instruction IX.1.7, IX.5.5

concept I.6.1, *III.3.6*, *III.3.8*, III.3–4pas.

concept activation *III.3.5*, *VII.3.15.1*

conceptual connectivity *I.2.12*, I.2.10, I.4.4,
I.4.11.2, I.7.3, IIIpas.

conceptual dependency: language theory
centered on the underlying structures of
actions and events I.6.12, III.4.11

conceptualization *III.3.15ff.*

conceptual memory *III.3.16*, III.3.24,
III.3.29, IV.1.4

conceptual-relational network *III.4.22*, V.6.2

concord VIII.2.11

conflation: mixing entities by losing
differentiation VI.3.29.4, VIII.2.44

conjunction *II.2.15.11*, II.2.20.3, V.1.4.8,
V.7.1.1, V.7.3

connection vs. segmentation II.2.5, III.2.6

connectivity I.2.12, *I.4.4*, I.6.8, II.1.14,
II.2.39f., IX.6.1;s. conceptual c.;sequential
c.

constituent: element forming a part of a
structured entity II.2.4; s. immediate c.

constitutive vs. regulative I.4.13

constraints: controls on a system's
workings I.5.5.2, IV.3.15

containment-of *III.4.7.13*

content words II.2.20.2, *II.2.23*

context *I.3.4.5*, I.3.5.2, I[1], I.4.11.3ff.,
III.3.11.11, IV.1.23.4, IX.5.5

context-free grammars: those with axioms
and categorical rules only II.2.13, IV.1.9

continuity I.4.3, *I.4.4*, I.6.4, II.2.14, III.1.7,
III.2.6, III.3.7, III.4.41, IV.3.17.10

contrajunction *II.2.15.11*, II.2.20.3, II.2.24,
V.1.4.8, *V.7.1.3*, V.7.5

contrast IV.3.4.7

contrastive linguistics IX.6.2

control: means of affecting selections,
decisions, or operations of a system I.1.7,
I.2.11, I.3.4.7, I.3.5.2, I.3.5.8, I.4.4,
III.1.4.1, V.1.1, VII.2.3

control center II.2.9, II.2.11f., III.3.6,
III.3.11.2, III.3.24, III.4.4, III.4.6,
III.4.14, III.4.21, III.4.27f., VI.3.5,
VI.4.8, VII.1.8.1ff., VII.2.9f., VII.2.30,
VII.3.34f.

control flow I.2.12, III.4.7, III.4.21, III[10]

control levels of expression VII.2.16ff.

conversation I.7.8, VIII.1pas.; s. face-to-face
communication

conversational maxims: principles of
participating in ordinary conversing
VIII.1.6ff., VIII.1.24

conversational texts *VII.1.8.8*

core grammar: one dealing with the most
powerful options and rules of a language
I.4.9, II.2.3, II.2.28

co-reference III[17], *V.1.4.3*, V.4.pas.

co-referential-with *III.4.7.32*

co-text *I.3.4.5*, *I*¹, IV.3.5
counter-example: data which does not
follow a regularity I.2.5, I¹⁰, III.4.36
counterfactual: opposed to propositions
held to obtain in a world III.4.12, III.4.18
count-nouns III.4.5
creativity I.5.3.3, V.2.6, VII.2.39, IX.1.3,
IX.7.3
cue II.2.19, III.4.17, *IV.1.4*, IV.1.7,
IV.1.23.1, IV.1.24, VI.1.6, VII.1.10ff.,
VIII.2.30f.
current I.3.4.7, II.1.4, *II.2.8*, II.2.16, V.1.7
current controls I.3.4.7, I.3.5.2, V.1.1
cybernetic regulation I.4.3, *I.4.4*, I.6.8,
IV.1.21, IV.1.26
cybernetic system: one governed by self-
regulation to maintain stability I.4.3,
I.6.2, V.1.1, VII.3.41

D

damaged structure: one of which a part is
masked by noise or disturbance II.2.21,
II.2.38
data-limited processing: processing where
efficiency cannot improve with practice,
due to the nature of the data VIII.2.15
data-oriented studies I.1.11
decay: loss of data over time III.3.17,
VII.3.29.5, VII.3.36, VII.3.41, VIII.2.44
decidability I.6.13, III.1.1ff.
decision: choice of an operation I.3.3,
I.4.5.2, VII.2pas., IX.4pas.
declarative knowledge *III.3.2*
decomposition: operation of processing via
minimal units III.2pas.
deconstruction 0.8
deduction *III.6.5*
deep structure: an underlying configuration
having a basic, axiomatic format II.1.6,
II.1.10.2, II.1.13, II.2.9, II.2.32
default *I.3.4.3*, I.3.5.2, I.5.5, III.1.5, V.3.14,
VI.4.10f.
default entity *V.3.3.6*, V.5.4.3
definite article V.3pas.
definiteness *V.1.4.2*, V.3pas.
degree of generality III.3.3, III.3.23
deictic IV.3.12, *V.4.1.5*
delinearization: replacement of surface
linearity with underlying relational
configurations II.1.14, II.2.9
demonstration sentence I.3.5.3, III.4.7.3

depth of processing: s. processing depth
depth-first search *I.6.7.3*, VI.4.20, VI.4.27,
VI.4.31
derivational: a model building all
manifestations by combining or
transforming simpler versions II.2.6,
II.2.30, II.2.34, IV.4.11
description: procedure of defining the traits
of an object of study I.1.8.3, I.1.10,
IX.2.5
descriptive texts *VII.1.8.1*
design: optimal use of materials I.4.14,
IV.4.12, VI.4.34, VII.2.37
design criteria I.4.14, I.5.5.10, IV.4.12,
V.7.10, VIII.2.19
desirability VI.4.10, VIII.2.24.2f.
desires IV.2.3.7, VI.4.10, VIII.2.14
determinacy: I.4.4f., I.6.3, *III.3.15*, III.3.24,
III.3.28, IV.1.5, IV.4.6, V.3.7f., VI.1.7ff.,
VI.1.12, VIII.1.4.1; s. non–d.
determinateness operator *III.4.12.7*
determiner *II.2.15*, III.4.23
development phase *VII.2.8ff.*, VII.2.12ff.,
VII.2.30
didactic texts *VII.1.8.7*
differentiation: discovering dissimilar traits
of entities as a means of identification
I.4.2, III.3.23, IV.2.3.6, IV.2.6.5,
VI.1.4.1ff.
directionality I.2.12, III.4.7, III.4.22, III¹⁰,
IV.1.12, VI.1.4
direct object II.2.15, *II.2.15.2*
discontinuity I.4.5.5, I.5.5.15, *I.6.9*, IV.1.12,
VII.2.33, VII.3.15, VII.3.32, VIII.2.37,
IX.3.5
discontinuous elements II.2.31
dicourse *I.1.3*, VI.4.2
discourse action I.4.4, *III.4.26*, *VI.4.2*,
VIII.1.8
discourse analysis 0.9, I.1.3, *I*², VIII.1.2.2
discourse model: configuration of mutually
related text-world models IV.3.9,
VII.1.8.8, VIII.1.4
discrepancy I.4.5.5, I.5.5.15, *I.6.9*, IV.1.12,
IV.4.7, VII.2.33, VII.3.13, VIII.2.37,
VIII.2.42
discreteness I.6.3, I.6.15, III.1.7, IV.3.1
disjunction *II.2.15.11*, II.2.20.3, II.2.24,
V.1.4.8, *V.7.1.2*, V.7.4, VIII¹³
dispensible elements: those whose abscence
does not impair connectivity II.2.20.6,
II.2.30

distribution *III.4.5*
distributionalism I.2.3, I.4.10, III.3.1
distributive pro-form: one referring to each
  of a group of entites singly V.4.4
dividedness *III.4.5*
domain-specific *VII.1.7*, VII.1.9
dominance VI.3.1, VI.3.14, VII.1.1.4,
  VII.1.7, VII.2.8
downgrading *IV.1.11ff.*, VII.2.33
dummy II.2.15, *II.2.15.6*, IV.3.10, V.5.4.2

E

ease of processing: s. processing ease
economy I.4.4, III.3.7, III.3.18, IV.4.11,
  V.1.7, VI.1.4, VIII.2.39, VIII.2.45
economy principle V.1.7, V.2.3
education I.7.9, IXpas.
effectiveness *I.4.14*, I[14], IV.1.9, IV.1.26,
  IV.4.12, V.4.3, V.7.10, VI.4.14, VII.1.4.3,
  VIII.2.19, IX.2.5
efficiency *I.4.14*, I.6.6ff., II.2.19, III.4.14,
  IV.1.9, IV.1.26, IV.4.12, Vpas., VI.3.7,
  VII.1.12, VII.2.13, VIII.2.19, VIII.2.39,
  IX.2.5
elaborated code *V.5.6*
electrical signal I.6.14, III[4]
element I.1.6, I[3]
ellipsis I.4.5.1, I.4.11.1, I[9], *V.1.4.7*, V.5.10,
  V.6pas.
embedding: insertion of subordinated
  phrases into a clause I.3.5.3, II.2.27
emotion I.1.13.1, IV.2.3.2, IV.2.6.6
emotion-of *III.4.7.20*
empiricalness I.1.16f., I.3.5.4, III.2.2
enablement-of *III.4.7.15*, VII.3.24
encoding I.6.14
entity: any identifiable item of any kind
  V.3.3ff.
entry conditions *II.2.2*
entry operator *III.4.12.3*
episode: experienced sequences of events or
  states IV.1.4;s. story e.
episodic entites *V.3.3.3*
episodic knowledge VIII.1.4.5, IX.1.4
episodic memory *III.3.16f.*, III.3.24, IV.1.4,
  VI.1.4
episodic strategies III.3.26, VII.2.14f.
epistemic curiosity IV.1.12
epistemology: theory of knowledge III.3.11
equivalence VII.2.34

equivalent-to *III.4.7.30*
ergatives VII[6]
errors I.5.4, II.2.14, II.2.33, III.3.12,
  VII.3.14ff., IX.4.8
evaluation I.4.14, I.5.5.11, IX.2.5
event *III.4.4*, VI.3.2ff., VI.3.14, VII.2.12
existential quantifier *III.1.3*, *V.3.12*
exit operator *III.4.12.4*
exophora *V.1.4.6*, V.5.pas.
expectation: disposition of a processor
  toward certain occurrences II.2.11,
  IVpas., IX.7.4
experience III.4.3, VIII.1.4.5, VIII.2.16f.
explanation I.1.8.4, II.1.10.4, IX.2.5
explosion I.6.9, III.3.23;s. combinatorial e.
exposition VIII.2.11
expression *III.3.5*
expression phase *VII.2.8ff.*
extensional meaning *I.2.8.2*, V.3.1
external controls *I.2.11*, I[7]

F

face-to-face communication I.4.11.5, VI.2.6
facts *IV.1.23.1*
failure *I.6.7*, III.4.23, III.4.30, IV.1.12,
  VI.3.11, VI.4.18, VI.4.20, VI.4.34
feature: distinguishing trait of an entity
  III.2pas.
feature overlap III.3.27
feedback: reactive input back into a system
  from the environment VIII.1.5
fictional text IV.1.23.3, VI.1.12
figure vs. ground *IV.2.5*,IV.2.6.1, IX.4.7
final state: end condition of an actualized
  system II.2.22, VI.4.4, VIII.2.6
first-order informativity *IV.1.8ff.*
focus: directional center of attention
  IV.2.6.1, IV.2.6.6, IV.3.1, IV.3.10,
  IV.3.17.9, V.5.5, VI.3.14, VII.1.8.4f.,
  VII.3.33, IX.4.7
foreign language teaching IX.5pas.
forgetting I.4.5.4, VII.3.31
form-of *III.4.7.10*
format: manifest arrangement of data
  I.3.4.2, I.4.11.1, I.6.10, III.3.2, III.3.9,
  III.3.15, IV.1.5, V.1.1, VII.2.6.2
forward downgrading *IV.1.12*
forward planning *VI.4.8*
forward repudiation *IV.3.12*
forward search *I.6.7.1ff.*

found poem *VII.1.12*
fragment *I.3.4*, IV.3.13
frame I.7.6, IV.4.7, *VI.1.2ff.,* VI.2pas.,
  VII.1.8.1, VII.2.13f., VII.2.30ff.,
  VII.3.29.2
frame attachment VI.2.pas, VII.2.32
frequency III.3.14, IV.2.2
function *I.1.6*, I.5.3.1, V.3.5, VII.1.8.5
function words II.2.5.2, II.2.20.3, *II.2.23*
functional sentence perspective *IV.3.3ff.,*
  IV.3.13
fuzziness *I.1.6*, I.4.4, II.1.4, III.3.6, III.3.26,
  III.4.12, III.4.39, V.3.10ff.
fuzzy parsing *III.4.15, IV.1.10,* V.4.9
fuzzy set: set with probabilistically defined
  membership VII.1.5, VII.1.7, VII.2.5

G

gambler's fallacy II[13], *IV*[2]
gap I.6.4, *I.6.9*, VII.3.15.3, VII.3.19f.
gapping *V.6.4*
garden-path sentence *II.2.33ff.*
generalization: expanding statements from
  individuals to whole classes I.1.8.2
general problem-solving I.6.7, *I*[21], IX.1.4.1,
  IX.1.7
generative linguistics: the study of how
  language manifestations are produced
  I.1.11, I.1.16, *I.1.18*
generative semantics: a version of
  transformational grammar with logical
  propositions as base structures 0.5,
  I.1.13.3, I.2.6, I.6.11, II.1.6
gestalt psychology: psychology concerned
  with processing input in integrated
  chunks IV.2.5, VI.4.6
gist: approximative summary of a textual
  world III.4.35
given vs. new knowledge I.4.12, IV.3.3,
  IV.4.4
global: applied on a large scale VIpas.,
  VII.2.10f.
goal: intended future state of the world
  I.2.17, I.4.11.3, I.4.14, I.5.5.3, I.6.1,
  VI.4pas., VIII.1.4.3, VIII.2pas.
goal state: intended end state of an
  actualized system I.6.7.1, VI.4.4, VI.4.8
gradation: differentiation by small degrees
  I.3.4.4

grammar *I.1.15ff.*, I.3.2
grammar state: a surface state of a
  sequencing system II.2.8
grammatical: allowed by a grammar
  I.1.16ff., I[16]
grammatical dependency: structure with at
  least two grammatical elements, one of
  which cannot stand alone I.4.4, II.1.14,
  II.2.6ff., II.2.11, II.2.15, III.4.21, V.6.3
graph theory: study of the mathematical
  and electrical properties of networks
  III.3.10, III[4]
ground: s. figure vs. g.

H

head II.2.9, *II.2.15f.,* III.4.14
helper character VIII.2.10.1, VIII.2.26ff.
heuristic: a method of discovery I.3.4.9,
  VIII.1.18
hold stack: a temporary data store for
  current elements II.2.10, II.2.14
human activities: I.1.5, I.4.10, I.5.6, I.7.10,
  IX.4.9.3
hypothesis: a provisional statement II.2.9,
  II.2.14, III.3.12, IV.2.9, IV.3.17.4
hypothesis merging III.4.14, IV.1.4

I

iconic: aspect of signs that outwardly
  resemble their designations IV.2.8
idea *VII.2.9*
idealization: model ignoring manifest
  details III.4.35
ideation phase *VII.2.8ff.,* VII.2.30, IX.7.4
identification I.1.8.1
if added vs. if needed *I.6.9*
imagery VII.3.5
immediate constituents: components
  extracted by binary division of structures
  II.2.31
immediate constituent analysis *II.2.31*
implicature *VIII.1.6.6*
incomplete structures II.2.36
indefinite article V.3pas.
indefinite entities *V.3.5*
indefiniteness V.3.13ff.
indirect object II.2.15, *II.2.15.3*
induction *I.6.5*

inference *I.6.4*, I.6.8f., I.6.13, III.4.1,
III.4.24, III.4.29ff., IV.3.17.3, V.6.8,
V.7.7, VI.3.7, VII.3.15.3, VII.3.18ff.,
VII.3.29.6, VIII.1.21f., VIII.2.45
infinite regress *III.2.2.8*
infinite set I.1.15, II.1.5
inflection: alteration of a surface element in
conformity with the grammatical
dependency in which it occurs II.2.2ff.,
II.2.5.5
inform IV[6], VI.4.14, *VIII.1.8*
informant: a language user who judges
linguistic samples I.1.17.2
informativity *I.4.11.7*, I.4.12, I.7.4, III.4.1,
IVpas., V.1.5, VI.1.12, VII.2.16.3
inform reason VI.4.14, VI.4.21ff., VI.4.27ff.,
VIII.2.26
inheritance *III.3.19*, VI.1.11, VI.3.4, VII.1.9,
VII.2.36, VIII.2.24
initial state: beginning state of an actualized
system I.6.7, II.2.22, VI.4.4, VIII.2.6
initiation operator *III.4.12.1*
instance: member of a class III.3.19, III.3.28
instance-of *III.4.7.24*
institutionalized entities *V.3.3.5*
instruction *I.3.4.6*, II.2.9, III.3.6, VI.1.3f.
instrument I.4.11.3
instrument-of *III.4.7.9*
integrated theory I.6.2
integration: merging new entries with
storage I.6.5, I.6.9, III.3.11.3, III.3.13
intelligence *I.5.6*, *IV.3.18*, IX.1.5
intensional meaning *I.2.8.2*, V.3.1
intention: processing disposition that a
future occurrence should appear III.1.4
intentionality *I.4.11.3*, I.4.12f., VI.4.8,
VIII.1.6.1
interaction I.1.7, I.2.7, I.4.11.2, II.1.4,
VI.4.2, IX.8.2
interdisciplinarity I.3.5.10, IV.3.18,
IXpas.
interestingness III.1.4.3, *IV.1.8*, IV.4.12,
IV.4.18, VI.1.12, VI.4.18, VII.2.9,
VII.2.15, VIII.1.11, IX.7.3
interference: use of one language affected by
knowledge of another IX.5.6
intermediate states: those between the initial
and final states VI.4.4, VI.4.8
internal controls *I.2.11*, I[7]
intersection of sets: elements shared by sets
III.1.6

intersection of spreading activation III.3.24
intersystem *I.2.11*, I.4.1, III.4.3
intertextuality I.3.4.10, *I.4.11.6*, I.4.12, I.7.7,
VII.1.4, VIII.1.1, IX.6.4
intonation 0.9, IV.2.6.2, V.6.7, VII.2.6
intuition: undeclared belief or disposition
I.1.17.2
invention IV.3.14
invoke VI.4.14, VI.4.23, *VIII.1.8*
invoke theme VI.4.14, VI.4.23, VI.4.27,
VI.4.30
involvement: degree of activation of
processing resources IV.2.6.6

J

journalism IV.4.1, IV.4.10
junction *II.2.15.11*, *V.1.4.8*, V.7pas.,
VIII.2.37
junctives: surface signals for junction
V.7pas., VII.2.36, VIII.2.38

K

kernel: basic, irreducible sentence in early
transformational grammar I.1.15
keyword system *III.4.15*
kinship terms III.2.4
knowledge: content of human cognition
and meaning I.5.5.3, IIIpas; s. episodic k;
world k.
knowledge of the world: s. world knowledge
knowledge space: a configuration of
mutually accessible content I.6.1, I.6.10,
III.3.6, IV.1.25, VII.3.41
knowledge state: a state in an actualized
conceptual system III.3.7

L

lack of knowledge inference III.3.19,
III.3.21
langue vs. parole *I.1.14f.*, IX.2.4
learning IV.1.8, IV.2.2
learning system *I.4.3*, IV.1.22, IV.1.23.4
least-effort principle IX.3.3
level I.1.15, *I.2.1*, I[5]
lexical solidarity III.4.37

lexicon *I.2.8.2*, I.6.8, II.2.16, III.4.23
linearity: strictly serial formatting I.2.9.2
linearization: imposition of surface linearity
  upon underlying relational configurations
  II.1.4, VII.2.16.1f., IX.7.4
links: access paths between nodes II.2.8,
  III.3.7, III.4pas.
LISP: bracketed character-string computer
  language VII.3.42
list: enumerative data format III.3.9, V.6.2
literal expression: one with obvious
  reference to a world IV.1.17, VII.2.38
literary studies IX.7pas.
literary texts IV.1.5, IV.1.8, IV.1.22, IV.4.10
literary theory I.4.8
litigation VIII.1.3
load: current amount of data to be
  processed II.1.12, VII.2.20, VII.2.25
local: applied on a small scale VI.1.1
location: spatial definition of an entity with
  respect to others VII.3.21f., VIII.2.39
location-of *III.4.7.6*
logic I.2.9, I.3.2, I.4.11.2, I.6.2, *III.1.1ff.*,
  V.3.1, V.3.12
logical world *I.6.3*, III.1.3ff.
long-term memory storage II[10], III.3.16
loop: doubling back to an earlier state of
  an actualized system VIII.2.36

M

machine translation I.6.14, II.2.16, IX.6.1
macro-state *II.2.9*, II.2.17, II.2.25, III.4.14,
  III.4.27, VI.1.1, VI.4.7
macro-structure: a global structure III.4.27,
  VII.2.10, VII.2.15, VII.2.28, VII.2.38,
  VIII.2.24.2, VIII.2.42
management: controlling actualization for a
  particular motivation I.1.8.7, I.3.4.6,
  IX.2.1, IX.4.9.4; s. situation m.
manifestation *I.1.8*, I.5.3.2, I.5.4
mapping: correlating levels of an actualized
  intersystem I.2.10, I.3.3, I.3.5.1, I.6.12,
  III.3.5, III.3.24, III.4.10, III.4.16ff.,
  IV.1.23.4, IV.3.4.4, IV.3.14, IV.4.12,
  V.5.4.2, VII.1.8.5, VII.2.3, VII.2.16ff.,
  VIII.1.21, IX.4.3, IX.7.4
marker: an arbitrary feature assigned to an
  entity by an investigator III.2.1, III.4.33
Markov chain *IV.1.2*

mass nouns III.4.5, III[13]
matching: comparing entities or
  configurations III.4.36, IV.2.3.5; s.
  pattern-m.
material resources VI.4.3, VIII.2.39ff.,
  VIII.2.41
meaning: content conveyable via signs
  IIIpas.
meaninglessness *IV.1.14*
means-end analysis *I.6.7.1*, II.2.18, VI.4.8,
  VI.4.19
mediation: access via interposed entities
  I.4.11.5f., VIII.1.2
memory I.3.4.9, I.5.1, III.3.16, V.4.13
mentioned entities *V.3.3.1*
meta-action *VI.4.2*, VI.4.25, VIII.1.2
metaclass *III.3.20*, V.5.4.1, VI.1.11
meta-language: language for
  communicating about language III.2.1.5
metaphor I[23], III.3.20, IV.1.17, VI.1.10,
  VI.1.13
metatopic: topic attained by invoking a
  metaclass of a discourse entity VIII[3]
micro-state II.2.9, II.2.25, VI.1.1, VI.4.7
micro-structure: a local structure VII.2.11
minimal units: smallest entities incapable of
  further reduction I.1.15, III.2.1ff.,
  VII.1.1, VIII.2.1
miscues *VII.3.14ff.*, IX.3.1
mobility IV.2.3.1, IV.2.6.1
modality *I.2.8.2*, III.4.18
modality-of *III.4.7.27*
mode: means of representation or
  transmission III.1.1; cf. compatible m.
model: cognitive correlate of a domain
  under study I.1.6, I.1.12ff., IX.4.9.3; s.
  discourse m.; situation model; text-world
  m.
model-building I.6.1
model space: an integrated configuration
  inside a model III.4.27, III.4.29
modification: a change which retains some
  material or function within the whole
  I.4.3, VIII.2.30, IX.7.3
modifier *II.2.15*
modularity *I.2.7*, I.6.3, II.1.1ff., III.1.7
Montague grammar I.1.13.2
mood: grammatical differentiation of
  modality III.4.18
morphemes: minimal units of meaning-
  changing form I.4.10, I.7.1, II.2.1ff.

morphology *I.1.15,* II.2.3, III.2.1
motion-of *III.4.7.8,* VI.3.3, VII.3.28
motivation: disposition that an action
   should be performed IV.1.3, IV.1.12,
   IV.4.10, V.2.4, VII.1.8.4, VII.2.37,
   IX.4.5, IX.7.3
motivational statement VII.2.22,
   VIII.2.23ff., VIII.2.32
multistable system *I.4.3*

N

narration I.7.8, VIII.2pas.
narrative texts III.4.6, V.7.6, *VII.1.8.2,* VII[1]
natural language: one used in spontaneous
   communication by a society I.2.9, I.3.2,
   I.6.2, I.6.15, IV.1.2, V.7.7
near miss VI.1.6
negation: assertion that a proposition is
   invalid IV.1.25, VIII.1.23, IX.2.2, IX[2]
network: structure of nodes and links
   II.2.8, II.2.10, III.3pas., III.4pas., VI.3.2,
   VIII.2.35, IX.1.7; s. conceptual-relational
   n.; semantic n.
nodes: content-loaded points in
   representational space II.2.8, III.3.7
noise *III.4.26,* IV.2.8
non-determinacy I.6.13ff., III.4.19, IV.2.9,
   V.5.4.4, VI.1.8f.
non-text: language manifestation devoid of
   textuality I.3.4.4, I.3.5.5, I.4.14, I.5.5,
   IV.1.23.2, V.4.12
normality postulate *VI.4.11*
normal ordering IV.2.3.1, IV.2.6.4, VII.2.14
noticing *III.3.14*
noun phrase: a noun head plus at least one
   dependent element I.3.2, II.2.9
numerical: expression of countability II.2.23

O

object *III.4.4,* V.3.9
observation I.1.8, I.2.5, VI.1.14
occurrence: an element in an actual system
   I.1.3, I.1.16, I.3.4.5, I.3.5.3, I.6.8, III.4.6,
   III.4.22, IV.1.1
operator: a signal modifying the status of a
   relation or configuration III.4.12ff.
opposed-to *III.4.7.31*

opposition I.4.2, I.6.8
options: simultaneously available elements
   of a virtual system I.3.3, I.4.1f., I.5.5.1,
   III.3.17, IV.1.8, V.5.6
orders of informativity I.7.4, *IV.1.6ff.,*
   IX.3.6
ordering IV.2.6.4; cf. normal o.
originality *VII.2.12*
outline *VII.2.12, VII*[4]
outward downgrading *IV.1.12*
outward repudiation *IV.3.12*
overpower VI.4.14, VI[10], VIII.2.11
overriding: a normally disallowed
   occurrence imposed on actualization
   I.3.4.3, II.1.13, IV.1.5, IV.1.23.4

P

paradigm: (a) accepted outlook of a science
   I.1.1, IX.1.9; (b) a virtual system of
   forms capable of occupying a
   grammatical slot II.2.2f.
paradigmatic *I.2.2,* II.2.3
paradox: self-contradictory proposition
   III.1.2
paragraph III.4.28, IV.4.2, IV.4.6ff.,
   VII.3.32
parallelism: recurrent formatting IV.4.4,
   IV.4.7, VII.3.14.1
parallel processing I.6.12, *III.3.9,* III.4.14,
   IV.1.4, VII.2.3
paraphrase: different formatting for the
   same content II.1.11, III.3.11.10, VII.2.19
parole: s. langue vs. p.
parsing: the mapping phase that leads
   directly to or from surface structure II[2],
   III.4.15, IV.1.10, VII.2.18ff.
part-of *III.4.7.11*
participants: people in interaction or
   communication I.4.6, VI.1.3
passive: sentence format with the affected
   entity as subject II.1.13, IV.1.5, IV.2.6.4,
   VII.2.23
pathway: access route I.6.7ff., VI.4pas.,
   VIII.2pas.
pattern-matching I.6.6, II.2.22, III.3.11.5,
   III.3.15, III.3.28, IV.4.5, V.7.1, VII.2.30,
   VII.2.36, VII.3.29.1
peer group: group of people on socially
   equal basis V.5.7

performance I.1.17.3, I.5.2ff.
performatives *VI.4.2*, VI.4.23
perspective: selective viewpoint on a data
   configuration III.3.2, III.3.11.7, III.3.26,
   VI.1.2, VI.3.13, VIII.2.7
phonology *I.1.15*, I.5.1, III.2.1, VII.1.1ff.
phrase II.2.22, *III.4.26*
phrase structure grammar: grammar
   based on abstract symbol strings
   II.1.2
plan I.2.12, I.4.4, I.4.11.3, *VI.1.3ff.*, *VI.4.4*,
   VI.pas., VII.2.13ff., VIII.1.2.1,
   VIII.2.11ff.
planblock *VI.4.8*, VI.4.18, VI.4.34
planner *I.6.7*
planning phase *VII.2.8ff.*, VII.2.28,
   VIII.2.12
plexity *III.4.5*
poetic texts IV.1.5, *VII.1.8.5*, VII.1.11,
   IX.6.4
possession VI.4pas.
possession-of *III.4.7.23*
postdiction *III.1.7*
power I.5.3.3, II.2.27, II.2.29, *IX.5.4*
pragmatics *I.2.6*, I.2.12, VII.1.5
precondition *VI.4.3*, VI.4.20, VI.4.29
predicate: (a) whatever is asserted about an
   argument III.3.3; (b) stretch of a
   sentence dependent upon a verb agreeing
   with the subject IV.3.4.1, IV.3.4.6,
   IV.3.10, IV.4.4, IX.4.6
predicate calculus: a logic for formalizing
   predication I.6.2
prediction: (a) scientific activity of
   foreseeing manifestations I.1.8.5; (b)
   processing disposition that an occurrence
   will happen I.5.5.14, VIII.2.12
preference *I.3.4.3*, I.3.5.2, I.6.12, I^{22}, II.2.8,
   II.2.17, III.4.5, III.4.10, III.4.14,
   III.4.16ff., III.4.37, V.1.7, V.3.14,
   VI.4.10, VII.2.18
presupposition I.3.4.10, IV.3.4.3, IV.3.5f.,
   VIII.1.22
primary concept *III.4.4*, III.4.14
primitives *III.2.3*, III.4.6
probability I.3.5.2, I.6.13, II.2.8, II.2.11,
   IV.1.1, IV.3.15, VII.1.5
probability operator *IV.1.5*
problem *I.6.7*, III.4.23, VI.3.11,
   VIII.1.11ff., IX.3.5
problematization *VII.1.8.4ff.*

problem-occasioned inference *I.6.9*, III.4.30
problem-solver *I.6.7*
problem-solving *I.6.7*, II.2.6, II.2.8,
   II.2.30f., III.3.11.11, III.4.17, IV.1.10,
   IV.3.17.1, V.6.8, VI.3.8, VI.4.7, VII.2.11,
   VII.2.17, VII.2.30, VII.3.13, VIII.2.6,
   VIII.2.23, VIII.2.46ff., IX.4.10; s. general
   p–s.
problem space *I.6.7*, VI.4.20
procedural attachment *II.2.19*, *III.4.1*,
   III.4.17, III.4.37, VI.1.5, VI.4.8, VII.2.13,
   VII.3.6, VIII.2.5, VIII.2.19
procedural knowledge *III.3.2*
procedural semantics: an account of
   meaning in terms of processing
   operations III.3.pas.
procedure: statement of operations I.3.5.9,
   I.5.3.2, I.5.5ff., I.7.1
processing: cognitive operations upon data
   I.3.5.8, I.6.6, I.7.3, III.3-4pas., VII.3pas.,
   VIII.2.15
processing depth I.4.14, *III.3.5*, IV.1.6,
   IV.3.17.6, V.7.8, VIII.2.15, IX.3.3
processing ease I.4.14, IV.1.6, IV.3.17.5,
   V.7.7f., IX.3.3
processing interaction I.6.12, II.1.4, IV.2.3
processing resources I.4.14, I.6.7.2, VI.4.3
production of texts I.5.5.6, I.6.1, III.4.19,
   VII.2pas.
pro-forms I.4.5.1, I.4.11.1, *V.4.1ff.*, V.4.pas.
program *II.2.2*
progression: configuration of successive
   occurrences I.3.4.7, VI.1.2ff.
projection operator *III.4.12.6*
pronoun III.4.23, V.4.1.5ff.
proper names III.1.3
proposition I.6.10, *III.3.3*, III.4.4, V.6.1f.,
   VII.3.6
proposition list V.6.1, VII^{11}
protagonist *VIII.2.7*, VIII.2.9ff., VIII.2.25
protocol: statement by a test person of data
   acquired and recalled VI.2.4, VI.3.15,
   VII.3.2, VII.3.31ff., VIII.2.42ff.
prototype *III.3.27*, *V.3.3.7*, V.3.10, V.3.15,
   V.5.4.4
pro-verb *V.4.7*
proximity operator *III.4.12.5*, III.4.32
pseudo-cleft sentence *IV.3.11*, IV.3.14
psycholinguistics: discipline investigating
   the psychological reality of linguistic
   models II.2.4, II.2.5.6

purpose VII.3.28
purpose-of *III.4.7.17*
pushdown stack: data store in which each
  entry is placed on the top of a list,
  pushing others down a notch II.2.10

Q

quantification *I.2.8.2, III.1.3, V.3.3.7,* V.3.12
quantity-of *II.4.7.26*
question answering IV.3.6f., IV.3.4.8,
  VIII.1.20ff.
question test *IV.3.6*

R

rank I.4.1, *I*[5], III[12]
readability VI.1.3, VII.2.24, IX.1.8,
  IX.3.2ff., IX.4.9.2
reading I.4.8, IX.3pas.
real world *I*[17], III.3.3, *IV.1.23.1*
recall I.5.5.11, III.3.11.10, VI.3pas.,
  VII.3pas., VIII.2.42ff., IX.3.6
receiving I.5.5.7, I.6.1, II.2.20.12, VII.2.29
recognition: test of deciding whether a
  sample was part of a previous
  presentation VII.3.29.1
reconstruction: (a) scientific activity of
  building artificial correlates of a
  manifestation I.1.8.6; (b) recall via
  rebuilding previous input VI.3.12, VII.3.1
recurrence *V.1.4.1,* V.2pas.
recurrence-of *III.4.7.33,* III[17]
recursion *II.1.5,* II.2.9, II.2.25, II.2.27,
  VI.3.3
reductionism: simplification of a domain by
  ignoring certain aspects I.1.4
redundancy *VII.2.18ff.,* VII.2.24, VII.3.35,
  VII[13], IX.3.6
reference *I.2.8.2, III.1.2ff.* III.3.3, V.2.2,
  V.4.1
referent: a text-world entity accessed via
  reference III.3.3, V.2.2, V.4pas.
registers *VIII.1.3*
regulation I.4.3, I.5.5.14; s. cybernetic r.
reinforcement: in classical conditioning, a
  strengthening of a response to an
  arbitrary stimulus via outside motivation
  IX.5.3

relation I.6.1, III.3–4pas.
relational entities *V.3.3.9*
relation-of *III.4.7.4*
relevance I.4.4, *I.4.14,* III.4.23, IV.3.8,
  V.7.1.4, VI.3.12, VI.4.1, VI.4.8, *VII.2.8f.,*
  VII.2.15, VIII.1.6.2, VIII.1.6.6, IX.7.3
repair: text revision to remove
  unsatisfactory structuring VII.2.6
reproduction: recall via direct output of
  previous input VII.3.1
repudiation *IV.3.12,* V.4.6, V.6.7
residual meaning *III.2.2.4,* III.4.2
resolution VIII.2.11
resource: VIII.2.11.1; cf. material r.;
  processing r.
resource-limited processing: processing
  where efficiency is limited by the amount
  of processing resources that can be made
  available VIII.2.15
restricted code *V.5.6*
revising II.2.34, IV.4.11, VII.2.6, IX.4.5
rewrite rule: a notation where the left-hand
  structure is replaced by a more intricate
  one to the right VIII.2.3
rhetorical choice *VII.2.38*
ritual VIII.1.3
role VI.1.3, *VI.4.13*
routine: operation performed regularly
  without special signals II.1.9, III.2.5
rule: a regularity applying to an entire class
  of structures or operations I.3.5.9, I.6.2,
  I.6.8, II.2.11, III.1.1, V.3.14, IX.2.2

S

salience *III.3.14, IV.2.2,* IV.2.4, IV.2.6.2,
  VII.3.5
scene: visual input at one time III.4.9,
  IV.2.6.14, V.5.6
schema *VI.1.2ff.,* VI.3pas., VII.1.8.2,
  VII.2.13, VII.3.29, VII.3.37ff, VIII.2.2,
  IX.3.4
schema attachment VI.3pas.
scientific texts *VII.1.8.6*
script I.7.6, *VI.1.3ff.,* VI.4.13, VIII.1.4.3
search: operation to obtain needed data or
  access I.6.7ff., III.3.25, IV.1.12, VI.3.9,
  VIII.1.2; cf. breadth-first s.; depth-first s.
secondary concepts *III.4.4*
second-order informativity *IV.1.11ff.*

segmentation: subdividing manifestations
under study II.2.5, III.2.6
selection: choice of a systemic option I.4.1,
I.6.14, VII.2pas.
self-contextualization I.4.7, IX.7.5
semantic distance: the number of nodes
and links between two points in a space
III.3.11.4
semantic memory *III.3.27*
semantic network *III.3.7, III³*
semantics of syntax *I.2.9.1*, V.1.2
semantics proper *I.2.6, I.2.8.2*
semiotics: study of signs I.1.3, I.2.6
sender I.6.14
senses II³, *III.3.5*
sentence *I.3.1ff.*, I.3pas., I.6.11, I⁸, II.1pas.,
III.4.25f., VII.1.1
sentence boundary I.3.4.9, II.1.12, II.2.5.4,
III.4.25, III²²
sentence sequence 0.4
separable graph III.3.10, III⁴
sequencing *II.2.1*, II.2pas., VII.2.16.2
sequential connectivity *I.2.12*, I.4.4,
I.4.11.1, I.7.2, IIpas.
serial processing *III.3.9*, III.4.14
serious problem *I.6.7*, IV.1.6, IV.1.12,
VI.4.8, VI.4.18, VI.4.20
set *III.1.6*
set theory: branch of mathematics dealing
with sets III.1.6, III¹
shallow structure: a configuration in which
grammatical dependencies are shown via
direct linkage II.2.9
short-term storage: a rapidly decaying
memory store II¹⁰, IV.2.8, VI.2.1
significance-of *III.4.7.28*
sincerity conditions VI.4.29, VI.4.34
situation I.3.4.5, *I.4.11.5*, *III.4.4*
situationality *I.4.11.5*, I.4.12f., V.6.8,
VIII.1.1
situation management: controlling
actualization of a totality of current
states I.3.4.6, I.5.5.12, V.5.3, VI.4.2,
VII.1.4.7
situation model: a participant's cognitive
correlate of the current situation I.6.1,
VIII⁸
situation monitoring I.3.4.6, I.5.5.12
slot: position to be filled in a sequence
I.2.2
sluicing *V.6.5*

space: domain in a network III.3.11.6; cf.
knowledge s; model s.; problem s.
specification *III.3.19*, III.3.27, VI.3.4
specification-of *III.4.7.25*
specific entities *V.3.3.2*
speech acts: subclass of discourse actions
with conventionalized preconditions
VI.4.2
spoonerism *II.2.1*
spreading activation *I.6.4*, I.6.13,
III.3.11.11, *III.3.24*, III.3.28, III.4.1,
III.4.4, III.4.37, IV.2.8, IV.3.14, IV.4.6,
V.1.3, V.3.7, V.6.8, VII.3.2, VII.3.15,
VII.3.20, VII.3.29.6, VIII.2.45
stability I.3.4.7, I.4.3, I.4.8, II.2.14, IV.1.21,
V.1.7, V.4.11, IX.8.3
stability principle *V.1.7*, V.4.11, V.7.5
state: condition and data present in a
system at one time I.3.4.7, III¹¹, III¹⁴,
VI.3.2ff.; cf. final s.; goal s.; initial s.;
intermediate s.
state-of *III.4.7.1*
statistics IV.1.2
status: classificatory characterization
II.2.24, III.2.5
steal VI.4.14, VI.4.21ff., VI¹⁰
stimulus-response: a simplistic model of
human behavior as a pairing of outward
event and internal action VI.4.1, VI.4.6,
IX.3.1, IX.5.2
storage II.2.5.7, III.3.7, III.3.16ff., VII.3.31;
s. long-term memory s.; short-term s.
story VII.2.22, VIII.2pas.
story episode *VIII.2.9ff.*, VIII.2.22ff.
story-telling strategies *VIII.2.8ff.*
story-understanding strategies *VIII.2.21ff.*
story-world *VIII.2.6*
strategy I.5.3.2, *I.5.4*, II.2.4, VII.3.29,
IX.1.4ff.
stretch of text: the portion of surface text
being processed or studied III.4.26, V.2.6
strength of linkage *III.3.15*, III.4.12,
III.4.36, IV.1.15
structural description: the dominant
cognitive interest of conventional
linguistics I.1.8, II.1.2, II.1.10.3, II.1.12,
VII.2.4
structure *I.2.12*
style *I.2.10*, I.4.10, IV.1.23.4, VI.1.13,
VII.3.10ff., IX.7.4
stylistic options *VII.2.38*

subclass *III.3.19*, III.3.22f., III.3.27f.
subgoal: intermediate goal state leading toward a major goal I.6.7.2, VI.4.32
subject: (a) noun agreeing with the predicate verb in a sentence II.2.15, IV.3.4.1, IV.3.4.6, IV.3.10; (b) test person in experimentation VI.2.1ff., VII.3.4ff., VIII.4.2ff.
subordination *II.2.15.12*, II.2.20.3, II.2.26, V.1.4.8, V.6.6, *V.7.1.4*, V.7.6ff., VII.2.22
substance-of *III.4.7.12*, VII.3.28
substitution: activity of replacing elements within a structure III.4.38, V.1.3, V.6.1
success *I.6.7*, VI.4.4, VI.4.9, VIII.2.27
successor arithmetic: a logic formulated for arithmetical operations VII.3.42
summary I.5.5.11, III.3.11.10, III.4.27, III⁴, VI.3.14, *VII.2.12*, *VII⁴*
superatom III.3.6
superclass *III.3.19*, III.3.22f., III.3.27f., VI.1.11, VI.3.4
superclass inclusion *VII.3.15.2*, VII.3.17
superlatives V.3.2, *V.3.3.8*, V.3.11
supertopic *VIII.1.15*
surface: manifest aspect of a text I.4.4, I.4.11.1, I.6.13, II.1.4, IV.3.2, V.1.5, VII.2pas., VII.3.3
symbol: sign whose relation to its significance is arbitrary III.1.1, III.3.15, VI.4.2
synchronic viewpoint *I.3.4.7*
synonyms *III.3.5*
syntactic approach *II.2.4*
syntagmatic *I.2.2*, II.2.3
syntax of semantics *I.2.9.2*, V.1.2
syntax proper *I.2.6*, *I.2.8.1*, V.1.2
system *I.1.6*
systemic I.1.14, I.5.5.2, *I³*, II.2.2
systemization *I.1.6*, III.3.16, III.3.27

T

tag: subsidiary link label taken from the surface II.2.18, V.7.6
tagmemics: linguistic model of slot-and-filler analysis on all levels I.1.10, IV⁵
taxonomy *I.1.15*, II.2.11, III.3.9
tense: grammatical differentiation of relative time III.4.18
termination operator *III.4.12.2*

test-operate-test-end model *VI.4.5*
text: occurring sign configuration possessing textuality I.1.1f., I.4.11, etc.
text-internal pattern matching IV.4.5, V.7.1, VII.2.36, VIII.2.13, VIII.2.29
text linguistics Opas.,
text-presented knowledge I.4.11.2, III.4.1, VII.3.29ff.
text-structure/world-structure theory *I.6.2*
text types I.4.11.6, I.7.6, IV.1.23.3, V.6.2, *VII.1.7*, VII.1pas, VII.2.8
textual competence *I.5.5ff.*, I.5pas.
textuality I.3.5.5, *I.4.11ff.*, I.4pas., II.2.35
textual world (text-world) *I.6.1*, I.6.4, *III.4.1*
text-world model *I.6.1*, I.6.4, *III.4pas.*, V.4.4, VII.2.37, VII.3.20, VII.3.31ff., VIII.1.4
theme: recurrent world-knowledge in discourse; cf. invoke t.
theory I.1.12.1ff.
third-order informativity *IV.1.12ff.*, IV.3.15, IV.4.6
threshold of termination *I.6.1*, I.3.4.3, I.6.4, II.2.27, III.3.3, III.3.23f., IV.1.6, VII.2.7, VII.2.10, VII.2.38
time: temporal definition of an entity with respect to others V.7.6f., VII.3.23, VIII.2.40
time-of *III.4.7.7*
tolerance I.4.11.3f.
tone group *III.4.26*
top-down: input from inside the processor's store I.6.5, VI.1.1, VI.1.5, VIII.2.5
topic *III.3.11.9*, *III.4.27*, IV.3.1ff., IV.3.4.10, IV.3.9, IV.3.13, V.3.8, V.4.10, V.5.8, VII.2.13, VII.2.20, VII.2.30, VII.3.7, VIII.1.2.2, VIII.1.9, VIII⁷
topic sentence *III.4.28*
topography: spatiality of a data domain III.3.11.3, VIII.2.4f.
trace abstraction: retention of surface cues VI.3.16, VII.3.3, VII.3.11, VIII.2.48
trade-off: III.2.5, III.3.18, III.3.23, V.4.13, V.6.10, VI.4.11ff.
traditional grammar IX.2pas.
transfer *IV.2.2*
transformation: conversion of data or format I.6.2, I¹⁸, II.1pas., VII.2.19
transformational grammar: a language model of autonomous syntactic conversion 0.5, I.2.5, I.4.9f., II.1pas., VII.2.1

transition *IV.1.2*, IV.1.5, V.7.5
tree: a hierarchical format branching from the top downward II.2.34, VII.3.42, VIII.2.3, VIII.2.24.2
trial-and-error VI.4.6f., VIII.2.27
truth *I.2.8.2*, III.1.1, IV.3.8, V.3.1, VI.4.34, VII.1.8.3
Turing machine: a tape-driven processing automaton II.2.13
turning point VII.2.22, *VIII.2.7ff.*, VIII.2.16, VIII.2.26, VIII.2.31
turn-taking *III.4.26*, VII.1.8.8, *VIII.1.2.1, VIII.1.18ff.*
typicality *III.3.14f.*, III.3.24, III.4.12.8, IV.1.15, IV.4.6, IV.4.10, V.3.7f., VI.1.7, VI.1.12, VIII.1.4.1
typology: classification via idealized representatives III.4.2, VII.1.1f.

U

ultrastable system *I.4.3*
underlying: at greater processing depth I.6.11, II.2.2, III.3.5, III.3.11.10
unique entities V.3.3.4, V.3.6
universals IV.3.17ff., VIII.2.18, IX.6.3, IX.7.5
universal quantifier *II.1.3*
universe of discourse *I.1.4*, VII.2.30, IX.7.5
unstable goal VI[15], VIII.2.11.2, VIII.2.22
updating *I.6.4*, I.6.13, III.4.1, III.4.13, III.4.31, V.3.12, VI[8], VIII.1.5
upgrading *IV.1.11*, IV.1.19
utility *VI.4.7*
utilization 0.6, I.1.1, I.3.5.6, II.2.11, III.3.7, III.3.17, III.3.24
utterance *III.4.26*

V

vagueness III.2.3
valence theory *III.4.8*
value assignment VIII.2.7, VIII.2.21.5, VIII.2.28.1ff., VIII.2.31ff.
value-of *III.4.7.29*
variables I.3.4.8, IV.2.33, VIII.1.12
verbal duels VIII.1.3
verbatim VI.3.9, VI.3.12, VII.3.3, VII.3.16
verb phrase II.2.15, II.2.17
virtual system I.3.4.1, *I.4.1*, I.5.5.1, I.6.8, II.2.11, III.3.5, IV.1.5, IV.1.24, IX.2.5, IX.3.3f., IX.6.2
vision III.3.13, III.3.18, IV.2.8, VII.3.25
voice: grammatical differentiation of event participants II.4.18
volition-of *III.4.7.21*
von Restorff effect *IV.2.2, VII.3.8*

W

Waltz effect IX.8.3
well-formedness *I.2.4*, I.4.2, I.4.10, I[10], II.2.13, II.2.37ff., IV.2.8, V.3.14f., V.6.1
words *III.3.5*, III.3.8, III.4.22, V.1.3
word-class II.2.11, II[11]
world *I.6.3;* cf.logical w.; story w.; textual w.
world-knowledge I.4.11.2, II.2.19, III.3.13, III.3.18, III.4.23f., VII.3.29ff.
world-knowledge correlate III.4.30, *III.4.36*, VII.3.20, VII.3.29ff.
writing V.5.6, VII.2pas. IX.4pas.
zero organization *I.5.3*, I[15]
Zipf's law *V.4.1.3, V.7.6*